THE REPORTER'S HANDBOOK

An Investigator's Guide to
Documents and Techniques

Third Edition

THE REPORTER'S HANDBOOK

An Investigator's Guide to
Documents and Techniques

Third Edition

Steve Weinberg

*Under the Sponsorship of
Investigative Reporters and Editors Inc.*

ST. MARTIN'S PRESS

NEW YORK

Editor: Suzanne Phelps Weir
Manager, publishing services: Emily Berleth
Publishing services associate: Kalea Chapman
Project management: Omega Publishing Services, Inc.
Text design: Lee Goldstein
Production supervisor: Joe Ford
Cover design: Rod Hernandez

Manufactured in the United States of America.
0 9 8 7 6
f e d c b a

For information, write:
St. Martin's Press, Inc.
175 Fifth Avenue
New York, NY 10010

ISBN: 0-312-10153-8 (paper)
       0-312-13596-3 (cloth)

Library of Congress Cataloging-in-Publication Data

Weinberg, Steve.
    The reporter's handbook : an investigator's guide to documents and
  techniques. — 3rd ed. / Steve Weinberg : under the sponsorship of
  Investigative Reporters and Editors Inc. (IRE)
        p.   cm.
    Rev. ed. of: The reporter's handbook / under the editorship of
  John Ullmann and Jan Colbert (Investigative Reporters & Editors Inc.).
  2nd ed. c1991.
    Includes bibliographical references and index.
    ISBN 0-312-13596-3
    1. Investigative reporting—Handbooks, manuals, etc. 2. Public
  records—United States—Handbooks, manuals, etc. I. Investigative
  Reporters and Editors, Inc. II. Title.
  PN4781.R38   1995
  070.4'3—dc20   95-16817
                                                                CIP

Contents

PART TWO

Investigating Individuals, Institutions and Issues

PART THREE

Putting It All Together

Preface

*I*s every journalist an investigative journalist?

Not even journalists agree on the answer.

The board of directors of Investigative Reporters and Editors Inc., eleven experienced journalists, once found themselves discussing the cover of a pamphlet explaining the organization's services. The discussion centered on how to word the cover: "Every journalist *is* an investigative journalist" or "Every journalist *should be* an investigative journalist" or "Every journalist *can be* an investigative journalist."

It would be wonderful to say every journalist *is* an investigative journalist, but it would be untrue.

Many journalists are transmission belts for official proceedings. They attend a city council meeting, write on a notepad or tape the meeting, then edit their material to fit the space or time allotted. Such journalists are not investigators for these reasons: They follow somebody else's agenda; they fail to capture what took place in private among city council members, staff and interest groups; and they do not check land records, contracts or other potentially revealing documents upon which the council's decisions are based. They act more as stenographers than curious, skeptical reporters and editors.

So, is it wise to desire that every journalist *should be* an investigative journalist? Probably not. Some reporters and editors must be available to produce features about how cats now outnumber dogs, service pieces on how to purchase an energy-efficient refrigerator, and—yes—provide a deadline account of the previous evening's city council meeting.

That leaves the premise of this book: Every journalist *can be* an investigative journalist. There is nothing magical about becoming one. It requires intense curiosity about how the world works—or fails to work. Such curiosity is accompanied by skepticism stopping short of cynicism or nihilism, abetted by undying outrage that expresses itself through comforting the afflicted and afflicting the comfortable. Such traits lead to exposés, not because of luck, but because "chance favors the prepared mind." There are no lazy lucky reporters. If vital traits are present, the rest is teachable.

That established, is it possible to define "investigative journalism"? Here is a tentative definition: "The reporting, through one's own initiative and work product, matters of importance to readers, viewers or listeners. In many cases, the subjects of the reporting wish the matters under scrutiny to remain undisclosed."

Let us analyze that definition. Investigative journalists rarely follow somebody else's agenda. They decide what is worthy of coverage, rather than attend a meeting merely because somebody in authority convened it. They will cover a city council meeting, for example, if it might provide background for a larger project; that the meeting might yield a daily news story is incidental. If they must cover the meeting because of their beat, they will be alert for material to use in a future project.

The element of the definition that most divides investigative journalists is whether secrecy and evasion must be present. Many journalists believe that unless somebody in power is concealing information, a story cannot be called investigative. This book takes a more expansive view. If a journalist decides to examine the mortgage lending of local banks—with an emphasis on whether potential minority borrowers receive unequal treatment—it may be that no banker in town is hiding anything. In fact, some bankers might be cooperative. Yet the story qualifies as investigative—the reporter took the initiative, pulled together information from documents and human sources, eventually enlightening the audience about a practice that affects everybody, directly or indirectly, in the lending area.

Gene Roberts, while editor of the Philadelphia Inquirer, subscribed to the expansive definition as he inspired his staff. Roberts said investigative journalism is "not so much catching the politician with his pants down or focusing on a single outrage"; instead, it is digging "beneath the surface so we can help readers understand what's going on in an increasingly complex world."

ACKNOWLEDGMENTS

This book owes a large debt to the two previous editions. As noted elsewhere in the text, John Ullmann, then executive director of Investigative Reporters and Editors, conceived the first edition. He served as primary editor with help from Steve Honeyman, then a graduate student at the University of Missouri School of Journalism. For the first edition, these journalists volunteered their expertise as authors of sections or as nonwriting consultants: Donald Barlett, David Burnham, Richard Cady, David Chandler, Aurora E. Davis, Al Delugach, Robert Dubill, James Dygert, Margaret Engel, Bill Farr, Walter Fee, Jeanmarie Lang Fraser, Gilbert Gaul, Bob Goligoski, Robert W. Greene, Robert Hahn, Daniel P. Hanley Jr., Stephen Hartgen, Maile Hulihan, Bill Hume, Elliot Jaspin, Harry Jones, Peter Karl, George Kennedy, Dick Krantz, Jonathan Kwitny,

Jay Lowndes, Randy McConnell, Mike McGraw, Clark Mollenhoff, Alan D. Mutter, Mark Nelson, Jonathan Neumann, David Offer, Allan Parachini, James Polk, Robert Porterfield, Robert L. Peirce, Wendell Rawls, Patrick Riordan, Keith P. Sanders, Sally B. Schilling, Bruce Selcraig, Leonard Sellers, Dale Spencer, James Steele, Richard Stout, Jack Taylor Jr., Jack Tobin, Jerry Uhrhammer, Chris Welles, Linda L. Wertsch and Robert D. Woodward.

By the time of the second edition, Ullmann had left IRE, but served as co-editor from Minneapolis, where he was working as a newspaper editor. Jan Colbert, an IRE staff member as well as a journalism professor at Missouri, was the other co-editor. Gerry Everding, a former student worker at IRE turned St. Louis journalist, coordinated the fact checking. Section authors who added their names to those from the first edition included John Bender, James K. Gentry, Tom Hamburger, Harry Hammitt, Kathleen Hansen, J. Harry Jones Jr., Dolly Katz, Penny Loeb, Myrta Pulliam, Fredric N. Tulsky, Reagan Walker and Nancy Weaver.

For this third edition, Suzanne Phelps Weir served as lead editor at St. Martin's Press, assisted first by Elizabeth Toomey and later by Susan Chiu. Rich Wright of Omega Publishing Services found and fixed more problems in two months than I thought possible for any editor. At IRE, Rosemary Armao, Tracy Barnett and Brant Houston, three superb journalists, provided feedback. Tora Stoneman, Caron Carlson and Lisa Robbins, then graduate students at the School of Journalism, reacted to drafts of chapters, and helped by conceptualizing chapters, conducting research and assisting with fact checking. Students in the investigative reporting class at the Missouri School of Journalism provided encouragement and served as test audiences for many chapters, as did faculty colleagues.

Four journalism professors who teach and practice investigative reporting commented on the manuscript as reviewers for St. Martin's. All four—Jean Chance, University of Florida; David Protess, Northwestern University; Sherry Ricchiardi, Indiana University's Indianapolis campus; and Christopher Simpson, American University—provided helpful feedback.

Rhonda Glazier, Missouri School of Journalism newspaper librarian and database searcher extraordinaire, provided reaction to the book's first section. Cheryl Reed, police reporter at the Dayton Daily News, volunteered her knowledge to provide a detailed critique of Chapter 9. Subject matter experts from government agencies, universities, trade associations, and private-sector businesses agreed to read sections for errors of commission and omission. Especially helpful were Steve Forsythe, John Galliher, Bill Hager, Bill Haws, Hal James, Tom Schauwecker, Julie Simpson-Burris and Steve C. Smith.

Thousands of additional journalists (many of them IRE members), scholars and librarians—some knowingly, some unknowingly—contributed to the knowledge that informs this book. Of those, some are named in the text, many are not—for reasons of readability and space. My debt to all of them is great.

The greatest debt of all, however, is owed to friends and family who suffered my inattention through yet another book. Those suffering most of all were my wife, Scherrie Goettsch, and my children Sonia, Seth and Kendra.

About This Book

*F*rom its creation in 1975, Investigative Reporters and Editors Inc. has encouraged high-quality journalism based on sophisticated information-gathering and compelling presentation. Any print or broadcast journalist can be a voting member; anybody else can subscribe to IRE's magazine, buy its books, attend its conferences, visit its headquarters.

The founders, more or less convened by Indianapolis Star reporter Myrta Pulliam, had no idea if there would be much enthusiasm. At IRE's first conference during June 1976 in Indianapolis, several hundred journalists showed up, surpassing IRE expectations.

The meeting generated a special energy for a reason besides the turn-out—just days before, assassins had fatally wounded Arizona Republic investigative reporter Don Bolles with a car bomb. How to respond? wondered the assembled journalists. The answer: Form a team of reporters and editors from around the nation to finish Bolles' work. That would show potential murderers they can kill the journalist, but not the investigation.

The team—some volunteers using vacation time, others paid by their employers, all led by Bob Greene of Newsday—pieced together a series about corruption in Arizona and offered it to news organizations at no cost. The effort brought recognition to IRE, not all of it positive. Some journalists criticized the Arizona Project, calling it "gang-bang journalism." Some of the subjects mentioned in the series threatened to sue for defamation. Eventually, IRE found itself in court.

IRE survived the criticism and the lawsuits, found a home during 1978 at the University of Missouri School of Journalism, hired John Ullmann as executive director and collaborated with St. Martin's Press to publish the first edition of this book in 1983.

It was Ullmann's conception. As he taught journalism at the University of Missouri, he says, "I was asked by students where to find records related to stories they were pursuing. There must be a book listing the most useful government documents, I thought, so I spent several weeks looking. I didn't find one."

Ullmann hired a graduate student, Steve Honeyman, to help him line up journalists to contribute chapters. They received help from some of the best investigators in the world. "The Reporter's Handbook" became the cookbook for journalists, providing recipes for delving into the activities of individuals, institutions and issues. Just as it made no sense to prepare a gourmet dinner without consulting recipes by master chefs, so it made no sense to investigate without consulting "The Reporter's Handbook."

The first edition became outdated in places, so Ullmann, by then an editor at the Minneapolis Star Tribune, lined up Jan Colbert of the IRE staff to help coordinate a revision. The second edition appeared in 1991.

The earlier editions of this book were grounded in despair. Ullmann said, "We in journalism don't know as much about reporting as we think we do. We like to say among ourselves that 'investigative reporting' is redundant, that all good reporters are investigators by definition. . . . Most of us don't know as much about investigating as a second-year lawyer, a second-rate insurance investigator or even a rookie cop. . . ."

I shared that view when I replaced Ullmann as IRE executive director in 1983, and still held it when I stepped aside in 1990. One solution was to improve an already useful version of "The Reporter's Handbook." This edition is different in significant ways.

First, it is written by one author. The narrative drive resulting from one author makes up, I hope, for losing the diversity of styles. I have borrowed from the journalists who helped with the earlier editions, so there should be no loss of expertise. I have also borrowed from journalists not mentioned in previous editions.

The examples are drawn from articles written for the IRE Journal, the organization's magazine, which I have edited since 1983; investigations submitted to the annual IRE contests; presentations at IRE conferences; interviews of journalists; correspondence between myself and journalists the world over; accounts in professional magazines (most notably Columbia Journalism Review) and nonjournalism periodicals (Washington Monthly and Mother Jones deserve special mention); memoirs by journalists; biographies of journalists; journalism textbooks; investigative books; and occasionally my own reporting.

Second, the coverage is broader. The earlier versions contained almost nothing, for example, on investigating financial institutions, utilities and insurance companies, sectors that touch almost every life in significant (and sometimes harmful) ways. The earlier versions also contained no separate chapters on issues, such as the environment and transportation. There are more references to international journalism and computer-assisted information gathering.

Third, the book is organized differently. There is a logical progression for those reading it front to back. For readers planning to dip in and out, each chapter—when used in conjunction with the detailed index—can stand alone. The documents and techniques explained in Part One (through Chapter 5) are meant to enhance any investigation on any topic covered in Part Two.

Fourth, the index is far more detailed. It is the key to using this book. The investigator who desires a quick answer might not find the information in what would seem to be the logical chapter; the index should point the reader to the right pages.

To keep this book affordable, I had to limit the number of pages. That decision has had consequences:

First, some topics (agriculture, national defense, etc.) are mentioned only incidentally. I made the choices based on what most journalists cover, combined with what I think most needs investigating.

Second, many case studies are told in short form; fuller accounts are available (from IRE, commercial databases, public and newspaper libraries, bookstores, periodicals or the journalists themselves) for readers who want to know more.

Third, many resources are discussed more briefly than I would like. In such instances, I have included references in the text that readers can mine on their own to acquire more depth. There is no bibliography at the end of each chapter but there is a chapter-by-chapter bibliography at the end of the book.

Fourth, the book does not include addresses, telephone or fax numbers. That saves space, and avoids the problem of the book becoming outdated before it reaches its audience. I have included enough information for readers to locate addresses, telephone or fax numbers on their own.

Fifth, I had to abandon my original plan to reproduce documents and layouts of computer tapes.

IRE's address is 100 Neff Hall, School of Journalism, University of Missouri, Columbia, Mo. 65211. The telephone number is 314-882-2042. The fax number is 314-882-5431. The electronic mail address is jourire @muccmail.missouri.edu. The author and the journalists on IRE's staff would appreciate hearing about outdated or otherwise inaccurate information, as well as gaps in coverage.

PART ONE

The Basics: How to Investigate Anyone or Anything

INTRODUCTION

Paper Trails and People Trails: An Overview

*J*ames Steele and Donald Barlett, the investigative duo of the Philadelphia Inquirer, talk about a "documents state of mind" as the key to producing projects. Robert Caro, newspaper reporter turned author who has transformed investigative biography, believes taking time to research is the key, because "time equals truth."

Although investigative journalists rarely think of themselves as theorists, they do have watchwords such as "documents state of mind" and "time equals truth" that rise to the level of theory. The variations on a theme come together in a technique best described as "working from the outside in." If the theory were rendered graphically, it would resemble concentric circles, with the outermost circle labeled "secondary sources," the middle circle called "primary documents," and the inner circle "human sources." The main subject—sometimes unwisely called the "target"—of the investigation is the center.

Like every model meant to simplify the world, this one has complications: If the subject has previously escaped scrutiny by journalists, the secondary source material will be scarce or nonexistent. Some sensitive subjects undertaken by investigative journalists yield no primary documents—nothing has been written down, what was written down has been destroyed, the documents are in a private repository, the keeper of the information fears somebody's privacy would be invaded, business secrets are involved, the information is classified for military, diplomatic or law enforcement reasons. This is not meant to be discouraging. It is simply the way things sometimes are. Good investigators overcome the obstacles.

Choosing a Subject for Investigation

Before attempting to operate from the outside in, the investigator must choose an appropriate subject. Some are always appropriate, including government corruption, unsafe workplaces, quality of classroom instruction, shoddy construction, costs of medical care, to name a few. Others have heightened relevance to a geographic area (coal mining safety in West Virginia) or a specialized audience (bureaucratic inefficiency at the Federal Communications Commission for readers of Broadcasting and Cable magazine).

How do investigators get started? A tip might come from a long-time source, or a stranger. Other times a news story done on general assignment or a regular beat cries for in-depth treatment. Unfortunately, many beat reporters never try projects because they have become used to accepting the official version from sources they have no wish to alienate.

It does not have to be that way. Daily reporting is a lode of project ideas. Bob Woodward is proof. He started on a weekly newspaper in the Maryland suburbs of Washington, D.C. By using "routine" assignments to start building projects, he worked his way to the Washington Post. There, he combined ideas from his beat with his penchant for digging. Leonard Downie in his book "The New Muckrakers" describes how Woodward "assigned himself" to uncover "small-to-middling scandals" such as supermarkets selling fatty meat and pharmacies dispensing outdated drugs and mislabeled prescriptions. Those stories prepared him for the Watergate exposé, which appeared to be no more than a minor building break-in at first.

The only way for journalists to discover whether they have the temperament and talent for investigations is to try one.

The Research Hypothesis

Here are questions to ask on the way to launching a project: How is something supposed to work, and how well is it actually working? Who wins and who loses? Why? How?

Newspaper editor Tom Honig wrote in the IRE Journal that he has discovered "most good investigations come down to one of two things— either a process did not work or people did not follow the guidelines. . . . If a baby dies, was it one Child Protective Service worker who screwed up, or is the whole system failing?"

Beginning with a tentative hypothesis is different from starting with a closed mind. The best investigators search as assiduously for contradictory evidence as they do for supporting evidence.

The Outer Ring: Secondary Sources

When a reporter is working from the outside in, information already published or broadcast can serve as a starting point for answering basic questions. Such information is secondary source material. If independently verified, it can be a signpost. For example, a newspaper article from six years ago mentions a hearing by a legislative subcommittee, with testimony from a local labor union leader. That article might lead a current-day journalist to seek a hearing transcript and interview the union leader.

Many news organizations retain an indexed clipping library going back many years, or enter published stories into a computerized database. Many published stories are accessible for a fee on third-party computerized databases. Secondary-source materials from television and radio are increasingly available in a technological age. Details about secondary sources are in the next chapter.

Having a "Documents State of Mind"

Secondary sources are most useful when they lead to primary documents. The legislative hearing transcript would be a primary document, as would a real estate deed, political candidate's campaign finance report, lawsuit, insurance policy, discharge certificate from the military. Documents can lie just like human sources can lie, because, after all, documents are prepared by humans. However, unlike humans, documents do not talk back, do not claim to have been misquoted.

Primary documents are more readily available than many investigators realize. The best journalists possess the "documents state of mind" articulated by Steele and Barlett; they assume that somewhere a record exists. If the documents state of mind comes with difficulty to a fledgling investigator, she can think about the paper trails in her own life. From birth, she started generating a paper trail, including a birth certificate and hospital admission/discharge. As she grew, she left behind school records, from report cards to yearbook entries. She obtained a driver's license for a car titled in her name, then received automobile insurance. She received student loans and college scholarships.

After graduation, she put together a resume and completed job applications. She began charging purchases to her credit card, wrote personal checks, applied for insurance, paid for licenses (hunting, fishing, gun ownership, pets, piloting a plane), bought property upon which she built a house, paid personal and property taxes, filed state and federal income tax forms, registered to vote, donated money to political candidates, rented cars while on business, became involved in a dispute with a neighbor that led to a lawsuit in the local courthouse, married, gave birth, divorced.

Institutions—whether government agencies, private corporations, not-for-profit charities or some hybrid—leave paper trails much as individuals do. For example, the articles of incorporation for a business can be likened to an individual's birth certificate. There are extensive paper trails on issues, too. See Chapter 2 for a fuller discussion of primary documents.

Human Sources

Documents serve many purposes, one of which is helping locate human sources. Too many investigators contact only the obvious sources, those in current positions, while ignoring "formers"—the former spouse, former professional colleague, former accountant, former neighbor, former minister, and so on. The formers often have scores to settle or outdated knowledge. But formers can risk candor, have had time to reflect and may have kept documents.

One reason human sources are so vital is that documents take on new meaning when explained by insiders and experts. As a result, there is reason to refrain from key interviews until the paper trail is nearly complete. Information in documents often serves as the basis for questions during the interview; because a journalist might get only one interview with a source, it is best to wait until most documents are in hand. When it comes to interviewing the main subject of the investigation, documents serve as a reality check, helping determine if the subject is lying or is ignorant about certain matters. See Chapter 5 for more information about people trails.

Research Techniques

During the information-gathering stage, freelance journalist Dennis King merges paper and people trails through what he calls parallel backgrounding and indirect backgrounding. Other top investigators work the same way, but no one has explained it better than King in his book "Get the Facts on Anyone: How You Can Use Public Sources to Check the Background of Any Person or Organization."

About parallel backgrounding, King says that when the subject is connected to an institution, the organization will leave its own trails. By following those trails, investigators might locate new information about the subject. For example, personal documents about Mr. Smith may contain no negative information, but city public works files on his contracting firm might include information suggesting bid rigging.

"The same principle also works in reverse," King says. "If your main target is a business enterprise or nonprofit organization, you may gain startling insights by examining the personal backgrounds of its principals or officers. That seemingly innocuous annual report of your local community development corporation may appear in a different light once you learn that the city has padlocked two buildings owned by the executive director because of illegal gambling on the premises."

King defines indirect backgrounding as "parallel backgrounding on a grand scale." An investigator might find the subject is tied to economic or political interests. The way to understand the relationships is to analyze the larger environment. King's research on a West African nation visited often by a New York businessman helped identify possible Libyan connections of the businessman. In another case, King's journey into the history of the Teamsters Union and organized crime families led to a better understanding of Lyndon LaRouche.

Organizing the Information, Writing and Rewriting

As an investigator consults secondary sources, primary documents and human sources, the information gathered becomes overwhelming if it is left to accumulate. It makes sense to evaluate the information weekly, making preliminary choices about what is valuable. The potentially valuable material can be entered into a chronology, whether of a person's life, an institution's history or an issue's progression. Creating a chronology does not mean writing the story chronologically, although that might be the best decision. Rather, the chronology is meant to organize large amounts of information in a linear way to help illuminate links among factors that might otherwise seem unrelated.

For example, a city council member tells an investigator he never participated in closed-door sessions eighteen months earlier about rezoning land owned by a partnership involving his wife. He was 1,500 miles away visiting relatives. The reporter investigating the rezoning enters that detail in the chronology, thinking nothing more about it. Then, three months later, the reporter is reading minutes of a long-past meeting held by a neighborhood association concerned about the rezoning. As the reporter enters details from those minutes into the chronology, she notices that the city council member is mentioned as speaking at the meeting— during the period he claimed to be visiting relatives. The reporter investigates further, discovers that the council member lied and writes how the council member did indeed influence the rezoning. Without the chronology, the reporter might never have discovered the lie.

One caveat about chronologies: Information excluded early in an investigation might take on relevance later, as the reporter learns more about the subject. As a result, all information collected must be reevaluated from time to time during the reporting stage and even after the first draft is written.

Every piece ought to involve rewriting. It can make the difference between a project falling flat or making a high impact. High-impact writing is the topic of Chapter 22.

Thinking Through the Conventional Wisdom

Sound information-gathering, organizing and writing techniques mean little if the underlying logic of the investigation is faulty. Too many investigators accept the conventional wisdom about an individual, institution or issue.

Journalists should look for answers about how and why things are as they are. Mary Kay Blakely, writing in the Los Angeles Times magazine, practiced that kind of thinking as she contemplated the problem of homelessness in an affluent society. The homeless "were not dropped on our streets by a deus ex machina," she wrote. "They arrived through human actions and social choices," which included government urban renewal that destroyed low-income housing but failed to replace it with something desirable and affordable; elimination of unskilled jobs that supported families; and deinstitutionalization of the mentally ill along with the simultaneous reduction in funding for community-based mental health programs.

Cutting through the conventional wisdom is difficult, but it can be done. When the Star Tribune of Minneapolis–St. Paul decided to investigate whether rapists are punished effectively, the reporters and editors studied past projects. The team determined that many of the previous projects had been flawed for four underlying reasons. As described by John Ullmann in his book "Investigative Reporting: Advanced Methods and Techniques," the reasons were:

> Short follow-up periods. Many studies followed sex criminals for only a year or two after their release, not enough time to draw meaningful conclusions.
>
> Faulty study groups. Much of the research has focused on only a handful of sex criminals—too few to draw conclusions. Others have lumped all types of sex criminals together—rapists with incest offenders, for example—even though their patterns are as different as apples and oranges.
>
> Poor counting techniques. Many studies noted only subsequent convictions or returns to prison, failing to count such reliable indicators as arrests.
>
> Erroneous time calculations. Many studies were sloppy in calculating the time frames in which sex criminals committed later offenses; for example, many didn't deduct the time a rapist was in prison and therefore unable to commit another rape.

The Star Tribune team grounded its investigation in accepted principles of sound social-science research, such as studying a sample of adequate size. Perhaps the best book by a journalist for journalists on employing social science techniques is "The New Precision Journalism" by Philip Meyer.

Some of the best books about questioning the conventional wisdom come from nonjournalists. My favorite is "After the Fact: The Art of Historical Detection" by historians James West Davidson and Mark Hamilton Lytle. The authors reexamine historical happenings by questioning underlying assumptions about them. Among the techniques they explain are photographic analysis, psychohistory, oral history and theoretical models. A companion volume is "Historians' Fallacies: Toward a Logic of Historical Thought" by David Hackett Fischer, who explains 11 types of fallacies. A complementary book about logic, aimed specifically at reporters and editors, is "How Do Journalists Think?: A Proposal for the Study of Cognitive Bias in Newsmaking" by S. Holly Stocking (a newspaper reporter turned journalism professor) and Paget H. Gross (a psychology professor).

By concentrating on unconscious bias and backing their examples with research from numerous academic fields, Stocking and Gross raise warning flags. An illustrative passage:

> A reporter who regularly writes "people" stories may theorize about hunger and poverty from the perspective of the individual (hunger and poverty numb the soul), giving little attention to the social and economic causes. . . . The reporter who writes more consistently from a social and economic perspective, on the other hand, may generate theories that are more "macro" or "structural" in nature (the causes of the current hunger crisis are embedded in our social, political, or economic system).

Journalists must confront what they think and become aware that they have brought certain assumptions to their subject. During an investigation, everything should be questioned.

The Paul Williams Way

Paul N. Williams, an investigative journalist from Omaha and a theorist of the craft at Ohio State University until his death in 1976, set forth an idealized description of investigative reporting fuller than anything I have seen since. Because Williams' posthumous book, "Investigative Reporting and Editing," is out of print, his thinking is summarized here.

Williams recognized that theorizing would be anathema to journalists:

> The fundamentally intellectual nature of the discipline eludes many would-be Bernsteins, Steffenses, Hershes and Tarbells. Because some reporters have a

tip, can surround it with circumstantial evidence and can dash off a sensational story, they think they will blow the lid off the town. Instead, they come
up with a one-day, one-source story that falls flat. They then complain about
public apathy because nobody reacts. They have failed the test of finding out
everything their readers need to know. They have failed to pull everything
together.

To pull everything together, Williams said, investigators ought to follow a procedure with 11 major steps (and numerous substeps). Williams
outlined those steps. What follows is his outline, adapted by me with
some commentary:

1. Conception

The search for investigative ideas is "unending," Williams said in his
book. Ideas can

> "come from anywhere—legal advertisements, estate sales, bankruptcy no-
> tices, transfers of business executives, company and professional newsletters.
> The bulletin of the local dental society, for example, once provided one of my
> reporters . . . with a story. He read a one-paragraph item about disciplinary
> action being proposed against two dentists. Why? He asked questions, found
> some public records, and established that the two had been milking Medicaid
> with false billing, and that the local prosecutors were waffling about whether
> to file charges.

A. One-Time Tips

Williams said never to discard a tip without screening—it might be
the kernel of a story. Williams looked for proof of facts that gave credence
to the tipster's claim. That might mean a few calls to reliable sources to
intuit whether or not the tip is plausible. Often, checking a tip means
visiting the courthouse, the library or some other records repository.

B. Listening to Regular Sources

For general assignment and beat journalists, developing regular
sources is necessary. They need to leave the office, meet sources face-to-
face, listen to conversations in elevators and restrooms, cover government
meetings that no other investigator attends. For freelance investigators
who jump from topic to topic, regular sources are likely to be friends or
social acquaintances. Every person an investigator meets knows something the investigator does not, and therefore is a potential source.

C. Reading

The best investigators read local and national newspapers every day,
watch television news and listen to radio, look at a range of magazines, visit

bookstores and libraries and place their names on mailing lists maintained by government agencies, corporations, charities and other organizations.

D. Using Breaking News Stories

A curious investigator will accumulate a thick file within a month simply by paying attention to breaking news, then asking why or how something described briefly in a story happened.

E. Following Up on Angles From Other Stories

Williams related an example involving a reporter investigating a political kickback scheme. A source mentioned a young man being intimidated by a probation officer. The reporter made a note, then returned to the tip several months later. It turned out that the intimidator was more than a probation officer. He reported directly to the mayor and to a judge who was the mayor's former law partner. The reporter documented that the subject also drew $1,500 a month as a consultant to the police department, plus receiving questionable fees as a security consultant to a municipal agency. He was eventually convicted of income-tax evasion.

F. Direct Observation of the World

"Sit and stare at the wall and ask what things happen in this town that affect a lot of people but are never written about," Williams advised. "What institution—public, educational, nonprofit, corporate—manages to stay out of the news?" Banks, savings and loans, credit unions, insurance companies, law firms, accounting firms, hospitals, labor unions and other major employers are usually among the institutions escaping scrutiny.

2. Feasibility Study

A. What Obstacles Exist?

Williams mentioned some to be considered: "Are records available? Will sources talk about the subject? Is there time to do the job properly before, say, the next election or the next session of the legislature or the next meeting of the city planning board? Do you or your colleagues know how to interpret the technical material related to the story? . . . Will the target of the investigative story apply pressure on people not to talk? . . . Will he sue?"

B. Can One Reporter Do It All?

If not, are resources for assistance available? Those resources might involve other reporters, editors, a researcher, a student intern, a librarian who handles database searching and outside experts.

C. Is There a Downside for the News Organization?

Is it likely there will be a lawsuit, withdrawn advertising, a readers' boycott? Disturbing answers should not derail a planned investigation, but should be thought through. Editors must be part of this discussion.

D. Can the Investigation Be Kept Quiet?

Is there a strong possibility that competing news media might print or broadcast something before the project is ready?

3. Go–No Go Decision

Is it likely that an investigation will yield at least a minimum story?
Williams quoted Bob Greene of Newsday on the minimum-maximum thinking: "We received information that the Metropolitan Transit Authority had bought an airport here on Long Island, then leased it out to a fixed-base operator at incredibly advantageous terms to the operator. We got a copy of the contract. . . . What had been run as a private business at a $250,000 annual profit . . . was running $600,000 in the red. So we said all right, we have a minimum and a maximum here—the minimum is that we can show there's been a huge waste of taxpayers' dollars . . . and the maximum is that we can show somebody's been paid off."

4. Basebuilding

How will the investigator go about learning the norms of the individual, institution or issue to gain historical and contemporary perspectives?
To understand how something works, it is necessary to learn how it is supposed to work. Williams told of how a reporter started looking at an insurance agency. He found it had advanced $163,000 to finance one of its directors as a general agent for the company. "The transaction was listed in a state-required report and meant little . . . until he discussed it with an expert source," Williams commented. The expert said such an advance was unusual. "This discovery of self-dealing became a basic reference point for . . . subsequent stories about an ingenious circular hustle involving the insurance company and a small bank in Washington acquired by California promoters."

5. Planning

A. How Will Information Be Collected and Filed?

A chronology of an individual's career, an institution's existence or an issue's evolution is usually a powerful organizational tool. All documents and interview notes should be painstakingly cross-referenced among relevant topic files.

B. Who Will Perform What Tasks, and on What Schedule?

Those tasks include reporting, filing, writing, copyediting, photography, graphics, accuracy checking and libel readings.

6. Original Research

A. Following the Paper Trail (See Chapters 1, 2, 3 and 4 of this book.)

B. Following the People Trail (See Chapter 5 of this book.)

7. Reevaluation

Should the investigation continue to move ahead? Should it be filed for now? Or should it be dropped permanently?

8. Filling the Gaps

Key interviews and additional documents work should be targeted at answering the questions that have not yet been answered.

9. Final Evaluation (See Chapter 23 of this book.)

10. Writing and Rewriting (See Chapter 22 of this book.)

11. Publication and Follow-up Stories

More Books With Insight Into the Investigative Process

In many ways, Williams' book has no equal. But there are many other books with insight into the byways of investigative journalism. The following list, which is not exhaustive, consists of books that consciously try to teach the theory and practice of investigative journalism. Some are out of print, which means visiting libraries and used book stores. The Bibliography for this chapter contains fuller information about each book:

Anderson, Jack, with James Boyd, "Confessions of a Muckraker."

Beaty, Jonathan and S.C. Gwynne, "The Outlaw Bank: A Wild Ride Into the Heart of BCCI."

Behrens, John C., "The Typewriter Guerrillas: Closeups of Twenty Top Investigative Reporters."

Benjaminson, Peter, and David Anderson, "Investigative Reporting," second edition.

Bernstein, Carl, and Bob Woodward, "All the President's Men."

✓Buchanan, Edna, "The Corpse Had a Familiar Face: Covering Miami, America's Hottest Beat."

Campbell, Richard, "Sixty Minutes and the News."

Cheshire, Maxine, "Maxine Cheshire, Reporter."

Cook, Fred, "Maverick: Fifty Years of Investigative Reporting."

Downie, Leonard Jr., "The New Muckrakers."

Duzan, Maria Jimena, "Death Beat: A Colombian Journalist's Life Inside the Cocaine Wars."

Farber, Myron, "Somebody Is Lying: The Story of Dr. X."

Filler, Louis, "The Muckrakers."

Gaines, William, "Investigative Reporting for Print and Broadcast."

Hume, Brit, "Inside Story."

Keeler, Robert F., "Newsday: A Candid History of the Respectable Tabloid."

King, Dennis, "Get the Facts on Anyone."

✓ Meyer, Philip, "The New Precision Journalism."

Miraldi, Robert, "Muckraking and Objectivity: Journalism's Colliding Traditions."

✓Mitford, Jessica, "Poison Penmanship: The Gentle Art of Muckraking."

Mollenhoff, Clark, "Investigative Reporting."

Patterson, Margaret Jones, and Robert H. Russell, "Behind the Lines: Case Studies in Investigative Reporting."

Penn, Stanley, "Have I Got a Tip for You, and Other Tales of Dirty Secrets, Political Payoffs and Corporate Scams: A Guide to Investigative Reporting."

Phelan, James, "Scandals, Scamps and Scoundrels: The Casebook of an Investigative Reporter."

✓ Protess, David, et al., "The Journalism of Outrage: Investigative Reporting and Agenda Building in America."

Ricchiardi, Sherry, and Virginia Young, "Women on Deadline."

✓ Rose, Louis J., "How to Investigate Your Friends and Enemies."

Steffens, Lincoln, "The Autobiography of Lincoln Steffens."

Taibbi, Mike and Anna Sims-Phillips, "Unholy Alliances: Working the Tawana Brawley Story."

Tarbell, Ida, "All in the Day's Work."

Thiem, George, "The Hodge Scandal: A Pattern of American Political Corruption."

Yocum, Robin, and Catherine Candisky, "Insured for Murder."

For readers wanting to move beyond the list above, categories to consider include:

Journalism textbooks aimed primarily at university students. There are dozens with useful chapters on investigative reporting. Three of the books listed above (Benjaminson/Anderson, Gaines, Mollenhoff) are textbooks produced specifically for classroom instruction. They are on the list because they are devoted entirely to investigative journalism. Some textbooks more narrowly focused on writing, ethics and libel are mentioned in the appropriate chapters of this book.

Histories of specific journalism organizations. Keeler's history of Newsday contains an ample section on investigative journalism at that newspaper. Sections in histories of other institutions are less ample, but still worthwhile.

Overviews of turn-of-the-century muckraking. The Filler book listed above mixes discussion about reporting techniques with the muckrakers' philosophies; other overviews pay less attention to technique.

Autobiographies by journalists and biographies of journalists, in the United States and internationally. There are hundreds. The few listed above offer large amounts of useful information.

Anthologies of reporting and writing. Among the most useful is "Best Newspaper Writing," an annual collaboration between the American Society of Newspaper Editors, Reston, Va., and the Poynter Institute for Media Studies, St. Petersburg.

Accounts of specific beats or cases. Buchanan's book is just one of many by journalists about the crime beat. The Beaty/Gwynne book about the BCCI banking scandal is one of several on that case; the authors have made their information-gathering techniques the focus, while the other books did not.

Reference books on information-gathering. There are dozens aimed at the masses. The King and Rose books are by journalists. Authors of similar books also have valuable information to offer, but do not approach their subject from an investigative journalist's perspective.

Any book that takes an in-depth, appropriately skeptical look at an individual, institution or issue. Books with endnotes or footnotes are especially useful, because they inform readers about the location of information. James Bamford's "The Puzzle Palace," about the National Security Agency, is an outstanding example. Hundreds of in-depth studies are mentioned in the subject-specific chapters of this book.

Chapter *1*

SECONDARY SOURCES

Working From the Outside In

*M*ike Berens demonstrated the value of secondary sources while reporting on the death of a prostitute in Ohio. Berens, a reporter at the Columbus Dispatch, began to wonder whether a serial killer might be at work. It was a hunch based on past stories Berens had read about murdered prostitutes, combined with a comment years earlier by an FBI agent that some serial killers prey on prostitutes because they tend to be transient and are therefore sometimes not missed for weeks.

From his newsroom, Berens used a personal computer to log on to Vu/Text, a computer database owned by Knight-Ridder Newspapers. In its memory bank, Vu/Text contains the full text of daily newspapers across the country. Berens began with Ohio newspapers, keying in the words "prostitute" and "body." That search turned up 60 stories.

One of the 60 piqued Berens' interest. From the Associated Press, it told of a woman's body found outside Cincinnati; she had last been seen alive at a Youngstown truck stop. That sounded similar to a case Berens already knew about. While pondering the similarity, Berens found a United Press International story about the disappearance of a different prostitute from the same Youngstown truck stop.

Because all the bodies had been found along Interstate 71, Berens expanded his search at the suggestion of a Dispatch librarian to include the words "highway" or "interstate." That search located references to three more murders in Ohio of truck-stop prostitutes; each showed characteristics similar to the three cases already in Berens' files. One characteristic was that the women's bodies apparently had been dumped directly from a truck cab, so Berens decided to discount cases of murdered prostitutes where the victims had been dragged or concealed.

He expanded the Vu/Text search to newspapers in other states, turning up references to similar murders, spanning six years, of prostitutes in Alabama, Illinois, Indiana and New York. With evidence in hand to back his hunch, Berens built on his findings using traditional reporting techniques. He worked the telephone, visited truck stops, canvassed sheriffs within Ohio and elsewhere whose officers patrolled interstate highways. Law enforcement officers from widespread jurisdictions eventually formed a task force based on Berens' work; they began investigating what had appeared to be unrelated murders as the probable work of a serial killer.

While researching a different type of story, James Steele and Donald Barlett of the Philadelphia Inquirer wanted to learn the identity of a corporation receiving a tax break from Congress that was intentionally left unidentified by the lawmakers. All the reporters could deduce from the legalistic phrasing of the bill was that the company had incorporated in Delaware on Aug. 10, 1928, and had incurred various debts, including $400 million of subordinated debentures at 12.5 percent due June 1, 2001.

Barlett and Steele discussed their needs with an Inquirer librarian. She knew something Barlett and Steele did not—which computer database was most likely to contain an answer. She entered the debt numbers into the Dow Jones News Retrieval database. Voilà! a story about a specific corporation offering debentures with the correct face amounts, interest rates and due dates. A check of a business directory showed that the corporation, under a previous name, had incorporated in Delaware on the appropriate date in 1928. Steele and Barlett had the information they needed to grill members of Congress about the special-interest tax break.

Using Newspapers

Both Berens and the Inquirer team used secondary-source material—defined as already-published information—to generate investigative pieces. Daily and weekly newspapers, television and radio programming, magazines, newsletters and books are a vital first step for investigators looking into individuals, institutions and issues.

All secondary-source information should be independently verified. An investigator must check later issues of the publication for corrections, dissenting letters to the editor and clarifying follow-up articles, then nail down accuracy by talking to the original sources. But secondary sources can provide an invaluable starting point.

In fact, local newspapers are the only sensible place to begin on some stories. No other source has published references to a large bank headquartered in the middle of Missouri as often as the Columbia (Mo.) Daily Tribune and Columbia Missourian have. Nobody has covered a controversial Kansas City–based financier like the Kansas City Star, complemented by suburban newspapers as well as the Kansas City Business Journal. Nobody covered the corrupt Missouri second-injury fund, part of the state workers compensation plan, like the St. Louis Post-Dispatch. The references from those newspapers could serve as first steps for journalists in Texas looking into a former officer of the Columbia bank, journalists in Wisconsin examining how the financier's dealings have affected investors in Milwaukee or journalists in Washington, D.C., seeking to determine whether states other than Missouri have similar corruption in their second-injury funds.

Besides news stories, local papers publish seemingly routine information that can help investigators: society columns telling who was seen with whom (associations may prove damning later, as when the subject of an investigation denies knowing so-and-so), rewritten news releases with details about individuals, advertisements placed by businesses and professionals that might come back to haunt them when the claims made therein fail to pan out.

Letters to the editor can be mined, too. While investigating the background of a murder suspect, a Columbia Daily Tribune reporter recalled a letter to the editor written by the suspect while imprisoned for a previous offense. By searching his newspaper's files, he unearthed the letter from three years earlier; in it, ironically, the prisoner said his sentence was too harsh, that he was no threat to society because he would never act violently.

My favorite page (professionally speaking) of the local daily is "For the Record." I start with the obituaries, checking names of survivors. Those names sometimes reveal connections among persons who previously seemed unconnected. That is especially true when blood relatives have different last names. If the deceased is Harold P. Burnside, a powerful low-profile businessman, I might learn from the obituary that Gayle O'Connor (married name) is his sister. That in turn might lead to a story about how O'Connor, as a zoning board member, cast the deciding vote on a rezoning request from her brother's development company without revealing her conflict of interests.

Birth and marriage notices also help determine relationships that might not surface otherwise. The birth notices tell of new parents with different last names: Carla D. Crane and Michael R. Storm are the parents of a seven-pound girl born March 2 at Regional Hospital; I knew both parents separately as news sources, but had no idea they lived together. Marriage license listings serve a similar purpose: Leslie Anne Logan, 30, of Columbia, and George Jacob Tice, 33, of Columbia.

Next I look at lists of alleged and actual lawbreakers. Under "Arrests," I read about people like Stephen C. Cronan, 49, child abuse, $15,000 bond; and Ginger L. Roberts, 38, passing a bad check, $1,000 bond. What the listings do not say: Cronan is a minister; Roberts is associate provost of the university.

Page two carries a separate heading, "Drunken Driving Dispositions," with items such as Mark R. Sokol of 2221 Florida Circle, who "pleaded guilty, was sentenced to 30 days in jail, fined $50 in court costs and $10 for driving without a seat belt. Execution of sentence suspended on condition defendant be placed on two years unsupervised probation and complete drivers' school." Again, this is not necessarily a story, but what if he works as a school bus driver? What if he is the son of the police chief and received special treatment? What if his case is just right for a project on disposition of drunken driving charges?

Away from the record page, the legal notices (covering disposition of wills, divorces, child custody disputes, personal name changes, auctions of property when the borrower has failed to make payments, government agency requests for bids on products or services and more) have tipped me to what became investigations or have helped complete investigations under way.

Anything might provide grist for the investigative mill. The suggestive wording of a newspaper classified advertisement under "houses for rent" helped a reporter for KOMU-TV in Columbia prove that a landlord was trying to force nude modeling and prostitution on tenants. The reporter read back ten years in the classifieds to document a pattern of behavior. Eventually, the local prosecutor charged the landlord with a crime.

To use local newspapers most profitably, investigators must know which publications cover which geographic areas. For this information, they can consult the Editor & Publisher International YearBook, New York City; it lists daily and weekly newspapers state by state, city by city. In some cities, there are newspapers for specific neighborhoods as well as newspapers aimed mainly at workplace, ethnic or religious groups. In St. Louis, for instance, there are newspapers aimed at Italian-Americans, Korean-Americans, African-Americans, Chinese-Americans, gays, Jews and Lutherans. Many of those can be found in the Editor & Publisher Yearbook, too, as well as in the National Directory of Community Newspapers, Minneapolis, or Bacon's Newspaper Directory, Chicago.

Once the appropriate local newspaper has been identified, an investigator must gain access to its materials. "News Media Libraries: A Management Handbook," edited by Barbara P. Semonche, is a useful guide. As it explains, published articles are accessible through hard-copy or computerized libraries, commercially printed indexes, commercial computer databases—or sometimes a combination.

When a library contains hard-copy clips, an in-person search is advisable, because the file might include unpublished material of value. For example, at some newspapers parents are asked to fill out birth announcement forms, which are filed with published clippings about the father, mother and/or child. One space on the form asks for mother's maiden name. If the maiden name is Jacobs and the married name is Foster, that might be the bit of information the investigator needs to crack the ownership of a land trust registered as FosJac Corporation. Other forms that find their way into the clipping files include engagement, wedding and anniversary sheets.

Members of Investigative Reporters & Editors use the IRE network when accessing files of distant newspapers whose stories do not appear on computerized databases. They check their IRE membership directory, then call the appropriate person at the distant newsroom. One alternative is the distant local public library, where sometimes the staff clips the hometown newspaper, then files the clippings under topic headings.

Newspapers covered by commercially available print indexes include the American Banker, Atlanta Constitution and Journal, Boston Globe, Chicago Tribune, Christian Science Monitor, Denver Post, Detroit News, Houston Post, Los Angeles Times, Nashville Banner and Tennessean, New Orleans Times-Picayune, New York Times, St. Louis Post-Dispatch, San Francisco Chronicle, USA Today, Wall Street Journal and Washington Post. Many of those print indexes, if not in a nearby library, are available from University Microfilms Inc., Ann Arbor, Mich. The availability of distant newspapers on commercial computer databases and CD-ROMs is covered later in this chapter.

Broadcast Sources

Some broadcast news programs are also the subjects of hard-copy indexes and available on computer databases. Television News Index and Abstracts—covering the national evening news from ABC, CBS and NBC, including, recently, ABC's "Nightline" and CNN's "PrimeNews"—is produced by the Vanderbilt University Television News Archive, in Nashville. Public television's "MacNeil-Lehrer News Hour" is covered in a print index while also being available on a commercial computer database. A source for television news transcripts from a range of stations and networks is Journal Graphics, Denver. The full text of some news programs is available online from Burrelle's, in Livingston, N.J.

Magazines and Newsletters

Investigators mining secondary sources should search already existing listings of periodicals. Ulrich's International Periodicals Directory (R.R. Bowker-Reed Reference Publishing, New Providence, N.J.), devotes three of its five volumes to magazines, one to U.S. newspapers and one to serials that include annual reference works. The Standard Periodical Directory from Oxbridge Communications, New York City, has similar scope.

Periodicals come in many forms: general-interest magazines, newsletters, newspapers, trade journals, in-house publications, association organs and local, state or federal government-generated printings. Other guides to periodicals cover titles in a particular field; many of those are published by H.W. Wilson Company, Bronx, N.Y., including the Index to Legal Periodicals, Business Periodicals Index and Education Index. Brand-new publications can be tracked through the Library of Congress' New Serial Titles.

Because the directories often list individual editors for each periodical, investigators can request someone by name when following up; that somebody is likely to have developed expertise during years of covering a narrow part of the world. Editors of specialized publications are often generous with their knowledge, sharing industry norms as well as specific tips. While researching a congressman, I learned that he owned a large fishing tackle company. By consulting a periodicals directory, I learned that a half-dozen covered the fishing tackle industry. I called their editors; by doing so, I tapped into information that yielded the lead for my story: The company was under investigation by the U.S. Justice Department for possible violations of import laws. The specialized publications had reported the story, but no general-circulation outlet had.

While exploring secondary sources, investigators should look for newsletters, which are normally distinguished from magazines by their lack of advertising. There are thousands of newsletters, some so specific that they cover just one law or one agency.

The Newsletter Publishers Foundation, Arlington, Va., has been promoting its little-known dailies, weeklies and monthlies in journalism magazines. One advertisement, headlined "Exclusive," says

> Behind many military stories lies a common theme—interservice rivalry. But the rivalry burst into the open with an Air Force proposal to take over all the Army's long-range anti-aircraft and anti-missile programs. As first reported in Defense Daily, the proposal was formally made in a private face-to-face meeting between the services' top generals. And if adopted it could have major implications for Army and Air Force missions in a time of shrinking defense budgets . . . Defense Daily, published by Phillips Business Information Inc. of Potomac, Md., helps us show what subscription newsletters are all about. No pretty pictures. No crossword puzzle. Just needed news and information for interested subscribers.

In her book "Poison Penmanship," Jessica Mitford emphasizes the importance of specialized publications, but distinguishes between those intended for broad public consumption (such as the Journal of the American Medical Association) and those not (such as Medical Economics), about which Mitford says, "In its glossy pages, you will find many a crass and wonderfully quotable appeal to the avarice of the practitioners of the healing arts." Discussing her investigation of the funeral industry, Mitford points out the gap between funeral directors' public postures in advertisements aimed at customers and their trade publications such as Mortuary Management: "Here were undertakers . . . talking to each other, in the secure belief that no prying outsider would ever have access to their inner councils."

Reference Books

An investigator consulting the catalog of Gale Research, Detroit, will find the Encyclopedia of Associations. It contains details on thousands of trade and professional groups, social welfare and public affairs organizations, labor unions, fraternal and patriotic clubs, plus religious, sports and hobbyist gatherings. The Encyclopedia of Associations has proved useful on almost every project I have conducted. Like many of Gale's books, the encyclopedia is now searchable on-line. Similarly useful is National Trade and Professional Associations of the United States and its companion State and Regional Associations of the United States from Columbia Books, Washington, D.C.

Reference works containing biographical information are so prevalent that there are indexes to the indexes. One of the best is Gale Research's Biography and Genealogy Master Index. It contains hundreds of thousands of citations to biographical articles from biographical dictionaries and who's whos. Another resource is Biography Index from H.W. Wilson Co., covering profiles that have appeared in periodicals, obituaries, references in book-length biographies, autobiographies, diaries and collections of letters.

Dennis King says, "Never assume a person is not listed, no matter how humdrum his or her life might be." If a subject has been listed over a stretch of time, it is useful to compare the most recent information with older versions. The older entries might list previous addresses, former spouses dropped from recent editions or show a gap of a year in a life, which the investigator might then check.

Biographical listings less obvious than Who's Who include local, regional and national social registers for the upper classes; government handbooks with biographies of elected and appointed officials and their top aides, as well as privately published versions; college reunion directories; regional, statewide or national listings of members sharing a trade or profession, such as those kept by medical organizations and their parent, the American Medical Association.

What appears to be a noncontroversial listing might contain a key tidbit. As King explains, "The date of birth might help you in ordering driver's license abstracts and other public records concerning the subject. The name of a parent or former spouse may lead you to court papers regarding a divorce or probate of a will. Information about [the] subject's educational background may guide you to college yearbooks, a master's thesis, or a doctoral dissertation."

When well-known reference books fail to provide the needed information, a check of American Reference Books Annual, published by Libraries Unlimited, Englewood, Colo., is wise. An excellent alternative is the Guide to Reference Books, published by the American Library Association, Chicago.

Dissertations and Theses

University libraries house doctoral dissertations and master's theses—part secondary source, part primary source—rarely thought of as a source by even experienced journalists. Freelance reporter Jack Tobin said his project about low graduation rates of college athletes "was aided immeasurably when I discovered that a former UCLA fullback had written a doctoral dissertation at another school on that precise topic." Doctoral and master's students often receive unparalleled access to institutions because they are seen as nonthreatening. The smart investigator assumes a thesis or dissertation has been composed on the project at hand, then finds it by using the hard-copy or on-line versions of Dissertation Abstracts International or Masters Abstracts International, published by University Microfilms, Inc.

Books

Despite all the resources mentioned thus far, sometimes the key for an investigator is one good book. To find books illuminating an individual, institution or issue, the journalist should follow the library search steps of Thomas Mann on pages 28–30. To increase chances of locating the most contemporary book, the investigator should look beyond a library catalog search, as it may take some time for a new book to be catalogued.

Guides to already published or about-to-be-published books include Books in Print and Books Out of Print from Bowker-Reed Reference; the magazine Publishers Weekly, New York City, especially its compilation issues of upcoming books; Kirkus Reviews, New York City; Choice, from the Association of College and Research Libraries, Middletown, Conn.; and Book Review Digest from H.W. Wilson Co. The Reader's Adviser from Bowker-Reed Reference lists the best of recent and older books in a multivolume set.

When an investigator locates a useful book, it is wise to contact the author to request any relevant information that may not have found its way between covers but resides, unpublished, in a file drawer.

Secondary Sources on Computer Databases

According to BiblioData, Needham Heights, Mass., publisher of the Newspapers Online directory, several hundred U.S. and international dailies are searchable in full text on one or more computer databases.

Computer database vendors that allow searching of newspapers offer other resources as well. Investigators can grasp the universe by consulting the Directory of Online Databases, from Gale Research. A recent edition lists about 5,000 databases accessible through about 700 vendors.

Nora Paul at the Poynter Institute for Media Studies categorizes vendors as superstores, boutiques and hybrids. The superstores include Dialog, Nexis/Lexis, Dow Jones News/Retrieval, DataStar, NewsNet and DataTimes. These vendors provide access to databases produced by hundreds of organizations. Each superstore offers access to some of the same resources—for example, the Washington Post is available through many of them—but each has exclusive access to other resources. (For many years, the New York Times was available only through Nexis/Lexis, and Dow Jones News/Retrieval could say it was the only database to carry the Wall Street Journal, the New York Times *and* the Los Angeles Times.)

Paul defines boutiques as "database vendors that specialize in providing access to certain types of information"—only television news transcripts or driver's records, for example. A variation on the boutique is local government as vendor. In Dade County, Fla., the county's computer services department provides access to everything from civil court records to parking tickets to property assessment records.

Hybrids—such as CompuServe, America Online, GEnie, Prodigy and Delphi—provide access to information similar to what is available from superstores, but also offer bulletin boards for communicating with people of like interests, not to mention online shopping, airline schedules and games. The hybrids offer gateways to certain superstores, so both can be searched on the same subscription and with greater ease thanks to the gateway's menus.

Full-text databases are usually preferable to those providing citations or abstracts only. Full text means passing references to the main subject will show up. The passing reference might hold the key to the investigation. While searching full-text databases for references to Armand Hammer, I found his name in footnotes to judges' opinions and near the bottom of feature stories; some of those footnotes and bottom paragraphs became starting points for entire new sections of my biography.

No matter which vendor an investigator chooses, the cost consists of some combination of six components: a long-distance charge (some vendors offer local tie-in telephone numbers); a connect charge levied by the system vendor, usually a per-minute rate common to every database; a charge for the number of minutes spent on-line in a particular database based on an hourly rate, which typically falls between $30 and $100; a display charge, varying from database to database within the same vendor, determined by how many and what types of records are called to the screen during a search; a fee for the number of items printed in hard copy or downloaded onto a disk during a search; and a monthly fee or monthly minimum.

Comparing prices across vendors can be difficult. A librarian at USA Today believed she could save money by reducing usage of Nexis/Lexis, substituting vendors such as CompuServe. Indeed, she found that retrieving an article cost $6.13 on CompuServe and $14.95 on Nexis. But when she performed a similar test with an article from a different publication, the costs on CompuServe and Nexis were almost the same. Some of the best money-saving tips come from Nora Paul in her booklet "Computer-Assisted Research: A Guide to Tapping Online Information."

Whatever the cost, learning about computer databases is vital: They are often superior to print indexes not only because of broader coverage and full text, but also because the searcher can combine terms, such as "organized crime" and "waste haulers," capturing only items mentioning those terms together. A print index such as the Readers' Guide to Periodical Literature from H.W. Wilson Co., on the other hand, allows a searcher to check just one term at a time. Fortunately, even the Readers' Guide is now searchable online.

Another point: A recent print version of Encyclopedia of Associations shows 14 entries in its index under "homeless"—mostly organizations with that word in their name. An on-line search of the same encyclopedia yields at least 80 references, because the text of the organizations' entries is included. The text lists areas of emphasis; "homeless" shows up in the text even when it is not part of the organization's name.

Increasingly, information available from computer databases cannot be found in print indexes. That is true not only for some secondary sources, such as privately published newsletters, but also for certain primary sources from government agencies. The U.S. Geological Survey discontinued its paper copy of Selected Water Resources Abstracts, allowing private providers to make it available in electronic format only. Another resource with no hard-copy equivalent is Mednews, which includes statistics and news from the federal Centers for Disease Control and the Food and Drug Administration amid original columns about AIDS and other health topics.

The Internet

A network of computer networks, the Internet is the broadest ranging repository of electronic information. In 1980, the Internet had about 200 connected host computers; now the number is in the millions.

Journalists have started discussing the Internet in their own publications. Joe Abernathy wrote in the Columbia Journalism Review that

> once you have an account on any machine connected to the net you can make remote use of any other machine connected to the net, anywhere in the world. You might remotely access the catalog of the City University of New York library, the White Sands Missile Range library of computer software, or a repository of pending legislation.

A Kansas City Star reporter used the Internet's Fedworld gateway to pull up the electronic bulletin board of the federal Food and Drug Administration. It was not an idle search—he was investigating FDA mishandling of a toxic warehouse fire that contaminated food. While perusing the bulletin board, he noticed an obscure reference to the agency awarding contracts to the same companies that had botched disposal of the contaminated food.

Some commercial on-line services offer gateways to the Internet. That is fortunate, because the network is not user friendly. When the Chronicle of Higher Education offered its resources on the Internet, including "a schedule of congressional hearings of interest to the men and women of academe," a summary of instructions read like this: "Internet users with Gopher software may find 'Academe This Week' at chronicle.merit.edu. Other Internet users may find 'Academe This Week' under 'All the Gopher Servers in the World.' For more information, send an electronic-mail message to help@chronicle.merit.edu."

Although the Internet is difficult to learn, the effort is worth it. One guide is the Directory of Electronic Journals, Newsletters and Academic Discussion Lists from the Association of Research Libraries, Washington, D.C. An example of an electronic journal—440 are mentioned in a recent edition—is the Education Policy Analysis Archives, covering schooling at all levels in many nations. An example of a discussion list is the Forensic Medicine and Sciences Interest Group, which shares information about presenting evidence in court while serving as an expert witness. Bruce Maxwell's book "Washington Online: How to Access the Federal Government on the Internet" is jargon-free and filled with illuminating examples.

Database Searching in the Real World of Journalism

Whether accomplished through the Internet, Nexis/Lexis or some other vehicle, computerized searches enhance deadline stories as well as long-term projects. For instance, when one businessman emerged as a figure in the Iran-Contra scandal during the Ronald Reagan–George Bush administrations, journalists knew almost nothing about him. The wire services described him only as a mysterious entrepreneur. Curious, a Los Angeles Times searcher typed the name into the Nexis database, where he learned that the "mysterious" businessman had been involved in a huge Canadian bankruptcy. The bankruptcy files provided voluminous information.

Another instance: When a chartered airplane crashed shortly after takeoff from Reno, Nevada, killing 70 passengers who were returning to Minneapolis from a gambling trip, reporter Joe Rigert collaborated with a Star Tribune librarian to learn about the accident record of that model plane. The librarian, figuring newspapers elsewhere might have reported crashes, searched Nexis. He started by linking the names of the manufacturer and model with "accidents" and "crashes." The computer informed him that more than 100 articles contained those linked words. Some were indeed news accounts of earlier crashes; others were follow-ups about investigations by the National Transportation Safety Board and Federal Aviation Administration.

Rigert plugged the results into his story: "The NTSB . . . had found that the [model] had the worst fatal accident rate per hours of flight of any aircraft in common use for a 10-year period. . . . The database search also turned up reports over the years of the plane crashing or being forced to make emergency landings because wings or propellers fell off."

That a librarian rather than a reporter took the lead in searching is common. Librarians are specialists in devising search strategies, as well as being fluent in specific databases. Searching inefficiently can be costly in two ways. First, an inefficient searcher might end up with incomplete or misleading results. Second, an inefficient searcher might end up spending more money than anticipated by failing to narrow the terms adequately. Searching databases while writing my Armand Hammer biography, I learned that entering just his last name would yield not only articles about my subject, but also references to a tool used to pound nails, plus anything from the sports world using the word as a verb, as in the Dodgers "hammered" the Mets on the baseball diamond.

A novice searcher who cannot rely on an experienced librarian has options. The best is achieving fluency—most vendors offer training. A second option is gaining access through an institution that subscribes on a flat-rate basis, which means the cost per year is predetermined no matter how many hours are spent on-line. A third option is searching on a computer loaded with a CD-ROM (compact disk, read-only memory). A compact disk contains the same type of information found on-line, but is not updated as frequently.

The University of Missouri library, in my hometown, has many CD-ROM databases. An example is the CD-ROM version of Medline, with articles from thousands of journals covering biomedicine, nursing, dentistry and reproductive biology. Some of the most helpful CD-ROM databases are produced by Information Access Co., Foster City, Calif., including the National Newspaper Index and InfoTrac, which mixes general-interest and scholarly periodicals. Perhaps the most comprehensive directory is CD-ROMs in Print from Mecklermedia, Westport, Conn.

■ USING LIBRARIES EFFICIENTLY

Whether searching hard-copy resources or computer databases, too many investigators fail to use libraries. The IRE Journal asked Thomas Mann, a Library of Congress reference specialist, to discuss research for investigative journalists. Mann, author of "A Guide to Library Research Methods" and "Library Research Models," suggests researchers follow seven steps. Although an experienced library user, I tried Mann's suggestions. They enhanced my research results immediately.

1. Find the best search terms by using controlled vocabulary subject headings. An investigator who enters a library to learn about the "death penalty" is wrong to assume that all the relevant information is grouped under that term. The best material might be found under "capital punishment," "legal execution" or some other term.

Once a researcher has found a useful book, the bottom lines of the title page should be checked for a "tracing," the subject heading assigned to that title. It can be used to find other books.

The most systematic way of finding the right subject heading is to consult the thick red books found in any major library, the Library of Congress Subject Headings. A recent four-volume edition contains about 12,000 personal name headings, 2,800 corporate headings, 27,000 geographic headings and 151,000 topic headings.

"This is the list of acceptable terms, with cross-references from the ones that don't work to the ones that do. For example, 'death penalty' will tell you to see 'capital punishment' instead," Mann says. "Unfortunately, very few researchers . . . seem to know that these books exist. Most just jump into the catalog with whatever terms they happen to think of, rather than find the headings that are formally acceptable." The volumes show narrower terms than the original one. For example, the heading "divorce" yields a narrower heading "children of divorced parents." The heading "suicide" refers investigators to "youth—suicidal behavior." The holdings of many libraries can be searched simultaneously through online public access catalogs. Mecklermedia publishes the OPAC Directory to help searchers in getting started.

2. Systematic browsing. Browsing library shelves can turn up otherwise-overlooked books. It works best if the researcher understands that books on the same topic are scattered throughout the building. Books about drug abuse have a home base in the HV5800 classification (social pathology) of the Library of Congress system. But drug abuse books also appear in AS35 (societies), BV4470 (pastoral theology), LB1044 (teaching), QP37 (human physiology), several H classes (social sciences) besides HV, several KF areas (U.S. law), several R classes (medical) and under Z (bibliographies about drug abuse).

3. Key word searches in manual indexes. "What do you do when you want sources on 'managing sociotechnical change' and there is no good subject heading that corresponds to this topic?" Mann asks. "Or on 'urban sprawl'? Some topics fall between the cracks of the formally approved subject headings; others represent subjects that are too new to have been established in the system. While browsing may work to some extent in circumventing the lack of such headings, key word indexes usually work better."

Mann says the best are published by the Institute for Scientific Information, Philadelphia: the Science Citation Index, Social Sciences Citation Index and Arts and Humanities Citation Index. These indexes cover academic and professional journals, indexing articles by key words. "They enable you to look up any exact words to see if two or more of the precise terms you want have appeared in the title of a journal article," Mann says. "You can thus look for the exact word 'sociotechnical' to see if it is paired with 'management' or 'planning.' It is."

4. Citation searches in manual indexes or on-line. The basic citation sources are the Institute for Scientific Information indexes named in step three. "With a citation search," Mann says, "you have to start with a known source. It can be a book, a magazine or journal article, a dissertation, a conference paper—whatever. It can date from last year or 200 years ago—that does not matter either. A citation search will tell you if someone has written a later journal article that cites the source in the footnote." While researching Armand Hammer, I looked up a book he had written in the 1930s. By learning who had cited it since, I found information that would have escaped my attention otherwise.

5. Searching published bibliographies. Many journalists never consult bibliographies, even though they list hundreds of relevant published works that would take months for the journalist to compile. After finding the Library of Congress subject heading, an investigator can plug it into these two formats in the library's main catalog: "SUBJECT HEADING—Bibliography" or "SUBJECT HEADING—Geographic subdivision—Bibliography."

Starting with the broad topic "criminology," an investigator will locate bibliographies on arson, capital punishment, embezzlement, family violence, gangs, gun control, juvenile delinquency, halfway houses, organized crime, parole, prisons, probation, rape and work release, to provide a sampling. An alternative is to use the appropriate search term in the Bibliographic Index, published by H.W. Wilson Company, a listing of published bibliographies, including those with 50 or more citations at the end of books and journal articles. The first cousin to the bibliography is the directory. About 16,000 directories are listed in Directories in Print (Gale Research).

6. Computer and CD-ROM searches. These are covered elsewhere in this chapter (see page 27) and in Chapter 2 (pages 42–44).

7. Talk to human sources who can explain the paper trail.

Mann's employer, the Library of Congress, is the ultimate repository for secondary-source materials. From the Library's various reading rooms, it is possible to request a large percentage of books and periodicals printed in English and other languages.

The library allows searches of Scorpio, the in-house database, which guides access to secondary sources as well as many primary documents. It contains most books written in English published in the United States since 1978; periodical articles on thousands of topics, going back to 1976; congressional files by topic, bill number, committee, subcommittee, or member of Congress; plus a list of experts from about 15,000 organizations. The library's information office handles requests for reports from the Congressional Research Service—which usually go only to members of Congress—as well as interviews of subject-matter experts at the library.

The Library of Congress is not the only national library useful to investigators. The National Library of Medicine in Bethesda, Md., and the National Agricultural Library, Beltsville, Md., house collections and experts rarely consulted by journalists.

Most federal agencies operate subject-specific libraries in their Washington-area headquarters, which contain a mix of secondary and primary source information. In the Environmental Protection Agency library, I found privately published periodicals previously unknown to me; I also found EPA-generated information about hazardous-waste sites that I had not seen published anywhere. Federal agency libraries are listed in Gale Research's Subject Directory of Special Libraries and Information Centers. Volume one of the three-volume set lists business, government and law libraries; volume two covers computer, engineering and science libraries; volume three is devoted to health sciences libraries.

Mann suggests checking with reference librarians, "especially if you think you already know what the best sources are. We can almost always suggest additional sources you have never heard of, and that you would never find on your own."

Chapter 2

PRIMARY DOCUMENTS

Obtaining the Best Evidence

The newspaper clipping is dated now, but it is still my favorite example of how a journalist can enhance a story by following the trail of primary documents—which contain the most reliable evidence available.

It was 1984. Brooks Jackson, then a Wall Street Journal reporter, heard rumors that U.S. Sen. Gary Hart, a presidential candidate, had inexplicably falsified his age, making himself appear a year younger than he was.

Many reporters would have asked Hart's press secretary, sought comment from the Republican opposition, then published an inconclusive "on the one hand, on the other hand" article. Not Jackson. In his 22-paragraph story, Jackson cited these sources:

- ☐ Hart's certificate of birth, which showed his name as Gary Hartpence;
- ☐ His voter registration in Denver, where he moved to practice law in 1968. It turned out to be the earliest document unearthed by Jackson that showed the incorrect birthdate of Nov. 28, 1937, rather than 1936.
- ☐ A statement of candidacy for reelection to the U.S. Senate. Hart swore to its truth in front of a notary public. The statement gave Hart's birthdate as Nov. 28, 1937;
- ☐ A book by Hart, where he writes, "In 1937, the year I was born . . .";
- ☐ Driver's license applications at the Colorado Division of Motor Vehicles, which showed the wrong birthdate;

☐ Hundreds of newspaper articles from 1972 mentioning Hart because of his role as director of George McGovern's presidential campaign. Hart apparently did nothing to correct the wrong age in those articles;

☐ The biography provided by Hart to the Congressional Directory, which listed the wrong birthdate in every edition since his election;

☐ Hart's entry in Who's Who in America, provided and verified by him. The date had been incorrect since Hart's original listing;

☐ An application for a commission in the U.S. Navy Reserve, submitted by Hart, which showed the incorrect birthdate;

☐ Hart's student records from college and divinity school, which showed the correct birthdate, as did his file at the Denver Bar Association and personnel records at the U.S. Justice Department, where he worked after graduating from law school.

Documents can be revealing in high-impact ways. As Jackson's digging demonstrates, sometimes documents are inaccurate; after all, they are completed by human beings who can be forgetful or deceptive. But even when documents are incorrect, an investigator can use them as Jackson did for the Hart story.

Freelance investigative journalist Bruce Selcraig wrote this to me while a U.S. Senate staff member looking into the transportation of toxic waste:

Document A is the yearly report filed by the receiver of the waste. . . . In this case, it is the Northside Sanitary Landfill. In this report, Northside is telling how much waste it supposedly received from one company during the past year. The company is Titan Oil.

Document B is the yearly report filed by the generator of the waste. . . . In this report, Titan Oil is telling how much waste it had transported to a certain facility. The facility is Northside.

You catch on, obviously. The two should match perfectly. But Northside said it received 1,517 pounds of waste from Titan, and Titan said it sent 10,187,500 pounds to Northside. . . .

It makes sense to examine relevant papers before interviewing people during the research process. Mike Baxter and Jim Savage of the Miami Herald illustrated the benefit of doing so during their investigation of an obscure housing developer supposedly involved in bilking the federal government. As recounted by Leonard Downie in "The New Muckrakers," Baxter and Savage received a tip about the developer's allegedly illegal behavior. But as they interviewed the obvious human sources (other developers, real estate agents, federal housing officials), the investigators kept coming up blank. Nobody seemed to know anything about the developer in question. Miami Herald clipping files didn't yield anything either. The city directory listed the supposed developer as proprietor of a hearing aid business.

It was too soon to interview the subject; if he lied how would Baxter and Savage be able to contradict him? Baxter, believing in his heart that the tipster was reliable, decided to dig through land records at the local courthouse, looking for any transactions with the developer's name. He found them. In fact, day after day, week after week, Baxter turned up land records linking the developer to the Federal Housing Administration. When Baxter and Savage finally interviewed their subject, they were prepared to detect his lies based on the knowledge they had gained from documents.

No reference book lists every document available at every government agency and in every library, not even superb guides such as "Introduction to United States Government Information Sources" by Joe Morehead and Mary Fetzer. There are thousands of types of documents. Lou Rose, of the St. Louis Post-Dispatch, author of "How to Investigate Your Friends and Enemies," has mined many of them. He says,

> There are people I've constructed who I've never met. I can tell them, totally from the public record, when and where they were born, the color of their eyes, how many cars they own, what they paid for them, where they borrowed the money for them, how often they trade cars, whether they have been divorced, whether they've gotten traffic tickets, how long they've owned their home, the whole history of their real property, what their credit reports are.

That is what a New York Times reporter did on deadline after the arrest of a suspect on charges of murdering five people on a Long Island Railroad commuter train. By combining documents research with human sources, he found the accused's birthdate, parents' names and living circumstances, siblings' names, primary and secondary schools attended, jobs held, workers' compensation history, marriage and divorce dates, college record and evidence of the California gun purchase prior to the mass killing in New York.

The Three "I"s

Which documents a journalist seeks first depends on whether the story is mainly about an individual, institution or issue (the three "I"s). Every project falls primarily into one of those three categories.

During an investigation of an individual, a journalist probably will examine the subject's property holdings, driver's license, automobile registration, voter's registration, plaintiff or defendant status in lawsuits and divorce proceedings, to name a few possibilities. An investigation of an institution might pass over those documents, instead examining records from government agencies such as the National Labor Relations Board and the Equal Employment Opportunity Commission. An investigation of an issue (for instance, disposal of nuclear waste) would pass over such items as driving, voting, divorce and NLRB records, concentrating instead on Nuclear Regulatory Commission filings plus congressional and state legislative hearings.

After deciding which "I" to focus on, the experienced investigator will consider which level of government (federal, state, county, city, special district) to explore first. Returning to the nuclear waste example, the Nuclear Regulatory Commission is a federal agency with headquarters in Washington, D.C. Most states lack an equivalent agency; regulation of nuclear power plants is accomplished primarily by the federal government. So the investigator will seek documents at the federal agency's headquarters and at its closest regional office. There is no point spending time at state agencies until determining what the federal agency will yield.

On the other hand, if the investigation involves an insurance company, the experienced investigator knows the federal government plays a small role. The appropriate state insurance commission would be the place to start. Picking the correct level of government is *not* a matter of common sense. There is nothing inherently logical about nuclear power plants being regulated by the federal government or insurance companies by state governments.

To decide whether the federal government is involved, the quickest guide is the U.S. Government Manual. It is available from the U.S. Government Printing Office in Washington, D.C., or almost any library. If an agency's entry in the U.S. Government Manual looks promising, the next step is contacting a public affairs officer to request the agency's annual report and studies relevant to the investigation, including those prepared because of congressional laws.

Having decided which level of government to mine first, an investigator should search *all* branches of that government. Every level has three branches—legislative, executive and judiciary. If that sounds like basic civics, it is. Unfortunately, many investigators fail to use their civics to gather the best evidence.

The Nuclear Regulatory Commission, for example, while an executive branch agency, is implementing laws approved by Congress, the legislative branch. That means it makes sense for the investigator to read the debates leading to passage of the laws affecting the NRC as recounted in the Congressional Record, a daily account of U.S. Senate and House of Representatives activity. Furthermore, it is quite likely that laws and NRC rules have been challenged. So the investigator can look for lawsuits naming the Nuclear Regulatory Commission, starting with U.S. district courts.

■ THE SOCIAL SECURITY NUMBER AS DOOR OPENER

An individual's Social Security number, because it is used as a quasi-national identifier, can help in finding documents within any level or branch of government. A Social Security number tells an investigator where the subject lived when applying. Because so many people apply in their state of birth, the knowledge gained can save an investigator time when searching for a birth certificate. The first three digits show state of issuance:

001–003	New Hampshire	440–448	Oklahoma
004–007	Maine	449–467	Texas
008–009	Vermont	468–477	Minnesota
010–034	Massachusetts	478–485	Iowa
035–039	Rhode Island	486–500	Missouri
040–049	Connecticut	501–502	North Dakota
050–134	New York	503–504	South Dakota
135–158	New Jersey	505–508	Nebraska
159–211	Pennsylvania	509–515	Kansas
212–220	Maryland	516–517	Montana
221–222	Delaware	518–519	Idaho
223–231	Virginia	520	Wyoming
232–236	West Virginia	521–524	Colorado
237–246	North Carolina	525, 585	New Mexico
247–251	South Carolina	526–527	Arizona
252–260	Georgia	528–529	Utah
261–267	Florida	530	Nevada
268–302	Ohio	531–539	Washington
303–317	Indiana	540–544	Oregon
318–361	Illinois	545–573	California
362–386	Michigan	574	Alaska
387–399	Wisconsin	575–576	Hawaii
400–407	Kentucky	577–579	District of Columbia
408–415	Tennessee	580	Virgin Islands
416–424	Alabama	580–584	Puerto Rico
425–428	Mississippi	586	Guam, American Samoa, other Pacific territories
429–432	Arkansas		
433–439	Louisiana		

Special cases: Vietnamese and other refugees entering the United States received California numbers 568–30 through 568–58 between 1975 and 1979.

North Carolina received 232–30 from West Virginia. Before 1963, workers covered under the Railroad Retirement Act received 700 through 728 no matter what the state of residence at the time of application.

The fourth and fifth digits, called the group number, divide geographic areas into more manageable chunks for the Social Security Administration. In theory, a group number could range from 01 to 99, but some are intentionally unassigned; an investigator checking the validity of a number should ask the Social Security Administration whether the group number is false.

A Lawrence (Mass.) Eagle-Tribune reporter wrote in Uplink, the newsletter of the National Institute for Computer-Assisted Reporting, about how he obtained a state government computer tape of area welfare recipients, complete with Social Security numbers. With that tape in house, he asked a different Massachusetts agency for a computer tape of workers' compensation awards.

His intention was to learn how many welfare recipients winning worker's compensation claims illegally failed to tell the welfare office. But the second agency said it would have to omit Social Security numbers. The reporter protested. The agency then said it would provide the Social Security number, but only after it removed names and dates of birth. Knowing he already possessed that information from the first agency, he agreed to the compromise. Eventually he was able to report that 99 percent of welfare recipients receiving workers' compensation were cheating.

◼ Primary Documents as Entry Points

If a Social Security number is unavailable, there are other entry points to information gathering. Something as innocuous as a voter's registration application in Missouri shows state of birth (helping an investigator narrow the search for a birth certificate), age, previous place of residence, length of residence at the current address and occupation. When Des Moines investigators John P. Dolan Jr. and Lisa Lacher compiled the Iowa Public Records Manual, the looseleaf notebook ran to thousands of pages. To unify the manual, Dolan and Lacher created Dr. Willoughby F. Wrighteous. They show how almost every aspect of Wrighteous' life can be illuminated through documents.

Investigators in jurisdictions besides Des Moines benefit from local records manuals. One of the best is Access, a guide to documents in Boone County, Missouri. A library science professor at the University of Missouri served as editor. Access has since been updated by the Freedom of Information Center, School of Journalism, University of Missouri. Investigators anywhere might find a local guide, especially in a newsroom or a journalism school. If none exists, guides from elsewhere can suggest records to be found locally.

The Uniform Commercial Code Example

When an individual borrows money and promises to repay on schedule, the lender, wanting legal protection, might file a Uniform Commercial Code statement. It is called "uniform" because it has been in use by every state but Louisiana since the early 1950s. The statement is filed under the borrower's name. It is found at the office of the county recorder of deeds or the secretary of state's office in the capital.

I have used Uniform Commercial Code statements to document who is doing business with whom. For example, while checking a rumor that a local politician voted to shift the city's money from one local bank to another in exchange for favorable personal loans, I found bank officials invoking confidentiality. So I looked at UCC filings under the name of the politician as a first step in establishing a borrower-lender relationship. I have also used UCC forms to learn the address of a borrower unlisted in telephone directories; the name of a borrower's spouse or business partner; dates of transactions plugged into a chronology about my subject's rise or fall; and property owned by the borrower, listed as collateral, of which I had been unaware.

Dennis King emphasizes UCC forms as a tipoff to further investigation: If the borrower lists an airplane or yacht as collateral, those can lead to other documents. If the collateral listed is a painting, that knowledge could initiate inquiries into the subject's relationships with art dealers. When a UCC filing reveals the subject borrowed from a marginal finance company, that suggests the subject has a poor credit rating.

While investigating government contracts to supposedly minority-owned construction companies, reporters have consulted UCC forms. One reporting team heard companies owned by whites were using minority persons as fronts to gain government contracts. So they looked for UCC filings by lenders who provided money to the minorities. Then they looked for follow-up transactions between minorities and white contractors suggesting the contractors were assuming financial responsibility for the original loan. That could be an indication the minority contractors lacked adequate capital to meet the payback requirements.

From UCCs to Tax Documents

If an individual or institution has borrowed money (as evidenced by UCC filings or other documents), is the borrower having difficulty repaying the loan? An experienced investigator will explore that possibility. Borrowers sometimes end up with liens placed against their property by the Internal Revenue Service or a state agency due to unpaid taxes. The lien is generally filed at the recorder's office in the borrower's home county, although in some states federal tax liens are filed in one office while state tax liens are filed elsewhere. The personal property–real property distinction also might determine where an investigator will locate the documents.

When Donald Barlett and James Steele of the Philadelphia Inquirer examined 20,000 tax liens during an investigation of the Internal Revenue Service, they found a physician who owed more than $900,000 in income taxes and an insurance executive who owed more than $2 million. Debtors often end up paying far less than owed. Settlements for reduced payments are filed at an IRS regional office or IRS headquarters. Settlements, liens and UCC filings can lead investigators to tax cases that end up in court, where the documentation is rich. U.S. Tax Court, tax cases in district courts and bankruptcy courts will be treated more fully in Chapter 10.

If a borrower fails to pay local property taxes, the property can be sold at auction. Every week in my local newspaper, I scan unpaid property auction notices. Frequently the debtor is prominent in the community. Then I visit the appropriate county or city building to find the underlying documents, which help determine if the potential exists for an investigation or a daily news story.

Birth and Death Records in the States

Another category of primary documents is "vital records": birth, death, marriage and divorce certificates. They help locate sources as well as provide information about subjects under investigation. Researching a biography of the elusive writer Hunter S. Thompson, an author began her magazine profile of him by reprinting his birth certificate data. When the Washington Post published a feature about the previously unknown half-brother of U.S. President Bill Clinton, the graphic included a reproduction of the half-brother's Texas birth certificate.

As with all documents, the information contained in vital records might be misleading. After analyzing death certificates for Harper's Magazine, a reporter gave an example: the pianist Liberace's doctor had listed subacute encephalopathy, a brain disease, as the cause of death, but the coroner, citing autopsy findings of a form of pneumonia found in patients with AIDS, rejected the certificate; the coroner said Liberace's doctor had known the truth all along. The lesson: Investigators must try to verify information in primary documents.

In many states, vital records are kept at the county level and in the capital. Ease of access varies from state to state. The federal Department of Health and Human Services publishes a guide to birth and death record locations in the states. So do private publishers, including the Consumer Education Research Center, South Orange, N.J. Private companies are crossing state lines to gather vital statistics in ways that make searching more efficient⁄For example, Cambridge Statistical Research Associates, Irvine, Calif., offers a CD-ROM containing millions of death records compiled from social security master files. ⁄

Depository Libraries

Federal and state depository libraries allow investigators to find lots of primary documents in one location. The U.S. Congress Joint Committee on Printing publishes A Directory of U.S. Government Depository Libraries; it lists about 1,400. Depository libraries decide which documents to order from the government; those designated as regional depositories must carry certain items as well as provide interlibrary loan and reference services. Every federal depository carries the federal budget, census of housing and population, the Congressional Record, U.S. Government Manual, Federal Register, a monthly catalog of the Government Printing Office, subject bibliographies, Weekly Compilation of Presidential Documents, U.S. Supreme Court decisions, U.S. Code (laws divided by subject matter into 50 titles) and Code of Federal Regulations (regulations meant to implement the laws).

It is harder to generalize about state government depository libraries. In Missouri, the library is operated by the secretary of state's office. Public libraries in St. Louis and Kansas City are full depositories, as are libraries on eight university campuses. Another 28 libraries are partial depositories—they are a mix of public and campus sites. The state library issues a monthly checklist of new publications, plus a cumulative "Missouri State Government Serial Publications." More and more libraries can access each others' catalogs from remote computer sites.

The Monthly Catalog of United States Government Publications, covering materials from all branches of government back to 1895, is a sensible starting point for finding government documents. Listings are primarily by subject; since 1974, author and title have been indexed, too.

Wise investigators supplement the Catalog when aiming at comprehensiveness. As explained by Judith Schiek Robinson in "Tapping the Government Grapevine: The User-Friendly Guide to U.S. Government Information Sources,"

> Although the monthly catalog is the most comprehensive listing of federal documents, it has omissions which should be noted. [It] does not index individual articles in government periodicals [that is handled separately by the Index to U.S. Government Periodicals], provide abstracts, index federal specifications or comprehensively list government audiovisuals, databases,

technical reports and certain agency special publications, such as those of the National Aeronautics and Space Administration or the Department of Defense. One particular danger of becoming too fond of the monthly catalog is forgetting its poor coverage of technical reports. Overlap between the monthly catalog and the National Technical Information Service's Government Reports Announcements and Index, the most comprehensive index of technical reports, is only 10 percent.

The technical reports referred to by Robinson are intended for experts, but can be useful to journalists. Most are sponsored by three agencies: the Defense Department, Energy Department, and National Aeronautics and Space Administration. They publish their own indexes, too—the Defense Technical Information Center index, Energy Research Abstracts supplemented by its computerized Energy Data Base, and Scientific and Technical Aerospace Reports, respectively.

The National Technical Information Service offers more than 2 million reports at any given time. They are divided into subject categories (examples are health care and transportation), which are in turn divided into hundreds of topics. Many are derived from overseas research. Reports are available from the sponsoring agency, the funding recipient or NTIS, U.S. Department of Commerce, Springfield, Va.

Proceedings of technical/scientific conferences are rarely consulted by journalists, even though many proceedings break new ground. Proceedings throughout the world are indexed. The Institute for Scientific Information, Philadelphia, publishes the Index to Scientific and Technical Proceedings, covering thousands of meetings annually. Here is an example from the "Forestry" category: "International Symposium on Fire and the Environment—Ecological and Cultural Perspectives." The specific presentations listed would excite any journalist interested in covering natural resources. In addition, ISI publishes Current Contents, which reproduces table-of-content pages from hundreds of scientific journals.

Once a journalist has located a promising technical report, the task of evaluating the information begins. Is it biased? Incomplete? The task is difficult, but the best investigators tackle it with delight. That is the essence of investigative reporting—cracking the code to produce a new understanding.

Scientific proceedings are often filled with statistics. Journalists usually shy away from numbers, a tendency that can lead to shortchanging their audiences. The American Statistics Index, from Congressional Information Service, Bethesda, Md., details comprehensible federal sources; it even covers charts and tables appearing in largely nonstatistical government publications.

Investigators will find background, statistical or text, by consulting subject bibliographies compiled within agencies, then distributed through the Government Printing Office. An example is the bibliography Water

Pollution and Water Resources, which lists three pages of government publications, including "America's Wetlands: Our Vital Link Between Land and Water" and "Quality Criteria for Water."

Congressional hearings and publications are especially valuable for journalists. A superb guide is the Congressional Information Service Index, published in Bethesda, Md. It allows investigators to search by topic, congressional committee, institutions mentioned prominently, or individuals testifying. It is available in hard copy or on-line. By using it, I found hearings in which members of Congress questioned Armand Hammer, plus references to him and his corporations. Depository libraries carry congressional committee hearings and reports in hard copy or on microform.

The National Archives Systems

Besides the Library of Congress and its satellite depositories, a government repository filled with primary documents is the National Archives. Journalists mine the archives rarely because they think of it as containing "historical" records. But much of the history is recent, with relevance for contemporary investigations. The Guide to Federal Records in the National Archives of the United States, from the Government Printing Office, makes that clear.

The main archives building is in downtown Washington, D.C., supplemented by a new building in College Park, Md., that has relieved overcrowding. The saying chiseled into the stone above the downtown entrance should be a watchword for journalists: "The Past Is Prologue." While researching the Hammer biography, for example, I found documents showing how my subject, then still alive—and therefore not "historical"— had sought favorable government rulings for his business ventures. One of those documents was a passport application that helped verify a crucial point made by a human source. The ins and outs of obtaining passport applications and other documents are explained in Prologue, the archives' magazine.

Documents of local interest are located in regional archives. With the exception of the archives in Anchorage, each region covers at least three states. While researching the Hammer biography, I located a 1905 bankruptcy case involving Hammer's father at the federal records center in Bayonne, N.J. It yielded information about family relationships as well as showing the tendency of Hammer's parents to shade the truth, much like he did in his own life. Each state government operates its own archives, as do institutions such as universities.

The National Archives administers military and some civilian personnel records separately from records centers at two sites in St. Louis.

Perhaps the most thorough guide is "How to Locate Anyone Who Is or Has Been in the Military: Armed Forces Locator Directory" by Richard S. Johnson, an Army lieutenant colonel. Michael Jennings, a Louisville Courier-Journal reporter, used military records to locate the father he had never known. All Jennings had to start with was a common name; hearsay that his father had met Jennings' mother while he was a Marine stationed in North Carolina toward the end of World War II; and a newspaper reference to his father's having served in China. Jennings' account of his search, reprinted in the book "1993 Best Newspaper Writing," included this passage:

> An officer at Camp Lejeune suggested I try the Marine Corps Historical Center in Washington, D.C., the archive for muster rolls—the monthly rosters of all Marines on duty. . . . I visited the historical center . . . and picked up a pamphlet on the Marines operations in North China from 1945 to 1949. From it I learned that in June 1946, the month before my birth, the Marines in China reorganized into three units with an authorized strength of 24,252 men. . . . Within four hours, I found my father. . . . A footnote said that on July 24, the day after my birth, [he] left Tientsin for discharge in the United States.

Tracing the military record backward, Jennings learned something else: his father was a deserter sentenced to military prison. With that information in hand, an alternately hopeful and heartsick Jennings shifted the search to determine if his father was still alive. But that is another story.

Besides military records, the National Archives system encompasses the presidential libraries, from Herbert Hoover through George Bush, which contain documents of interest to contemporary investigators. While researching the Hammer biography, I found references to him in every presidential library. A project on the closing of a local military base would benefit from records in each presidential library back to the year of the base's opening. An explanation about the evolution of the presidential library system is/"Records of the Presidency: Presidential Papers and Libraries From Washington to Reagan"/by Frank L. Schick with Renee Schick and Mark Carroll.

Primary Documents on Commercial Computer Databases

However useful the materials in presidential libraries, the mostly manual retrieval systems there are a contrast to records found today in government databases offered by commercial vendors and by government itself. Investigators searching for documents from a distance because of time or money constraints can do as well as if they were present at the counter of a government agency.

Database vendors publish state-by-state lists of documents covered on-line. By consulting the Lexis/Nexis Library Contents and Alphabetical List, an investigator learns that Lexis covers UCC filings in many states. Lexis and its competitor Westlaw, St. Paul, Minn., are best-known for their on-line state and federal judges' opinions. These include opinions not found in hard copy; the Sixth Circuit U.S. Appeals Court in one recent year issued 550 opinions in hard copy and computer formats while making 2,250 opinions available by computer only.

But Lexis and Westlaw offer so many other primary documents—from the legislative and executive branches as well as the judicial branch—that they are changing the nature of investigative journalism.

Westlaw, for example, offers these primary documents from Missouri: Supreme Court cases (back to 1923); appellate court cases (back to 1944); attorney general opinions (1977); state taxation administrative cases (1979); public utilities reports (1953); current Uniform Commercial Code filings; required filings by corporations and partnerships; insurance regulation cases; all state statutes; and the status of proposed legislation while the legislature is in session.

When it comes to the federal government, the database services offer pending legislation in Congress, compilations of U.S. laws and regulations, plus decisions by many agencies, including attorney general opinions, Office of Government Ethics rulings, and Federal Election Commission advisories. As already noted, the Internet can be used to find many primary documents from the federal government. The reference book The Federal Internet Source from National Journal, Inc., Washington, D.C., lists many of those documents.

Reporters who once found the prospect of traveling to records repositories in county after county (Texas has 254), state after state daunting, now find much of what they seek sitting at a computer terminal. They still have to travel to examine the complete files, but the computer searches provide enough information to make intelligent decisions about which trips to schedule.

The Government's Own Computer Databases

Author Matthew Lesko has called attention to the possibilities in The Federal Data Base Finder: A Directory of Free and Fee-Based Data Bases and Files Available from the Federal Government. A sample entry, from the chapter covering the Department of Health and Human Services, is

"U.S. Cancer Mortality Rates and Trends." The computer file contains cancer mortality rates county by county. The data could be the beginning of a project on why a county is above or below the national average. The national statistics could help document a relationship between cancer and toxic chemical dump sites in a geographic area.

The National Technical Information Service provides a "Directory of U.S. Government Data Files for Mainframes and Microcomputers." It lists computerized record sets from federal agencies, divided into dozens of topics. An example is the Regional Air Pollution Studies, documenting emissions in selected cities hour by hour for three years. The National Technical Information Service also manages Fedworld, a gateway to mostly free government agency bulletin boards. One of the most useful is the USDA's Agricultural Library Forum, accessible on its own or through Fedworld. One of the features it offers is bibliographies on topics of interest to journalists, such as rural health care, nutrition, cancer, poverty, and toxic waste. Government CD-ROMs include the National Economic, Social and Environmental Database produced at the U.S. Commerce Department. It contains a mix of data from the Census, the Justice Department, even airline on-time statistics for individual airports.

When it is practical, newsrooms are linking directly to government computers. The Dayton Daily News linked a newsroom personal computer to Montgomery County government computers. The newspaper paid the county for maintenance on the hookup, plus a monthly fee for a dedicated telephone line. The equipment, including a modem and a device allowing the newsroom computer to emulate a county dedicated terminal, cost a minimal amount. With a few keystrokes, the staff can examine property tax records, deeds, mortgages, civil court dockets, divorce cases and domestic violence filings.

When a Dayton Daily News reporter received a tip from a college student that an immigration lawyer had left town with her money, he tapped into county records from his newsroom desk. He learned that the lawyer had recently purchased a $305,000 home with a $275,000 mortgage, and more recently had taken out a $40,000 second mortgage. He had also bought a $40,000 automobile. It seemed he spent more than he could afford, because a federal tax lien of $36,825 had been placed on his home and a lien of $22,504 on his business. Creditors had sued him; the names of the lawyer's own attorneys showed up on the newsroom computer screen. The reporter also learned about a divorce five years earlier. Because the county's computer database only summarized court records, the reporter telephoned the court clerk, gave her the case numbers and arrived at the courthouse later that day to pick up the waiting folders.

The use by investigators of government-computerized information has given rise to the term "computer-assisted reporting." The conundrum with computers is access to the information. The next chapter discusses access difficulties, along with solutions.

■ PUTTING IT ALL TOGETHER
WITH PRIMARY SOURCES

However documents are gathered, it takes a mind trained to discern connections for the information to yield its meaning. In that spirit, this chapter ends with a timeless account by Patrick Riordan, based on a real project. While he was a Miami Herald reporter, Riordan wrote a chapter for an earlier edition of this book. It is reprinted here, lightly edited:

You're methodically researching your project on the monorail the county wants to build at the new zoo, when your editor starts flailing her arms. The police have an update on a bust at a disco last night. They found marijuana, cocaine and Quaaludes. A Colombian citizen was among those arrested. The police are cooperating with the Drug Enforcement Administration, but not with you. They're giving out nothing beyond the arrest sheets.

There are unanswered questions: Who owns the disco? What else does this person own—land, buildings, cars, boats, airplanes? What's the disco owner's economic background? Has the owner ever been accused of a crime? Does the owner use corporations to hide behind? Is there a limited partnership involved? Who are its investors? How much did they invest?

Public records could answer every one of those questions in a few hours. Let's suppose the police won't even tell you the name of the disco owner. You can still find it. You have the address of the disco from the arrest sheet or the phone book. Go to the office of the tax collector, or the office where deeds are kept on file, and convert the street address into a legal description of the property. In an urban area, that will be a block number and one or more lot numbers in a particular subdivision.

For example, suppose the disco is located at 3000 Coral Blvd. in Miami. Either by asking a clerk or by using the county real estate plat map yourself, you find that 3000 Coral Blvd. is in Miami's Urban Estates subdivision and that your particular address corresponds to Lots 5, 6 and 7 of Block 5. With that information you can find the owner in one of two ways.

The easy way: If your county keeps abstract books, tract indexes or a property index, look up the book page, computer screen or microfilm reel for your subdivision until you come to Block 5. Then go to the last entry under Block 5 and work backward. The first entry you come to for Lots 5, 6 and 7 is the most recent. It reflects the current owner. The harder way: If you don't have abstract books for each subdivision, work through the tax roll. You may need to convert the legal description of the land into a folio number, composed of the block and lot numbers, a code number for the subdivision and municipality and other code numbers for section, range and township—terms you'll encounter more often when you're researching rural acreage. Each piece of property in your county has a unique folio number. The folio number shows who's paying the taxes. About 99 percent of the time, it is the owner. No matter how you get the name of the apparent owner, it is a good idea to double check. Go to the office where the deeds are kept. It is the recorder's office in some states, the registrar of deeds, clerk's office or official records office in others.

In this case, the current owner appears to be something called Taca Corp. Ask for the grantor and grantee indexes (also known as the official records index, the deed index or the index to real estate transfers). To find the owner's deed to the disco property, look up Taca Corp. in the grantee index. There you will find a reference to Book 289, page 34. Find Deed Book 289 on the shelf or in a microfilm drawer. Turn to page 34, and you've got the deed. Taca Corp., it appears, acquired title to the property from Charles Candyman, a name that's vaguely familiar. The corporation owes $50,000 on the property to First Smuggler's Bank and Trust Co. That is its first mortgage. It also owes another $375,000 to Candyman, payable in quarterly installments over 10 years. That is the purchase-money second mortgage. You note in the grantor and grantee indexes that Taca Corp. seems to have several other deeds on file. But before proceeding, you decide to learn a little more about Taca other than its property holdings.

The courthouse office where licenses are kept sheds little light on the subject. Taca holds the local business license in its corporate name. You could check the utilities office to see who pays the water and electricity bills, but you decide to pass for the moment. You call the secretary of state in the capital to ask for the corporate information office. It will give you a lot of information on the phone and send you more by mail. [Since Riordan wrote that passage, many secretary of states' records have become available through commercial computer databases.]

Always ask for current officers and directors, including their addresses; corporate address (also called the registered address); name of the registered agent; nature of the business in which the corporation engages; whether the corporation is up-to-date on its franchise tax; and the date of incorporation. From the original articles of incorporation, you can get the names of the people who formed the corporation, the attorney who handled the paperwork, the notary public who notarized the corporate charter and, sometimes, a more detailed statement about the business in which the corporation engages.

In this case, one name jumps out at you: It is Charles Candyman, who sold the disco to Taca. He turns out to be the president of Taca, its registered agent and one of its original incorporators three years ago. His lawyer, a well-known criminal defense attorney, is Taca's corporate secretary—a little out of his line. Call another agency in the capital, the Uniform Commercial Code office. Taca, you discover, owes a restaurant supply company for its kitchen and bar equipment at the disco, but that's all. Now you call the Alcoholic Beverage Commission or whichever agency licenses bars in your state. The agency will have in its files a list of stockholders of the disco if it has a liquor license.

It turns out that there is only one stockholder—Candyman. A picture is emerging. The disco where the police found the drugs has a complicated corporate structure, but only one man behind it all. That man receives large sums of money in the form of mortgage payments. This could be a clever scheme to steal from the business, then declare bankruptcy. Or it might be Candyman's way of establishing a large, on-the-record taxable income for IRS consumption, in order to conceal his real income from drug smuggling.

Back to the deed books. Those other transactions involving Taca now become much more interesting than they were before. You get copies of all deeds involving the company. With each deed the pattern grows stronger. In your county alone, Taca owns 50 acres near the new free-trade zone, a key parcel next to the seaport and two old downtown hotels in the path of a new convention center, along with three condominium apartments and the disco where the drugs were found. You extend your research. The Uniform Commercial Code office does not have any record of loans on cars, airplanes or boats. Maybe that's because Candyman paid cash for his smuggling vehicles. You call the motor vehicle records office in the capital and explain the general nature of the inquiry.

A state employee looks up Candyman and Taca. Candyman owns a new Seville in his own name with no lien on it. He paid cash. Taca owns three large, straightbody trucks and a jeep, all free and clear. The Department of Natural Resources (or the agency that licenses boats in your state) looks in its files for Candyman and Taca and discovers three Donzi speedboats, each capable of outrunning anything owned by the U.S. Customs Service.

The state Department of Transportation looks up Candyman and Taca. The corporation, it seems, owns two aircraft: a plush, radar-equipped Piper Aztec, suitable for spotting ships at sea and hauling cocaine, and a Convair 220, capable of hauling 10,000-pound payloads. Taca begins to look like a smuggling conglomerate. At the local courthouse, you look up Taca in the index to see if anyone has ever sued it. There's only one case: a patron who slipped and fell on the dance floor, settled out of court.

You look up Candyman and find a divorce file. The property settlement contains a reference to Taca Investors, Ltd. You double back to the deeds office and look up Taca Investors, Ltd., kicking yourself for missing it the first time. You find three deeds and a limited partnership declaration. According to the deeds, the partnership owns an apartment building, rural acreage that includes a landing strip and some ocean-front land with a canal leading to a privately maintained channel where smugglers have been arrested before. Best of all, the declaration of partnership lists Candyman, his lawyer and a city council member as limited partners. The general partner is Taca.

According to the declaration, each investor put up one-third of the investment. But only the general partner, the corporation, can be held financially accountable, and its liability is limited by the state corporation laws. One last stop—at the criminal-court building—confirms what you thought you remembered: Nine years ago Candyman was convicted of selling 600 pounds of marijuana and a kilo of cocaine to an undercover cop. He's got a record as a dealer; he's tied to a public official; he owns boats, planes, trucks, a landing strip and a secluded harbor, all of which he paid cash for; and his criminal defense attorney is his business partner.

You put it all together and call a friendly cop. You tell him what you have. The cop trades you a little information in return: Candyman is about to be arrested, along with five of his lieutenants. The officer asks you to hold the story until Candyman is arrested. You spend the time polishing the writing. Everything you have is tied to a public record. Everything is documented and almost certainly libel-proof.

Chapter 3

COMPUTER-ASSISTED INFORMATION GATHERING AND OTHER ACCESS TOOLS

Secondary and primary sources of information are the life-blood of investigative journalism—when they are available. If access is shut off, investigating becomes more difficult or impossible, as Elliot Jaspin knows.

When Jaspin, of the Providence Journal, asked the Rhode Island Housing and Mortgage Finance Corporation for its computer tape containing records of 30,000 loans, alarm bells rang at the agency. The director of the agency—which sells tax-free bonds to finance mortgages meant to help lower-income home buyers—ordered an employee to delete portions of the tape. The director had plenty to hide, including a secret fund he was using to grant favorable mortgage terms to politically connected people like the governor's daughter.

As Jaspin said later, the director thought he could get away with the deletions for at least two reasons:

> The first was that no one would take the time to leaf through 30,000 mortgage records. That's not unreasonable—a reporter examining one mortgage every five minutes would complete his task in 73 weeks. . . . The second assumption was that because of general computer illiteracy, no one would even know how to look at the electronic record. Again, that's not unreasonable. . . . For the most part, news [organizations] use computers as glorified typewriters.

Jaspin detected the fraud because he was one of the few journalists at that time (1985) who knew how to work with nine-track computer tapes. For him, it was a mission: "The government's use of computers to monitor its operations gives us, in turn, the opportunity to monitor the government. But we can only do this if we devote the time and resources to a long-range, well-financed and well-staffed computer program."

Computers as More Than Sophisticated Typewriters

Today, journalists in hundreds of news organizations are using computer tapes, tape cartridges, CD-ROMs and other technology as part of their information-gathering. Many of them learned the techniques from Jaspin after he established a computer-assisted reporting institute at the University of Missouri School of Journalism. The National Institute for Computer-Assisted Reporting, now under the direction of Investigative Reporters & Editors, publishes Uplink, a monthly newsletter; produces books summarizing projects that benefitted from computers; and presents hands-on workshops in Columbia or in newsrooms.

The National Institute for Advanced Reporting at the Indianapolis campus of Indiana University also offers training. So do the journalism schools at Columbia University in New York City and the University of North Carolina as well as the Transactional Records Access Clearinghouse at Syracuse University. In some newsrooms, training occurs internally. The Raleigh News and Observer is in the forefront of news organizations training as many editorial personnel as possible to use computerized information on a range of stories.

Most journalists are not intuitive about computers; learning how to acquire, read and analyze computerized information is like learning a foreign language. It takes determination and lots of practice. But just as students of foreign languages can take heart from those who have gone before them, so can investigators. "Don't be discouraged if it takes awhile to load your first tape," says Penny Loeb of U.S. News and World Report.

> It took us two weeks. It will load eventually. Pick a project you know you can finish, possibly one done somewhere else in the country. Working through the entire process, from obtaining the tape to analyzing the information and writing the story, will give you a real understanding of computer-assisted journalism.

After the learning curve has flattened, investigators must remember that information on computer tapes is just a beginning, Loeb says: "The story will almost always take longer, maybe twice as long. Once you have analyzed the information, you have to find out the whys of what you found."

To reduce time spent and aggravation incurred on the way to a worthwhile story, Loeb emphasizes obtaining

> the record layout before getting the tape. Analyze it and decide what stories you could do with that information. Always check the tape information against a sample of paper records. That way you will know your wonderful discovery of overpaid taxes or tiny fines for gross abuses is real, not a computer glitch. . . . Find experts who work in the field you are probing. Some have probably analyzed some of the data you are looking at.

Occasionally it makes sense to pull back from high technology. Writing in Uplink, Ronald Campbell of the Orange County (Calif.) Register discussed his search of a computer database on bus inspections in California, a search spawned by a fatal accident:

> The story, and the endless research that went into it, illustrate what I call seduction by technology. Entranced by the siren song of high tech, I pursued a story long after my instincts told me it was not there. . . . I was easy prey for [a] myth—gather enough facts and you are bound to find a great story. All reporters play hunches, looking under rocks for something odd. With computers comes the temptation to look under every grain of sand on the beach. . . . Had I faced a similar quantity of paper records, I instantly would have turned away for a reality check. I would have called some experts, read some reports and chosen one or two angles to explore. Instead I plunged into the database with all the direction of a near-sighted man on a foggy night.

That is a caution, not meant to discourage. Many newsrooms prepare to minimize unsuccessful computer-assisted projects. The St. Paul Pioneer Press newsroom keeps government computer tapes loaded for regular use, including arrest records, drivers licenses and violations, political contributions, census data and a roster of public employees. A reporter tries to update them at least every six months.

■ GEORGE LANDAU ON SOFTWARE

Investigators must choose the best software to extract the needed information. George Landau at the St. Louis Post-Dispatch groups software into three categories: database managers, statistical packages and geographic information systems.

Database managers help investigators search, sort and group data. About the searching function, Landau says, "With the right software, computers can find needles in haystacks. . . . In a matter of seconds, for example, a PC could extract from a master database of death certificates a list of everyone who had died from brain cancer." About sorting: "Using the same database, you could have the computer list those brain cancer victims by ZIP code. You could also sort by name, age, weight, or whatever else is in the database." About grouping: "If you wanted to identify the ZIP code with the most brain cancer deaths, you could tell the software to 'group' on ZIP code, counting up the occurrences within each ZIP, then displaying the resulting list in descending order of frequency."

Concerning statistical packages, Landau says they contain "built-in formulas that can be used to isolate cause-and-effect relationships in a sea of variables. Such software would allow you to analyze court records, for example, to show a link between sentencing and defendants' race— independent of defendants' age and sex, the kind of victim and crime and the specific judges and attorneys involved."

As for geographic information systems, Landau says they allow

mapping of any data with a geographic component, from real estate records to census counts. Analyzing the 1990 census, for example, can be daunting if you don't have software to plot the hundreds of census tracts in a metropolitan area. With a geographic information system, the computer can instantly color each tract to reflect data values—for example, red for tracts that saw increases in median income from 1980, blue for tracts that saw a decline. . . . A good [system] can also plot anything that has a street address. In St. Louis, we used software . . . to "pin map" a database of 18,000 vacant lots. By merging the pin map with a map of the city's 28 political wards, we were able to publish a ranking of vacant lots by ward.

Spreadsheets are another type of software used by journalists; they put numbers in rows and columns, then do calculations on them. A journalist can add, subtract or figure out percentages in less time than it would take with a calculator.

As journalists become comfortable with the software, they can create their own databases from scratch. That is what the Allentown (Pa.) Morning Call did while investigating voided tickets for police who were parking illegally all over town.

The local parking authority refused to release its computer tape, so the reporter sat at the authority's office for two weeks entering data from 2,000 canceled tickets into spreadsheet software loaded into his own laptop computer. He read handwritten notations on the back of tickets, then summarized the reasons for the illegal parking in a special field he had built into the spreadsheet. After finishing the first stage of data entry, he determined, through documents work, which ticketed vehicles were owned by the city and which were private vehicles.

When it was time to write, the reporter used his software to determine which police officers had received the most tickets, how many they received near police stations and the like. The software allowed sorting alphabetically by name, by location and by number. If he needed to refer back to a specific ticket, the software located it in a second or two.

Getting Around Obstacles to Access

The biggest obstacle to computer-assisted reporting is not hardware or software. Rather, it is the same obstacle facing investigators on projects without nine-track tapes: restricted access to government information. Access to paper documents always has been difficult for journalists, even though governments are subject to freedom of information acts. The irony is that just when journalists thought they had reached accommodations with recordkeepers over access to paper documents, disagreements arose over computer tapes.

As Jaspin has sarcastically noted, laws that give the public a right to see information seem straightforward

> until you come to computers. It's a little-known fact that public documents go through a process similar to transubstantiation as soon as they are placed on computers. Government officials have repeatedly said a paper document, which everybody agrees is public, no longer becomes public when they put it on a computer. . . . Why do computer tapes have this magical property? I think that what has happened here is that when I buy a computer tape containing all the state's records, the state suddenly loses control over the analysis of information. To say the least, they don't like that.

Jaspin's strategy to gain access works like this:

> First thing I will do is get the paper records. For example, if I wanted to get [a computer tape of] drivers' licenses, I would go in and get one person's driver's license record. Then I go back and say "How are your records kept on computer?" And generally they are pretty happy . . . to explain to me "Well, we have this thing here and whirls here and lights flash there" and I take notes. . . . Then I come back and I say "Okay, I got the technical specs, and . . . I want it this way, and it's a public record because here's the paper record I got from you folks. Now give it to me."
>   Then they go through a period of fits and moaning at which point you say to them "Here's the state privilege of information act; it says you have got to give it to us." Now at that point they usually cave in. If they don't cave in—this is absolutely key to our operation—it is as certain as the sun comes up that we're going to file a lawsuit.

Obtaining a paper record first is not always possible anymore. A Houston Chronicle series about access told of a local police department entering crime reports into computer terminals with no paper back-up. In the past citizens could read reports at no charge. But citizens now had to pay, sight unseen, for computer printouts. Another police department no longer separated public information from private in computer printouts. Each had to be reviewed by a police lawyer.

David Armstrong of the Boston Globe says money often is a sticking point, as when an agency agrees to provide information on a computer disk; however, it will cost $36,000. Armstrong's response:

> In most instances, the agency attempts to take advantage of the reporter's perceived lack of computer knowledge. . . . Always require a detailed estimate. You want to know Central Processing Unit time cost per hour, the cost per hour of a programmer, and all other costs for which you are being billed. Now that you have that information, here are some favorite, and real, shenanigans to look for. . . . Agencies have attempted to bill the newspaper $60 per hour and up for the work of a government computer programmer. Just do some simple math and calculate the rate out to an annual salary ($117,000). . . . Obviously, no programmer in government is paid that much.

Brant Houston, who directs IRE's CAR institute at the University of Missouri, has probably encountered every ploy to limit access. But he says the overall situation is improving, with some agencies actually promoting use of their computerized information. The Nuclear Regulatory Commission's NUDOCS computer database, for example, is easy-to-use, accessible, up-to-date and accurate. It can be searched from a newsroom or home computer over a toll-free long-distance telephone line. A Cleveland Plain Dealer reporter, who used NUDOCS to help document hospital deaths from overradiation, recommends it for stories about the environment, hospitals, universities, radioactive waste and nuclear power.

State Access Laws

Whether information is computerized or not, each state has its own access laws and regulations. Because investigators often need information from states other than their own, compilations of those laws are helpful. The Reporters Committee for Freedom of the Press in Arlington, Va., publishes a compilation, "Tapping Officials' Secrets." As Congress debated whether to restrict release of drivers' license information in all states, journalists consulted "Tapping Officials' Secrets" to determine that 18 states already restricted access while 32 states practiced openness.

State press associations, usually located in the capital or the largest city, stay current on access laws. Many publish updates in newsletters, as well as printing the law on wallet-sized cards for easy reference. Because press associations must pay attention to so many matters besides access, in many states freedom of information foundations have formed. Two of the most active are the Iowa Freedom of Information Council, based at Drake University, and the Freedom of Information Foundation of Texas, in Dallas.

The Freedom of Information Center at the University of Missouri School of Journalism receives publications from state press associations and other access groups. The center's files are unmatched in their documentation of access controversies. The Brechner Center for Freedom of Information at the University of Florida is another first-class repository.

Journalists must worry about access to meetings as well as to documents. State open meetings laws and federal laws (Government in the Sunshine Act, Federal Advisory Committee Act) are generally satisfactory as written. They are difficult to enforce, however, because telephones, facsimile machines, electronic mail and networked computers make noncompliance simple. So journalists cultivate sources who can provide warning of closed meetings or provide summaries afterwards.

The best meetings laws allow those petitioning for openness to recover attorney fees. If the cost of achieving openness is too dear, few will try. Laws should permit fining and jailing of violators, as well as invalidating actions they took behind closed doors.

The best laws, furthermore, provide for advance notice of government meetings; journalists must take the responsibility of placing their names on mailing lists, checking bulletin boards in public buildings, then showing up if they expect to be taken seriously. One way to stay on top of federal meetings is to read the Congressional Record and the Federal Register: Congressional committees and subcommittees announce meetings in the Congressional Record; federal agency subgroups and advisory committees announce meetings in the Federal Register.

When journalists know about closed sessions in advance, they should enter and refuse to leave, forcing officials to physically evict them or open the meeting. Courtrooms, however, can be an intractable problem; the judiciary generally is exempt from access laws. Some judges are laws unto themselves, closing proceedings arbitrarily. Furthermore, when journalists want access to closed meetings, they are dependent on judges to rule in their favor, making it awkward for news organizations to challenge the judiciary's own secretiveness.

Because so many public officials are part of the problem, investigators need to understand why they are so determined to prevent access to what should be the public's business, then try to change those attitudes. Occasionally public officials speak openly about the downside of secrecy; journalists should ally with them. A strategy adopted by some journalists when denied access is to persuade the city attorney, county attorney or state attorney general to call the recalcitrant official. If that fails, a top news executive should ask the mayor, county commissioner or governor why the government is keeping the contents of the documents from the public. It is a dense politician who misses the drift of a conversation like that.

Federal Access Laws

The federal government is usually more formidable on access issues than state or local governments. The reason is simple: being a freedom of information bureaucrat is a full-time job in the federal government, so they are more sophisticated at foiling journalists.

But if journalists give up before using access laws, the bureaucrats have won by default—which is precisely what they want. Harry Hammitt says the first weapon in a journalist's arsenal is knowledge of congressional laws, related agency regulations and court cases. Hammitt, editor of Access Reports, Lynchburg, Va., is an expert on the Freedom of Information Act, having worked as a journalist, lawyer and access bureaucrat within a federal agency.

Congress approved the Freedom of Information Act in 1966. It applies to executive branch agencies, but not to Congress, the courts or the president's immediate staff. It places the burden on agencies to show why information could be withheld; requires them to publish in the Federal Register procedures for filing FOIA requests; instructs them to maintain reading rooms with indexes for locating information; tells them to establish uniform, reasonable fees for locating and duplicating records; sets time limits for responding to requests, appeals and lawsuits; and allows recovery of court costs by a prevailing requester.

After learning the law, requesters must figure out what information is needed and which government agency has it. An FOIA request to see a file should not be made unless absolutely necessary: The investigator should check the agency's public reading room and consult its public affairs office. For example, the Nuclear Regulatory Commission publishes announcements of released material and can locate previously processed FOIA requests by number, requester and topic. Some agencies keep copies of the most requested documents in their reading rooms. When an agency's files are often used, such as the FBI's, somebody might have categorized them for a broader public. Gerald K. Haines and David A. Langbart did that in their book "Unlocking the Files of the FBI: A Guide to Its Records and Classification System."

If forced to file a request, journalists should establish their media credentials to obtain a fee waiver or reduction. Demonstrating how release of the records will contribute to public understanding of government operations might help.

Even though the law states that the requester need only "reasonably describe" the records sought, the request should be specific, quoting titles and dates of documents, if possible. When the topic is broad, the request letter should break it into categories. It might be preferable to file a separate request for each category: Agency personnel are daunted by massive requests that appear likely to evolve into problems for them; such requests go on the back burner because of the perceived difficulty in responding.

An investigator should maintain a record of the request and any related correspondence. It makes sense to pay for a return receipt to have proof of delivery. The 10 working day reply time, which an agency can extend another 10 days to review large amounts of records or consult other agencies, does not begin until the request reaches the proper office within the agency.

Contacting the agency frequently to track the request is a good strategy, as long as the line between persistence and obnoxiousness is never breached. It is best to develop a relationship with one person handling the request. I have made special trips to the agency to meet the FOIA bureaucrat. That personal touch was appreciated. In a few instances, I walked out with documents in hand.

Because of overlap in the government, an investigator should request information from all custodians who might have the documents. Author Scott Armstrong requests the same records from different agencies, finding that one will release information withheld by another. It is also wise to ask each agency if any other government entity has requested information on the subject. For instance, the Equal Employment Opportunity Commission might be investigating allegations of discrimination by a corporation and therefore request a Labor Department report on the relationship between the union and the corporation. Where the federal government overlaps with the states, an investigator should make requests to pertinent state agencies to obtain any federal information forwarded to the state.

In the end, even if investigators do everything correctly, requests for information may ultimately prove futile, because an agency determined to withhold information can find reasons for doing so. The reasons are the FOIA's nine exemptions, covering national security; confidential business information; law enforcement records; banking documents; oil and gas data; records withheld under another statute; internal memoranda from the early stages of discussion; personnel matters; and invasions of privacy. The exemptions sound broad and they are, if that is how an agency chooses to interpret them.

After an FOIA request is denied, an appeal is required before going to court. The appeal will be decided by someone higher in the agency; the agency has 20 working days to respond, but, as with original requests, appeals invariably take longer than the statutory limit.

Although agencies do not require a justification for appeals, it is wise to include supporting evidence such as relevant court cases and previously published references to the material being sought. When the investigator has obtained agency records through another source, the agency should be sent copies to support the argument. An investigator can challenge the adequacy of the original search if there is reason to believe that the agency has more records than it admits. The investigator should consider having a lawyer co-sign the appeal so the agency can see the case is serious. The letter can contain a threat to sue if information continues to be withheld, but the threat should not be hollow.

Assuming a reasonable case to begin with, the chances of getting information through litigation are good. If an investigator cannot get financial backing from a news organization, public interest groups, law schools or individual lawyers can be appealed to for help. Starting points for such help are American Civil Liberties Union chapters, the Reporters Committee for Freedom of the Press and state press associations.

FOIA suits can be filed in any of three locations: where the plaintiff resides; where the documents are located; or the U.S. District Court for the District of Columbia. Many requesters prefer to file in the District of Columbia because that court has the most experience with FOIA suits and is less likely to misinterpret the law.

The Justice Department produces publications that provide guidance to agencies. FOIA Update educates government personnel about the law. Some of those personnel belong to the American Society of Access Professionals, Bethesda, Md., whose members might give friendly advice. The Freedom of Information Case List is an annual compilation relating to the FOI, Privacy, Sunshine and Federal Advisory Committee acts. Copies are available from the Government Printing Office or at depository libraries.

Other useful publications include "How to Use the Federal FOI Act," from the Reporters Committee for Freedom of the Press; "Litigation Under the Federal Open Government Laws," American Civil Liberties Union Foundation, Washington, D.C.; and "A Citizen's Guide on How to Use the Freedom of Information Act and Privacy Act in Requesting Government Documents," from the U.S. House of Representatives Government Operations Committee.

While writing my Armand Hammer biography, I consulted those resources as I pressed agencies to release documents. Sometimes the agencies were willing, but Hammer threatened lawsuits to halt release of information. In one instance, he sued the U.S. Securities and Exchange Commission to prevent it from releasing documents. Overcoming the obstacles turned out to be time-consuming and expensive. But I am glad I persisted. The information I eventually received helped me, and therefore my readers, approach the truth.

Chapter 4

ACCESS TO INFORMATION ABOUT OTHER NATIONS AND ACROSS NATIONAL BORDERS

*M*ore and more journalists are working together as they research across national boundaries. While researching the Armand Hammer biography, I received help from journalists in France, Israel, England, Ecuador, Canada, the Soviet Union, China, Norway and Australia.

A few English-language books serving as models of multinational information-gathering are "Desperados: Latin Drug Lords, U.S. Lawmen, and the War America Can't Win" by Elaine Shannon; "The Samson Option: Israel's Nuclear Arsenal and American Foreign Policy" by Seymour Hersh; "Yakuza: The Explosive Account of Japan's Criminal Underworld" by Alec Dubro and David Kaplan; and "The Lords of the Rings: Power, Money and Drugs in the Modern Olympics" by Andrew Jennings and Vyv Simson.

It is a truism that the world is growing smaller as it becomes easier to communicate across national borders. Previous editions of this book said almost nothing about access to information in other nations. This chapter is devoted to helping investigators find information in the United States involving international matters, plus locating paper and people trails in other nations.

Finding Information Across National Borders

Gaining access in most other nations often means overcoming obstacles. Two obvious obstacles are distance and cost. Sometimes language is a third. Usually these obstacles can be overcome. The obstacle that sometimes cannot be overcome is the closed nature of other societies. As inadequate as U.S. access laws can be, they are less restrictive than laws in other nations, although a few (Canada and Sweden are examples) do have some tradition of openness.

To begin their quest, investigators can tap into human networks. Investigative Reporters & Editors has members in dozens of nations; their names are easy to find in the IRE membership directory. Organizations patterned after IRE include the Canadian Association of Journalists in Ottawa; Gravande Journaliste, Stockholm; Australian Centre for Independent Journalism, Sydney; and the Center for Investigative Journalism, Manila. Some journalists are communicating across borders through electronic mail.

Using individual and organizational contacts, investigators can determine which journalists in a given nation have looked into specific subjects. The investigators can ask who has mastered information-gathering in general in a given country.

International journalists can also provide perspectives on their cultures. That is what Aida Bustos of the San Diego Union-Tribune did on a panel about covering Mexico at an IRE conference:

> The process of gathering news south of the border is much the same as here. You still have to talk to the right people, go to the right places and come up with sound conclusions. But the process of reporting is going to be slower because very often you are going to have to talk to key people in person. . . . Be prepared to go office hopping to get your information. Do not expect to get a lot of information over the phone, particularly if people do not know you personally. . . . Try to get things done as early as possible because you hit that dead zone in the middle of the afternoon. . . . People leave for lunch at about 2 P.M. and may be gone anywhere from two hours until the next day. . . . Get home numbers because you are likely to need them. Also, get the cellular phone numbers of people you interview. Often, government officials are more available on their cellular phones than their regular ones.

In a few nations, investigators have written guides to following paper and people trails. Examples are British Sources of Information by Paul Jackson and Finding Canadian Facts Fast by Stephen Overbury. Belmont Publishers, Washington, D.C., identifies thousands of agencies and officials in its Worldwide Government Directory. The U.S. Internal Revenue Service publishes "Sources of Information From Abroad," which explains, nation by nation, where types of documents are stored and whether they are normally accessible.

Commercial database services have eased finding international information. On Lexis, an investigator can search court cases from England, Australia, New Zealand, Northern Ireland, Ireland, Scotland, Ontario (Canada), the European Communities' Court of Justice and France. Many national and international wire services, as well as individual overseas publications, are available. Examples include Agence France Presse, Kyodo News (Japan), Xinhua News Agency (China), Asian Wall Street Journal, Africa News, Current Digest of the Soviet Press, Hungarian Observer, Jerusalem Post and Warsaw Voice. Information Access Co. produces the on-line service Globalbase, covering business publications from dozens of nations. University Microfilms Inc. compiles the Transdex index, based on materials originally published outside the United States and translated into English. It is based on the U.S. government's Joint Publications Research Service files.

Directories of publications are becoming increasingly international. Ulrich's International Periodicals Directory covers more than 140,000 magazines, newspapers and annual directories, a significant number of which are non-U.S. titles. Monitor Publishing Company, New York City, compiles the International Corporate Yellow Book. It contains telephone and fax numbers and addresses for about 1,000 non-U.S. corporations.

Governments throughout the world publish documents listings, much as the U.S. government publishes its Monthly Catalog. Barbara L. Bell's An Annotated Guide to Current National Bibliographies is a starting point. In the Library of Congress card catalog, headings such as "NAME OF COUNTRY—executive departments," "NAME OF COUNTRY—officials and employees," "Administrative agencies—NAME OF COUNTRY" and "Legislative bodies—NAME OF COUNTRY" can lead to valuable resources.

Sometimes there is no need to cross borders. In U.S. government files resides information about international individuals, institutions and issues. That is especially true at the departments of State, Defense and Commerce. The International Trade Administration, part of the Commerce Department, assists U.S. companies in developing exports. As a result, the agency compiles files on overseas companies and markets.

Overseas companies sell stock in American financial markets, which means the companies are regulated by the Securities and Exchange Commission, the same agency that oversees U.S. companies trading their stock publicly. The overseas companies file SEC Form 6-K, an annual report that shows officers, directors, changes in ownership and wholly owned businesses.

Business-oriented publications compile lists that can provide journalists with story ideas or specific sources. The Wall Street Journal publishes lists of the world's 100 largest publicly traded corporations, 100 largest banks, 50 largest insurers and so on. Forbes, Fortune, Business Week and other publications compile similar lists.

International angles can be documented through sources inside the United States. Looking at the North American Free Trade Agreement, a Wall Street Journal reporter showed how Mexico was financing a campaign to promote the trade accord, and itself, to Americans. Conceiving and implementing the campaign was a list of U.S. political heavyweights. The reporter consulted lobbyists' registrations at the Justice Department to show that the Mexican government and businesses hired two dozen U.S. lobbying, public relations and law firms on behalf of the trade pact, at a cost of about $15 million for each year of the campaign.

When investigators want to expose corruption across national lines, there are sometimes ready-made sources to consult overseas. The Wall Street Journal reported on a nongovernmental organization founded in Berlin. Its intention: to teach business ethics around the globe. A test case for the organization involved nine French railroad locomotives sold to Ecuador. The locomotives turned out to be too heavy for Ecuadoran tracks. Ecuador's vice president became convinced that bribery had led to the inappropriate sale, so went to the organization. One of its founders, a German citizen who had directed East African programs for the World Bank, said "Most people think anyone trying to attack corruption is naive, a spoiler, unrealistic. Well, I'm none of these things. I'm a hard-nosed manager and I think the time is right to do something practicable."

Numerous international agencies provide documents and human sources to help investigators. The International Atomic Energy Agency is one example. More than 32,000 groups can be found in the Yearbook of International Organizations, published by K.G. Saur, a division of Reed Reference Publishing, and edited by the Union of International Associations, Brussels, Belgium. The best-known is the United Nations. Books in Print of the United Nations System lists thousands of UN-related monographs, available through the distributor UNIPUB, Lanham, Md. Some of the publications have obvious applicability on issue stories. Examples include "Recommendations on the Transport of Dangerous Goods"; "The World's Women 1970–1990: Trends and Statistics"; "Taxing Energy: Why and How"; and "International Statistical Classification of Diseases and Related Health Problems."

Another United Nations title, "The Consolidated List of Products Whose Consumption and/or Sale Have Been Banned, Withdrawn, Severely Restricted or Not Approved by Governments," figured in an international investigation for E Magazine by Diana Hembree and William Kistner of the Center for Investigative Reporting, San Francisco. The story ran under the headline "The Shell Game/It's a Tale of Two Countries and One Pesticide." The subheadline posed this question: "In the United States, Shell's No-Pest Strips vanished from stores years ago—after scientists found a carcinogenic ingredient—but in Mexico the dangerous fly killers still hang over baby cribs and kitchen counters. Does Shell have a schizophrenic social conscience?" In its publication, Muckraker, the Center for Investigative Reporting published an article by Hembree telling the story behind the story. It is reprinted here:

William Kistner was shopping at a corner store in Mexico City when he noticed something unusual. . . . Kistner was doing some traveling after winding up an article on the chemical compound DDVP, or dichlorvos, invented by Shell Chemical Co. and once the most common household pesticide ingredient in the United States.

He knew that Shell's DDVP pest strips, which emitted an invisible cloud of bug-killing fumes, had disappeared from store shelves in the United States years ago after controversy over their cancer risk. So he was surprised to find an almost identical DDVP pest strip being sold in the neighborhood store—this one manufactured by Shell Mexico.

Still more unsettling was the label: Although Shell pest strips in the United States had warned consumers not to use the pesticide strips in kitchens or around infants, the Shell Mexico pest strip featured a drawing that suggested consumers hang the strips in kitchens and—among other places—above a smiling baby in a crib.

Who was responsible for the Shell Mexico label, which so directly contradicted the health warnings on U.S. pest strips? Why didn't the same safety standard apply to everyone? And how dangerous *was* DDVP?

Seeking to answer such questions led Kistner and me, via telephone, to five countries (including Italy, where scientists paid by Shell had tested DDVP pest strips on infants in the 1960s), to the Environmental Protection Agency, Shell employees and medical researchers, and finally to the London branch of Royal Dutch Shell, a Netherlands-based multinational. . . .

We began with the question of DDVP's potential dangers. EPA documents classified DDVP as carcinogenic in animals, and neurotoxic and mutagenic in laboratory studies. Published medical studies obtained through the Nexis Medline computer database had also linked DDVP in bug sprays to childhood leukemia and aplastic anemia, a rare and sometimes fatal blood disease, so several hematologists were contacted for interviews. Among them was [a researcher at] UCLA, who found Shell Mexico's label instructions "unconscionable" and "potentially very hazardous."

To see whether Shell Oil Co. was consulted on the label, we called its Houston headquarters, where [a] public relations official . . . confirmed that pest strips were definitely not safe to use around infants. Told about Shell Mexico's label, he seemed taken aback, but explained that the two companies were entirely separate. And since Shell Chemical no longer made the pest strips, he added, its records on that product were no longer available.

But there was another possible way to find out who was responsible for the label: The company's product registration file from the EPA would contain any written requests from foreign governments for the label. An EPA official informed us, however, that part of the file had disappeared ("it happens sometimes"), and only a few dog-eared documents remained.

We then turned to Shell Mexico. Contacted by phone in Mexico City, [a] Shell Mexico [official] repeated that the two companies were entirely separate, adding that Shell Mexico, like Shell Oil Co., was a wholly owned subsidiary of Royal Dutch Shell.

Shell Mexico had, we were told, been making the pest strips for well over 20 years, and, according to a fax from the company, the label with the pest strip above a baby that Kistner saw in Mexico City had been used since 1968. Shell Mexico took full responsibility for its label, which local authorities and unspecified "advisors" had approved: "Our advisors confirm that taking into account all the known evidence there are no reasons for any changes in the recommended uses" [for the DDVP pest strip].

And who were these mysterious advisors? Shell Mexico would not disclose their identity, but company officials noted that they consulted regularly with Shell International Petroleum Maatschappij in the Netherlands. After being transferred from office to office in the pre-dawn hours (SIPM's work day began about 2 A.M. Pacific time), one of us finally reached a Shell International Petroleum official in London, who confirmed that a department in SIPM does approve labeling for all of Royal Dutch Shell's wholly owned products—including DDVP no-pest strips.

Several days later, he called back to tell us that this department had "almost certainly" approved Shell Mexico's label in 1968, and that the Mexican company had again contacted it for advice about the same time we contacted it concerning the label. Reached in Holland, [an] SIPM [official], who tracks Shell product regulation in various countries, said he saw nothing wrong with Shell Mexico's label. "The DDVP substances are not hazardous to humans, but specifically hazardous to flies . . ." This opinion was contradicted by stacks of medical studies available through the EPA and library medical journals—all of which are readily accessible, it would seem, to a giant multinational like Royal Dutch Shell. But although EPA data showed the cancer risk from lifetime exposure to DDVP was one in a hundred, an extremely high figure, Shell long denied the potential hazards of the invention. This stance reflected an underlying theme of our story: what happens when the testing of pesticides for health effects is left up to chemical companies alone. As one scientist told us, "Until we have someone else doing the studies, the corporations will control the results."

The National Security Obstacle

A special access problem for investigators revolves around information classified on grounds of "national security." When the existence of classified documents is kept secret, how can journalists know what to request? In the United States, classification is governed by presidential executive order, a unilateral action falling outside congressional approval.

Most U.S. journalists have done nothing to push for declassification, bowing instead to the Defense, Justice, State and Energy departments, Central Intelligence and National Security agencies that keep millions of documents—generated on public time, using taxpayer dollars—off limits. When journalists do request access, the courts almost always uphold the government.

Occasionally, persons with legitimate access to classified documents will leak them. Otherwise, investigators must use common sense to posit the existence of classified documents, then request a declassification review, a procedure separate from a Freedom of Information Act request.

Historians, political scientists and other scholars have used declassification review far more often than journalists to throw open previously classified files. According to the government's Information Security Oversight Office, in a recent year agencies received 4,268 requests to declassify documents that were marked "Top Secret," "Secret" or "Confidential." As a result of such requests, agencies declassified 81,986 pages in full; 146,796 pages in part; and retained classification in full on 18,121 pages. Unfortunately, documents continue to be classified at an alarming rate.

Sometimes documents are declassified by the government before outside investigators make requests. The difficulty is in learning what has been declassified, since the documents were secret in the first place. The National Archives helps by devoting a few pages in its magazine Prologue and its newsletter The Record to "accessions and openings." Another resource is the Declassified Documents Reference System, from Research Publications, Woodbridge, Conn. It consists of abstracts indexed by subject, backed by a microfiche collection of the full documents.

■ SO-CALLED PERSONAL PAPERS AND ORAL HISTORIES

A little-known obstacle to open government in the United States involves the Library of Congress and National Archives, which contain collections of classified personal papers generated by federal officials. Much of the closed information involves international affairs.

The term "personal papers" is misleading. It has come to mean that U.S. presidents, members of Congress, cabinet secretaries and Supreme Court justices control access to documents generated on government time at public expense—papers no common-sense definition would consider "personal."

Access to presidential and vice presidential materials improved recently with congressional passage of the Presidential Records Act. But those materials are still closed until five years after the end of the administration or until the National Archives staff has completed processing, whichever is earlier. Some parts of the collections remain closed much longer.

Many "personal papers" with significance for journalists are housed at the Library of Congress. While leaving the Reagan administration, Secretary of Defense Caspar Weinberger shipped his papers to the Library of Congress, but he retained power to deny access to investigators. He drew selectively from the documents to write his memoirs, which were partially unverifiable as a result.

Most journalists began to realize the potential of the Weinberger papers only after the special prosecutor appointed to look at the Iran-Contra scandal gained access. The documents, the special prosecutor said, suggested President Reagan and Vice-president Bush knew more about the scandal than they had admitted. I studied the Weinberger case and other "personal papers" abuses in "For Their Eyes Only: How Presidential Appointees Treat Public Documents as Personal Property," commissioned by the Center for Public Integrity, Washington, D.C.

Universities are often chosen as sites for the papers of members of Congress, executive branch officials, judges and corporate titans from around the world. Sometimes influential individuals do nothing with their papers, instead allowing interviewers to tape record their thoughts. Unfortunately, the speakers often place those oral histories out of reach until after their deaths, or even longer. But sometimes access is immediate. I have used oral histories (some of persons still alive, some by persons now deceased) to add depth to international investigations, including a biography of Armand Hammer. One of the best-indexed oral history collections is at Columbia University. Others can be located by consulting Allen Smith's Directory of Oral History Collections or Meckler Publishing's Oral History Index: An International Directory of Oral History Interviews. The National Union Catalog of Manuscript Collections, compiled by the Library of Congress, helps locate personal papers.

Because of the delays and gaps in guides to personal papers, savvy investigators call sources who might know where a collection resides: in somebody's attic, a university library, a presidential library, the Library of Congress. For example, if they call the archivist of the U.S. Senate, they learn that office keeps track of where current and former senators have donated their papers. The same is true for the U.S. House of Representatives archivist.

Personal papers, oral histories and other normally private information can be found in family genealogy collections. Among the best indexes are Genealogies in the Library of Congress: A Bibliography and A Complement to Genealogies in the Library of Congress, both edited by Marion J. Kaminkow. Many such indexes are described in The Source: A Guidebook of American Genealogy, edited by Arlene Eakle and Johni Cerny. Although The Source is aimed at amateur genealogists, not investigative journalists, its emphasis on paper trails and people trails makes it worthwhile. The next chapter examines people trails in greater depth.

Chapter 5

PEOPLE TRAILS

Finding and Interviewing Sources

After investigators have learned about individuals, issues or institutions from secondary and primary documents, it is time to interview people. Despite the detail in this book about documents research, the paper trail alone is usually inadequate. According to Steve Luxenberg, projects editor at the Washington Post:

> Records are a means to an end, not the end in itself. A record is often conclusive proof of something, but records can also be wrong. They can lead you to a certain set of facts, but they can also lead you astray. What I'm saying is this—use your common sense. Think about what the records are saying. Above all, call the people who created or maintain the records, and ask them to explain them. Call the people whose lives are being described in the records, and give them a chance to say what the records mean . . .
>
> Records don't tell you why something happened, they just tell you what happened. An example: I did a story about a Baltimore man who was selling land in New Mexico on the promise that it contained vast oil and gas reserves. Records proved that he sold the land; records proved that he made such promises. But no records proved whether oil and gas existed in vast quantities. The seller had a geology survey (his own records) to prove his contention. Only by looking at other, more objective, geological surveys and by talking to experts could I suggest that his promises were phony—without that combination, I had no story.

Many journalists concede their shortcomings when it comes to finding documents. But few admit to shortcomings in locating and interviewing sources. Too often, they are overestimating their abilities. One unrecognized shortcoming is that many investigators fail to cast their net deep enough in a big enough lake when fishing for sources. As an example, consider an investigation of the president of a local business. A journalist hears rumors of how the president has driven away high-level managers who disagreed with him; abused corporate perquisites; sexually harassed female employees; and ordered that cheaper parts be used in products, possibly endangering consumer safety.

The journalist's informant is a former company vice president who passed along hints at a block party attended by the journalist because they live in the same neighborhood. Now working for a supplier of the former employer, the informant will not provide documentation and does not want to be mentioned by name, but does agree to answer questions from the journalist later, off the record, about whether the investigation is on course.

The journalist checks secondary and primary documents mentioned in previous chapters. During a month of off-and-on searching, enough information is found to approach the paper's editor about working on the project full-time. The editor says yes.

"Formers" and "Currents"

At this point, the journalist should look for people in two categories: "formers" and "currents." Most journalists do well finding currents, but ignore formers, who can be difficult to track down. For the project under discussion, the journalist should seek interviews with current *and* former company directors; current *and* former employees at all levels who have had contact with the president; current *and* former sources at past places of employment, especially the subject's personal secretaries and executive assistants; current *and* former executives at competitors; current *and* former labor union leaders who have organized or tried to organize the company's workforce; current *and* former company suppliers; current *and* former in-house and outside lawyers, accountants, stockbrokers as well as other licensed professionals providing services to the company.

From the president's personal life, the journalist should seek current *and* former neighbors; current *and* former leaders at the subject's place of worship; current *and* former country club members, including golfing and tennis partners; current *and* former colleagues from clubs or lodges; current *and* former social friends; current *and* former spouses; children; brothers, sisters, cousins, aunts, uncles, nieces, nephews and their families.

The journalist should never assume a desired source will refuse to talk. People may harbor reasons for granting an interview that no logic on the journalist's part could divine. Naturally, some want to paint a positive picture. That is fine. A journalist should never turn down an interview with a knowledgeable source just because the source will talk about "only good things."

Why? First, nobody is all bad, so anecdotes revealing good qualities might add balance and insight. Second, while supplying positive anecdotes, the source might mention something previously unknown to the journalist. ("You know, George is so generous he is paying his former wife $5,000 a month child support when the court ordered only $3,500.") Suddenly the journalist knows about a former wife and a child who had not shown up in records searches. Or the interviewee might mention other seemingly innocuous information that fills in a piece of the puzzle. ("When we were neighbors on the east side, George loved golf so much he bought 10 acres adjacent to the Regal Country Club and built himself a couple of pitch and putt holes.") Suddenly the reporter understands the origin of George owning land that 15 years later became the site of a lucrative shopping center seemingly unrelated to his main occupation.

As Mike Baxter and Jim Savage at the Miami Herald tried to establish a link between an alleged shakedown artist and a U.S. senator who allegedly sanctioned shakedowns of building contractors hoping for help from the Federal Housing Administration, they obtained names of the senator's former employees from the newspaper's Washington correspondent. One, a former assistant press secretary, recalled seeing a document from the shakedown artist come over the fax machine in the senator's office. She remembered the document years later because of its candid content and because the senator's administrative assistant had made a big deal of her not mentioning it to anybody.

Experienced investigators, understanding the value of formers, maintain files of who has moved where. Sources of that information include local and national newspapers (the Wall Street Journal column "Who's News" is filled with comings and goings that yield formers who could be consulted later); magazines; industry or institution-specific newsletters; press releases about comings and goings at businesses, government agencies, philanthropic groups, universities; and word of mouth.

Some formers have scores to settle, and therefore might exaggerate or lie. It is the journalist's responsibility to find those exaggerations and lies—after listening to the source. There is no point in shunning formers just because they might prove to be partially unreliable. After all, currents can be just as unreliable.

When a source seeks out a journalist first, there is also reason for caution. But journalists should find time for tipsters. An Atlanta Journal-Constitution reporter was glad he did. His tipster was a landowner who had leased property to a mining company seeking kaolin, white clay used in a variety of products. The landowner appeared in the newsroom, where five reporters and editors brushed him off before he reached another reporter's desk. The tale the reporter heard was the beginning of a kaolin industry exposé.

Tools for Finding People

Once identified, sources must be located. When the whereabouts is not readily available, there are resources that increase chances of success:

Telephone Directories

It is puzzling how many investigators fail to consult the phonebook. At IRE, I received queries about whether I knew the telephone numbers of Bob Woodward or Seymour Hersh. My callers assumed famous journalists would be unlisted. I had the numbers of Woodward and Hersh—they were listed in the Washington, D.C., directory.

That same resource works for many formers, who leave jobs without leaving the metropolitan area. There are on-line computer databases and compact disks combining thousands of hard-copy telephone directories, making it easier than ever to locate formers. CD-ROM national telephone directories include PhoneDisc, from Digital Directory Assistance Inc., Bethesda, Md.; ProPhone from ProCD Inc., Marblehead, Mass.; and MetroSearch Library, a CD-ROM from Metromail Corp., Lombard, Ill. One on-line version is Electronic White Pages from DirectoryNet Inc., Atlanta. Supermarket database vendors offer alternatives—Phone*File on CompuServe and Finder on Lexis. Local libraries collect hard copy or microfiche telephone directories from around the nation.

The penny-wise investigator will use toll-free numbers. American Telephone & Telegraph publishes a directory of 800 numbers. Calling 800-555-1212 might yield a number not listed in the directory. Often 800 numbers are unlisted, so a journalist can ask a source inside the workplace whether such a number is available. If a distant organization has no toll-free number, an investigator can at least save money on directory assistance calls by using the National Directory of Addresses and Telephone Numbers, published by Omnigraphics Inc., Detroit, or Gale Research's similar National Business Telephone Directory.

City Directories

Because so many telephone numbers in the United States are unlisted (as high as 65 percent in some cities), investigators must frequently go beyond telephone directories to locate sources. Commercial companies, most notably R.L. Polk, Detroit, produce city directories for thousands of locales in the United States and Canada. Public and newsroom libraries often have current and past volumes.

The directories are arranged alphabetically, like the phonebook, but also list names of adults at the same address as well as their occupations; telephone numbers in order (so 874-2221 would follow 874-2220); plus street-by-street, block-by-block listings. Each feature has its uses. An investigator with a telephone number but no name connected to it can look in the ordered phone numbers section to learn the name. The street-by-street listing provides names of neighbors; with a name, it is easier to start a conversation when phoning cold or knocking on a door unexpectedly.

Jack Tobin, an investigator for Sports Illustrated, found a former neighbor of a subject through a city directory, then visited her. "A nosy neighbor can be a great source," Tobin said. "I was trying to find someone who had moved out of an apartment building 20 years before. The manager was no help, and tenant records went back only five years. Instead of a record, I found a tenant, an elderly woman, who for years had had little to do but keep track of her fellow occupants. She knew my target and where he had gone."

Workplace Directories

Once I wanted an unlisted telephone number for a reclusive subject. I knew the subject's wife taught at a local school. So I called a friend who taught in the public schools, asking her to look up the wife's name. There it was, complete with the otherwise unlisted telephone number. I called, and the reclusive subject answered. Most workplaces have internal telephone directories. It makes sense to save back issues—what better way to identify formers than to look up the auditor in 1988 and in 1995, see the names are different, then locate the departed auditor?

Computers open new possibilities. At the St. Paul Pioneer Press, the newsroom has in-house access to a computer database of all city employees. After a gas line explosion resulted in injuries and property destruction, the database yielded names of the public works department backhoe operators. By calling them one by one, the staff found the worker who had operated the machinery that damaged the gas line.

Many workplaces produce in-house publications that chart departures and hirings. That has been true at every place I have worked. Several years after I left the Des Moines Register, I wrote an article about the newspaper for Columbia Journalism Review. One of my sources was a daily newsroom announcement sheet that included personnel comings and goings.

Informal Networks of "Formers"

I left the Des Moines Register about the same time as a few of my colleagues. We were friends, and occasional dissidents, together. If an investigator were trying to find us years later, calling the Register might be fruitless. If just one "former" could be located, the investigator could find the others. Formers' networks revolve around workplaces, as well as churches, neighborhoods, social organizations, high schools, universities and professional societies. Some organizations consist entirely of formers—one is the Association of National Security Alumni, whose members are former employees of the Central Intelligence Agency and other usually impenetrable workplaces. The group has its own publication, Unclassified.

Other Documents and Records

Voter registration records can lead to a local address, as can pilots' licenses. Drivers' license records are especially efficient for this purpose—drivers' license databases are statewide (voter registration, in contrast, is county by county) and the majority of Americans 16 or older have a license. The records are kept in the state capital; the agency is named the Department of Motor Vehicles or something similar.

In many states, it is possible to request an individual's license information in person, by mail, by tapping into the agency's database on-line after an account has been established or by obtaining a computer tape from the agency. If the subject fails to show up in the drivers' license database, the motor vehicles department might have information about transferred licenses, indicating which state received the records upon the subject's application there.

When people are trying to escape detection, clues are nonetheless left by using a variation of their name, or a nickname, or a mother's maiden name. It seems to be human nature to link oneself with one's past. A Boston detective found a suspected murderer 25 years after the killing by starting with his given name, nickname (Stacey) and mother's maiden name (Griffin). The name being used by the suspect? Stacey Griffin.

When no single document or technique provides the answer, combining resources might. Jack Tobin related how he located a "former." His account is reprinted here, lightly edited:

> The call for help came from a lawyer friend. He was trying to untangle a dispute over a will. The signer, of course, was dead. So were the lawyers who had drafted it and the secretary who had typed it. The only person who might still be alive to testify about the signer's soundness of mind was another secretary, who had witnessed a codicil to the will. Her name was Jane Smith. That's all we knew, and it was one of the most common names among the more than 10 million people in the Los Angeles area. I found her. Here's how.
>
> To begin with, I made the assumption that Jane had been employed in the office of the long-dead lawyer who had drafted the will. Using an employee to witness a will is a common practice in law offices. My first stop was the archives of the Los Angeles central library, where I asked for the 1940 edition of the Polk's City Directory. Four Jane Smiths were listed as secretaries. I started a separate notebook page for each. Then I tracked each Jane, going forward in the directory year by year. R.L. Polk and Company gave up trying to keep track of Los Angeles' exploding and transient population not long

after World War II—a great loss to reporters. But I had addresses from the last edition, so I could use the telephone book. That led me forward a few more years before each trail disappeared.

One of the last city directories had listed an employer of one Jane Smith. It, too, was a law firm, now defunct. From the Yellow Pages of that year's phone book, I got the names of the firm's member-lawyers. The bar association was able to supply the home address of a retired partner. Yes, he remembered Jane. No, he had no idea what had become of her. But he did remember that she had gotten married and he recalled her married name. The county recorder's office keeps the marriage license file. Jane Smith's husband had come from another state. A call to the motor vehicle department there turned up his driver's license, with his current home address. I made another call. A man answered. I made my inquiry. After a pause, I was talking to the right Jane Smith.

Whistleblowers

The Jane Smiths of the world often fade into the crowd. That is not as likely with whistleblowers. They are currents or formers who seek attention or find themselves thrust into the spotlight. Their importance in exposing wrongdoing is recognized by a federal law, the Whistleblower Protection Act.

Many are sincere and correct in their assertions, having become whistleblowers reluctantly after failing to change the organization through more mainstream or acceptable channels. Some are correct but less sincere, glorying in publicity. Others are sincere, but ultimately incorrect, perhaps coming forward because of mental instability or greed; whistleblowers can receive monetary awards under the federal False Claims Acts if the government collects a penalty. A few whistleblowers are both insincere and incorrect. All those possibilities put a burden on investigators.

Many state legislatures have approved whistleblowing laws protecting public employees; some states also provide protections for private-sector employees. The federal and state protections yield a rich public record— not only about the individual whistleblower, but also about the alleged corporate or government transgressions that led to the whistleblowing.

A report in the National Law Journal about one case shows the extent of the public record. Triggering the account was a ruling by the U.S. labor secretary voiding settlements between employers and whistleblowers that restrict a whistleblower's right to contact government agencies. The specific case involved an electrician for a nuclear power plant contractor. The electrician reported safety concerns to the power plant's confidential, in-house investigative program. Shortly afterward, his confidentiality somehow was breached; the contractor forced him to resign. From then on, every step yielded documents for journalists.

He filed a wrongful termination complaint with the Labor Department. Before his complaint went to a hearing, he signed an agreement restricting his testimony in judicial proceedings concerning the nuclear plant. The electrician later challenged the agreement, saying his attorneys had pressured him into accepting it. The Labor Department held the restrictive terms violated the public interest. The U.S. Circuit Court of Appeals reversed on technical grounds. The labor secretary's decision took care of the technical objections.

Investigators seeking whistleblowers are in the best position if they have covered an institution or an issue for a long time. Without that advantage, an investigator must explore other routes. If the employer is unionized, union representatives might serve as a contact between the journalist and whistleblower. An investigator can stay in touch with personnel in charge of organizational hotlines and can mine sources at the federal Office of Special Counsel, federal Merit Systems Protection Board, inspectors general in many government agencies and congressional committees. Lawyers who regularly represent whistleblowers can help. An investigator can also call watchdog groups such as the Government Accountability Project in Washington, D.C., and Cavallo Foundation, Cambridge, Mass.

Book-length accounts by whistleblowers include those of A. Ernest Fitzgerald, a civilian Air Force engineer. Accounts of whistleblowers by journalists include "Serpico," Peter Maas' book about a New York City police officer who talked openly about corruption. Myron Peretz Glazer and Penina Migdal Glazer, in "The Whistleblowers: Exposing Corruption in Government and Industry," relate findings from their study of 64 ethical resisters and their spouses.

Outside Experts

Journalists can benefit by interviewing outside experts who, unlike whistleblowers, do not have to worry about recognition leading to disciplinary action. Experts are especially prevalent at universities, which often publish directories of faculty willing to talk to journalists. But some who advertise themselves as knowledgeable are biased or outdated. As a result, a journalist might do better to call the appropriate university department, explaining what information is sought, then contacting the professor suggested by the chair.

In her book "Poison Penmanship," Jessica Mitford tells how she used a university nutrition scientist while researching the propriety of drug company experiments on prisoners. The accounts of the companies' research baffled Mitford. The write-ups discussed "Cleocin HFC levels" of volunteer prisoners. Those levels helped "determine antibiotic levels in various tissues" based on consumption of 150 milligrams of Cleocin q.i.d. followed by collection of sebum and semen. What was going on? Mitford's expert told her the prisoners were being forced to masturbate to produce semen samples, then having their arms cut all the way to the muscle tissue for various injections. The expert said such experimental designs would never be allowed at his university.

Knowing the difficulty investigators have choosing experts, the State University of New York at Stony Brook established ProfNet, an electronic-mail system matching journalists and academics. Similarly, the Scientists Institute for Public Information, New York City, is a far-flung think tank, whose experts have agreed to share their expertise with journalists.

Think tanks are the first cousins of universities as places to locate experts. Many of the best known are in Washington, D.C., including the American Enterprise Institute for Public Policy Research and the Brookings Institution. A second geographic locale filled with think tanks is California; the Hoover Institution at Stanford University and the Rand Corporation in Santa Monica are examples. David M. Ricci puts their expertise into perspective in "The Transformation of American Politics: The New Washington and the Rise of Think Tanks." James A. Smith, author of "The Idea Brokers: Think Tanks and the Rise of the New Policy Elite," estimates the number of freestanding think tanks at 1,200, supplemented by thousands of university-affiliated research institutes.

Research Centers Directory from Gale Research contains a subtitle spelling out its reach: "A guide to more than 13,000 university-related and other nonprofit research organizations established on a permanent basis and carrying on continuing research programs in agriculture, astronomy and space sciences, behavioral and social sciences, biological sciences and ecology, business and economics, computers and mathematics, education, engineering and technology, government and public affairs, humanities and religion, labor and industrial relations, law, medical sciences, physical and earth sciences, and regional and area studies."

Logging onto any computer bulletin board with a query to like-minded users is almost sure to produce replies. Nora Paul of the Poynter Institute for Media Studies says there are three types of electronic bulletin boards available to journalists:

> Commercial boards are services such as CompuServe, Delphi or America Online. They provide . . . forums or special interest group areas where users discuss particular topics. They will charge monthly or hourly for the time you are connected to the service.
>
> Linked boards are networks of individually run bulletin board services that share the messages posted to a specific board with other boards through an echo mail network. . . . Among the largest . . . are Fidonet, with more than 400 specific topic areas for messages [and] RIME (Relaynet International Message Exchange). . . . Through linked boards, a person dialing into a local bulletin board service can retrieve and read messages posted around the world.

Stand-alone boards are generally sponsored by an association or a government agency. They contain information and allow messaging on specific topics. Examples: Greenpeace's Environet and the U.S. Department of Commerce's Economic Bulletin Board. [Many of these bulletin boards. . . . can be found on the Internet.]

Paul says bulletin board services have four main features. The first is the message area, which tends to be subject-specific. Paul says:

By reading the messages from people in the "Living With AIDS" forum on CompuServe, or the "Ask a Cop" area on a Fidonet bulletin board service, you will be reading comments by people intimately involved in the subject. You can get story ideas; you can message them to find out what they might think about a particular issue; or you can tap into their network of contacts by asking if they know of people familiar with a particular topic.

The second is electronic mail, which allows a user to send a message to a designated person or group. The third feature is conference areas: "Users of a bulletin board service can arrange to meet in a conference 'room' at a certain time and then conduct real-time conversations. People meeting in the conference room can immediately read the comments, questions and responses of others in the room." The fourth is the library, where people can place documents, articles or software on the system to be uploaded by other users of the bulletin board.

When going on-line is impractical, no problem. There are so many print directories of organizations housing experts that a listing could consume dozens of pages. Two that are powerful when used together are the Washington Information Directory from Congressional Quarterly Inc. and the Encyclopedia of Associations from Gale Research. Specialized groups have their own organization, too, the American Society of Association Executives, Washington, D.C.

Most organizations of significant size have public information officers with their own specialties. Sometimes investigators obtain what they need from public information officers. It is not always useful to go to the top anyway, because bosses are frequently unaware of what is happening in the ranks. There is some truth to the maxim "The higher you go, the less they know."

In his book "Writing for Your Readers," Donald Murray makes the point with an insightful paragraph:

In the accident ward you will notice doctors deferring to one nurse; at the garage one mechanic is called over for an expert diagnosis; at the fire one fireman is consulted to decide if the roof is safe; at the Senate hearings the names will look at a staff member for direction.

The type of leaders described by Murray are the sources investigators should be seeking out, despite their middling status.

Yet it is often vital to interview top executives—because they are the focus of the project, have unmatched knowledge or their place on the organization chart makes them accountable.

■ POWER STRUCTURES, OBVIOUS AND OBSCURE

Often it is clear who has ultimate authority. But sometimes titles and organization charts can be deceptive. In some cities, the mayor is a figurehead, with major employers calling the shots from their closed weekly luncheon. In some universities, the chancellor is a rubber stamp for the board of curators. A journalist should be able to discern and then penetrate power structures. Some journalists, backed by some social scientists, dismiss power structures as conspiratorial rubbish. My experiences covering government, corporations and universities suggest otherwise.

For those interested in the debate over power structures, one of the most interesting summaries is in "Who Rules America Now?" by G. William Domhoff. Philip J. Trounstine at the San Jose Mercury News has written extensively about power structures. Here are key parts of an article he did for the IRE Journal:

> There are lots of ways of finding out who's who in any community. Sociologists and political scientists have debated for years which way is best. . . . In 1978, the Detroit News came up with a massive, 10-month study that entailed a complex, computerized network analysis of some 1,200 interconnected leaders. The paper hired consultants and invested huge amounts of resources. . . .
>
> For those of us with less extravagant editorial budgets, there is another way to study power that yields substantially the same structure. It is a modification of [an] original reputational model that I have developed. . . . The model does not attempt to state who are the most powerful or influential persons in town. It promises and delivers instead those who are perceived as the most powerful by the influential themselves. That is why political sociologists call it a reputational model. It measures reputation for power. . . .
>
> Three characteristics make this model good for [journalists]: One, it reveals behind-the-scenes leaders—those who may never surface publicly but who exert pressure, wield influence or exercise power quietly and effectively. It does this better than any of the other popular methods. Two, it leaves the reporter and the [newsroom] in their traditional role—you don't declare people powerful; you report that their peers say they are powerful. Three, it is relatively cheap and quick—three or four months of full-time work by one person. . . .
>
> You start by pulling together every conceivable list you can get your hands on. Political organizations, corporations, banks, neighborhood groups, churches, civic organizations—absolutely any forum that you think plays some role in your community. Study local histories and back

newspaper clips. Who surfaced in [controversies over] issues? Who led fights? Who founded businesses and philanthropic projects? Who ran campaigns? Be especially careful to seek minority group leaders and women. They will seldom appear among the most powerful so you have to guard against bias at the outset by making sure you have included them in the original stages.

Create a [file] for each person, listing relevant information. One side benefit of this is that after the study is done, you will have the best . . . file in the newsroom, especially if you include phone numbers. Be sure to check the country clubs and other exclusive groups; if your community has a social register, use it. . . . Do not be afraid to add or cut names if you are convinced it is the right thing to do. I try to be as inclusive as possible, working with about 200 names. . . . The next step . . . involves selecting about 15 initial judges to cut the list down to size. This is probably the most critical stage of the process and the step most fraught with subjectivity.

The idea is to choose people you . . . consider close to and knowledgeable about power and influence in your community. But the list must also be broad-based. Key city or county bureaucrats, chamber of commerce insiders, minority community leaders, United Way fund-raisers, socialites, grass-roots organizers, bankers, news media executives, education leaders, labor leaders, behind-the-scenes politicians, religious leaders, elected officials—all these should be considered. Be sure to have women [and minorities] among the initial judges.

Now you need to draw up a form to use as a questionnaire. . . . The first task for the judges, interviewed individually and confidentially, is to work from the list of names, placing the top 30 leaders in approximate rank order. The idea is to get them to think in terms of across-the-board power and influence—political, economic, cultural and social issues. Those in the top ten will get three points; those in the middle ten, two points; and those in the third ten, one point.

From [sociologist Floyd] Hunter's original work I have devised the following series of questions. You could come up with others:

☐ If a project were before the community that required decisions by a group of leaders, which ten could put it over?
☐ Name the ten persons most effective at initiating projects.
☐ Name the ten persons most effective at stopping projects.

In discussion with respondents, I explain that a project could be anything—political, social, economic or cultural. The idea is to think of those who individually and collectively best fit the category. They can overlap.

Be sure also to tell judges that they are not limited by the initial list of names. If someone they think of belongs on the list of 30 or on any list of ten, by all means include them. The study is open-ended and it is possible you may have overlooked someone.

I also ask judges to name the person who has the most power, the person who exercises the most power, the most influential person in town and the top leader in town. Each person named gets five points. By asking questions this way it is possible to distinguish subtle differences among leaders and power holders. After the judge has completed the form—this takes about 45 minutes to an hour—I generally discuss some of the choices with him. My experience is that only if you guarantee confidentiality will people openly discuss those named as powerful. But if you do, you will get remarkably candid insights. After the second stage is completed, tally the results. You should come up with a cluster of people—from 20 to 40 names—that appear to stand apart from the others.

Let us say it is 30 names. Alphabetize that list, draw up a new questionnaire and you are ready for round two of interviews. This time you want to narrow the choices more exactly. I ask each person to list, in precise rank order, the most powerful and influential persons in town. Be sure to tell them they are not bound by the list. Number one gets ten points, and number ten gets one point. This time I ask, If a project were before the community that required decisions by a group of leaders, which four could put it over? Each person named gets five points. [I then follow with the same questions as before.] I also throw in, Name the most underrated leader. Name the most overrated leader. Name the most trusted leader. Name the least trusted leader.

These lead to even more fascinating discussions. No points are assigned to the answers, but the questions yield new dimensions for the final stories. . . . After interviews with as many of the 30 as possible—I have never found fewer than 27 . . . willing to participate—you once again tally the results. In my experience, there is generally a small group that stands apart from the others. . . .

In both Indianapolis and San Jose, I found ten persons at the top. In Indianapolis, the differences between the 11th and 32nd persons were not that significant. In San Jose, there seemed to be a second cluster, and so I presented the group in three tiers. In Indianapolis, where leadership is a tight-knit group, no names were added in sufficient numbers to demand that they be added to my list of 32. In San Jose, eight persons received enough recognition that it made sense to expand the final list . . . to 40. . . .

Hunter has done scores of studies throughout the country. He says the mayor always winds up in the top ten because of his or her position, even when he or she is not much of a real power. Often your readers will not know who some of the top ten are. I have found that many reporters have never heard of some of the people, or if they had heard of them, they had no idea they were influential. Both those situations are good reasons for doing power structure stories.

The studies can be found in the IRE Resource Center under "Who's Who." On a less ambitious scale, investigators can compose profiles of individuals in the power structure as a way of educating readers, listeners or viewers. A Seattle Times reporter did that when she wrote a feature about a consultant involved in opposing limits on downtown Seattle skyscrapers, keeping the professional baseball team from moving to another city and helping New York investors buy the landmark Pike Place Market without significant opposition. Yet his name was little-known to those outside the power structure.

■ *Interviewing Those In and Out of Power*

Once an investigator has located potential sources, inside or outside the power structure, the next steps are learning about the subjects, scheduling interviews in a logical order if the schedules of those involved allows, eliciting information on the record, condensing it fairly and accurately— all without burning bridges for future investigations. The process is filled with trouble spots. But there are techniques that can ease the difficulties.

One technique is diligence through the years. Writing in the IRE Journal, newspaperman Tom Honig said:

> Keep up your source list. Use your computer at work to store as many names and phone numbers as possible. When you do an interview or meet someone at a party, enter the name and anything else that is pertinent—including the name of family members. Then, when a bank in your town fails and you have already met someone who has worked there for 15 years, you can call the house: "Hello, Blanche? I met your husband Jerry at last month's chamber of commerce cookout. Will he be home soon?" That is a lot better than "Mrs. Johnson, I am from the Daily Blat. I would like to talk to your husband about how his bank went broke." Clipping and filing secondary source references helps—local newspaper articles, the New York Times [which is indexed by personal name at Roxbury Data, Sparks, Nev.], and other sources.

There are entire books on techniques that will help an interview go smoothly. Among the best are "The Craft of Interviewing" by John Brady; "Interviews That Work: A Practical Guide for Journalists" by Shirley Biagi; "Creative Interviewing" by Ken Metzler; and "Before the Story" by George M. Killenberg and Rob Anderson. Interviewing chapters within broader books are equally valuable, such as chapters 10 and 12 of "Investigative Reporting" by Peter Benjaminson and David Anderson.

■ *Interviewing*

The Research Stage

An interview might focus on the person being interviewed, the institution about which the person has special knowledge, or an issue. Whatever the emphasis, the interviewer needs to know as much as possible going in.

Walt Harrington of the Washington Post Magazine has a specific goal: "To understand people as they understand themselves. One of my profile subjects . . . a man whose son had committed suicide, described better than I ever could what I hope to discover—'Your thoughts when you say your prayers in a quiet room.' Yes, exactly."

In his book "American Profiles: Somebodies and Nobodies Who Matter," Harrington says,

> I try to approach each subject, whether a vice president or a retarded man, from the same cast of mind—the belief that each person, famous or obscure, is at once ordinary and extraordinary in his own way. My job is to discover those ways.
>
> Always, I begin my research looking for continuities or rifts in each person's life that might help clarify how he or she came to be the person he or she is. I look for the social context—how a subject's sex, race, age, religion, or social class might have shaped his or her life. I look for the individual context—how family and personal experiences might have shaped a subject.
>
> Yet I am not one who believes that everything that came before explains everything about us now. . . . Too much magic or monstrosity occurs in passage. . . . I believe it is the interplay and struggle between being and transcending our social categories and personal experiences that makes us who we are. It is called character.

Developing trusting, reliable sources can be hard work. Reporter Lisa Hoffman shared her techniques with the Missouri Group for their book "News Reporting and Writing." One tip—think of beat sources as extended family:

> To become part of the family, you must convince your sources that you're a human being and that you're interested in them as people, too. I take them out to lunch or for drinks. I ask about their spouses and children and tell them about the fight I had with my boyfriend and the movie I saw Saturday night. I bitch about my editors and grumble about the play of a story. Many have only a "Front Page" perspective of the news business, and most are fascinated by how the process really works.

Hoffman ignores top-down protocol when it interferes with the quest for truth: "I check each morning with the secretaries who answer the phones, open the mail, prepare the dockets. Like most mothers, they're the ones who keep the household running. They also know first what is going on."

To be accepted, interviewers should speak the special language of their potential sources. If an outsider wanted to chronicle the work of journalists, it would be necessary to understand terms such as "scoop," "lead," "managing editor," "field producer" and more. Similarly, an interviewer relying on a physicist should understand quarks; one looking into airline safety should understand stress fractures before asking questions of an engineer. Lack of such preparation will result in lack of access or unsuccessful interviews.

Conducting an investigation divorced from a regular beat increases the difficulty of research. But by relying on the documentary and human sources covered in this book, supplemented by going to the beat reporter for help, an investigator should be prepared.

Looking for Credentials Fraud in Résumés

Investigators should check a source's résumé line by line for exaggerations or falsifications. Common sense goes a long way in uncovering fraud. As private investigator Edmund J. Pankau says in his book "Check It Out!," "Personal references are almost always chosen by the job applicant, so if that person is a fraud, you had better not depend on those references, because they could even be an integral part of the scam." The telephone number of a supposed past employer might be the number of a friend or answering service that has been paid to lie.

False identities are so easy to create that when a Hartford (Conn.) Courant reporter set out to adopt one for himself (as part of a newspaper project), he had little trouble becoming someone who had died 31 years earlier as a four-day-old infant. False identities are usually assumed by resourceful criminals. More common is a partially falsified résumé by a generally responsible person.

One case involved Washington Post reporter Janet Cooke, who was awarded a Pulitzer Prize for an investigation of a preteen drug addict. It turned out that Cooke's story was fabricated, and so was some of her résumé. She lost her job and her Pulitzer after a wire service reporter discovered the résumé falsifications while making routine calls to prepare a feature story.

Many assertions on a résumé can be checked with ease. College degrees can be verified with a call to the campus registrar. For example, if a subject mentions military service, an investigator should check the local courthouse for military discharge Form DD 214. The IRE Resource Center has articles filed under the heading "Credentials Fraud."

Getting Ready to Pop the Questions

During preparation for interviews, the investigator should look not only for lies, but also for neutral and positive information. Some of the information can be used as an icebreaker, to show some intersection between the reporter's life and the interviewee's. People frequently say "It's a small world" because it is. Knowing the interviewee collects stamps is an icebreaker, especially if the interviewer does the same. Or perhaps the connection will be the subject's daughter attending the same college the investigator attended two decades earlier.

Neutral information might relate to an institution or issue connected with the source. An interviewer knowledgeable about the interviewee's employer or specialty (such as nuclear waste disposal) will impress the source, whose prior experience with journalists may have left the impression that they tend to be inadequately prepared.

The positive information might relate to the interviewee's accomplishments. The interviewer should work such matters as a local award or the publication of a book into the conversation. Flattery can be a door opener; furthermore, mentioning the matter is one more way to demonstrate preparation. Documents discovered during preparation can come in handy during the interview. Journalist Jerry Uhrhammer says, in John Ullmann's book "Investigative Reporting: Advanced Methods and Techniques," that

> reluctant witnesses are more willing to talk if they are being asked about documents and what those documents mean. This approach has an added advantage—if you get good documentation, it often obviates the need for a human source, named or unnamed, in the story. This can appeal to someone who may have key knowledge of what's happened but doesn't want to be publicly associated with the story.

Getting in the Door

When time permits, I rarely use the telephone to set up an interview. Instead, I write a letter. Why? It can be hard to reach a source on the telephone; many are shielded by switchboard operators, secretaries, administrative assistants and answering machines. An investigator might avoid the screeners by calling early in the morning or past the dinner hour, when workaholic sources are alone in the office. An elusive source who happens to pick up the telephone might talk out of curiosity, politeness or habit.

But even when an investigator gets through by telephone, it may be an inopportune time for the source; perhaps the source is having a bad day at work or experiencing personal problems. Besides, telephone conversations leave room for misunderstandings. The words disappear into air; if, months later, the source denies parts of the conversation, the investigator may have no convincing way to contradict the assertion—short of taping phone conversations without permission.

Writing letters is one way to circumvent these difficulties. Most sources see mail intended for them. Furthermore, most people read their mail when in the mood to do so; letters are not as intrusive as telephone calls. They can reread the letter, too, mulling it over. The words do not disappear as in telephone calls: you have a paper trail. In those rare instances when my letters go unanswered, I send a telegram. It gets attention and conveys that I am serious, thus often producing a response.

The wording of the letter is crucial. Reporter Olive Talley says "I formulate what is going to be my standard explanation of what the story is about, and I tell everybody the same thing. . . . That way, if people you talk to compare notes, they will have heard the same story."

While formulating my wording, I avoid words like "interview" and "investigation." Instead, I use phrases such as "I would like to talk with you to fill gaps in my research." When I have reason to believe sources are reluctant or hostile, I explain why it is in their interest to talk. That involves first guessing why a source would talk to any journalist, then figuring out why you. Investigator Don Ray has listed potential reasons. On the matter of why a source would talk to any journalist, Ray says, "She has to, it's her job; she believes strongly in her cause; she wants to defend herself against rumors; she hopes the exposure will help her career." On the matter of why a source would talk to a particular journalist, Ray mentions, "She believes you really understand and care; she is impressed with your previous work; she believes you have information to share."

When I believe it is the only route, I promise that, if they are cooperative, sources can read my manuscript for accuracy. Many journalists believe this will lead to censorship or lawsuits, but these objections are misguided. I have made the offer to hundreds of sources. Many of them, who had no reason to talk, granted an interview only because I made the offer. After the interview, the practice has led to increased disclosure as sources, reviewing the manuscript, recall information never mentioned during the original session. It also has meant improved accuracy, as sources point out factual errors or misinterpretations. It is rarely painless, but not once has it backfired.

A survey based on social science techniques might be the best way to make contact with reluctant sources. While investigating government contracts to possibly phony minority-owned construction companies, a Minneapolis Star Tribune team devised a sound questionnaire, then asked every one of the 400 minority contractors certified by the city government to answer. Many did, including some who would have refused to answer questions in isolation apart from the survey. The answers showed a pattern that strengthened the eventual stories.

For investigators unwilling to try the strategies mentioned so far, there are other techniques. It can help to tell reluctant sources that somebody they respect will vouch for my integrity and accuracy as a reporter. But I use this strategy only after making sure that the third party will come through. I also ask the third party to have the source call me, so I can explain firsthand what I am doing. Sometimes the intended subject has heard about my interviewing from sources I have already approached. If the feedback is complimentary, that might melt resistance.

Often, though, the feedback will be a warning. That is why some investigators go to the main subject early. Mary Hargrove, a newspaper reporter and editor, says the timing of interviewing high-level sources is especially sensitive: "If they hear from 12 other people that you're looking and you're not talking to them, you really make them skittish."

If every tactic has failed and I am interviewless, I send questions in the mail, taking the stance: Here they are. If you answer them, great. If not, the story will proceed without you. Occasionally the sources—fearful of their views being omitted or intrigued by the questions—call. When necessary, I put aside my manners, showing up unexpectedly at the potential source's office or home. I have been granted entry because of my persistence or because the source is curious beyond restraint about what I want. A variation on that theme is contacting elusive sources when they are away from their home city—at a professional conference or on vacation.

A positive mental attitude might tip the balance. Reporter Eric Nalder says "As a warm-up, maybe during your morning shower, imagine a successful interview. Reporters who don't believe they will get the interview . . . usually fail. As far as I'm concerned, no one should ever refuse to talk to me. It works."

When it works, the time and place of the interview become important. Sometimes they are beyond the investigator's control because it is necessary to fit the subject's schedule. But when the investigator has a say about the site, the options should be weighed carefully. Meeting the source at home makes sense if the investigator wants a glimpse of the source's personal life. The subject's office makes more sense if the investigator plans to focus on the work life. The office is ruled out, though, when the source does not want to be seen by colleagues. If the investigator works in a newsroom, that might be a satisfactory site. But when confidentiality is an issue, the journalist should be wary, because fellow journalists or a nonjournalist visitor might disclose the meeting. It is almost always a bad idea to meet at a restaurant. Inevitably, during a key question or answer, the server will interrupt. Other problems include notetaking (difficult while trying to eat), tape recording (background noise), and arguing over who pays for the meal.

Asking the Questions, Dealing With the Answers

The first few minutes of the interview should be devoted to breaking the ice. This is the time to mention the small-world commonalities that were the fruit of preinterview research, to talk the talk about the institution or issue at hand. It is also wise to repeat where the investigation is headed and to go over any ground rules previously discussed. Such a review can minimize misunderstandings later.

Impressions created during the small talk are important. Nalder says "Never approach your subjects as though they seem menacing or likely to clam up. Appear innocent, friendly, unafraid and curious. If you are a hard-boiled, cynical reporter who talks out of the side of your mouth, you will need acting lessons."

The order in which the investigator asks the questions can be crucial, and so some time should be spent before the interview carefully ordering the questions. Sometimes chronological ordering makes the most sense, allowing sources to explain their actions chronologically. A chronological account also might help the investigator discover lapses and gaps in logic.

I move from nonthreatening questions to threatening. I never apologize for the threatening ones or request permission to raise an unpleasant subject; asking them is my job. Besides, there are no embarrassing questions—just embarrassing answers.

Some of the questions are meant to elicit atmosphere more than facts. I ask sources what they were wearing at the time of a key event, what they remember about the meeting room, whether it was storming or sunny outside. The details might help construct a compelling narrative when it is time to write. Because answers lead down unexpected paths, the investigator must be flexible. Usually, however, it is possible to stick to the questions in the order written.

When a source goes down a path that seems unproductive, the interviewer must know how to get back on track. Michael Schumacher, in a Writer's Digest article headlined "Creative Interviewing," uses this example from author Gary Provost:

> I'll let people go on for a while, and then I'll try to get them back to the point in a way that doesn't sound as if I'm saying "shut up and let's get back to the point." I try to make a question sound as if it's related to what they're talking about. For example, let's say I wanted to talk to Dan Wakefield about writing fiction, and he's telling me about a time when he was in Cuba, writing a nonfiction piece for the New York Times. I might say something like "Did you ever think of writing a novel about Cuba?" I'm really trying to get him back to a discussion about whether he prefers writing novels over nonfiction, but it sounds as if we're discussing Cuba.

To keep an interview moving productively, the structure of questions is vital. If the investigator wants full-blown answers, open-ended questions should be asked and those that can be answered yes or no should be eliminated. If an open-ended question ("What are your plans after you retire from the Senate next year?"), results in a useless response, the investigator can ask a second question that forces the source to focus ("What would it take for you to return to teaching at Harvard?"). To elicit feelings, the interviewer can ask "Describe your state of mind when you decided to quit." To get details for local color, "Take me back to the day before the murder, walk me through the scene."

Some types of questions are unwise. "Did you embezzle the money, or did your partner do it?" is a double-barreled question. What if the subject answers yes? Or no? Yes or no to which part of the question? "Don't you think" questions, as in "Don't you think your corporation's policy on overseas payments is illegal?" are not so much questions as counterproductive mini-lectures.

Leading questions are risky, but like most risks, they occasionally yield results. Journalist Oriana Fallaci became well known for asking risky, leading questions. When interviewing the Pakistani president, she alluded to antagonism between him and the Indian prime minister, then asked, "You two really can't stand each other, can you?" The intemperate response led to a story for Fallaci.

An investigator should leave no easy out: Rather than ask whether the subject fired the whistleblower, ask why. That puts the source in the position of explaining rather than issuing a simple, and perhaps disingenuous, denial. When such tactics bring silence, talented interviewers let the silence linger. Reporter Tad Bartimus says the "pregnant pause" is one of her favorite interviewing tools: "Most people abhor silence. It makes them nervous. . . . Often an interviewee, in an attempt to fill a silent void, will volunteer information that astounds both the talker and the listener. 'My God, I've never even told my husband that,' said one shocked interview subject. 'Good! Now we're getting somewhere,'" Bartimus remembers thinking.

While the source is talking, I make eye contact. I nod my head. I make reassuring noises such as "uh-huh," "yes," and maybe say "fascinating" or "how interesting." When appropriate, I ask "How?" or "Why?" or "What do you mean by that?" Eventually, I ask for documentation in an indirect way like "How do you know that?" I hope such questions will produce a response along the lines of "I am going to show you how I know."

It is a good test of the source. Many make assertions that turn out to be based on rumor, not fact; many fail to distinguish between what they actually know and what they assume. When researching my biography of a then elderly Armand Hammer, I had to press aging sources to distinguish between what they knew about him 65 years earlier, and what they had read or heard after Hammer became famous. A few sources told me about incidents that never happened or that could not have happened during the year they claimed it had.

It is important to figure out what is not being said, as well as what is. Reporter Bruce Selcraig notes, "It might be significant if the mayor speaks to you routinely about his family yet never mentions his wife, or a successful businessman talks for hours without crediting his partner."

Selcraig tests for lies in confrontational interviews. He asks questions for which there is only one true answer. He listens for admissions of guilt that are lies in themselves. A bank teller might say "I occasionally took money from the drawer," when actually embezzling from hundreds of accounts. A different kind of lie is the carefully worded response: "If I ask, 'Are you taping this conversation,' and you reply, 'No,' it could mean that someone else is taping it, someone else is listening and transcribing it or that you were taping it but stopped."

Notetaking and Other Matters of Accuracy

An investigator who is a weak notetaker or wants proof of every word said should tape record the session. Few sources are nervous about that; those who are should be offered a copy of the tape or be encouraged to do their own taping. In circumstances where taping is impractical or likely to stifle candor, the investigator should know shorthand, or devise a personal shorthand based on proper names, words and phrases likely to come up.

If the notetaking still fails to keep up with the subject's words, the interviewer can ask—once in awhile—for the source to repeat what was said, perhaps flattering the interviewee by saying "That last point was so fascinating I want to make sure I have it word for word." Another tactic is to ask a throwaway question, completing the notetaking from the previous answer while the source rattles on about an irrelevant matter.

If the investigator expects the interview to be on the record but the source invokes off-the-record, background or some other unacceptable condition during the session, there are countermoves. One possibility is to listen respectfully, then later interject "That information you shared earlier is fascinating. Is there any way I can quote you about that?" Another possibility is to find out from the source whether documents or other persons might reveal the same information.

An investigator can stand on principle, telling the source that everything must be on the record because that was the original verbal or implied contract. Standing on principle is easier for an investigator if there is no prior relationship with the source and if there is little likelihood of such a relationship developing in the future. But burning bridges is never sound policy if an alternative can be found.

As the interview winds down, it is wise to say "Is there anything I didn't ask that you want to discuss?" I also ask whether there is anybody else I should interview, any books, articles or reports I should read. A seemingly cheeky, but usually answered, question is "Who are your three closest friends? What three people do you fear most as your enemies?"

When the project is likely to continue for months after I have conducted an interview, I contact my sources periodically to let them know about my progress. This courtesy is appreciated and sometimes leads sources to call back with additional information. On the beat, it is wise to contact sources after an unflattering story to ask if they had problems with the piece and what responses they have gotten. Such a call might keep a bridge intact. That is what interviewing is about—building bridges and keeping them repaired to get as much information as possible.

PART TWO

Investigating Individuals, Institutions and Issues

Chapter 6

INVESTIGATING GOVERNMENT

The Legislative Branch and Those Who Try to Influence It

*U*ntil this point, The Reporter's Handbook has been offering advice relevant to virtually any investigation. From this point forward, the chapters will be topic-specific. Readers delving into the topic-specific chapters are reminded here that using the documents and techniques mentioned through Chapter 5 will increase the power of their information gathering.

The best investigators pull together information from paper trails and people trails. Novices (and those more experienced who are in need of inspiration) should study the endnotes of first-rate investigative books to see what I mean.

I have done just that numerous times. For this example, I will cite the endnotes in Erik Larson's book "Lethal Passage: The Story of a Gun." On the paper trail, Larson used documents from every branch and level of government, as the best investigators do. From the legislative branch of the federal government, he relied on congressional hearings and General Accounting Office studies. From the federal executive branch, he used, among other documents, notices in the Code of Federal Regulations and memos from the Bureau of Alcohol, Tobacco and Firearms. From the federal judicial branch, Larson mined U.S. district court and bankruptcy court records. Court cases helped him delve into criminal proceedings as well as civil matters.

A similar recitation could be given for the branches of state and local governments. Larson interviewed government sources from all branches and levels as he followed the people trail in his quest to fully understand documents.

As noted in the earlier chapters of this book, not all information resides in government files and the brains of government employees. Larson found information in the files of private businesses (including numerous gun manufacturers and dealers) and private-sector interest groups (such as the National Rifle Association, Handgun Control and the Violence Policy Center). Furthermore, he mined secondary sources such as newspapers, newsletters, magazines, books, medical journals and broadcast transcripts. He dug into historical archives to gain perspective.

Moving from history to the technological present, Larson found information on government computer tapes of gun sales and purchases. To make sense of the numbers he asked lots of questions and he observed sources for days, weeks or months until he understood what made them tick.

End of exhortation. The topic-specific chapters begin with legislatures.

Legislators elected by the populace assume a huge responsibility. Their decisions allocate millions of dollars, benefit or harm businesses and individuals, determine the fabric of society. Yet the policymaking role of elected representatives—whether part of the U.S. Senate and House, state legislatures, county commissions or city councils—rarely receives sustained scrutiny by investigative journalists.

Unfortunately, correcting the problem is complicated. For investigators, there are no easy answers: How effectively are legislators representing constituents? How should effectiveness be measured? If a U.S. representative pushes through a $500 million dam for his district, should the representative be praised for bringing jobs and safety from floods to constituents or criticized for wasting tax dollars on a narrow segment of the population while harming the natural ecology? When the legislator takes money from dam construction lobbyists, is he accepting support from like-minded individuals or selling favors to special interests?

Similar questions arise at all levels of government. If a city council member votes to award a paving contract to the low bidder who is also a business partner, should the council member be censured for a conflict of interests or held blameless because the law requires awards to legitimate low bidders? Projects based on such thorny questions are listed under "Conflicts of Interests" at the IRE Resource Center.

This chapter is not built on a unified strategy for investigating the legislative branch. Instead, I have divided this immense subject into manageable subtopics. Each could be a self-contained investigation. Alternately, two or more subtopics could be combined as part of a broader investigation—for example, the subtopic of payments from lobbyists to legislators could be combined with how legislators handle their committee assignments.

The possibilities for investigations of elected representatives are endless and exciting, partly because the real scandal is what is *legal*. Paul

Williams, speaking of state legislators, put it well in "Investigative Reporting and Editing":

> Because their salaries are rarely above those of skilled blue-collar workers, they are subject to temptation and leverage from well-funded lobbyists and their corporate, professional or union backers. A financially hard-pressed legislator may suddenly find credit easy to get when banking bills are before his committee; if he is on the health and welfare committee, he may find his doctor making house calls and then staying to talk about medical-insurance legislation; or members of the house painters' union may want to show their gratitude by redoing his house free of charge, with paint donated by a major wholesaler. In examining the legislative process, your major problem is one of tracing subtle or ephemeral relationships that are kept secret. The use of public records to build personal profiles is a key.

Following the Dollar

Following the dollar from outside interests to legislators is one way to start, looking at the givers (political action committees, lobbyists and individuals) as well as the recipients. Campaign contribution and expenditure reports are more accessible than ever. Because of that, journalists are able to write more informative stories than in decades past.

In other respects, however, little has changed over the decades. As Brooks Jackson, author of "Honest Graft: Big Money and the American Political Process," says,

> The influence of big money on American politics is nothing new, as I was reminded by Louise Overacker's classic volume "Money in Elections," published in 1932. . . . She concluded that spending limits were futile and only encouraged concealment, that efforts to raise enough money in small donations usually didn't work, and that public financing was the best solution.

In her book "Politics and Money: The New Road to Corruption," Elizabeth Drew explains why she considers her topic a year-round beat:

> While a good deal of attention has been paid to the growing costs of political campaigns, the real point is what the raising of money to pay for those campaigns does to our politicians—and to our political system. It is driving the politicians into a new form of political corruption. It is making it very difficult for those who wish to avoid this corruption to do so. The pressures, real and imagined, on the politicians to raise large sums of money and to prevent large sums of money from being spent against them have become a full-time preoccupation on Capitol Hill, affecting the politicians' conduct of their job to a greater degree than ever. These pressures have provided new opportunities for the lawyers and lobbyists who try to shape national policies and have

brought to their activities a new level of sophistication and a new energy. The pressures of money have made it more unlikely than ever that politicians will take difficult positions, exercise leadership.

Charles Peters stresses the insidious special access money can buy. In his book "How Washington Really Works," Peters says,

If the other side can't get similar access, a lobbyist's views may be all the official ever hears. Especially on smaller issues, where a decision either way won't rock the ship of state too much, whichever side gets to the congressman usually wins. . . . Even when the congressman hears other views, the voice of a friend is likely to stand out in the cacophony of opinions. More insidiously, the psychology of access plays on the fact that most government officials are basically decent people who want to be . . . liked. Faced with a . . . fellow human being who wants something very much, with perhaps only an abstract argument on the other side, the natural reaction is to be obliging. That's why if you are a lobbyist, just getting through to a high official and presenting your case . . . no favors involved . . . gives you a good chance for success.

A former U.S. senator says the impact of special-interest money is everywhere. The result might be as obvious as a vote favoring the contributor's wished-for tax loophole. Or it might be more subtle, such as a speech never delivered or a bill stuck in subcommittee by a chairman paid handsomely through PACs from throughout an industry.

The dual reality of legislators wanting money and special interests wanting access has made fund-raising a mini-industry in Washington, D.C., and in state capitals, too. Compiling the invitation list to a fund-raiser is an exercise in crassness. If a legislator serves on the Agriculture Committee and favors sugar price supports, the lobbyist organizing the fundraiser will invite sugar producers. If the legislator opposes sugar price supports, the candy manufacturers will be on the guest list instead.

Fund-raising events should be grist for investigators more often than they are; at the least they can provide raw material for stories about influence peddling. Journalists smart enough to stay on top of the phenomenon usually are not invited, but they can put out the word to sources in Washington and in the home district of their desire to be notified. Investigators documenting fund-raisers after the fact can look for FEC reports of contributions on the same day from donors in the same industry. Society page stories in the Washington Post or the hometown newspaper also help track fund-raisers after the fact.

Knowledge of fund-raisers can help journalists build projects that document how many hours of each day legislators devote to filling the coffers. The average U.S. senator raises tens of thousands of dollars a week every week during a six-year term. The average U.S. House member raises thousands a week over a two-year term. Such devotion to fund-raising seems likely to have a negative impact on legislating and constituent service—a good story in itself.

The best stories go beyond raw dollars, to why an individual or institution donates—and what they get in return. For example, whenever a candidate receives a contribution from outside the district, journalists should be asking why a nonconstituent cares enough to give. If lots of individuals and corporations within the same industry are donating to the same member of Congress, it is vital to understand the industry. How do the donors make their money? How are they taxed? What government activities could harm them? Some of the most poignant such stories are in the IRE Resource Center under "Campaign Finance," "Congress," "Elections," "Political Action Committees," "Politicians" and "State Government/Legislatures."

Campaign Finance Records

Investigators can track campaign dollars by studying the contribution and expenditure reports that are required at every level of government. Reports for congressional and presidential candidates are at the Federal Election Commission in Washington, D.C. Each contributor is identified by name, town, state, ZIP code, amount given, date given, which election given for (primary or regular), occupation and place of employment. It is not necessary to visit Washington. FEC records are available on-line from the agency. In addition, the FEC offers computer tapes containing contributions of $500 or more. The agency also customizes computer printouts for individual requesters.

Federal candidates are required to report contributions of $200 or more from individuals, plus all contributions from political action committees, political party committees and bank loans. Individuals can give $1,000 to a candidate in a primary and an additional $1,000 in the general election, up to $25,000 total to all candidates in one calendar year. Institutions cannot give directly to candidates. Instead, they form PACs, which can give up to $5,000 to each candidate of their choice.

Every committee has a treasurer identified in the filings. The treasurer is a potential source; if the treasurer is prominent or unsavory, that might be a story in itself. Many treasurers are not sophisticated Washington types, and therefore might talk candidly about FEC investigations or other sensitive matters.

An investigator can examine expenditure reports in the same office as the contribution records. The Nashville Tennessean found a local congressman using contributions to pay rent on a building he owned. Furthermore, he created two computer companies, which then leased equipment to the campaign. The campaign treasury bought him a luxury automobile, pickup truck, mobile phone and furniture for his home, as well as employing his sister.

Nongovernment groups enhance FEC information in ways helpful to investigators. The National Library on Money and Politics, in Washington, D.C., assigns codes to every PAC based on its legislative interest—agriculture, highway construction and so on. By matching those codes to congressional committees, the library makes it easier to determine if PACs are donating to legislators because of committee assignments. The library is part of the Center for Responsive Politics, which publishes studies based on FEC data.

Despite the watchdogs, election law violations often go unpunished. The FEC's strength is compiling contribution and spending records. Its weakness—partly because it is headed by political appointees—is enforcement. One type of incumbent violation rarely policed is the use of "personal" staff from the House or Senate office—staff paid with taxpayer dollars—in a reelection campaign. The violation most common among challengers is failure to file timely, complete reports.

To monitor enforcement, an investigator can examine advisory opinions, audits and completed actions. Investigators should examine the index of FEC rulings on alleged violations. Large contributors have often violated federal campaign laws; an alert reporter can find out what they did and how the FEC handled it. Letters from contributors' attorneys might be part of the public record. When a Thomson Newspapers' Washington correspondent looked at large individual contributors from Pennsylvania, he found several had violated the $25,000 annual limit. Why had the FEC failed to discipline the violators, he wondered. When he asked the agency's vice chair, she gave the standard bureaucratic reply that the FEC lacked resources.

Not all the corruption is in federal campaigns. Coverage of how state legislators, county commissioners and city council members raise and spend money should be more attentive.

"Bankrolling the Legislature" said a headline over a series in the St. Paul Pioneer Press. "Money Gushes Through State Politics," read the headline's next deck. "Last election, candidates for the Minnesota legislature spent a record $9 million on their campaigns. Where does that money come from, and what role does it play when lawmakers meet to decide the state's future?"

The investigation found a correlation between campaign contributions and legislative success:

> Minnesota's biggest special-interest groups gave $1.3 million to lawmakers
> . . . and were rewarded by winning 41 of their top 50 legislative priorities. . . .
> The newspaper asked the state's biggest campaign contributors to rank their
> priorities at the state capitol during the . . . session. The computer-assisted
> study then examined how the groups fared on those issues, and how much
> help they got from the legislators who received their contributions.

Many states have campaign finance disclosures patterned after federal law. State election offices are in the capital city. They are sometimes complemented by obscure agencies ready to be mined by journalists. The state capital bureau chief for the St. Louis Post-Dispatch reported that the Missouri State Ethics Commission levied substantial fines and ordered 16 candidates off the ballot during its first year of existence.

■ THE MANY POCKETS OF A POLITICIAN'S COAT

Writing for the IRE Journal, Viveca Novak of Common Cause magazine provided a campaign finance primer. The article is reprinted here, with minor editing:

Federal campaign contribution ceilings . . . are not as limiting as they may appear for the hungry politician and the creative donor. There are many legal ways for contributors to fill a politico's pockets, and other ways that are legally questionable.

Contributions of $100,000-plus to presidential campaigns, for instance, still occur. Companies can give virtually unlimited amounts to state accounts or foundations begun by members of Congress that are not required to report to the Federal Election Commission. Special interests fly members of Congress to Hawaii and other hardship posts to earn bogus honoraria, sometimes bringing their families along for the ride.

The FEC makes available an abundance of campaign contribution and expenditure information that federal candidates must submit, though the agency is pitiful on the enforcement end. Finding the other channels the money takes—the ones not reported to the FEC—is a tougher reporting job.

The key in both cases is knowing what to look for. At least as important as knowing who is giving and how candidates are spending is figuring out why. Large contributions often result in some individuals or special interests having more access to decisionmakers than others—and money usually means, at the very least, access. It is hardly a mental leap to figure the big givers want to be beneficiaries of policy decisions in statehouses, Congress and the White House—and they often are.

There are four common money games. First, soft money. When people wrote big checks to Richard Nixon's Committee to Reelect the President, they expected something in return—special consideration for themselves or their businesses. Some of this was spelled out in the Watergate hearings and led to reforms in campaign finance law. But these soft money donations continue. They allow the national political parties to raise money and direct it to state affiliates, where it is used for such activities as get-out-the-vote drives. This money is not supposed to be spent to directly influence a specific federal election, but that is the effect.

Second, bundling. Obviously, giving a candidate a $200,000 contribution is going to make a bigger impression than giving $1,000. One way to do that legally is to convince other people to write $1,000 checks, gather them together, and hand them over in one lump. Corporations do this, although they are not supposed to coerce employees to write checks. To check, look for contributions, for example, from General Electric employees all recorded on a single day or within a short period. The FEC computers allow an investigator to run a principal place of business search, which involves punching in the name of a company; what comes back is a list of all contributors who named the company as their workplace.

Individuals, not just corporations, do this as well. I looked into a Brooklyn rabbi . . . unknown in Washington until the 1980s, when he began fund-raising for various Republicans. He collects checks from individuals in Orthodox Jewish communities throughout the United States and gives them to members whose views he finds helpful. Trading on his cachet, he then is able to get Congressional or White House support for friends' projects—though [he] seems to enjoy, as much as anything, the perquisites that come with his fundraising stature, such as giving invocations at Washington events. Bundlers are supposed to register as intermediaries at the FEC, but seldom do. One FEC service that did help me in this case was a search that produces a list of all the contributions from a given ZIP code. The ZIP code search is great for other story ideas, like finding out what neighborhoods give most heavily to whom.

Third, member PACs. Many members of Congress, while raising money for themselves, give some of it away to other members. They can do this by reaching into their campaign treasuries or by starting their own PACs, thereby opening another pocket to be lined by willing donors. The amount spread around like this increases with each election. The contributions are easy to find at the FEC in the disbursements section of a member's campaign account or PAC. Why do they do it? Some of the most generous donors have been members running for House or Senate leadership positions. This raises questions about vote buying.

Roll Call, a Capitol Hill newspaper, reported that . . . for example, [a] senator . . . gave $86,500 to his colleagues; he then won the chairmanship of the Senate Republican Conference, beating his opponent by just one vote. Besides Roll Call, the monthly magazine Campaigns and Elections covers campaign finance. . . . So do the publications of many private and public interest groups, including Common Cause and Public Citizen. Lists of PACs can be found in numerous publications . . . A book with insight into PAC decisionmaking is "Risky Business?: PAC Decisionmaking and Strategy," edited by Robert Biersack, Paul S. Herrnson and Clyde Wilcox.

Fourth, independent expenditures. Such expenditures by the National Security Political Action Committee paid for the infamous Willie Horton ads in the 1988 presidential campaign. The term describes any spending on behalf of a candidate by a separate individual or committee. To be legal, the spending—for instance, the development of an ad and the purchase of television time—must not be coordinated in any way with a candidate's campaign. There is not supposed to be any back and forth about if and when, for instance, the American Medical Association will buy an ad in support of a candidate. Unlike direct campaign contributions, there is no limit on independent expenditures. They are, however, reported to the FEC.

A number of independent expenditures are made not in favor of candidates, but against them. Much of this money goes into negative campaigning. It is worth trying to figure out if particular independent expenditures are really independent, or linked too closely to a campaign. Sometimes an investigator will find that the candidate and the group doing the independent spending use the same consultants and other personnel, which should raise questions.

Since Novak wrote her piece, not-for-profit foundations have become increasingly popular among members of Congress. The Wall Street Journal reported how one congressman established the Commission on Savings and Investments in America, which sought tax-deductible contributions from banks, brokerage firms and finance companies. The impetus appeared to be changes in tax law making it more difficult for corporations to deduct lobbying expenses. Donating money to a foundation would still be deductible, as long as it did not cross the line between educating legislators and attempting to influence them. In an earlier edition of this book, Gerry Everding told of one U.S. senator who established several tax-exempt voter registration groups shortly before an election. The groups were ostensibly nonpartisan, but inside sources conceded they were registering only voters favoring the senator's political party. A major contributor to the questionable tax-exempt group was a savings and loan executive on whose behalf the senator had interceded with regulators.

Another practice involves unsecured or favorable-rate loans from financial institutions, other corporations or individuals to legislators. Such loans are difficult to detect unless they are disclosed voluntarily. The loans, like many benefits offered to legislators, are not always initiated by outsiders determined to wield influence. Frequently legislators solicit the special treatment.

Wealthy legislators and challengers probably do less soliciting—many have few reservations about contributing their own money instead of relying on outsiders. One recent study of Congress showed that 17 percent of House members and 28 percent of senators were millionaires. A one-volume overview of legislators' money and everybody else's money in politics is "Congressional Campaign Finances: History, Facts, and Controversy" from Congressional Quarterly Books, Washington, D.C. A step-by-step investigative manual for journalists is "Follow the Money Handbook" by Larry Makinson at the Center for Responsive Politics, Washington, D.C.

The World of Lobbyists

Beyond looking at campaign contributions, an investigator can examine other methods employed by lobbyists to reach legislators. Often it makes sense for a journalist to start at the beginning by learning how newsworthy lobbyists arrived at their calling, and how they built and consolidated their influence. In Public Citizen magazine, Nancy Watzman explained ten stages on the road to becoming an effective lobbyist: Get experience in the legislature or executive branch, become especially knowledgeable about a specific issue, find wealthy international clients to supplement domestic accounts, skirt revolving-door rules, raise lots of money for legislators, give lots of gifts to policymakers, form coalitions with impressive (and often misleading) names, manufacture what appears to be grass-roots support, disclose as little as possible, renew contacts and reputation by reentering government periodically.

It helps to know who is defined as a lobbyist and who is not. At the federal level and in many state capitals there are concrete definitions of who must file regular reports. In Washington, D.C., lobbyists are defined as those who receive or expend money to influence legislation, or who otherwise seek to push or block bills. Many corporations employ full-time lobbyists (almost always called by some other term, such as "vice president for government relations"). So do labor unions, universities, professional organizations and government units. A variation is to hire lawyers and public relations firms to lobby part-time. In addition, special interests are frequently represented in Washington, D.C., or state capitals by trade associations. An oil company with its own full-time lobbyists in state capitals and Washington, D.C., plus Washington lawyers and public relations practitioners on retainer, will also belong to the American Petroleum Institute.

Lobbyists trying to influence Congress are supposed to register with the secretary of the Senate or clerk of the House. About 6,000 are registered at any given time; they are supported by thousands of secretaries, administrative assistants and the like whose names never show up on registration forms. The form asks for a business address, the name and address of the employer in whose interest the lobbyist is working, duration of employment, amount of salary or retainer, plus expenses allowed by the employer. The magazine Congressional Quarterly Weekly Report and the official Congressional Record publish registrations on an occasional basis. In addition to the registration document, an investigator can check quarterly reports of income and expenditures.

The law is so riddled with loopholes and so poorly enforced that lobbyists themselves estimate that about 75 percent of lobbyists never register; almost none of them is punished for that failure. Despite the loopholes, it makes sense to check registrations to learn which individuals and groups are active in which controversies. A look through just one month's registrations turned up 59 businesses, 49 trade associations, 4 labor groups, 4 local governments and 10 citizens' groups. One example that could spawn a project for a Texas journalist, higher education reporter or environmental investigator: the University of Texas registering as a lobbyist on a crude oil windfall profits tax. To determine players beyond the registrations, it might help to check with the American League of Lobbyists, in Alexandria, Va.

Former members of Congress (who have their own association based in Washington) can be especially effective lobbyists because of special access to the floor of the chamber, favors they did for other legislators while still in office and their adeptness at appealing to pet projects of current legislators. Larry Van Dyne of The Washingtonian magazine captured the personal side of legislating; if a legislator's spouse contracts Parkinson's disease, suddenly the legislator is willing to sponsor a bill increasing funding for research. Van Dyne said "Nobody in Washington understands this sentimental side of politics better than lobbyists, who stand ready to exploit even the smallest advantage. Which congressmen have arthritis? Whose wife has breast cancer? Who rides a bike to work? Whose child is dyslexic? He who knows these secrets about the lives of politicians knows where to find the soft spots in their hearts."

Lobbyists working on behalf of international governments are supposed to file separately under the Foreign Agents Registration Act, regulated by the U.S. Justice Department. Investigators have found former U.S. representatives and senators, cabinet members and a director of the Central Intelligence Agency lobbying for governments whose interests appear to be at odds with those of the American citizenry.

Reporters at the Center for Public Integrity used the registrations while researching "The Trading Game: Inside Lobbying for the North American Free Trade Agreement." Charles Lewis and his team commented that

> We have publicly criticized the way in which [the] records are collected and the way in which disclosure is enforced. . . . Nonetheless, the imperfect FARA documents are an invaluable resource. . . . Thousands of pages . . . were broken down into tens of thousands of facts—names, numbers, contacts made. . . . These facts were then entered into a database. . . . In this way, we were able to glean intriguing new insights. . . . We were, for example, able to . . . ascertain the top ten U.S. officials most frequently contacted by Mexican officials or their paid representatives.

Washington Representatives, published by Columbia Books, Washington, D.C., with more than 15,000 listings of special-interest advocates, is considered a more reliable guide to lobbyists than the official filings with the government. Another frequently consulted volume is Gale Research's American Lobbyists Directory. "Public Interest Profiles" from the Foundation for Public Affairs, Washington, D.C., lists individuals who consider themselves more altruistic than corporate lobbyists, but who are lobbyists nonetheless.

Many states require lobbyists to register, but, as at the federal level, the definitions contain loopholes. Tens of thousands of lobbyists are registered in state capitals. Yet much of the money they spend on travel, gifts and entertainment goes unreported. The lobby disclosure laws often are so confusingly drafted that it is hard to discuss who should report what. The magazine mentioned Illinois, where "representatives from Las Vegas descended on the state capital for rounds of meetings with state legislators. Casino operators told reporters they spent $5.3 million lobbying for a pro-gambling bill. Lobby disclosure reports, however, indicated expenditures of just $24,000."

The Raleigh News and Observer made good use of lobbyist registrations, however imperfect, in North Carolina. A story by Van Denton opened like this:

> At Vinnie's Steakhouse and Tavern, it's easy to tell when the General Assembly is in town. "The bar is packed full," says [the] general manager of the North Raleigh restaurant. Inside . . . state legislators can fancy themselves a part of the capital's power clique to which Vinnie's caters. . . . If legislators don't want to pay a nickel, they don't have to. Because just as much as legislators enjoy going to Vinnie's and other classy Raleigh restaurants, lobbyists hired to influence them enjoy buying them steaks and Scotch. Vinnie's was the most popular spot in town on expense reports filed . . . by 486 corporations, trade associations and other interest groups that spent $3.3 million lobbying the General Assembly. . . . One legislator . . . chairman of the House Commerce Committee, dined there at least 12 times before and during the legislative session as a guest of lobbyists for banks, savings and loans and mortgage companies.

A book showing how influence peddlers can poison a state legislature is "What's In It for Me?" by Joseph Stedino with journalist Dary Matera. Stedino, a convict turned government agent, posed as a mobster wanting to legalize casino gambling in Arizona. Working a sting through the Phoenix district attorney, Stedino's payoffs to legislators resulted in criminal charges. A more subdued account is "The Art of Legislative Politics" by Tom Loftus, former speaker of the Wisconsin general assembly. Numerous books about lobbying in Washington, D.C., are listed in the Bibliography under Chapter 6.

From the diversity of books about lobbying comes the message that investigators who disregard information from and about lobbyists are foolish. At the least, the information is worth reading to learn the conventional wisdom held by special interests on vital issues.

■ Financial Disclosures of Legislators

When an investigator is trying to determine the impact of special interests on legislators and their staffs, required annual financial disclosures can be consulted. Roll Call began with required disclosures to document that a leader of the U.S. House had received special treatment while buying and selling stocks that were part of corporate initial public offerings.

An obvious question is whether legislators' lifestyles surpass what common sense suggests. The Nashville Tennessean showed how a U.S. representative entered Congress with assets worth $15,000 and a previous salary of $10,000 annually; six years later his assets, according to his financial disclosure, exceeded $2 million.

Committee assignments are often the focal point for conflicts of interests that can be illuminated by the financial disclosures. At one point, a third of House Agriculture Committee members owned farms. Could they be objective about federal farm policy when personal enrichment was at stake? From one viewpoint, it makes sense for, say, a banker to sit on a banking committee. Why not bring the legislator's real-world experience into play? From another viewpoint, such a committee appointment is an obvious conflict. Journalists need to uncover these potential conflicts. After that, voters can decide how much they think it all matters.

It is fruitful to check whether the incumbent continues to receive income from a previous job, and how many hours are spent at that job. The time taken by the job could affect performance in office, or it could be that the job is a fiction providing the employer with access to an influential legislator. The job checks should not stop with the legislator; an investigator can find out whether a politician's friends and relatives have been benefiting from legislative decisions. For example, is the politician's sibling a lawyer whose clients win government contracts due to favoritism?

Because honoraria can be quantified accurately—as opposed to some other income—such payments are a sensible category to explore. Honoraria are often connected with travel sponsored by special interests. Public Citizen magazine examined reports of privately funded trips for U.S. senators, then wrote a study about the abuses titled "On the Road Again." One senator characterized such travel as an attempt by special interests "to get you on the airplane, to get you at the dinner table, to get you on the golf course. It's to be able to peddle a message."

Senators and representatives once could use honoraria for personal items. Now they are supposed to donate honoraria to charities. Investigators should be asking the announced recipients whether they have received the donations. Furthermore, investigators should ask why a legislator designated one charity and not another. As Jean Cobb noted in Common Cause, " While giving to the needy is a worthwhile cause, it can also be used as a source for building support. You may want to check which causes a member gives to and whether there are any relatives or business associates on these boards."

Financial disclosure forms will not answer every question. Cobb reminded fellow investigators that "sometimes what is omitted from the forms is of greater interest than what appears. One U.S. senator failed to disclose loans he received from a California businessman, and also failed to mention debts forgiven by the same businessman." To fill in the gaps, basic research is necessary. One resource is "The Opposition Research

Handbook: A Guide to Political Investigations" by Larry Zilliox Jr. of Investigative Research Specialists, McLean, Va.

U.S. Senate financial disclosures are filed with the Office of Public Records. The reports come from incumbent senators, candidates, officers and employees of the legislative branch; principal assistants to senators; employees designated to handle political funds and some other highly paid employees. Most categories require disclosure of financial dealings affecting spouses or dependents. House of Representatives financial disclosures are filed by members, candidates, officers or employees making more than the GS-16 government salary, plus any employee designated as a principal assistant to a representative. Reports are filed with the Office of Records and Registration.

Many states require financial disclosures by legislators. At all levels of government, journalists should ask legislators to go beyond the limited disclosure in the forms by supplying federal and state income tax returns.

Resources and Perquisites in Office

Legislators are not totally dependent on special interests, outside jobs and investments. Election brings with it resources legislators can use for selfish ends or in the public interest. Members of Congress receive an annual salary ($133,600 as of 1994). When they leave office, they receive generous taxpayer-funded pensions.

Their personal income is dwarfed by their office allowances, which also come from the taxpayers. Each House member currently receives hundreds of thousands dollars annually to run the office. Part of that total can be devoted to salaries for full-time and temporary assistants. Each senator receives funds for personal staff plus additional money for staff assigned to legislative committees. Depending on the state's population, the annual amount for personal staff plus committee assistance can run into the millions of dollars. Both House members and senators are allowed to hire relatives, which provides an opportunity for investigators to determine whether such legal nepotism is being abused.

Details about staffing are available from the House Administration Committee and the Senate Rules and Administration Committee. Perspective is available from "Congressional Pay and Perquisites: History, Facts, and Controversy," published by Congressional Quarterly Books. If the knowledge of staff members is power, then there are some mighty powerful staffers. That is the premise of Michael J. Malbin's book "Unelected Representatives: Congressional Staff and the Future of Representative Government," and Harrison W. Fox Jr. and Susan W. Hammond's "Congressional Staffs: The Invisible Force in American Lawmaking." An insider account comes from John L. Jackley, "Hill Rat: Blowing the Lid Off

Congress." In state legislatures, staff members tend to accumulate lots of power, because those elected serve only part-time.

Staff turnover on the Hill is heavy, meaning investigators have little trouble finding "formers" to talk. Many are disgruntled. Investigators can keep up with formers and currents on personal and committee staff by consulting the Congressional Staff Directory, Mount Vernon, Va., or The Almanac of the Unelected: Staff of the U.S. Congress, Almanac Publishing, Washington, D.C. Investigators can also check staffers' own organizations, such as the Administrative Assistants Association of the U.S. House of Representatives, House Legislative Assistants Association and Senate Press Secretaries Association.

Staff sources might be especially helpful during reelection campaigns, pointing out improper deployment of aides. As Knight-Ridder national correspondent Frank Greve demonstrated in Washington Monthly,

> At least 70 incumbents summoned two or more federally paid Washington aides to their districts late in their campaigns, House expense records indicate. Typically, lawmakers claimed, "official business" required their aides' presence. Just as typically, that business ended on election day. . . . Because publication of House office expense records lags three months or longer behind outlays, it is impossible for challengers, or reporters, to learn during a campaign's heat whether aides remain on the federal payroll. The ethics manual states that [members of Congress] "should keep careful records documenting that campaign work was not done on official time." But many don't, and some lawmakers . . . refuse to disclose what leave or vacation time aides took for campaign work.

The Riverside (Calif.) Press-Enterprise documented the same kind of campaign abuse with state legislative staff.

Names of key legislative staff can be found in each state's government manual and in the State Legislative Staff Directory, from the National Conference of State Legislatures, Denver. Campaign consultants for each candidate will probably have some knowledge of strategy, aboveboard or otherwise. The American Association of Political Consultants, Washington, D.C., might be able to supply potential sources.

Between elections, as well as during campaigns, practices out of touch with common-sense ethics pervade Capitol Hill. Ward Sinclair of the Washington Post said that looking through congressional expense records is like "tripping through a great mail-order catalog of life's amenities. If it exists, it's almost certain that a member of the House bought it—under the rubric of 'official purpose,' of course."

Some investigators consider perquisites to involve such small sums of money that they prefer to concentrate on corrupt policymaking. Other investigators, believing the perquisites to be a moral outrage, write regular exposés. They rely on the clerk of the House reports of members' expenditures, as well as those published by the secretary of the Senate.

Disclosure of travel is required by legislators, officers or employees who accept trips or travel expenses outside the United States from a foreign government. Some foreign travel is underwritten by U.S. taxpayers as House members and senators venture overseas in connection with their committee assignments. Supporters of such travel call the trips "fact-finding missions"; opponents call the trips "junkets." The word "junket" seems appropriate when an already defeated member of Congress is the traveler, billing taxpayers before leaving the House or Senate. By consulting the travel forms, Roll Call determined that 13 of 76 lame-duck U.S. representatives took a foreign trip—a higher percentage than legislators who had won reelection. Journalists who cultivate travel agents might receive advance notice of interesting journeys. The American Society of Travel Agents, in Alexandria, Va., can provide names of its members broken out by location of business.

Congressional Quarterly Weekly Report found the true cost of foreign travel is often higher than what House and Senate members report. The official reports often exclude air transport and escort officers provided by the Defense Department or some other government agency. Furthermore, overseas travel is often absorbed into the expense reports of House and Senate committees, making it difficult to determine which individual members of Congress should be debited for spending taxpayer funds.

Monitoring is needed at all levels of government. When nonsalaried city council members travel on legislative business, they often request a travel advance—documented for an investigator on a pretravel authorization request form. Upon returning, the local legislator files a travel expense voucher. In Columbia, Mo., examination of such forms by journalists has led to resignations and reprimands of council members due to travel expense abuse, including reimbursement for a spouse. In Florida, the Fort Myers News-Press found fifteen local officials had traveled to five hurricane conferences in one year, then profited on reimbursements because of lax accounting.

Constituent Service and Reelection

All those expenditures can have a positive side from a journalist's perspective; they pay for staff members—especially administrative and legislative assistants and committee staff subject experts who are often knowledgeable sources.

Legislative staffers who share the casework files are invaluable. Some senators receive 10,000 constituent letters daily, in addition to the 5,000 or so pieces of mass mailing from special-interest groups. Lots of complaint letters about the same problem might take an investigator down paths that would never have been discovered otherwise. Or an individual letter might provide an investigator with the case needed to tell a story in a compelling, convincing manner. Investigators needing quick background on constituents can consult Congressional Quarterly's Congressional Districts in the 1990s: A Portrait of America and The Almanac of State Legislatures.

From a Bill to a Law

Although many members of Congress pride themselves on constituent service, the highest profile part of elective office is legislating. A few books have captured the intricacy, mundaneness and occasional drama of legislating, especially "The Dance of Legislation" by Eric Redman (about a national health service bill); "Congressional Odyssey: The Saga of a Senate Bill" by T.R. Reid (about waterway user fees); "Blue Skies, Green Politics: The Clean Air Act of 1990" by Gary Bryner; "Lessons From the Hill: The Legislative Journey of an Education Program" by Janet M. Martin; and "The Bill" by Steven Waldman (about President Clinton's national service program).

Memoirs by current or former members of Congress, while rarely devoid of self-serving passages, can provide insights into the process. Some of the most educational are by Tip O'Neill, John Tower, Jim Wright, Morris Udall and Donald Riegle. Biographies of contemporary legislators can provide insights, too. Examples are Nadine Cohodas' biography of U.S. Sen. Strom Thurmond, Mark Kirchmeier's examination of Sen. Robert Packwood, Jerry Roberts' chronicle of Sen. Dianne Feinstein and Lee Roderick's life of Sen. Orrin Hatch. Political scientist Richard F. Fenno Jr. has specialized in the genre, writing "When Incumbency Fails: the Senate Career of Mark Andrews," "Learning to Legislate: The Senate Education of Arlen Specter," "The Emergence of a Senate Leader: Pete Domenici and the Senate Budget" and "The Making of a Senator: Dan Quayle."

Although legislation sometimes strays from paths described by books, certain steps are normally completed. Congress publishes booklets about the process, including "Enactment of a Law: Procedural Steps in the Legislative Process." Every bill introduced in a legislature has a primary sponsor; many carry the names of cosponsors. Every day of publication, the Congressional Record and some state legislatures' services run a list of bills introduced. Sponsorship might be meaningful, although many bills are introduced for show—to satisfy campaign contributors or assuage popular sentiment at home.

An investigator can ask around to learn whether a sponsor really believes in a proposal or introduced it halfheartedly, maybe even hypocritically. In her book "Senator," Elizabeth Drew says of one legislator, "He does not take on a large number of issues, and those that he takes on tend to be ones that make an important point—and also ones on which he feels he has a reasonable chance of winning." He is contrasted by Drew with a senator of whom it is said, "If 25 of the 50 bills he introduced were never heard of again, he didn't give it another thought."

Whether a legislator is serious about bills introduced is usually related to why the legislator sought particular committee assignments. Some legislators seek seats on the Armed Services Committee or a military appropriations subcommittee to protect bases in their districts. They see their role as essentially local. Other legislators try to avoid selfish local politics, being more interested in setting broad policy. Some Armed Services Committee members, for example, do not have military bases in their districts.

Members of legislatures signal their interest in particular issues by starting or joining caucuses and legislative service organizations, which have quasi-official status in the House and Senate. Not so incidentally, membership might attract special-interest donations and impress constituents. Investigators can mine the groups on issue stories. In the U.S. Congress there are many including those promoting the arts, animal welfare and rural health.

Authorizations and Appropriations

Policy can be influenced from appropriations committees as well as from subject-specific committees. Legislatures usually separate policy-making from funding when establishing committees. The authorizing committees prepare grocery lists; the appropriations committees decide what will be purchased—one new hydroelectric dam or four, eight new bombers or 15—and at what price. Sometimes the appropriators strike an item from the list altogether or provide only minimal seed money.

A seat on an appropriations committee is perceived as unglamorous by outsiders who think budgets are boring, but insiders understand the influence attached to such an assignment. A program might be authorized only once every several years. But money must be spent every year, with supplemental appropriations requested if the original amount turns out to be inadequate. Richard Munson's book "The Cardinals of Capitol Hill" demonstrates the power of the appropriations subcommittee chairs in the House and Senate.

Sometimes appropriations come through a side door through a formula rather than an unambiguous dollar allocation. A New England senator will offer a seemingly innocuous amendment making "degree heat days" a criterion for heating oil aid to low-income persons. In effect, the senator is trying to take part of the allocation from another region and channel it to his or her own. Spencer Rich of the Washington Post said the appropriations formula game hides "a grubby reality. The formula that seemed fairest and most equitable to each senator usually turned out to be the formula that helped his state to a bigger slice of the pie." R. Douglas Arnold's book "Congress and the Bureaucracy: A Theory of Influence" explains geographic allocation from a scholarly perspective.

So much of legislating consists of elected representatives grabbing as much funding and special consideration as possible for their districts, and damn the overall consequences. As one member of Congress said, "Angels in heaven don't decide where highways are going to be built. It's a political process." The jargon for such behavior is "pork-barrel politics." Investigators have filled books with egregious examples of such behavior. They include Brian Kelly's "Adventures in Porkland: How Washington Wastes Your Money and Why They Won't Stop," and Martin L. Gross' "The Government Racket: Washington Waste from A to Z." But because voters at home benefit from the deals, they tend to reelect their legislators while simultaneously crying about the big deficits and higher taxes that flow from those deals. Almost all legislators try to win pork for their districts; an overlooked truism is that there are no fiscal conservatives in Congress. The reality, though, is that some legislators have more integrity or power than others when it comes to pork, so the costs and benefits are distributed unequally.

Another type of often irrational spending is the entitlement program, indexed to the rate of inflation or some other indicators beyond legislative control. Examples include Social Security, Medicare, unemployment compensation, veterans' benefits and federal employee pensions. Because of entitlements, hundreds of billions of dollars in government budgets are not reviewed annually. Investigators can try to match benefits and needs; many programs seem to ignore the truly needy. A book to stimulate thought about the relative equity of entitlements is "Who Gets What From Government" by Benjamin I. Page.

Overall, there is much sleight of hand in the legislative budget processes, as legislators place spending off the books in transparent attempts to make deficits look smaller. One common tactic is the loan guarantee, a government obligation to pick up the cost if private-sector financing fails. Despite their invisibility, Robert Samuelson of the National Journal said off-budget programs "are as real as the Washington Monument. They certify the ingenuity of politicians and bureaucrats, who crave the best of both worlds—extra plums for constituents without the extra pain of higher taxes." Richard Forgette's book "The Power of the Purse Strings: Do Congressional Budget Procedures Restrain?" provides detailed insights.

Investigators who understand the process look not only for the use of power in the authorization-appropriations realm, but also for hypocritical legislators who approve the authorization (satisfying proponents of the program), but oppose funding (satisfying detractors of the program while hoping proponents will fail to notice). Numerous groups keep tabs on legislators' voting records in an attempt to ferret out such hypocrisy. From the U.S. Chamber of Commerce to Americans for Democratic Action, voting scorecards are available. Rarely do groups keep track of every vote, instead choosing issues of importance to their membership. Sometimes the ratings that result are intellectually dishonest. A special-interest group will choose votes that make members of one or the other political party appear to be antibusiness, antilabor or whatever. As a result, investigators might need to check legislators' complete voting record by using the official Congressional Record or tabulations in Congressional Quarterly Weekly Report.

Legislating Through Committees

Besides looking for hypocrisy in the authorization and appropriations cycles, investigators look for hypocrisy in legislative hearings. Hearing records can be unmatched resources for information gatherers. But sometimes the hearing is stacked to reflect the views of the chair. If the tobacco subcommittee of the Agriculture Committee holds a hearing on whether cigarette smoke is dangerous to nonsmokers and the witnesses discount the dangers, an investigator should check whether tobacco interests are contributors to subcommittee legislators, whether constituents are dependent on tobacco industry jobs or both.

Placement of witnesses on the hearing schedule can be a tipoff. Witnesses appearing in the morning tend to receive more attention from legislators and journalists. Later in the day, legislators drift to other duties and journalists leave to file daily stories. Near the end of the witness list is the likely placement if the committee chair disagrees with the views to be expressed.

Legislative hearings can be shams in so many other ways. For instance, Congress has an intentionally inefficient delineation of committee and subcommittee jurisdictions. Dozens of committees and subcommittees have some say over surface transportation legislation, making it difficult for any one committee to act definitively. The blurring of jurisdictional lines provides more members of Congress a chance to grab publicity on any given issue. The occasional books on congressional hearings provide rich detail. One bird's-eye account is "Men of Zeal: A Candid Inside Story of the Iran-Contra Hearings" by Senators William S. Cohen and George J. Mitchell. Overviews include "Congressmen in Committees" by Richard F. Fenno Jr. and "The Politics of Finance: The House Committee on Ways and Means" by John F. Manley.

If a bill starts moving through overlapping jurisdictions in both the House and Senate, there are many stages that bear scrutiny by journalists, including the committee mark-up, committee report, setting of debate rules, discussion on the chamber floor and the conference committee to iron out House-Senate differences. Each of those stages yields useful documents. "Congress Today" by Edward V. Schneier and Bertram Gross describes the stages clearly. Congress' in-house bill tracking arm, the Legislative Information Service, is available to outsiders by telephone or on-line. Legi-Slate, an online service in Washington, D.C., provides prepared testimony from every hearing and verbatim coverage of selected hearings.

 ## Committees and the Function of Oversight

No matter how effective a legislator might be in pushing bills, serving on committees is supposed to be about more than getting laws approved. It is also supposed to be about monitoring the impact of laws, a function called "oversight," as in "overseeing" the results. When oversight hearings are conducted honestly, they can be forums for truth telling. James Hamilton includes such examples in his book "The Power to Probe: A Study of Congressional Investigations."

But "oversight" has a second, unintended, meaning—as in failing to do anything at all. ("I meant to take out the garbage; that was an oversight on my part.") Oversight is thankless. It does not win many votes at home. It requires penetrating the bureaucracy, which will fight back or cause delay. Besides, the subcommittee chair with responsibility for oversight is often the person who most strongly supports the program in question.

Executive branch agencies run thousands of programs. Maybe six per agency per year receive in-depth congressional oversight. When subject to scrutiny, program directors can do a great deal to cast fog rather than shed light. Charles Peters, a one-time bureaucrat, admitted in his book "How Washington Really Works" that "I felt it was my duty to conceal from Congress any fact that might reflect adversely on my agency. The congressmen . . . were usually ill-prepared . . . and seldom asked me the right questions. When they did, it appeared to be accidental, and they failed to ask the right follow-up questions."

Joel D. Aberbach captures the essentials in his book "Keeping a Watchful Eye: The Politics of Congressional Oversight." A more specific treatment is Frank J. Smist Jr.'s "Congress Oversees the United States Intelligence Community, 1947–1989." David Schoenbrod explains the increased need for oversight as Congress abdicates on the specifics of legislation in "Power Without Responsibility: How Congress Abuses the People Through Delegation."

The Connection Between Legislating and Personal Character

Scrutiny of legislators must go beyond campaign finances, conflicts of interests that affect legislating and avoidance of oversight. Personal character must be explored, too. The fact that a candidate is having extramarital affairs might or might not be worthy of publication. But what if the politician lies about it? If lies are told about personal matters, what other lies might the candidate tell, perhaps lies directly related to the candidate's political agenda or performance.

The Miami Herald reporters and editors who exposed U.S. Senator and Democratic presidential candidate Gary Hart's extramarital relationship with Donna Rice said the main issue was not Hart's sex life. Rather, it was whether he was telling the truth about being a faithful husband. Something similar can be said about the abuse of alcohol and other drugs or sexual orientation. Is the legislator open about the situation, or in denial that leads to lies?

Until the early 1970s, journalists almost always refused to disclose illicit sex or drugs among legislators unless the conduct was so egregious that it led to criminal charges. In retrospect, the past standard seems wrong, as it becomes clear, for example, how John F. Kennedy's sexual conduct affected his performance in the U.S. Senate and in the White House. Standards have obviously changed since then, as explained by Larry J. Sabato in "Feeding Frenzy: How Attack Journalism Has Transformed American Politics."

The Dallas Morning News reported a lie by a U.S. senator about his place of residence. That senator filed for a homestead tax exemption in Washington, D.C. But to legally represent Texas, the senator was supposed to maintain his home there. So the reporter checked the Texas address used by the senator. It turned out to be the residence of a friend.

Sometimes the conduct is unequivocally criminal. A U.S. representative, for example, pled guilty to accepting $12,000 from the family of a federal prisoner who wanted to transfer the prisoner to a less strict institution. He also pled guilty to accepting below-market rental of a house and filing false tax returns. Another U.S. representative faced criminal charges for accepting $35,000 to help a company in his district renew its contract to provide meals at a military base. "Congressional Ethics: History, Facts, and Controversy" from Congressional Quarterly Books examines the consequences of such behavior for legislators within their chambers and among the voters. More theoretical approaches can be found in "Political Ethics and Public Office" by Dennis F. Thompson and "Thinking About Political Corruption" by Peter DeLeon.

Two reference books establish the conventional wisdom about a legislator's character and its connection to his job performance: The Almanac of American Politics (National Journal, Washington, D.C.) and Politics in America (Congressional Quarterly Books, Washington, D.C.).

If a would-be legislator is running for the first time, the investigator can examine the candidate's reputation in past jobs. If the past job was in the public sector (including a lower-level legislature), reports might be available from an agency inspector general, a state auditor or the like. The investigator can talk to fellow employees, employers, family members, neighbors, ministers, school classmates, teachers—the usual range of currents and formers set out in Chapter 5. The wise investigator will also check every line on the politician's résumé, looking for exaggerations or outright fabrications.

Using Congressional Information for All Manner of Investigations

In addition to being stories in themselves, legislatures and legislators can be marvelous sources of information for investigations about individuals, institutions and issues.

Congressional committee documents and the Congressional Record are helpful for all manner of projects. Committee documents are often encyclopedic. An example is the House Ways and Means Committee's "Overview of Entitlement Programs." Nicknamed "the Green Book," it topped 1,800 pages in a recent edition. The report tells investigators much of what they need to know about Social Security, Medicare, adoption assistance and other federal programs covering large subgroups of the U.S. population. To keep up with the release of hearing books and other committee publications, investigators can subscribe to Congress in Print from Congressional Quarterly, Inc.

The Congressional Record is especially useful for its word-by-word transcription of House and Senate floor debates. The Record is available at depository libraries, on some commercial computer databases or by mail subscription. It is indexed by the government, but an index from the National Standards Association, Gaithersburg, Md., is easier to use.

When a bill does become law, it enters the United States Code, where it is placed into one of 50 subject-matter chapters called "titles." Compilations published privately can be easier to use than the official government version. The United States Code Annotated (referred to as the USCA) is a product of West Publishing Co., St. Paul.

The Research Arms of the Legislature

The research units of legislatures can be invaluable resources. Best known to investigators is the General Accounting Office, frequently identified as "the watchdog arm of Congress." Its staff (many of them lawyers, engineers and accountants) writes about 1,000 reports annually on public policy issues. The individuals working on each report are identified by name and title on the final page.

Although GAO reports are treated by many daily journalists as self-contained stories, they should be a starting point, not the final word. That is especially true for the reports initiated at the request of a member of Congress. It is human to tell one's bosses what it is presumed they want to hear; although GAO employees are generally candid in person, their reports are sometimes couched in language so low-key it muffles the outrageousness of the misconduct.

A value of GAO reports is the specificity of recommendations for reform. An investigator delving into an issue can make compliance with GAO recommendations part of the report. One recent four-volume GAO report mentioned 2,334 unresolved recommendations.

Journalists can ask GAO public affairs staff for regular mailings of full reports or of monthly summaries. Annotated bibliographies of GAO documents on numerous controversies are available; for example, the bibliography on environmental protection contains hundreds of references, such as "Hazardous Waste: Status of Private Party Efforts to Clean Up Hazardous Waste Sites." A quarterly magazine, the GAO Review, is useful for its explanations of how the agency operates and for its mentions of hirings, promotions and departures among staff members who have an advantage over even the most talented investigative journalist—subpoena power. Context is available in Frederick C. Mosher's books, "The GAO: The Quest for Accountability in American Government" and "A Tale of Two Agencies: A Comparative Analysis of the General Accounting Office and the Office of Management and Budget."

The Congressional Research Service, part of the Library of Congress, is funded with tax dollars, but staff members will not release their research to the public unless authorized by the member of Congress or the committee requesting the information. One way around the obstacle is to request specific issue briefs from a member of Congress. The briefs are listed in the CRS publication Update. The magazine CRS Review provides highlights from CRS analyses that tend to be the talk of Congress.

At the beginning of each congressional session, CRS provides each committee with a list of programs under its jurisdiction that are ready to expire, along with a companion list of topics the committees might want to examine in depth. During each session, CRS compiles Major Legislation of the Congress. Some topics are singled out for in-depth treatment called legislative histories; an example is "A Legislative History of the Clean Air Act Amendments." Those can be found through the privately published Congressional Information Service Index, or the Monthly Catalog of U.S. Government Publications. One classic is the "Medicaid Source Book: Background Data and Analysis," a 700-page study by the CRS for the House subcommittee on health and the environment. Like GAO, the Service has specialists in almost every topical area imaginable, including education, housing, labor, employment, banking and veterans affairs. Congressional Information Service Inc. publishes an index to the CRS's major studies and issue briefs.

The Office of Technology Assessment helps Congress evaluate the impact of scientific advances on government policy. The office is more subject to political influence than many of its employees would like— policy is set by a board consisting of three Democratic and three Republican senators plus three Democrats and three Republicans from the House of Representatives. The congressional board hires OTA's director.

The Congressional Budget Office is the legislative branch counterpart to the White House Office of Management and Budget. The Budget Enforcement Act sets caps on discretionary spending and contains pay-as-you-go rules for entitlements and taxes. So if the CBO projections are more conservative than OMB's, Congress must live within the CBO limits. The director is appointed by Congress and can be removed by resolution of either chamber. The director's first responsibility is to help the Senate and House budget committees. The next priority is to aid appropriations committees in both chambers, as well as the Senate Finance Committee and the House Ways and Means Committee. Many of the CBO studies transcend cost analysis to discuss policy implications. Examples are "Federal Options for Reducing Waste Disposal," "Rising Health Care Costs: Causes, Implications, Strategies" and "The Economic Effects of the Savings and Loan Crisis."

State legislatures have support arms, too, but these are usually more sparsely staffed than those of Congress. In Missouri, the Committee on Legislative Research combines with the House of Representatives Computer Service to provide an index of bills organized by chronological number and name of sponsor. Wakeman/Walworth, Inc., of Alexandria, Va., publishes numerous newsletters tracking issues in state legislatures. Some are as narrow as alcoholic beverage control. Others are as broad as taxation and revenue policy.

The National Conference of State Legislatures in Denver publishes Inside the Legislative Process, containing comparative data, state by state, on legislative organization, committee procedures and bill processing. Numerous publications by the conference help investigators put seemingly localized issues in perspective. The organization's catalog lists reports about the arts, tourism, cultural resources, corrections, criminal justice, economic development, education, employment, labor, insurance, fiscal affairs, health, human services, natural resources and environment.

Legislatures are windows on the world, and journalists have the responsibility of peering in those windows, and of keeping them disinfected so that rot does not set in.

Chapter 7

INVESTIGATING GOVERNMENT

The Executive Branch

*E*xecutive branch agencies have long names that conjure up arcane duties. Behind the facade, though, are government bureaucrats (called public servants by their partisans) whose decisions affect huge numbers of lives in tangible ways every day.

One investigation of a seemingly arcane agency began with a listing in the Miami Herald Sunday real estate column: notice of a $100,000 mortgage loan on generous terms to the director of the regional Federal Housing Administration office. Reporters Mike Baxter and Jim Savage looked into the loan, writing a brief story about the connection between the favorable terms and approval of a questionable housing project proposal by the federal administrator.

Little did Baxter and Savage know the story would evolve into a scandal about the operations of an entire agency, bringing down a U.S. senator along the way. Their exposé became the basis for a chapter in the book "The New Muckrakers" by Leonard Downie Jr.

The original real estate story led to Baxter and Savage receiving an anonymous tip: The federal regional office was giving favored treatment to one developer of government-subsidized single-family housing. The reporters asked their builder sources about the alleged favored treatment. To their surprise, nobody knew anything about the builder allegedly benefitting. A check of the city directory showed him only as proprietor of a hearing-aid dealership.

Many reporters would have given up then, but an inner sense told Baxter and Savage to continue, an inner sense fed by agency stonewalling about releasing documents. When the Herald finally obtained the documents, though, the alleged kingpin builder barely showed up in them.

Still, the investigation continued. As Downie relates, Baxter and Savage "became convinced, as their real estate contacts had told them, that [the builder] was somehow hidden in several places on that FHA list in the disguises of several unfamiliar corporations." While Savage explored other angles, Baxter visited the courthouse to run the paper trail on corporations receiving FHA money.

It was work that many journalists avoid because they perceive it as boring, but Baxter

> became caught up in his sleuthing through the courthouse records. He began finding real estate corporations that [the builder] was on record as controlling, although none of these corporations turned up on the FHA list of subsidy commitments. At the same time, he found that many of the corporations on the FHA list did not turn up in the telephone book, other city directories or the courthouse corporation records.
>
> These mysterious companies did appear from time to time in the land records, however. They bought land for the projects that the FHA office had approved. . . . The names signed as officers of these corporations were unfamiliar, but Baxter noticed that the notaries used by all the mysterious corporations were the same.

What Baxter and Savage had uncovered was a sophisticated scheme of corruption involving an executive branch agency, a developer and—it turned out—a U.S. senator from Florida.

Delving into executive branch conduct does not always yield such blatant corruption. But digging is a no-lose activity: If a taxpayer-supported agency is performing well, that is a story in an age of skepticism about government. If, on the other hand, taxpayer money is being squandered, that is by definition newsworthy.

There is no grand strategy for investigating the executive branch. As in the chapter about legislatures, what follows are the building blocks of manageable, discrete projects. They can be combined to constitute larger projects when appropriate or desired.

Probing an Agency's Mission

The wise investigator begins with the U.S. Government Manual and similar manuals for the state, county and city. Reading about each agency, the investigator asks: How does the agency define its mission, and how well does it carry out that mission? The investigator will notice the breadth of each agency's mission—granting licenses, setting rates, establishing industry-wide rules, supervising performance, imposing sanctions on individuals and institutions. Agencies are like total governments in miniature, with quasi-legislative and judicial powers to complement their executive duties. Such wide authority makes abuses of power all the more devastating. That is reason enough for journalists to pay more attention to agencies.

David Burnham shared thoughts about scrutinizing bureaucracies in the IRE Journal while writing his book "A Law Unto Itself: Power, Politics and the Internal Revenue Service":

> I had decided [years earlier] that my principal role as the New York Times reporter assigned to cover the system of criminal justice was to describe the reasons why the agencies within this system often failed to achieve their stated goals. This approach to reporting about the police worked equally well with the IRS. The stated goal of the NYPD—to make the streets safe for all New Yorkers—was terrific. But like all human institutions, the NYPD frequently came up short. People were mugged. Houses were burgled. Women were raped. Why? Was it because the department had been given an impossible mission? Was it because the department had been given inadequate resources? Was it because many police officers cared more about receiving their weekly paycheck than providing public service? Was it because a large number of cops were corrupt? Quite obviously, the failures of the department can be blamed on all of the above and a number of other factors, too.
>
> My game plan—trying to tell readers why the NYPD did not achieve its stated goals—was the rationale behind my decision to write an article about "cooping," the widely accepted practice of sleeping while on duty, especially while working the midnight to 8 A.M. shift. . . . Like the NYPD, the IRS has been given an impossible mission and inadequate resources. Like the NYPD, the IRS suffers from a number of lazy, poorly trained, underpaid and incompetent managers. Like the NYPD, the IRS always is vulnerable to corruption and political fixes. The inevitability of these problems in large organizations does not mean society can afford to shrug its collective shoulders and accept them.

Probabilities of Corruption

Like Burnham, Paul Williams was one of a few journalists to combine a theory of bureaucracy with real-life digging. Writing in "Investigative Reporting and Editing," Williams said:

> To be a successful investigative reporter, you need to assume that the institutions of government are under constant and pernicious attack by both external forces seeking special advantage and internal operators who figure that graft is one of the perquisites of office. . . . You need also to assume that within these institutions, most of the people are still either essentially honest, unaware of what's going on, or merely jealous of the grafters and graftees. This majority comprises your best resource, your best hope for doing reporting that will effectively describe our systemic problems.

Williams quotes Lou Rose of the St. Louis Post-Dispatch:

> When I see someone in a position to take graft, I try to think of all the worst things they could be doing. What are the inherent possibilities here, what is every single advantage that somebody could get out of this? You've got to train your mind not to accept anything at face value. Put down every single thing you can think of, no matter how incredible it may seem, and then gradually go down the list and cut them off—this can be done in this case, this can't be done, this is a possibility but can I prove it?

Campaign finance corruption, usually reported in the context of the legislative branch, is just as ripe for exploration in the executive branch. Lobbyists do not spend all their time trying to influence legislators only. That is especially true of special-interest contributions to governors, county executives, mayors and other local government executives whose actions can enrich donors. In Baton Rouge, the Morning Advocate determined that two-thirds of the contributors to the incumbent mayor were doing direct business with the city government. The newspaper's investigators made the determination by matching campaign contributions with payout vouchers.

An especially ingenious campaign contributions scam occurred in Jefferson City, Missouri's state capital. After Terry Ganey of the St. Louis Post-Dispatch broke it open, he wrote for the IRE Journal that "the fraud was shocking, widespread and well-hidden. . . . What started out as an obscure workers' compensation fund had become a gold mine for a few insiders. An exclusive club of lawyers and doctors had learned how to milk a system known as Missouri's Second Injury Fund. Their trail led to the doorstep of the state attorney general . . . the Republican candidate for governor." Because almost every state maintains a similar fund to supplement compensation for on-the-job injuries, Ganey explained the scam:

> Lawyers specializing in workers' compensation cases filed claims against the fund on behalf of injured workers. Defending the fund against these claims were special assistant state attorneys general. . . . Because thousands of claims were filed each year and because the expense of litigation often exceeded the value of the claim, 95 percent of the claims were settled by the lawyers involved. The Post-Dispatch first looked at the fund because unusually large contributions were flowing to [the] attorney general's . . . campaign from a small group of St. Louis lawyers filing claims against the fund. Soliciting the contributions from the claimants' lawyers was . . . one of [the attorney general's] appointees assigned to defend the fund. . . .
>
> The Post-Dispatch requested Second Injury Fund settlement documents from the state Division of Workers' Compensation. After some resistance from the state attorney general's office, a computer tape containing 11,647 settlements became available. The analysis showed that lawyers who contributed to [the attorney general] obtained substantially larger settlements from the fund for their clients than those lawyers who did not contribute. Larger settlements meant larger fees, since the lawyers' compensation was always

25 percent of the settlement amount. . . . The data-analysis story touched a raw nerve among a group of lawyers in St. Louis. They knew about specific claims with problems. Requesting anonymity, they began to tell their stories: How [a] workers' compensation attorney [who was the] largest individual campaign contributor obtained $65,000 in settlements for himself for a fall in his office and for hurting his shoulder while closing a file cabinet drawer.

Scholars who see executive branch misbehavior as institutionalized include Peter DeLeon in "Thinking About Political Corruption" and John T. Noonan Jr. in "Bribes." An alternate view—that corruption is particularized, not generalized—can be found in Charles T. Goodsell's "The Case for Bureaucracy."

Uncovering Conflicts of Interest

Investigators can begin a corruption check by examining financial disclosures by executive branch supervisors. They must be filed with the designated agency ethics official under the federal Ethics in Government Act; many states have similar laws.

When journalists at the Center for Public Integrity in Washington, D.C., started digging into the Office of the U.S. Trade Representative, they learned from disclosure forms that two top officials held stock in tobacco companies while pushing to open foreign markets to the deadly substance. A savvy investigator will also examine disclosures in search of corporate directorships. When an agency official is a bank director, for example, it is legitimate to ask whether the bank has interests pending before the agency. Looked at from a different perspective, what is in the directorship for the official: Cash payments? A lucrative job after leaving government?

The federal Office of Government Ethics, Washington, D.C., can help with inquiries about executive branch conduct. Disclosure forms filed there allowed the New York Times to report the personal wealth of President Bill Clinton and Hillary Rodham Clinton, identifying specific bond, stock and mutual fund holdings. Perspective is found in Robert N. Roberts' book "White House Ethics: The History of the Politics of Conflict of Interest Regulation."

Sometimes conflicts are disclosed in places other than annual financial forms. A careful reader of the Congressional Record will spot disclosures by executive branch officials, as mandated in various laws. An example is the Interior Department secretary supplying Congress with disclosures of bureaucrats who have responsibilities under the Energy Policy and Conservation Act. A separate Congressional Record notice the same day revealed campaign contributions by four presidential nominees for ambassadorships; a law requires such disclosures to guard against wealthy citizens buying ambassadorships secretly.

The Federal Register contains equally informative disclosures. When a new secretary took over the Energy Department, the Federal Register contained a notice explaining that agency officials are prohibited from "knowingly receiving compensation from, holding any official relation with, or having any pecuniary interest in any energy concern." The appointee, it turned out, received a survivor annuity through her husband's employment at a utilities company. But Energy Department ethics officials allowed her to keep the annuity, as long as she excused herself from decisions involving the particular utility.

One common conflict is the revolving door between government and the private sector. It is difficult to monitor—the comings and goings are frequent and intentionally low profile. Some of the conflicting interests are so egregious, however, that journalists need to make the effort. Two organizations of "formers" might be able to help journalists understand the mindsets of those who choose the revolving doors: The National Association of Retired Federal Employees and the Council for Excellence in Government, both in Washington, D.C.

The Office of Government Ethics is supposed to oversee federal post-employment conflicts, but it is largely toothless. When Bill Clinton became president, he vowed to stop the use of government as a stepping stone to riches in the private sector. But the Wall Street Journal reported, less than a year into the Clinton administration, that the White House deputy chief of staff was departing for a $500,000 annual salary at the U.S. Telephone Association. The article said that the president required some senior appointees to sign a pledge promising not to lobby the offices where they work for five years, but that pledge did little to prevent officials from joining organizations lobbying Congress.

With the Office of Government Ethics so often neutralized, an investigator looks for alternate pathways. For example, the Defense Department's Standards of Conduct Office supplies the Senate and House Armed Services committees with a list of military retirees or former civilian employees taking jobs with defense contractors. I knew about the list because I had studied laws and regulations, including Title 10, Section 2397, of the U.S. Code. It requires Defense Department military and civilian employees above certain levels to file a report if hired by a major defense contractor above a certain pay rate. One year when I examined the list, 1,623 defense officials had moved to private industry jobs. Only 79 had moved from private industry to government defense employment.

Alfred E. Eckes, who served on the U.S. International Trade Commission, provided an account of the phenomenon for Chronicles magazine. He told how he

watched the revolving door spin round and round. Friends and colleagues briefly punched tickets in the public sector and then left to enjoy foreign lucre. . . . One day a senior attorney in our general counsel's office came in to shake my hand; he was departing for the green fields of private law. . . . The next business day he reappeared in the commission hearing room to represent a foreign client in an ITC proceeding. . . . Some of the most revolting episodes have involved presidential appointees, especially fellow commissioners. [One] gained notoriety when he traveled to Japan and signed a private agreement to represent Japanese business interests before he had resigned his government post. Several of [his] successors learned from his public example and sought foreign clients more discreetly. During the 1980s eight commissioners departed from the ITC. Four of the five who remained in Washington, all professionals in mid-career, registered as foreign agents or represented foreign interests before the commission within two years of resigning their public position.

From time to time massive corruption at the cabinet or regulatory agency level goes unnoticed by journalists, despite warning signs. The rotten core of the U.S. Department of Housing and Urban Development remained unexposed for years during the Reagan and Bush administrations. The HUD secretary presided over a multibillion-dollar bureaucracy that gave a significant percentage to wheeler-dealers while millions of Americans lacked decent housing. The secretary escaped prosecution, but when a top assistant was found guilty of accepting a bribe, conspiracy and perjury, she became the eleventh person convicted in connection with the HUD mess.

Scrutinizing the Top Executive

Even if corruption is absent, agencies often operate inefficiently or insensitively. One of many ways for an investigator to scrutinize agencies is paying attention to what is happening at the top of the executive branch—in the White House, governor's mansion or mayor's office. At the least, that is where the tone is set for the rest of the executive branch.

The chief executive's pronouncements are a starting point. For example, presidential executive orders, which are legally binding despite never receiving congressional approval, appear first in the Federal Register, the Monday through Friday publication of the executive branch. The obscure orders can have far-reaching impact. When President Ronald Reagan issued Executive Order 12291, he centralized review of pending agency regulations within the Office of Management and Budget. Furthermore, OMB could require a cost-benefit analysis as part of the justification for the proposed regulation. With a stroke of his pen, Reagan had altered operations of the executive branch.

Executive orders, speeches, news conference transcripts, proclamations and remarks to White House visitors appear in the Weekly Compilation of Presidential Documents, available through a Government

Printing Office subscription or a government depository library. The official documents can be supplemented with insider memoirs; independently researched biographies of past presidents, vice presidents, Cabinet secretaries and regulators; as well as exposés. Two overviews, administration by administration, are "Fall From Grace: Sex, Scandal and Corruption in American Politics from 1702 to the Present" by Shelley Ross and "Presidential Saints and Sinners" by Thomas A. Bailey.

Books by and about governors who still held office on the publication dates include Robert S. McElvaine's biography of New York Governor Mario Cuomo, a biography of Texas Governor Ann Richards by Mike Shropshire and Frank Schaeffer, Dwayne Yancey's biography of Virginia Governor Douglas Wilder, plus Thad L. Beyle's "Governors and Hard Times." Book-length studies of local chief executives include a biography of Los Angeles Mayor Tom Bradley by J. Gregory Payne and Scott C. Ratzan, plus memoirs by New York City Mayor Ed Koch and Detroit Mayor Coleman Young. Entries in the IRE Resource Center under "Governors," "State Government," "Mayors" and "City Government" are worth consulting.

There are also resources for placing current state and local government actions in context, including the National Governors' Association, National Association of Counties, National League of Cities and U.S. Conference of Mayors, all in Washington, D.C., plus the Council of State Governments, in Lexington, Ky. Independently written books such as "County Governments in an Era of Change," edited by David R. Berman, can supplement the national associations.

Whether the top executive is efficient or inefficient, corrupt or honest, covering the position meaningfully requires going beyond that lone figure, beyond official pronouncements and the press secretary. Effective investigations centering on the government's chief executive hinge on gaining access to the policymakers and support staff who rarely receive sustained attention—aides who are liaisons to the legislature; staff members who recommend political appointees; operatives in the office of the vice president or lieutenant governor, who are often bitter about the chief executive; assistants to the chief executive's spouse. Their information can be supplemented by sources lower in the hierarchy, especially secretaries, chauffeurs and custodians—not to mention all the "formers" who held those positions.

Cabinet Secretaries and Regulatory Commissioners

Of all the agencies that the president oversees, the most sprawling are the 14 Cabinet departments; many state governments are organized similarly. Because many Cabinet appointees are already public figures before being tapped by the chief executive, which means that investigators can find telling information about them. Some have written books that can be mined for insights; when President Clinton took office, Publishers Weekly magazine printed a list of books by his Cabinet nominees.

Top executive branch appointees require Senate confirmation. The confirmation hearing record is filled with information about the nominee. The process is scrutinized in Stephen L. Carter's book "The Confirmation Mess: Cleaning Up the Federal Appointments Process."

Combining confirmation hearings with other resources, a few investigators have produced book-length exposés of agencies and their top bureaucrats. "The Puzzle Palace," James Bamford's book about the National Security Agency, may be the best of the genre. Mike McGraw, Jeff Taylor and other members of the Kansas City Star staff produced a series, "Failing the Grade," that devastatingly dissected the Agriculture Department. Biographies of former FBI director J. Edgar Hoover, with their timeless lessons about management, demonstrate how an investigator can explicate executive branch conduct in ways that transcend one agency. Memoirs of Cabinet secretaries and other high-ranking executive branch officials contain insight into policymaking. An example is "Taking Care of the Law" by former Attorney General Griffin Bell.

The Permanent Bureaucracy

Below the highest levels, many government officials remain in the bureaucracy their entire working lives. The careerists often know more than the easy-come, easy-go presidential appointees. When Des Moines Register reporter James Risser read about suspensions of grain inspectors at the Port of Houston, he sought out career bureaucrats to learn the story behind the story. The Agriculture Department is so far-flung that the grain division staffers were not even in the main building. Rather, they worked at a remote shopping center in a Maryland suburb. "I think it was the first time a news reporter had come to their office in years," Risser said. Those interviews turned out to be an early step in Risser's series about corrupt inspections of American grain exports.

Like the Agriculture Department, every Cabinet department has its divisions and offices, each of which has a degree of autonomy as well as its own bureaucratic culture. The Justice Department, for example, is divided into 14 largely decentralized divisions.

Journalists should determine whether top administrators allow the power centers to flourish, or institute rigid centralization. Each approach has its advantages and disadvantages for government employees, for those directly regulated and for the general citizenry that pays through taxes. An enlightening discussion occurred in a Regulation magazine article written by Wendy L. Gramm, former chair of the Commodity Futures Trading Commission, and Gerald D. Gay, CFTC chief economist during Gramm's tenure. They explain how they changed the agency's overall culture more readily than their counterparts at other agencies had been able to do. The reasons included a staff that was young and therefore not so entrenched; a relatively small workforce, making communications easier; a receptive, intelligent mix of backgrounds, including lawyers, economists and accountants; a regulated sector with the option of escaping CFTC scrutiny by relocating offshore, thus causing the agency to examine all decisions with special care; and congressional committees with little interest in micromanaging an agency whose mission they barely understood.

Publications that cover executive branch activities and cultures include Federal Times, Springfield, Va.; Governing, Washington, D.C.; and Government Executive, Washington, D.C. Some publications are valuable for their focused coverage on one agency—an example is OMB Watch, Washington, D.C. Investigations focusing on one agency abound in the IRE Resource Center. The Federal Staff Directory, Mount Vernon, Va., lists tens of thousands of "key federal executives," with nearly 3,000 of them profiled. Carroll. Publishing Co., Washington, D.C., publishes executive branch directories for all levels of government. Details about personnel can be gained in many ways. After a Hartford (Conn.) Courant reporter sought information from the employment applications of city workers, a judge ruled the city had to grant the request.

In the permanent bureaucracy, an investigator should cultivate the lowest-level employees on the organization charts, such as typists and custodial workers. They hear lots, see lots, can supply copies of documents if so inclined and sometimes have little loyalty because of their low pay and status. Agency telephone directories can lead to such sources. For example, the directory for the U.S. Department of Housing and Urban Development contains a section for the general counsel. In that section are names of secretaries to the general counsel, with their direct telephone numbers, as well as names and direct lines of every secretary to every deputy general counsel. The directory lists personnel in HUD's 10 regional offices, too. The importance of regional office personnel entered public consciousness during investigations of President Clinton's role in the Whitewater-related land dealings. Three government employees of the Resolution Trust Corp.'s Kansas City regional office received suspensions because of their activities in the Whitewater affair. At massive agencies like the Agricultural Stabilization and Conservation Service, decisions on how to spend billions annually are made at the grass-roots by committees of farmers who decide the recipient of payments. The Wall Street Journal exposed how a local farmer ASCS committee in Georgia doled out huge amounts to those who grew and then destroyed squash to qualify for payments under a crop disaster program.

Agency publications such as DOE This Month are filled with names of currents and formers (as explained in Chapter 5) who could help nail down an investigation; in fact, that publication—and similar publications in other agencies—has a column headed "Retirements," which lists the retiree's name, specialty and years of service.

As vacancies occur, personnel officers try to hire competent people, but often fail. When investigators are checking inefficiency or corruption within an agency, part of the inquiry ought to focus on hiring and firing practices. Does the agency offer salary and benefits in line with comparable private-sector jobs? If not, what does the agency say to the brightest applicants, those who have a choice between government and industry? Once somebody is working within the agency, what incentives exist to encourage peak performance? When an employee is inefficient or corrupt, how do higher-ups find out about the problem? How do they handle it?

The conventional wisdom is that civil service employees are impossible to fire, no matter how incompetent or corrupt. Once again, the conventional wisdom is wrong. Firing can be relatively easy if managers follow certain procedures, especially documenting problems in detail as soon as they begin. Instead, many managers give passable evaluations while complaining privately. Finally, an especially egregious incident causes the manager to act. But by then the worker's file fails to reflect serious incompetence, causing union officials or hearing judges to question the agency's case. Journalists should look for inept management handling of legitimate cases, just as journalists should look for valid charges by workers of unfair treatment. Neither situation benefits taxpayers. Many government agencies are so convinced that traditional employees are inefficient and corrupt that they have moved to award operations to businesses in a movement called privatization. When journalists have delved into specific privatization operations, though, they often find less service for more money. The San Francisco Bay Guardian determined that animals in the local zoo were suffering from neglect because the private company taking over from the city on a lucrative management contract was laying off experienced zookeepers who had worked for the city. The bottom line had taken precedence over the animals. Employee labor unions often oppose privatization, making union members and officials potentially talkative.

In exploring the executive branch, there are so many positions to consider. Within agencies are public affairs specialists, statisticians, legislative liaisons, advisory committee members, legal counsel, budget and procurement officers, consultants and auditors. The rest of this chapter will explain how to investigate their performance and develop them as sources.

Public Affairs Personnel as a Gateway to the Bureaucracy

Investigators should use public affairs personnel for basic information-gathering. They have their own organization, the National Association of Government Communicators, located in Alexandria, Va. News releases, despite spin meant to make the agency look good, can contain information of value. That is especially true if the release mentions action against an individual or institution, such as the Missouri Department of Natural Resources release headed "Confirmed or Uncontrolled Hazardous Waste Disposal Sites." Accompanying the release was a multi-page description of each site, plus maps.

Agency libraries and reading rooms are filled with in-house periodicals, specialized outside periodicals and summary documents such as the agency's annual report to the legislature. Public affairs staff work with agency statisticians and economists to produce documents such as "Residential Electric Bills in Major Cities"; some agencies house numbers-crunching subdivisions, such as the Bureau of Labor Statistics and National Center for Health Statistics.

Through public affairs staff, investigators can identify the unofficial lobbyists within agencies—the employees in the office of legislative liaison. Their mission is to convince the legislature that the agency is doing a good job and therefore entitled to more money to do an even better job. Some legislators become dependent on the liaisons, asking them to draft bills affecting the agency. That dependence raises questions about the statutory independence of the legislature, and so ought to be reported. It certainly has the potential to compromise meaningful legislative monitoring of programs that might result from the bills.

Agency liaisons sometimes influence legislators when it comes to advisory committee appointments. Some advisory bodies to executive branch agencies are for show; others have influence on policy. Either way, they are good stories, but many journalists never think about them. Gale Research's Encyclopedia of Governmental Advisory Organizations contains thousands of such bodies at the federal level alone. The Federal Advisory Committee Act requires the U.S. president to submit an annual report to the House and Senate on each body.

After studying defense contracting, Gordon Adams wrote in his book "The Iron Triangle" that

> advisory committees can be one of the most significant channels of communication between the industrial and the executive side. . . . They may discuss technical issues or broader policy problems, as some sample names suggest: the Moab District Grazing Advisory Board to the Department of the Interior . . . the Navy Resale Advisory Committee to the Department of Defense. . . . The work of these committees is often crucial to the formation of government

policy, [including] issues like atomic weapons development, the Three Mile Island nuclear [power] near-disaster and the future of national forest lands.

Public affairs staff serve as spokespeople for lawyers from the general counsel's office, publicizing some of the legal battles—as plaintiff and defendant, civil and criminal—that typically engage a government agency. One fertile area for investigation is how often the agency settles cases on terms favorable to the other side, rather than to the majority of taxpayers. If settlements are frequent, why is that so? If settlements are rare, what is the record of the general counsel when cases go to trial?

The Orange County (Calif.) Register started with one case, a lawsuit by a prisoner in the county jail. The county government's lawyers settled confidentially. The reporter pursued the story until he learned the settlement terms. He then started researching what turned out to be a 17-part examination of lawsuits against the government. The number of lawsuits is quite likely to increase: The Public Risk Management Association, Arlington, Va., made up of local and state government officials, says budget cutbacks make it harder to fund prevention, such as street repairs, that could reduce court awards and settlements.

Some legal disputes are heard within agencies before reaching the judicial branch of government. Administrative law judges are executive branch employees with a great deal of independence, as a Legal Times story demonstrated. It explained how the U.S. Mine Safety and Health Administration had penalized operators of 800 mines for tampering with equipment that measures hazardous airborne particles in the shafts, thus endangering worker safety. The fines levied by the agency totalled $5 million. The operators appealed to the Federal Mine Safety and Health Review Commission, which houses 13 administrative law judges who can uphold or overturn the regulatory arm. The story reported how one of those judges ruled that the agency had to prove that "intentional tampering was the only reasonable explanation for the altered sample[s] . . . not just the most probable." The ruling meant the agency had to split the aggregate case into 800 separate trials to meet the new burden of proof, a costly enterprise that pretty much guaranteed the suit would not be pursued. Sometimes agency administrative law judges end up hearing disputes that reach into other nations, as when a California biotechnology company complained to the U.S. International Trade Commission about alleged patent infringements by two rival companies, one of them based in Denmark. The plaintiff took its case to an administrative law judge at the ITC because the agency has the authority to prohibit imports from entering the United States.

The Federal Administrative Law Judges Conference, Washington, D.C., can provide perspective, as can the American Bar Association sections on Administrative Law and Regulatory Practice, plus Government and Public-Sector Lawyers.

The Budget and Management Watchdog

Every agency has a budget staff. Keeping track of each agency is an executive branch superagency such as the White House Office of Management and Budget or counterparts in state and local government executive branches. The superagency recommends which individual agencies receive budget increases and which budgets are cut. Those decisions signal the administration's priorities—or its compromises with special interests. The superagency also tracks whether individual agency expenditures during the year are consistent with administration policy.

One spending practice that should spawn journalistic inquiry is an agency going on poorly thought-out spending sprees during the last month of a fiscal year. The reason is to prevent a reduction next year on the grounds that the agency had no need of its full budget. A related psychological reason is that some agency managers forget they work for the citizenry. Instead, they view ever-increasing budgets, even when unjustifiable objectively, as the path to promotion. In such an atmosphere, budget meetings called solely to plot increases replace working harder with less money to better serve the public. If a budget increase looks politically unpalatable, an agency might request a lesser amount—but only after legislators have agreed quietly to approve a supplemental appropriation later in the year. The Association of Government Accountants, Alexandria, Va., and the Governmental Accounting Standards Board, Norwalk, Conn., might provide comment on that practice, as well as on others that journalists may want to question.

Sometimes a superagency will discover untoward practices. But the scrutiny of individual agency budgets is often minimal; the agencies can overwhelm the relatively understaffed watchdog. In his book "How Washington Really Works," Charles Peters says if overmatched OMB examiners manage to cut through obfuscation, agencies have "yet another way of dealing with the problem—offering the OMB investigator a higher salary to come work for the agency. When this is done by a private government contractor, the impropriety is obvious. But it's done all the time within the government." Books that can assist understanding include "The Federal Budget: Politics, Policy, Process" by Allen Schick and "The Budget Puzzle: Understanding Federal Spending" by John F. Cogan, Timothy J. Muris and Allen Schick.

Making Sense of Agency Budgets

A budget is a key document for looking into waste, fraud and abuse; it allows an investigator to practice a tenet of the craft—following the dollar.

Budgets are about two things: Where the money comes from (revenue) and where the money goes (expenditures). At the local agency level, revenue usually comes from taxes on property, income and retail sales; fees for garbage pick-up and other services to individuals; fees collected from businesses for licenses; fees paid by utilities and other monopoly franchises; penalties such as traffic tickets and court fines; trickle-down state tax revenues (which might or might not surpass the total paid in by local residents); trickle-down federal funds; sales of tax-exempt bonds to investors; and interest on investments.

Each category presents investigation opportunities for journalists. For example, rather than being invested at a good rate, revenue might be in a low interest-bearing account at a local bank controlled by a relative of the mayor. A journalist need not be an accounting genius or a mathematics wizard to ask "how" and "why" about every revenue item.

Expenditures are harder to categorize, because each unit spends money for highly specific reasons. However expenditures are categorized, they should be viewed, at least in part, as a political statement. Every expenditure reflects somebody's priority—some forces inside and outside the agency won, while other insiders and outsiders lost. "Favoritism" and "revenge" (by the mayor, governor, president, agency director) are words to remember when deciphering reasons for expenditures.

Budgets can be hugely misleading to the uninitiated. Journalists need to inquire which agencies or programs are absent from the budget. As Stanley E. Collender explains in his book "The Guide to the Federal Budget,

> There is no standard list of reasons as to why some program is not included in the budget totals; the decision is almost always political and can be changed depending on the year and the situation. For example, until 1981 the purchase of oil for the strategic petroleum reserve was on-budget, that is, any spending was included in the budget and the deficit was affected accordingly. In 1981, the Reagan Administration proposed and Congress agreed to take this spending off-budget. There was no specific reason for this other than the fact that the price of oil had increased and the White House did not want the deficit growing by as much as would have occurred. Rather than propose to increase revenues or cut other programs to control the deficit, Reagan proposed to take the spending off-budget. In 1985 this program was put back on the budget again by Congress.

Other omissions are obvious yet rarely discussed by journalists for their audiences. Public employee pensions are an example. Many governments have not provided for future pension liabilities in current budgets, even though the money will have to be paid out as employees retire. That means gigantic obligations that would drive up deficits are being hidden by budgetary sleight of hand.

Governments use three kinds of budgets. The general operating budget covers day-to-day commitments; the capital improvements budget covers long-term, tangible items such as buildings and streets; the debt service budget covers payments to investors and lenders on financial obligations incurred in previous years.

Tracking a budget effectively is a year-round job. In a guide for journalists at the Memphis Commercial Appeal, Walter Dawson and Jimmie Covington advise,

> Don't wait for the new budget to come out. Get started now with the current budget so you'll become familiar with it and be ready to address any changes from it to the new budget. The current budget also gives you a chance to practice your knowledge and questions on your sources, letting them get to know you and how much you're just dying to talk figures and bonds and debits and credits. . . .
>
> Find a mid-level person in the budget office and take him to lunch to find out how he helps put the budget together. . . . Talk to the finance director, the person who is in charge of the budget process. Ask her about the bigger picture—is it financially wise for the city to keep property taxes low while increasing the city's debt through bonds? . . . Most states have an auditing division with some oversight responsibilities on local budgets. If possible, travel to the capital and get to know these people face to face.

In "Investigative Reporting and Editing," Paul Williams offers additional wisdom by quoting New York City budget director Frederick O'Reilly Hayes about avoiding the simplistic "compared to last year" budget story. As Hayes said,

> This approach has obvious limitations. Usually the increases . . . account for only 5 to 10 percent of the total budget, and reductions are even smaller. . . . [If we] only look at these pluses and minuses, we are accepting on faith the other, larger part of the budget—for example, our attention might be directed to a police chief's request for ten additional detectives and a proposed 5 percent pay increase, but not to the uses of the 900 officers already on duty. Like an iceberg, the largest part of the budget escapes our gaze.

In almost every government's budget there is a major project that never should have been funded. Downtown convention centers are commonly in that category. With an average occupancy rate below the break-even point of approximately 50 percent in city after city, why do government officials in places such as Mobile, Ala., or Erie, Pa., think they can attract enough business to justify spending tens of millions of dollars? When governments sell bonds to finance construction, are buyers of those bonds in danger of being hurt by default years or decades later? The SEC is requiring more muni-bond disclosure than in previous decades. Issuing governments are supposed to release annual financial updates to supplement what had been provided at the time of sale; issuers are also supposed to release information on material events, such as the closing of a major employer or a large airline withdrawing service from the local airport.

In their book "Reinventing Government: How the Entrepreneurial Spirit Is Transforming the Public Sector," journalist David Osborne and former city manager Ted Gaebler suggest new ways to think about budgeting:

> Normal government budgets encourage managers to waste money. If they don't spend their entire budget by the end of the fiscal year, three things happen—they lose the money they have saved; they get less next year; and the budget director scolds them for requesting too much last year. Hence the time-honored government rush to spend all funds by the end of the fiscal year. By allowing departments to keep their savings, [the city of] Visalia not only eliminated this rush, but encouraged managers to save money. The idea was to get them thinking like owners—If this were my money, would I spend it this way?

Expenditures are not the only problem for watchers of waste, fraud and abuse. Sometimes agencies need to be scrutinized for what they sell as well as what they buy. Government agencies regularly dispose of supposedly surplus equipment at prices that benefit purchasers rather than the general taxpaying public.

For example, as noted in Auction Block magazine, based in Houston, the U.S. General Services Administration sells

> confiscated and surplus boats, vehicles and miscellaneous. Vehicles are late model sedans, station wagons, pickups, vans, 4×4s, buses and heavy trucks at various locations. Each sale usually consists of about 30 to 125 vehicles. Most sedans are three-year-old fleet vehicles, some with very low mileage. . . . Sealed bids often include miscellaneous office and computer equipment, salvage vehicles, excess machinery, jewelry, aircraft parts, aircraft, electrical and plumbing supplies.

The investigator needs to ask whether the material should be reallocated to agencies that could use it.

Who Gets the Money, and How

A significant portion of an agency budget is devoted to paying outsiders—consultants and contractors. If an agency relies on them heavily, an investigator needs to ask why. Is the agency demonstrably understaffed? Adequately staffed but operating inefficiently? There are questions of impropriety, too: Are outsiders being paid because of their connections instead of their skills?

When Washington Post reporters Ted Gup and Jonathan Neumann delved into consulting contracts, they learned more than two-thirds had been awarded without competitive bidding. Commerce Business Daily—the official government publication advertising contract opportunities—went largely unread in the private sector because so many awards had been decided before the notification appeared. Government officials who awarded and monitored contracts accepted favors from contractors. In one case, the contractor lived with the government employee heading the office that supervised the contract. In another instance, a contractor hired prostitutes for the official who monitored the firm's troubled contracts. Gup and Neumann also found that the government awarded contracts to companies for data used in regulating their own products.

The Post duo found violations any reader could understand: A Cabinet department paid a consultant for work performed Sept. 31; September has just 30 days. Promised reports had never been delivered. When delivery occurred, reports remained unread or unimplemented.

Similar problems occur when procuring tangible goods. Every day government agencies spend taxpayer dollars for everything from paper clips to automobiles. The potential for abuse accompanies every contract. Investigators have concentrated on Defense Department procurement because the amounts are so huge, the waste and fraud so prevalent. One case study that documents fraud across government branches and agencies is "Feeding Frenzy: The Inside Story of Wedtech." This book, about a manufacturer bilking government agencies, is a collaboration between Washington correspondent William Sternberg and one-time Wedtech vice president Matthew C. Harrison Jr.

Many corporations are dependent on government contracts. Government Executive magazine publishes a booklet, "The Top 200 Federal Contractors." Despite the large amounts of money to be had, those who try to observe the rules often give up in disgust. The chief executive officer of one supplier explained in the Washington Post why he would no longer seek contracts after 20 years of selling paint to the government. He blamed the General Services Administration, the purchasing arm of government:

> The officers responsible for procuring paint are separate from those involved in contract administration, thus ensuring turf wars and lack of accountability for results. . . . These contract administration officers know almost nothing about the paint they are purchasing, since they lack any chemical or engineering background.

The executive said overly specific, 20-year-old government specifications were irrelevant to military paint applications, where technological advances occur continually. As a result, the government denies itself newer, better products.

Investigators trying to explain items like $400 hammers should explore not only corruption and inefficiency by the agency and contractor, but also built-in factors. Those could include government accounting standards (it might be that all the long-distance telephone calls necessary to close the contract were included in the cost) and socioeconomic policies (such as accepting a higher unit price from a minority contractor).

Contracting problems at all levels of government are so rampant that they should be a full-time beat. In Oklahoma, commissioners in dozens of counties accepted kickbacks from suppliers on road-building projects. Harry Holloway and Frank S. Meyers chronicled the case in their book "Bad Times for Good Ol' Boys: The Oklahoma County Commissioner Scandal." The section on the anatomy of corruption is a roadmap for investigators looking at suspicious contracts anywhere:

> A commissioner would act as his own purchasing agent and conduct the purchase of materials for the road and bridge program. Orders involved such things as gravel, sand, culvert pipe and lumber. . . . The requirement that the counties buy from a bid list was no barrier to the kickback system for two reasons. First, the "lowest and best bid" loophole would allow commissioners to contract the favored supplier, even if that supplier was not the low bidder, on the grounds that the supplier was the lowest *and* best bidder. Second, the suppliers jacked up their bids to cover the cost of their kickbacks. . . . In this perverse system the commissioners even had an incentive to use poor-quality materials. Frequent breakdowns meant frequent opportunities to order supplies, with their accompanying kickbacks.

The Contracting Process

Journalists tracking contracts can study completed projects in the IRE Resource Center under headings such as "Bids," "Bribery," "Conflicts of Interests," "City Government," "County Government," "State Government" and "Contractors." Experienced investigators know there are well-established procedures to examine. The progression looks like this, with any single step or the full cycle grist for projects:

Informal Cost Estimates

Government officials somewhere write down estimates, even on non-bid items. An investigator should obtain the estimate, then determine whether the contract as awarded was below, at, or above the estimate. If there is a significant discrepancy between the estimate and the actual cost, an investigator ought to figure out why. If there is never an advertisement for bids, an investigator should inquire whether the government agency is violating rules. One dodge is dividing a bulk purchase into units small enough to avoid competitive bidding. A review of small purchases during previous years might reveal a deliberate plan to shift non-bid business to a political contributor, social friend or a company in which the government administrator has a financial interest.

Notice of Bid

Local, state and federal rules prescribe how much notice be given to potential bidders, as well as the media through which word must be spread. The most common medium is a general circulation newspaper. An example from my hometown newspaper said: "Invitation to bid. The Boone County Commission will receive mailed sealed bids until . . . Feb. 17 for furnishing Boone County with . . . asbestos survey and pre-demolition abatement. . . . Bid specifications may be obtained from the . . . county clerk." That legal notice should alert a journalist to ask why the county is seeking asbestos removal, whether removal might cause health problems, why it was not deemed necessary earlier and what safeguards bidders must institute to protect employees.

Bid Specifications

Investigators should determine whether specifications favor a particular supplier by excluding all but one brand of equipment. Narrowly drawn specifications ought to be a red flag. Who sought the narrow description, and why? Did a potential supplier help the agency write the terms? As bids arrive, an investigator can run a check on each company. Does it owe back taxes to the city, county or state? Do its officers, directors, stockholders, lawyers, accountants or other key players have suspicious links to members of the government awarding the contract? Has it failed to finish jobs satisfactorily in the past? Are there post-contract audits to document past problems? Have any lawsuits resulted from alleged poor performance?

Requests for Proposals

Governments sometimes use RFPs instead of bid notices when seeking flexible, open-ended contracts, especially for consulting services. That flexibility can benefit taxpayers, but it also leaves extra room for abuse.

Product Preferences

Rules often mandate that governments select locally produced goods if bids are equal to, or maybe even higher than, distant suppliers. Are governments twisting the purposes of local preference to award contracts on the basis of friendship or payoffs? Or, alternately, are they ignoring local preference rules when it suits their agenda to do so?

Minority Contracting Requirements

Government agencies must make reasonable efforts to contract with minority-owned businesses. In my hometown, a construction company advertised in the legal notices that it sought minority or female-owned subcontractors for at least 5 percent of the work on a university classroom building. Such a requirement is subject to abuse, especially in geographic areas devoid of minority contractors. White-owned contractors have been caught placing minorities as fronts in subcontracting firms, then using those illegally planted fronts to win the overall job.

Audit Requirements

Rules call for government contracts to be audited at intervals during the job and at completion. Sometimes the audit is performed by an independent outside firm; sometimes internal government auditors are allowed to do the checking. Whoever performs the audit, journalists should obtain a copy, checking to see if taxpayer money is being spent legally and wisely.

Bid and Performance Bonds

A bond posted by the prospective supplier is supposed to assure the government that the supplier will accept the contract if its bid is selected. The bond is forfeited if the supplier rejects the contract offer. Later, a performance bond covers the agency if the supplier fails to fulfill the contract. The bonds usually cost the supplier a percentage of the contract's dollar value. Journalists should ask whether the bonding company is monitoring contractors and whether it is paying the government if default occurs. The Public Contracts Law section of the American Bar Association can provide perspective through its publications, Public Contract Law Journal and Procurement Lawyer, as well as through members willing to talk.

An investigator tracking contracts has to be alert to all manner of scams. For example, the apparent low bidder might turn out to be a bad deal for taxpayers. At the Rocky Mountain News a reporter looked into a company that had won a Denver computer services contract. Bid documents showed that firms competing for the contract promised to pay property taxes on the hardware they supplied. But the winning company never paid those taxes. Companies that planned to pay the taxes lost to a company failing to pay. It turned out the supposed low bid was costing taxpayers money.

Another scam can be tracked through change orders. A low-bid contractor hired to remove concrete from a city street suddenly "discovers" that it is six inches thicker than premised in the bid. As a result, he convinces the city to issue a change order allowing an extra charge. The potential for dishonesty is especially high because change orders are not subjected to competitive bidding. Even when the change orders are for relatively small dollar amounts, they can add up quickly as a percentage of the total contract. On a $129,000 street repair job in Columbia, Mo., the contractor requested change orders for costs "incurred in repairing a private sanitary sewer line not shown on the plans which was hit during excavation"; additional costs incurred "while repairing a hole in an existing box culvert caused by the removal of an abandoned storm drain whose existence was not known"; and "removing unsuitable material from the subgrade." The change orders equalled more than $5,000, about four percent of the new contract total.

The best tactic for the investigator unfamiliar with contracting is to take a well-defined government task—for example, the awarding of an office supply contract by the school system or the hiring of an architectural consultant by the city council—and examine it step by step. The investigator should begin with the enabling law and the executive branch regulation implementing the law.

Ted Wendling of the Cleveland Plain Dealer did just that while looking at food bids solicited by seven school districts. Writing in the IRE Journal about finding $1 million of excessive food costs, Wendling said school administrators "were engaging in bid-splitting, in which they were paying different prices for the same foods." That was not all: "We found [cases] in which the district accepted the low bid, even though it didn't meet specifications and was lower only because it didn't include sauce, an essential ingredient."

Executive Branch Thievery

If executive branch employees are not involved in sweetheart deals with outside contractors, those employees might be stealing directly from the government. Tracey Kaplan of the Los Angeles Times explained how Los Angeles County created an eight-person office to ferret out fraud among the 84,000 employees by auditing randomly selected telephone extensions, going through trash cans and conducting photographic surveillance:

> No fraud is too small to ferret out, it seems. A health department employee was counseled recently for stealing newspapers from a vending machine. But interviews with the investigators and their official reports show the other end of the spectrum . . . there was the manager in the Department of Childrens' Services who resigned after investigators discovered he spent more than $500,000 on unauthorized computer services for the department and falsified records. . . . Then there was the "paper caper." Investigators tailed a Depart-

ment of Mental Health employee and took photographs of him selling boxes of county-owned photocopy paper to local printers. He was fired.

Expenditures to cover bills from office and car telephones should be scrutinized. A review of telephone bills by the St. Paul Pioneer Press showed the fire chief had made hundreds of dollars of personal calls from his car, including regular calls to a local tavern. Many public officials carry credit cards, billing travel expenses directly to the government. Hotel bills charged to the government often contain telephone numbers called from the room. Expense reimbursement vouchers help an investigator determine an official's whereabouts on a specific date.

Absenteeism is at the center of some scams. Employees might call in sick regularly while feeling fine or might be marked as at work all day when they showed up for the first 30 minutes only. Government agencies in a national survey reported absenteeism at more than twice the rate of private-sector employers.

Sometimes the thievery goes by the name "nepotism." A reporting team at the Beaver County Times in Pennsylvania noticed familiar last names being hired by a city government and a school district. The names were the same as those sitting on the city council and board of education. The team also found relatives with dissimilar names who were hired due to nepotism—daughters using married names, sons-in-law, brothers-in-law, cousins. In its IRE awards entry, the team said few of the government bodies "advertised job openings, reserving them instead for family members."

The IRE Resource Center contains numerous projects involving journalistic surveillance of government employees. The discoveries included four-hour lunches, going shopping or fishing while being paid with tax dollars and neglecting important duties such as inspecting the safety of bridges or commercial buildings. Many of those investigations are filed under "Public Workers."

The Twilight Zones of Government: Public Authorities and Self-Regulatory Organizations

When it comes to monitoring the executive branch, perhaps the hardest type of agency to track is the "public authority." Kevin Johnson of the Los Angeles Times explained their reach:

> When even the simplest things in life become too expensive, unmanageable or just too much trouble, Californians for generations have responded with heavy doses of government. When swarms of disease-carrying mosquitoes accompanied soldiers home from World War II, mosquito abatement districts

became the bureaucratic rage. The early solution to a shortage of hospital beds in 1945—hospital districts. Even in death, government has been able to find new life. In the 1920s, upset by the deterioration of local cemeteries, residents throughout the state worked to guarantee a future of respect for their burial grounds. How? Special cemetery districts, of course.

Johnson counted 3,000 public authorities in California, with a collective annual budget of $14 billion. The U.S. Commerce Department counted 33,131 special districts nationwide.

Robert Caro's biography of Robert Moses, "The Power Broker," shows how one bureaucrat took public authorities to new heights (or new depths). Donald Axelrod's book "Shadow Government: The Hidden World of Public Authorities and How They Control Over $1 Trillion of Your Money" shows how Moses' concept spread. The most practical primer for journalists is by Diana B. Henriques. "The Machinery of Greed: Public Authority Abuse and What To Do About It," contains accounts of her own investigations (for example, of the New Jersey Housing Finance Agency) and investigations by other journalists. Examples akin to those cited by Henriques are in the IRE Resource Center under "Public Authorities." Thomas H. Stanton's book "A State of Risk," about costly but off-budget government-sponsored enterprises such as the Farm Credit System, explains similarities and differences between the enterprises and public authorities.

Self-regulatory organizations are either the essence of capitalistic democracy or self-serving shams concocted by powerful industries in concert with corrupt government agencies, depending on the viewpoint of the observer. A prominent example is the New York Stock Exchange, which has dispensation from the SEC to manage its own affairs, including meting out its own discipline of stockbrokers. The Commodity Futures Trading Commission, with congressional consent, has given self-regulatory authority to the National Futures Association, Chicago. It blew its own horn in ads talking about zero tolerance for misconduct, openness to public inquiries and the best regulation at the lowest cost. Journalists should be scrutinizing such claims.

Inspectors General

Executive branch agencies are more likely to perform efficiently and honestly if audited from inside. Most federal agencies, plus many state and local agencies, house such an office. At the federal level, the auditor is usually called the inspector general, and the most visible document produced by the office is the semiannual report. As prescribed by Congress in the Inspector General Act, the report is supposed to discuss deficiencies in agency programs along with proposals for corrective action; identify previous proposals that have not been implemented; summarize items referred to prosecutors; and list audits issued during the six-month reporting period. Inspectors general often concentrate on programs with large dollar values (e.g., the USDA's inspectors general monitor the $24 billion food stamp program) or that are especially vulnerable because guidelines have changed recently, or are new, or have a reputation for weak management. If inspectors general are not concentrating on such programs, why not? Investigators need to analyze historical patterns to look for oddities—the retailer whose food stamp sales suddenly double, the employee claiming far more money on far more expense vouchers than ever in his employment history.

Journalists should stay alert for wrongdoing more urgent than what is mentioned in the semiannual report; inspectors general, in cases of "particularly serious or flagrant problems, abuses or deficiencies," are supposed to immediately contact the relevant agency head, who in turn must tell the appropriate congressional committees within seven days. In his book "Monitoring Government: Inspectors General and the Search for Accountability," Paul C. Light demonstrates the huge quantities of information that journalists can seek, but cautions that inspectors general are not always unbiased, unrestrained investigators.

When Leslie Henderson wrote about inspectors general in the IRE Journal, she mentioned the value of their reports to investigations in four newsrooms. The Des Moines Register used Agriculture Department inspector general information while delving into sanitation violations by a company supplying 42 percent of the meat for the school lunch program. The Washington Post cited Environmental Protection Agency inspector general audits in an investigation of wastewater treatment plants. At the Milwaukee Journal, reporters used an inspector general's audit of the Department of Housing and Urban Development to show that the agency was running its local programs poorly. The Chicago Sun-Times, working with the Better Government Association, found information in inspector general files showing that the Farmers Home Administration had reversed loan rejections after members of Congress intervened on behalf of unqualified applicants.

Most auditing of grants to localities is done locally; at the Department of Housing and Urban Development, for instance, 4,400 recent annual audits of 40,000 grants were issued by the inspector general. The others were contracted out to local accounting firms. Sometimes appointed or elected state officials become involved; the National Association of State Auditors, Comptrollers and Treasurers, in Lexington, Ky., can provide perspective.

Audits contain two sections: the management advisory report and the financial statement. The first section shows compliance (or noncompliance) with laws and regulations; deviations from sound business practices; and the program's degree of effectiveness. The financial statement includes the balance sheet, listing assets, liabilities and fund balances on a particular date (usually the final day of the fiscal year); a statement of revenues, expenditures and encumbrances during the year; and a statement of changes in financial position during the year. The touchstone of the second section is the opinion, which takes one of three forms: the unqualified, or clean opinion; the qualified opinion, rendered with reservations; and no opinion because records do not permit the auditor to make adequate judgments.

Journalists need not wait for audit reports. There are documents and people to consult every step of the way. What follows is the chronology of one $600,000 federal grant, to restore a city's abandoned cotton mill for use as a community center.

The first document is the city's application, which includes a contact person, a list of other grants already received from the federal agency and a budget separating expenses into nine categories.

The second document is the federal agency's approval, with a proviso that at least 10 percent of the grant will go to minority-owned businesses and that at least 26 percent of the laborers hired belong to a minority group.

After receiving approval, the city advertised for bids, studied the bids received and made an award. As renovation progressed, the city filed monthly "employment utilization reports" documenting the breakout of the workforce, plus "minority business enterprise utilization reports" providing details of contracts and subcontracts to minority-owned businesses.

Periodically, the city asked for permission to amend the project, such as using money to demolish a building separate from the old mill.

At various stages, the city submitted a "project performance report." The reports told of progress, but also outlined problems with specific subcontractors.

Eighteen months after renovation began, the city christened its community center. But it was three years before the city submitted its final report (showing a cost overrun of $240,000, funded with other than federal money). The independent auditor completed its report two months later, and the federal agency inspector general reviewed the independent audit five months after that.

■ USING THE FEDERAL REGISTER

The Federal Register is a tool for investigators interested in monitoring the executive branch, much as the Congressional Record is for the legislative branch. The Register appears every working day; some issues contain 1,000 pages of small type. It is searchable in hard copy (with a daily table of contents by agency, plus monthly and annual cumulative indexes) or on-line.

A Federal Register notice can lead immediately to a story. The Chronicle of Higher Education used a notice as the basis for an article headlined "New Policy of Naming Scientists Who Are Found Guilty of Fraud Renews Debate on Federal Role." The story noted the Public Health Service used the Federal Register to publish names of 14 scientists found guilty of misconduct since the creation of the Office of Research Integrity.

For documents-minded investigators, Register notices from the Office of Management and Budget can be especially useful. Under the Paperwork Reduction Act, every document agencies use to collect information must be approved by OMB on Standard Form 83. For instance, IRS Form 211, "Application for Reward for Original Information"—filed by citizens who want a reward for supplying information that "led to the collection of taxes, penalties, fines and forfeitures"—carries OMB Clearance Number 1545–0409.

The Federal Register designation for such approvals is "Public Information Collection Requirements Submitted to the Office of Management and Budget for Clearance." In a Register submission from the Health Care Financing Administration, the agency told OMB it wanted to collect information for a study of nursing home and home health care needs of Medicare and Medicaid patients; the annual form would be completed by state and local governments. An investigator wanting to know more could call an HCFA telephone number printed in the Federal Register notice, or the person named at OMB's Reports Management Branch. OMB lists approved forms in a monthly inventory. It is arranged in alphabetical order by agency name, then broken down further according to the agency's internal units.

A particularly valuable issue of the Federal Register is the semiannual agenda of regulations published by each agency. A recent edition contained 50 pages of proposed regulatory initiatives from HUD alone. Each agency lists a real person and a direct telephone number. The agenda items are divided by program office (for example, Office of Public and Indian Housing; Office of Fair Housing and Equal Opportunity), then divided by stage of development (pre-rulemaking actions, proposed rules that have been published, recent final rules that have been published, recent completed actions).

The permanent titles of the Code look like this:

1. General Provisions

2. Vacant

3. The President

4. Accounts

5. Administrative Personnel

6. Vacant

7. Agriculture

8. Aliens and Nationality

9. Animals and Animal Products

10. Energy

11. Federal Elections

12. Banks and Banking
13. Business Credit and Assistance
14. Aeronautics and Space
15. Commerce and Foreign Trade
16. Commercial Practices
17. Commodity and Securities Exchanges
18. Conservation of Power and Water Resources
19. Customs Duties
20. Employees' Benefits
21. Food and Drugs
22. Foreign Relations
23. Highways
24. Housing and Urban Development
25. Indians
26. Internal Revenue
27. Alcohol, Tobacco Products and Firearms
28. Judicial Administration
29. Labor
30. Mineral Resources
31. Money and Finance: Treasury
32. National Defense
33. Navigation and Navigable Waters
34. Education
35. Panama Canal
36. Parks, Forests and Public Property
37. Patents, Trademarks and Copyrights
38. Pensions, Bonuses and Veterans' Relief
39. Postal Service
40. Protection of Environment
41. Public Contracts and Property Management
42. Public Health
43. Public Lands: Interior
44. Emergency Management and Assistance
45. Public Welfare
46. Shipping

47. Telecommunication

48. Federal Acquisition Regulations System

49. Transportation

50. Wildlife and Fisheries

Each title is broken out into chapters, which usually bear the name of the issuing agency. Chapters are divided into parts covering specific regulatory areas. Parts are divided into sections. An example: Title 8, Aliens and Nationality; Chapter 1, Immigration and Naturalization Service, Department of Justice; Part 235, Inspection of Persons Applying for Admission; Section 235.10, U.S. Citizen Identification Card. The U.S. government's booklet "The Federal Register: What It Is and How to Use It" contains a useful example of tracing a brief reference in a newspaper article to the actual law and regulations.

Books about executive branch rulemaking can make the Federal Register come alive. A study of a regulation from start to finish is "Smoking and Politics: Policymaking and the Federal Bureaucracy" by A. Lee Fritschler. Overviews of the process include George C. Edwards III's "Implementing Public Policy" and Cornelius M. Kerwin's "Rulemaking: How Government Agencies Write Law and Make Policy."

The federal system is pretty much duplicated by state governments. In Missouri, for example, the Missouri Register is published twice monthly by the Administrative Rules Division in the secretary of state's office; 154 agencies publish regulations to implement legislative actions. The Missouri Code of State Regulations is actually thicker than the compilation of the laws. The Bureau of National Affairs, Washington, D.C., publishes the Directory of State Administrative Codes and Registers to guide an investigator through each of the 50 systems.

It is time for journalists to begin reading—and reporting on—the documents that those in power publish to establish the rules governing daily life.

Chapter *8*

INVESTIGATING GOVERNMENT

Education

*M*eg Laughlin expected to write a feature about an elementary school receiving a national excellence award. The eventual story in the Miami Herald turned out to be quite different.

The published article instead focused on a principal determined to win national honors at any cost. Laughlin discovered that the school's test scores had improved partly because the principal exempted students who spoke poor English, even though those children were required to complete the examination. Attendance statistics had been doctored to hide numerous absences. The upshot: The principal, demoted, ended up teaching social studies in a different school. As for the excellence award, the U.S. Education Department revoked it. The moral: Things are not always as they seem in school.

School administrators get skittish about journalists asking questions and wanting to sit in classrooms. While researching a series about the quality of education in Mississippi, Jackson Clarion-Ledger reporters found working as a pair helped. They took turns, one being led around by the principal, who wanted to show off the new gym or auditorium, the other observing the classrooms freely. They saw teachers reading verbatim from books in hot classrooms while squirming students tried to follow along. The reporters interviewed students and listened to hallway conversations. They checked the students' tattered books for dates of publication.

Lisa Gutierrez of the Lansing (Mich.) State Journal notes that it rarely makes sense to cover education in the traditional way—by attending school board meetings. Writing in the Gannett Company magazine Gannetteer, she commented: "Meetings reveal what administrators want the public to know, not necessarily what it should know. Meetings don't tell you that the budget cuts being discussed mean students will keep using history books written in the 1960s." It is the "why" that interests Guti-

145

errez the most: "Why can't Johnny or Jane read when they graduate? Why do children need middle schools?"

To learn the why, Gutierrez cultivates teachers as sources. "The most important books I own are school district directories with home phone numbers for employees." Another important source is parents. Gutierrez attends the opening PTA meeting of each school year, making sure to hand out business cards. "They won't always call you first, but you can count on a few good whistleblowers in the bunch," she said. Another locale for sources is the state department of education. She suggests getting to know the numbers people, the ones who conduct opinion polls on education, the ones who keep statistics about dropouts and test scores.

Her favorite sources are the students. "If you can't talk to young children and teenagers, stay away from education reporting," she said. Gutierrez is able to find stories in what other reporters might consider fluff: her assigned feature on a Hispanic graduation ceremony became a way to discuss why Hispanics drop out of high school at almost twice the district average.

Project ideas can flow from materials gathered by schools as they prepare for accreditation, a process almost all schools—elementary, secondary and postsecondary—are required to complete. The state government sets accreditation standards for public elementary and secondary schools. If accreditation is granted provisionally or denied, the schools will have to submit follow-up reports about problems. The Association of Chief State School Officers, Washington, D.C., can help sort out state-by-state rules.

Accreditors are not the only ones evaluating schools. Government advisory committees, blue-ribbon private panels and public-spirited foundations make recommendations every year on improving quality. The reports, stacked high and dating back for decades, focus on the same problems over and over. It would be useful for a reporter to take a study such as the 1992 "National Education Goals Report: Building a Nation of Learners," then compare it to the local schooling situation.

Covering Compulsory Education Versus Higher Education

The breadth and depth of paper and people trails in education can be seen by skimming books such as Marda Woodbury's "A Guide to Sources of Educational Information" or "American Higher Education: A Guide to Reference Sources" by Peter P. Olevnik et al. Then there is the Educational Resources Information Center (ERIC), managed by the U.S. Education Department; it consists of 16 clearinghouses on separate topics, including early childhood, vocational and higher education. ERIC's resources are available through print indexes, CD-ROM or on-line. University-based institutes that study education supplement the ERIC clearinghouses.

Education at the preschool, elementary, junior high and high school levels is usually covered separately from post–high school education. Many specialized publications divide along those lines as well. For instance, Education Week, based in Washington, D.C., covers elementary and secondary schooling. The Washington-headquartered Chronicle of Higher Education concentrates on the postsecondary world. The National Directory of Magazines listed 525 publications about education in a recent edition. The main forum where education reporters and editors share ideas across the divide is the Education Writers Association, Washington, D.C.

This chapter will focus first on compulsory education, then on higher education. That said, there are many intersections, like the Scholastic Aptitude Tests that drive high school curricula in areas with many university-bound students, and the second-rate writing programs in secondary schools that lead to many college freshmen requiring remedial writing instruction.

Schools are big money operations, which means that they can be scrutinized like other government programs—by "following the dollar." An investigator can begin with the budget, comparing line items and totals with previous years to see what shifts in emphasis have occurred. All educational institutions purchase goods and services, from test tubes for chemistry class to drug abuse workshops for high school teachers. An investigator should look at what goods or services require bids (see Chapter 7), then monitor the process.

Most of all, money in education is supposed to be a means to an end—learning. The most important story for an education reporter at any level is about quality of learning. A reporter sitting in the back of the classroom should be asking questions, some of them radical to the education establishment: Does it make sense to group children by age, when they learn at different rates and in different ways? Does it make sense to teach discrete subjects, with mathematics class never relating to science, with English class never relating to social studies? Would it result in more learning if teachers lectured less and involved students in extended discussion frequently? Why force students to change teachers every year?

Some journalists do ask those questions while trying to bring the big picture into focus. When the Lexington Herald-Leader examined public schooling in Kentucky, it found a system placing politics ahead of children's needs, with nepotism prevailing over merit, old classroom methods being adhered to despite research showing better ways and corrupt undercollection of tax money used to support schools.

It is hard to accurately measure the quality of a school system. But here are some things to look at.

Student Test Scores

Elementary and secondary student scores are released every year; it is the responsibility of journalists to keep the scores in perspective. They should be sure to measure across time, at least three years, as one-year dips and rises are nearly meaningless. Beth Shuster of the Los Angeles Daily News suggests checking "for any schools that suddenly show dramatic results. Check into why . . . did they suddenly receive better instruction? Were the kids coached for the test? Or did someone at the school change wrong answers to right ones?"

No matter what the results, there are eternal questions to ask, such as who decides which tests to use and which to reject? How much do the tests cost to acquire and score? Are comparable school districts using tests that yield more sophisticated results?

Even if scores have dropped district-wide, the superintendent will probably find a way to emphasize the positive, perhaps by focusing on schools where improvement has occurred. When there is reason to doubt the district's interpretation of the scores, a journalist can talk with experts at the education department of a local university or the state education department in the capital. If local experts are viewed as protective of the local schools, there are experts in distant universities who can help, as well as sources at the International Test and Evaluation Association, in Fairfax, Va., and groups nationally that serve as watchdogs of the testing industry, including FairTest, of Cambridge, Mass.

Placing children in classes on the basis of standardized tests needs questioning. Professor Stanley Greenspan and Washington Post reporter Jacqueline L. Salmon, co-authors of the book "Playground Politics," wrote that standardized testing is unfair and ineffective:

> Most standardized tests don't pick up on many of the skills that really count in the "real world"—creativity, persistence, dedication, problem-solving abilities, the ability to think on your feet even when tense and anxious, a gift for seeing the "big picture" and a gut-level instinct for making the right move.

Related books worth studying include "Testing, Testing: Social Consequences of the Examined Life" by F. Allan Hanson, "Underachievers in Secondary Schools: Education Off the Mark" by Robert S. Griffin and "None of the Above: Behind the Myth of Scholastic Aptitude" by David Owen. The organization often criticized in such books, the Educational Testing Service, Princeton, N.J., has its own body of evidence supporting tests, which should be looked at to ensure balance and fairness.

Discipline of Students

In some districts, one of ten students is absent on an average day due to suspension for violent or other antisocial behavior. While suspended, many of these students roam the streets, unsupervised, sometimes committing crimes, individually or as part of gangs. The parents are nowhere to be found; they never show up for conferences called by teachers, never answer notes sent home, never return telephone messages.

In city after city, students who have not been suspended are greeted at the school door by metal detectors and armed security guards. Dress codes appear in the hope that they will somehow discourage gang activity. In classrooms and principals' offices, paddling and other forms of once-abandoned corporal punishment are practiced in desperation. School districts try conflict-resolution classes, hoping the message will take hold. In the Boston Globe magazine, Sara Terry examined classroom moral upgrade programs. Thomas Lickona devoted an entire book to the topic, "Educating for Character: How Our Schools Can Teach Respect and Responsibility." As more schools offer character development and values classes, journalists should be asking questions such as: Who chooses the values to stress, and how? Can such a theoretical approach possibly improve discipline?

When faced with an immediate discipline problem, teachers cannot wait patiently for theory to take hold. How do individual teachers keep order in the classroom? Is there a written policy adhered to uniformly throughout the school district? Alternately, is discipline ad hoc and therefore unpredictable—extreme in its sternness or in its laxity? Are the teachers receiving support from parents, or are parents and teachers working at counter-purposes? Irwin A. Hyman's book "Reading, Writing and the Hickory Stick: The Appalling Story of Physical and Psychological Abuse in American Schools" raises these and other interesting points.

When a knife or gun is brandished, can a teacher remove the student immediately? Or must the student be allowed to remain in class while the matter is appealed to higher levels? How does the Individuals With Disabilities Education Act, a federal law, figure in? It is meant to prevent certain children from being shunted from school to school because of disruptive behavior. But is the law serving its purpose when a student caught with a gun is allowed to remain because the student's parents claim that their child suffers from attention-deficit disorder?

Reporters looking into discipline need to ask about the conscientious students: Do they have trouble studying during school hours because of disruptions? How safe are the hallways? A project about discipline will involve lots of interviewing, and many of those interviews will yield contradictory information. As a result, the investigator will have to convince parents and students to open their school records to scrutiny, so there will be documentation to resolve contradictions among verbal accounts.

One sensitive question to explore is whether some teachers and administrators abuse authority by singling out racial or ethnic groups for punishment. Jonathan Eig of the Dallas Morning News found that black students received corporal punishment more frequently than white or Hispanic students. Some of his evidence was anecdotal; some came from reports submitted by schools to the U.S. Office for Civil Rights in the Education Department. The question became whether the uneven discipline was justified or grounded in bias.

Misbehavior often is related to trouble at home. When teachers and administrators hear rumors about sexual abuse, domestic violence, divorce and extreme poverty during the school day, do they ignore it, pretending it has no connection to effective learning? If they intervene, in what manner? Do they contact those at home directly, call the police, contact a government social worker, work with an in-school or district-wide counselor? Organizations such as the American Association for Counseling and Development, Alexandria, Va., and the National Association of School Psychologists, Silver Spring, Md., can help journalists figure out whether a local situation is the norm.

Some misbehavior is tied to alcohol and other drug abuse. Police officers in the narcotics division might discuss their perceptions of the school drug problem. It is necessary to verify the alleged problem with arrest reports, records of overdoses, results of locker searches and interviews with students in treatment. There are drug counseling centers and an Alcoholics Anonymous office in most communities that can offer insight.

Misbehavior might also be linked to sexual experimentation; today problems extend beyond unexpected pregnancies and treatable venereal diseases. With the appearance of AIDS, sex education is more necessary, and controversial, than ever. An investigator can see if local schools provide AIDS information to students; AIDS education might include dispensing condoms on school property. A related controversy is whether teaching sexual abstinence should be part of the curriculum. Whatever the policy, did parents have a chance to express their views, maybe even in a binding vote? Should schools be reflecting majority family values, or leading the way no matter what the popular sentiment?

Student Retention

In many schools, students automatically progress to the next grade, no matter how poor their academic performance or how disruptive their behavior. In other schools, such students must repeat grades. An investigator can compare a high school's pass-on, repeat and dropout rates, daily attendance and graduation percentages with national and state averages. Beth Shuster of the Los Angeles Daily News suggests caution, however, when interpreting such statistics: "Try to see why one school has a high rate while others are much lower. Often, reporting differs among administrators, and sometimes schools are lax in keeping track of students with high absenteeism." In some schools, if a student shows up for first hour then skips, the student is counted as present for the whole day. That variation on absenteeism could be considered as effectively dropping out.

Putting faces on the dropouts and the perpetual absentees will tell a compelling story no matter what the explanation. Are talented students leaving school? Is it because classes fail to challenge them? It might also suggest inadequate in-school counseling. In some high schools, the student-counselor ratio is 500 to 1. A profile of individual counselors and a few of their advisees can have high impact. Students being promoted to the next grade—without regard to whether or not they're qualified to pass—to make retention rates look better than they should be are also compelling subjects for profiles. Lawsuits in which students claim injuries resulting from being rushed along or from instructional negligence can help document allegations.

Because most journalists are college-educated, they tend to know few persons who drop out of high school. Yet in Missouri, to take one example, 12 percent of the population never begins high school. Of those starting, 15 percent fail to finish. That is a lot of human beings. Journalists need to put the situation in context: For many lower-income children, there is no reason to believe good grades and other signs of learning pay off in society. Deborah Meier, head of alternative public schools in East Harlem, New York City, said, "If being good at school comes naturally, it's a nuisance worth putting up with. After all, it brings praise, and being competent feels good. But if you're not good at it, it's one long arduous task, full of humiliation and confusion. Then the absence of a reason is cruel."

The Wall Street Journal captured the culture of failure at a Washington, D.C., high school by focusing on a few high-achieving students ostracized by classmates and peers who had already dropped out. The tormentors had no shame: Every source spoke on the record.

Knowing dropout rates can lead to other questions: For those who leave, is there any hope later, such as an easily accessible program leading to a high school equivalency diploma? Many school districts ask students why they drop out, so can provide statistics about the reasons. If female students are quitting because of pregnancy, maybe the district needs a better program to enable them to finish school.

A few of the useful books about high school troubles (and occasional successes) are "South of Heaven: Welcome to High School at the End of the 20th Century" by Thomas French; "Small Victories: The Real World of a Teacher, Her Students and Their High School" by Samuel G. Freedman; and "Horace's School: Redesigning the American High School" by Theodore R. Sizer.

Teacher and Administrator Competency

When Chicago Tribune team members examined the city's schools, they found a fourth-grade classroom in which all 22 students had to attend summer school. The reason? Their teacher was so incompetent that the children failed to learn enough to move to fifth grade. Four previous schools had tried unsuccessfully to remove the teacher from classroom work.

Journalists covering education should examine the quality of teaching. There are ways. States set a minimum score to pass the National Teacher Examinations, prepared by the Educational Testing Service in Princeton, N.J. A check can be made of a state's certification standards, including how they compare with other states. In Mississippi, reporters found the required score was so low that only 3 percent of those taking the test nationally would have failed. Perspective is available from the book "The Validity Issue: What Should Teacher Certification Tests Measure?" by Michael L. Chernoff, Paula M. Nassif and William P. Gorth.

Many teachers are required to undergo periodic testing and recertification, giving investigators another benchmark. Are those tests biased against teachers from specific racial or ethnic groups, making it difficult for them to find jobs? If the student population is diverse but the teacher ranks lack diversity, what impact does that have on instruction? The Stockton Record in California documented the widening gulf between teachers and students: 80 percent of the teachers were white, versus 50 percent of the students, with teachers earning three times as much as the average local family of color. While checking demographics, it might prove interesting to find out how many of the teachers have school-age children of their own. Do those children attend public school in the same district? How many teachers actually live in the district in which they teach?

To increase diversity, among other reasons, about half the states allow certification without a degree from an education college. The organization Teach for America is in the forefront here. Many education colleges themselves are not accredited by the National Council for Accreditation of Teacher Education, Washington, D.C., whose imprimatur is probably the most recognized. Journalists should ask whether training is demonstrably inferior at unaccredited schools than in those institutions that have won accreditation from the council or some other legitimate group. Other changes being tried include adding a fifth year to college teacher training, having candidates spend more time in schoolrooms instead of university lecture halls and emphasizing more liberal arts training. Is any of this working?

However teachers prepare, what do they learn about how children acquire knowledge? Keeping gifted children interested? Teaching below-average children in classrooms where there is no tracking by ability? Handling discipline problems? Do the techniques imparted in university classrooms work in real life? If not, how do teachers adapt? Are continuing education courses part of the solution?

To some extent, investigators can answer such questions by interviewing current and past education professors, classroom teachers, administrators, parents and students. The American Association of Colleges for Teacher Education, in Washington, D.C., can shed light on such matters. But all the interviewing in the world is no substitute for extended observation, in education colleges and children's classrooms.

Mary Ellen Schoonmaker quoted a principal in a Columbia Journalism Review article headlined "The Beat Nobody Wants": "Teachers and the complexities of their lives are not represented. People don't know what it's like to have 170 kids in a high school each week. It's a backbreaking, bonebreaking job." Teacher burnout is a problem, as Barry A. Farber explains in his book "Crisis in Education: Stress and Burnout in the American Teacher." Teachers' viewpoints are told by Catherine Collins and Douglas Frantz in their book "Teachers Talking Out of School." To get a handle on the pressures facing teachers, author Tracy Kidder immersed himself in an elementary school classroom for a year to write his book "Among Schoolchildren." Emily Sachar of Newsday did her extended observation from the teacher's desk, spending a year in the front on an eighth-grade mathematics classroom. She chronicled that year in her book "Shut Up and Let the Lady Teach."

Certain teachers are hard to observe because they duck their problems by staying away from school a lot. The Atlanta Business Chronicle found that on an average day, 6 percent of the city's teachers called in sick. That absenteeism affected learning; substitute teachers are usually less effective than the regular instructors. In some states, substitutes are not required to hold a college degree. In the classroom, substitutes are usually unmonitored, their performance never measured. Furthermore, absenteeism costs a school district financially—$14,000 a day according to the calculations in Atlanta.

Some advocates say low teacher salaries are a factor causing burnout and affecting the overall quality of instruction; others say salaries are adequate. The National Education Association and the American Federation of Teachers, the two major unions, both based in Washington, D.C., compile national salary data. State teachers associations have their own salary databases, magazines and issue briefs—not to mention their political machinery that gives money to politicians, provides volunteers during the election years and lobbies effectively.

Some states are linking teacher pay to a merit scale. Too often, journalists write about the beginning of the experiment, then fail to determine whether it is producing the intended results. One possibility is tracking a few teachers from the time they enter the merit program until they retire.

The occasional profiles of those teachers could be supplemented with district-wide or statewide statistics.

Some teachers never achieve competency; some competent teachers have other shortcomings. Journalists need to be vigilant in tracking cases of incompetence and moral turpitude. Administrators often try to keep disciplinary proceedings secret. The disciplined teacher often leaves quietly, moving to some other school where other children then become vulnerable to the same kind of harm.

The harm might be avoided if state licensing agencies, school districts and individual schools checked applicants' backgrounds adequately. An investigator should delve into a district's procedures for checking potential teachers, and should also find out how the district handles requests for information about problem teachers trying to move away.

In Florida, the Winter Haven News-Chief discovered more than three dozen convicted felons, including child molesters, had lied about their pasts to win teaching certificates. The reporter gleaned his information from teacher discipline files at Florida's Department of Education. When the Detroit News checked computer tapes of 450,000 Michigan convictions against a tape of 97,000 teachers, a reporter found 200 teachers whose criminal records were unknown to school officials, who were taking applicants at their word. The IRE Resource Center contains similar investigations under the "Teachers" heading. An extended example is "Secret Lessons," a book by prosecutor Don W. Weber and St. Louis Post-Dispatch reporter Charles Bosworth Jr.

Teacher-coaches should be scrutinized with extra care. They have more opportunities for taking advantage of students than the average teacher. Furthermore, their sins tend to be overlooked or forgiven in an atmosphere of winning at all costs. Los Angeles magazine reported how a coach got away with his sexual transgressions; a similar story about a different coach appeared in Texas Monthly. Journalists should question the traditional assumptions about the value of high-school athletics, as Andrew W. Miracle Jr. and C. Roger Rees do in their book "Lessons of the Locker Room: The Myth of School Sports."

Many principals and district-wide superintendents served as teachers (and often coaches) first. Were they well prepared for the switch? What exactly did the preparation consist of? To whom are administrators accountable? When a new principal is needed, a new district superintendent needed, does the search committee encourage applications from local candidates? Or are excellent local candidates ignored during the excitement of a high-profile, high-cost national search?

The ultimate supervisors of principals and superintendents are usually elected, unsalaried school board members. They are likely to be dependent on the administrators for information, a system that often reduces board members to nothing more than rubber stamps for everything from curriculum changes to salary increases for those very administrators. In my hometown, the schools superintendent makes four times the salary of the average teacher. A few districts have moved to erase such imbalances by indexing administrator salaries so that they are no more than twice the teacher average.

Thomas Toch, education reporter at U.S. News and World Report, has examined many of the 15,200 public school boards in the United States, 94 percent of which are elected. He says local democracy is working poorly, and believes such boards will be replaced in more and more districts. Some districts have shifted to school-based management, allowing a council of teachers, staff and parents to choose principals and vote on policy questions. When that is the case, do the councils represent the diversity in the student body and the community at large?

Where traditionally chosen boards still prevail, journalists should refrain from viewing all school board members suspiciously—many are unselfish, civic-minded people serving, after all, without pay. That said, journalists should ask school board members, what is in it for them? Are they interested in steering school district contracts, administrative jobs and teaching positions to business partners, friends and relatives? Are they planning to enrich themselves through kickbacks from suppliers? Do they have instructional agendas they would like to impose on classroom teachers? These are not theoretical situations; the IRE Resource Center contains examples of each abuse cited here, and others.

Other problems are obvious, too. Although 30 percent of public school students are nonwhite, only 6 percent of the 97,000 local board members are nonwhite. In an increasing number of school board races, candidates are running on single-issue platforms, with low voter turnouts making it more likely they will be elected. Board members are being sued more often by students, teachers and staff; those lawsuits are discouraging some of the best people from serving.

Organizations grappling with such matters include the National Middle School Association, Columbus, Ohio; the National Association of Secondary School Principals, Reston, Va.; the National Association of Elementary School Principals and the National School Boards Association, both of Alexandria, Va.

Instructional Materials, Tracking and Class Sizes

In many districts, teachers, administrators, parents or school board members (or some combination of those four groups) sit in a room, behind closed doors, choosing textbooks. Despite their deliberation, they too frequently choose books that are factually inaccurate, poorly written and/or biased. An investigator should ferret out which books were chosen, which rejected, and why. Textbooks are a business proposition as well as a pedagogical one. Are textbook publishers or wholesalers inappropriately involved in the selection process by courting or even bribing those who make the decisions?

Three common controversies in textbook selection are portrayals of the Vietnam War, racial/ethnic minorities and Darwinism. Debates about Darwinism versus creationism get mixed into the controversy about religion in the classroom. If a majority of parents want religion worked into the curriculum, should the school board accede? Alternately, if a minority of fundamentalist parents is able to gain control of the school board, should that minority be able to place their religious beliefs in classrooms? Perspective is available from Warren A. Nord's book "Religion and American Education: Rethinking a National Dilemma."

Even when textbooks are chosen openly and honestly, controversies abound. For instance, how do teachers of reading choose among textbooks that rely on completely different theories? Each academic discipline has its own philosophical disagreements about how and what to teach. No textbook can satisfy everyone. Teachers in most disciplines have their own organizations, such as the National Council of Teachers of Mathematics, Reston, Va., and their own publications, such as American Biology Teacher from the National Association of Biology Teachers, also in Reston.

Journalists Jack Nelson and Gene Roberts examined textbook controversies in a 1962 book, "The Censors and the Schools," before each became among the most celebrated investigators of an era. More recent books on the subject include Harriet Tyson's "A Conspiracy of Good Intentions: America's Textbook Fiasco," and James W. Loewen's "Lies My Teacher Told Me: Everything Your American History Textbook Got Wrong."

As schools become increasingly dependent on computer hardware and software, selection committees will hold the same type of power as those choosing textbooks, and therefore will also need to be monitored by journalists. The use of computers in schools raises the issue of disparities in computer access. Schools attended by wealthy families and with parent-teacher associations good at raising money tend to have more computers than schools in low-income areas. Should those disparities be allowed? Or should central administrators step in to equalize the situation, thereby perhaps discouraging neighborhood school initiative?

If a computer manufacturer offers machines at little or no cost, should the school board accept, thereby helping the company build its customer base to the exclusion of competitors? Corporations are influencing the availability and content of instructional materials in classrooms by supplying them free in times of tight budgets. Everything free has a price—in this case, embedded messages meant to favor the corporate suppliers. An energy company videotape about the environment says a major oil spill has done no permanent harm to area wildlife. A food conglomerate's science class kit promotes its sugary snacks. Some manufacturers approach schools about distributing products through the children. Should schools say yes to serving as marketing mechanisms? If so, should they seek payment for their role?

Local businesses get their messages into schools through the noblest sounding of programs, such as Partners in Education. A business "adopts" a school. The arrangement seems sincerely altruistic, but in some cases the motivation is building goodwill on the way to increasing corporate profits or influencing the content of classroom instruction. Perspective is available from the National Association for Partners in Education, in Alexandria, Va.

Disparities and inequities exist within, as well as among, schools. Different instructional materials are used for different tracks, a term denoting clustering of students based on classroom performance and standardized test scores. The majority of schools track students, but the decision of the majority has failed to diminish the debate. Journalists looking at tracking should be especially alert for placements based on race, ethnicity or class. Another question flows directly from the placements: Are students in the lower tracks given the opportunity to move to college preparatory classes if it turns out the original placement was mistaken? Anne Wheelock's book "Crossing the Tracks: How Untracking Can Save America's Schools" is one of many capturing the debate. Parents of children designated as gifted often favor tracking, on the grounds that placing gifted children with slower learners drags down the brightest.

Parents of gifted children are often advocates for expanding the curriculum beyond reading, writing and arithmetic to include music, drama, dance and painting. Sometimes foreign language instruction and physical education are lumped into the debate. Groups such as the American Council on the Teaching of Foreign Languages, Yonkers, N.Y., and the National Art Education Association, Reston, Va., can help investigators produce enlightening stories on the place of the arts in the curriculum. Is the conventional wisdom about the arts falling outside the basics misguided? When schools do offer arts classes, teachers often complain about lack of specially equipped classrooms and overcrowding. Some of those teachers end up buying supplies out of their personal savings. A journalist who obtains store receipts from those personal purchases has one element of a good story.

On behalf of students who will never escape the lower tracks, have no desire to attend college and care little about arts instruction, an investigator should delve into how well schools provide vocational training. Are the programs set up so that participants avoid the "dummy" label? Do the programs offer employers the quality and quantity of workers needed? Is there preparation for high-technology industry as well as for traditional manual labor jobs? State employment agency officials can be asked their views, as can employers themselves. The officials of industries that have decided against locating in the area should be questioned about whether the worker pool and overall educational quality were deciding factors. Journalists needing perspective on local practices can contact the National Association of State Directors of Vocational/Technical Education Consortium, Washington, D.C.

The New Orleans Times-Picayune found that the personnel manager for one of the city's largest employers never received a call from the schools about job openings or advice on what training to offer. That same newspaper illustrated educational problems by reproducing job applications submitted to a local employer. When asked their city of residence, some applicants wrote "New Orlance" or "New Orlennes." Another wrote the type of work desired was "aney tihig open."

Many such applications come from graduates of the school system; others come from those who never completed twelfth grade. Such obvious inadequacies should lead an investigator to ask about adult education classes, including those aimed at achieving basic literacy. Who teaches the classes? How are they funded? What are the dropout and job placement rates? Perspective is available from the American Association for Adult and Continuing Education and the National Clearinghouse on Literacy Education, both in Washington, D.C.

Investigating class size is less complicated than some other instructional issues. Because it is a quantitative matter, there are fewer shades of gray. Journalists writing about class size should know about state laws, district policies and any other guidance for help in establishing compliance or noncompliance. When class sizes are larger than allowed by law, who takes the blame? If parents and teachers push for legal compliance, are they told budgetary constraints make compliance impossible? What then?

"Special Needs" Students

In the broadest sense, every student has special needs because every student is unique in some ways. But in most schools, "special needs" is used to refer to children who are mentally or physically impaired. Federal regulations identify more than a dozen disabilities; about one of every ten students receives support from government programs for the handicapped. The National Association of State Directors of Special Education, Alexandria, Va., and the Council for Exceptional Children, Reston, Va., are among the resources for journalists. An investigator should inquire whether the school district ignores special needs children, forcing them into distant state schools, private schools or home schooling.

If the local school district does have a program, are the special needs students segregated or mainstreamed? Mainstreaming, sometimes called inclusion, means taking classes with nondisabled students of the same age at the neighborhood school. Either approach—segregation or inclusion—

raises thorny questions. If a school district chooses inclusion, how does it afford the extra costs in an era of stretched budgets? How do teachers with little experience in such situations cope? Are other students slowed in their learning because of the attention that must be spent helping special needs peers?

U.S. News and World Report found too many students being placed in special education because of government financial incentives. The results: Students with relatively minor learning disabilities unfairly labeled as impaired learners, a bloated bureaucracy including a separate transportation system and unhappiness among parents and teachers.

Wisconsin Public Television found that children with special learning needs were not being educated adequately. Research on the Madison school district's programs took time, partly because parents and teachers were reluctant to talk on camera for fear of retribution. The reporter used federal and state court records, complaints at the Office of Civil Rights, state and federal regulations covering special education and articles in academic journals. He suggests enlisting help from parents with learning-disabled children. The parents can provide access to their children's school records and lead the investigator to teachers willing to discuss the problems.

There is plenty of documentation to examine. Aleta Watson of the San Jose Mercury News quoted an exasperated school district business manager:

> "This is a J50," [he] said, flipping through a 24-page special education report the district must file to get federal funding for its handicapped students. "We do it three times a year." Even though the school district has only 300 special education students, their records—some folders three inches thick—fill eight file drawers in the central office.

Some families, rather than being deprived by bureaucracy, use expansive definitions of special needs to take unfair advantage of benefits that should be reserved for the most critical cases. One such abused program is the Social Security Administration's supplemental security income. Some parents teach their children to fake disabilities or withhold medicine to qualify for Supplemental Security Income cash payments. Some local governments encourage Aid to Families with Dependent Children recipients to switch to all-federal SSI benefits. Journalists should document such shifting, as well as checking how many requests under SSI are granted or denied and for what reasons. Among the books explaining the problems and solutions are "Schooling Without Labels: Parents, Educators and Inclusive Education" by Douglas Biklen, "All of Us Together: The Story of Inclusion at the Kinzie School" by Jeri Banks and "Succeeding Against the Odds" by Sally L. Smith. Also useful is the reference book The Special Education Sourcebook: A Teacher's Guide to Programs, Materials and Information Sources by Michael S. Rosenberg and Irene Edmond-Rosenberg.

Desegregation, Multiculturalism and Gender Equity

A different category of special needs is created by a segregated society; minority and female students sometimes receive inferior educations, no matter how motivated they are to learn.

Many school districts are considered officially desegregated. An investigator should determine whether official desegregation is a reality, or an illusion. Where the public schools are open to all, many white children attend all-white private schools, creating de facto segregation. The white children remaining in the public schools are almost all from low-income families, creating a different kind of segregation—by economic class.

To understand the history of school desegregation, a journalist can read "Simple Justice" by Richard Kluger. Busing of students outside their neighborhoods is part of any discussion on desegregation. There are hundreds of books about busing; one that frames the debate is Christine H. Rossell's "The Carrot or the Stick for School Desegregation Policy: Magnet Schools or Forced Busing."

In schools where there are significant numbers of blacks and whites together, a journalist, through extended observation, can determine if desegregation means true integration. For instance, do students from different races and ethnic groups mix in the lunchroom, or do they cluster exclusively at race-specific tables? If they cluster, what role, if any, should teachers and administrators play in encouraging mixing? Are faculty and administrators racially and culturally diverse?

Even where social integration appears to have occurred, the schools are sometimes academically unequal between races. After the Louisville Courier-Journal found that the schools did not provide racial breakouts of test scores, it obtained access to raw data from the school system's computers. Analyzing the data, the newspaper reported that black students scored below average in most grades in reading while white students were above average in all grades. The same gaps existed in math, college entrance tests and first-grade failures. The reporting took on extra richness because the newspaper's team knew that school districts receiving federal funds file Forms 101 and 102 with the U.S. Education Department's Office of Civil Rights. The reports include statistics on race and gender of students, numbers of students in special education programs and student suspensions.

Whatever the level of integration, government agencies and many parents expect schools to promote multiculturalism in the classroom and extracurricular activities. An investigator can examine whether multiculturalism has become a front for resegregation, in which every race and ethnic group has its own curriculum, its own extracurricular clubs. An observant journalist will check such details as whether authentic ethnic food is served in school lunchrooms, and whether all students are encouraged to try it.

Gender equity should be part of the mix: In physical education classes and after-school athletics, are female students given the same options as male students? Do interscholastic sports for females receive funding equal to male sports? The National Association for Girls and Women in Sports, Reston, Va., has information that will help with perspective. Are females encouraged or required to enroll in industrial arts; are males encouraged or required to enroll in home economics? Books that examine the situation are "Failing at Fairness: How America's Schools Cheat Girls" by Myra Sadker and David Sadker, and "Multicultural Education: Issues and Perspectives" by James A. Banks and Cherry A. McGee Banks.

School Choice

Sometimes students attend schools outside their neighborhoods because of mandatory busing to achieve desegregation or because of centralized special needs classes. Other times, the reasons are dicier, as when parents use permits to get their children into schools outside of their neighborhoods because of alleged child-care arrangements or by claiming medical problems. Some parents fake their addresses.

Beyond such individual situations, school choice has become a sociopolitical movement. In his book "School Choice: The Struggle for the Soul of American Education," Peter W. Cookson Jr. asks and answers such questions as: Should families be able to decide which schools their children attend on the basis of any factor except neighborhood? Is it true that increased competition among schools for students leads to higher-quality education, as school choice advocates claim? Are school choice laws logistically feasible and economically viable? What happens to schools not chosen by many families? Do they react by innovating in an attempt to regain enrollment? Or do they fall further as the best students with the most caring parents leave?

Nonteaching Employees

It takes more than teachers and administrators to make a school work. But because support personnel tend to be poorly paid, schools often attract less than the cream of the labor force. That means story possibilities.

School bus drivers sometimes are child molesters, or have alcohol-related arrests while behind the wheel. Journalists have obtained lists of bus drivers from school districts or transportation companies, then matched names with state motor vehicles databases that show speeding tickets, alcohol-related offenses and other violations.

Even if the drivers are safe, the buses may not be. WCBD-TV, Charleston, S.C., revealed, according to the IRE Resource Center abstract,

> safety problems on school buses . . . including bad brakes and tires, dangerous seats, windshields recalled for safety problems and faulty governors designed to keep bus speed down as required by law . . . maintenance shop staff were performing shoddy workmanship and the supervisor was using the garage for his personal projects.

That situation raises questions about why the bus company received a transportation contract in the first place, and whether anybody within district administration was monitoring the contract. When school districts use taxi companies to supplement buses, do they know whether the cabs and drivers are safe? Is the school district receiving a fair price from the taxi company?

School lunch programs are sometimes a haven for board members and administrators to hire family members or persons suggested by local politicians. The jobs may not always pay well, but the work is generally not taxing and the hours are short. Hanging around the lunchroom seeking information on personnel is a good time for the reporter to check out the food. Many school lunches taste bad and also lack nutrition, but it does not have to be that way. Journalists can consult the Community Nutrition Institute in Washington, D.C., plus the American School Food Service Association and the Snack Food Association, both in Alexandria, Va., for perspective.

Custodians, playground supervisors, secretaries and other support personnel also should be scrutinized for efficiency, and to make sure they want to be around children for the proper reasons. No reporter can check the record of every such employee, but spot checks are practical. At the least, a reporter can write about the school district's own system of checking. That story might stimulate sources to come forward with specific cases, which a reporter can then check one by one or allow to accumulate until the reporter believes a critical mass has been achieved. The Dallas Morning News found 185 employees (of 16,000 total) in the city's school district who had been convicted of felonies in Dallas County or who had received probation on a felony charge.

School Buildings

The title of a study from the Education Writers Association says it well: "Wolves at the Schoolhouse Door—an Investigation of the Condition of Public School Buildings." An investigator who looks at buildings from the inside will often notice significant problems. Why did administrators allow such deterioration? Where will the money come from for repairs? If repairs are left undone, what physical dangers might result? What harm to learning is likely in such an environment? Is there air conditioning in classrooms to use on 100-degree days? How often does it break down, and how long does it take to get it fixed? If some schools have air conditioning and others do not, why?

Overcrowding is common. Journalists should visit as many schools in the district as possible, looking for tangible evidence of overcrowding. One rough but objective measure is square feet per student. In general, newer schools are less cramped than older buildings. Are all those newer buildings in the richer areas of town?

Asbestos within schools has proved to be a problem. A federal law, the Asbestos Hazard Emergency Response Act, requires districts to inspect for asbestos, then devise a removal or abatement plan. Some state laws were in place before the federal law, but many were more lax. Journalists can ask whether their state has been granted a waiver because the law is as stringent as the federal. The National Conference of State Legislators conducted a state by state compliance study. Has the district complied? If not, has the government punished the district? KTHI-TV, Fargo, N.D., found not a single local school had been inspected and that the government had done nothing to punish the schools for violating the law. The Chicago Sun-Times checked 6,000 Illinois districts, finding, according to the IRE Resource Center abstract, "that the schools have been asked to do too much in too little time; Environmental Protection Agency regulations have led many districts to hire incompetent asbestos removal companies; Catholic schools cannot afford the multimillion dollar removal cost, while city schools cannot keep up with the EPA-dictated schedule." Amidst the controversy, journalists should ask whether asbestos hazards have been overstated. Is covering exposed asbestos an adequate response, rather than the far more expensive, hazardous process of removal?

Some school buildings are asbestos traps. Others are dangerous because of radon gas, as KOA Radio discovered in Denver and the North Jersey Herald and News discovered in its circulation area. Yet another hazard can come from chemical use inside the buildings and on the grounds; WYFF-TV, Greenville, S.C., discovered that children were becoming ill from inappropriate indoor cleaning or outdoor turf chemicals dispensed by unqualified or unsupervised workers.

School buildings might be fire traps, too. An investigator should find out how recently a certified fire inspector has done a thorough check. WFLA-TV, Tampa, found state education department fire standards failed to meet local government standards. When inspections occurred, they were done by school district employees who had incentives to look the other way when confronted by fire hazards. The San Francisco Examiner discovered missing fire extinguishers and doors that had been padlocked in violation of local safety rules.

Who Pays for Education?

Keeping buildings safe, reducing class sizes, supplying up-to-date textbooks—all that requires money. A district's revenue stream affects what occurs in the classroom, even if there is no direct correlation between dollars spent and quality of education. While wrestling with the relationships among revenue, expenditure and quality of education equation, an investigator must first determine how much money schools have available to educate students.

It is most sensible to break out expenditures school by school. Many investigators have done their calculating at the district level rather than the individual school level. The trouble with that approach is that many districts allocate expenditures unequally from school to school. Whether this is done intentionally or unconsciously, often schools in well-to-do neighborhoods fare better than schools in lower-income neighborhoods, an equation that favors political clout over need.

In at least 16 states, courts have ruled that the property-tax system violates principles of fairness; as of 1994, courts were facing such decisions in another 14 states. But few states have found an alternative that makes a clear majority happy. One of many books about the controversy is Richard Lehne's "The Quest for Justice: The Politics of School Finance Reform." State lotteries have been one of the most highly touted "solutions." But lotteries shift some of the burden to the poor, who sometimes spend more money on lottery tickets than their household budgets can bear in the vain hope of escaping destitution quickly. Politicians sometimes use the lottery as part of a shell game, reducing appropriations to schools by the same amount that gambling income yields—leaving schools right where they started financially.

The most complete view of income, and outgo, often can be obtained from information made available because the school district is selling bonds to generate money. An offering statement, sometimes called a prospectus, discloses the district's finances to members of the public who are considering buying the bonds. Bond-rating agencies establish the creditworthiness of the district, thus influencing how well the bonds sell. Any drop in the bond rating should warrant a story and further investigation of the cause for the drop. The principal independent bond-rating agencies are Standard & Poor's Corp. and Moody's Investors Services, both of New York City.

Besides cash from property taxes and bond sales, a school district might generate revenue from landholdings. An investigator can find out about school-owned property by running the name of the institution through the county assessor's or recorder's office. Jackson Clarion-Ledger reporters found school districts failing to take advantage of state land set aside to be leased out for their benefit. The reporters showed that thousands of acres were under lease for pennies an acre annually. That was great for the leaseholder, but not for the school district's treasury. Among those with low-rate leases were individual school officials acting as entrepreneurs, government units and a private golf course.

In some locales, the largest percentage of funding comes from a central appropriation (usually tax revenue allocated by the legislature to state education agencies), supplemented by the federal government (usually earmarked by Congress to be channeled through executive branch agencies to local districts). The nature of funding sources can point to many possible stories. For example, a school district can be overly dependent on federal funds, making them especially susceptible to unforeseen budget cuts. Another school district may fail to take advantage of federal money, depriving its students of opportunities. The National Association of State Budget Officers, in Washington, D.C., can provide perspective.

While studying the revenue flow, the alert investigator will look at the other side of the ledger, concentrating on expenses that seem unrelated to quality education. Any budget entry might be interesting. The Kansas City Times went over the district's budget line-by-line; they found the superintendent had spent $13,352 to furnish his executive suite. In contrast, the money spent for science equipment and supplies that year was $1,400. Examining expenses submitted by school board members may show unusual or unsubstantiated expenditures. The examination should include long-distance telephone calls and reimbursements for out-of-town trips.

A St. Louis Post-Dispatch reporter examined hundreds of expense vouchers and receipts to uncover the fact that the superintendent had spent $62,000 in two years on travel expenses, far more than his $15,000 annual limit. She also determined that the superintendent had overcharged the school district for lodging by comparing the number of nights in hotel rooms claimed by the superintendent with the hotel records and his itineraries.

Contracts awarded by elected or appointed school boards include those for construction, transportation of students, teacher training, food for the lunchroom and supplies. As with any contract, the investigator should check whether those in charge are skirting the law by awarding no-bid contracts or if the bid solicitation is tailored for a specific vendor.

In New York City, a contract for construction of a high school went $50 million over budget. An investigation by state officials led to revelations of bid rigging, bribes and phoney construction company invoices paid by board of education employees who apparently were parties to the falsification. At the time that arrests took place, a New York Times reporter quoted an investigator explaining why the inquiry took nine years: The board of education, she said, "has loads of bureaus and lots of people with titles that don't match their jobs. There were officials with very important-sounding titles that did not have much real power, and others with lowly titles but a lot of important responsibility. It was very hard to figure out."

■ PRIVATE SCHOOLS

Compared to public schools, private schools are tougher to investigate. Most states do provide minimal information about accredited private schools, allowing an investigator to compare class sizes, test scores, teacher salaries and elective offerings.

Finding out about unaccredited private schools can be more difficult. A local private school association might supply some information. County health and fire departments should share information about the school buildings. Many private schools are not-for-profit and tax exempt. That means they might file a Form 990 informational tax return with the Internal Revenue Service, a document worth consulting. The federal Office of Educational Research and Improvement collects and disseminates private school information as best it can.

Groups that can provide perspective are the National Association of Independent Schools, Boston; Council for American Private Education, Washington, D.C.; and National Catholic Education Association, Washington, D.C. About half of the private schools in the United States are affiliated with the Catholic church. The rest are affiliated with other religions, military academies and college preparatory institutes, or are specifically for disabled children.

Home Schooling

About four-fifths of the parents who school their children at home do so because of religious beliefs. Others are motivated less by religion per se and more by the fear of secular humanism. Still others have no specific religion or ideology to promote, but turn to home schooling because they believe the public schools provide second-rate education.

Investigators can check whether the state education department issues guidelines for home schooling; about two-thirds of the states do. Some states treat home schools similarly to private schools, with no certification required for teachers. Differing treatments by states of home schools raise questions: If a student wants to enter public school before completion of twelfth grade, or if a home schooled student plans to enter college, what documentation must parents show about coverage of certain subjects? What if a home-schooled student appears to be way ahead of his public-school peer group, but does poorly on standardized tests because of inexperience with such tests? Does the home-schooled student miss important socialization? If parents are teaching racial discrimination, hatred of homosexuals or other doctrines that would be unacceptable in public school classrooms, should authorities be able to intervene?

Resources include the National Center for Home Education, Paeonian Springs, Va., and Home School Legal Defense Association, Purcellville, Va. Magazines chronicling the movement include Growing Without Schools, Cambridge, Mass., and Home Education Magazine, Tonasket, Wash.

Preschools and Other Day Care

Research suggests that children's minds are pretty much formed by age three. If that is true, preschools and nursery schools are obviously important. Yet many do little to educate, acting more as a babysitting service than as an incubator for developing minds. In many states, even when the preschool itself is licensed, teachers are under no requirement to seek training; nationally, only about one in four possesses a child development associate's credential.

Much of the journalistic emphasis in recent years has been on child abuse and neglect in preschools. One book on the topic is "Nap Time" by Lisa Manshel. Horror stories can be found under "Day Care Centers" in the IRE Resource Center. Such allegations must be investigated, but should not completely replace coverage of the day-to-day learning environment.

Coverage of preschools could address many questions: Should preschool programs tie into local kindergarten curricula? If so, how do preschool and kindergarten teachers and administrators coordinate their activities? Should the teaching be child-centered, in which children are permitted to roam among activity areas filled with hands-on materials? Or should it be teacher-centered, in which adults pour knowledge into children as they sit at desks drilling on predetermined topics? Is there some happy medium? How should early childhood educators deal with children's varying levels of readiness, determined partly by heredity, partly by home life and partly by previous childcare experiences? If some local preschools have been established specifically for children whose families depend on welfare, does that type of economic segregation make sense educationally?

Unannounced visits by journalists who know the law can lead to good stories. When a writer for the Progressive magazine observed a center, she quickly noticed two violations—uncovered electrical outlets and a teacher-child ratio worse than one to ten. Journalists can talk with local health department workers about whether the children have been immunized properly. During that discussion, a journalist can ask what else the health department worker has observed. ABC Primetime Live managed to take hidden cameras into 18 day-care centers, and let them record all day. The footage showed babies neglected for hours, physical abuse, withholding of food and children who become ill from filthy conditions.

The St. Paul Pioneer Press found that Minnesota's three largest child-care chains had been cited for about 1,700 violations in one year. The main problems were too many children per worker, inadequate worker training and damaged or dirty equipment. The licensing division of the state Human Services Department kept a file on each center. Inside the files were inspector reports, correction orders, responses from the alleged violators and details on the qualifications of each day-care employee.

Books providing perspective include "Head Start and Beyond: A National Plan for Extended Childhood Intervention," edited by Edward Zigler and Sally Styfco and Sue C. Wortham's "Early Childhood Curriculum." The magazine Day Care and Early Education provides insight, as does material from the Association for Childhood Education, in Wheaton, Md., and the Child Care Action Campaign, in New York City.

Beyond High School

For five years, an administrative assistant employed at the University of Missouri Graduate School embezzled money by stealing from research grants allocated to professors and by fabricating travel vouchers. Her superiors, learned people with Ph.D.s, suspected nothing. Internal and external audits failed to catch irregularities. The scheme ended only when the embezzler confessed on her own, apparently because of a guilty conscience. By that time, $650,000 had vanished.

An alert journalist might have uncovered the embezzlement by scrutinizing publicly available financial statements. Short of that, regular inquiries about newly hired employees might have turned up intriguing pieces of information before any money was taken: The administrative assistant had been let go by previous employers because of suspicions that she was embezzling, she had been romantically involved with a prominent university executive and she maintained a lifestyle her salary alone never could have supported.

Although universities are perceived as hallowed places, the criminality at the University of Missouri is not unique. An investigation of a state college by the Daily Oklahoman revealed that the president and chief financial officer had embezzled more than $400,000. The reporters examined account ledgers, invoices, teacher retirement files and minutes of regents' meetings to uncover improper use of college credit cards, the funneling of money through a dummy corporation and the creation of a questionable retirement fund.

Two reporters delving into financial records at the University of Minnesota medical school uncovered irregularities. Nikhil Deogun wrote in the IRE Journal about how Maura Lerner and Joe Rigert of the Star Tribune proceeded:

When their efforts . . . to investigate the university's fund-raising activities were thwarted (the university initially granted access and then did an about-face), Lerner, the higher education reporter, and Rigert, an investigative reporter, started looking at research projects for conflicts of interests . . . compromising the integrity of universities.

At the University of Minnesota, every time a professor gets outside money for research, he or she is required to file an application, called Form BA-23. The application asks faculty members if they might have a conflict of interests with the industry for which they plan to do research. (For example, do they own stock in the company?) The document is invaluable. . . . Aside from listing potential conflicts, researchers must describe the project and report if human subjects will be used, how much lab space is required and what university resources are needed.

Of the 24 cases of conflicts disclosed by researchers, one looked especially intriguing to Rigert. . . . [An] associate professor of surgery was a founder, major stockholder and paid consultant of the company sponsoring his research. The success of his research, then, would enrich not only the company but himself. . . . After interviewing medical experts, reading journal articles on wound-healing drugs and reviewing transcripts of papers presented at conferences, Rigert and Lerner realized they were looking at a story about conflicts of interests *and* questionable research.

The stories published led to the resignation of the physician-researcher. By then the reporters were examining another case of possible research fraud, involving a university-affiliated child psychiatrist. He eventually ended up being convicted on criminal charges.

The stories kept coming. Lerner and Rigert received anonymous calls about improprieties in a drug program run by the university's surgery department. Documents from the U.S. Food and Drug Administration showed violations in testing and selling. Most important, Deogun wrote, "the surgery department and its world-renowned chief . . . had not reported deaths or injuries that may have resulted from the drug. Through a source at the Mayo Clinic, Rigert learned [the chief] had sent an urgent letter to medical centers telling them to stop using [the drug]."

After the Star Tribune articles appeared, Deogun wrote,

The university acknowledged serious problems and ordered its own investigation. Soon, three federal agencies, including the FBI, were investigating. . . . Two months later, the star of the University of Minnesota medical school . . . was forced to resign as surgery chief, a post he had held 25 years.

Higher Education: The Big Picture

Any journalist who looks into handling of funds or research-related conflicts of interests at any university is certain to find stories. But those are just two of dozens of subjects that deserve scrutiny. It is time to stop treating universities as sacred cows, and to begin to conduct investigations that never lose sight of the ultimate question: quality of education.

Some writers have entered the attack mode. Broadsides against higher education include Roger Kimball's book "Tenured Radicals: How Politics Has Corrupted Our Higher Education" and Charles J. Sykes' "ProfScam: Professors and the Demise of Higher Education." The credibility behind their indictments varies from point to point, but their books, and others that have achieved less attention, are worth reading for an understanding of why many university graduates are disenchanted with higher education. There are also hundreds of books presenting less outraged but nonetheless critical overviews of universities. Every week, the Chronicle of Higher Education publishes a listing headlined "New Books on Higher Education."

Enrollments at American colleges and universities have grown by huge percentages since World War II, making higher-education investigations more relevant than ever. On the other hand, higher education is far from universal: about 20 percent of the adult population has completed a degree. But because taxpayer dollars go to higher education, almost everybody has a stake.

Of universities granting two-year, four-year or graduate degrees, about half are public, meaning they are heavily subsidized by government, charge relatively affordable tuitions and are relatively open about accepting high-risk students. Two-year public community colleges enroll about 60 percent of students, receive about 20 percent of state appropriations, yet are nearly ignored by journalists. Private universities tend to charge higher tuitions because they receive smaller government subsidies, and they can be more selective about which students attend. Some are affiliated with religious denominations.

Another category in the higher-education mix is the for-profit proprietary, or trade, school emphasizing vocational education; many are part of commercial chains, and they tend to have bad reputations. An investigation by the Detroit News shows why. As the IRE awards entry said,

> Nearly 75,000 Michigan students each year enroll in trade schools, paying millions of dollars in tuition and other fees. In return, only four in ten end up graduating and finding a job in their field of training. Most of those jobs are entry level, often paying minimum wage. . . . For the other 60 percent—the majority low-income students—the dream of becoming financially independent . . . is shattered. Half of those dropped out of school before ever completing a class.

Other investigations are listed under "Trade Schools" in the IRE Resource Center.

Each type of school has its own associations, accrediting bodies, publications and books written about it. For example, trade schools belong to the Career College Association, Washington, D.C. The American Association of Community and Junior Colleges, Washington, D.C., publishes Community College Journal. Perspective can be gained from the book "The Diverted Dream: Community Colleges and the Promise of Educational Opportunity in America" by Steven Brint and Jerome Karabel.

National and state-by-state statistics are available in the Chronicle of Higher Education's annual "Almanac Issue." Another source of overview information is the Higher Education Directory, from Higher Education Publications Inc., Falls Church, Va. The magazine Lingua Franca, Mamaroneck, N.Y., is useful for its in-depth features about the realities and textures of university life.

At the local level, every campus is teeming with secondary and primary documentary sources, not to mention hundreds of articulate human sources. One resource that too many investigators overlook is the student newspaper. It might be amateurish, it might be less accurate than a professional newspaper, but it is almost always filled with tips unavailable elsewhere.

University Revenues and Expenditures

Following the dollar is a sound procedure, as emphasized in earlier chapters. Universities are big-budget enterprises. Income arrives from state legislative appropriations, congressional funding funneled through the U.S. Education Department plus other federal agencies, tuition and fees from students, gifts from institutional and individual donors, athletic revenues and sales by university-owned businesses.

Much of the income can be tracked, even when the university is uncooperative. For example, gifts from overseas must be reported to the Education Department as part of legislation intended to track foreign influence. The reporting form is public. Many institutions have violated the law; those violations are stories in themselves.

Myths about university budgets have taken hold, such as athletics being an automatic money maker. A report by the National Association of College and University Business Officers, Washington, D.C., "The Financial Management of Intercollegiate Athletics Programs," suggests otherwise. A different angle is available from the National Collegiate Athletic Association, Overland Park, Kan. Some reporters have had to file freedom of information requests or lawsuits to obtain athletic department budgets. It is fair to assume that when athletic department officials are resistant to reasonable access requests, it is because they have something to hide.

In an era of budget cuts by legislatures, reporters should ask what has changed on campus as a result of less money being allocated. Are there noticeable differences compared to the years when budgets increased?

Are the changes ones that allow the campus to do the same, or even more, with less? As suggested in the Education Reporter, published by the Education Writers Association, "Look at orders for new library books and the numbers of journal subscriptions; these concrete numbers can make good stories, and help personalize the debate. Why should the library get [the] Journal of Finnish Literature rather than the professor who needs it?"

When wanting more money, the local university might play the pork barrel game, asking legislators to earmark funds for a specific project that escapes competitive merit reviews. Many university officials say they find lobbying for pork-barrel projects unseemly, but they do it anyway. The Chronicle of Higher Education publishes lists of projects earmarked by Congress. A typical entry reads: "New Hampshire College. $1 million from the Department of Housing and Urban Development to develop a technology center on business information."

Many universities have lobbyists who have moved to Washington, D.C., or the state capital from the campus. When Rutgers University opened a Washington office, its lobbyist estimated the institution already received $150 million annually in student aid and research grants. He planned to stay in regular contact with the New Jersey congressional delegation. Schools without full-time lobbyists have worked out other arrangements. The University of Texas hired a former congressional staff member as assistant vice chancellor. Although based in Texas, he would be traveling to Washington often. Other universities pool resources to hire a lobbyist; Cassidy and Associates said it represents several dozen. Some universities are hiring public relations firms, on the theory that a high media profile is good for business. At least six public relations firms are specializing in representing universities for hefty fees. A journalist, by spending a week or a month observing university lobbyists and public relations representatives, is sure to end up with a story that will change the image of universities as isolated, ethically pure institutions.

Some universities have such a large endowment that they make substantial money investing it, and while there is nothing wrong with this on the face of it the moral dimension of how the money is invested is worth reporting. In the 1980s, many universities received criticism for investing in racially repressive South African economy. A second moral dimension revolves around the costs of managing the endowment. When a reporter from the Wall Street Journal looked into who managed university endowments, he learned that some managers are paid more than anyone else on campus. One Harvard University money manager received more than $1.2 million annually; a colleague received about $740,000. The top money manager at Stanford University received about $576,000.

Compensation of high-level administrators and some professors also can be hard to justify. When universities say they are simply being competitive with private industry, a reporter should check that assertion. Many university officials have had difficulty adjusting to an era of tighter budgets, failing to understand how upset taxpayers will be at what is perceived as lavishness. The Columbia Daily Tribune triggered public outrage when a reporter disclosed the University of Missouri system president and the main campus' chancellor each spent more than $26,000 for new cars, driving up the price nearly $3,500 by insisting on immediate delivery, instead of waiting a month for delivery. Presidents and chancellors of other universities are driven around by chauffeurs while their students struggle for scholarship money.

Other components of higher education worthy of scrutiny include:

Students, in the Classroom

Who is admitted, who is turned away? Should a state university give preference to in-state residents, whose families' taxes help support the institution? Or to out-of-state students willing to pay higher tuition in a time of budget cutbacks? Is the admission process weighted in favor of students who have no need of financial aid to pay tuition? Is the process working, based on retention and graduation rates? The National Association of College Admissions Counselors, Alexandria, Va., can provide perspective.

Journalists have to put the numbers in context. As Alexander W. Astin of the Higher Education Research Institute at the University of California-Los Angeles explained in the Chronicle of Higher Education,

> a simple retention 'rate' tells us a lot more about who an institution admits than about how effective its retention practices are. . . . Regardless of where they attend college, the least well-prepared students—those with C averages in high school and SAT composite scores below 700—are five times more likely to drop out . . . than are the best-prepared students.

Additional perspective is available from the American Association of Collegiate Registrars and Admissions Officers, Washington, D.C.

Tied up with admission and retention is affirmative action. Joel Dreyfuss and Charles Lawrence III's book "The Bakke Case: The Politics of Inequality" wrestles with the question of race-based affirmative action by examining a now-famous legal challenge. The Chronicle of Higher Education publishes statistics on enrollment by race at about 3,300 universities. Affirmative action means more than consideration for persons with certain skin colors. Scott Jaschik at the Chronicle of Higher Education learned about universities violating rights of women and the disabled by requesting "letters of finding" from the Education Department's Office for Civil Rights. In each case, Jaschik wrote, the federal government

> reached an agreement to bring the college into compliance with the law. The colleges generally do not have to acknowledge guilt as part of the agree-

ments, but must promise to make certain changes in policies by specific dates. The department has the option of seeking to cut off federal funds to institutions found to be violating civil-rights laws.

Students from disadvantaged backgrounds are less likely to enroll if financial aid is unavailable. Is financial assistance available to all needy students? If not, how is the scarce money allocated? What percentage of tuition revenue is allocated by the university for financial aid, compared to amounts flowing from governments and other nontuition sources? How much of the total is available to non-needy students as incentive to enroll?

Financial aid falls into three general categories: grants (including scholarships and tuition waivers), part-time employment and low-interest loans. How many students have loans tied to the Student Loan Marketing Association (Sallie Mae), a private company chartered by the U.S. Congress as a government-sponsored enterprise? How do Sallie Mae loans compare with those made by banks, state funds or universities themselves in terms of payback rates? With the U.S. Education Department making more and more direct student loans at Congress' direction, how is the picture changing for local companies? What is the default rate on student loans? Does the university do anything effective to collect delinquent loans? Journalists can consult the Postsecondary Review Entity in each state. That unit, mandated by Congress through the U.S. Education Department, is supposed to investigate institutions with high loan default rates. In Missouri, the responsibility fell to the already existing Coordinating Board for Higher Education in the state capital. Journalists are sometimes able to learn names of defaulters by checking lawsuits, including those in the local small claims court.

If desperate for funding or just greedy, have university officials or students defrauded the state or federal government by claiming benefits for those who are actually ineligible? The Detroit News exposed how students with little or no Native American heritage were receiving preferential treatment simply by checking a box on enrollment forms. Each type of financial aid has its procedures, which an investigator can learn by reading the legislation that created the aid and regulations implementing it. Background can be obtained from the National Association of Student Financial Aid Administrators, Washington, D.C.

Star athletes receive financial aid, whether they need it or not. A reporter should ask the next question: Do the athletes receive additional special treatment to keep them eligible for competition? Improprieties in sports programs are a staple of investigative reporters. In "Behind the Lines: Case Studies in Investigative Reporting," authors Margaret Jones Patterson and Robert H. Russell explain how Arizona Daily Star reporters Clark Hallas and Robert Lowe revealed corruption in the University of Arizona football program. What about graduation rates for students athletes in each sport? On many campuses, athletes graduate at much lower rates than other students. An added wrinkle is that white athletes almost always have higher graduation rates than black athletes. Why is that? Where graduation rates for athletes are far better than average, a journalist should ask whether grading for athletes is the same as for nonathletes.

Grading in general, not just grading of athletes, is worthy of inquiry. Are so many students receiving A's and B's that good grades are devalued? Is grading inconsistent from course to course within the same department? From department to department? How do graduate schools evaluate grades of undergraduates while deciding whether to admit them? What happens when students transfer from a two-year community college to a university? From a program in one discipline to the same discipline at a different university? From one discipline to another? How do potential employers evaluate grades from different departments and different universities?

Has the university received reports of cheating on classroom examinations or take-home assignments? How has it dealt with the allegations? Universities convene disciplinary boards—consisting of faculty, students and administrators—that can provide case studies. Journalists rarely pay attention to those proceedings. The Student Press Law Center, Washington, D.C., can help gain access.

Students, Outside the Classroom

When crime occurs, does jurisdiction belong to the university's security force? Are they competent law enforcement officers? Do they carry guns? What firearms training do they receive? How often are students the criminals instead of the victims? Does the university keep and release information about campus crime as required by federal law? Does it try to hide student crimes by shunting them to student courts ignored by journalists? Perspective is available from the International Association of Campus Law Enforcement Administration, Hartford, Conn., and from the book "Campus Security and Law Enforcement" by John W. Powell, Michael S. Pander and Robert C. Nielsen. The Student Press Law Center publishes a booklet, "Access to Campus Crime Reports," that suggests how to deal with universities refusing to cooperate with inquiries about crime. Scott Jaschik at the Chronicle of Higher Education suggests reporters walk the campus after dark, looking for poorly lit areas and other obvious trouble signs. "Try walking into a dormitory with no identification and see how far you get," Jaschik says. "If you get in and it is clear that anybody can get in, you may have a great campus crime story regardless of what the statistics show."

Many universities are major property owners, not just on the campus, but throughout town. Are some of the properties rented to students? Does the housing meet fire and other safety codes? Are dormitories integrated by race, or is there de facto segregation? Does the university help students living off-campus distinguish honest landlords from those who are predatory and supply legal advice in connection with evictions, unreturned security deposits and unsanitary conditions? Questions about safety and segregation apply to fraternities and sororities, too. Hank Nuwer's book "Broken Pledges: The Deadly Rite of Hazing" discusses another kind of hazard connected to Greek houses.

Are all student organizations, Greek or otherwise, allowed to use campus facilities, no matter what the organization's political viewpoint, sexual orientation, racial or ethnic composition? If not, on what basis does the university grant legitimacy or illegitimacy?

Are services for students adequate? Can a student receive mental health counseling whenever needed, or are those who have been raped, have drug problems or who are contemplating suicide on weekends forced to wait until 9 A.M. Monday to get help? Is the student health center staffed with capable nurses and doctors, or by those nobody else would hire? The United States Student Association, Washington, D.C., can help with perspective.

Faculty

How are faculty recruited and hired? Is classroom performance observed firsthand before an offer is made? Are student evaluations scrutinized? Upon hiring, are salary and benefits much higher than similar jobs in the local private sector? If so, how can that be justified? Do faculty members paid with tax dollars contribute any services to the town and the region? For example, do law professors take pro bono cases for indigents? Do medical professors treat patients without health insurance? Do education professors help public school teachers and students? One extreme example of such intervention is Boston University running the school system in Chelsea, Mass.

Are new faculty ever hired into tenured jobs? If so, how can a lifetime job guarantee be justified before the professor's worth is proven? Terry L. Leap's book "Tenure, Discrimination and the Courts" explains the process. If the faculty member is hired without tenure, what is the agreement about when tenure will be considered? A tenured professor means a big commitment for a university administration and for those paying the bills. Such a commitment should signal to journalists that every tenure case at the local university is worth tracking. Each is filled with drama, from personal rivalries to questions of academic policy. Yet journalists rarely pay attention. How about endowed chairs for faculty? Few individuals or corporations establish such chairs without an expectation of payback. Does the contract for the chair indicate a conflict of interests?

When scrutinizing faculty, journalists should pay attention not only to teaching style, but also to the context of courses. A study of syllabuses can be the beginning of an interesting story on what students are—and are not—being taught. Do professors assign their own textbook, then collect royalties from sales to captive students? Is the reading list current? Is a controversial political, economic, religious, gender-based or other societal viewpoint presented without countervailing evidence? Should classroom teaching include a moral component? If so, does that belong in the course, or does it belong in a separate required or optional ethics class? Who should decide what values are taught? Do the course materials reflect multiculturalism, or is everything presented from a white, Anglo-Saxon, upper-class point of view? If the cliché is true that the winners write history, should the course include the viewpoint of the losers?

When the university hires adjunct faculty members to supplement or substitute for regular faculty, are they provided with office space to enable them to meet conveniently with students? Are they paid enough per course to make a serious commitment to teaching? Is there any attempt to measure their ability as teachers before a contract is offered?

If faculty bring research credentials with them, do they give short shrift to teaching, making their lectures perfunctory or relying too heavily on graduate assistants? If teaching assistants are used, how qualified are they? Do they speak the same language as the majority of their students? What screening and training do they receive from the university before entering the classroom? If a faculty member is absent frequently, is she ignoring her students while involved in lucrative outside consulting?

Faculty research projects should yield extensive documentation. Universities often publish lists of research contracts recently consummated; at the University of Missouri, the list is in each issue of a Graduate School newsletter. Each line shows the faculty member receiving the money, the title of the research project, the sponsor and the amount. Grants are not free money for campuses; overhead costs are considerable. The University of Missouri estimated that government-funded research by professors cost the campus $13 million annually for overhead, consisting largely of building use and administrative support. Federal auditors have questioned the overhead costs that universities ask the government to reimburse. One of the most publicized conflicts, reported in depth by the San Jose Mercury News, involved a university that appeared to ask for indirect costs reimbursement to maintain a yacht and build a new bed for the campus president. The controversy led to a revised ceiling on the rate universities can charge the government. Most of the indirect cost controversies involve the Department of Health and Human Services, although through a quirk of precedent some universities deal with the Office of Naval Research.

If human subjects are involved, the researcher must file forms showing consent and alleviating concerns about mental or physical harm. At the University of Missouri, the Institutional Review Board, consisting of faculty members appointed by the administration, scrutinizes the documentation. Animal research often spawns controversy and internal review as well. A reporter should ask whether research projects involve financial conflicts of interests or pressures from supervisors or sponsors to produce inaccurate data. A campus' scientific integrity officer might be helpful.

A university's conflict of interests policy can be invoked by a journalist in a variety of real-world situations. The University of Missouri policy contains fascinating detail, such as this paragraph: "Official university stationery may not be used in outside business, personal or other private or political activities. . . . However, for use in such activities, faculty may have printed at their own expense personal business stationery carrying their academic title, university address and phone number."

Research means time away from the campus. How do faculty spend their months while on paid sabbaticals or other leaves? Reporters can review reports from professors after they have completed a leave, or interview the professors directly about what they accomplished, asking for documentation to back up the statements. While doing their research, have they been abusing taxpayer-financed telephones, fax machines, photocopiers and other perquisites?

Journalists should be alert for other forms of moral turpitude. Too many professors try to take advantage of students, sexually or psychologically. How does the university administration handle sexual harassment? How is consensual sex handled when the professor is an authority figure to a student? Is moral turpitude grounds for firing? Do firings actually occur?

Sometimes upright faculty members are treated unfairly. The American Association of University Professors in Washington, D.C., represents faculty on many campuses, which means there will probably be a local chapter to consult. It places universities on its censured list for mistreating professors. The organization's magazine, Academe, tips off journalists to many disputes between faculty and administration. The American Association of University Women, Washington, D.C., can add a valuable perspective. The National Education Association and the American Federation of Teachers, best-known for representing faculty below the college level, have organized numerous campuses.

Support Staff

Secretaries, administrative assistants, custodians, laboratory technicians, computer programmers, bookkeepers, building supervisors, locksmiths, groundskeepers, power plant operators, parking attendants, campus police, librarians—without them a university could barely function, yet they are usually ignored by journalists. Are they paid a living wage? Are they treated with condescension? Have staff members found it necessary to unionize because of perceived or actual second-class treatment? If so, officials of the union locals might be good sources.

Are staff given enough budget to keep the physical plant from deteriorating? If not, is the short-term neglect penny wise and pound foolish for taxpayers? Reporters can gain perspective from the Association of Physical Plant Administrators of Universities and Colleges, in Alexandria, Va. More generally, what do support staff know about teaching, research, administration and other university functions that those in power may have a reason to hide?

Administrators

Is the university top-heavy with academics turned administrator who never enter classrooms or research laboratories because they are so busy attending self-important meetings and filling out paperwork? How do they explain their absence from classrooms and laboratories, the reasons for the university's being? Is the administrator-faculty ratio out of kilter with similar universities? If so, what is the explanation? Are there so few female and minority administrators as to suggest conscious or unconscious hiring biases?

Are the highest-level administrators (president, chancellor, vice presidents, provost, deans, department chairs, athletic coaches) promoted from within, based on merit? Or are they hired from outside, gypsy administrators who come in at big salaries (plus free housing, free car and other perquisites), only to leave a few years later for an even bigger compensation package? Is the university paying scarce dollars to a professional headhunting firm to find outside candidates? The Chronicle of Higher Education polls universities to document administrative salaries. Those universities with nonprofit status might report their highest salaries to the Internal Revenue Service on Form 990.

Governing Boards

Usually called trustees or curators, how and why are the members of an institution's board chosen? In many states, the governor appoints curators of public universities, placing them in the political realm. Do they serve for altruistic reasons, to promote their educational ideology, to direct contracts to friends, to promote their own careers? Do they ever mingle with students, faculty, administrators and staff? Are they usually alumni who have a preexisting familiarity with the campus? Or is it wiser to choose mostly nonalumni, thereby avoiding preconceptions and cozy relationships? At private universities especially, does a large financial contribution buy a spot on the board? Do lawyer-trustees end up with a share of the university's lucrative legal business? Do contractor-trustees end up with profitable building contracts?

Many governing boards are rubber stamps for the campus president or chancellor. As rubber stamps, they grant huge compensation packages and golden severance parachutes. The Sacramento Bee reported that University of California regents provided an outgoing campus president with a million-dollar retirement package, then tried to cover up the largesse to minimize the public relations harm.

To counteract the vested local interests of specific university governing boards, what role should be played by statewide, politically appointed governing boards? Should such a board make sure that each campus has a distinct role, thereby pushing for elimination of duplicative programs on nearby campuses? Should the boards automatically serve as advocates for the highest possible funding? Or should they be skeptical of funding requests from individual campuses? Are the coordinating boards themselves a wasteful level of bureaucracy? In some states, there has been intense debate about abolishing the boards. A reporter wanting perspective can contact the Association of Governing Boards of Universities and Colleges, Washington, D.C. Its book by Clark Kerr and Marian L. Gade, "The Guardians: Boards of Trustees of American Colleges and Universities," is especially helpful.

Accreditation Documents as a Source of Information

Accreditation of universities by knowledgeable outsiders can be an investigator's check on quality of education. The University of Missouri, for example, is examined by the North Central Association of Colleges and Schools, Commission on Institutions of Higher Education, Chicago. It is one of six such regional organizations. Specific academic units receive accreditation separately. The Missouri School of Journalism is accredited by the Association for Education in Journalism and Mass Communication.

When dealing with public institutions, obtaining the accreditor's full report—sometimes running to hundreds of pages—should pose few problems because of access laws. If a private university refuses to provide a copy, the state agency for higher education may have been given it. Another approach: If the university operates a teaching program on a military base, the base commander or educational liaison officer may have a copy.

These documents often emerge during the accreditation process:

The Self-Study

Compiled by a faculty-administration committee at the university, this provides an internal look at strengths and weaknesses in curricula, faculty credentials, administrative operations, financial stability and the gamut of other issues the university faces. Self-studies usually must be obtained from the university.

The Visiting Team Report

A typical report will include a recommendation on accreditation status; a statement on the university's mission and whether it has been achieved; an evaluation of the short and long-range planning mechanisms at the school; an assessment of administrative performance, particularly if the school faces morale or financial problems; an assessment of general education patterns; a judgment on financial stability; an analysis of development activity; an analysis of faculty credentials overall; a comparison of faculty salary levels with those at competing institutions; the role of faculty in governing; an analysis of students' academic credentials, geographic spread, educational interests and retention rates; and evaluation of the physical plant. This report is likely to be more objective and hard-hitting than a self-study.

The Final Action

The accrediting association's governing body's final action may be obtained from the accrediting association or the individual school.

Follow-up Reports

Accrediting associations might require universities to submit follow-up reports on trouble spots—such as a weak core curriculum or financial instability—within a year to three years after accreditation is extended. A university may receive full accreditation for 10 years, but a follow-up report may prompt downgrading to provisional accreditation or withholding of further accreditation.

An alternative to accreditation reports is the scorecard required by legislatures as part of the accountability movement. Joye Mercer reported in the Chronicle of Higher Education that the West Virginia report card

offers 275 pages of information on public colleges, including narratives on each college, statistics on enrollment over the past six years, the age of undergraduates and college budgets. Then the report compares the institutions according to several criteria, including scores on college entrance exams, students' cumulative grade-point averages, campus crime rates, and, where applicable, the amount of sponsored research.

Sometimes the most comprehensive document is a university's catalog, which amounts to a prospectus. A catalog usually contains the accreditation status; a mission statement; admissions procedures, including necessary high school rank and standardized test scores; policies on the release of student information; requirements for majors and graduation; tuition, room, board, book and other fees; financial aid and eligibility requirements; counseling and advising services; student organizations; residence hall policies; descriptions of the campus physical plant; health care; officers and trustees; faculty and their academic background; and alumni association information.

Why the diverse education establishment is considered a second-rate beat by so many journalists is beyond my comprehension. Reagan Walker, education reporter at the Nashville Tennessean, says the beat is exciting, spilling over as it does into "government, crime, social issues, features and a lot of other topics." Beth Shuster at Los Angeles Daily News makes a similar point: "Covering education in Los Angeles touches everyone—from taxpayers without children to parents to politicians. The beat is at turns political, academic and investigative. It's rarely routine and almost never boring."

Chapter 9

INVESTIGATING GOVERNMENT

Law Enforcement

David Freed, a Los Angeles Times reporter, was listening to a deputy district attorney explain a case pending against two accused armed robbers. Police, he said, had observed the men as they robbed a store and beat two employees.

But why, Freed asked instinctively, did the police stand by instead of moving in to prevent bloodshed? The prosecutor, apparently surprised by the question, said he had no idea. Freed, curious, went elsewhere to seek an answer.

His simple question turned out to be the start of something big. When Freed had completed his research, the headline over his story read: "Citizens Terrorized as Police Look On."

Freed discovered it was standard procedure for the 19-person Special Investigations Section of the Los Angeles Police Department to observe armed robbers and burglars committing their crimes, arresting them only after the victimizing of shopkeepers and homeowners. In effect, the detectives were using unsuspecting citizens as live bait.

Freed also discovered the SIS unit was killing suspects at a rate higher than common sense dictated. A majority of those suspects had been shot in the back. Freed found his information by studying arrest warrants and other criminal court records in a dozen courthouses. He reviewed a decade's worth of police reports and press releases involving more than 600 incidents in which suspects had been wounded or killed by Los Angeles police.

Give a young man or woman a gun, a night stick or other armaments of police work, plus a license to use them, and some are going to abuse the privilege. Excessive force by police has been the topic of hundreds of investigations by journalists, many of them available in the IRE Resource Center.

Documenting incompetence and corruption requires hard work and skill no matter what the topic, as every chapter in this book suggests. In some ways, however, investigating law enforcement is the most difficult topic of all.

One reason is the hostility law enforcement officers exhibit when journalists are around. To many police officers, who rightly perceive their jobs as life-threatening on a daily basis, reporters are welcome only if they are openly pro-police. That is why such a large percentage of books about policing are written by authors who are content to be transcribers (such as Connie Fletcher in her fascinating but uncritical oral history "What Cops Know: Cops Talk About What They Do, How They Do It, and What It Does to Them" and E.W. Count's "Cop Talk: True Detective Stories From the New York Police Department") or who have covered the beat long enough to be more or less accepted (such as Edna Buchanan of the Miami Herald, author of "The Corpse Had a Familiar Face" and "Never Let Them See You Cry"; Mitch Gelman of New York Newsday, author of "Crime Scene"; and Robert Blau of the Chicago Tribune, author of "The Cop Shop.")

Reporters who cast a critical eye on a knight in blue are shunned, misled or even harassed. Because law enforcement agencies tend to be run according to a military-like mentality, members close ranks against outsiders more emphatically than bureaucrats inside other institutions. Even a journalist who writes about a crime increase based on the police department's own statistics is perceived as attacking the integrity of law enforcement—though common sense says that to draw such a conclusion would be no more logical than blaming an increase in garbage on trash collectors.

Adding to the difficulty police reporters face is their inability to get the other side of the story. Often the accused will not talk for fear of the police. Even if they want to talk, the accused are often kept away from reporters by the jailers. Journalists are reduced to working through the accused's lawyer (see Chapter 10). But in the hours after an arrest, the suspect might not have a lawyer yet. Later in the incarceration, it still makes sense to approach the accused by mail, with an addressed, stamped envelope enclosed. Many accused persons have little contact with their lawyers. As a result, the accused feel ignored. Talking to a journalist might be desirable after awhile.

Still another hurdle for police reporters is the polarization of the audience: a large segment automatically sides with police because of the belief that extreme tactics are warranted against criminals. It's the killers and muggers and rapists out there you ought to be after, not the men and women who go out and risk their lives every day to keep our city safe, say those members of the audience. They unequivocally support the police because of statistics like those uncovered by the Fort Worth Star-Telegram—in its home county, nearly one of every 80 persons walking the streets is a felon who has avoided imprisonment; one of every 16 homes is burglarized; one of every 30 vehicles stolen. A smaller segment of the audience believe police cannot normally be trusted.

However, it is dangerous to generalize, as always. In the United States alone, there are about 12,500 local police departments; 3,000 county sheriffs' departments; statewide police departments; 60 federal government law enforcement units (with the Federal Bureau of Investigation receiving the most attention); plus thousands of specialized police departments for universities, subway systems, airports, parks and public housing complexes.

Cheryl Reed, a Dayton Daily News police reporter, suggests finding out if a department is accredited. If not, why not? "The Law Enforcement Accreditation Association is a great reference, and supplies most of the standard operating procedures used by most police departments," she says. "A reporter should get copies of these procedures to see if their departments are up to standards."

Private-sector security agencies do not fit under the government umbrella. But their function in the community is similar, and they provide plenty of story opportunities for journalists. They are shadow police forces in certain neighborhoods, often lacking the civil rights or weapons training of officers on the public payroll. A Time magazine investigation found the security guard industry has become a dumping ground for unstable, violent people, some of whom have criminal records. On the local level, KSEE-TV of Fresno, Calif., reached similar conclusions.

The same forces that have led to larger roles for private security guards has led to private investigators assuming roles once reserved for police officers. The Los Angeles Times reported that municipal police used to respond to reports of workplace drug use by sending in a trained undercover officer. But, as crime rates grew and police forces shrunk because of municipal budget cutbacks, corporations began hiring private detectives to do the undercover work. Many were former police officers who knew what they were doing and had the trust of regular law enforcement agencies. The Times found that California was home to about 7,400 licensed private investigators, triple the number from 15 years earlier. With the need for more and better trained law enforcement officers everywhere, sometimes journalists end up solving crimes, through persistence.

The next sections of this chapter will examine the individuals who carry guns while enforcing the law. How are they chosen and trained? How good is the agency for which they work? The chapter will also cover how police handle different types of crime, from murders to traffic violations.

Before proceeding, it is important to note that the focus on police in this chapter should not obscure the remainder of the criminal justice system, the topic of the next chapter. David C. Anderson, a New York Times specialist in law enforcement, likens the system to a funnel in his book "Crimes of Justice: Improving the Police, the Courts, the Prisons": "At the top a broad flood of crimes challenges and mobilizes the police, courts and correctional system. At the bottom is the apparent result of all their labors—a relative trickle of convicted felons actually sent to prison."

Monitoring Individual Law Enforcement Officers

As in most occupations, the majority of law enforcement officers and civilian employees are honest and efficient. When a significant minority are not, however, the consequences can be devastating for individual citizens, neighborhoods or entire cities.

It is not easy for a journalist to determine how good a police officer or department is. The same is true when it comes to assessing any bureaucrat or bureaucracy, of course—the vital difference, the one that makes journalistic inattention to police matters especially upsetting, is that police are bureaucrats with guns. Journalists should be monitoring police officers from recruitment to retirement. Techniques include direct observation, studying arrest (and eventual conviction) rates, tracking day-to-day prevention efforts, talking regularly to sources in neighborhoods, knowing leaders of the police union, reading personnel files, checking for investigations by the police department's Internal Affairs Unit, and following lawsuits in the local courts.

Recruitment

The Fort Lauderdale Sun-Sentinel wrote about an officer with five arrests in his past, not an ideal candidate for police work. But Florida's police certification commission granted him a license. More than a decade later, the officer in question was still on the force, despite 11 acts of serious misconduct.

Reporters should check screening protocols at the local police department. Are resumes checked carefully? Do applicants undergo lie detector tests about their backgrounds? drug testing? psychological testing? Alan W. Benner's essay "Psychological Screening of Police Applicants" is a starting point for journalists delving into recruitment. It is part of the book "Critical Issues in Policing," edited by Roger G. Dunham and Geoffrey P. Alpert.

Journalists should be especially alert for problems at the hiring stage when the department is expanding. Rapid expansions are usually a political response to public fear about crime, or to court-ordered affirmative action meant to remedy shortages of female and minority-group officers. After a rapid expansion in Miami, about 10 percent of all officers ended up imprisoned, fired or otherwise disciplined. Groups such as the National Black Police Association, Washington, D.C., and the International Association of Women Police, Decatur, Ga., can provide perspective. Large group hirings often mean large group retirements decades later. When numerous officers retire simultaneously, training and overall role modeling fall to less experienced officers. Journalists should be alert for negative consequences in those situations.

Police Academy Training

A police officer's competence is determined partly by the training received in a police academy. Yet journalists almost never inquire about the local academy. It makes sense to write a feature about the academy to become familiar with the training; a reporter could practice immersion journalism by undergoing training with the recruits.

Many states have a central academy; in some states, though, there are certified academies run by individual police departments. In New York City, academy training is six months, followed by six months of field training before assignment to a precinct.

Physical conditioning is one part of training. Reporters should be alert for conditioning trainers going overboard. The Central New Jersey Home News found abusive conditions at an academy after a recruit collapsed and died. New York magazine found the other extreme. Standards had dropped so low—partly to accommodate recruits hired to meet diversity goals—that obesity was more common than usual. The magazine found some recruits too weak to pull the trigger of a revolver. Poor initial physical conditioning is almost sure to spawn out-of-shape police as they gain seniority. On any police force, there is a group of officers that resists regular workouts. Journalists should inquire how the central administration deals with that phenomenon.

Besides physical conditioning, a sound curriculum covers how to investigate specific types of crime at the scene and afterwards; use of force, including guns and high-speed chases; report writing; interrogation techniques; constitutional law; undercover work; counseling in domestic violence and hostage situations; plus sensitivity training to help officers understand the opposite gender, other races, religious and ethnic groups. The essay "Learning the Skills of Policing" by David H. Bayley and Egon Bittner in the Dunham-Alpert anthology is a useful starting point, supplemented by the career guide "Police Officer" by Hugh O'Neill, Hy Hammer and E.P. Steinberg. The American Society for Law Enforcement Trainers, Twin Lakes, Wis., might be a useful source.

Without first-rate academy training, officers are more likely than not to be dangerous to society. For example, if they do not learn in the academy how to handle their cars during high-speed chases, they will have to learn during a chase. As Michael J. Berens of the Columbus Dispatch discovered, such on-the-job training can be fatal.

Columbus police received only four hours of behind-the-wheel training, most of it at 30 miles per hour or less. None of the training cars had been equipped with antilock brakes, even though police cruisers have such brakes, which can be dangerous if pumped like traditional brakes. Berens found officers received far more gun training, even though police cars killed more people than guns did.

Files from the National Highway Traffic Safety Administration showed eight police pursuit–related deaths in Ohio during the year studied by Berens. But that number, Berens learned, should have been 21. To discover discrepancies, he had to crosscheck with media reports, local fleet maintenance and hospital records. Nationally, the agency documented an average of 292 deaths annually resulting from police chases. Berens found that number to be at least 25 percent too low.

Chases are not an occasional occurrence, Berens discovered. One occurs nearly every minute of every day somewhere in the United States. In Columbus, Berens found 744 chases over four years, most of them beginning with minor traffic violations. No officers had been disciplined despite numerous transgressions of the chase policy.

Raises and Promotions

Like every bureaucracy, law enforcement agencies are filled with personal favoritism, political intrigue, inefficiency and corruption. Are the most deserving officers receiving raises and promotions, or are factors such as friendship and affirmative action inordinately influencing decisions? "Making Rank: Becoming an American Police Sergeant," an essay in the Dunham-Alpert anthology by John Van Maanen, provides perspective.

The Chicago Sun-Times found that the Chicago police department based its performance evaluations more on quantitative criteria—sheer number of arrests—than on qualitative measures, such as effective crime fighting. The Village Voice found that a New York City police union had a good deal of power in influencing raises and promotions, power that often worked against the public good, given the union leadership's ties to criminal elements.

Continuing education, or lack of it, can spawn trouble. When an officer is taken off the street and given an administrative job, is there any internal training? The qualities of an outstanding patrol officer are sometimes the same qualities of a terrible administrator. Outside continuing education can go awry, too. The Boston Globe found police taking advantage of a statewide program to get better educations. The reporting team said "the noble idea of encouraging police to seek higher education has turned into a much abused, $12 million-a-year program in Massachusetts, providing hefty pay increases to many officers for securing quick and easy college degrees." One small school was issuing more graduate degrees in criminal justice than any major university in the country; it required little reading or writing in its courses. At another school, police officers were falsifying attendance records for absent colleagues.

While delving into job-related benefits, journalists should examine workers' compensation claims. Police suffer many legitimate injuries, physical and mental. But some take advantage of the workers' compensation insurance system for public employees by filing false claims, maybe with the help of a corrupt physician or lawyer. Reporters for the Hartford Courant and Boston Herald found that some claims qualified police for 100 percent of their wages, tax free, meaning they could increase their pay by staying off the job. Newsday found lifetime payments to disabled officers somehow able to work as lifeguards, lift weights and play softball.

Police pensions also tend to be generous, with taxpayers footing the bill. Journalists should ask whether retirement after 20 years is counterproductive if the retired officers then double dip by moving to a police agency elsewhere. Would it make sense to restructure the incentive system so that more experienced officers stay beyond the initial 20 years?

The Top Command

When journalists delve into the background and current performance of the police chief, they almost always end up with an informative story.

How the top person got the job may be revealing. Did the chief come up through the ranks? If so, who were the chief's patrons? What did performance evaluations say? What were the strengths and blind spots noted on the way up—for instance, did the chief ever handle an investigation of violent crime? If that experience is lacking, can the chief effectively supervise homicide detectives?

If hired from outside the department, who chose the chief—an unbiased city manager interested in quality leadership or a calculating city manager interested in dominating an indebted employee; politicized city council members who placed connections above law enforcement skills; business leaders who behind the scenes pushed for the most dogmatic law-and-order chief? The St. Louis Post-Dispatch found that a new police chief took office after secretive lobbying by business leaders. That story led to a look at the department's entire top management; previously confidential evaluations indicated political connections mattered more than policing skills. In instances where the top person is elected—the case with many county sheriffs—is appropriate law enforcement experience a factor? Is the agency used as a center for patronage and nepotism? U.S. marshals in each state are chosen on a patronage basis by the senior senator of the president's political party or the senior U.S. House member of that party. How many marshals and their deputies have previous law enforcement experience? Are they able to effectively protect federal courtrooms, guard informants in the Witness Protection Program and track down fugitives?

Unsurprisingly, corruption sometimes goes to the top. Book-length treatments include "Terror on Highway 59" by Steve Sellers and "Praying for Sheetrock" by Melissa Fay Greene. The IRE Resource Center is filled with examples. The Milwaukee Sentinel, checking a tip from a deputy sheriff, found deputies transferred to unfavorable assignments after arresting the sheriff's friends; dismissal of drunk driving charges due to political favoritism; and transporting of sheriff's cronies to major league baseball games in squad cars.

At WZZM-TV in Grand Rapids, Mich., a reporter received a tape of a telephone conversation in which the sheriff instructed a jail employee to transport government surplus food to the sheriff's home. The reporter discovered that the sheriff had a contract with the county to cater meals at the jail; the surplus food, used illegally, helped the sheriff increase his profits.

To gain perspective on management techniques, a reporter can consult numerous sources, including the International Association of Chiefs of Police, Alexandria, Va.; its magazine, Police Chief; the Alexandria-based National Sheriffs Association; and the Police Executive Research Forum, Washington, D.C. Not all the attention should be paid to the top person. Assistant chiefs, district commanders and stationhouse sergeants usually escape journalists' scrutiny, even though those middle managers can have a significant impact on an entire city or specific neighborhood.

Discipline of Wayward Law Enforcement Officers

Because police wield life and death powers, weeding out irresponsible ones is vital. But a dilemma is built in. Honest officers are reluctant to speak up for fear of being shunned. No bureaucracy is good at investigating itself; as a result, departmental internal affairs divisions are prone to coverups. Yet an outside investigator is unlikely to receive cooperation from clannish officers; that is one reason citizen review commissions are also often ineffective. These conundrums are discussed more fully in Douglas W. Perez's book "Common Sense About Police Review."

Examining the Florida system, the Palm Beach Post found the state licensing-disciplinary commission had only six staff members to review cases and three lawyers to consider prosecution. Before the commission, consisting of 17 unpaid appointees, could consider a complaint prepared by the staff, a state administrative law judge had to rule on the quality and quantity of evidence. Because the administrative judges heard cases from other state agencies, too, there was a backlog. Meanwhile, officers accused of brutality or other dangerous behaviors remained on the job. The commission's open caseload stood at 1,200. (Such problems are common to state licensing agencies, as explained in Chapter 11.)

Fred Schulte and Margo Harakas looked at errant police in great detail in the Fort Lauderdale Sun-Sentinel series, "Above the Law: Cops Who Betray the Badge." The reporters obtained computer tapes from the commission with information on more than 100,000 current and former officers. The data originated with the state's 400 police agencies, which must notify the commission when officers are fired or when any of 70 types of police misconduct are confirmed.

"Commission tapes contain a termination code for each job," Schulte explained in the IRE Journal.

> The codes tell us that about 10 percent of departures (about 8,000 since 1980) came amid misconduct or evidence that the officer was unfit. We also picked out scores of cops fired more than once, or reported to the commission for revocation twice or more. Knowing the names of problem officers saved us time later when we visited police departments to review personnel files.
>
> [A] second database enabled us to review 1,600 police commission cases since the early 1980s. . . . We found the commission took no action in 60 percent of its cases, which typically dragged on for two years; about 40 percent of 223 cop crimes weren't reviewed by prosecutors; sex crimes were the most common reason for license revocations; other violence against women was occurring regularly; blacks appeared to be singled out for disciplinary action. Margo Harakas and I spent a week in Tallahassee reviewing commission evidence. The files gave us dozens of horror stories to wrap around our statistics.
>
> Our next step was to find bad cops who had not been reported to the licensing commission. We reviewed hundreds of yellowed newspaper clips naming troubled officers and had a librarian search electronic clips. We found 400 accused cops not known to the commission. Many had been suspended or fired by a city, prompting a news story. Some didn't stay fired. A few agreed not to sue to get their job back if officials would expunge records of their misdeeds and say they had resigned. Several police departments admitted that they failed to report bad colleagues despite laws requiring them to do so.

At the federal level, agencies have professional associations and unions that might provide information about specific cases from the viewpoint of those being disciplined. One example is the FBI Agents Association.

There is no national registry of bad law enforcement officers, meaning one who runs amok can move to another city or state without obstacles to rehiring. To make matters worse, prosecutors are reluctant to bring charges against police officers, because they worry about harming their long-term relationship with the officers they need day in, day out. Furthermore, when citizens—tired of waiting for prosecutors—enter the court system with excessive force lawsuits of their own, they lose two of three cases on average. Brutality is hard to prove without sympathetic witnesses and most potential witnesses worry about retaliation from the police. Jurors, average citizens who put their hopes in the police to stop crime and protect them and their families, want to believe the best about officers, so are reluctant to convict. Jerome H. Skolnick and James J. Fyfe provide an overview in their book "Above the Law: Police and the Excessive Use of Force." Sometimes brutality occurs during interrogation of suspects. Journalists should ask if local police departments have instituted a policy of videotaping interrogations to minimize mistreatment. If not, why not?

Despite the difficulty of proving brutality, the IRE Resource Center is filled with investigations by talented, persistent journalists. Some cases become the subject of books, such as Edward Humes' "Murderer With a Badge: The Secret Life of a Rogue Cop"; Jan Golab's "The Dark Side of the Force: A True Story of Corruption and Murder in the Los Angeles Police Department"; and Howard Swindle's "Deliberate Indifference: A Story of Murder and Racial Injustice."

■ EDNA BUCHANAN'S TIPS

Police reporter Edna Buchanan provided tips on tracking excessive force for the Bulletin of the American Society of Newspaper Editors. She suggests keeping an especially close watch on the midnight to 8 A.M. shift, where problem officers are often assigned. Though they are the officers most in need of supervision, that is exactly what they fail to get, because the most talented administrators are home sleeping. The cover of darkness is an added temptation. Furthermore, a city is relatively quiet on the midnight shift, allowing officers from all over to converge on a trouble call; as they congregate, they may play off each others' fears and aggressiveness, creating what is in effect a police mob.

Buchanan warns journalists to be skeptical, but not dismissive, of excessive force complaints registered by career criminals, who are eager to deflect charges against them by accusing those who made the arrest. Another warning sign is an alleged victim who contacts lawyers and journalists before filing a complaint with the police department's internal affairs division. For such questionable victims, Buchanan suggests asking if they will submit to a lie detector test or examination by a neutral physician.

Use of force does not always mean brutality, Buchanan says: "Good cops doing their jobs and stepping on toes will generate complaints; many lousy cops putting in time until the pension never do a thing and have clean records." The proficient officers who use force to subdue suspects manage to keep from crossing the line, Buchanan says: "The difference between the force necessary to subdue and force that maims, breaks bones and sometimes kills is easily discernible."

Internal affairs units conduct investigations other than those involving brutality. In Columbia, Mo., for example, the internal affairs division looked into allegations from a department store that a moonlighting officer, employed as a security guard, had shoplifted two shirts. Although acquitted in a court of law, the officer lost his job for allegedly lying.

Cadging is a common offense that journalists can document. It occurs when police officers stop at fast-food restaurants, grocery stores and other business establishments, especially those open round-the-clock. Store managers welcome the visits on one level, because a police presence discourages robbers. The visits are less welcome when police expect free merchandise in return. Honest officers discuss cadgers among themselves. Journalists who have trusting relationships with the honest officers can learn names. An alternate method is to hang out in the businesses during the hours when cadging is most likely to occur; observant, patient journalists might see the practice for themselves.

Evaluating an Agency: Preventing and Investigating Crimes

Each type of crime has different roots, different types of perpetrators and victims, different investigation techniques. Federal laws alone identify about 3,000 crimes. All that makes the challenge of covering law enforcement even greater for journalists.

Murder

The Washington Post conducted an investigation of 1,286 homicides in Washington, D.C., committed during a three-year stretch. Trying to figure out how many ended in apprehension and conviction, the newspaper found that the major difficulty encountered in their investigation was the separate record-keeping systems of police, prosecutors and courts. Victims' names from police files were useless at the courthouse, where recordkeeping was by defendant's name.

When the newspaper finally finished compiling the information, it found no arrests in 40 percent of the homicides; in cases with arrests, charges were dropped in one-third; of defendants going to trial, one-third were acquitted. Half the murders occurred on the midnight shift, which was staffed by fewer detectives than the other two shifts.

When reporters chronicle murder investigations, they rarely explain the "why" behind the progress or lack of it. Their failure is often grounded in their ignorance of police investigative procedure. Reporters can overcome their ignorance by enrolling in police administration courses (offered by colleges with criminal justice degree programs); studying police manuals; and reading books such as "Homicide: A Year on the Killing Streets" by Baltimore Sun police reporter David Simon, or "Criminal Investigation" by James W. Osterburg and Richard H. Ward, former New York City policemen turned academics.

Reporters should ask: How well did police record the crime scene through photographs, sketches and notes? How well did they collect and preserve physical evidence, allowing them to reconstruct the crime, identify the substance or object used to kill and link a suspect to the victim or crime scene? Have police considered all possible motives, including financial gain, sexual gratification, spurned love, removal of an impediment (a blackmailer, unwanted child, elderly parent preventing the takeover of a family business) and self-protection (during an interrupted burglary, for instance)? With evidence in hand and motive in mind, how thoroughly have detectives followed people trails and paper trails to gather further information? Because they are considered the elite within the department—and because of the overtime pay that accrues from long hours—do homicide detectives refuse to ask for help even when it's needed? Are police reports written in a way that shows how many murders were committed by strangers to the victim? This is vital information to a populace terrified by random shootings. The Tacoma News Tribune was troubled that police records failed to designate drive-by shootings, leaving journalists to rely on possibly unreliable anecdotal evidence. The police wanted to know more, too, so began collecting the information. Analysis of the first year's worth of data found drive-bys occurred about once every other night, not three or four times a night, as the anecdotal evidence suggested. Furthermore, the data showed drive-by shootings were concentrated in a few parts of the city, usually where gangs hung out or crack houses existed. In other words, the bullets were rarely aimed at strangers. But police in some jurisdictions suggest that at least 18 unreported drive-by shootings occur for every one that is reported.

As they investigate, do police step over the line? The Philadelphia Inquirer examined 400 murder cases and found that in about 80 cases judges ruled detectives had acted illegally by beating confessions out of suspects. Court records yielded medical reports and eyewitness testimony.

Because every murder is inherently interesting, journalists should fight the tendency to publish or broadcast "murder briefs," with violent deaths dispatched in a few matter-of-fact paragraphs. Every murder is major to the victim, and to relatives, friends, neighbors, schoolmates and coworkers. Cheryl Reed suggests spending time in the deceased's neighborhood, talking to neighbors, asking whether the victim had a criminal record? What were his virtues?

Autopsy reports and death certificates can provide detail for stories. The local coroner or medical examiner therefore should be cultivated as an adjunct to police.

In many counties, coroners are elected; they are often funeral home directors or other persons without medical training. Funeral directors have an especially poignant conflict of interests: They want to sell a funeral to the family, making it tempting to rule a death natural. As Joel Brinkley of the Louisville Courier-Journal wrote in the IRE Journal:

> Suppose some bit of evidence, such as an empty pill bottle beside the bed or an open jar of rat poison, catches his eye and suggests the death might not be natural. Will the funeral director/coroner investigate and call the police, upsetting the family and risk losing a several thousand-dollar funeral? Maybe. Maybe not.

In some counties, especially those with urban areas, there is an appointed medical examiner rather than an elected coroner; medical examiners are often physicians trained in forensic pathology. Journalists should inquire whether a medical examiner has other specialized training that might help increase the certainty of the diagnosis. Specialties include forensic serology (the study of blood), forensic odontology (teeth, dentures, bite marks) and toxicology (poisons).

Missouri has elected coroners in 104 counties, appointed medical examiners in the other 11 counties. The coroners perform autopsies in about 3 percent of all deaths, medical examiners in 13 percent, according to an investigation by St. Louis Post-Dispatch. The IRE Resource Center contains a "Medical Examiner" heading that encompasses coroners. The book "Coroner" by Thomas T. Noguchi, former Los Angeles County medical examiner, contains useful insights. In her book "The Corpse Had a Familiar Face," Edna Buchanan provides two fascinating examples of how the Dade County–Miami medical examiner solved two different murders through a combination of scientific knowledge, common sense and intuition.

Reporters should check whether the coroner's findings at the early stage of an investigation disagree with the preliminary findings police have announced. Medical examiners and coroners are in a peculiar position, balancing on the tightrope between law and medicine. They are responsible for determining the deceased's identity plus the time and cause of death, which are medical questions; they also determine the legal issue of the manner of death: The *cause* refers to the medical reason for death, such as heart failure or a knife wound. *Manner* refers to the circumstances—natural, accidental, homicidal or suicidal.

Despite many successes by coroners and medical examiners, investigations in the IRE Resource Center show incompetence and corruption, too. As a result, killers literally get away with murder, or innocent people are convicted. The American Academy for Forensic Sciences, Colorado Springs, Colo., and the International Association for Identification, Alameda, Calif., can provide perspective.

Juvenile Criminals

About 30 percent of arrests for violent crimes nationally involve persons under age 18. Unless police, prosecutors and judges agree that a youthful perpetrator should be tried as an adult, names of the accused are normally confidential. The idea is to give juveniles a chance to turn their lives around before being publicly labeled as criminals.

But what if the offense is not the first? Should journalists push to find the accused's identity, then publish the name or names regardless of law or custom? It is a balancing act between the rights of an individual and the larger community.

Police cannot be expected to take the lead in preventing crime by juveniles. Parents, other relatives, neighbors, social workers, school teachers and employers share the responsibility. That said, it is appropriate for journalists to ask what role police are playing in prevention. Have police identified any root causes of juvenile crime? Are the proposed solutions ones that have failed in the past? If so, why stick with them? If the proposed solutions are new, where did they originate? Have they succeeded in other jurisdictions? The Youth Law Center, Washington, D.C., and the National Center for Juvenile Justice, Pittsburgh, are two of many organizations that can provide perspective.

What happens to juveniles after arrest will be described in the next chapter of this book.

Rape

Rape can turn into homicide. If it does not, the victim's life, while not over, is devastated. Catching rapists should be a top priority for law enforcement officers. Author James Neff wrote in the IRE Journal about how to evaluate rape investigations. His advice is reprinted here with minor revisions:

> What percent of your city's rape reports are deemed unfounded? FBI statistics say the national average is 9 percent; a significantly higher number is cause for alarm. For instance, Oakland police showed a 24 percent unfounded rate until an expose by San Francisco Examiner reporter Candy Cooper revealed that detectives wrote off the complaints of victims who were

drug abusers, prostitutes and others whom police felt had inappropriate life-styles. Victims were not even given the courtesy of an initial interview. These women were the very group most vulnerable to sexual violence. Are the overworked sex crimes detectives in your city doing likewise?

As sex crimes soar, so has the number of therapists. There are now more than 1,100 therapists specializing in working with sex offenders, says the head of the Association of the Behavioral Treatment of Sex Abuse, an orga-nization of therapists based in Portland. He says only 20 percent are qual-ified. Most therapists are not required by state laws to have any sort of academic degree or accreditation. Which raises the question—are your local courts sending sex offenders to qualified therapists? How are court referrals handled? Who gets the work? What are the ties to the referring judges?

See if a correlation exists between the time victims take to report rapes and the subsequent rates of indictment. Among some law enforcers, a persistent stereotype exists of the distraught, emotional victim being the "good victim." Often law enforcers don't take seriously a three-day-old complaint of a somewhat emotionless victim, even though this is quite normal.

Eliminating treatment of sex offenders is a trend today; it is a good move if you want more rape victims. Look for a correlation.

When faced with serial rapists, are police working together in a task force to apprehend a criminal crossing districts, precincts and city lines? Or are they playing politics, hoarding information, impeding the investigation?

Have the detectives been trained, especially in victim interviewing meth-ods? What are the staff turnover rates in the unit, its caseload and clearance rates? How do they compare to those of other cities' sex crime units?

When detectives are stumped by a serial rapist, have they checked the neighborhood police blotter for reports of suspicious persons, trespassers, peeping toms, nearby break-ins—all characteristics of stranger rapists? Voy-eurism very often is the gateway crime for rapists. Check the blotter or file investigation cards yourself to see what turns up. With an in-house arrest database obtained from police, as exists in the St. Paul Pioneer Press news-room and many others, journalists can do some of the checking themselves.

Besides Neff's tips, suggestions can be found in "Practical Aspects of Rape Investigation," edited by Robert R. Hazelwood and Ann Wolbert Burgess, as well as Chapter 22 of the "Criminal Investigation" text by James W. Osterburg and Richard H. Ward. As with all crimes, there are many perspectives for a journalist to understand. Nancy Ziegenmeyer explains the perspective of the raped woman in "Taking Back My Life," written with Larkin Warren. Kevin Flynn, a Rocky Mountain News re-porter, captures the perspective of a rapist's wife in his book "The Unmasking: Married to a Rapist." Helen Benedict explains the traps of insensitivity journalists enter in her book "Virgin or Vamp: How the Press Covers Sex Crimes."

Because many rapists are former husbands and boyfriends, the crime is sometimes related to domestic violence. Ugly romantic relationships occasionally lead to false rape reports by the so-called victim. Every police officer knows that. The possibility that a rape report is fictitious puts police in a difficult situation. How they deal with that conundrum has the makings of an insightful project.

Domestic Violence

Battered spouses often do not behave in ways that are "logical" to police. Why do they stay with the batterer, instead of walking out? The answer is complicated. Journalists should delve into what training police officers receive in recognizing and dealing with batterers and their victims. Background is available from numerous books, including Ann Jones' "Next Time, She'll Be Dead: Battering and How to Stop It."

With the 1994 arrest of former football star O.J. Simpson on murder charges, domestic violence became a hot media topic. As journalists delved into Simpson's past, they learned that five years before the murder of his former wife, he had been arrested on a battering charge. Prior to that, there had been at least eight domestic violence calls, none of which ended in an arrest. Journalists should consider reporting such situations before somebody dies.

Stalking may also be a form of domestic violence. Stalkers sometimes end up raping and murdering their victims. Journalists should know how anti-stalking laws are written and enforced locally. Is a complaint from the prey enough to imprison somebody, or must the prey demonstrate physical harm before police will make an arrest? If physical harm is the standard, will police officers do anything to protect a probable victim? Journalists should also determine whether police examine domestic violence scenes for indications of child abuse. Is there a constructive relationship between police and social service agencies in such cases?

Hostage situations are sometimes connected to domestic violence, as the perpetrator holds a weapon on the significant other or a child. Even when no hostage is involved, police usually fear domestic violence calls because of their volatility. A common occurrence is for a family member to call the police, who show up and brave danger throughout the incident, with the end result that the caller refuses to press charges. The Dunham-Alpert anthology contains a helpful essay by Joel Garner and Elizabeth Clemmer, "Danger to Police in Domestic Disturbances—A New Look." A useful book is Lawrence W. Sherman's "Policing Domestic Violence: Experiments and Dilemmas."

Narcotics

The war on drugs has been fought for decades, with no victory in sight. Perhaps legalizing drugs would put victory within reach, perhaps not. Perhaps school-based programs such as Drug Abuse Resistance Education (DARE) will have a long-term positive impact. Those are legitimate, albeit speculative, stories.

Investigative journalists could inform the debate with a minimum of speculation by digging into experiences of other nations that have tried innovative solutions, as well as by chronicling experiments in the states: The National Association of State Alcohol and Drug Abuse Directors, Washington, D.C., might be helpful. The main province of journalists, however, is documenting how domestic law enforcement agencies are dealing with drug-related crime.

Hundreds of books about the national and international drug wars have been published. Two of the best journalistic efforts are "Desperados" by Elaine Shannon of Time magazine and "Kings of Cocaine" by Guy Gugliotta and Jeff Leen of the Miami Herald. Books by former U.S. Drug Enforcement Administration officials provide different perspectives, including Robert M. Stutman's "Dead on Delivery: Inside the Drug Wars, Straight From the Street" and Michael Levine's "Deep Cover: The Inside Story of How DEA Infighting, Incompetence and Subterfuge Lost Us the Biggest Battle of the Drug War." One of the many scholarly books that shed light is Steven R. Belenko's "Crack and the Evolution of Anti-Drug Policy."

Drugs are mainly a cash business. Anyone trying to figure out how the cash reaches the ultimate profiters has to understand money laundering—through banks, otherwise legitimate retail businesses (which falsify receipts to account for the cash flow) and offshore entities. The job of law enforcement is to detect money laundering techniques so criminals have difficulty enjoying their illegal proceeds. Ann Woolner's book "Washed in Gold: The Story Behind the Biggest Money-Laundering Investigation in U.S. History" can provide insight. (Money laundering goes beyond drug profits, as discussed elsewhere in this book, especially in Chapter 16.) Journalists should ask whether law enforcement agencies are handling the spread of new narcotics while trying to combat the standbys. Spin magazine documented the infiltration of methcathinone from a Michigan laboratory into the street and underground residential culture within a few years during the early 1990s. Is there any way law enforcement agencies could have acted differently to cut off the spread of the addictive substance?

Drug crimes are especially difficult to solve for lots of reasons: First, the drugs involved keep changing. Second, because persons on both sides of the transaction willingly break the law, they rarely have incentive to call the police. Furthermore, patrol officers have so many other responsibilities during their shifts that minor street dealers go undisturbed. Specialized narcotics officers, meanwhile, are concentrating on big busts of wholesalers.

All that suggests that when journalists write about narcotics arrests, they should figure out who did not get arrested. Many police officers say that despite huge numbers of imprisoned dealers and users (about 60 percent of all federal prisoners and 20 percent of state prison inmates), the most powerful and violent perpetrators tend to escape incarceration.

On the drug detail, the potential for corruption of police is huge. Looking the other way in return for bribes—bad enough—is being replaced by police being paid off in drugs or stealing drugs from dealers to set up their own rings. Writing in an issue of Media Studies Journal about covering crime, a former undercover narcotics agent says she became an addict while making drug buys with taxpayers' money. She adds that every undercover agent she knew developed an addiction. That explains why many law enforcement agencies require undercover officers to undergo unannounced urine tests. Journalists should inquire about the testing policy, the results, and administrative sanctions against officers who fail.

Another temptation among police is to make unfounded drug accusations or overly aggressive arrests, enabling them to seize property in a proceeding known as forfeiture. A forfeiture law might allow an entire farm to be seized because marijuana plants are growing there, and it can be done before the grower is convicted or acquitted. A forfeiture law might allow seizure of an automobile after a routine traffic stop simply because the driver is carrying lots of cash. The police choose to assume that the cash is the fruit of a drug sale.

Forfeiture laws operate on the assumption of guilty until proven innocent. Reliable nationwide statistics on forfeiture are nowhere to be found, although the U.S. Marshals Service houses a seized assets division that makes educated guesses, broken out state by state. The incentive for an overzealous seizure policy is transparent: Law enforcement agencies use the assets thus acquired to enhance their budgets. Dishonest individual officers might fill their own pockets with cash or seized material goods.

At the St. Louis Post-Dispatch, an investigation of the drug forfeiture program began when a reporter overheard a county prosecutor's secretary talking to a caller whose automobile had been seized. The secretary said she would look up his case. The reporter watched as she opened a drawer jammed with index cards representing suspects whose cars, cash or other property had been confiscated without any determination of guilt.

Joined by a partner, the reporter began investigating. The key was obtaining previously secret settlements between law enforcement agencies and suspects. A few police officers, horrified at their agencies' forfeiture practices, provided documents. The reporters also obtained information from court cases, which led them to victims of forfeiture laws and the victims' sometimes talkative lawyers.

Drug cases are worthy of scrutiny for yet another reason—because they rely heavily on police use of informants. That is always risky, because informants tend to be unreliable by definition. Many have criminal records, and are informing in return for reduced prison time. The Columbus Dispatch found informants facing drug trafficking and related murder charges fabricating evidence in exchange for favorable judicial dispensation, cash payments or both. "Professional" informants, especially those who are incarcerated and thus in a position to report jailhouse talk, finger cellmates. Judges, despite knowledge of the questionable arrangements, often look the other way. The trouble is, many of the accusations, made for mercenary reasons, lead to wrongful convictions. (The phenomenon of wrongful convictions, and what journalists can do about them, is covered in the next chapter.) The National Law Journal reported that some confidential police informants cited in affidavits for search warrants turn out to be fictional. Police officers fabricate the confidential sources, then bamboozle prosecutors and judges to sign on. If the resulting searches lead to incriminating evidence, the burden is on the defendant and the defense lawyer to somehow demonstrate that the search warrant should be ruled invalid. But proving that a confidential informant never existed is a difficult task. Journalists can play a role by examining records in criminal cases relying on confidential informants. A close examination might uncover discrepancies, such as informants claiming they bought drugs from a postal service employee at work when in fact the employee was five states away that same day on documented official business.

Vice

Because drug transactions involve willing parties, they are sometimes referred to as victimless crimes by legalization advocates. Prostitution is also frequently referred to as a victimless crime; talk of legalization is common. But vice officers see prostitutes forced into the business by bullying pimps, sometimes to support drug and alcohol addictions. They see those infected with the AIDS virus engaging in sex for money without warning their partner. They see prostitutes beaten and robbed by customers. They see the prostitutes' customers (also lawbreakers) beaten and robbed by prostitutes and pimps. Some of the altercations end in murder.

Prostitutes, pimps and johns are vulnerable to corrupt or brutal police officers. Some squeeze prostitutes on the beat, taking a percentage of earnings in exchange for no arrest. Others demand free sex. By working human sources and looking for complaints filed with the police or in court, journalists might uncover officers taking advantage of their vice assignments.

To supplement people and paper trails, journalists can observe the life of the streets firsthand. They will see how prostitutes organize their soliciting around the schedules of vice officers. A lot of business can be conducted during half-hour shift changes. Vice officers understand the prostitutes' routine, though, so occasionally alter the time of shift changes. Prostitution and other antisocial activity thrive in parks, buildings and other public spaces designed without safety in mind. Are architects and planners working on designs that minimize secluded stairwells, blind corners and other problem crannies?

One of the most controversial duties of vice officers is policing pornography. When does a book, video or live show cross the line of constitutionally protected free expression to become illegal? Does pornography, however defined, incite its consumers to commit sex crimes?

Combatting pornography that features children is less controversial. The criminals who produce and the pedophiles who consume the material are despised by all segments of society, making their apprehension a matter of widespread support. Tamar Hosansky and Pat Sparling's book "Working Vice" contains a section about how one police department tracks down pedophiles. Almost every type of vice investigation is covered in the book, which is essentially a biography of Cleveland police officer Lucie J. Duvall. The section about the connection between bars and crime explains why police spend so much time trying to find liquor license violations as a way to close the bars, thus reducing neighborhood vice crime.

■ Organized Crime and White-Collar Crime

Organized crime syndicates are often involved in drugs and vice. The pervasiveness of syndicates should dictate investigations, but much of what is reported about organized crime, especially the so-called Mafia branch, is sensationalized. Occasionally, journalists' investigations of the Mafia do move beyond the machine-gun slayings, expensive suits, neat-sounding nicknames and competition for the title of family boss to the guts of the matter—money. Seemingly legitimate businesses controlled by Mafia families should be the focus of coverage, in accord with the maxim "follow the dollar."

Books with that emphasis include Jonathan Kwitny's "Vicious Circles: The Mafia in the Marketplace," Ralph Blumenthal's "Last Days of the Sicilians: At War with the Mafia," Peter Reuter's "Disorganized Crime: Illegal Markets and the Mafia" and William Knoedelseder's "Stiffed: A True Story of MCA, the Music Business, and the Mafia." Crime organizations with their generations-ago roots in Italy and Sicily today tend to be diverse conglomerates that control retail and wholesale businesses. The organizations also seem to have a stronghold in some labor unions, profiting by extorting money from employers in exchange for labor peace.

Organized crime operations in the United States with roots in Colombia, China, Russia and Vietnam tend to be less diversified than their historically Italian/Sicilian counterparts. The Colombian combines, for example, are well-known for buying and selling illegal drugs. That said, many organized-crime enterprises know no ethnic or national boundaries, making it especially challenging for investigators to identify them with precision.

Not all organized crime involves guns and physical threats. White-collar criminals practice organized crime in the suites, not in the streets. When they are policed at all, the policing usually comes from a government agency not normally associated with law enforcement, such as the U.S. Securities and Exchange Commission. Those bureaucracies might be overzealous when using their criminal authority for behavior that could be handled in civil forums. Should all insider trading of corporate securities, for example, be treated as criminal just because Congress approved a law criminalizing such behavior during a period of societal norms that have since changed?

White-collar crime, more frequently called "enterprise crime," involves a network of individuals linked together in an illegal relationship. Books that explain enterprise crime include "The Criminal Elite: Professional and Organized Crime" by Howard Abadinsky and the similarly titled "The Criminal Elite: The Sociology of White-Collar Crime" by James William Coleman.

Journalists should ask law enforcement agencies what is being done about enterprise crime, especially now that it frequently occurs via computers in cyberspace. Does the agency have a detection policy? Or does it simply wait for disgruntled insiders to blow the whistle? Are any officers trained in uncovering enterprise crime? Is surveillance—through undercover infiltration, wiretapping, neighborhood stakeouts—part of the crime-fighting strategy? Are investigators using a powerful law, the Racketeer Influenced and Corrupt Organizations Act (RICO), as well as laws aimed at money laundering, to full advantage? At a level involving less physical danger but huge amounts of money are consumer credit scams aimed at corporations that think they're selling to legitimate businesses. One organization that can provide case studies is the National Association of Credit Management, Columbia, Md.

Missing Persons

Some of the most spectacular missing persons cases involve planned hits by organized crime syndicates. But there are thousands of less sensational cases that deserve attention. Families of missing persons are almost always upset at police. In the early stages, family members perceive police as overly skeptical that foul play is involved. In later stages, if police believe the missing person might indeed have met with violence, family members become upset that the case remains unsolved.

Journalists can explore police policy on missing persons reports. Do police wait at least 24 hours before checking, based on the unvarying assumption that the "missing" person might have disappeared voluntarily? If that is the policy, is the assumption sometimes counterproductive? At what age does the policy kick in—16, 18 or 21? When police receive a missing person report about a child, they usually operate differently. Should that mode of operation be the norm for persons above the age cut-off, too? When the missing person turns out to be a runaway under legal age, to whom do police refer the juvenile?

The Osterburg-Ward text contains a six-page checklist for missing persons cases. A journalist could use the checklist to determine whether police have been thorough.

Burglary

Crimes against persons are a higher priority for police than crimes against property. But property crimes may outnumber violent crimes by ten to one. Property crimes are rarely solved, which can leave negative impressions about police among the citizenry.

Burglaries leave police in a dilemma. If the department is overworked, does it make sense to respond promptly to every burglary call, especially when the amount of stolen property is small and nobody has been injured? Do police feel they must respond immediately to every private home or business burglar alarm, when studies indicate that as many as 97 percent are false? What perspective is available from the National Burglar and Fire Alarm Association, Bethesda, Md.? Osterburg and Ward address some of those questions in Chapter 23 of their textbook. Connie Fletcher's book "What Cops Know" contains additional insights in the property crimes chapter; another insightful—and insider's account—is "Burglars on the Job: Streetlife and Residential Break-ins" by Richard T. Wright and Scott Decker.

One type of burglary of special interest to journalists working in large cities and resort areas involves items stolen from hotels and motels. Are they staffed by private security guards as well as covered by city police? If so, how effectively do they share their jurisdiction? Do they undercount or completely suppress burglary reports so as not to damage tourism? ABC-TV News aired an investigation showing lapses in hotel security, leading to guest vulnerability. Burglaries are sometimes inside jobs, staged so the purported victims can file false insurance claims. If a business or home is protected by a private security firm, that firm might use its knowledge of the premises and its ability to disconnect the alarm system temporarily from the main office to perpetrate the crime.

Another angle on burglary is the destination of the stolen property. Journalists should examine pawn shops, flea markets and street-corner vendors. What is their policy on accepting undocumented goods? WCBD-TV, Charleston, S.C., discovered flea markets and pawn shops that accepted goods they knew were stolen.

Automobile theft is one category of burglary with a high recovery rate when the motive is a joy ride. But journalists too often ignore more interesting automobile thefts. The first is theft with owner consent. The owner's motive is ending up with a new car paid for by insurance; the thieves end up with a car for personal use or sale for profit to a chop shop, which disassembles it, then sells the preordered parts. If a reporter becomes interested in a particular auto theft—perhaps because the apparent victim is prominent—one inquiry should be whether the victim had fallen behind on insurance payments. The insurance company would have the definitive documents. Other paper trails could include lawsuits concerning payment or scope of coverage, and Uniform Commercial Code financing statements. Private companies such as Carfax, Fairfax, Va., can help journalists track a vehicle's history if the investigator can supply a vehicle identification number (VIN). The history will indicate odometer fraud, undisclosed rebuilding resulting from salvage and other suspicious activity. Carfax pieces together its histories from state motor vehicle department title documents and odometer readings registered at vehicle auctions.

A persistent reporter can uncover chop shops, which are often in league with salvage yards, auto salesrooms, auto auctioneers, body repair garages and insurance companies. A Time magazine story about a chop shop in a Pennsylvania industrial park is an example of what can result.

Another potential story is corruption in the state motor vehicles department when a car is stolen for resale rather than for parts. The thief or an accomplice will quite likely alter the VIN. To make the transfer virtually foolproof, the next step is bribing a clerk at the motor vehicles department to produce fake papers.

More auto thefts are turning violent due to carjacking—stealing an already occupied vehicle while it is at a light or parking space. Journalists should ask what strategies police have developed for preventing and solving carjackings. The International Association of Auto Theft Investigators, Horseshoe Beach, Fla., can provide perspective.

Arson

Police officers frequently know little about arson. Their academy trainers assume the fire department will take the lead. But because police are often the first on the scene of a suspicious fire, they should know about collecting evidence. Arson is yet another property crime that maims or kills human beings.

A journalist should document the cooperation or dissension between police and fire department investigators, known as marshals. The journalist can study police and fire department arson reports going back several years. How frequently do their conclusions disagree? If disagreement exists, might it stem from inadequate training of police or payoffs to fire inspectors by the beneficiaries of the arson? A useful organization is the National Association of Fire Investigators, Hoffman Estates, Ill.

Chapter 24 of the Osterburg-Ward text is a starting point for understanding how an arson investigation should be conducted. A book by Peter A. Micheels, "Heat: The Fire Investigators and Their War on Arson and Murder," provides an education through interviews with eight fire marshals. "Last American Heroes: Today's Firefighters" by Charles W. Sasser and Michael W. Sasser is based on observing one Miami Beach firehouse. The newsletter "Public Safety and Justice Policies," Alexandria, Va., tracks fire department issues played out in all 50 capitals in the context of larger law enforcement issues. The IRE Resource Center contains projects under the headings "Arson" and "Fire Departments." One of these projects, by the Providence Journal-Bulletin, showed that of 6,033 arsons reported in one year, only 19 resulted in prison sentences. Those statistics on their face suggest either corrupt or inept investigators and prosecutors.

As journalists investigate suspicious fires, they should consider all motives. One is to collect insurance money on the building, so the journalist should investigate whether the owner has incurred unexpected financial obligations: back taxes, alimony and child support payments? Has the building owner lost a business license, zoning case, property tax appeal or major investor? Is the building in violation of code, meaning city inspectors have ordered expensive renovations? Were the owners planning to go out of business anyway? Is there reason to believe a disgruntled current or former employee set the fire? If the fire occurred at a personal residence, is it possible the owner planned to apply insurance proceeds to business debts? If the journalist finds witnesses—neighbors, tenants, competitors, business partners—who saw the owner remove contents of the building before the fire, that could be valuable testimony.

Not all cases of arson are connected to business difficulties. Other motives include pyromania, vandalism, revenge against an unfaithful spouse or concealment of another crime—such as incineration of a body after a murder. The Star Tribune in Minneapolis documented an arson ring led by a fire chief, his brother, plus 15 associates (including an insurance adjuster and construction company executive), who had reported 51 fires during a 25-year span. What about other fire department capabilities: response time, rescue skills, and adequacy of staffing? The Kansas City Times showed the city fire department was unprepared to handle emergencies linked to hazardous chemicals. When firefighters work in an area with lots of wooded land, have they received special training in fighting brush and forest fires? Those types of fires are sometimes acts of nature, but frequently are caused by arson, too.

Bombings

Arson sometimes involve explosives. Does the police department house a bomb squad, or at least have one officer on staff with specialized training? If so, is the training up-to-date? Who provided it? Osterburg and Ward in their "Criminal Investigation" text distinguish between frequently unsuccessful reactive bombing investigations (with a concentration on the detonation site) and more successful proactive investigations (with a concentration on gathering evidence that might prove involvement of a likely perpetrator). Knowing that distinction would have helped journalists investigating the New York City World Trade Center bombing.

After police hear about a bomb threat, do they follow the most sensible procedure, one that protects potential victims without scaring them unduly in the event of a hoax? Journalists can compare how different police departments handle bomb threats.

Traffic Patrol

Automobiles are not classified as weapons, but they are among the most lethal in history. Police assigned to traffic patrol try to alleviate the carnage. It can be dangerous work. In Connie Fletcher's book "What Cops Know," traffic officers relate how a stop for a broken headlight might lead to a confrontation with a murderer. Such incidents happen often enough that journalists should understand the anxiety of officers working what seems to be a routine assignment. Journalists should learn how police recruits are taught to handle traffic stops in the academy, then determine whether officers are following the procedure to minimize dangers.

Hit-and-run accidents are a variation on lethalness almost always difficult to solve. During one year in California, there were 331 hit-and-run deaths, according to a Los Angeles Times investigation. There is usually no motive, no reliable witness—a hit-and-run happens so fast that witnesses see only a blur. Other obstacles to solving such cases include expired plates and unlicensed drivers (about 10 percent in California, or 2 million people). One reason some drivers fail to stop is that they are undocumented aliens scared of imprisonment or deportation.

Catching drunk drivers is part of the traffic patrol's work. Questions surrounding enforcement of DUI laws include whether or not police should set up sobriety checkpoints at which every passing driver is pulled over and tested. The handling of drunk driving cases will be mentioned in the next chapter and Chapter 18.

Police scandals sometimes have their roots in traffic patrol. Officers might work out a sweetheart deal with a towing company. When the traffic patrol sees an accident requiring a tow truck, the same rig gets the call every time. WJZ-TV in Baltimore found such a questionable relationship between police and a towing company, plus one between the towing service and a body shop charging exorbitant prices. The IRE Resource Center contains other, similar examples.

Speed traps set to ensnare motorists going too fast sometimes lead to ticketing of motorists who were obeying the law, as police realize they can abuse their authority to raise revenue, not to mention harass or sexually abuse those they stop in an exercise of raw power. Journalists should examine the number of tickets written per year by each officer: Is there a quota system from on high? Are some officers way above it? So what?

Another scandal involves targeting minority motorists for traffic violations, even when they are not breaking any law. The purpose of the harassment is to discourage minorities from driving that route in the future. The Belleville News-Democrat heard from a former Illinois policeman about the practice. A reporter went through nearly 19,000 tickets that indicated the driver's race to document the allegations. Blacks received tickets five times more frequently than whites in the locale most likely to deter them from entering the city. The situation was aggravated by the percentage of black police officers—zero—and the proximity of Belleville to East St. Louis, an almost all black city.

If a traffic stop leads to an arrest for a non-traffic offense, journalists should ask whether police had legitimate reasons for their search. What is police policy? What do prosecutors say? Have juries or judges set defendants free as a result of traffic stops that result in non-traffic charges?

Canine (K9) Corps

Police use dogs to harass and harm minorities, too. In the relatively rare instances when investigators have delved into the use of police dogs, they have found an inordinate number of unleashings against minority citizens.

Journalists should check whether police departments in their jurisdiction use dogs. Are the dogs trained well? Are the officers taught that dogs can be as lethal as guns? Brutality complaints sometimes cite dogs and their police handlers. In fact, one of the most wrenching police brutality investigations ever done by a journalist involved dogs.

William Marimow of the Philadelphia Inquirer was the investigator. His colleague David Preston wrote about it in the IRE Journal:

> Marimow received a telephone call from a law enforcement official who alleged that a handful of the K9 unit's 125 officers were ordering their dogs to attack innocent, unarmed citizens without justification. . . . He tracked down victims and witnesses of K9 attacks, pored over court testimony and medical records and traced cases through the criminal justice system.

After receiving the original tip, Marimow heard from a local attorney who said that two other lawyers had witnessed a K9 attack. Then a newsroom colleague told Marimow about an attack on the son of a family friend. Four months after the first tip, Marimow published a story. Calls about other attacks poured in. Before Marimow had finished, he knew of more than 350 unwarranted attacks. Two officers and their dogs accounted for 50 of those. In such situations, the United States Police Canine Association, Delray Beach, Fla., can provide perspective.

Civil Rights and Community Relations

A disproportionate number of K9 attacks victimize innocent black males. Many police departments have negative images in black and other minority neighborhoods. Journalists should look into what law enforcement agencies are doing to alleviate those images, and into whether the image is justified. Is the department hiring officers who reflect the diversity of the jurisdiction where they work? Are officers—from all ethnic, racial and religious backgrounds—trained in dealing with sensitive, sensitized portions of the population? If community relations positions exist, are the officers assigned to them full-time? Or is the community relations work an add-on, occasional responsibility? When trouble refuses to die down, do local police ever consult the Community Relations Service of the U.S. Justice Department?

Process Servers

Serving legal papers on suspects, witnesses or defendants is a law enforcement function almost never noticed by journalists. When a person is trying to resist being served, what techniques are officers taught to boost the success rate? Do warrants for probation violations stack up at the police department because they are a low priority, having come from a different part of the criminal justice system? When warrants go unserved, do criminals who are supposed to be on the receiving end of those warrants commit new mayhem? Failure to appear in court on a specific date is one of the most common crimes in the United States, but police rarely locate—or even try to locate—those who skip.

Evidence Rooms

If evidence is misplaced, destroyed or stolen, a guilty person might go free. Yet journalists almost never inquire about the handling of evidence. A Kansas City Star story told of 13,000 guns jutting from shelves and dangling hangers in a police subbasement. The story also noted "evidence bags stuffed with pills, pot, speed and LSD spill[ing] from shelves in a long, store-sized room." Kansas City police were trying to control internal theft from the storage areas. How often do officers take guns and other pieces of evidence for personal use? What happens to officers who are caught?

The Seattle Times documented the mishandling of a cotton swab carrying evidence of child molestation. As a result of the mishandling, the swab ended up contaminated and the alleged molester ended up with an acquittal due to lack of physical evidence.

Crime Site Technicians, Crime Laboratories

In "What Cops Know," Connie Fletcher quotes an officer:

> Policemen are notorious for screwing up crime scenes. The first thing they do is pick up the gun—in order to prevent the victim from killing anyone else, I guess. It's inherent in the policeman. I wish I could tell every cop who ever gets called to a scene, "The best place for your hands at a scene is in your pockets."

To minimize screw-ups, every officer should have specialized training. It also helps to have professional fingerprint lifters, sketch artists, computer artists and photographers at the scene. The Osterburg-Ward text includes a chapter, "Physical Evidence: Discovery, Preservation, Collection, Transmission" that should help journalists formulate questions.

After the evidence has been collected at the scene, it sometimes goes to a crime lab. An inefficient or ineffective laboratory will mean failure to convict. WCCO-TV, Minneapolis, investigated a vehicular homicide in which poor work by the state crime lab caused trouble for the prosecution. The Seattle Times found crime labs with such huge back-ups that they had stopped accepting samples for analysis, leaving police and prosecutors unable to proceed against suspected criminals.

Polygraph operators might be attached to the crime lab; wherever they fall within the organization chart, their capabilities and the use to which their lie-detector results are put should be grist for journalists. The same is true for DNA analysts, who are becoming an increasingly important factor in police work. Is DNA analysis as conclusive as law enforcers testify? Or is it still in the experimental stage, with room for error due to inexact equipment and poorly trained, overworked technicians?

Patrol Officers, Dispatchers and 911 Operators

The Fort Worth Star-Telegram reported that the police department received a call every 39 seconds. With 942 officers, it had a ratio of 2.1 officers to every 1,000 citizens, which is below average for large cities. As a result, some calls labeled "emergency" failed to receive the desired emergency response.

The story tracked one emergency call, from a woman with a two-year-old daughter who rang 911 to report four men trying to break into her home. When the call arrived, the 911 operator (one of seven on duty at that hour) sent the information to one of four police dispatchers working that shift. But no on-duty patrol officer was available. One-third of all calls received did not meet the police department's own response-time goals. Response times are often excellent in some parts of the city (usually the most affluent), yet substandard in other parts (usually the poorest, most crime-ridden). The Pittsburgh Press documented such disparities by using computerized records of 911 calls after listening to complaints from neighborhood groups with anecdotal evidence about slow police responses. Many law enforcement agencies erase 911 tapes after a month or two, so journalists must move quickly if they want tapes to explore a specific case or overall response quality.

Even the best response times cannot help a caller whose location is unknown. Journalists should examine the quality of the local 911 system, asking whether it is enhanced so it does not have to rely on callers to provide their location.

Journalists who learn about police patrol will discover how patrolling means hours or days of boredom followed by minutes of terror and anxiety. They will also learn it is a creative, formless activity, grounded in instinct and suspicion. They will learn about ineffective techniques—officers who arrive with sirens blaring are either poorly trained or are intentionally warning suspects of their arrival. It is well known among police that some of their colleagues let perpetrators escape to avoid paperwork and testifying in court. New York magazine documented the paperwork involved in one minor marijuana arrest on the street. The paperwork, transport of the prisoner and meeting with the assistant district attorney kept one patrol officer away from his beat for six hours, three of them at budget-busting overtime pay rates.

Studious journalists will come to understand why patrol officers take time away from the street after each dispatched call. This gives them a chance to do preventive work, looking in on local drug dealers, for example. Many arrests come from such initiative. Even though it makes response time statistics look bad, many officers think it is necessary. They also have to find time during their shift to write reports. If reports are dashed off, their low quality might make it more difficult or impossible to obtain convictions. If they phone in reports, they might wait an hour for an operator who is simultaneously handling nonemergency calls from citizens. Naturally, such waits adversely affect response time to new calls.

Quick response is mostly about apprehension. But police patrols should also be set up to maximize prevention. The current debate centers on the manner of patrol—motorized vehicles (cars, motorcycles) that have the virtue of speed but separate officers from their communities or means that increase contact (bicycles, horses, on foot). Closer contact is at the core of the community policing movement. A recent examination by the New York Times magazine appeared under the headline "One Cop, Eight Square Blocks." Two useful books are "Cop" by Michael L. Middleton and "Community Policing: How to Get Started" by Robert Trojanowicz and Bonnie Bucqueroux.

An emphasis on community policing might lighten the burden of maintaining police cars that never should be away from the street. Journalists found Fort Worth was operating 272 patrol cars, one-third with more than 80,000 odometer miles over their lifetimes. They were all scheduled to run nearly 24 hours a day. But at any given time, between 30 and 40 were off the street for maintenance. Are police officers allowed to drive patrol cars home after the shift? Is the take-home program working, by giving the appearance of more officers all over town? Are police abusing the program by using the cars for strictly personal matters?

While checking usage and maintenance records, journalists should ask about equipment inside the cars. For instance, are they equipped with computer terminals so officers can run license plate numbers and ask for rap sheets while in pursuit or at a crime scene?

Community policing, even when carried out enthusiastically, is no panacea because it does not automatically reach into private places away from street view. Robberies in office suites, rapes in public housing elevators, drug deals in the basement of a home generally escape notice. There are ways for police to address crime in private places, but those take planning.

Lawrence Sherman's essay in the Dunham-Alpert anthology explains how planners can map each type of crime, determine possible causes, then decide how to reallocate resources according to the causes they can affect. For example, are lots of homes being burglarized? Maybe the most effective strategy is helping residents buy stronger door locks and window bars. Are women being snatched from the street, taken to abandoned buildings and raped? Maybe part of the solution is to convince women to alter their daily patterns; another part of the solution might be to tear down or secure the buildings.

Records Divisions and Public Information Officers

Journalists are by definition interested in the accessibility and completeness of police records. Complaints initiated by citizens and those initiated by police themselves ought to be organized logically. Too many departments organize them only by time of day and date. That is of little help to journalists or other citizens who have only the name of the complainant or alleged offender.

Journalists should scrutinize the logic of reporting forms. Do they capture the relationship between the victim and the offender? If not, how can police know whether they are fighting crimes involving people who know each other or strangers? Because acquaintance crimes and stranger crimes are handled differently in both the prevention and apprehension stages, such information ought to be considered vital.

Are crime statistics charted by neighborhood, rather than citywide only? Citywide statistics do not allow police to plan their crimefighting according to each precinct where officers are stationed. For example, a citywide drop in aggravated assaults might mask a big jump in knife fights between black and Vietnamese gangs within a particular precinct.

Public information officers can help journalists figure out how reports are organized, plus assist with accessibility to the documents or computerized databanks. Public information officers ought to be consulted and trusted until they prove themselves untrustworthy.

check PD for 1995 stats —

The Meaning of Crime Statistics

The U.S. Justice Department's Sourcebook of Criminal Justice Statistics often paints a different picture from the other major national source, the Federal Bureau of Investigation's Uniform Crime Reports. The FBI data exclude unreported crimes. If an automobile is stolen but never reported, statistically it is as if the theft never happened.

Furthermore, the FBI data cover only eight categories: murder and nonnegligent manslaughter, rape, robbery, aggravated assault, burglary, larceny/theft, motor vehicle theft and arson. Another problem with the data is that law enforcement agencies funneling information to the FBI have varying systems of crime statistics management. Justice Department data try to account for unreported as well as reported crime.

Numbers can lie locally as well as nationally. Pam Zekman of WBBM-TV, Chicago, found the police department was wrongly taking credit for a lowered crime rate. It made no sense to her that crime was decreasing when so many people she knew had been victimized.

Zekman's hunch turned out to be correct. Officers, anxious to please their superiors, were marking legitimate crime reports—especially rapes, robberies and burglaries—as "unfounded." By comparing that "unfounded" designation to statistics from departments in other cities, Zekman determined Chicago police had used the term from 6 to 50 times more frequently than police in New York, Los Angeles and St. Louis. In some areas, police discourage citizens from reporting minor crimes. That discouragement makes the geographic area appear safer than it actually is and reduces police paperwork. Journalists can inquire into police practices that discourage citizen reporting, such as refusing to accept complaints by telephone.

The Tacoma News Tribune performed a computer analysis of violent crime data that shattered myths. For example, the assumption that military personnel were more likely to commit crimes turned out to be mistaken: they had half the level of reported violent crime as the rest of the population. Even local police expressed surprise at which neighborhoods had the highest number of reported crimes.

Adam Berliant, computer-assisted reporting expert at the Tacoma News Tribune, suggests starting with computerized information at the local, not the state, level. The most appropriate local agency is probably the one that submits statistics to the FBI.

A reported crime is considered cleared by police if it results in an arrest or the gathering of enough evidence that an arrest could have been made if not for external factors. But a high clearance rate is not necessarily cause for celebration. Many arrested suspects turn out to be innocent, admitting to previous crimes in the hope of receiving lenient treatment for the current crime.

Law Enforcement Budgets

As mentioned in previous chapters, journalists can learn a lot from scrutinizing budgets. That holds true for budgets of law enforcement agencies.

In the case of police, overtime payments may indicate the shifts on which additional officers are needed to combat crime increases or which specialists are spending extra hours combatting a particular type of crime that has spiralled out of control.

Another example: From the budget, journalists can determine how much money is used to pay informers, then ask, when informers are used, are they already in prison or under threat of imprisonment? Does their potentially tainted testimony hold up often enough to make payment sensible?

Contracts should be scrutinized, too, as at any taxpayer-supported agency. The Grapevine Sun in Texas received a tip from a police officer resulting in a story describing questionable spending for repair and maintenance of city police vehicles. The stories told how the chief funneled business to a local garage where his son-in-law worked, paying excessive prices for parts and labor. The reporter relied on repair shop invoices, vehicle maintenance logs, request-for-repair forms filed by police and monthly department expenditure reports.

People Trails

As in any bureaucracy, current and former employees should be cultivated as widely and deeply as possible. Sources in other law enforcement agencies can provide perspective, especially if the agencies have worked together on solving crimes that cross jurisdictional lines.

Private detectives can be sources about what is going on inside police departments. They do favors for uniformed police and sometimes receive favors in return. Detectives will sometimes help journalists, too, by obtaining unlisted telephone numbers, running credit checks and finding missing persons. Journalists should expect to pay expenses for such assistance at least some of the time.

Prosecutors can help. If either the prosecutor's office or the police department is in need of reform, there is always the chance one will blow the whistle on the other. Police often dislike prosecutors because they will not file charges unquestioningly. Prosecutors often become angry at police for bringing poorly prepared cases. Each side possesses files on specific cases that journalists would not normally see. The same is true for public defenders and defense attorneys in private practice. Prosecutors and defense attorneys as sources are treated more fully in the next chapter.

Victims, witnesses and those arrested can be interviewed even without police cooperation. Cheryl Reed of the Dayton Daily News checked the criminal record of a 20-year-old murder victim after hearing he had been found in a known drug area. She obtained his rap sheet through a newsroom computer hook-up to a local law enforcement network. The rap sheet showed the victim's criminal history as well as the name and telephone number of his mother. Reed interviewed the victim's family before police had even released his name to the public.

The St. Louis Post-Dispatch asked a convicted murderer for access to his records, which contained insights into the crime. The 31-year-old man, who first killed when he was 14, signed a release giving the newspaper medical and conduct records that had accumulated during 16 years in prison.

Other types of sources who get close-up views of police conduct include coroners, medical examiners, funeral home directors, emergency room doctors, nurses, ambulance personnel, citizens crime commissions, scholars in university criminal justice departments, psychologists and psychiatrists who examine the accused, informants, pawn shop employees and gun dealers.

Paper Trails

Police department organization manuals spell out paper trails if read carefully. If a journalist can somehow get access, the National Crime Information Center, coordinated by the FBI, contains a wealth of data. Records are entered by local law enforcement agencies. Each state maintains a control terminal, which is supposed to help with data input and retrieval. The NCIC files include missing persons; wanted fugitives; stolen and retrieved but unidentified guns; missing stocks, bonds, cash, license plates and boats. The computer system is off limits to journalists, so convincing an inside source to help becomes a legal and ethical matter.

Search warrants filed in local courthouses are not off limits; they can help journalists break open a case. The San Francisco Bay Guardian used search warrants while investigating the apparently unnecessary fatal shooting by police of an Oakland, Calif., resident in his home. "According to the seven-page warrant," the story said, "police were looking for equipment used to alter the encoded magnetic strip on credit cards and any goods purchased with the stolen or altered cards." The warrant named the man's wife, who was not home at the time of the fatal raid. The raid turned up no such evidence, and the dead man's wife never was arrested.

If police conduct a warrantless search, that is a story in itself. The Las Vegas Review-Journal investigated incidents in which the police failed to obtain search warrants. Three officers eventually faced criminal charges in connection with the death of a man during a warrantless search.

Local jails keep books listing people who have been incarcerated there. The books contain such information as the person's name, date of birth, address, gender, race and physical description; the name of the arresting agency; date of commitment to the county jail; who made bond and how; discharge date; and the suspected offense. The book usually is indexed chronologically. Read carefully, it can break stories. For instance, a prisoner admitted in battered physical condition who is soon given medical attention might have been a victim of excessive force by police.

All those records build and build. Crime will never go away.

Chapter *10*

INVESTIGATING GOVERNMENT

The Judicial System

*L*awrence W. Sherman's essay, part of the book "Critical Issues in Policing" notes that "police have historically viewed their responsibilities as ending when they have made an arrest. Recent research suggests, however, that what police do both before and after an arrest has substantial impact on the likelihood of the arrest resulting in a conviction."

That is an important point; journalists on the crime beat should follow police work through prosecution and sentencing. But by then police are not the only parties determining the outcome of an arrest. Others who can make or break a case include prosecutors, public defenders, private-practice defense attorneys, judges, law clerks, bail bondspeople, witnesses, jurors, victims and jailers.

Experienced journalists visit courthouses often to talk to participants, view criminal and civil case filings and observe trials in progress. Those journalists know they will usually find valuable, unduplicable information.

Every chapter in this book contains references to legal documents that aid all manner of investigations. The focus of this chapter, however, is on investigating the justice system itself. Like any branch of government, it can perform honestly and efficiently, or corruptly and inefficiently.

As with other branches of government, resources for learning about the system are immense: books both popular and academic; bibliographies; Ph.D. dissertations and master's theses; legislative hearings as well as studies by support arms such as the General Accounting Office; executive branch reports, especially overviews from the Bureau of Justice Statistics in the U.S. Justice Department; court decisions; newspaper, magazine and newsletter articles; and television and radio segments. Examples are scattered through this chapter.

"Crime and the American Press" by Roy Edward Lotz examines journalists' practices as they try to understand the system. So does "News Making in the Trial Courts" by Robert E. Drechsel. Drechsel shadowed a newspaper reporter on the courts beat, then conveyed the immensity of the task:

> It includes 36 state and local judges and their staffs; 72 attorneys in the county attorney's office and 20 in the city attorney's office; 50 public defenders; about 20 private criminal defense attorneys . . . court administration staff; the U.S. attorney's office (12 prosecutors); four federal judges and their staffs; three federal magistrates; bankruptcy court; the FBI; the Drug Enforcement Administration; the Secret Service; the Minnesota Supreme Court . . . the state Lawyers Professional Responsibility Board; and the state Board on Judicial Standards.

A few common-sense precepts help when investigating so many institutions. Investigations have faltered because journalists failed to recognize one or more of the precepts. The precepts below are adapted from "The Reporter and the Law" by Lyle Denniston, one of the most talented legal reporters anywhere.

First, most law is practiced outside of courthouses. The vast majority of controversies, whether in criminal or civil matters, are settled before a judge is involved. "Much of the time and energy of the [legal] profession is and must be spent . . . avoiding contests in court," Denniston says. The best journalists will shed light on matters that never reach court as well as those that do.

Second, precedent usually determines the results of criminal and civil cases. Law tends to be predictable because rulings in previous similar cases are so controlling. "Only when a precedent simply will not fit does the judge or attorney feel truly free to strike out on a new path," Denniston says.

Third, procedure is vital to understand. The prescribed steps are rarely exciting. But a journalist who fails to learn the order of those steps will be lost.

Fourth, a legal dispute is self-contained, limited to its own facts. "If it does become a mechanism through which law itself grows or changes, that is really quite incidental to its own purpose . . . to get a result between its particular contestants," Denniston says.

Fifth, those contestants are expected to act as adversaries. Each side is trying to win through prescribed means. Some approximation of the truth is supposed to emerge from the adversarial proceeding. A journalist who forgets that the adversaries see truth from their own peculiar angle is a dangerous journalist.

The Judicial System as a Political System

Legal cases are about precedent and advocacy. Sometimes they are about politics, too; Fredric N. Tulsky, a reporter at the Philadelphia Inquirer, explained that expertly in the previous edition of this book. Tulsky, who holds a law degree, has since moved to the Los Angeles Times. In his "Courts" chapter for the earlier edition, he explained that like city hall, legislatures or the presidency, the courts are a political system.

To begin investigating the courts, a journalist must know how judges are chosen. Whatever the selection process, judges are politicians in robes, a consideration often overlooked by journalists. Similarly, prosecutors are politicians in suits who serve as officers of the court.

In the federal system, judges and prosecutors are appointed by the president and confirmed by the Senate, often with the backing of the state's U.S. senators, representatives and other officials of the political party holding the White House. The injection of party affiliation emphasizes the political nature of the jobs. The St. Louis Post-Dispatch investigated the selection of a Missouri state court judge for the federal bench. The name emerged from a nominating committee appointed by a St. Louis representative with clout at the White House. The newspaper reported how the representative chose the nominating committee, how the committee conducted its search, what the committee seemed to have missed in the judge's controversial past and why so many politicians seemed upset at the choice.

Once confirmed, federal judges and prosecutors play a role in appointing subordinates who also exercise power—for example, Bankruptcy Court judges and assistant prosecuting attorneys.

In the state system, judges and prosecutors are either appointed (usually by the governor, with legislative approval) or elected by the voters. Supporters of the elective system say it is more likely to include minorities and women in office. Supporters of the appointive system say it minimizes politicization of the courts and leads to higher-quality officials.

What other impact does the political process have on the court system? One obvious consequence is that campaigning for election or appointment as a judge requires money. In an elective system, the bulk of the campaign contributions almost always comes from lawyers, who will eventually be bringing cases to the judge they supported.

Judges' campaign finance reports are public record, but are often overlooked by journalists. One exception was the work of Sheila Kaplan when at Common Cause magazine. While judgeship races were "once the K-Mart of political elections," she wrote, lawyers and other special interests began contributing large sums. Kaplan described a Florida lawyer solicited for a contribution on behalf of a incumbent judge running for reelection, just days before trying a nonjury case before that judge. She also reported that as two huge oil companies were pitted against each other in a multimillion-dollar Texas lawsuit, the law firms representing the oil giants combined to contribute almost $400,000 to Texas judges, including state Supreme Court justices not even up for reelection.

In Philadelphia, where voters elect trial court judges, sample ballots are sometimes distributed by ward leaders. A Philadelphia Inquirer series demonstrated the failings of such a system. The series quoted one judge, who was seeking election to a higher court, telling political party officials at a ward meeting, "They say you're not supposed to do favors in the courtroom. . . . That's not the rule in my courtroom. Just don't get caught."

Inquirer reporters studied campaign finance reports of successful judges over a five-year period, noting lawyers who were campaign officials, those who were contributors and those who were both. They obtained, from court administrators, computer printouts for the same years. The printouts listed the cases assigned to each judge and identified the attorneys arguing each case. The newspaper discovered that defense lawyers active in campaigns for municipal court judges won 71 percent of their cases before those judges, while only 35 percent of all municipal court defendants won their cases.

Other journalists have documented connections between campaign finances and attorneys who receive lucrative case assignments from judges as trustees, guardians ad litem, special masters or arbitrators. An Indianapolis Star bankruptcy court investigation found cronyism at work as judges awarded $14 million of professional fees over a four-year period. Much of that money went to attorneys with political ties to, or financial relationships with, the judges.

After documenting the conflicts of interests, journalists can ask what the lawyers actually accomplished for their fees. Detroit News reporters studied abuses by attorneys appointed to represent indigent defendants on their appeals. The vouchers submitted by those lawyers showed charges for visits to incarcerated clients. Comparing the vouchers to visitor cards on file at the state prison, the reporters found requests to be paid for dozens of consultations that never took place.

When judges are appointed rather than elected, campaign contributions are still a factor. A Los Angeles Times team reported how 118 lawyers who contributed to a California gubernatorial campaign became judges after the candidate won. Those 118 made up one-fifth of all the governor's judicial appointments.

The court system provides additional political rewards. The courts often escape civil service regulations. Thus, they become a repository of patronage positions for judges and the political parties to which they belong. In Philadelphia, reporters identified more than 2,000 court jobs excluded from civil service. Journalists should ask how people get those jobs: Do minimum qualifications exist? Are tests required and administered fairly? Do court administrators give undue weight to letters of support from politicians?

The Inquirer series showed the $55 million annual court payroll included relatives of at least 30 of the city's 120 judges, as well as relatives of court administrators. The deputy court administrator, with four relatives on the payroll, said he was "just sorry I can't get more of my family members on the court." The series described a judge's intervention when a court administrator disciplined a habitually tardy employee who happened to be the judge's son.

Corruption in the Courts

Given the politics imbedded in the judicial system, journalists should expect imperfections. That does not mean journalists should expect to prove judges, prosecutors, clerks and other judicial employees are taking payoffs. It is valuable enough to tell readers and viewers what their officials are doing. Reporters can use paper and people trails to question judicial conduct, whether money changed hands or not.

There will be times when journalists do learn of payoffs. A Philadelphia Inquirer reporter heard from sources that the FBI possessed evidence of judicial wrongdoing. The FBI had been investigating a local union it believed was engaged in extortion and had received court authority to plant wiretaps in the union hall. The surveillance led to the discovery of union members filling envelopes with cash for judges at Christmas. At least 14 judges, according to sources, received from $300 to $500.

The reporter wrote an initial story, based on his sources as well as the Code of Judicial Conduct, adopted by the state Supreme Court. Those standards, as in most states, are based on American Bar Association rules. In Pennsylvania, the code prohibits the "appearance of impropriety" by a judge; local bar association leaders said the alleged gifts appeared to violate that canon.

The Inquirer waited for May 1, the deadline for judges to file financial disclosure forms covering the previous year. Judges must list gifts of $200 and more or face misconduct charges. On that date, two Inquirer reporters went to the state court administrative office, expecting to see competitors. Instead, the reporters found themselves alone in the office; they reported the next morning that nine judges had disclosed receiving cash the previous December from union officials. Two other judges invoked the Fifth Amendment on the forms, refusing to answer the question. One judge had filed his form in January, before the newspaper disclosed the FBI probe, and listed no gifts. In April, he filed an amended form listing the union gift.

Some offenses committed by judges are more serious. The National Law Journal reported on the conviction of an Illinois judge for taking bribes to fix murder cases. The article quoted the prosecutor as saying that in the courtroom, "for the right price, you could get away with murder. We thought we had seen it all, but [this] judge . . . took us to new depths." An earlier Chicago scandal, dubbed Operation Greylord by investigators, involved convictions of 15 judges among more than 80 bribe-taking or bribe-giving lawyers and court officials. James Touhy and Rob Warden's book about the scandal, "Greylord," provides fascinating detail.

While waiting to investigate the occasional dramatic payoff scandal, journalists can uncover story after story simply by paying attention to each step of the legal process.

Between Arrest and First Court Appearance

After arrest, suspects are taken to the police station to be finger-printed and photographed. A criminal-records check is conducted. Police might begin interviewing the suspect. The jail book can help journalists keep track of comings and goings.

Suspects often spend considerable time in holding cells. The local public defender, private-practice defense attorneys, prison society officials, current and former jailers, former prisoners and their relatives can help answer pertinent questions: What are the conditions like in those cells? What kind of food and medical care are available to prisoners? Are jailers trained to identify epileptics, diabetics and the mentally ill, treating them appropriately? How long before suspects see a magistrate? Journalists should look at the average time, especially checking delays on Saturday nights. How do the waits compare to other jurisdictions? What do court rulings say about such delays?

Making Bail

Journalists rarely pay attention to whether the bail system is working as intended. That is a big oversight. Making a suspect pay bail before leaving jail is supposed to increase the odds that the suspect will show at trial. No show, no refund. A judge can set bail at any amount deemed reasonable. A defendant who cannot raise the money stays in jail until trial. One way to raise the money is through a bailbondsperson, who makes a profit by charging what amounts to interest on the loan. The defense attorney can ask the amount be lowered or that the suspect be released without paying—on their own recognizance, in legal jargon. The prosecutor can oppose bail on the basis of danger to the community or risk of flight or ask for a higher amount than the judge sets.

The Sarasota Herald-Tribune found judges releasing suspects on their own recognizance, even in cases where the suspects had prior criminal records. The article said that

> For many, no-release bail was granted despite a Florida law that is supposed to dissuade judges from granting [it] to defendants on probation or awaiting

trial in other cases. The logic of the law is simple—criminals should pay for one crime before being free to commit another. But a computer analysis of court records by the Herald-Tribune finds that Florida's laws on pretrial release are ripe for abuse.

The newspaper examined 2,430 cases during a year's stretch. The reporter asked judges why they were allowing hardened criminals— some with records of forfeiting bond to become fugitives—to leave custody with no payment. In many cases, the judges said they had no idea of an accused's criminal history at the time of the bail hearings. The unanswered question: Why did they fail to demand the information before making a decision?

The bail system obviously favors wealthy defendants: Is the discrimination against poor defendants so egregious as to violate civil rights? Prosecutor Steven Phillips, in his book "No Heroes, No Villains: The Story of a Murder Trial," says about the inability to make bail:

> There is the anguish of separation from one's family and the special torment of being unable to assist in the preparation of a defense. An accused person desperately needs to go out into his community and help his attorney (usually a mistrusted outsider in that community) to find the witnesses who will bolster the defense. This cannot be done from a jail cell. Statistics have long shown that a jailed defendant is far more likely to be convicted and sent to prison than a defendant who makes bail.

How many suspects are charged with other crimes while free on bail? How many bail bonds are forfeited? Does the court system collect forfeited bonds efficiently? If not, how much money are taxpayers losing? The IRE Resource Center contains investigations that demonstrate why it is wise to seek answers. WCAU-TV, Philadelphia, found suspects waiting days to see a bail judge, even though many had not been charged with committing a crime. The Hartford Courant discovered that on average black and Hispanic suspects paid twice as much as whites to be released on bail even when they had similar records and backgrounds. The Shreveport Times exposed a sheriff who failed to collect bond forfeitures. WDIV-TV, Detroit, determined that criminals jumping bond rarely had to worry about being pursued; 12 law enforcement officials were expected to handle 22,000 fugitive cases statewide.

Bond companies need to be scrutinized because of their crucial role in the criminal justice equation. The Dallas Morning News chronicled the bankruptcy of the largest bond company in the urban area, which cost Dallas County more than $2 million in lost revenue. Bailbondspeople hoping to earn money from capturing fugitives employ bounty hunters. In their book "Working Vice," Tamar Hosansky and Pat Sparling describe a bounty hunter for a Cleveland bailbondsperson: "The work was free-lance. No health coverage, no guaranteed salary. If someone jumped bail, and about 20 percent did," the bounty hunter received a call. He earned a commission for every capture.

Initial Appearance in Court

The first court appearance after filing of a criminal charge is called the preliminary hearing or the arraignment. The criminal charge might emanate directly from police working with the prosecutor, in which case a judge is supposed to decide if enough evidence exists to move toward trial. Other times, the police and the prosecutor appear before a grand jury consisting of citizens chosen from voter lists, driver's license databases or some other registry. If the grand jury believes the evidence is sufficient, it will issue an indictment.

Prosecutors generally prefer grand juries over preliminary hearings in front of judges. Grand jury proceedings are one-sided, held in secret and generally easy to manipulate. In an open courtroom preliminary hearing, the prosecution will have to share discovery material with the defense, thereby eliminating the advantage of a head start. The preliminary hearing for O.J. Simpson on murder charges was an example of an open, substantive proceeding.

A journalist should know the rules regarding grand juries. If the prosecutor has discretion, how is the decision to call a grand jury made? Is the grand jury representative of the community? What happened inside the grand jury room? Is there reason to believe the prosecutor and prosecution witnesses told less than the whole truth to obtain an indictment? If the prosecutor bypassed the grand jury in a discretionary situation, why?

Laws governing grand jury activity vary from state to state, and federal grand juries operate under yet another set of rules. One common denominator: Grand jury proceedings are held behind closed doors. Reporters can sit outside grand jury rooms to see which witnesses go in and out, asking them what they said. If a reporter believes that is time well spent, all entrances and exits should be observed; some rooms are set up so that witnesses who enter from one door can leave through a different door.

In many states, witnesses are forbidden by law from revealing what went on inside the grand jury room. Grand jurors are almost always legally restrained from talking. There are exceptions. In California state courts, grand jury transcripts are available after an indictment. After a grand jury examined evidence in the murder case involving O.J. Simpson, journalists apparently assumed the transcripts were sealed upon request of the prosecutor or the defense. A reporter for the Los Angeles Daily

Journal, assuming nothing, asked the judge if he could see the transcripts. The judge handed them over immediately, giving the reporter a scoop and the public new information.

Furthermore, some grand juries leak, thanks to a friendly prosecutor, juror or judge. The court clerk's office will have names of the grand jurors. Subpoenas issued for witnesses are public record. Witnesses might be reimbursed their expenses from public funds, which means their names should be available through the voucher system.

Not all indictments become public immediately. Some remain secret while authorities look for the accused. (Grand juries sometimes issue reports that go beyond criminal conduct of an individual. The reports, called presentments in legal jargon, deal with government malfeasance. For example, a report could discuss the extent of organized crime's influence in a city, or unsanitary conditions at the county jail.)

If charged, a suspect can plead not guilty, guilty or "nolo contendere" (I do not contest it). One reason for pleading nolo contendere is to avoid liability in the civil courts. As explained in the book "You and the Law," from the American Bar Association;

> Let us say a nursing home operator is accused of the crime of abusing patients. If the operator pleads guilty, anyone who sues . . . for civil damages will not have to prove that the abuse occurred. However, if the operator pleads nolo contendere, the civil court will have to decide whether the acts alleged took place.

Sometimes a suspect is confused about how to plead—as more and more defendants do not speak English, the criminal justice system has failed to adapt. When interpreters are supplied, they can still cause problems: The San Jose Mercury News found that incompetent interpreters denied non-English speaking defendants their right to understand what was happening to them.

Pretrial Hearings

A defendant might file motions contending the state improperly obtained evidence. The motion will be heard at a pretrial hearing. At this stage allegations of police misconduct are commonplace, which makes it difficult to understand why pretrial hearings are ignored by so many journalists.

Philadelphia Inquirer reporters studied transcripts of pretrial hearings from homicide cases. They documented a pattern of police beating confessions out of suspects. Examining a three-year period, the reporters found 80 cases in which judges refused to allow confessions into evidence. How a defendant has been treated by police pits the defendant's word against several officers. Certain judges routinely accept the police version, no matter how suspect the story or how many times the same officers have offered a similar account in other cases. Other judges may be overly suspicious of police officers, so refuse to admit critical evidence. Journalists should learn which judges are which. They can begin by asking lawyers about judges' reputations. After conducting that informal survey, journalists can go to court files to learn if the reputations are valid.

A pretrial controversy might revolve around admissibility of lie detector tests; a journalist should assume the results are inconclusive, then can seek perspective from the American Polygraph Association, of Chattanooga, Tenn., or the National Training Center of Lie Detection, New York City. Other pretrial motions might involve dismissing the case, delaying a hearing date, reducing the charges to a lesser offense, moving the trial to another locale, reconsidering the amount of bail, determining whether a defendant is mentally or physically competent to stand trial, challenging the composition of the jury, providing taxpayer money for investigators requested by a public defender and replacing a judge because of alleged bias.

Assigning Cases to Judges

Federal courts, and some local systems, use a random-assignment method, in which cases are assigned by lottery to judges in roughly equal numbers. This system is favored by some because it discourages shopping, in which attorneys use their influence to place their cases before a favored judge. On the other hand, such a system can cause backlogs. Some judges will be sitting idly if cases they have scheduled settle or break down unexpectedly. So some court systems create calendar rooms that feed out cases one-by-one for trial as judges become available.

Where judge-shopping is possible, a journalist can determine whether certain lawyers appear before certain judges more often than chance would suggest. Do those lawyers fare particularly well before those judges? When the answer is yes, the journalist must determine whether there are business or social connections between judge and lawyer.

To present a snapshot of the system's functioning, the Philadelphia Daily News planned a descent on the city's 41 common pleas courts for one day. They found judges showing up late then working only briefly, as well as absent defendants, victims and lawyers. Other lawyers were present, but scheduled to be in two different courtrooms at the same hour. The sloth and inefficiency, combined with a large number of cases, gave the impression of a system about to break down.

Investigating Judges

An investigator can begin scrutinizing judges by determining how often their decisions are overturned by appellate courts. Legal Times, Washington, D.C., studied reversal rates for all 17 U.S. District Court judges in the nation's capital. The publication found one judge had been reversed 39 percent of the time, more than twice the average; another judge had not been reversed even once. A high reversal rate does not prove incompetence or corruption, but might be an indicator of a problem.

A reporter calculated the costs in money and time of one reversal, in a drug-selling case. During the trial, the judge refused to let the defense attorney cross-examine a police officer. The appellate court ruled the judge had erred, so ordered a retrial. The new trial ended with a deadlocked jury. So a third trial occurred, ending in a not guilty verdict. The result of the original error was a defendant in limbo for years, $22,000 in jurors' fees, plus the extra efforts of two public defenders, three prosecutors, three trial court judges as well as an appellate judges' panel—all paid for with public funds.

Another relatively simple-to-document story involves a judge's work habits. Many hold court a few hours in the morning, take long lunch recesses, then go home early to golf. Meanwhile, plaintiffs and defendants wait months or years for rulings or trials because of a supposedly overcrowded court docket.

WCCO-TV, Minneapolis, used its projects team to document such a travesty so skillfully that it became a featured case in the investigative reporting primer by Peter Benjaminson and David Anderson. As the textbook authors note,

> The story is an excellent example of television's strengths as an investigative medium. It is one thing to read about judges playing golf when they should be working. It is another thing to watch them play golf when the on-screen clock shows that they are playing during working hours on a workday. It is one thing to read about how the judges squirm when confronted. It is another to watch them do so on camera.

Some judges work long hours on a regular basis, but still rule slowly. They may simply have an inhuman case load, or may be indecisive, not particularly bright, undergoing family difficulties, having trouble communicating with their law clerks.

By talking to lawyers, law professors, clerks and fellow judges, a journalist can gauge whether a judge is considered to favor plaintiffs or defendants. In a multijudge trial district or on a multijudge appellate court, disagreements and rivalries are common, meaning journalists can find talkative sources. Rivalries among judges, perceptions of favoritism toward plaintiffs or defendants, might not be stories by themselves, but the information might find its way into a later project.

In her book "Unequal Protection," Judge Lois Forer acknowledges that there is behind-the-scenes talk. Speaking of a family court judge she considered incompetent, she mentions his bad temper, political ambition, undistinguished record as a lawyer, embitterment at his assignment and the fact that he had no children himself.

By hanging around courthouses, journalists can pick up on animosities between judges and particular lawyers. The ABA Journal published an article about two law partners in Kansas who were embroiled in a feud with a judge. It became questionable whether persons represented by those lawyers could receive an unbiased trial in front of the judge.

Judges who issue many citations against lawyers, witnesses, plaintiffs and defendants might be abusing their authority. Journalists should know which judges issue more contempt citations than average, then inquire why. Similarly, does a judge abuse authority by refusing to step aside from a case (recusal is the legal term) when convincing evidence of a conflict of interests is presented by the plaintiff or defendant?

Many states require candidates for judgeships and sitting judges to file reports detailing personal finances. A check with the state elections commission or other appropriate state agency could be the start of a story about conflicts of interests. Financial disclosures of federal judges, except for U.S. Supreme Court justices, are handled by the Administrative Office of the U.S. Courts, Washington, D.C. U.S. Supreme Court data is available from the court's public information office.

A beginning point for stories on federal judges is the Judicial Staff Directory, updated regularly by Staff Directories Ltd., in Mt. Vernon, Va. The biographical information suggests where to look next. Texas Lawyer found a judge who had extensive business dealings with a bank that appeared before him in court as plaintiff and defendant. Even if the judge's rulings appear to be balanced, what do judicial ethics say about the appearance of impropriety? Other conflicts might arise from a judge's past affiliations. By which firms was the judge employed while a lawyer in private practice? Does the judge favor former partners in the courtroom?

Conscientious judges tend to isolate themselves socially to avoid even the appearance of conflicts. Guidelines are vague when it comes to how a judge should conduct private life. Social isolation as a solution, however, can lead to understandable frustration, which might show up in courtroom behavior. Insights into the dilemmas can be gained from reading what judges read, including Judges' Journal, published by the American Bar Association's Judicial Administration Division.

As the allusion to socializing suggests, personal qualities matter in a judge. If a reporter hears that a judge sexually harasses court personnel, the reporter should explore whether the judge rules fairly in sexual harassment cases. If the judge frequents prostitutes, can he rule fairly in prostitution cases? If the judge is racist, are rulings made in racial discrimination cases fair?

When a judge's behavior seems to be out of line, the state bar association, a quasigovernmental body (such as the Missouri Commission on Retirement, Removal and Discipline of Judges) or the U.S. Justice Department might investigate. After the investigation, a report might be available at the state Supreme Court or the U.S. Congress. Occasionally, a judge is forced from the job. The Illinois Courts Commission removed a judge who handled traffic and other misdemeanor cases, calling him a "mean-spirited judicial tyrant." Alert journalists could have documented his behavior long before the commission made its findings. Sometimes complaints lead to cover-ups rather than removal. The Seattle Post-Intelligencer found compelling evidence that a judge had forced teenage boys to have sex with him. The Washington State Commission on Judicial Conduct knew of the problem, but allowed the judge to remain on the job.

"Taming the Storm," Jack Bass' biography of U.S. District Court Judge Frank M. Johnson, Jr., shows how a journalist can write insightfully about an active jurist. Print and broadcast reporters should make a habit of profiling sitting judges, even when no misconduct is evident. Such features build reporter-subject relationships, and sometimes bring tipsters forward with allegations of wrongdoing. "The Benchwarmers" by Joseph C. Goulden is a rare example of a book-length exposé.

Ratings stories, such as a jurisdiction's 10 worst judges, can enlighten at the same time they get the community talking. The IRE Resource Center contains numerous ratings-based stories in the "Evaluations" section of its "Judges" category.

Investigating Prosecutors

The obligation of a prosecutor in representing the citizenry is to seek justice, not just convictions. But prosecutors are politicians, too; federal prosecutors are appointed by the administration in power with the consent of the Senate. Most local prosecutors are elected. So everything significant they do or fail to do ought to be examined in a political context as well as in a legal context.

Journalists can learn about federal prosecutors by reading Senate confirmation hearings. Both federal and local prosecutors can be backgrounded further through examination of law school performance plus past legal jobs, whether in private practice or the public sector. The traditional paper and people trails discussed in chapters 2 through 5 should be mined as well.

When federal prosecutors or their assistant attorneys misbehave, the Justice Department's Office of Professional Responsibility (OPR) is supposed to investigate. Many of the allegations come from defense attorneys, especially in drug and white-collar crime cases, who believe they are being harassed to discourage vigorous representation of their clients. The Washington Post found that the OPR tended to treat misconduct charges against prosecutors lightly.

Somewhat similarly, local prosecutors might need to be disciplined by the state attorney general, usually an elected official. When St. Louis Post-Dispatch reporters exposed the corrupt activities of the city prosecutor, the state attorney general entered the inquiry. The National District Attorneys' Association, Alexandria, Va., and the National Association of Attorneys General, Washington, D.C., can provide perspective, as can the book "State Attorneys General: Powers and Responsibilities," edited by Lynne Ross.

Journalists should examine the backgrounds and performances of the assistant prosecutors, and the prosecutor's hiring practices. Does the prosecutor go back again and again to a former law firm or law school to hire assistants, perhaps bypassing more qualified lawyers? Does the prosecutor look for disparate legal philosophies, and seek assistants with experience as defense lawyers, who will thus understand the adversary? If assistant prosecutors lose case after case on behalf of the citizenry, does the prosecutor fire or transfer them?

One measure of a prosecutor's performance is how many cases go to trial. There is no magic percentage that makes a prosecutor capable. But if almost every case goes to trial, something is amiss, because many cases brought to prosecutors by police are flawed. On the other hand, if almost no cases go to trial, it is possible that too many criminals are getting off too lightly with plea bargains.

Journalists should not assume that plea bargaining is unwise. But the more a system depends on closed-door dealing, the more likely instances will arise in which someone with connections receives special treatment. Journalists should ask whether certain lawyers negotiate successful plea bargains far more frequently than the average. Do certain judges reject plea bargains submitted by certain prosecutors in certain types of cases?

Related to plea bargaining is undercharging. Many prosecutors have blind spots when it comes to the seriousness of certain crimes. For example, does the prosecutor treat driving while intoxicated offenses as minor, even though a car is a lethal weapon?

The opposite of undercharging is overcharging. Journalists should look for cases that go to trial, but end in convictions on something less than the original charge. If, in case after case, the prosecutor brings an aggravated assault charge that ends up in a misdemeanor assault conviction, this suggests that the prosecutor is overcharging. Some prosecutors routinely prosecute on the stiffest possible charges to cultivate a "law-and-order" image. Defense attorneys are natural sources for information about this phenomenon.

Prosecutors, being human, show interest in some types of cases more than other types. Recognizing this, journalists can examine how a prosecutor handles specific categories.

What about white-collar criminals, for example? When workers die on the job because of management negligence, is a corporate homicide charge filed? Do embezzlers in large corporations or computer hackers compromising entire systems have nothing to fear from a prosecutor? How about cases of consumer fraud, as in telephone boiler room operations, or physicians who bilk Medicare and Medicaid patients as well as the governments that pay those bills? What about income-tax evaders? When refusing to bring charges in complicated white-collar crime cases, prosecutors often mention lack of money and time. Why does that answer seem valid in corporate cases, when it would never find acceptance in the case of a street thug?

If a 35-year-old woman visits the prosecutor's office to allege the molestation and murder of her best friend by her father 25 years earlier, how does the prosecutor react? Does the prosecutor automatically believe the allegations when supported by the woman's therapist, and therefore file criminal charges against the father, despite his sincere-sounding denials and the lack of physical evidence? Does the prosecutor automatically disbelieve an allegation made on the basis of repressed-memory therapy so many decades later, or largely avoid taking sides by encouraging that the complaint be addressed in a civil lawsuit?

How a prosecutor reacts to difficult cases such as those involving repressed memory says a great deal. The repressed memory example is not a random choice; such cases are proliferating. Some of the many new books addressing the controversy are "Remembering Satan" by Lawrence Wright; "Unchained Memories: True Stories of Traumatic Memories, Lost and Found" by Lenore Terr; and "Once Upon a Time: A True Story of Memory, Murder, and the Law" by Harry N. MacLean. If children are involved, a relevant book is Lucy S. McGough's "Child Witnesses."

When prosecutors are trying to decide whether to bring charges in any kind of case, do they handle witnesses with consideration, rudeness or condescension? After a charge is filed, are witnesses prepared for the ordeal ahead? Do prosecutors overuse subpoenas to force reluctant witnesses to speak? Do prosecutors offer new identities in witness protection programs when there is reason to fear for a witness' safety? If so, do witnesses receiving new identities run wild, without supervision, committing new crimes? The IRE Resource Center contains a "Witness Protection Program" category.

If the witness is also suspected of a crime, do prosecutors too readily grant immunity? Will judges and juries believe witnesses who have so much to gain for saying what the prosecutor wants to hear? There is a saying for such occasions: When you prosecute the devil, you're probably going to have to go to hell for your witnesses. The saying is especially apt in prosecutions of street gangs and rings of drug dealers.

When an expert witness seems useful, how frequently do prosecutors (or defense attorneys) take that step? Such witnesses might charge hundreds or thousands of dollars per day. Does the prosecutor have a budget to pay such fees? Is there reliable research showing that expert witnesses make a difference with judges and juries? How does the prosecutor choose expert witnesses when so many people claim to be expert in a certain area? There are so many "experts," in fact, that companies exist to help lawyers make choices; perhaps the largest is Technical Advisory Service for Attorneys, Inc., of Blue Bell, Pa. If the defense also has retained an expert witness, what does the prosecutor say about the experts canceling out one another? The Expert Witness Journal, based in Miami, can be a useful resource, helping track emerging issues such as expert witnesses being sued by their own clients or by parties on the opposing side.

The IRE Resource Center contains numerous entries under "Criminal Justice" and "District Attorneys." Dozens of true-crime books contain useful sections about prosecutors. For example, Howard Swindle's "Deliberate Indifference" starts with a case of fatal police brutality, but along the way provides insight into the conduct of prosecutors—not to mention judges, juries and defense lawyers. A smaller number of books actually focus on the prosecution, including Timothy Sullivan's "Unequal Verdicts: The Central Park Jogger Trials," "Heavy Justice" by J. Gregory Garrison with Randy Roberts, and James Stewart's "The Prosecutors."

Investigating Defense Attorneys

The role of the defense attorney can be hard to accept. As law professor Susan Estrich wrote in the Los Angeles Times, everybody involved in a criminal case is bound by law and custom to tell the truth, except the defense attorney, who is "not pledged to tell the truth, seek the truth, let alone be bound by it. . . . If [the client] is innocent, that means advocating the truth. If he is guilty, it means attacking it. . . . They are pretty free to obstruct the search for truth in any way they can, within the rules of evidence."

In criminal cases, a journalist should distinguish whether the accused is represented by a court-appointed public defender or a private-practice attorney chosen and paid by the accused. If the accused has been certified as indigent, and therefore entitled to a public defender, that tells the journalist something useful. Such representation is not always noble. Some private-practice lawyers seek appointments to defend indigent criminal defendants so that there will be a chance to submit padded bills, enriching themselves at the public's expense.

The entrance of a public defender opens the story line of whether they are less competent, less successful, than private-practice attorneys. The stereotype of public defenders is one of youthfulness, disdain for high pay and idealism that explains why they want to defend "people like that." Like most stereotypes, it contains some truth and some silliness. One quantifiable measure that can affect quality of representation is the lawyer's caseload. The private-practice defense attorney might be handling half-a-dozen criminal cases simultaneously, while the public defender might have dozens or hundreds. The National Legal Aid and Defender Association, Washington, D.C., can provide perspective.

Judge Lois Forer, in her book "Criminals and Victims," says that the public defender's caseload does matter, because

> preparation cannot be very thorough. . . . Most cases which do come to trial are completed in one to three days. These are not the cases about which journalists write books detailing massive investigations and lengthy interviews with the victim, witnesses, suspects and police.

Private-practice defense lawyers often care a great deal about money, which should lead a journalist to inquire about clients being overcharged. Sometimes private attorneys bilk the court itself. The Miami Herald found bill-padding and other fraud among lawyers appointed to represent indigent defendants whom the public defender's office could not accommodate. Some bills to the court claimed more than 24 hours of work in a single day.

The probity of a private-practice lawyer depends partly on the culture of the law firm where the lawyer is employed. One of many books about private-sector law firms is Lincoln Caplan's "Skadden: Power, Money and the Rise of a Legal Empire."

In their fervor to represent clients, defense attorneys sometimes file motions that fly in the face of social order and common sense. The St. Petersburg Times and the Ann Arbor News, among other media outlets, discovered that with the help of pliant defense attorneys and judges, clients could use state laws to wipe out their criminal records, even for crimes such as murder, drug trafficking and rape. Assuming such representation is legal, should it be considered ethical? After all, a successful expungement means a convicted rapist can teach school without having to tell the district about past criminal conduct.

Much of what defense attorneys do is try to keep clients out of court and try to keep prosecutors from pressing charges, especially in cases of corporate crime. When a case does move into court, trial tactics are worthy of scrutiny.

For example, is the defense attorney mounting a mental illness or insanity defense for an accused murderer? That defense might mean acquittal, but might pose a danger to society if the mentally disturbed person kills, maims or robs again after release. On the other hand, long-term confinement to a mental institution might be more beneficial than prison. Perspective on this complicated tactic can be gained from Michael T. Perlin's book "The Jurisprudence of the Insanity Defense." Every year the National Law Journal publishes a special section, "Winning," consisting of interviews with top lawyers who are admired (or reviled) within the profession for their tactics.

As with the subject of prosecutors, true-crime books shed light on the tactics of defense attorneys. A few books focus specifically on defense attorneys, including Emily Couric's "The Trial Lawyers" and Joseph C. Goulden's "The Million-Dollar Lawyers."

The National Association of Criminal Defense Lawyers, Washington, D.C., can provide perspective. So can publications like the National Journal of Criminal Defense, Houston, and those produced by the Criminal Justice and Litigation sections of the American Bar Association, Chicago. The Martindale-Hubbell Law Directory is organized alphabetically by state and city and covers almost every lawyer and law firm.

Choosing a Jury

Prosecutors and defense lawyers in criminal cases must decide whether their chances would be helped or hurt by a jury trial. In most felony cases, the accused has a right to a jury. Plaintiffs and defendants must choose between a judge trial and a jury in civil cases, too. The number of jurors is usually six or twelve. The use of a jury raises questions: Why did a judge-only trial seem less desirable? Has either side retained a consultant to select jurors? If so, how much does the consultant earn? Who is paying the fee? What is the consultant's record in previous trials? Does hiring a consultant contribute to a dual system of justice—one for the rich, one for the poor? Does it subvert the jury system, which is supposed to be a random selection of peers in the community? The American Society of Trial Consultants, in Towson, Md., can provide perspective.

Whether suggested by a consultant or for some other reason, racial discrimination is sometimes present in jury selection. The Dallas Morning News found local prosecutors excluded 90 percent of eligible blacks from jury service in felony and capital murder cases. The Miami Herald found racially balanced juries. But additional reporting showed the balance was unintentional: Prosecutors excluded blacks, while defense attorneys excluded whites.

Exclusions are the result of two traditions: one for cause, one involving peremptory challenges. Cause involves discernible bias, such as when potential jurors say they distrust government prosecutors or believe most defendants are guilty—why else would they have been arrested? Lawyers can make unlimited challenges for cause as long as the judge believes the challenges are valid.

Peremptory challenges mean lawyers on both sides are allowed to exclude a certain number of potential jurors without stating reasons to the judge. When lawyers eliminate potential jurors with special knowledge about the topic of the case, are those lawyers going for the lowest common denominator? If the jurors are ill-informed, is justice served? In some jurisdictions, judges ask all the questions during jury selection, which is called "voir dire." In other jurisdictions, lawyers for both sides pose the questions. Neither system is ideal.

The makeup of a jury is beyond total control of the judge and the lawyers, especially when the pool of jurors comes solely from registered voter lists. In many locales, at least 40 percent of the citizenry have not registered to vote. Journalists should ask whether a significant percentage of nonregistered citizens come from ethnic or racial groups complaining about underrepresentation on juries. Are some citizens refusing to register specifically to avoid jury duty? Have decisionmakers improved the system so that voter registration lists are supplemented by driver's license databases, welfare rolls and telephone directories?

Journalists should delve into whether all jurors in the pool have an equal chance of being called. Paula DiPerna, author of "Juries on Trial: Faces of American Justice," noted that her 72-year-old mother had never been summoned, even though she voted every year of her adult life in the New York–Connecticut area. The younger DiPerna, on the other hand, had received multiple notices from state courts, but never from the federal courts.

Once a name is drawn from the pool, will that person be automatically exempted if she chooses to be? Some jurisdictions exempt lawyers, physicians, firefighters, police officers, embalmers, pharmacists, parents of infants. Do such exemptions decrease the chances of choosing a representative jury?

Because jurisdictions pay only a few dollars a day for jury service, potential jurors often receive exemptions on the basis of lost income. Journalists should explore the exemption policy for economic hardship. Does it leave a panel of mostly middle-aged, middle-class people working for employers who cover lost wages during jury service? Should all employers be required to cover lost wages? Alternately, should governments be required to pay at least minimum wage for jury service?

No matter how the jurors are chosen, is it responsible to assume that jurors understand the process? Do judges explain rather than letting jurors decide cases based on misconceptions? For example, opening arguments by lawyers do not constitute evidence, yet jurors are supposed to listen carefully. Do the jurors understand the legal standing of those opening arguments? Is it clear to jurors that if the defendant has a previous criminal record, they probably will never hear that information, on the grounds it might be prejudicial? To aid jurors in following the trial, a few judges allow notetaking and direct questioning of witnesses. A journalist should question why so many judges oppose those measures.

Stephen J. Adler addresses these and other controversies in his book "The Jury: Disorder in the American Courts." Unfortunately, most journalists fail to win the access Adler had. One extreme way to gain access is to serve on a jury, then write about the case. William Finnegan did that for the New Yorker. After hearing a subway mugging case, Finnegan harbored doubts about the accused's guilt. He originally voted against conviction, but was on the short side of a 10 to 2 ballot. Finnegan and the other doubter eventually came around. The defendant went to prison. But Finnegan, beset by uncertainties, reported independently by talking to law enforcement officers, lawyers, witnesses and eventually the defendant.

One of many insights from Finnegan's article:

> We started discussing the [defendant's] alibi, and were soon busily contravening [the] judge's . . . instruction that we "must not, under any circumstance, indulge in speculation or guesswork, nor are you to consider anything outside the evidence." We guessed and speculated about the lives and motives of the alibi witnesses, trying to put "the evidence" into some narrative context that made sense. . . . We had no idea who [the defendant] really was. We did not even know whether he had a criminal record, whether he was a career mugger, or what. It was right . . . that we did not know such things—[he] was charged with this crime, and not others—but it was also frustrating, and the disputed facts before us would make sense only if we could imagine the worlds around them. And so we told each other stories.

Some judges try to forbid reporters from contacting jurors even after the verdict is in. In a growing number of cases, jurors' names and addresses are withheld from the media. Protecting their privacy might be admirable, but Legal Times reported "some defense lawyers and jury consultants . . . say that veiling the identity of the jurors strips the defendant of the presumption of innocence" because the unusual policy injects a fear factor leading to conviction. One reason journalists might want to interview jurors is to discuss the possibility of jury tampering by the defendant or the defendant's partisans. The Wall Street Journal pulled together numerous known instances of tampering to demonstrate a disturbing phenomenon. The truly successful tamperers, though, are the ones never caught. With sustained interviewing, a journalist might ferret out previously unknown tampering.

The Trial

How quickly do cases get to trial? Justice delayed can be justice denied. Criminal suspects have constitutional protection on this issue: Every federal defendant and many in states have the right to a "speedy" trial. Journalists should explore whether the deadlines are being met; at the same time, they should inquire whether expeditious handling of criminal cases is causing a backlog for civil cases.

In Pennsylvania, for example, state Supreme Court rulings called for defendants to be tried within 180 days of arrest, discounting delays for which the defense was responsible. But the flood of cases coming into the system, combined with prosecutors who opposed plea bargaining, made it unrealistic to meet that deadline. Thus, courts modified the rule: If the delay was the prosecutor's fault, the defendant could expect to be released. But if the problem could be attributed to overcrowded courts, delays could legally exceed 180 days.

Such delays may seem trivial in the abstract. But many defendants remain in jail until trial because they cannot afford bail, not because they have been convicted of anything. On the other hand, in any system suffering from jail overcrowding, there are going to be suspects released, pending trial, who commit new crimes.

One caveat: Speed has its downsides. Lawyers might need additional time to prepare adequately. That is especially true for a public defender with a heavy caseload who meets the accused for the first time at the preliminary hearing.

Court administrators tend to be overly concerned with the raw numbers on backlogs. After all, their job is to see that backlogs diminish or at least appear to be diminishing. But achieving justice and disposing of cases are not always synonymous. One way to manipulate the statistics so that no backlogs appear is overloading judges' dockets.

In Philadelphia, judges assigned to Juvenile Court found as many as 50 cases listed for hearing each day. Attorneys and defendants who go into such overscheduled courtrooms have plenty to say about the quality of justice that results. Court reporters, the professionals who take down every word of the proceeding, hear all and see a lot. They can be tapped for their horror stories, but rarely are. The National Court Reporters Association, in Vienna, Va., can help locate sources.

Every stage of the proceedings in the courtroom can raise questions for the journalist. Does it make the most sense to present a brief or a lengthy opening statement? Some experts say an opening statement of more than an hour will confuse jurors. Other experts say the opening statement is the best time to establish a coherent theory of the case, no matter how long it takes. How well have the lawyers used visual aids? Do they credit the received wisdom that jurors believe 15 percent of what they hear and 85 percent of what they see? What about closing arguments: Should they be extensive, to remind jurors of all the evidence? Or should they be brief, because jurors are anxious to begin deliberations and go home?

Deploying witnesses effectively is also vital. The National Law Journal explained why a defense lawyer decided against letting his client testify. In fact, the lawyer called no witnesses, preferring to make his case through damaging cross-examination of the government's witnesses. The lawyer said, "Whenever you put the defendant on, that takes the jurors' eyes off the prosecution and shifts the focus and puts the burden onto yourself. I wanted to focus on the prosecution's weaknesses." The lawyer conceded it was risky, "But I thought they had not made out a case. And this says starkly as you can that you are giving the back of your hand to the prosecution's case."

A proposed jury instruction is submitted by each attorney to the judge, who has the discretion to accept, modify or reject it. In general, jury instructions deal with points of law and set the boundaries within which the jury must make its decision. Sometimes a proposed instruction rejected by the judge forms the basis for the appeal by the losing party.

Understanding jury instructions and other procedural matters is important. In addition, the best journalists become expert in the specific subject matter of the case. For example, when covering domestic violence cases, journalists should understand the application of the "battered woman syndrome" if they are to follow what the prosecutor is doing, how the defense tries to combat the strategy and why the judge rules in a particular way on motions and objections raised by both attorneys.

To understand courtroom dynamics, journalists should try to put themselves in the place of the various parties. Most victims and witnesses find trials frightening and confusing. Judge Lois Forer has written eloquently about the phenomenon, pointing out that the defendant, quite likely a criminal, is able to consult with his attorney in the courtroom, while the victim must remain outside the courtroom, unaware of the testimony, except when called to the stand.

During a rape trial, for instance, the victim may have to rush to a nine o'clock trial after getting the children off to school. When she arrives at the courthouse in 100-degree, humid weather, she cannot find a parking place. She enters the courtroom, hot, frazzled and unaccompanied by the prosecutor, who, after all, represents society, not the victim.

She has heard nothing of the trial to that point, while her attacker, seated next to his attorney, knows every word that has been said. The night of the attack he was dressed in ripped jeans, had not shaved in two days and reeked of alcohol. Now he is wearing a new suit, is clean shaven, bathed and sober. The victim takes the stand, where she has to identify the leering defendant, then relate a degrading sexual attack on the most horrifying night of her life in front of 12 strangers serving as jurors, an imposing judge, courtroom spectators and maybe a television crew and audience, if the court is one that allows televised trials. How many stories about the courts explain that reality?

If a trial is televised, journalists should be alert for grandstanding by the judge, attorneys and witnesses. Paul Thaler's book "The Watchful Eye: American Justice in the Age of the Television Trial" is a primer. The Court TV cable channel allows journalists to learn about the legal system from home while also looking for positive and negative impacts of cameras in courtrooms.

■ WRONGFUL CONVICTIONS

Journalists must be alert to guilty verdicts that are miscarriages of justice. It is not easy to second-guess a jury or judge. But some defendants do get railroaded, and by reexamining the facts journalists might be able to right a wrong. Even if the wrongful conviction rate is just 1 percent, that still means 15,000 human beings each year are in prison for something they did not do. It also means thousands of actual perpetrators are free, maybe killing, stealing or raping again.

Journalists should question everything. Is the prosecution built on people who may be unreliable, for reasons the jury never learned? On police testimony that can be disproven? What evidence was withheld, either because it was unavailable or because of the judge's rulings?

Elements that suggest problems include coerced confessions, failure to run DNA tests where practical and to conduct careful analyses of them, information from paid jailhouse informants, inadequate lineup procedures that lead victims and witnesses to identify the wrong person, prosecutors and sheriffs worried about election returns.

On the other hand, a journalist deep into a case should never assume that new evidence presented is true. If a prosecution witness is recanting previous testimony, that does not mean the new version offered is true. Is the witness being pressured to change the story? Has the witness been given a lie detector test? Such a test may not prove anything. But if someone refuses or takes one and fails, it should give pause.

It can be wearing work. John Woestendiek of the Philadelphia Inquirer said after six months of checking out an alleged wrongful conviction: "It seemed that all I had done . . . despite the new witnesses I found and the questions I raised, was make an educated second guess." Yet right after putting that case behind him, Woestendiek heard from a man who claimed that his son, a convicted murderer, was innocent. Woestendiek heard the father mention allegedly overlooked evidence, such as the son signing for a registered letter about the time the murder was occurring miles away. Checking out such specifics convinced Woestendiek to pursue the case. Eventually, the decision was reversed and the convicted man was set free.

The IRE Resource Center contains stories about wrongful convictions. An article by Mike Masterson and Martin Yant in the IRE Journal says there should be more stories. Masterson has published newspaper articles that led to wrongful convictions being overturned. Yant wrote a book, "Presumed Guilty," about the problem. Here is part of their Journal piece:

> News outlets across the nation carried the story of two black men who spent more than 17 years in a California prison for a murder they did not commit. They finally were freed thanks to facts uncovered by a former Seattle newspaper reporter and a religious organization. Experience has shown their case, unfortunately, is far from unusual.

This most recent revelation of injustice within the criminal justice system makes it clearer than ever that journalists must question the motives and inner workings of those criminal justice systems.

In the California travesty, the two men gained their freedom after New Jersey–based Centurion Ministries and Pulitzer Prize–winning former Seattle Times reporter Paul Henderson (now a private investigator) interviewed witnesses from the trial and unearthed crucial police reports not introduced at the trial. Centurion Ministries is dedicated to freeing wrongly convicted people.

The two men were wrongly convicted of murdering an off-duty sheriff's deputy in a California gas station restroom without a shred of physical evidence. After Henderson and Centurion disclosed the new evidence, a Superior Court judge freed both men, calling the police mishandling of the case and the coercion of several young witnesses "reprehensible."

Why weren't journalists ferreting out the police reports and witnesses when these California men were originally charged? Did they simply accept the official version, as has become the practice in many newsrooms?

Henderson, who won his Pulitzer Prize for clearing a rising junior executive from a wrongful rape conviction, left the Times in the mid-1980s. It is his impression that only a few papers in the country today will dig deeply into issues of injustice.

"I'm not sure why that is," he said. "I found it very difficult (as a reporter) to interest my old newspaper in any type of criminal justice advocacy. They seemed to view such travesties with great skepticism and trepidation."

An example occurred with the release of a man from wrongful rape and murder convictions in Little Rock, Ark., because stories in the Arkansas Democrat proved his innocence three months after his trial. Yet as the stories demonstrating the man's innocence broke, the sheriff who arrested the man, the prosecutor who put him away with two life sentences and the technicians at the Arkansas State Crime Laboratory formed a united front to insist on his guilt and try to save face.

Unfortunately these are by no means isolated incidents. Masterson, then of the Arkansas Democrat, pored over transcripts of old court records, which clearly revealed that Arkansas' most notorious convict could not logically have committed the murder of a police officer. He had spent more than two decades behind bars when the reporting prompted the 8th Circuit Court of Appeals in St. Louis to order a federal evidentiary hearing in Little Rock.

Every attorney and reporter had access to the same stacks of testimony from these three hearings, which lay unresearched for more than 20 years. After Masterson finally looked into these records, it took less than a week for him to raise questions serious enough that the federal appeals court reversed its own mandate and ordered a third trial. Today, the man is free and living in another state.

Too often, reporters overlook sinister aspects in these travesties. For a criminal justice system (police, lawyers, crime laboratories and courts) to wrongly convict an innocent person of a crime, the odds are great that a conspiracy has to exist between at least two of the parties.

A significant part of one Arkansas case was how two experts from the state crime laboratory provided "facts" that turned out to be virtually the opposite of the truth. It should stretch the envelope of any reporter's sensibilities to believe both men were simply inept in their findings.

In another Arkansas case, the police had to knowingly alter their testimony from one hearing to another to accommodate the "facts" as they changed over time. For instance, during the second trial, although the police officer had been shot through the heart by a single bullet, police testimony had one bullet going out to the crime laboratory and two being returned.

"Most convictions are valid and everything falls into place," said Henderson. "Unfortunately, there are a percentage of convictions, no one knows how large, that are wrong. There is routine deceit practiced."

Two of the best books about wrongful convictions are "St. Joseph's Children" by Terry Ganey and "Gone in the Night" by David Protess and Rob Warden. One overview is "In Spite of Innocence: Erroneous Convictions in Capital Cases" by Michael L. Radelet, Hugo Adam Bedau and Constance E. Putnam.

The Victims of Crime

When prosecutors fail to win a conviction, a common reason is uncooperative victims. David C. Anderson, in his book "Crimes of Justice," notes that about 70 percent of dismissed charges stem from complainants refusing to testify:

> Such behavior is not hard to figure. Victims of an angry exchange between friends, relatives or neighbors either thought better of pursuing the case after their anger subsided or [they] preferred to do so outside the law. In some cases, the victims may also have felt intimidated by the criminals.

Journalists should document the phenomenon. When victims make contact with the criminal justice system, they must realize they initiate investigations that consume taxpayers' time and money. If victims later choose to halt the investigation, the time and money have been lost. Furthermore, society is harmed another way—the assailants are free to strike again.

Journalists should examine claims of victimization skeptically. Many victims are not blameless. They place themselves at danger by seeking prostitutes, drug dealers or a two A.M. shot of whiskey. Such behavior does not excuse criminal behavior by the assailant, but it ought to find its way into the story. Although victims must be scrutinized, usually they are victimized twice over, first by the assailant, then by the system.

One type of revictimization occurs when victims of a crime are not notified about dropped charges, probation, parole of expungement of the perpetrator's criminal record. Suddenly the assailant, frequently unpunished, is back in their lives without their knowledge. In some jurisdictions, victims have the right to see their assailants tried speedily, can make a statement at the time of sentencing and parole hearings, and generally participate at any other stage. Journalists can study the impact of these changes on trial outcomes, probation proceedings and other aspects of the process.

Another type of revictimization occurs when expected payments fail to appear. The San Jose Mercury News discovered that two-thirds of court-ordered restitution payments never reached victims. The Provo Daily Herald found Utah's Crime Victims Reparation Fund was accumulating a large reserve by investing money, while the intended recipients suffered. As journalists scrutinize restitution programs, they should ask: Is restitution supposed to come from a taxpayer-supported fund or from the criminal? Which variation seems most equitable? Which philosophy has worked better? Perspective can be provided by the National Association of Crime Victim Compensation Boards and the National Organization for Victim Assistance, both in Washington, D.C., plus the National Victim Center, in Arlington, Va. Richard H. Saldana's book "Crime Victim Compensation Programs" can help journalists determine how each listed program is supposed to work.

The irony of uncompensated victims is obvious. Taxpayers support imprisoned assailants at the rate of $20,000 or more annually, supplying meals, education and health care that might be superior to anything previously experienced by the prisoner. Meanwhile, the victim who may have been injured or incapacitated receives nothing from taxpayers.

Sentencing

Before imposing sentence in a criminal case, the judge normally orders a presentencing investigation by a probation officer, social worker or psychologist. The big question is unanswerable: Is the accused going to commit another crime? The reports are normally closed to reporters without the aid of a source. Sometimes the person convicted will open the report to a journalist upon request.

The sentencing decision can cause anguish, even among seemingly emotionless judges. In her book "Criminals and Victims," Judge Lois Forer says the decision comes down to in prison or out of prison, with either choice unsatisfactory and unfair to somebody. "Out" will cause the victim mental anguish. "In" might irreparably harden an offender who has never had a chance in life.

In some jurisdictions, judges can impose varying prison terms within a range (for example, one year to ten years for aggravated assault), based on a defendant's history, the nature of the crime and any peculiar circumstances. The theory is known as indeterminate sentencing. It is grounded in a belief that prison rehabilitation can succeed, and does so at varying rates. When education is part of the sentence, journalists should ask who provides it, why them, what is the course content and how well is it taught? How many convicts complete the coursework, and how many of them end up with jobs because of the schooling they receive?

If rehabilitation seems to have succeeded, in, say, two years, the judge should have discretion to release the criminal. If there is no indication of rehabilitation, the judge can refuse early release.

For less serious crimes, the judge chooses among a monetary fine (perhaps including restitution to the victim), community service, a suspended sentence, a jail term, probation, or some mix of those five. All five choices raise questions worthy of exploration by investigators: Are fines too low to act as a deterrent, or so high that they constitute excessive punishment? Are the fines collected? If not, how much are taxpayers losing? Are community-service sentences helping needy people in meaningful ways? Is there any monitoring of hours worked and quality of performance?

Diversion programs, usually run by the prosecutor's office, are a possibility. They precede a trial, and successful completion of the program means avoiding a conviction. For example, first-time drug offenders might be allowed to attend a heroin users' rehabilitation program. Journalists should observe such programs to determine whether they are really making a difference and serving the public's interest.

A judge's philosophy plays a critical part, leaving defendants' and victims' fates tied to the luck of the draw when judges are allowed to exercise discretion. Journalists should look for sentencing patterns of individual judges and of the entire court. Are white-collar crimes treated lightly? Studies indicate only about one in five embezzlers serves prison time and most avoid restitution to victims. Is that because embezzlers tend to come from middle- or upper-class, college-educated backgrounds, similar to judges, who cannot imagine themselves in a brutal prison setting?

Detroit Free Press reporters found that sentences varied widely for similar manslaughter convictions across Michigan. Two similar killings would earn one defendant probation and another six years in prison. Using state Department of Corrections computer tapes containing information on 30,000 sentences, the reporters fed data into their own computers, looking for manslaughter convictions. They found 199; through additional court records, police reports, newspaper clippings and interviews, the reporters documented the disparities.

Many such projects document ugly discrimination in the judicial process. The Florida Times-Union, for example, determined that defendants killing whites received much longer prison sentences than defendants killing blacks. Among the books providing perspective are "Unequal Justice: A Question of Color" by Coramae Richey Mann and "Gender, Crime and Punishment" by Kathleen Daly.

The sentencing practices of some judges is not obviously discriminatory based on race or gender, but is so idiosyncratic that the judges should be exposed. WAGA-TV, Atlanta, found a judge forcing defendants to attend $70 counseling sessions with a private-practice therapist who was treating the judge for his own disorders.

To eliminate inexcusable idiosyncracies and inconsistencies—including racial discrimination in sentencing—some state and federal laws specify maximum and minimum terms. For federal crimes, the U.S. Sentencing Commission, Washington, D.C., is supposed to determine sentence ranges. The agency instructs judges how to consider each convict's criminal history as part of the mix. However, judges are allowed to depart from the formula if they believe mitigating circumstances exist.

When no flexibility is allowed, it might be because the crime falls into a category requiring mandatory sentencing. Along with its advantages for society at large, mandatory sentencing has drawbacks. First, it does not eliminate disparities, because many defendants subject to mandatory sentences plea bargain instead. That shifts decisionmaking from the judge, who exercises it publicly from the bench, to prosecutors, who exercise it in closed conferences. Second, when a prisoner's sentence has been served, the prisoner must be released, even if the prisoner is possibly a menace to an individual or group and prison officials and judges think the release is unwarranted.

In a few dramatic instances, judges have refused to follow the guidelines, breaking the law or resigning instead. That opposition might be heartfelt, but it also might contain an element of pique. After all, it is a rare judge who wants to relinquish authority. Judge Lois Forer's book, "A Rage to Punish: The Unintended Consequences of Mandatory Sentencing," is a starting point to gain an understanding of the controversy. Private groups with their own perspectives abound, such as Families Against Mandatory Minimums and the Sentencing Project, both based in Washington, D.C.

On any story involving the judiciary, the Administrative Office of the U.S. Courts has information. "Federal Offenders in the U.S. District Courts" is an annual statistical report about the disposition, sentence, type of counsel, age, sex and prior records of federal criminal defendants. The publication can be especially useful for measuring the consistency and quality of justice dispensed in a given area.

Appeals

Prosecutors want to appeal what they consider to be unfair court decisions. So do defendants. State courts handle several hundred thousand appeals annually; federal courts handle about one-tenth the amount, still a considerable number. Journalists should ask which prosecutors engage in questionable tactics or outright misconduct, which often wins a conviction but leads to a reversal. Another compelling question is which judges are overturned most? Because about 80 percent of civil appeals and 90 percent of criminal appeals fail, it is especially significant if a trial court judge's rulings are overturned again and again.

Occasionally some of the work has been done; for example, the Chicago Council of Lawyers issued an evaluation of the Seventh U.S. Circuit Court of Appeals, including commentary on each of its judges. The appellate courts matter more than ever: In 1950, about one of every 40 trial court decisions came up on appeal; in 1990, the ratio was one of every eight.

An appeal usually includes claims that the judge mistakenly interpreted the law at trial. The specifics might focus on admission of hearsay testimony, illegally obtained physical evidence or improper instructions to the jury. Because appeals deal only with matters raised at trial, journalists must study the written record from the lower court. As explained by U.S. Court of Appeals Judge Frank M. Coffin in his book "On Appeal: Courts, Lawyering and Judging," lawyers often fail to create a record in the trial court that will allow an appeal to be granted. Journalists can point out those errors of omission and commission by lawyers.

Journalists should attend oral arguments for cases of special interest. Not much new information is conveyed by the lawyers during oral arguments; their time is limited by the court, and they are frequently interrupted by the judges. Nonetheless, oral arguments can be decisive. As Coffin notes, the function of written briefs is to show the court how to decide in one's favor; the function of oral arguments is to make the court want to decide in one's favor.

Appeals from prisoners have automatic interest, yet are frequently ignored by journalists. For the prisoner who has been convicted and sentenced, there are not many options. Direct appeals and collateral attacks on the conviction (maybe because new evidence has surfaced) represent their last hope.

It has become routine for prisoners to contend that their own attorneys failed to provide effective representation. The Philadelphia Inquirer, in its massive courts investigation, found a new twist. A reporter was in court when he happened to see an experienced defense attorney take the witness stand to describe errors he had made at trial, such as failing to call witnesses who would have provided an alibi. The startling testimony caused the reporter to find out if he was watching an isolated case or part of a pattern.

He learned numerous prominent attorneys had admitted errors that would have been avoided by first-year law students. None of the attorneys had been disciplined. Their testimony would seem to ruin their reputations. But sources said, to the contrary, unethical attorneys engaged in such testimony to get business: It gave them the reputation among prisoners as attorneys who would do what they had to for their clients. Further research showed, ironically, the state Supreme Court had indirectly helped create such testimony by setting tough standards for granting a new trial.

Because journalists pay so little attention and because of a tradition conferring automatic wise man status on appellate justices despite their being politicians in robes, unaccountable baronies are common. At the Providence Journal-Bulletin, a team exposed widespread misconduct after one of the reporters received a tip. The investigation led to the resignation of the Rhode Island Supreme Court's chief justice. Books such as "Rationing Justice on Appeal: The Problems of the U.S. Courts of Appeal"/ by Thomas E. Baker and /"The Politics of State Courts"/by Harry P. Stumpf and John H. Culver can help explain the culture. The National Center for State Courts, in Williamsburg, Va., can provide additional perspective.

At the federal level, when Clarence Thomas joined the U.S. Circuit Court of Appeals, there was almost no in-depth coverage, even though appeals courts issue life-and-death rulings every week. U.S. Supreme Court justices, on the other hand, do receive scrutiny. When Thomas joined the Supreme Court, journalists rushed to investigate sexual harassment charges and other alleged transgressions by Thomas. This discrepancy between appeals court and Supreme Court coverage has no logic to it.

Journalists have an obligation to penetrate the Supreme Court's secrecy. Disclosure will not come easily from within. As Chief Justice William Rehnquist once told journalists, "The difference between the judiciary and the other two branches of government is that we do not need you people." Tony Mauro of USA Today is one of the best reporters at getting behind the secrecy while explaining why his revelations matter in places like Columbia, Mo. In one story, Mauro explained how an Ohio prisoner's name mistakenly found its way onto the Supreme Court's list of people who could be subject to the death penalty because their applications for stays of execution had been rejected.

Journalists outside Washington, D.C., should follow Mauro's lead by learning everything there is to know about a local case that has progressed to the Supreme Court. That can be done by reading the lower court files plus documents filed with the Supreme Court, interviewing all parties involved, then traveling to Washington to hear oral arguments in front of the nine justices.

The breakthrough Supreme Court book showing the interplay of personalities, procedures and issues was "The Brethren," by Bob Woodward and Scott Armstrong. David G. Savage used a similar approach more recently in "Turning Right: The Making of the Rehnquist Supreme Court." The solicitor general, appointed by the U.S. president and confirmed by the Senate to represent the federal government at the Court, is the subject of a book by Lincoln Caplan, "The Tenth Justice." Another viewpoint is contained in "The Solicitor General: The Politics of Law" by Rebecca Mae Salokar. Congressional Quarterly publishes reference books about the court, including The Supreme Court A to Z: A Ready Reference Encyclopedia.

Probation, Parole, Commutations and Pardons

Even after a prisoner has lost all hope of overturning a conviction, imprisonment is not a certainty. Being sentenced to probation is usually the preferred alternative—though not the victim's preference—because probation means relative freedom. For the judge, however, that relative freedom poses a dilemma. Most probation officers are so overloaded that supervision of probationers is almost nonexistent. Probation officers ideally act as social worker, employment counselor and classroom educator. Realistically, probation officers are passive paperpushers. Journalists should document the probation officer to probationer ratio, compare it to similar jurisdictions and follow an officer to understand what that kind of caseload really means day to day. The New York Times magazine did that with a Los Angeles probation officer, a 29-year veteran who tried to give individual attention to gang members despite huge obstacles.

Lawbreakers assigned to probation officers try to keep contact minimal, because a probation violation that gets noticed might mean prison. The notion that a probation officer can effectively serve as a social worker and cop at the same time is misguided. Because of the flawed reasoning, probation officers often are ineffective in both roles.

What training do probation officers receive? Do they receive meaningful supervision and continuing education? Are salaries adequate to keep veterans? Is burnout common, leading to troublesome turnover? What is the divorce rate for probation officers compared to that in the population at large?

Journalists should inquire about caseloads. If a probation officer is supposed to supervise more than 50 probationers, the journalist should ask why, then search for the horror stories almost sure to exist. Do probation officers know where their clients are residing? If the addresses are correct, can the probation officers answer with certainty how probationers are spending their days and nights? Are probation officers able to rely on technology to help their monitoring? For instance, has the court system invested in transmitters to be worn by probationers so the probation officer can determine from an electronic signal the client's whereabouts? An alternative technology involves an automatic dialer that calls the convict's home telephone at random times when he is supposed to be there. If he is indeed home, he can verify his presence by using a device on his wrist that plugs into another device on the telephone.

Journalists should investigative re-arrest rates, too. In many jurisdictions, more than half of probationers commit new crimes before the court has surrendered jurisdiction. Despite its failures, probation is imposed more often by judges who have to consider prison overcrowding and the failure of rehabilitation. There are about three times as many convicts on probation as there are behind bars. As David C. Anderson describes it in "Crimes of Justice," "You're guilty, the court . . . [says] to the young burglar or mugger, but we don't think you've done enough yet to deserve prison, and since we can't figure out anything else to do with you, we're going to let you go."

As with any topic, there are publications to consult, such as Federal Probation from the U.S. government, Probation and Parole from the New York Probation and Parole Officers Association, plus Probation and Parole Law Reports from a private publisher in Warrensburg, Mo. The American Probation and Parole Association, in Lexington, Ky., can provide perspective.

Unlike probation, release on parole comes only after a portion of a prison sentence has been served. Parole boards, at the federal level and within state governments, are frequently secretive, inefficient, corrupt, or all of those. They are often filled by political appointees with little inclination or background to do a good job. Because they are so politically sensitive, they let out prisoners too soon as the result of pressure from well-connected lawyers or clamp down too tightly after a sensational crime involving a recent parolee.

A classic investigation of parole and pardon corruption is "Marie" by Peter Maas. It chronicles the appointment of a woman to head the Tennessee Board of Paroles and Pardons, and how her discovery of wrongdoing led first to her dismissal, then to her decision to become a whistleblower against the governor and his operatives.

Looking at the Michigan system, the Detroit Free Press found that 6 percent of felons served full sentences, compared to 17 percent nationally. The parole board violated state law by releasing prisoners without jobs or educational plans as budget reductions led to fewer parole officers.

Some states have abolished parole boards, letting prison officials and judges determine the optimum release date. Journalists in states with parole boards could compare the effectiveness of their system with states that handle matters differently. One objection to elimination of parole is that it leads to loss of hope among prisoners, who then are more likely to be troublesome while incarcerated and prepare less vigorously for their release. The U.S. Parole Commission, in Chevy Chase, Md., produces an annual report that can provide perspective.

When a prisoner has exhausted parole possibilities and is politically connected, or retains a politically connected lawyer, there is always a chance the U.S. president or a governor will commute the sentence or issue a pardon. When such treatment occurs, there is almost always an interesting, and sometimes a scandalous, reason.

For years, I followed attempts by Armand Hammer to win a pardon from U.S. presidents. My reporting put me in touch with a U.S. Justice Department official called the pardon attorney. He helped as much as he felt he could while the case was pending, then released documents without delay after Hammer prevailed during the George Bush administration. At the state level, former California governor Edmund (Pat) Brown shared insights about pardons in a book, "Public Justice, Private Mercy," written with journalist Dick Adler.

New Orleans Times-Picayune reporters investigated the pardon of a convicted pimp who once operated a well-patronized French Quarter brothel. The man had been sentenced to five years for possessing stolen property, but was pardoned after sixteen months. The reporters learned the governor had been persuaded by a state legislator, who had been paid $2,000 by the convict and had failed to report the payment to the state ethics commission.

Based on that incident, the reporters probed pardon records generally. They went through the files of the pardon board, noting any political figures involved in the case, plus the attorneys handling the hearing. The hearing records, supplemented by interviews, showed the law firm of the governor's executive counsel had the busiest pardon-board business in the state. Over three years, that firm handled more than 100 cases before the board, and had won two of every three hearings.

Prisons

Prisons are not like the rest of the world. What is normal on the outside is usually turned on its head in prison. Journalists who have never tried to write about individual prisoners, or prisons as institutions, are in for a shock. Inhumanity is the norm. It is hard to portray, though, because access to documents and knowledgeable people is so difficult.

The warden and guards reign supreme. Journalists can view wardens as obstinate bureaucrats, or can view them as supervisors of dangerous convicts who most of us would not want to be around. Whatever a journalist's first impression, lack of cooperation from the warden means prison coverage will be unpleasant. Some state governments have turned prison management over to private companies, making wardens even less accessible.

Because wardens are so powerful, they ought to be scrutinized. How did they enter the prison bureaucracy? How did they receive their appointment to the current job? Have they articulated their philosophies about rehabilitation and punishment? Are their actions consistent with their philosophies? Records relating to the operation of the prison, including how it spends its budget, should be available from the division of corrections in the state capital, or from the legislative committees appropriating money.

How are guards hired? Do the minimum qualifications make sense, and are they adhered to? Is the pay adequate to attract intelligent, non-violent applicants for such a dangerous job? The hiring system is frequently a failure because the job is so unattractive. When shortages occur, guards might be recruited from the street in towns nearest the prison—without job references or aptitude checks. The recruits are often friends with prisoners, so smuggle in cigarettes, alcohol, drugs and weapons. One book that can help journalists figure out standards is the career guide "Correction Officer" by E.P. Steinberg.

Although prisons keep records on inmates, those records are usually denied to journalists on grounds of personal privacy and administrative efficiency. An inside source is usually necessary. That source can be an inmate, except that inmates cooperating with journalists often suffer unpleasantness from guards, administrators and sometimes fellow prisoners when the journalists are gone.

Jessica Mitford depended on information from prisoners for her book "Kind and Usual Punishment: The Prison Business." In the book's acknowledgments, she mentions

> over a hundred prisoners in penitentiaries across the country, who, at great risk and cost to themselves, have corresponded with me for the past three years, furnishing information I could not possibly have obtained otherwise. . . . Taken together, their letters convey as nothing else could the quality of prison life. . . .
>
> Some are intellectual treatises on the criminal justice system, some are factual descriptions of prison routines and procedures, some are full of despair, others witty or sardonic. . . . There is something deeply disquieting about corresponding with people behind bars. . . . One knows that each letter is scrutinized by the prison censor, possibly Xeroxed and put in the prisoner's file for the attention of the parole board, and that as a consequence of making injudicious observations about prison conditions the writer may well find himself . . . in deep trouble with the authorities, even risking extra months or years of confinement.
>
> Frequently my answers would be returned with the malevolent words "Refused by the Censor" stamped on the envelope. I found this totally infuriating, for my correspondent would likely have assumed I had not bothered to answer. There was nothing I could do to correct this impression. There is no recourse from prison censorship, no way of communicating with those inside once the authorities have decided not to permit it.

Are prisoners being treated in accordance with their constitutional rights? To find out, journalists should examine prison complaint files, interview recently released prisoners, plus check lawsuits filed by prisoners in federal and state courts. In many such lawsuits, the plaintiffs represent themselves (pro se is the legal term), using law books in the prison library for reference. Journalists should find out whether pro se cases are treated seriously. If not, the situation needs exposing.

One common rights violation is prison rape. Journalists' naivete and the sensibilities of audience members combine to keep prison rape out of the news, but it happens almost every day in almost every penal institution. Many prisoners, prone to violence anyway, are at the height of their sexual prowess. Having no normal outlet for their desire or need to control, they rape new inmates, often on the first night of incarceration. The inmates who cannot or will not fight back become sex slaves for years on end. The ones who do fight back end up in solitary confinement or with longer prison sentences, unless guards look the other way. Because the most violent inmates tend to be the "owners" of sex slaves, the theory is that the domination keeps aggressiveness in check. That aggressiveness might otherwise be aimed at guards.

Loretta Tofani of the Washington Post was covering a suburban courthouse when she wandered into a sentencing proceeding. She heard a lawyer say a prisoner had been gang-raped in the county jail. The lawyer's statement piqued Tofani's curiosity. The result, months later, was a three-part series.

"People have had the idea that men rape other men in jail and in prison," Tofani wrote in the IRE Journal.

"But the idea—at least in my own mind—was an abstraction without factual basis and without names and faces. The series was an attempt to describe the problem and its consequences in human terms.

. . . I found that commonly held assumptions . . . had a shaky foundation. Before the jail rape series was published, for example, it was easy for people to be unconcerned . . . because they assumed that the victims were criminals. . . . But as I asked questions of guards and judges, I learned an amazing fact— many of the victims had not been convicted of any crime. When I looked up the victims' court records, I learned something even more astonishing—the charges against many of them were for nonviolent crimes like shoplifting and driving while intoxicated. And when I visited the victims, I found that many had jobs: cook, salesman, repairman, waiter, a student and an Air Force lieutenant.

. . . The series reported that the rapes and sexual assaults occurred about a dozen times a week in the jail, according to guards, inmates and jail medical workers. . . . Most of the rapists had been in prison for years; they were in the county jail awaiting trial for violent crimes like armed robbery and murder. The jail guards . . . were unable, or unwilling, to stop the rapes, even when they were aware that rapes were occurring."

To locate jail guards, Tofani obtained names and addresses from sheriff's deputies who transported prisoners, court depositions in lawsuits filed by rape victims and an internal jail personnel list supplied by a friendly source.

Victims' names came from lawsuits when available. After that, Tofani cultivated jail medical workers, whose names she got from guards. When Tofani called on the medical workers at home, they refused to talk. "I kept going back to those houses, each time with a slightly different pitch. Eventually the door slammers turned into my most valuable sources. . . . The reason medical workers risked their jobs and decided to help me mainly was because they were troubled about the rapes. And they began to believe that a newspaper story might help change things." Tofani next convinced victims and rapists to talk, most of them on the record, proof that investigators should never assume a potential source will say no. Perhaps even more shocking is the number of suspects who die in local jails before being convicted or even formally charged. Mike Masterson documented the phenomenon in an Asbury Park (N.J.) Press series, "Dying in Custody." Some of the deaths had been falsely reported as suicides, Masterson's research suggested. As for the actual suicides, they raised questions about lack of supervision. After learning of jail deaths, journalists should ask whether guards, police or other prisoners are ever punished.

Another key question about prisons: Is anybody being rehabilitated? Journalists should inquire about in-prison educational programs, including those that could lead to a high-school diploma or a college degree; facilities for physical conditioning; spiritual guidance no matter what the choice of religion; psychological counseling for habitual sex offenders; treatment to alleviate drug addictions and control alcoholism; and vocational training, including help with job placement. If programs are operating, what follow-up do prison officials practice after release to determine whether the former convict has gone straight?

There is reason for skepticism when it comes to schooling, as suggested by the title of a book that Miriam Williford edited, "Higher Education in Prison: A Contradiction in Terms?" There is also reason for skepticism when it comes to health care. Investigation after investigation has shown needless deaths related to prison health care.

Results of one of the most compelling investigations appeared in the Dallas Morning News, which found the federal prison system to be a haven "for doctors of dangerous backgrounds, foreign doctors who had trouble with English and doctors too inexperienced or untrained to perform the tasks demanded of them." State prisons and local jails are often just as grim. A KPRC-TV team uncovered at least seven deaths in Houston's Harris County Jail that probably would have been prevented if the doctor-patient ratio had been better than one to 4,000.

When prisoners are healthy, are they being prepared for a productive life after release? Are prison industries training grounds, or slave-labor factories that profit the state? Furloughs and work-release programs are in principle humane and wise. But enterprising journalists will look behind the high-sounding motives to learn whether the programs succeed in rehabilitation and eventual job placement. That is especially relevant now that more prisons are charging inmates a daily fee for cell and board, a fee due soon after release if it is not paid during incarceration. Have local businesses actually hired ex-convicts? Does the chamber of commerce do anything to promote such hiring? Do government agencies reward businesses doing the hiring with tax breaks or work contracts?

Then there are the convicted criminals on the streets because of court-ordered releases due to prison overcrowding. Part of the story is why legislators and bureaucrats underestimated the need for prison cells so that dangerous criminals ended up back in the community. The numbers are staggering. One in every 35 adult white males, one in every nine adult black males and one in every four black males between ages 18 and 30 are incarcerated, paroled or on probation. In some states, corrections expenditures are the largest item in the budget.

Another part of the story is how judicial intervention led to overcrowding-related releases. As scholar John J. DiIulio Jr. notes, "In 1970, not a single prison system was operating under judicial orders to change and improve; today, [dozens] . . . operate under such orders. . . . For every instance where a judge's involvement led to a clear improvement in conditions, there is one where it clearly made things worse."

Although many citizens understandably oppose releases, the reality of prison overcrowding is grim. Journalists can do a better job of showing that reality by describing the conversion of prison athletic fields and libraries into unventilated sleeping quarters, the mixing of violent criminals with relative innocents, the spread of tuberculosis and AIDS among those incarcerated.

At the other end of the spectrum, some prisoners serve full terms while those in seemingly similar situations win release. Journalists who delve into the cases of the longest servers at the least end up with human-interest features. Too often, the story involves unequal treatment based on skin color or some other illegal factor.

Not all prison stories involve persons behind bars. For prisoners with families on the outside, do programs exist encouraging everybody to remain a unit during the incarceration? When spouses, children and other relatives visit, is there a private area to promote a constructive afternoon?

Journalists can get an overview of federal institutions by studying publications from the Bureau of Prisons, part of the U.S. Justice Department, for example, "Commitments and Discharges for the Month." Like other agencies, the bureau issues an annual report and a personnel directory. State prison agencies usually produce similar publications, annual reports and directories.

The National Prison Project, part of the American Civil Liberties Union Foundation, Washington, D.C., is a private organization interested in individual prisoners' rights and overall conditions. The organization has filed class-action suits on behalf of prisoners. Like all lawsuits, they can yield information that it would take journalists months to pull together on their own. The American Correctional Association, in Laurel, Md., speaks for prison administrators and staff. Like many professional groups, it has a library that can provide one-stop information gathering for journalists.

Some of the best books are "The Hot House: Life Inside Leavenworth Prison" by Pete Earley; "A Time to Die: The Attica Prison Revolt" by Tom Wicker; and the works of John J. DiIulio Jr. including "No Escape: The Future of American Corrections," "Governing Prisons" and "Courts, Corrections and the Constitution."

Writings of prisoners, especially those working on their institutions' newspapers, can inform projects. "Life Sentences: Rage and Survival Behind Bars" by Wilbert Rideau and Ron Wikberg collects pieces by two convict journalists incarcerated in the Louisiana state penitentiary.

Juvenile Cases

When an accused criminal is tried as a juvenile, the rules are different. The case is normally heard in a separate court with no constitutional right to bail, a jury trial or a public proceeding. The standard of proof is less rigid than "beyond a reasonable doubt." Those traditions might make it seem as if the system is stacked against youthful offenders, but in fact the opposite is true. Too often youthful offenders are dealt with so leniently that they go free, while society is terrorized.

Juvenile court judges are supposed to emphasize rehabilitation, not punishment. Does rehabilitation work? Rita Kramer's book "At a Tender Age: Violent Youth and Juvenile Justice" is pessimistic: "The obsolescent philosophy . . . gives far more emphasis to their youth than to their crimes." Kramer found the system worked sometimes when dealing with delinquents who had stolen hubcaps. But it failed when dealing with youthful murderers and rapists. The laxness "makes the courts a . . . sanctuary for the most vicious among the criminal young while paradoxically it fails . . . to reach . . . those who might be deterred from a life of crime."

Mark D. Jacobs' book "Screwing the System and Making It Work: Juvenile Justice in the No-Fault Society" reaches some of the same conclusions. A more narrowly focused book is Barry C. Feld's "Justice for Children: The Right to Counsel and the Juvenile Courts."

Peter Reinharz, chief prosecutor in New York City's family courts, says the juvenile justice system is at odds with common sense. Not even Reinharz or the judges who hear his cases know about the criminal history of youthful offenders; knowing that a 15-year-old murderer has been arrested previously for gun offenses would supposedly prejudice the prosecution and the judge against the youth. As a result, what is a second or fifth or tenth violent offense might be treated as a first offense.

Reinharz, writing for the Wall Street Journal's "Rule of Law" column, also marveled at the stupidity of making it illegal to fingerprint juveniles and nearly impossible to obtain a search warrant in juvenile cases and of forcing speedy trials despite the youthful suspect's lack of cooperation. Normally a suspect must be tried within 90 days of arrest. If an adult suspect fails to appear for a hearing, the time it takes to track the suspect down is not counted against the 90-day total. But in juvenile court, there is no such policy: "If a juvenile does not appear, the prosecution must demonstrate sufficient efforts to bring the absconder to court. If the court is not satisfied by these attempts, the case is dismissed. In effect, juveniles are rewarded for flouting the court." Journalists should inquire whether judges bring parents into the courtroom in an attempt to involve them in their childrens' lives. Does the court have flexible hours to deal with weekend and night-time transgressions? Do court officials work with school officials to seek classroom solutions rather than allowing dropouts to remain dropouts? Perspective is available from the National Council of Juvenile and Family Court Judges, in Reno, Nev., and the National Center for Juvenile Justice, in Pittsburgh, Pa.

No matter what sources a journalist consults, investigating the system will be an arduous task as long as police and court records about juveniles are closed to the media on the theory that youngsters in trouble have enough problems without adding public exposure. The exceptions to closure occur in one of two ways:

1. A judge allows access to files and hearings if the reporter agrees to withhold identification of the youth.

2. A judge rules that the youth should be tried as an adult.

Investigators unable to pierce the juvenile court's secrecy can find other sources, including juvenile divisions of police departments; domestic-abuse divisions within prosecutors' offices; local and state social service departments; officials of juvenile institutions; attorneys in private practice or part of a public defender's office; and child advocacy groups.

David Jackson of the Chicago Tribune spent years building trust through his reporting on juvenile justice. When he wanted records of individual cases to write a major series, the lawsuit he had to file was strengthened by the evidence of his performance. Jackson largely prevailed. He then built on the files released to him by obtaining permission from parents to view further documents about their children. The "Authorization to Release Information," on his newsroom's stationery, said:

I, _____ , give my consent to . . . the Illinois Department of Children and Family Services to release all . . . records pertaining to the care of my daughter, _____ , to David Jackson, a reporter for the Chicago Tribune. I further give permission for . . . staff members of DCFS to speak with Mr. Jackson about records and care. This authorization will be valid for 12 months from the date of signing and limited only to the information that I have requested be released to the Chicago Tribune. I understand I have the right to revoke this consent at any time.

The Indianapolis Star gained enough access into the local system to determine nearly 70 percent of the youths arrested in that city were repeat offenders. The Columbus Dispatch began a series on juvenile jails like this: "The deception begins with the name—Department of Youth Services. This state agency also calls a century-old prison a village; an eleven-by-seven cell is part of a cottage; guards are youth leaders; and a child handcuffed to a bed is being rehabilitated."

To obtain an overview of detention facilities, journalists can consult resources at the U.S. Justice Department and the American Correctional Association, in Laurel, Md. After learning the norms, journalists should observe juvenile detention programs firsthand, asking such questions as the length of time between arrest and disposition. If the interval is long, will youths fully understand the relationship between cause and effect? Are offenders of similar status placed together, or are 15-year-old murderers mixing with shoplifters? Are offenders under any court-imposed obligation to make restitution to victims? What are the qualifications of staff: Who would want such dangerous work at such low pay? The night and weekend staffs should receive extra-careful scrutiny; they are usually less well-trained than the weekday/daytime staff.

How much time do juveniles spend watching television, playing ping pong and standing in line for meals? Are the detained juveniles given the opportunity to complete courses toward a high-school diploma or college degree? If so, who are the teachers—those who received rejections from the public schools? Is there a meaningful effort to provide vocational education? How many youths die in custody by committing suicide, from inadequate health care, or at the hands of another inmate? Even when death is prevented, the reality almost always falls short of the promises. The official state manual for Missouri, under Division of Children and Youth Services, makes supervision of juvenile criminals sound ideal. The book "Reforming Juvenile Detention: No More Hidden Closets," edited by Ira M. Schwartz and William H. Barton, provides useful perspectives.

Closely related to juvenile court is family court, which handles cases of child and spousal neglect and abuse. Family court, called domestic relations court in some jurisdictions, is designed to follow a family for many years. That way, the judge can make decisions based on an understanding of the family history. The judge is frequently heavily dependent upon court-appointed investigators or private lawyers serving as guardians ad litem in cases involving termination of biological parents' rights through foster care and adoption. The Boston Globe magazine exposed greedy and incompetent investigators and guardians ad litem who hurried their cases to get paid more quickly, gave credence to unreliable hearsay and generally acted in ways that failed to place children's interests first. When lawyers served as guardians ad litem, they rarely had training in mental-health evaluation; however, when mental health professionals accept the assignment, they often are baffled by the workings of the legal system. There is frequent confusion over whether the main client is supposed to be the child, the biological family, the foster or adoptive family or the judge who does the hiring.

But as the IRE Resource Center demonstrates, family court has not been a panacea. Any journalist observing the parade of cases for a day can see that. Delays are common, recidivism prevails, judges make snap decisions without adequate information. Poor handling of child abuse cases is, sadly, common—first by executive branch social welfare agencies, later by courts—sometimes with fatal consequences. Family court has also failed to significantly reduce problems between spouses over timely child support payments. Courts have restricted enforcement powers. Unless prosecutors and social welfare agencies decide to make child support enforcement a priority through wage garnishment or incarceration, offending parents get away with their crime. Some custodial parents hire private bounty hunter companies to squeeze child support payments from current or former spouses who are violating court orders. If the private firms locate the offenders and secure payment, a flat fee or percentage of the payment constitutes the bounty. If offenders refuse to pay, the private company will turn over the case to a local prosecutor, then hope for legal action to commence.

Civil Cases

Unlike criminal cases, civil lawsuits are sometimes frivolous or uninteresting. Those cases ought to remain unreported by journalists. But many civil cases are important and interesting. They would be good daily stories as well as the impetus for investigative projects—if only journalists read them.

The sad truth is that most lawsuits are never read by journalists. Writing in Media Studies Journal, journalist/lawyer Peter A. Levin called for more attention to civil cases:

> While criminal cases received heavy coverage, I would venture to say that important cases on employment discrimination, sexual harassment, product liability, surrogate parents, right to die, prayer in schools, abortion and prison overcrowding—civil cases all—were being ignored.

Investigators needing further inspiration can turn to any of the major legal publications—American Lawyer, National Law Journal, Legal Times and the Journal of the American Bar Association—to find compelling stories based on civil cases. Some of the best pieces from American Lawyer are collected in a book, "Trial by Jury," edited by Steven Brill. Numerous other books are chronicles of one civil case. They include "Simple Justice" by Richard Kluger; "Roe v. Wade" by Marian Faux; "A Conflict of Rights" by Melvin I. Urofsky; and "Coals of Fire" by Thomas B. Littlewood.

Civil case files can be obtained from the court clerk, the lawyers or the plaintiffs and defendants. The paper trails are a journalist's dream; they are usually much more extensive than in criminal cases.

The docket sheet is the best place to begin. It includes all actions of the court, listed chronologically. A complaint, also called a petition, is the first document filed. Journalists should try to determine whether the complaint contains beliefs fervently held by the plaintiff, or whether it stems mostly from the initiative of a lawyer looking to generate income. If the plaintiff's lawyer is handling the case on a contingency fee basis, that means the lawyer is paid only if the plaintiff wins. Plaintiffs who could never afford a lawyer otherwise sometimes benefit from the contingency fee tradition. On the other hand, plaintiffs' lawyers accepting contingency cases are loathe to settle before trial if they think a larger award might be in the offing. If the lawyer guesses wrong, the client suffers, too.

Common early motions include those seeking dismissal before trial (summary judgment), alleging factual deficiencies, suggesting the plaintiff has no standing to sue at all or at least not in that locale and asking the court to reject evidence.

Each side learns about the other side's case through a process called "discovery." Intraoffice and interoffice memoranda, in hard copy or on computer disks, are fair game; discovery materials are not subject to the restrictive rules of relevance and admissibility. Discovery materials might also include depositions, which are sworn oral statements in question-and-answer format from a witness, taken before trial.

Sometimes settlement talks occur as part of the court proceeding; in other cases, the parties seek extra-legal help through arbitration, mediation or some different form of alternative dispute resolution. Journalists should inquire of local sources whether significant cases are going through arbitration and mediation outside the regular court system. Some judges are leaving the bench to join private mediation/arbitration companies at salaries higher than what the government pays. The not-for-profit American Arbitration Association, New York City, is the largest alternative to the courts; it now has competition from profit-making private corporations. If the best judges leave government service, that could cause trouble for quality justice. Another downside of the private system is unreported decisions and secret resolutions on matters of public importance. The Center for Dispute Resolution at the University of Missouri Law School can provide perspective, as can the National Institute for Dispute Resolution, Washington, D.C., the Dispute Resolution section of the American Bar Association and Martindale Hubbell's "Dispute Resolution Directory" with state-by-state listings.

Occasionally civil cases are filed as class-actions, involving hundreds or thousands of plaintiffs who claim to have been wronged in the same ways by the same parties. Class actions might be more lucrative for the lawyers than for those allegedly injured after the award, if any, is split into many small pieces. Thomas A. Dickerson's "Class Actions: The Law of 50 States" provides an overview.

Class actions are often aimed at major corporations, which in turn move to seal documents the disclosure of which might damage their image or business. Washington Post reporters found judges routinely granting confidentiality requests, also called protective orders. Such orders turn the public courts into bastions of private justice, limiting awareness of dangers ranging from unsafe fuel tanks to incompetent doctors.

Specialized Courts

Besides criminal courts, juvenile courts and general civil courts, there are others to investigate: local traffic, municipal, divorce, probate, and small claims courts, plus federal claims, military, tax and bankruptcy courts.

Traffic Court

St. Louis Globe-Democrat reporter Richard Krantz suspected something was awry at traffic court. He was right, as eventually he documented that an estimated $1 million yearly was being pocketed by court officials.

The key to the exposé was understanding the process, then watching closely. Krantz sat in court writing the name of every defendant called, who appeared, who did not and the disposition of each case. He then went to the clerk's office to compare what he had seen with what the records showed.

Krantz discovered case after case in which he knew defendants had failed to appear in court—but the file said the defendant had appeared and been given a sentence in which no money was paid. Krantz called the no-show defendants at home. From them, he heard the same illegal scheme described over and over: The defendant received a traffic ticket. On the court date, the defendant was approached in a hallway by a bail bondsperson or court clerk who offered to pay the ticket, thus saving the defendant hours of waiting. The defendant would be ushered inside the courtroom, pay a fine—for example, $20 for running a red light—then go home. But the money never reached the city treasury. In San Antonio, one traffic court judge became so disgusted at the extensive ticket-fixing that he supplied incriminating documents to a San Antonio Light reporter. He supplemented the leaks with an analysis of a computer tape showing all tickets and dispositions. Discretionary dismissals by judges showed up quickly.

Fixed traffic tickets cost taxpayers revenue, but are not life-threatening. Fixed drunk-driving cases, though, might end up as life-threatening. Many judges and prosecutors treat drunk driving with less seriousness than they do drug cases, even though alcohol can be just as lethal. Certain defense attorneys specialize in exploiting loopholes in drunk-driving laws on behalf of dangerous clients.

The IRE Resource Center contains investigations of drunk driving enforcement. The Albuquerque Tribune showed bonds were set too low to provide a deterrent. One of every four cases wound up being dismissed. Cases that led to a conviction yielded an average fine of $17. The few cases leading to jail terms averaged sentences of one week. Well-intentioned judges sentencing drunk drivers to counseling had no idea of the programs' ineffectiveness. Some drivers appearing in court had been there at least 20 times previously.

The Corpus Christi Caller-Times found that the courts were failing to tell the Texas Department of Public Safety about convictions, even though state law required notification. When courts revoked licenses, drivers operated without them, hoping police would fail to apprehend them. WTSP-TV, St. Petersburg, used surveillance to show persons with revoked licenses driving at will.

Municipal Court

In some jurisdictions, traffic cases are heard separately, as are other specific types of cases, those involving landlord-tenant disputes, for example. Many jurisdictions, however, mix all sorts of cases in municipal court. Because they are limited to violations of local ordinances, with the punishment minimal, it would seem an unlikely place for major injustices to occur. They occur anyway. For example, the Milwaukee Journal found poor people in jail, often without hearings, because they were unable to pay fines for jaywalking and disorderly conduct.

Divorce Court

Divorce files can yield details about individuals embroiled in the fallout from the marriage. Even no-fault cases—only about 10 percent of divorces go to trial—while accompanied by thin files, might contain a useful nugget. In Walt Harrington's profile of a divorce lawyer for the Washington Post Magazine, the subject says she never tires of her career: "It is like a soap opera."

Divorce court should be scrutinized as a system, an approach few journalists take. Domestic relations cases account for about one-third of all civil filings in state courts. The growth makes scrutiny more important than ever: Are the judges fair, considerate and well-schooled in the law? Does one gender or the other seem to suffer inordinately because of a particular judge's rulings? Are children given short shrift in custody or alimony proceedings? Is there a state law concerning levels of child support based on net income of the parent? If so, are judges allowed to vary from the formula by filing an explanation for the divergence? If not, how wildly do awards vary in similar cases? What happens if grandparents want visitation or custody?

Is mediation required in custody cases in an attempt to reduce destructive tensions? The Academy of Family Mediators, in Eugene, Ore., can provide perspective. When property disputes are involved, is all property fair game or only property acquired during the marriage? What about the house? What if one spouse is left without health insurance— will the court intervene? What about division of debts?

An investigation of divorce court in Chicago magazine emphasized the arbitrariness of the judges. Experienced divorce lawyers agreed with one who said "I could argue the same case before five different judges and get five different decisions." The arbitrariness was aggravated by the court's being a dumping ground for the least experienced judges or those veterans unable to secure an assignment to a more prestigious division.

Reporter Penelope Mesic added, "What is scariest . . . is the seemingly absolute powers of the judge in this area of law. He or she can inquire into your sex life, freeze your bank account, have you evaluated by a psychiatrist, order you to sell your house or forbid you to see your children." Those coming to court were not allowed to avoid judges known to be incompetent or hostile; cases were assigned randomly by computer.

The New York City Department of Consumer Affairs produced a report focusing on questionable conduct of divorce lawyers, especially those representing the poorer of the parties, which usually means the woman. The report found lawyers demanding huge sums of money on the brink of the trial or settlement; failing to refund retainer fees despite having done little work; charging unreasonably large fees; refusing to return files and personal papers; abandoning clients when their money runs out and filing excessive motions to pad billable hours. Some lawyers representing males understated or hid assets, which ought to be punishable as perjury. The Charlotte Observer, after analyzing hundreds of divorce cases with property at issue, concluded that the wealthier spouse sometimes dragged out the proceedings for years as the other party scrimped and sometimes approached grinding poverty.

Background can be found in the book "Unequal Protection: Women, Children and the Elderly in Court" by Judge Lois Forer and from the Family Law section of the American Bar Association.

Probate Court

When wealthy or controversial people die, experienced journalists make sure to check probate court (called surrogate's court or perhaps some other name in certain jurisdictions). If the deceased left a will that has been filed with the court, it is normally a matter of public record. If the deceased died without a will, the heirs might be fighting, and the dispute might spill over into court.

Lawyers named to handle the estate, either by the deceased before dying or by a probate judge after death, can walk away with huge fees for little effort. With the client dead, the beneficiaries distracted by grief and often unschooled in the ways of probate, there may be nobody to protest legal looting of the estate. Journalists need to learn whether the state regulates fees by law, or whether probate fees are privately negotiated case by case.

Probating a will is usually a simple job, which involves gathering assets of the deceased, paying bills (including taxes owed), investing the remaining assets temporarily, then paying those assets (plus money earned while invested) according to the will as validated by a probate court judge. Journalists need to be alert for cozy arrangements between probate lawyers and judges that enrich one or both while cheating the estate. The Houston Chronicle found just such a situation in local probate court.

Public administrators—sometimes elected, sometimes appointed by probate judges—are supposed to safeguard the assets of persons believed to be mentally incompetent. But unless judges supervise public administrators, the property of the incompetent is sometimes wrongly appropriated. WGN-TV, Chicago, found a public administrator making about $500,000 annually for doing almost no work. Secret buyers snatched up real estate offered by the public administrator at bargain prices; judges failed to keep track of how the public administrator disposed of personal belongings.

Paul Rubin of New Times, a Phoenix alternative weekly, uncovered what he called

> a pattern of abuse inside Maricopa County Probate Court that cost elderly victims and their heirs hundreds of thousands of dollars. County judges and commissioners rubber-stamped excessive fees and new wills that routinely meant more money for a prominent attorney and his private fiduciary. The probate court exercised little control over private fiduciaries, appointed by judges as guardian-conservators for elderly, incapacitated clients.

Legal notices in local newspapers can help investigators keep up with estates about to be probated. When a famous or powerful person dies, reporters ought to check with the probate court automatically. After FBI director J. Edgar Hoover's death, his will shed light on his relationship with FBI official Clyde Tolson. Rumors about a possible homosexual relationship between them had circulated for decades, a rumor made important because of Hoover's gay-bashing while the most visible law enforcement officer in the world. Hoover's will provided proof of a close personal relationship with Tolson. Journalists James P. Cole and Charles C. Thompson explained in the IRE Journal how a $142 bill filed by a Memphis pharmacy in probate court against Elvis Presley's estate helped them prove the rock star died after mixing various drugs.

It is worth checking whether many families, especially wealthy ones, bend the law to avoid probate. They might be motivated by how long probate takes, a desire to keep details of their estate from the media or by fees that must be paid to the court, lawyers and appraisers. Some persons use their wills to set up trusts before dying. After the will enters probate court, the terms of the trust can be protected from the scrutiny of journalists and other curious members of the public. The Real Property, Probate and Trust Law section of the American Bar Association can provide perspective.

Small Claims Court

Disputes in this court involve so little money that investigators tend to overlook it. That is a mistake. Many of the disputes are interesting; some involve influential citizens. It is traditional to enter the court without a lawyer; how disputants fare on their own—and how they are treated by the judge—can be a story in itself. Paperwork is minimal; rules are streamlined. Judges rule on the spot. There are no juries.

Journalists looking into the court's performance should determine whether winners are able to collect their judgments. If difficulty occurs, does the judge or court clerk help? Do losers frequently appeal, thereby defeating the purpose of the court as a place for quick resolution of small disputes? How long do appeals take to be decided? "Everybody's Guide to Small Claims Court" from Nolo Press, Berkeley, Calif., can provide perspective.

Even when a journalist has no interest in a small-claims case, the court should be a place to check to establish a relationship between two parties or learn about the holdings of a subject under investigation.

U.S. Claims Court

Individuals and institutions who believe they have been wronged by the federal government sometimes end up in this court, which is almost completely ignored by journalists. Many of the cases involve huge contractors—each a major employer somewhere—battling the government over sums that run into hundreds of millions of dollars. Judges appointed for life hear cases in Washington, D.C. They issue rulings available at the court, in law libraries, by subscription from private publishers or from online commercial computer databases.

U.S. Tax Court

Tens of thousands of cases are filed annually in this court. Most involve income tax disputes, but the court also deals with estate, gift, excise, pension plan and Individual Retirement Account tax cases. Journalists should always check tax court when backgrounding individuals and corporations.

All cases involve the Internal Revenue Service on one side and an individual or corporate taxpayer on the other side. Each case began with a notice of taxes owed from the IRS and a decision by the taxpayer to dispute the assessment. Taxpayers who decide to pay the disputed amount and then contest it end up in a U.S. District Court. Their motive for paying first is avoiding penalties if they eventually lose. In a recent year, 2,296 tax cases were filed in U.S. District Court, while nearly 15 times that many were filed in tax court. About 90 percent of tax court cases end in pretrial settlements, sometimes instituted by the IRS under a procedure called "offers in compromise." Investigators should question whether settlements let off wealthy taxpayers too easily. When cases go to trial, the IRS tends to prevail.

U.S. Tax Court consists of judges sitting in Washington, D.C., and hearing cases in other locales. They are suggested by the Treasury secretary, appointed by the president, evaluated by the American Bar Association and confirmed by the Senate (the Finance Committee rather than the Judiciary Committee) for 15-year terms. Associate judges hear smaller cases, involving amounts of less than $10,000. To help with the case load, the chief judge can appoint retirees as senior judges. There are no jury trials.

Filings, including normally confidential tax returns, and final decisions are available by visiting the court. Decisions are also available in law libraries and online. Commerce Clearing House's Tax Court Reporter is a private service updating filings weekly. The "Tax Report" on page one of the Wednesday Wall Street Journal contains briefs based on U.S. Tax Court decisions. The Taxation section of the American Bar Association can provide perspective.

U.S. Bankruptcy Court

Bankruptcies filed by individuals or corporations provide detailed information about the party in question. Journalists should check for bankruptcies in the past of any subject. They will walk away with the subject's Social Security number, bank accounts, landholdings, personal property (such as jewelry), stocks, bonds and income.

The most significant story is usually how an individual or business wound up bankrupt. Fraud is often a factor. Creditors, while biased sources, are often cooperative. Because they are usually innocent victims, they and their lawyers are enraged. One way to meet creditors, or at least their lawyers, is to attend a creditors' meeting. While listening to creditors' gripes, journalists should examine whether they contributed to the problem by making it too easy to borrow money. Credit card companies, for example, complain about being stiffed because of bankruptcy laws coddling debtors. But those same credit card companies solicit former bankrupts. Rick Desloge of the St. Louis Business Journal suggests concentrating on unsecured creditors, those in the last group to receive payment—office supply and photocopier companies are often among them.

Desloge has used bankruptcy court files in imaginative ways. After the arrest of a fugitive St. Louis business executive, Desloge found a document in bankruptcy court showing the executive's children rented a truck before the capture. They used the truck to remove property from the South Carolina apartment where the arrest eventually occurred, indicating that the businessman suspected law enforcement agencies were closing in. As a result of that suspicion, he was able to hide valuable property before apprehension. Another bankruptcy document showed the businessman writing checks worth $330,000 to his son during a three-month period.

The court itself needs scrutiny, too. Is the judge allowing a corporation to hide behind Chapter 11 of the bankruptcy code to keep creditors—some of them in dire need of payment—at bay while the company continues its profligate ways? Others needing scrutiny are lawyers supposedly supervising the bankrupt. The Indianapolis Star found cronyism and payoffs surrounding appointments of supervising lawyers by judges; unethical private contacts between lawyers and judges; and lax oversight of bankrupt firms, as assets that should have been used for creditors dissipated.

Wall Street Journal reporter John R. Emshwiller wrote about a Philadelphia lawyer who was

> a federal bankruptcy court trustee, in charge of millions of dollars of debtors' assets. He was also a crook. . . . [He] pleaded guilty to multiple counts of embezzlement, bankruptcy fraud and money laundering in connection with stealing more than $2 million from eight bankrupt small businesses that were in his charge. . . . In the past six years, about 40 bankruptcy trustees, attorneys or their employees have been convicted of stealing money from debtor accounts. Federal regulators have also gone after dozens of other court officials civilly for alleged misconduct ranging from conflicts of interest to mishandling of funds.

One source on fraud is the executive office of the U.S. Trustee, an arm of the U.S. Justice Department. That office is supposed to assure the creditors are fairly represented as the case moves through the courts.

Some Chapter 11 filings come from solvent corporations seeking the court's protection from product-liability or environmental claims. If a company is worried about having to pay millions of dollars because of a defective birth control device or harm to citizens from asbestos in buildings, it will ask a bankruptcy judge to limit or delay the claims. Other companies want to break a union contract or escape pension obligations.

Not all questionable filings involve corporations. WJXT-TV, Jacksonville, demonstrated how individuals retained lavish homes and lifestyles while refusing to pay creditors. Each state has its own rules on what assets a debtor can shield from creditors. Journalists should check to see whether the bankrupt, using either federal law or state law, has avoided paying tax claims, student loans, child support or alimony.

To school themselves, journalists can consult do-it-yourself books such as "How to File for Bankruptcy" by Stephen Elias, Albin Renauer and Robin Leonard. The Practicing Law Institute, New York City, commissioned Bankruptcy Judge William C. Hillman to write "Personal Bankruptcy: What Every Debtor and Creditor Needs to Know." Many such books reprint bankruptcy court forms, alerting journalists to what they will find in the files.

The Administrative Office of the U.S. Courts publishes overviews of bankruptcy proceedings. The Bankruptcy Law Reporter, from the Bureau of National Affairs, Washington, D.C., is a useful resource. The American Bankruptcy Institute, Washington, D.C., can help provide perspective.

U.S. Military Courts

Cases involving the military services have special relevance to journalists covering local bases and the Pentagon. For journalists working far away from bases and Washington, D.C., at least a few cases in the military courts will have relevance, if for no other reason than that they involve people with roots in the community. The Dallas Morning News studied hundreds of cases. The conclusions, as stated on an IRE contest entry:

> The U.S. military disregards its own laws to convict service members of crimes—and sends a disproportionate number of minorities to its toughest prison. The investigation uncovered cases in which commanders intimidated witnesses or stacked courts-martial panels with conviction-prone officers. Defendants are convicted with evidence that experts say would never stand up in a civilian court.

The Journal of the American Bar Association explained the military justice system in an exposé of a military lawyer who had falsified his legal credentials.

A general court-martial is akin to a felony trial in civilian courts. The judges are officers who are senior in rank to the defendant; nonofficer defendants can request enlisted service members to sit on the judges' panel. A special court-martial is convened for offenses that involve less incarceration than offenses brought to a general court-martial. A summary court-martial is for less serious offenses still. The U.S. Court of Appeals for the Armed Forces, Washington, D.C., with judges appointed by the president and confirmed by the Senate, handles cases involving dishonorable or bad conduct discharges, carrying more than a year of imprisonment.

Because the prosecutor, known as the Judge Advocate General, for each military service evaluates the judges, critics of the system say independence is compromised. John Murawski of Legal Times explained the controversy like this: "Imagine a court system where the judge owes his job—and his next assignment—to the office prosecuting the case." Journalists trying to determine if a military judge is sufficiently independent will have to examine rulings case by case.

Each service (Army, Air Force, Coast Guard and Navy-Marine Corps) has its own mechanism for handling first-level appeals, clemency and parole requests. The judges can be military officers or civilians. The Judge Advocates Association, Washington, D.C., can provide perspective.

Court Budgets, Court Operations

Courts spend taxpayers' money, much as legislatures and executive branch agencies do. Every court has a budget based on legislative appropriations, filing fees and fines collected.

State supreme courts supervise lower courts to some extent; most states also have an administrative agency to serve as a support arm for locally based courts. The National Center for State Courts, in Williamsburg, Va., provides useful overviews, as does the Institute for Court Management, in Denver.

The Bay Guardian of San Francisco exposed corruption and excessive spending at the Judicial Council, the administrative arm of California courts. The chief justice of the California Supreme Court allowed law firms and corporations to contribute money to the Judicial Council and to his travels around the world. Those same contributors were simultaneously appearing before the supreme court in a variety of disputes.

At the federal level, the Administrative Office of the U.S. Courts disseminates information. Like any bureaucracy, it sometimes withholds information, too. An investigation of the agency by Legal Times showed how researchers whose studies might reflect negatively on the judiciary had trouble obtaining information, and how efficient courts had been slowed down by the Administrative Office's failure to implement computerization of information effectively. The Federal Judicial Center is a related research agency, concentrating on computer systems, continuing education, litigation process, jury management, sentencing and probation.

The American Judicature Society, Chicago, is a broad-based court reform organization. It keeps files on judges who have been investigated and disciplined. Its magazine, Judicature, deals with problems in local, state and federal courts. It also publishes a number of specialized reports dealing with court issues.

Using Courts for Other Stories

It cannot be stressed enough: Court files provide a mountain of documents to use in stories that have nothing to do with the court system. One guide to finding the most appropriate court is the Directory of State and Federal Courts, Judges and Clerks, compiled by Kamla J. King and Judith Springberg along with the staff at the Bureau of National Affairs library, Washington, D.C.

As Jack Tobin wrote about court documents in an earlier edition of this book, wealthy, influential, reclusive Howard Hughes had no driver's license, never voted and owned almost nothing in his own name. But he was sued for slander by a former aide. The aide won at trial, lost on appeal, then settled out of court. "The real winners," Tobin said, "were all those who hungered for details of the life of the world's most famous recluse. The exhibits in the case filled a room. They amounted to millions of pages of testimony, depositions, accounting reports and tape-recorded conversations."

Any reporter studying an individual or corporation should check state and federal court cases. That used to be time-consuming and almost always frustrating. Court records were localized. In-person visits to hundreds or thousands of courthouses were necessary. Lexis, Westlaw and other computer databases—discussed more fully in chapters 1 and 2—have simplified searching.

Some on-line databases covering court cases are free; for instance, the Administrative Office of the U.S. Courts offers an online hook-up to the Public Access to Court Electronic Records (PACER) system, allowing journalists to search just-issued and older opinions from certain jurisdictions. The same office offers free remote access to the Bankruptcy Voice Case Information System.

When computer databases are impractical, there are numerous hardcopy resources at public libraries, law schools and law firms. The most common is the series of "Reporters" compiling decided cases from virtually every federal and state court. Some compilations are chronological—all the cases decided in 1993 and 1994, for example. Others are topical, organized by subject matter. For example, U.S. District Courts are covered by five chronological reporters (Federal Supplement, Federal Reporter Second Series, Federal Reporter, Federal Cases and Federal Rules Decisions), plus five topical reporters (West's Federal Practice Digest Third Series, West's Federal Practice Digest Second Series, Modern Federal Practice Digest, Federal Digest and Decennial Digests). State courts are covered by at least one state or regional reporter and one state or regional digest.

As already noted, some cases go unreported in those official and semiofficial volumes, mostly because courts write unpublished opinions to save money. More disturbing, some court rulings are later wiped off the books through a process known as "vacatur."

As explained by Eva M. Rodriguez in Legal Times, "The losers accomplish this [vacatur] by coming to terms with the winning party, paying a lucrative settlement and getting the other party to join in asking an appeals court to wipe out the lower-court ruling." She showed how frequently sued corporations worry about appealing after losing at the trial level. "The solution: Get rid of the original ruling and its nasty precedential value." Next time the defendants are in court, they can say precedent supports their side, when in fact precedent would look different without vacatur. An article in Business Week told of an entrepreneur who sued a large national corporation and felt optimistic about his chances after locating a newspaper article about a similar case that the company had lost. But when the entrepreneur sought the judge's opinion in that previous case, he learned that the national company had settled, then convinced the court, with the plaintiff's acquiescence, to wipe the opinion off the books. The article called the practice "precedent snuffing." Proponents, including the federal government, say the procedure promotes settlements, clearing overloaded court dockets. Opponents say the practice corrupts the system by allowing wealthy losers to excise rulings that could cause them to pay damages in future lawsuits.

When investigators want to search beyond the official, incomplete "reporters," they can seek out narrative publications. One—of hundreds that could be mentioned—is the United States Law Week: A National Survey of Current Law, from the Bureau of National Affairs, in Washington, D.C. While focusing on U.S. Supreme Court cases, it also summarizes rulings from other courts as well as executive branch agencies. Most states and some cities are served by legal newspapers that publish lists of case filings, accompanied by feature articles. Missouri Lawyers Weekly, of Jefferson City, is an example.

Truth is sometimes the first casualty in a legal system that is grounded in advocacy. It is up to journalists to arrive at the best approximation of truth when the judicial system does not.

Chapter 11

WHERE GOVERNMENT AND PRIVATE SECTOR MEET

Investigating Licensed Professionals

While K. Connie Kang was covering the legal beat for the San Francisco Examiner, she kept hearing about lawyers breaking rules set for the profession by the state Supreme Court. She decided to investigate systematically. Reporters James A. Finefrock and Alex Neill joined the project.

Following paper and people trails, the team pieced together "The Brotherhood: Justice for Lawyers." The series demonstrated that the state's lawyer discipline system was slow, lenient and secretive. Eleven lawyers lost their licenses in California, in the same year that nearly 9,000 complaints came to the attention of legal disciplinary organizations. Convicted felons continued to practice law without their clients knowing of problems. The reporters looked at 70 cases in detail, naming names, to illustrate the larger themes.

■ *Licensing as a Window Into the World of Professionals*

Licensed occupations are mentioned throughout this book. The most significant for journalists and their audiences are lawyers; police officers; accountants; teachers and other school personnel; real estate salespeople; insurance agents; stockbrokers; social workers; bus drivers, airplane pilots and other transportation carriers; undertakers; physicians, nurses, pharmacists and at least 30 other categories of health care workers.

This chapter will provide a systematic way to think about obtaining information from the licensing process. As with other chapters, it will also suggest investigations of the process itself and the players in it. Such investigations are too rare. Without seeming cynical, journalists should assume that licensing boards with the power to discipline are inclined to protect their own.

The truth of that is documented by Stanley J. Gross in his book "Of Foxes and Henhouses: Licensing and the Health Professions." Gross shows how licensing is weighted more toward limiting entry into the profession than toward protecting the public. By controlling the supply of professional services, licensing boards can enrich existing licensees by shutting off competition. Once an individual's license is granted, it is rarely suspended or revoked, even if the licensee fails to keep up with changes in the field. The Council on Licensure Enforcement and Regulation, Lexington, Ky., might be able to put individual cases into perspective.

■ *Uncovering Individual Fraud or Misconduct*

As Myrta Pulliam pointed out in her chapter on licensed professionals for an earlier edition of this book, cases of fraudulent credentials abound: "There are pharmacists who are not licensed or qualified dispensing drugs. Other people claim to be counselors, psychologists and psychiatrists and are not."

California Lawyer magazine unmasked a self-proclaimed lawyer. He fooled not only clients, but also six attorneys hired by him and who worked alongside him day after day. When the San Francisco Chronicle reprinted the article, its headline said: "Everyone thought Fred Sebastian was a do-gooder lawyer until he was arrested. Then they discovered he wasn't a lawyer. He wasn't even Fred Sebastian." Chapter 5 of this book discusses résumé fraud. Checking the résumé of a person in a licensed occupation will often uncover fraud. Checking the licensing agency should be part of the résumé verification.

Sometimes the fraud is legally sanctioned. The St. Petersburg Times produced a series, "Hiding the Past," in which it discovered licensed professionals who had used the courts to wipe out records of guilty pleas and convictions. The newspaper found these types of licensed professionals with sealed convictions: teachers, day care workers, bus drivers, child psychologists, physicians, nurses, pharmacists, veterinarians, lawyers, police officers, security guards and private detectives. They wrote stories about case after case, including a title company president who had a criminal record because of stealing $88,000 from customers' accounts. When she petitioned to have that felony erased from her record, a judge said yes. Two months later, she sought a state license to run a new title company. On her application, she said she had no felony record; the expungement law allowed her to do that. Knowing nothing about her record, Florida's insurance regulators granted her a license. When those regulators later learned the truth from the Times, they said they never would have issued the license if they had known.

Investigators must determine first if an occupation is licensed or otherwise regulated in a way that information on individuals will be accessible. Because most licensing is done by states, an investigator can begin with the official government manual. In Missouri's manual, the Department of Economic Development is the first stop. Within the department is the Division of Professional Regulation. It, in turn, oversees 27 boards that license or otherwise regulate about 250,000 individuals in specific occupations.

Although the boards under the Division of Professional Regulation are numerous, an investigator should not stop there. For instance, insurance agents do not show up in the 27 categories. Does that mean insurance agents are unlicensed? No. In Missouri and other states, insurance agents fall under the jurisdiction of an insurance department, often part of the governor's Cabinet. Lawyers are not mentioned in the 27 categories, either. That is because lawyers are licensed by their professional association, the Missouri Bar, under the general supervision of the state Supreme Court.

An examination of the Missouri government's official manual shows the Agriculture Department licensing pesticide dealers and applicators; the Health Department licensing bedding manufacturers, frozen dessert retailers, emergency medical technicians and paramedics; the Revenue Department licensing dealers and manufacturers of automobiles, motorcycles, boats and recreational vehicles. The secretary of state's office licenses notaries public. Because notaries are sometimes involved in fraud by placing their seal on documents they should have questioned, journalists should check whether notaries are ever disciplined. The American Society of Notaries, Washington, D.C., can provide perspective.

Studying the small print in the state manual yields details that lead to questions:

Every board consists of persons from the occupation being licensed—at most, there is one "public member" per board. Is this an example of the fox guarding the henhouse? How likely is it that a board dominated by accountants will discipline a colleague? What if they know each other—will any of the board members declare a conflict of interests? Is the public member truly independent, someone willing to blow the whistle if necessary?

Officially, appointments to the licensing boards are made by the governor with state Senate consent. What role is played by the professional association? Are the governor and Senate likely to name members disliked by association leaders? Does political affiliation or political philosophy play a role in what should be a nonpolitical activity?

Boards earn all or much of their operating budget through licensing and renewal fees. Does that encourage disciplinary laxness, because more licenses and renewals mean more revenue? Most of the boards are part of a national network. The Missouri State Board of Accountancy, for example, is a member of the National Association of State Boards of Accountancy. Journalists should inquire: Why not make licensing of occupations national, rather than state-by-state?

When a journalist determines an occupation is not licensed by a state government, other possibilities should be investigated. Maybe that occupation is licensed in other states. A sensible place to check is the local government (which often is the exclusive licensing body for taxi drivers, to take one example) or the federal government (the U.S. Securities and Exchange Commission, for example, concerning stockbrokers, investment advisors and other financial professionals, in conjunction with their professional organization, the National Association of Securities Dealers or the stock exchange where they do business).

Sometimes institutions are licensed (bars, for example) even when the owner is not. The application for a permit to operate the bar, granted by the local government, is likely to contain personal information about the owner. Another example: States license employment agencies, even though they do not license the owners. By requesting a blank licensing form from the Missouri board regulating employment agencies, I learned owners must supply a signed employment history.

The Process

Step One: Licensing

To be licensed, a professional must meet certain standards. These might cover age, citizenship, residency, level and type of education, examination scores, field experience and moral character. State or federal statutes or municipal ordinances set out the standards. For example, to find out what the state legislature requires of accountants in Missouri, an investigator can read Chapter 326 of the codified statutes.

The application form contains specific information. How much is publicly available varies from state to state, city to city and even profession to profession within the state or city. Some boards have automated call-in systems for verification of whether an individual holds a valid license. Some states have reciprocity agreements, allowing professionals to practice if they are licensed in another state with similar standards. In such cases, the investigator can look for public files in one state that are closed in the other. Assuming that certain occupations require licensing might be a mistake. Most states do not license income tax preparers; neither does the Internal Revenue Service. State accountancy licensing boards maintain lists of disciplinary actions, but the lists are often inaccessible to the general public—and many tax preparers are not accountants anyway. Using a variety of resources—lawsuits, professional networks, word of mouth, placing newspaper and magazine ads requesting horror stories—a journalist can piece together a list of dishonest or incompetent providers.

Step Two: Performance Standards

Having received a license, professionals must adhere to performance standards or face losing the license through suspension or revocation. Again, investigators should first turn to the statutes. Most often, grounds for license revocation or suspension fall into the following areas: felony conviction, obtaining fees by misrepresentation, drug or alcohol abuse, mental incompetence (as judged by a court), physical abuse of patients or other dishonorable or unethical conduct that harms the public.

For example, real estate brokers in some states can lose their licenses for employing unlicensed salespeople, issuing an appraisal report on real property in which they have an interest without disclosing that interest, or violating federal fair housing laws, civil rights laws or local ordinances of a similar nature.

Those within the occupation know performance standards. Often outside groups will contain sources every bit as knowledgeable. For example, the American Association of Retired Persons has an interest in monitoring funeral home operators. As a result, the association hires staff members who become experts about undertaker conduct and misconduct.

Step Three: Complaints and Investigations

A complaint, either by a fellow professional or a member of the public, usually initiates an investigation. In some states, licensing boards have the power to start an investigation on their own initiative.

For instance, the state association of engineers may investigate a member, submitting its findings to the licensing authority, state attorney general's office or local district attorney's office for action. An operating-room nurse might report a surgeon who is botching operations. A hospital administrator suspends a doctor's privileges, then notifies the licensing board, which opens its own inquiry.

Because most professionals protect colleagues rather than blow the whistle on each other, such instances are infrequent. Journalists should ask professional associations (for example, the county medical association) and related institutions (such as hospitals) for examples of internal whistleblowing in the public interest. If no instances are forthcoming, that can be a story in itself.

When disciplinary bodies refuse to discuss individual cases, a journalist can ask for aggregate data. Such information can suggest where an investigator should look first. For example, divorce lawyers are the subject of more complaints than any other type of lawyer. Knowing that, a journalist might want to begin by talking to divorce lawyers and their clients. When checking court indexes for legal malpractice suits, the names of local divorce lawyers might be the most sensible to run first.

Many licensing boards will release complaint files, but only after the case has reached an advanced stage. In Missouri, I keep track of the boards' disclosures at the nearby university law library. It receives all disciplinary notices, then files them in binders placed on open shelves. Furthermore, I check filings at the Administrative Hearing Commission in the state capital. This quasi-judicial agency examines preliminary findings by the boards to determine if there is adequate evidence for a license suspension or revocation to proceed.

The right of privacy is at work here, which makes the issue messy. No journalist wants to oppose privacy. But journalists must make difficult determinations about when one professional's privacy is being carried too far. I have investigated a physician accused by 20 patients of sexual molestation in the examination room. Every one of those 20 complaints remained sealed from the public while the state medical board investigated. The investigation lasted years. Then the accused sued the board in the courts to halt the investigation, increasing delays. All the while, more unsuspecting patients were potentially subjected to the doctor's unwanted advances.

Despite my respect for individual privacy, I write about such egregious cases as soon as I can document the information satisfactorily. Patients who disbelieve the allegations or who decide the risk is tolerable can continue seeing that doctor. Other patients, meanwhile, may make an informed decision to stay away.

In such cases, journalists should ask whether the legislature has instructed courts to give deference to disciplinary decisions by licensing boards, prohibiting stays by judges. Has the legislature adopted a "preponderance of evidence" standard in professional discipline cases, rather than a "clear and convincing evidence" standard?

Journalists must be alert to disciplinary action in one state never being conveyed to the state where the license is based on reciprocity. The Wall Street Journal chronicled the case of a physician licensed in seven states who accepted a mild reprimand in New Hampshire despite repeated, serious accusations—if he agreed to practice in a different state.

Being alert to disciplinary actions from unexpected quarters can pay off in an important story. A North Carolina realtor ended up a convicted felon not because her licensing agency took action, but because a federal prosecutor charged her with violating a money laundering statute after the realtor allowed a client to pay part of a home purchase with $60,000 of undisclosed cash. The prosecutor said the realtor should have figured out that the cash came from illegal drug profits.

Professional Associations as Sources

Associations can help reporters obtain information about individual members and professional standards. Sometimes the information will come from paid staff, sometimes from volunteer board members, sometimes from publications. An example of an in-house publication is CPA Journal, a national magazine disseminated by the New York State Society of Certified Public Accountants. Independent specialized publications, covered in Chapter 1, should be consulted, too. Examples are the Public Accounting Report, based in Minneapolis, and the Journal of Accountancy, Jersey City, N.J.

Most organizations are set up to help their members or to promote a cause; information from them should be judged accordingly. There is usually no law or regulation compelling an association to release information about its members, but many will at least confirm whether a particular person is a member and, if so, supply standard biographical data about that person.

Large national and regional associations, such as those of lawyers, doctors and engineers, sometimes have state and local chapters. It is wise to check all levels. Some associations produce membership directories, available from their headquarters (or from a friendly local member). Investigators must remember, however, that information in directories is supplied by the member, and thus can be self-serving or even fictitious.

It is common to find that these associations work with governments to develop standards, then act as the primary policing body for the profession. A few examples—of hundreds that could be listed—are the American Institute of Certified Public Accountants, New York City, and the National Association of Realtors, Chicago. The Guide to National Professional Certification Programs, compiled by Phillip A. Barnhart, covers hundreds more.

Even if the association has no authority to sanction its members, it might have produced ethical guidelines—often called codes of professional responsibility—that can inform a journalist's investigation. Rena A. Gorlin edited a compilation, "Codes of Professional Responsibility," for the Bureau of National Affairs book division. It covers lawyers, doctors (including psychiatrists), accountants, engineers, realtors, insurance underwriters, arbitrators, architects, financial planners and social workers.

Numerous books place ethical codes in a larger societal context. An example is "Ethics and Professionalism" by John Kultgen. A philosopher, Kultgen studied ethics codes from 19 professional associations to illuminate his thinking. Some ethics books focus on one profession, such as Philip G. Cottell's "Accounting Ethics: A Practical Guide for Professionals."

In some licensed occupations, such as electricians and plumbers, practitioners are more likely to belong to a labor union than a trade association. When nonunion workers try for certain jobs, they are often frozen out. This occurs, too: A nuclear power plant, for example, is under construction. The immensity of the job means hundreds of out-of-state plumbers and pipefitters will be brought in. Because all are required to pass a state proficiency exam, copies of the tests start showing up on the job site, are sold through the operator of the local lunch wagon or end up in the hands of union officials. Investigators can check locally, starting with telephone directory Yellow Pages, to see if the craft involved has a union office nearby or can check state or federal labor departments. Labor unions as sources of information and as subjects of investigations are discussed more fully in Chapter 12.

Investigating the Protectors

While inquiring about waste in the District of Columbia government, the Washington City Paper entered the thicket of licensing boards. The investigation told how the Barber and Cosmetology Board had been at odds for a decade with a hair braiding salon it wanted to regulate. The owner said procedures for cutting and shampooing hair had no relevance to braiding. The board disagreed, and fined the owner. He took the fine to court. As that legal battle unfolded, the owner convinced the city council to set up a separate licensing board for braiders.

The article also chronicled the Board of Interior Designers saga. In its first eight years of existence, the board had received only one complaint, about overcharging for rugs. So, the question arose, why license and oversee interior designers? The answer seemed to be twofold: First, interior designers appreciated the prestige of being a licensed profession whose entry could be controlled. Second, the local government appreciated the fees generated by the licensing procedure.

When St. Louis Magazine assigned me to investigate dangerous doctors, I expected to focus on individual physicians who harmed patients but somehow retained their licenses. The more I learned, however, the more convinced I became that the focus should be on the state board overseeing physician conduct.

The place to start is with the law that created the board. What is the board supposed to be doing? Does it have an adequate budget? What regulations has the board approved to achieve the legislative mandates? Who are the board members and what are their backgrounds? Were they once, or are they still, members of the regulated profession and do they have vested interests in lackadaisical enforcement? How are staff investigators trained, and on what are they told to focus? How do their counterparts around the country go about their jobs? How do the cases fare that they take to court?

As journalists look at the board's effectiveness, they should ask whether certain types of violations are pursued, while other types are ignored. Useful categories to consider, no matter what the profession, are misrepresentation of qualifications, practicing without a valid license, hiring unqualified assistants, functioning outside the area of competence, impairment due to alcohol or drugs, overtreating a problem, undertreating a problem, overcharging, sexual assault or other sexual abuse and malpractice leading to injury.

Boards tend to inflate their number of disciplinary actions by taking credit for suspensions or revocations initiated by sister agencies in other states. The boards play down their reluctance to discipline for substandard performance, which is vital but subjective. It is easier to evaluate cases of stealing, drunkenness or a felony conviction in the courts (all of which can be proven by using objective criteria) than it is to decide if a surgeon made an improper incision during a four-hour, life-or-death operation. As a federal inspector general said, "If a surgeon was standing over my mother with a scalpel and I had a choice between a crook that was competent and a very honest physician that was impaired by drugs, alcohol or age, I would choose the crook. And yet we seem to be very much better at finding the crooks."

Sometimes the boards have attorneys on staff; sometimes they retain outside lawyers from the private sector or receive help from government-paid lawyers in the attorney general's office. While investigating the Missouri board overseeing doctors, I received useful comparative information from the national Federation of State Medical Boards, based in Fort Worth, Tex. The information told me whether the Missouri agency had more or fewer than the average number of investigators per 1,000 physicians, a higher budget than comparable boards, more or less quasi-judicial authority than average to discipline wayward doctors and much more.

Outside groups occasionally try to police the boards. Their data, comprehensive or anecdotal, can be a good starting point. While looking at dangerous doctors, I learned that the Public Citizen Health Research Group, in Washington, D.C., ranks disciplinary boards state by state, as well as publishing names of every known physician disciplined by the state or federal governments.

Chapter 12

INVESTIGATING THE PRIVATE SECTOR

For-Profit Businesses and Their Workers

*I*n his book "Investigative Reporting and Editing," Paul N. Williams provided multiple compelling rationales for covering the private sector as thoroughly and aggressively as government. First, private businesses are beneficiaries of government assistance, including industrial development bonds, tax forgiveness or deferral, research grants, depreciation allowances and direct subsidies. As a result, taxpayers everywhere have a monetary interest. Second, taxpayers' lives are influenced when they buy or government buys goods and services of shoddy quality or at inflated prices. Third, many citizens and governments invest in corporate stocks and bonds, giving them a stake in management performance. Fourth, businesses, through lobbying and campaign contributions, influence legislative and executive branch policymaking, often behind closed doors.

Even when journalists have heeded Williams, they often miss the big picture, frequently concentrating on the financial condition of one corporation. Such stories serve their purposes, but what is normally called the "business beat" ought to be much broader.

I prefer to think in terms of the "workplace beat." The life of almost every employed person is dominated by the job. People are usually at their place of employment at least eight hours a day, five days a week. They spend additional time dressing for work, time getting to work, getting home, unwinding, maybe completing a job-related task before going to bed, then perhaps dreaming about it all.

Yet most journalists do nothing to capture what is happening in local workplaces, day after day. This chapter is intended to help journalists complete projects focusing on the quality of work, as well as on a given corporation.

The entries in the IRE Resource Center under "Business," "Corporations," "Employment," "Job Training," "Labor Unions," "Product Safety" and "Unemployment" cover lots of ground. The structure of this chapter reflects that diversity. Some projects that could be categorized as business investigations are also found at other places in the text, such as the bankruptcy court section of Chapter 10.

Some types of businesses have such huge impacts on readers, viewers and listeners that they are treated in separate chapters of this book. Those are financial institutions (banks, savings and loans, credit unions, mutual funds); insurance companies (life, health, property-casualty); utilities (gas, electric, nuclear, water, telephone, cable television); health-care providers (hospitals, nursing homes, health maintenance organizations, home health-care companies); and not-for-profit organizations. Many of the sources and strategies in this chapter will be useful for investigating each or all of those.

Investigating a Takeover: One Prototype

James K. Gentry, then executive director at the Society of American Business Editors and Writers, was so impressed with an Akron Beacon Journal investigation of a corporate takeover that he used it to lead the Business chapter in the previous edition of this book:

When the Beacon Journal business editor checked the Dow Jones newswire for activity in Goodyear Tire & Rubber Co., he was surprised to see that trading exceeded 1.5 million shares for the day, more than twice the norm. The reason turned out to be takeover rumors. "Obviously something was going on and we knew we had to find out what," said Rick Reiff, a Beacon Journal reporter. The effort to identify the acquirer tested the staff's ability to think creatively, identify human sources and decipher Securities and Exchange Commission documents.

"Through some sources on Wall Street, I learned that Merrill Lynch was rumored to be the buyer," Reiff said. "But I couldn't confirm it so we didn't use the information right away." Besides, the activity subsided for two weeks. When it resumed, Reiff dogged the source he needed: the Goodyear specialist at the New York Stock Exchange, a floor trader who makes a market in the company's stock by matching buyers and sellers. The next morning Reiff was in New York talking with the specialist, who identified the Merrill Lynch broker on the other side. The broker volunteered that a single customer was buying all the shares.

Although Reiff was unable to identify the individual buyer, the information led to the first report that Merrill Lynch was acquiring shares for an unknown investor. The next break came a day later. A source inside Goodyear called to say James Goldsmith was the buyer. The newspaper prepared a profile of Goldsmith, based partly on materials acquired through a computer database search. Soon after, Goldsmith's Goodyear holdings moved above 5 percent so the British raider was required by Securities and Exchange Commission regulations to file a Form 13D, which identifies the acquirer of the stock and the target. The Beacon Journal had its confirmation.

In discussing investigations of the private sector, this chapter will emphasize resources not mentioned earlier in the book. But it is important to reread Chapters 1 through 5, because most of the paper, people and computer trails apply to private-sector investigations just as much as they do to investigations of government. Like government investigations, business/workplace investigations go beyond stories about institutions to encompass individuals and issues. The book "The Columbia Knight-Bagehot Guide to Business and Economics Journalism," edited by Pamela Hollie Kluge at Columbia University, conveys the richness of private-sector investigations. So does the Business Journalist, the magazine produced by the Society of American Business Editors and Writers at the University of Missouri Journalism School.

Journalists need all the help they can get, because appearances can be so deceiving. William Sternberg, Washington bureau chief for Thomson Newspapers, planned to write a feature article about a corporation in the South Bronx that had been praised by the U.S. president. Its founder had been named minority entrepreneur of the year by the U.S. Commerce Department. It had a listing on the New York Stock Exchange, received glowing reports from financial analysts, been audited by a national accounting firm, sold securities through a Wall Street investment banker, submitted disclosure statements to prominent law firms. But despite all the apparent scrutiny, many of its disclosures turned out to be lies, many of its contracts phony. As Sternberg wrote in the IRE Journal:

> Just because something is disclosed in an SEC document does not mean it is true. . . . Politicians who are on the take [from corporations] are not about to reveal it on their financial disclosure forms. . . . Documents that do not mean much the first time you see them can take on added significance once you have done more reporting and learned to recognize the red flags. It did not take us long to discover that virtually every time the company paid "consulting fees," some sort of bribe or other scam was involved.

Companies Whose Stock Is Traded Publicly

The most important initial question an investigator can ask is whether a business is required to file information with the U.S. Securities and Exchange Commission. If the company's stock is listed on a national exchange or there are more than 500 stockholders while assets are above $5 million, the SEC is probably involved. About 11,000 companies fit that description, including most of the nation's largest private-sector employers. Many join the Association of Publicly Traded Companies, Washington, D.C., to deal with the Financial Accounting Standards Board, SEC and Congress. (Millions of businesses do not fall within the SEC's jurisdiction; they will be covered more fully later in this chapter.) Individual investors have created their own organizations, including the Chicago-based American Association of Individual Investors.

When Business Week writer Chris Welles was working on a story about Kennecott Corp., he depended heavily on documents filed at the Securities and Exchange Commission. They included:

A prospectus from a recent debt offering—a mandated disclosure of financial information that must be given to all investors in new shares of a company's securities. The prospectus contained fresh data on Kennecott's copper-mine production.

An offering circular distributed to shareholders of Carborundum, a company acquired by Kennecott in a controversial deal. Kennecott stockholders expressed anger about the $568 million Kennecott paid to acquire Carborundum.

Court documents from litigation started by Kennecott stockholders over the Carborundum deal. Briefs by the plaintiffs contended, for instance, that an investment bank involved in the deal had serious conflicts of interests. Also in the court files were letters written to the court protesting the deal by several large investors in Kennecott stock. Welles interviewed several of them. One, the chairman of a mining company, said the Carborundum deal "was a very stupid move" and that "if I had recommended a deal like that to my shareholders, I would have felt like a real idiot."

Minutes from a Kennecott board of directors meeting revealing the haste with which the directors had considered the acquisition.

Other SEC Documents

Many reporters mistakenly ignore the most basic corporate document, the annual report. The report's physical attributes might reflect the financial health of the company. Two years of an automobile company's annual report are illustrative; the company reported a net loss of $1.7 billion in a 32-page, black and white, pictureless book. Two years later, it boasted about a $170 million profit in a splashy, multicolored report that included a portrait of the chairman. Most annual reports' letter from the chair are noteworthy for the amount of obfuscation, but a few CEOs are refreshing exceptions.

Reporters frequently find the annual report's most interesting information in the footnotes. A typical annual report to the SEC contains at least 15 pages of footnotes, many of them revealing to a knowledgeable journalist. For example, companies have improved their bottom line without earning a cent by revising upward the assumed rate of return on their pension funds. That means they need less cash to fund pensions and therefore can claim profit. That practice is revealed in financial statement footnotes toward the back of the annual report, not in the text at the front.

A banking corporation's annual report, in a footnote on page 40, referred to "certain related parties"—officers of its banks—who had received millions of dollars in loans that the company was writing off as delinquent. A separate document—the bank company's proxy statement to stockholders sent before the annual meeting—filled in the missing information with two and one-half pages of explanation, names of the relevant officers and the amounts of their loans.

The proxy reveals salaries and benefits paid to top executives. It requires so much disclosure that some private corporations thinking of going public with their stock refrain simply because they shudder at revealing salaries and benefits, little-noticed lawsuits and problems with environmental regulators.

Another key document is the prospectus, issued when the company is trying to raise money. Forbes editor Gretchen Morgenson checks the prospectus "because it tells what the risks are," she said.

> Those risks could be from competition, shareholder dilution in the offering, conflicts of interest in the offering, lawsuits pending that could have material effects, and insider shares eligible for sale in the future. It also tells what the company will do with the proceeds and gives good financial data.

About 180 different forms are used by the SEC, described in Title 17, the Code of Federal Regulations. A few worthy of special mention:

> Form 10K, Annual Report, which contains far more detail than the glossy, shorter version mailed to stockholders.
>
> Form 10Q, Quarterly Update.
>
> Form 8K, Current Update, covering changes in management, a shift of accountants and other "materially important" events.
>
> Schedule 13D, Report of Securities Purchase, filed when an individual or institution acquires 5 percent or more of a public company, buys or sells significant numbers of shares after that, or decides to control rather than simply invest in a company.

These transactions are of so much interest that publications, such as Barron's, publish lists of filings weekly. One type of transaction hard to police is insider trading. The SEC and the stock exchanges cannot know about and track down every unexplained run-up in stock prices or trading volume just before a significant change in a company's management or ownership.

Specific types of businesses and individuals—such as mutual funds, investment advisors and stockbrokers—have to file SEC forms designed especially for their activities. One example covers banks that handle the sale of bonds for cities raising money. The banks must register with the SEC on Form MSD. The form names employees involved in the sales, then state work experience, whether any have participated in fraud or faced disciplinary action. The purpose of Form MSD is to flush out bank employees unqualified to manage a city's investment.

SEC Today is a daily summary of major filings and actions involving individuals and institutions regulated by the commission. SEC Docket is a weekly compilation of new rules, changes to old rules and reports of disciplinary actions. Outside publications, such as SEC Compliance, Englewood Cliffs, N.J., can provide leads for journalists. SEC filings and other business information make up the heart of many online computer databases and CD-ROMs, including ABI/Inform, Business Index, and Disclosure.

Resources Outside the SEC

Federal Agencies

The paper trail on publicly traded companies does not end with the SEC. Some federal agencies, in fact, have jurisdiction not only over public companies, but also most private companies. Those agencies include:

The Federal Trade Commission, created to guard against anticompetitive behavior and deceptive business practices. For example, the commission might investigate whether the takeover of a small company by a larger one would increase chances that the small company would later be shut down.

The Consumer Product Safety Commission, created to guard against injuries from dangerous products.

The Small Business Administration, which gives seed money to women, racial and ethnic minorities, then monitors compliance with the terms of the grant or loan. Sometimes the money is channeled through a state government agency with similar goals. Journalists can look for local success stories, honest failures and outright fraud.

The Equal Employment Opportunity Commission, created to protect employees from discrimination on the basis of race, ethnicity, gender, age, physical and mental disabilities. A sweeping law called Americans with Disabilities Act has kept the EEOC busier than ever and caused consternation among employers. Alcohol use, smoking, poor eyesight and difficulties handling stress are among the conditions employees claim as disabling under the law. Employers are responding that sometimes those should indeed be disqualifying conditions. Journalists should be delving into how employers are implementing ADA provisions for reasonably accommodating worker disabilities. How does an employer decide the point at which such accommodation becomes an undue hardship? When workers are injured on the job, are they not only collecting workers' compensation benefits but also invoking the ADA if the employer refuses to assign new duties as a result of the disability? How are employers handling wrongful termination claims under the ADA? Is it wrong to dismiss an executive with terminal cancer if there is no noticeable change in the executive's job performance? If there is noticeable change? Such questions, while important, should not distract investigators from the most pervasive forms of workplace discrimination, which continue to be based on race, gender and age. Lawsuits abound. Interest groups such as the NAACP, the National Organization for Women and the American Association of Retired Persons can provide examples. Journalists can find disturbing exclusive stories by tracking not only Fortune 500 corporations, but also by checking for unlawful discrimination at types of organizations often ignored by the media, such as country clubs, charities and family-owned retailers.

The Environmental Protection Agency, created to reduce pollution of the land, air and water by institutions and individuals. Information disclosed to the EPA by individual businesses in almost every industry can help journalists learn not only about pollution, but about workforce safety, corporate investments and manufacturing processes. Writing about disclosure requirements in the National Law Journal, San Francisco attorney David R. Andrews commented:

> A competitor can learn a great deal from reviewing the list of chemicals used by a company or a list of wastes produced by each of the company's facilities. Emission quantities may be an indication of production rates or capacities, and with not that much extra information, even precise production data may be calculable.

The Federal Election Commission (covered in Chapter 6) oversees political action committees formed by businesses and labor unions to support or oppose candidates for the U.S. Senate, House and presidency. Many individuals employed by businesses or belonging to labor unions make contributions in their own names, too, in addition to funneling money through the committees. Individual contributions are also subject to Federal Election Commission scrutiny.

The Federal Reserve Board has a less direct but real impact, as explained by William Greider in his book "Secrets of the Temple: How the Federal Reserve Runs the Country."

Workplace regulation by the Labor Department (including, most prominently, the Occupational Safety and Health Administration) will be covered more fully later in this chapter.

Part of the regulatory agencies' mission is to promote social responsibility among businesses. Journalists interested in measuring social responsibility can check a corporation's file at the government agencies named above; consult magazines such as Business Ethics, Minneapolis; read books such as "Rating America's Corporate Conscience" from the Council on Economic Priorities, New York City; develop ties with watchdog groups such as the Investor Responsibility Research Center, Washington, D.C.; document the amount and direction of charitable contributions; and determine which politicians receive contributions from corporate political action committees. Journalists should also, without fail, check the courts for lawsuits involving corporations and other types of businesses as plaintiffs or defendants. One of many questions is how the corporation acts when a request is made to depose the chief executive. Does the corporation automatically oppose deposition, and does the court uphold resistance? Is the lawyer making a request to depose the CEO sincere, or hoping to extract a settlement through harassment?

State and Local Agencies

Generally not as aggressive or thorough as the SEC, states require varying degrees of disclosure from businesses. For example, in some states the attorney general collects information from consumer complaints, but tends to move slowly on those complaints. In Missouri, the attorney general receives tens of thousands of consumer complaints annually. Journalists almost never examine them singly or systematically, missing fascinating stories as a result. To view the big picture, journalists can consult the National Association of Attorneys General and the National Association of Consumer Agency Administrators, both in Washington, D.C. As noted in Chapter 7, almost every state executive branch function has a counterpart in every other state; they then band together to form a national organization.

Many state agencies collect information before a complaint arises. Sales of securities within a state require registration with the securities commissioner. The state commissioners have banded together as the North American Securities Administrators Association, Washington, D.C. Lines of business singled out for tailored licensing or other regulation include alcoholic-beverage manufacturers and their retail and wholesale outlets, supermarkets, barber shops, hospitals, nursing homes, savings and loan associations and insurance companies.

Municipal business licenses and related tax payments offer a wealth of information. In Columbia, Mo., for example, I can estimate from the amount of the license fee, say, $25, how much a local company grossed the previous year, because the amount of the fee is based on total reported revenue. Combined with other indicators (in Missouri, for example, for-profit corporations with assets over $200,000 pay a state franchise tax, and retail companies also pay tax based on a percentage of sales), I might be able to arrive at an informed approximation of how much even the most secretive company is taking in. Reference books might help validate the estimates. For example, state-by-state directories published by American Business Information, Omaha, contain sales volumes for many relatively small, privately owned companies. In many jurisdictions, the local government requires filing of a business tangible personal property return—the city of St. Louis form shows the number of employees; property leased, rented or loaned to others or from others; furniture and equipment and vehicles.

Construction permits for and fire inspections of the buildings housing private businesses can provide additional information. Traditionally, cities have heavily regulated certain types of private-sector activity, including restaurants (subject to special health inspections as well as rules cutting across all lines of business), street vendors, rental units, hotels and motels.

Sometimes local governments possess information about businesses through sad experience. David Lindorff, writing in the Columbia Knight-Bagehot primer, said this about business relocation incentives from local governments:

> Some jurisdictions will offer property tax holidays, others access to subsidized land, others job training tax credits. Still others have set up new business incubators in conjunction with local university research centers. Besides the fact that such programs invite corruption because of the amounts of money involved, typically the lack of public involvement in the decision-making process raises serious questions about whether the community gets what it pays for. Companies that get tax holidays often pick up and leave when the holiday is over. And even when a business stays, the cost per job to the community can be extraordinary.

Pulling It Together on the Paper Trail

Welles, while exploring the financial activities growing out of the Rev. Sun Myung Moon's Unification Church, gathered information from federal agencies other than the SEC (the Internal Revenue Service, Commerce and Defense departments, Immigration and Naturalization Service and Comptroller of the Currency); state agencies (fund-raising information filed with attorneys general in six capitals, annual reports in corporations divisions listing officers and directors); and local governments (real estate transactions). Welles talked about uncovering the church's international activities:

Perhaps the most useful single set of documents was obtained from the Department of Commerce about Moon-controlled corporations in South Korea. Previous articles on the Unification Church had speculated on Moon's corporate connections in Korea, but none had any hard information. During an interview with a Commerce official, I learned that for a modest fee it was possible for anyone to obtain reports from the American Embassy in Seoul on most major Korean companies engaged in international trade. I got copies of the reports on Moon's companies and was surprised at the detail they contained: sales, earnings, major products, number of employees, capitalization and major shareholders.

One overlooked source of information is advertisements. The promises made can be compared by the reporter with the reality of the product or service. Advertisements sometimes even point the way to detailed documentation that otherwise might have escaped notice. An advertisement to buy acreage in Colorado appeared in Forbes magazine; one of its own divisions was the seller. At the bottom of the enticing, promise-the-moon sales pitch was a dense paragraph of tiny type, reprinted here in full to illustrate all the available documentation:

> Obtain the Property Report required by federal law and read it before signing anything. No federal agency has judged the merits or value, if any, of this property. Equal credit and housing opportunity. A statement and offering statement has been filed with the secretary of state of the state of New York. The filing does not constitute approval of the sale or lease or offer for sale or lease by the secretary of state or that the secretary of state has in any way passed upon the merits of such offering. A copy of the offering statement is available, upon request, from Sangre de Cristo Ranches. A statement of record filed with the New Jersey Real Estate Commission permits this property to be offered to New Jersey residents, but does not pass upon its merits or value. Obtain the New Jersey Public Offering Statement and read it before signing anything.

When an investigator is starting from zero, good sources of basic corporate financial data are regularly updated reports from Standard & Poor's, Moody's and Dun & Bradstreet, which can be found in university and public libraries. Reports on companies and industries are issued by securities analysts with brokerage houses such as Merrill Lynch, Paine-Webber and Dean Witter. Because stockbrokers are reluctant to criticize corporations publicly, the analyses tend to be bullish. But they frequently contain industry data unavailable elsewhere. The best analysts in each industry are chosen each year by Institutional Investor magazine, New York City, as well as other publications.

Guidance through the useful but sometimes bewildering welter of documents, directories and other source materials is provided masterfully by Lorna M. Daniells' book Business Information Sources. Guidance through the statistics and accounting assumptions is provided by booklets such as Understanding Wall Street from the New York Stock Exchange, and How to Read a Financial Report from Merrill Lynch. Books abound, including Mark Stevens' exposés of accounting firms ("The Big Eight" and "The Accounting Wars") and Howard Schilit's "Financial Shenanigans: How to Detect Accounting Gimmicks and Fraud in Financial Reports."

Schilit, a university accounting professor, is one of a small group of independent financial detectives publicly questioning the rosy reports of high-growth companies. Analyzing one retail chain's reports, Schilit noted how it included installment purchases as revenue before sales were final and obscured cash-flow deficits in its net income figures. Though technically legal, Schilit said, "these aggressive accounting policies may distort the true financial condition." Schilit concentrates on companies whose stock prices have tripled in the past 18 months or those whose insiders sell stock just before the outbreak of bad news, whose boards of directors are stacked with those having ties to revenues, whose executive compensation arrangements are absurdly generous. When businesses cross the line from legal but questionable accounting to lawbreaking, a 400-page IRS book can be a nice companion. Titled "Financial Investigations: A Financial Approach to Detecting and Resolving Crimes," it is available through the Government Printing Office, Washington, D.C.

Human Sources

Written records lay the foundation for a business story, but human sources are essential to provide the richness of detail that make stories come alive. The explanation of using "currents" and "formers" in Chapter 5 of this book is essential for delving into private-sector institutions.

Books about specific businesses and industries, biographies of businesspeople and autobiographies by businesspeople abound; they can help journalists understand how humans shape corporate culture and vice versa.

Most insightful books about specific businesses and industries are done independently. ("Unauthorized" is the popular term.) Two of the best are "Under the Influence: The Unauthorized Story of the Anheuser-Busch Dynasty" by Peter Hernon and Terry Ganey and "Blood and Wine: The Unauthorized Story of the Gallo Wine Empire" by Ellen Hawkes. Two of the best about the human factor within industries are "Brokers, Bagmen and Moles: Fraud and Corruption in the Chicago Futures Markets" by David Greising and Laurie Morse and "Merchants of Grain" by Dan Morgan. (It is instructive to compare Morgan's book, which features Cargill Inc., with the authorized history of Cargill by Wayne G. Broehl Jr.) A thoughtful biographical approach is found in "The Big Boys: Power and Position in American Business" by Ralph Nader and William Taylor.

One of the most insightful memoirs is Dorman L. Commons' "Tender Offer: The Sneak Attack in Corporate Takeovers."

Even the best books sometimes give little attention to the range of people who allow businesses to function. The breakout of human sources within executive branch bureaucracies (Chapter 7) is pertinent. Private-sector corporations employ people to perform the same types of functions as in government, including public affairs, budgeting, accounting, auditing, contracting, legal affairs, personnel, internal security, secretarial and maintenance. As in the government sector, people performing those functions band together to form national associations that might help journalists. Private-sector examples are the American Corporate Counsel Association, Washington, D.C.; Financial Executives Institute, Morristown, N.J.; Institute of Internal Auditors, Altamonte Springs, Fla.; National Association of Corporate Treasurers, Washington, D.C.; and Employee Assistance Professionals Association, Arlington, Va.

Academics and other quasi-independent experts can be a good source. Most universities have faculty members with varied areas of business and economics expertise. Often they are good sources for local reaction to national developments or analysis of economic trends. Some of the professors might have worked at, or consulted for, the business being scrutinized. Think tanks, covered in Chapter 5, are worth checking on many business and labor topics.

Additional outside sources could include a company's current and former customers, suppliers, competitors, franchise holders, advertising agency executives, lawyers, accountants, bankers, institutional investors and lobbyists, as well as legislators and regulators concentrating on business issues.

Outside directors are potential sources. Many businesses place at least one person from outside the company on the board. Outside directors ostensibly have more independence than a corporate owner or manager. Although outside directors are paid for their service, and therefore presumably will exhibit loyalty to the company, they also assume legal and moral responsibilities on behalf of the public. If there is trouble, they should not lie about it to inquiring journalists. The National Association of Corporate Directors is in Washington, D.C. Directors and Boards magazine is one of many publications that journalists can read to gain insight. Outside directors are quite likely to have strong views, one way or another, about whether the chief executive should be receiving a million-dollar bonus this year on top of his $750,000 base salary. Outside directors are also likely to know about the company's top salesperson who has been soliciting and receiving bribes from outside suppliers while top management of both corporations look the other way.

Chamber of Commerce and Better Business Bureau executives can be helpful. Local business association executives tend to be protective of their members. But with patience, a reporter can win their confidence so they will talk candidly about troubled businesses. Local chambers have a national organization in Washington, D.C.; local better business bureaus have their national organization in Arlington, Va.

Trade associations covering specific types of businesses and workers can supply useful information. Almost every industry and every type of employee is represented by an association in Washington, D.C., and state capitals. Examples are the National Association of Convenience Stores and the International Brotherhood of Teamsters union.

Union members or nonunion employees can provide information. If the business is unionized, the officers of the local almost surely have amassed a thick file on all aspects of their employer and might share it. Union leaders will know which current and former employees are the most knowledgeable, articulate and willing to help. When there is no union to consult, a reporter can locate current and former employees in other ways. One method is to write down license plate numbers from the company parking lot, match the plates with their owners at the state motor vehicles department, then contact the employees by letter, telephone or in person. Another method is to visit a restaurant, bar or other establishment where employees gather after work hours.

The Dictionary of Occupational Titles, published by the U.S. Labor Department, is a listing of almost every job imaginable—more than 20,000—including salary ranges, descriptions and future prospects. When journalists are unsure whether they have found and interviewed all types of employees relevant to an investigative project, the reference book can be invaluable.

Management-Worker Relations

As told by Mike McGraw of the Kansas City Star in the previous edition of this book, police led a disheveled, unemployed father of three to a patrol car and shuttled him off for questioning. Left in the aftermath of what appears to have been his stress-induced temporary insanity were the bodies of his wife and young children. The police were not talking; the neighbors said they knew nothing; the editor was screaming for details before deadline.

A few miles away, in a state office building, there was a public record that included a tape recording of the father pleading for unemployment benefits during a hearing. It began with an admission that he was seeing a psychiatrist for depression after being laid off from his job. It ended with his screaming at the state unemployment compensation referee that unless something went his way soon, he could not be held responsible for his actions.

The need for investigating is everywhere: A building under construction collapses, killing 10 workers. Using sources listed in this chapter and elsewhere in the book, an investigator might find the construction companies involved had horrible safety records, including numerous previous accidents, and that past dangerous practices were never corrected. Government safety inspectors had been to the site but failed to catch problems that may have contributed to the collapse. A union official responsible for safety on the job had a conflict of interests because his son was the top officer of one of the contracting companies.

A military plane crashes halfway around the world, killing the entire crew. The Air Force blames the plane's avionics system, made in the reporter's hometown. By looking in the right places, she finds the company fired all its quality control inspectors the previous year to save money, that other employees had been complaining about flawed parts and that Pentagon auditors had given the company poor marks in previous site visits.

Not all workplace stories are so dramatic. Treatment of lower-level employees at local employers is a day-in, day-out story: What is it like to work as a secretary? A custodian? What daily challenges and insults do they face? Is the pay structure at the company equitable? Are managers trained to be sensitive in ways that also increase productivity? What is the likelihood of physical injury in the workplace? Of psychological injury? Is job burnout common? Excellent perspective that suggests numerous projects can be found in Juliet B. Schor's book "The Overworked American: The Unexpected Decline of Leisure."

Besides age-old workplace problems, employers and employees are trying to deal with new challenges such as quality child care, the AIDS epidemic's effect inside the office or factory, drug testing and invisible health threats. Books that touch on nearly every workplace issue include "Every Employee's Guide to the Law" by Lewin G. Joel III and "The Employee Rights Handbook" by Steven Mitchell Sack. The U.S. government's Monthly Labor Review is a good source for big-picture stories and trends, as is the statistics-based government publication Compensation and Working Conditions.

When workplace dissidents complain openly about problems, they are supposed to be protected by federal and state whistleblower laws. Whistleblowing as a phenomenon of benefit to journalists is discussed more fully in Chapter 5 of this book. One investigation that combined a corporation's finances, workplace ethics and whistleblowers in a near-perfect mix appeared in the Philadelphia Inquirer. The investigation exposed a scheme by a national convenience store chain to extort money from poorly paid employees by falsely accusing them of stealing.

Labor Unions

The National Labor Relations Board (NLRB) is a federal agency that investigates and prosecutes unfair practices involving unions and employers, unions and their individual members as well as employers and their employees—both union and nonunion workers. The board also tries to insure the integrity of elections in which workers can choose to unionize or throw out a union. The NLRB has broad jurisdiction in the private sector, intervening in situations such as a corporation cutting off pension credits of striking workers in the middle of the dispute. Disputes involving state and municipal employees (including school teachers) are handled by the individual states.

It is frequently useful for a journalist to know whether workers have attempted to unionize an employer. For an NLRB-sponsored election to occur, 30 percent of eligible workers must sign a petition. (The agency does not have jurisdiction over all employers that might be unionized— for example, a retail business would have to take in at least $500,000 annually and receive or send merchandise across state lines.)

The process of filing a charge works like this: An aggrieved member who feels discriminated against because of union activity, or who feels the union is not providing fair representation, files at the regional NLRB office. This can be done without the aid of a lawyer. The charge is a public document containing the employee's name, home phone number, employer, union local and a description of the complaint. It is assigned to an NLRB investigator, who interviews all the parties and witnesses involved. The investigator recommends to the regional director whether the charge has merit. If the board investigator finds no merit in the claim and the regional director agrees, the charge is dropped. The charging party can appeal the regional director's decision to the general counsel in Washington, D.C.

If the regional director believes the charge has merit, a complaint is issued, which is much like an indictment. The regional director then gives the other party a chance to settle the matter informally. If a settlement cannot be reached, a hearing before an administrative law judge is scheduled. The hearings are public; transcripts are available at board offices. The law judge issues a decision, also public, and either party can request a review of the decision by the five-member, presidentially appointed National Labor Relations Board in Washington, D.C. In turn, the NLRB's findings can be appealed to the courts and, eventually, to the U.S. Supreme Court.

A more or less typical case involved an employee of a chain discount store trying to organize a union local in Hinsdale, N.H. When store supervisors found out, they offered the employee a raise if she would desist. She persisted. She said she was then harassed, fired and challenged by her former employer when she tried to receive unemployment compensation. The worker filed an unfair labor practices challenge against the company. After hearing evidence, the agency issued a formal complaint to have the worker reinstated, with back pay. Such cases are interesting individually. An alert journalist will look at the cumulative picture, too, trying to discern patterns of management and labor behavior locally.

The best NLRB sources are the regional director and regional attorney. Individual investigators might be excellent sources who can say, for example, if internal board decisions about whether to pursue specific cases represent pro-union or promanagement biases. One method of contacting investigators is through local officials of the union that represents them—the independent National Labor Relations Board Professional Association. Board clerical workers can also be helpful; one way to get to know them is regular visits to board offices to check docket sheets for pending cases that might make good stories.

The Federal Labor Relations Authority and state public-employee relations boards provide the same services for federal, state and local government workers. The Federal Labor Relations Authority makes its decisions available by subscription through the Government Printing Office. When federal construction projects run into labor-management strife, there are special tribunals to issue decisions. An example is the Wage Appeals Board within the U.S. Labor Department. If contractors are trying to avoid paying the prevailing local wage on projects, the board might halt the avoidance. Wage determination cases are available by subscription through the Government Printing Office; journalists can buy volumes covering their section of the country only, if they prefer.

Some labor unions are giant entities in themselves, just as in need of scrutiny as employers. Although union membership has declined nationally in recent decades, about 17 million workers are still members. The most highly unionized sectors—although none has more than 50 percent unionization—are construction, transportation, public utilities, communications, durable-goods manufacturing and government itself.

Books about labor leaders and unions are weighted toward coverage of corruption, with the Teamsters Union the most exposed. "The Teamsters" by Steven Brill is a classic. Kenneth C. Crowe brought it up to date in "Collision: How the Rank and File Took Back the Teamsters." James Neff's biography of Teamsters leader Jackie Presser and Arthur A. Sloane's biography of Teamsters leader Jimmy Hoffa show what can be done given persistence and talent.

The Bureau of National Affairs, Washington, D.C., publishes an annual Source Book on Collective Bargaining and Employee Relations and a Directory of U.S. Labor Organizations—two of many reference books that can help journalists see the big picture. Many unions publish informative newspapers and magazines. Some of the best traditionally have come from the United Auto Workers, United Mine Workers, Service Employees International Union and American Federation of State, County and Municipal Employees. Print journalists might already be familiar with the Guild Reporter. The National Right to Work Committee, Springfield, Va., an anti-union organization, is one of many potential sources on union excesses.

Government documents about unions abound. The paper trail is a starting point when looking into inefficiency or corruption. The IRE

Resource Center is filled with investigations of union corruption. Here are a few of the documents used most heavily by the journalists who researched the stories:

Form LM-1 is a union's initial filing, which should include its constitution and bylaws, composition of members, name of parent body, expected annual receipts, names and titles of officers, date of the next union election, any fees or dues required and whether work permits are needed.

Depending on its annual receipts, a union files an annual financial report on Form LM-2, LM-3 or LM-4. It contains names and salaries of officers and most employees, receipts and disbursements, including those to charities, real estate purchases, trust funds and whether losses of funds or property were discovered. These reports can also be used to notify the government about the termination of a union through a merger, consolidation or dissolution.

Form LM-15 must be filed by a parent union 30 days after it suspends autonomy of a union local by putting it under "trusteeship" or "supervision." That might result from election irregularities, an attempt to control dissident members and officers or financial irregularities. Follow-up reports are required every six months explaining why the trusteeship was continued. Form LM-16 is required when the trusteeship is lifted, including the method of selecting officers left in charge. Reporters should watch such a development closely. Trusteeships can be abused by officials of parent unions who dislike leaders chosen by the local union or who want to bring members of a certain local in line with other locals.

Racketeering investigations by the U.S. Labor Department, sometimes in conjunction with the Justice Department, often involve unions. Federal agents, for example, might explore shakedowns in which construction companies pay off a union official before certain work is performed. A journalist with good sources can investigate rumors of such activities long before the federal agents arrive.

Mediation, Conciliation and Arbitration

When labor-management disputes mean work slowdowns or stoppages, journalists should look for the involvement of outside negotiators. The Federal Mediation and Conciliation Service is an independent federal agency—separate from the National Labor Relations Board and Labor Department—that is supposed to be notified by unions at least 30 days ahead of the expiration of labor contracts. The agency might assign commissioners based in Washington, D.C., or a regional office to help resolve disputes before or after strike deadlines. These commissioners, usually former management or union negotiators or officials, vary widely in background and abilities.

Arbitration services—some government-run, some private-sector operations—are available to settle disputes. They have already been mentioned briefly in Chapter 10 of this book, in the context of dispute resolution outside the courts. Although hearings by arbitrators are not normally open to the public, reporters can attend by permission. Accounts of past arbitration hearings can often be found in published volumes.

There are two types of arbitration. Grievance arbitration occurs when an employee challenges an action of management through the union contract and the matter cannot be settled by union and management officials. It is appealed to a third-party arbitrator who hears evidence and issues a decision. These hearings sometimes are public, but few reporters ask to attend.

Interest arbitration takes place when labor and management cannot agree on a new contract and usually occurs in the public sector. If strikes are prohibited (often the case with public employees) or both sides want to avoid a strike, they can turn to an arbitrator who will hold hearings and issue a decision.

Many states offer arbitration services to government employee unions; these decisions are often public. For example, an arbitration award may be the only document available detailing the disciplinary action of a police officer alleged to have stopped young women, whom he then sexually harassed. Charles J. Coleman and Theodora T. Haynes are editors of the annotated bibliography Labor Arbitration, with hundreds of references useful to investigators.

Safety and Health in the Workplace

Safety and health disputes are often at the center of labor-management disagreement. The problems have been around a long time, as evidenced by two classic exposés: Paul Brodeur's book "Expendable Americans" and "Bitter Wages" by Joseph A. Page and Mary-Win O'Brien for Ralph Nader's Study Group on Disease and Injury on the Job. A Wall Street Journal exposé by Tony Horwitz showed that in the mid-1990s, inhumane conditions exist in many workplaces. After himself working on a poultry plant assembly line, Horwitz wrote

> While American industry reaps the benefits of a new high-technology era, it has consigned a large class of workers to a Dickensian time warp, laboring not just for meager wages but also under dehumanized and often dangerous conditions. Automation, which has liberated thousands from backbreaking drudgery, has created for others a new and insidious toil in many high-growth industries: Work that is faster than ever before, subject to Orwellian control and electronic surveillance, and reduced to limited tasks that are

numbingly repetitive, potentially crippling and stripped of any meaningful skills or the chance to develop them.

Horwitz, through a combination of traditional paper and people trails plus firsthand observation, produced detailed evidence to support his melodramatic-sounding summary.

Because the problems are so pervasive, one of the most important U.S. Labor Department arms is the Occupational Safety and Health Administration (OSHA). It is divided into regional offices around the country, with area offices under them. Each area office is divided between safety inspectors (often former union construction workers or management safety experts), who investigate physical hazards, and health inspectors (often recently graduated industrial hygienists), who investigate health matters such as injuries from toxic chemicals.

States have the option of enforcing private industry safety and health themselves, as long as the rules are at least as stringent as federal rules. Sometimes the responsibilities are shared. OSHA conducts inspections of businesses based in Missouri, but so do state bureaucrats under certain conditions. For example, the Department of Health's Bureau of Environmental Epidemiology focuses on diseases associated with exposure to workplace chemicals. Because OSHA has no jurisdiction over federal government workplaces, some states have similar agencies to cover municipal and state workers. Federal workers are covered under agency-by-agency plans.

OSHA conducts three types of inspections: those that are programmed (companies in especially dangerous industries randomly picked by computers for wall-to-wall scrutiny); those resulting from a signed complaint by a worker or union official; those triggered by accidents, especially if someone is killed or at least five people are hospitalized or it is high profile.

Inspections frequently result in no citations. If a problem is found, the citation categories are "other-than-serious," "serious" and "willful." OSHA can request that the U.S. Justice Department conduct investigations, but usually depends on fines—based on the company's size, past record and maybe other factors—for serious or willful citations. The company has 15 days to contest the citations, request an informal conference or pay. An informal conference, usually held with the OSHA area director, often results in reductions of fines by as much as 80 percent in return for a promise by the company to abate the safety hazards. The agency's regional administrator might become involved if the proposed reduction is more than 50 percent.

If no settlement is reached, the company can appeal to the Occupational Safety and Health Review Commission, which assigns administrative law judges to hear arguments from OSHA and the company. When the commission upholds a law judge's ruling against a company, that decision can be appealed to the courts. The commission's decisions are available by subscription through the Government Printing Office.

After an accident, journalists should request the OSHA inspection report, including the inspector's handwritten notes. But journalists should not be waiting for accidents to happen. Instead, they should request employers' inspection histories from OSHA, then visit the work sites to see if the current situation is better or worse. One reason to make in-person visits is that numbers on OSHA reports can lie. Many workers suffer injuries that are never reported because of employer pressure.

Carol Countryman, reporting for the Texas Observer, told of a poultry company plant that discouraged reporting injuries to outside agencies through inducements: "Safety awards include . . . watches, thermoses and money. Everybody on the line gets an award if no one is injured. But if one person gets hurt, nobody gets the award."

A variation is the workplace bingo game, with cash prizes. Workers receive a token for each day they are present. If they miss work or if a colleague reports an injury, their chance to win the prize ends. Sometimes the bingo card is played by a work unit, rather than individual employees. That arrangement leads to peer pressure on all unit members to work hurt rather than seek treatment under workers' compensation or some other medical program.

When a worker who has been injured on the job gets up the nerve to leave the plant for a doctor's appointment, the employee might be charged a vacation day instead of the company absorbing the time away. Many employees do not have family doctors so end up visiting a physician loyal to the employer. The physician, unsurprisingly, says the injury is not serious enough to stay away from work.

A journalist touring the workplace can look for a posting of OSHA Form 200, listing a summary of all injuries and illnesses. If the form is not posted, a journalist can ask why, then request to see it. If there is trouble obtaining any reports from the employer or the OSHA area director, an appeal can be made to the regional director before invoking the federal Freedom of Information Act.

Most regional OSHA offices have a labor liaison (usually a former union official). A reporter should become acquainted with the liaison. To understand how OSHA inspectors view workplaces, a journalist can read the publicly available manual "The 100 Most Frequently Cited OSHA Construction Standards" for the most recent year. OSHA's magazine Job Safety and Health Quarterly is also useful for getting inside inspectors minds. State officials handling workers' compensation insurance claims can be helpful sources as well. (Workers' compensation is treated more fully in the insurance chapter of this book.) Other sources include university safety or health programs and occupational medicine clinics; specialized publications such as the Occupational Safety and Health Reporter, Washington, D.C.; and statistical services, such as OSHA Data, Maplewood, N.J., which sells computerized enforcement and compliance data back to 1972. Russell Mokhiber's book "Corporate Crime and Violence:

Big Business and the Abuse of the Public Trust" emphasizes criminality surrounding workplace health and safety. The book contains a 50-point program to fight corporate crime. Discussion of those points (for example, enactment of a federal homicide statute to be used against officers, directors and the corporation itself in certain cases of workplace deaths) could yield an educational sidebar to an investigative series.

Wage Enforcement

The Fort Lauderdale Sun-Sentinel found that local garment manufacturers were cheating employees by the thousands out of the minimum wage, overtime, medical benefits and compensation for job-related injuries. Similar investigations could be completed almost anywhere if journalists would just focus their attention.

Overseeing minimum and overtime wage provisions falls to the U.S. Labor Department's Wage and Hour Division within the Employment Standards Administration. Reports available to journalists show employers fined for failing to pay federally required minimum wages or premiums (time-and-a-half after 40 hours) in any one week. The reports often show a pattern of illegality, such as companies that deduct from workers' paychecks to make up for cash drawer shortages. Such cheating explains part of why approximately one in five employees of U.S. companies work full-time but earn less than what the government considers the poverty line for a family of four.

Journalists who examine complaints filed under a 1931 law called the Davis-Bacon Act might be amazed at the richness of the information. The original law was meant to please the labor unions that wanted contractors disqualified from construction projects involving federal money unless they paid the prevailing union wage. That shut out workers willing to work for less, many of them blacks, who had been denied union membership. Today enforcement of the law still excludes many minorities, as well as driving up costs to taxpayers on many federal projects. Part of the journalist's job is to document the legalized racial and ethnic discrimination. Another part of the job is to determine whether the higher wage to union workers is justified by greater skills and efficiency.

Journalists should be alert for local employers who want to pay less than minimum wage to workers deemed incapable of producing at the same rate as a "normal" worker. These usually include mentally retarded people whose work can be considered therapeutic. But abuses abound; the federal agency has granted permission to state agencies to pay less than the minimum wage to clients, such as veterans, producing at normal levels. Perspective on reasonable wages can be gained by subscribing to the federal publications called occupational compensation surveys.

The federal agency, sometimes working with state agencies (in Missouri, the Department of Labor and Industrial Relations Division of Labor Standards), investigates violations of child labor laws. When the Boston Globe looked for usually invisible child workers, it found them in sweatshop garment factories and on farms where they were in danger of being maimed by dangerous heavy equipment. But when employers employ and abuse underage workers they are rarely caught. Regulators are outnumbered, and often are unable to assign anybody full-time to violations involving children. In the few instances when fines are levied against employers, the amounts are so low that there is little or no deterrent value.

Federal and state agencies try to watch over migrant and seasonal workers, who are often as vulnerable as children. But journalists should not wait for understaffed and sometimes uncaring agencies to visit the fields. KGW-TV, Portland, Ore., found migrant workers in pathetic housing being paid less than minimum wage for backbreaking work around pesticides that were causing serious illnesses.

Government agencies are becoming increasingly aware of abuses revolving around corporations replacing regular employees with temporary or part-time workers to save money on wages and benefits. To discover such situations, journalists can develop sources at local employment agencies and temporary worker pools. Hanging around the entrances of those places early each morning is one way to meet talkative workers. The National Association of Temporary Services, Alexandria, Va., can provide perspective as well as help journalists locate the biggest or oldest local suppliers of workers. Robert E. Parker's book "Flesh Peddlers and Warm Bodies: The Temporary Help Industry and Its Workers" contains useful examples and theories.

When regular employees leave a job temporarily for sound family reasons, there are supposed to be wages available when they return. The federal Family Medical Leave Act applies to companies with 50 or more employees within a 75-mile radius; it is supposed to guarantee up to 12 penalty-free weeks of unpaid leave because of a birth, adoption or serious illness involving the worker or the immediate family. Journalists have found that many employers are ignoring the law by refusing leave requests, granting them but then failing to guarantee a job upon return or cutting off benefits.

The Labor Department has been upholding more than 60 percent of worker complaints under the law. An investigation by the Wall Street Journal began with complaint files at the Labor Department. The reporter supplemented those with a survey jointly conducted by a university and a management consulting firm; anecdotes from the National Association of Working Women, Milwaukee; cases brought by a law firm specializing in worker-management disputes; plus quotations from sources at Parent Action in Baltimore, National Coalition of Working Parents in Philadelphia and Families and Work Institute in New York City. When journalists write about hardworking families whose wages barely cover necessities, the articles too frequently treat the situation like it has been mandated from on high—like the weather, beyond the control of humans. The journalists who research these articles seem unaware that wages are the result of conscious decisions of corporate owners, their financiers, legislators dependent on corporate executives' campaign contributions, regulators hoping for highly paid private-sector job offers and judges who before appointment to the bench were established lawyers earning huge fees from corporations.

Pension, Health and Welfare Plans for Workers

Most of the pension-related investigations in the IRE Resource Center look at government employees who are being ripped off or doing the ripping off. Those are important stories, involving as they do billions of dollars of taxpayer money. But the emphasis on public employee pensions gives inexplicable short shrift to private-sector pensions. Every year, millions of workers find they will receive little or nothing at retirement time due to corporate ineptness or fraud combined with ineffective government regulation of business.

The Pension and Welfare Benefits Administration, part of the Labor Department, collects information about company plans for workers on Form 5500. Required under the Employee Retirement Income Security Act, the form details assets of the pension, health or welfare plan, number of participants, names of trustees that handle the assets, administrative costs and a breakdown of investments.

The law, approved as a result of corporate pension funds going bankrupt, limits the kinds of investments trustees can make. Only about 30 percent of retirees are covered by work-related pensions, an indication that the system is working poorly. Journalists should delve into which local businesses provide no pension coverage for workers, and why. They should also know which of the employers that do offer pensions are reducing benefits. The reports on Form 5500 are meant to provide information that will point out trouble before it is too late to intervene. The forms first are sent to the Internal Revenue Service, which evaluates them for continuing tax-exempt status, then to the Labor Department. Journalists interested in a specific company's pension should find out whether the Labor Department has audited the information disclosed. Because the Labor Department assigns just a few hundred auditors to track nearly a million pension plans, fraud has run rampant. An example: A bank invested $727,000 of its pension plan assets in securities issued by one of its affiliates. That was an improper investment jeopardizing the future payments to retirees. But it was never detected by the Labor Department. Rather, it surfaced through other means. Journalists who examine local companies' pension reporting forms will often detect problems never even glanced at by the government agency supposedly responsible.

Besides providing clues about how union and management can steal dollars from such funds (hiring a brother-in-law to administer funds at inflated costs or investing in a friend's venture), the forms are valuable for other stories. Some companies have declared pensions "overfunded" under federal regulations, dissolving them, purchasing less reliable annuities for remaining workers, then using the leftover assets as operating capital. Workers' future retirement funds are then dependent on the financial health of the insurance company providing the annuities.

Many pension funds, to the detriment of workers, have played a part in reducing the sales price of a dying company. For example, Company A owes millions of dollars to its underfunded pension plan, but agrees to a sale to Company B for cash and an agreement that Company B make good on the debt to the pension fund. Company B gets a bargain-basement price, fails to make good on the pension fund debt, then files bankruptcy and dumps the ailing plan on the government's taxpayer-financed Pension Benefit Guaranty Corporation.

Pension Reporter, Chicago, and Pension World, Atlanta, are two of many publications that can help journalists understand the issues, institutions and individuals involved. John A. Turner's book "Pension Policy for a Mobile Labor Force" is a good resource. Every interested party has its own advocacy organizations. Examples based in the Washington, D.C., area include the Association of Private Pension and Welfare Plans (employers), Pension Rights Center (employees) and the Society of Professional Benefit Administrators (third-party managers).

State Employment Security Divisions

An often overlooked source on companies, unions and individuals is the state unemployment office. A reporter can use unemployment records to find former company employees or former union members, look for local employment trends and determine why workers get fired or quit. The records can help plumb the depths of alcohol or drug-abuse problems among local employers.

The stories told range from an employee fired for sitting on the copying machine and selling the results to coworkers, to the firing of a slightly retarded dishwasher by a restaurant manager for dropping a small stack of dishes.

The system works this way: When workers are fired, laid off or quit for what they feel are valid reasons, they can claim unemployment benefits, which are paid out of the state's unemployment trust fund, financed by employer taxes. Validity might turn on whether the employer has issued an employee handbook, and, if so, whether the employer violated any provisions of that handbook. It is always worthwhile for a journalist to find out whether a handbook exists, then obtain a copy if it does. Some courts have ruled that the practices and policies in a handbook constitute an implied binding employment contract.

Contract or no contract with employees, which employers are the most aggressive in fighting unemployment claims? The more successful claimants against an employer, the more taxes the firm pays. Hence, many employers will try to keep costs down by challenging claims time after time.

The former employee makes an initial claim at the local unemployment compensation office. A claims officer interviews the claimant, and often the employer, who is given a chance to contest the filing. If disagreement persists, a hearing is held before an impartial referee. That decision can then be appealed to the state's employment security board of review and from there to the state courts. Journalists wanting detail should ask not only for the paperwork but also for the tape recording of the entire hearing. A tip: Workers who file unemployment claims might file other complaints elsewhere, such as with equal employment opportunity commissions. Those additional complaints might provide further insight into a local employer.

Workers may be disqualified from receiving benefits if state examiners disagree that a worker quit for "good cause." How each state defines "good cause," and the cases arising from those definitions, might be the genesis of interesting articles. For example, some states consider sexual harassment in the workplace good cause, but most do not believe sexual harassment allegations solely on the alleged victim's say-so. How about forced retirement or resignation in lieu of termination? Reductions in salary or work hours? Workplace toxins? Should an individual be disqualified from unemployment benefits because of refusing to accept a new job? On what grounds is refusal allowed while benefits are maintained?

Some workers fail to qualify for unemployment insurance on the face of it, including self-employed individuals and those on a commission arrangement, such as insurance and real estate agents. What happens to them when the bottom drops out? Some unemployed persons are denied government insurance payments because they are judged to be seeking work haphazardly rather than systematically. Are those judgments by the state fair and consistent or cruel?

Journalists should be checking state government sources to determine whether any local employers are refusing to pay the required amount into the unemployment insurance fund. Are state data collection systems compatible with federal income tax filings by employers? If not, the state will have far more difficulty tracking employers that cheat. Those that do cheat and get caught usually benefit from no publicity, because so few journalists track such cases. Yet it seems obvious that many local readers, listeners and viewers would be interested in learning about such conduct by a local employer.

A recent unfortunate phenomenon is unemployment that occurs when employers close their plants so they can move elsewhere in the country or across national borders. Frequently, employers making those moves are hoping to pay lower wages, offer fewer benefits and escape certain government regulations. They probably will worry little about the permanent impact on the community that gave them a home for so many years. A scathing look at the phenomenon is "Runaway America: U.S. Jobs and Factories on the Move" by Harry Browne and Beth Sims.

One overview of job loss is the book "Out of Work: Unemployment and Government in Twentieth-Century America" by Richard K. Vedder and Lowell E. Gallaway. Ways to track local and regional employment trends include three U.S. government publications available by subscription: "Area Trends in Employment and Unemployment," "Unemployment in States and Local Areas," and "Employment and Earnings." A helpful guide is the book "How to Maximize Your Unemployment Benefits" by Raymond Avrutis and Geraldine S. Wulff. The U.S. government guide Comparison of State Unemployment Insurance Laws provides useful detail; the newsletter Employee Policy for the Private and Public Sectors, Alexandria, Va., can also be helpful.

Labor Lawyers and the Courts

Labor law has undergone so many fundamental changes in recent years—and changes are still occurring—that the courts and labor lawyers have become excellent sources. Journalists should contact the state bar association for a listing of its labor law section, as well as the American Bar Association membership list for its section on Labor and Employment Law. Employment law newsletters published by law firms for their corporate clients can be an excellent source for keeping up with local decisions. A journalist can ask a court reporter colleague to look for employment-related lawsuits involving individual workers, companies or unions.

One expanding area involves civil suits taking the position that a job loss constitutes a breach of an oral, written or implied contract. They stem from the erosion of a legal theory called the "employment at will doctrine." The doctrine long held that the boss could fire workers for "good reason, bad reason or no reason at all." The contemporary lawsuits, usually filed by fired or demoted nonunion workers, often seek millions of dollars in damages. Other targets in the new world of labor law are unions, as worker members allege the union failed to represent them adequately in return for dues or that it failed to live up to its stated duty to help provide a safe workplace. As Mike McGraw of the Kansas City Star commented, "The way workplace law has been expanding, you're likely to find almost any kind of claim in the courts these days."

The School of Industrial and Labor Relations at Cornell University, Ithaca, N.Y., operates a book publishing company offering many relevant titles that mesh well with information from labor lawyers and lawsuits. An example is "Mutual Gains: A Guide to Union-Management Cooperation" by Edward Cohen-Rosenthal and Cynthia Burton. A rare book detailing management tactics from the inside is "Confessions of a Union Buster" by Martin Jay Levitt, with Terry Conrow. Modern-day union strategies are the subject of Hector L. Delgado's book "New Immigrants, Old Unions: Organizing Undocumented Workers in Los Angeles." The Journal of Labor Research, Fairfax, Va., is one of many periodicals with useful articles. General-circulation publications such as Business Week, Forbes and Fortune regularly publish articles that are worth reading. The Wall Street Journal is unmatched among national newspapers for its labor-management coverage. The Labor Relations Reporter from the Bureau of National Affairs, Washington, D.C., and Labor Law Reporter from Commerce Clearing House, Chicago, keep up with court cases, government agency rulings and other developments week after week.

■ THE MINTZ WAY

If Paul Williams served as the bard of investigators delving into the private sector, Morton Mintz served as the in-the-trenches scribe. When Mintz "retired" to freelancing after 42 years as a salaried reporter—the last 30 doing investigative work for the Washington Post—the IRE Journal published a retrospective of his journalism.

Mintz is not exactly an unknown. He wrote or cowrote 10 books, numerous magazine articles, and hundreds of daily stories and series for newspapers. He won many journalism awards. Yet he never became a household name the way Bob Woodward, Seymour Hersh or some broadcast journalists did.

In 1974, Mintz unveiled his mass media proposition: "If it's really important, it doesn't get the attention it deserves, or it gets it late or gets it only because some oddball pushes it." As examples, he cited filthy food plants, auto safety, corporate secrecy, insurance, medical devices and the like. In the preface to his book "At Any Cost: Corporate Greed, Women and the Dalkon Shield," Mintz explained the need for investigating the private sector about as well as it can be explained. The IRE Journal reprinted that preface, with permission. It is reprinted here in an edited version:

> The story of the Dalkon Shield lays bare the perils inherent in a system that allows corporations to profit even if they put human beings at risk.

The Dalkon Shield created a disaster of global proportions because a few men with little on their minds but megabucks made decisions, in the interest of profit, that exposed millions of women to serious infection, sterility and even death.

The problem is not simply that corporations have no conscience, but that they are endowed by law with rights beyond those allowed to individuals. Corporations too often act without compassion and, no matter what damage they cause, without remorse. Even worse, they cannot be held accountable, as people can be. You cannot lock up a corporation, or sentence it to hard labor or the electric chair. And too often, the law fails to look behind the corporate veil, to prosecute the individuals who make decisions and act in the name of the corporation.

In 1962, I wrote the story of thalidomide, the sedative-tranquilizer that caused several thousand children to be born without arms or legs. This was my unforgettable introduction to a brutal fact: corporations run by human beings regularly and deliberately undertake activities that cause grave environmental damage, or lead to large-scale disease, injury or death to those who make, use or are exposed to their products.

In the ensuing quarter-century, in the Washington Post and in books and articles, I have reported many more cases of knowing and willful misconduct involving a broad spectrum of industry: producers of medicines, contraceptives, mechanical heart valves, anesthesia machines, agricultural and industrial chemicals, food additives and colorings, infant formulas, toys, automobiles, tires, asbestos, coal, uranium, space heaters, washing machines, weapons systems. But not until my investigation of the Dalkon Shield did I have access to a factual record so panoramic in scope and so complete that I could reconstruct in faithful detail the origins and evolution of a catastrophic episode and could identify precisely who had done and who had concealed each morally dubious or indefensible act.

By mid-1985, more than 14,000 American women who had worn Dalkon Shields had filed lawsuits and claims against the manufacturer, the A.H. Robins Company of Richmond, Va. This flood of litigation has by now produced several hundred thousand pages of pretrial "discovery" materials, particularly company records and sworn testimony in depositions, as well as transcripts of trial testimony and other court documents. Starting in September 1982, and for more than two years thereafter, I reviewed literally tens of thousands of pages of these materials. I also conducted more than one hundred interviews and attended Shield-related judicial proceedings in three Minnesota cities and in Washington. Since 1973, when I covered a five-day hearing on IUDs held by a U.S. representative, I have also tracked the Dalkon Shield in hearings held by panels of outside advisers to the Food and Drug Administration.

These materials illuminate every aspect of the Dalkon Shield saga, from its origins in the mid and late 1960s to the present. They tell what happened, and how and why; what Robins executives knew, and when they knew it; which Robins officials contradicted each other (and, on occasion, themselves) under oath; and what evidence disappeared or was destroyed, falsified or covered up.

The documents do more: They take the observer to a vantage point from which he can peer into the chasm between the flesh-and-blood person and the paper corporate person. This chasm is widely perceived but rarely examined, for the fact is that the human being who would not harm you on an individual, face-to-face basis, who is charitable, civic-minded, loving and devout, will wound or kill you from behind the corporate veil. He may do this without qualm because he has been conditioned to drop a curtain between his private moral and religious self and his corporate immoral and irreligious self. And society at large accepts and, if only by its silence, validates such compartmentalization.

Is it not an atrocity and a sin—and should it not be a crime?—to commission, devise or implement an advertising campaign designed to induce children to smoke? To warn American but not foreign physicians that an antibiotic which causes an often fatal blood disease at significant rates should be used only in rare circumstances? To certify shoddy work on a nuclear power plant? To sell faulty weapons to the armed services? To sell in the Third World drugs that are banned in the United States for want of evidence that they are safe and effective? Such questions are rarely discussed in classrooms, schools of theology and business administration or newspaper editorials or opinion columns. Such questions never arise in presidential elections and probably never in congressional races.

Perhaps most dismaying, they seldom become sermon topics for mainstream clergymen and never for television evangelists. From Lynchburg, Va., the Rev. Jerry Falwell leads the Moral Majority in its crusade against abortion. In Lynchburg, Robins made millions of Dalkon Shields, thousands of which caused spontaneous septic abortions. Might Falwell have by now found this grist for a sermon?

The paradox by which immersion in the corporation washes away personal responsibility is perfectly captured in the figure of the builder and chairman of the Fortune 500 company that bears his name. A towering presence in American philanthropy, he has given away truly astonishing sums in gifts to a broad array of worthy causes. In 1969, he gave $50 million to the University of Richmond, an unrestricted gift said by the university to have been the largest gift ever made by a living person to an institution of higher education. Since then, he and his family have given at least $50 million more to the university, and additional millions to other universities and to diverse other causes. In December 1983, Town and Country magazine listed him among the top five of "The Most Generous Americans."

A Baptist, the chairman was nominated by the Richmond chapter of B'nai B'rith International for the Jewish service organization's Great American Tradition Award. At the presentation banquet in June 1982, the president of the University of Richmond was the principal speaker. "Truly the Lord has chosen you as one of His most essential instruments," he told Robins. "We applaud you for the high accomplishment of always exhibiting a steadfast and devoted concern for your fellow man. . . . Your example will cast its shadows into eternity, as the sands of time carry the indelible footprints of your good works."

But with the power to do great good goes the power to do great harm. Edward Ashworth Ross, sociologist and author of the brilliant, pithy "Sin and Society: An Analysis of Latter-Day Iniquity" (1907), saw this years before the chairman was born, and observed:

> The grading of sinners according to badness of character goes on the assumption that the wickedest man is the most dangerous. This would be true if men were abreast in their opportunities to do harm. In that case, the blackest villain would be the worst scourge of society. But the fact is that the patent ruffian is confined to the social basement, and enjoys few opportunities. He can assault or molest, to be sure; but he cannot betray. Nobody depends on him, so he cannot commit a breach of trust—that arch sin of our time. He does not hold in his hand the safety or welfare or money of the public. He is the clinker, not the live coal; vermin, not beast of prey. Today the villain most in need of curbing is the respectable, exemplary, trusted personage who, strategically placed at the focus of a spiderweb of fiduciary relations, is able from his office-chair to pick a thousand pockets, or imperil a thousand lives. Is it the great-scale, high-voltage sinner that needs the shackle?

Decades later, the chief U.S. district judge for Minnesota had to spell it out again in reprimanding the chairman and two other officers of the company:

> It is not enough to say, "I did not know," "It was not me," "Look elsewhere." Time and again, each of you has used this argument in refusing to acknowledge your responsibility and in pretending to the world that the chief officers and directors of your gigantic multinational corporation have no responsibility for the company's acts and omissions. . . .
>
> Today as you sit here attempting once more to extricate yourselves from the legal consequences of your acts, none of you has faced up to the fact that more than 9,000 [at that time] women claim they gave up part of their womanhood so that your company might prosper. And there stand behind them legions more who have been injured but who have not sought relief in the courts of this land. . . .
>
> If one poor young man were, without authority or consent, to inflict such damage upon one woman, he would be jailed for a good portion of the rest of his life. Yet your company, without warning to women, invaded their bodies by the millions and caused them injuries by the thousands.

Ross warned—in 1907—that the insistence on defining sin and misconduct in an industrial society in the same way as it was defined in the past was exacting a terrible price. He saw the absurdity of condemning what a man did in a bedroom but not what he did in a boardroom. The Dalkon Shield case judge repeated—in 1984—how we still haven't grasped that the man who assaults women from an officer chair is as grave a sinner as the man who assaults a woman in an alley. Surely the time has come to extend the definition of immoral conduct into the boardroom and the corporate office.

Chapter 13

INVESTIGATING CHARITIES AND OTHER NOT-FOR-PROFITS

Charities. The word has such a harmless sound. So harmless that most journalists never delve into their activities, locally or nationally.

Not-for-profit organizations. Not charities exactly, but existing to improve society in some way. If no profit motive exists, how much wrongdoing could be involved? So why investigate?

Foundations. They are a type of not-for-profit organization, often with charitable overtones. They are frequently associated with wealthy, prominent philanthropists. Why question how the rich give away their money?

Such thinking about charities, not-for-profits and foundations is misguided. Charities frequently spend donations unwisely, sometimes crossing the line from inefficiency into the realm of corruption. Even if run efficiently and honestly, they might be failing the populations they want to help. Increasingly, they charge fees for their services, violating the concept of charity that originally earned them their tax-exemptions.

Not-for-profits are often anything but, building up huge surpluses as they operate like other businesses. One of the primary reasons for their success is the advantage they possess by not paying taxes. Under tax law, they can accumulate surpluses as long as they do not distribute them as stock or dividends. Instead, they often spend surpluses on new buildings, large salaries and start-ups of commercial ventures.

Foundations are sometimes nothing more than questionable financial shelters for the wealthy, spending tiny amounts to benefit society while hoarding the rest, much of it tax-free. Some foundations, those not set up and controlled by individuals, are spinoffs from hospitals and other organizations that originally did lots of charity work. Often begun with donated corporate stock (the Ford Foundation, the Kellogg Foundation), they are still under the control of huge profit-making companies.

David Johnston created a non-profits beat at the Los Angeles Times, investigating the previously untouchable local United Way. He found secret, low-interest loans to five of the organization's executives. He also found an authoritarian executive director pulling down a huge salary, riding around in a telephone-equipped Cadillac and socializing at an all-white, all-male country club thanks to donors' charitable contributions. Before Johnston could do follow-up stories, his editors removed him from the beat because of perceived unfairness. His removal seemed to demonstrate the influence of charities. But Johnston's article in Columbia Journalism Review calling for greater scrutiny of non-profits—and explaining the techniques for applying such scrutiny—has influenced some reporters and editors in recent years.

A massive Philadelphia Inquirer investigation of the not-for-profit sector by Gilbert M. Gaul and Neill A. Borowski identified about 1.2 million tax-exempt organizations, and that number excluded churches. Their estimated total annual revenue topped $500 billion, which meant that the economy lost an estimated $40 billion in revenue due to tax exemptions. Meanwhile, Congress and the Internal Revenue Service keep adding tax-exempt categories, including mutual life insurance companies, health insurers, labor unions, credit unions, cemeteries, fraternal groups and trade associations. A professional football league, which conducted almost no unselfish activities and paid its commissioner more than $1.5 million annually, had tax-exempt status.

The investigation, reprinted as a book titled "Free Ride: The Tax-Exempt Economy," began with Gaul's curiosity. He had covered the changing nature of supposedly non-profit hospitals for a decade. Benefitting from tax exemptions, the hospitals were becoming more and more involved in commercial activities while providing little charity care. Gaul proposed a major study of the entire non-profit economy. Borowski, curious about an increase in tax-exempt real estate, joined Gaul. They built a paper trail from a number of documents.

Form 990 informational tax returns. These are filed annually with the IRS. Most groups that win tax-exempt status from the IRS in the first place (using Form 1023 or Form 1024) incur a legal obligation to file an informational tax return, even though they do not have to pay taxes. The only blanket exemptions are for churches and non-profit groups with less than $25,000 in annual revenues. Gaul and Borowski obtained some of the forms from the IRS, some from state attorneys general and some from the organizations themselves.

Audited financial statements of non-profits groups. Gaul and Borowski said in their IRE contest entry form that the audited statements

> were valuable supplements to the tax returns because they contained additional financial information, so could be used as a check against the Form 990s. Hospitals, for instance, often report smaller profits on their 990s than

they do on their financial audits through the use of accounting gimmicks that allow them to "reserve" income against future charges.

Unrelated business income is supposed to be reported on Form 990T. Some non-profits fail to report such income at all, or underreport it by overallocating expenses against revenues.

Offering statements for tax-exempt bonds. Tax-exempt bonds are sold by hospitals, universities and other organizations. Offering statements often contain historical and biographical information. Gaul and Borowski used bond sale filings to show how a Texas financier used charities to buy and dispose of Iowa nursing homes with tax-exempt bonds, making a profit of more than $6 million.

Local, state and federal court cases. The Inquirer team reviewed about 150 court cases involving non-profit organizations; in many cases, their tax-exempt status was being challenged. Federal bankruptcy court records contained revelations in some instances. So did cases on file at U.S. Tax Court.

IRS studies of the tax-exempt sector. These studies are available, as are statistics on IRS audits and revocations of organizations' tax-exempt status. The agency publishes a list, currently about 2,000 pages in length, showing organizations to which contributions are deductible. It is known by insiders as IRS Publication 78.

Sales tax exemptions. The reporters obtained information from state revenue agencies to determine the extent of lost tax revenue. They obtained and analyzed real-estate assessment records kept at the county level in a similar fashion.

Educational records from tax-exempt colleges. These records are compiled by the U.S. Education Department. The reporters compared the amount of charitable scholarships granted by colleges against the revenue lost to the greater society because of the institutions' tax exemptions.

Congressional hearings involving tax-exempt organizations.

Gaul and Borowski followed people trails as well, interviewing about 400 sources, including executives of tax-exempt groups, IRS bureaucrats, economists, state and county government regulators, legislators, academic experts, tax lawyers, health, education and welfare officials.

■ BEYOND THE BOTTOM LINE

Non-profit organizations yield more than financial stories. Some of the most sacred cows in newsrooms are doing widespread harm. In the IRE Journal, Elizabeth Marchak of the Washington Times told the story behind the story about exposing one sacred cow—the Boy Scouts of America. The story is reprinted here in part:

When Boy Scout leaders began to teach Scouts about sexual abuse in the late 1980s, they never mentioned that sometimes the abusers were the men who took them camping. After more than 10 months spent looking at 400 cases, we were able to document an organization-wide cover-up of sexual abuse in our five-part series "Scouts Honor."

Reporter Patrick Boyle, working with Database Editor Elizabeth A. Marchak, discovered the Boy Scouts of America went to great lengths to cover up hundreds of incidents of sexual abuse and the millions of dollars it paid in out-of-court settlements.

We narrowed our search to Scout leaders who abused Scouts. We eliminated some 50 cases because we weren't sure if the victims were Scouts. We left out other cases because we couldn't determine if the victim was a child. In case after case that we did use, a pattern emerged.

A Scout leader, often an upstanding citizen with a stable job, a wife and children, would molest a Scout, usually on a campout. Sometimes he got away with it several times.

Loyalty is part of the Scout Oath. The abusers used it to their advantage, intimidating victims so the incidents would be kept secret. Besides, some Scoutmasters told their victims, that's how everybody learns about sex.

Anguished parents whose nine or ten-year-old sons had been repeatedly masturbated or penetrated were usually persuaded that the problem could be resolved by the Scouts without help from the police. We found that pattern in all 50 states.

The Scouts' way of resolving the issue was almost formulaic. Scores of abusers were allowed to resign with letters that cited work or family pressures in exchange for promises of no prosecution.

Those forced to leave Scouting all got letters with the nearly identical wording, saying that Scouting was a "privilege, not a right." More than 90 percent of the letters were signed by the same person.

Those resignations often turned out to be no resolution at all, as many of the accused joined Big Brother or Little League or another Boy Scout troop.

Victims fared differently. Not once in the thousands of pages of court or Scouting documents did we ever find any national scouting official show the slightest concern over the victim's injuries or psychological well-being. Their primary interest, evidenced in dozens of letters, was to keep the incident out of the media.

If the parents did file a civil lawsuit, the Scouts' crack legal advisors arrived to help local lawyers craft an out-of-court settlement that generally required a gag order. The gags appealed to parents because they offered a way to resolve the problem, get money for much-needed counseling and protect their child's identity.

If the case did go to trial, the boys were again victimized by the Scouts. This time, no-holds barred courtroom tactics painted boys as sexually aggressive co-conspirators. It is a standard defense to argue that preteen boys initiated sex with Scoutmasters.

In 1989, a Fairfax, Va., victim and his parents turned down one of the Scouts' out-of-court settlements and its accompanying gag order. The settlement finally agreed to, minus the gag, gave us the first look at 15 years' accumulation of lawsuits and Boy Scout documents that filled nearly two file drawers.

Using 4th Dimension software for the Macintosh, we created a database for the lawsuits and sexual abuse complaints filed by parents. Being able to assign a number to each case helped enormously. In 88 percent of the cases, the abusers' names had been blacked out by the Scouts. More than 99 percent of the Scouts' names were missing as well.

Some documents gave us only state, date, council name, age of victim or victims and a couple of cursory letters making oblique references to a "leadership problem."

Other cases included thick files about repeat offenders or obviously disturbed men who repeatedly tried to join troops or write letters to victims detailing sexual practices.

We were able to determine which level of Scout leader was most likely to abuse (Scoutmasters), the most likely location for abuse (campsites), the types of abuser (for example, married men were just as likely as unmarried men), the most common response to the charge of abuse (bar him from Scouting but never report him), how many had previous police records (at least 8 percent), the most likely group to sponsor a troop (churches).

We added nearly 60 instances of abuse to our database after we found a Florida court case in which the Scouts were required to file a synopsis of 350 incidents where abusers were kicked out of Scouting from 1971 to 1986.

We knew we had some of these cases, but we wouldn't have been able to tell which ones without our own computer database. Searching the cases state by state, we compared the sketchy information we got from the Florida filing against what we had already—the abuser's title, age, city, Boy Scout council, dates and description of abuse and police action, if any.

In each case we had in our files, we found the Boy Scouts provided minimal or misleading information. For example, one case said a Scoutmaster had been "accused of involvement with young boys," yet we knew the man had been kicked out of Scouting for inappropriate sexual conduct.

We used the comparison technique when we called up the Vu/Text commercial database to search newspapers for "Boy Scouts and sex and abuse." We got more than 100 references from regional newspapers.

We turned to another computer database—DataTimes' regional newspapers—to give us leads on new arrests. The search put us on the phone for several recent cases—including two in Nebraska and one in Wyoming, previously unrepresented.

The Boy Scouts of America deserve some credit. They did try to keep unfit people out of Scouting. When they could not keep abusers out, or if they were sued, they became masters at public relations damage control.

When the Dallas Morning News called the Scouts for a year-end wrap-up, the organization's press official told the newspaper yes, there had been 416 cases of sexual abuse and no, the information was not hard to come by: The Scouts provided the Washington Times with all the information it wanted about every lawsuit.

Later, the press official told us he had made a mistake. Either way, admitting to 416 cases of abuse over the last 20 years is actually an effort at damage control. We know there are hundreds more cases and so do they.

But the Scouts are a cultural icon. Parents, teachers, parish priests and police officers from Maine to Hawaii will tell you there's no safer place for boys to become men than to progress from Cub to Eagle Scout. It is an image the Boy Scouts of America will always nurture even when it is not always true.

Boyle expanded the investigation into a book, "Scouts Honor: Sexual Abuse in America's Most Trusted Institution."

A Wall Street Journal reporter dug into a related sacred cow, the Girl Scouts—especially its dependence on child labor to generate much of its revenue through cookie sales. The reporter determined that the leading seller, age 11, in a Connecticut troop generated $498, but only $67 ended up in the troop's treasury. The rest went to support regional and central office paid administrators and staff.

The Bottom Line of Charities

A huge tax-exempt civil rights organization headquartered in Montgomery, Ala., sent thousands of heartfelt letters across the nation every month begging for funds. But the staff at the Montgomery Advertiser knew the group's lavish, modern headquarters contradicted the tone of the appeals. After investigating, the Advertiser staff found the organization had about $52 million in an endowment fund.

KOVR-TV, Sacramento, Calif., looked at a charity claiming to grant dying children their final wishes; the reporters found only three youngsters receiving benefits, as the organization retained about 99 percent of its donations.

"God Is My Landlord," a Village Voice investigation, introduced the concept of once small, pure not-for-profits—in this case a religious organization and its related housing operations for the needy—growing into big businesses almost entirely unregulated. The subject of the Voice article bordered on being a slum lord, but despite its unsavory practices, was still exempt from paying most taxes, rent control ordinances and labor laws.

Some not-for-profits—the Salvation Army is an example—have become a leading provider of social services in the community. All the not-for-profits lumped together might dominate the social services scene, taking over what was once clearly a government function and sometimes heavily funded by government contracts. According to the Chronicle of Philanthropy, Washington, D.C., not-for-profits employ nearly 7 percent of the U.S. work force. Gale Research's "Charitable Organizations of the United States" is a nearly comprehensive listing of those groups.

The big questions are obvious about charities, yet rarely asked by journalists: What percentage of the funds raised by a charity end up paying administrative costs? How much money should a charity spend to raise more money? What percentage of total donations actually goes into charitable activities? Is the charity helping the people it says it will help in the ways it says it will help? Are audited financial statements and other documents available immediately on request?

Help in answering these questions is available from insider groups such as the American Association of Fund-raising Counsel, New York City, and the National Association of Fund Raising Executives, Alexandria, Va. Guidelines are available from nonpartisan watchdog groups such as the National Charities Information Bureau, New York City; Philanthropic Advisory Service of the Council of Better Business Bureaus, Arlington, Va.; American Institute of Philanthropy, St. Louis; National Committee for Responsible Philanthropy, Independent Sector and Capital Research Center, all of Washington, D.C.

Generally, watchdog groups recommend that charities make available an audited annual report; spend at least 60 percent of annual expenses on the activities donors think they are supporting; keep net assets at a fiscally sound level, but not more than twice the current year's expenses or the next year's budget; and find otherwise unaffiliated board members who will volunteer their time to meet at least twice a year.

"Charities" and "nonprofits" are broad terms. A journalist should ask what section of the Internal Revenue Code an organization has used to gain its tax exemption. Knowing that will help a journalist determine which forms are supposed to be available and which activities are permissible. For instance, a tax-exempt private school is supposed to file IRS Form 5578 certifying that it eschews racial discrimination. Organizations receiving their tax-exempt status under Section 501-c-3 of the IRS Code can usually accept donations that are tax-exempt. Most organizations receiving tax-exempt status under any other section usually cannot grant tax exemptions for donations.

Foundations perform some functions of a charity, but are different in many ways. While many charities file an annual Form 990 with the IRS, foundations—especially those dominated by a wealthy individual—might file a Form 990-PF, which discloses its own kinds of information. The forms required by the IRS are normally available from the organization that files on its premises during normal business hours. But if a journalist would rather request the forms from the IRS or a state government watchdog agency, it often will speed processing if the employer identification number is in hand. "The National Directory of Non-Profit Organizations" from Taft Publishing, Rockville, Md., provides those numbers for about 300,000 groups. The same outfit publishes "Foundation Reporter: Comprehensive Profiles and Giving Analyses of America's Major Private Foundations."

When the Orlando Sentinel began investigating the "temples" of a charitable organization, the staff knew it was examining a sacred cow. Who could find fault with a fraternal organization raising money to operate orthopedic and burn hospitals for children? The year they conducted their investigation, the local chapter made an $81,000 profit. But, the journalists discovered, not a penny went to children's hospitals. Instead, it helped pay for members' entertainment, including upkeep of their private bar and restaurant.

The story began with a tip from an insider. But it was the Form 990s that nailed down the story. The forms showed that in most years, members spent more money on conventions and parties than on hospital operations. A fund containing money contributed for hospital endowments was making no-interest or low-interest loans to top officials. The organization's board of directors received free trips to exotic locales, plus expense accounts running into the tens of thousands of dollars apiece. Directors of non-profits are usually volunteers, but sometimes benefit by taking perquisites or providing services to the organizations for a fee. When too much of that dealing occurs, the board of directors can lose its effectiveness as a watchdog.

Here are some tips on how to read a Form 990 and its precursor, the document a group must file with the IRS to receive tax-exempt status (often Form 1023 or Form 1024):

Review all sources of revenue. What percentage comes from charitable donations? Government grants and contracts? Fees for services? Many nonprofits that once relied on philanthropy now exist mostly by charging fees—hospitals, for example.

Line 18 on Form 990 is a key. Nonprofits call their net income "excesses" or "surpluses." This is semantics. It is profit. Where do these funds go? Are they parked in a reserve, earning interest but not helping anybody directly? Is the money used as venture capital in a for-profit subsidiary?

Line 20 on the Form 990, "Other Changes in Net Assets," shows if a nonprofit transfers funds in or out of its organization. A schedule is required that provides additional details. This is one way of uncovering if a hospital is diverting assets to finance other activities.

Some nonprofits understate their profits by playing accounting games. This makes them appear poorer than they really are. For example, say a hospital routinely receives settlements from Medicare for patients treated in earlier years. How does it account for this money? If it puts it on the income statement, it boosts profit. If the hospital puts it on the balance sheet as a reserve, it becomes a liability. Another trick is to remove nonoperating revenue (gifts and investment income) from the financial statement by creating a separate tax-exempt foundation or parent corporation with its own financial statement. A hospital may report a surplus of, say, $10 million on its income statement, but earn income of $20 million to $30 million through its foundation. A reporter unaware of the foundation would have only half of the picture.

An organization can make it look as if it is spending more on do-good activities than it really is by using an accounting tactic called "joint-cost allocation." Fund-raising costs are allocated to program expenses on the grounds that the solicitation letters contain educational material. The educational material, however, might be as sparse as one sentence with statistics about cancer deaths if the charity is in the business of fighting cancer. Accounting rules exist to prevent such misstatements, but poor judgment or willful bending of the rules can result in misleading numbers. Conscientious investigators can study the rules, available from the American Institute of Certified Public Accountants and carrying headings such as "Accounting for Joint Costs of Informational Materials and Activities of Not-for-Profit Organizations That Include a Fund-Raising Appeal."

A schedule accompanying Part VI, Lines 80a-b, should list all the related organizations of a nonprofit, both tax-exempt and for-profit. This is one of the better ways to put together a corporate profile of a nonprofit network. It's also useful for determining whether a nonprofit is parking huge sums in another company.

Line 54 of Form 990 shows investments in stocks and bonds. Line 67a shows the funds a nonprofit has available for any purpose it chooses—the "Current Unrestricted" fund. It offers one indication of the wealth and discretionary cash nonprofits hold. A more complicated multiyear cash flow analysis is required to really get at the wealth issue.

Schedule A, Part III, Lines 2a-d, of 990s provides details of business transactions between board members and their nonprofits.

Some books and pamphlets aimed at charity insiders that can inform journalists include "Completing Your IRS Form 990: A Guide for Tax-Exempt Organizations" by Michael I. Sanders and Celia Roady, "The Law of Tax-Exempt Organizations" by Bruce R. Hopkins and "Protecting Your Organization's Tax-Exempt Status: A Guide for Nonprofit Managers" by Mark Bookman.

Foundations

Perspective on how foundations should and do operate is available from the Foundation Center, New York City. It keeps individual forms on file and publishes The Foundation Directory, covering thousands of groups with at least $2 million of assets or giving grants totalling more than $200,000 annually. A journalist can use the directory to learn about a foundation already under scrutiny or can troll the directory's geographic section to learn which local foundations exist that might be worthy of scrutiny. By consulting the directory, for example, a Milwaukee journalist would find a local foundation with more than $400 million in assets and a reputation as the leading funder of conservative political intellectual activity. Mpls. St. Paul magazine found that local foundations have become the lead players in the power structure as government budgets atrophied and for-profit corporations cut back philanthropy in hard times. The magazine documented construction projects and social policies emanating from foundation boardrooms.

A private foundation is a type of charity that gets a substantial share of its resources from investments and endowments, frequently from a single donor or a small group of donors. The IRS decides what is a private foundation and what is not. Generally, a foundation is a charity that gets less than one-third of its revenues from public donations, fees or government grants. But there are exceptions. The income is used to make grants to other organizations rather than disbursed directly for charitable activities.

Is the foundation mainly trying to do good? Or is it mainly trying to shelter the income of an individual or family from taxes? Sometimes tax avoidance is accomplished by shuffling funds between related foundations. Interlocking directorships might be a tipoff to questionable transfers.

Donors who give more than 2 percent of the foundation's annual income are called substantial contributors. A private foundation cannot enter into certain business transactions with "disqualified persons." Breaking the rule is called "self-dealing." Those disqualified persons include substantial contributors and members of their immediate families, foundation officials and their families, companies owned by disqualified persons and government officials. Banned transactions include property sales, leases or rentals, loans, transfers of foundation assets, sales of stocks, bonds or other securities.

A private foundation must limit its investment in any company in which disqualified persons also have an interest. If disqualified persons have controlling interest, their holdings and the foundation's holdings cannot equal more than 20 percent of the company's voting stock. If disqualified persons do not exercise control, the combined ownership can equal 35 percent.

A private foundation must pay out an amount equal to 5 percent of its total assets each year. The payouts can be in the form of program spending or grants to other charities. A 15 percent penalty tax is imposed on any shortfall. Gaul and Borowski found many give away the minimum 5 percent, "while earning much more on investments. With $163 billion in assets, they are operated like private banks, with elite, self-perpetuating boards of directors."

A private foundation cannot spend its money on certain things. It cannot lobby for or against legislation, cannot give grants to noncharitable organizations unless the foundation oversees how the money is spent. Numerous groups can provide perspective, including the Council on Foundations and the Association of Black Foundation Executives, both headquartered in Washington, D.C.

Fund-raising Techniques and Conundrums

If a charity uses volunteer fund-raisers, their labor is free. When a charity has decided against using volunteers, journalists should ask why.

No volunteers probably means professional fund-raisers, who tend to rely on telephone solicitations. Such solicitations are a special problem for journalists and regulators because when dishonesty occurs there is no hard evidence. Charities that use telephone solicitations only are immediately suspect; honest charities have no worry about putting their pleas for money in writing.

Professional fund-raising firms hired by legitimate charities might lie to potential donors about how the money will be used, will say they represent legitimate charities when they do not or will use names so similar to well-known charities that donors are almost certain to be confused.

Even honest fund-raising firms might cause distress for donors because of the huge percentages taken off the top. Journalists should find out if the fund-raising firm is working on a flat fee basis or under an arrangement involving a percentage of the money raised. Sometimes the flat fee is larger than the amount of money donated, putting the charity in a deficit position and leaving charity officials wishing they had worked out a percentage arrangement. But a percentage arrangement might lead a fund-raising firm to use high-pressure tactics, since there is a direct linkage between what donors pledge and what the firm clears. The most effective, reputable professional fund-raising firms end up with no more than 25 percent of the total.

Journalists should find out which options are being presented to potential donors. There should be lots of choices. For example, the University of Missouri tells donors about cash gifts, securities, real estate, tangible personal property, bequests, charitable remainder trusts, pooled income funds, charitable lead trusts and gifts of life insurance proceeds. When a donor is being given just one option, something might be amiss legally or ethically.

If the fund-raising agency being scrutinized is the local United Way, journalists should question donors. Are they giving with the understanding that their contributions are being channeled only to specific recipient charities within the United Way circle, or instead to groups traditionally outside the circle? Such widespread earmarking is a possible indication that local donors have lost their faith in the United Way to make appropriate decisions. Recent books about the United Way inform journalists about it, as well as about the charitable world in general: "The United Way: Dilemmas of Organized Charity" by Eleanor L. Brilliant and "The United Way Scandal: An Insider's Account of What Went Wrong and Why" by John S. Glaser. Other books focus on other groups but make many of the same points, such as "Unhealthy Charities: Hazardous to Your Health and Wealth" by James T. Bennett and Thomas J. DiLorenzo with its emphasis on the American Heart Association, American Lung Association and American Cancer Society. If a charity has local chapters, the volunteers and paid staff at that level are often helpful. Sometimes they talk because they are bitter about national headquarters' directives. The Wall Street Journal found litigation filed by local chapters of Mothers Against Drunk Driving against national headquarters over control of spending at the local level.

"The Guidebook for Directors of Nonprofit Corporations" by the American Bar Association can provide benchmarks for journalists to study, as can information from the National Center for Nonprofit Boards, Washington, D.C. Journalists should look for interlocking directorships among local nonprofits; those groups might be shifting money around through their common directors to deceive donors and regulators.

Unrelated business income is revenue from operations outside a nonprofit's main purpose as stated on its IRS registration. A common example is a university operating a bookstore in competition with commercial bookstores downtown and at the shopping mall. The commercial subsidiaries are legal, as long as they do not erase the organizations' mission for which they received tax-exempt status in the first place, and as long as they pay taxes on the commercial activities. Such income is supposed to be reported to the IRS on Form 990-T. The book by James T. Bennett and Thomas J. DiLorenzo, "Unfair Competition: The Profits of Nonprofits," investigates this phenomenon.

Tax-exempt bonds, mentioned prominently in the Philadelphia Inquirer series, are worth investigating. They are issued by quasi-governmental authorities (see Chapter 7) such as the New Jersey Economic Development Authority or the Health Care Facilities Finance Authority. So tax-exempt groups drain government treasuries even more by receiving tax breaks from bond sales.

As Gaul and Borowski note in their series,

> Many nonprofits operate just like for-profit businesses. They make huge profits, pay handsome salaries, build office towers, invest billions of dollars in stocks and bonds, employ lobbyists and use political action committees to influence legislation. And increasingly they compete with tax-paying businesses.

More and more nonprofit hospitals, they found, have shifted their attention to more and more commercial spinoffs—hotels, restaurants, health spas, laundries, marinas, parking garages.

Many state governments do not tax unrelated business income, but many are considering doing so due to the rise of charity-business partnerships. A common example is a charity asking donors to sign a credit-card contract with Visa, Mastercard or some other financial institution. The assumption among many donors is that the more they charge, the larger the proceeds to the charity. It might be, though, that the charity receives a set amount unaffected by the amount of credit-card charges, giving the charitable appeals a false ring.

Federal, State and Local Government Regulation

In some states, the regulation of charities and other not-for-profits is handled exclusively in the attorney general's office. Other states have established more targeted units, such as a consumer protection division, sometimes freestanding, sometimes within the secretary of state's office. Many state watchdogs require the IRS Form 990 to be filed along with a state form. Journalists can check with the National Association of Attorneys General and the National Association of State Charity Officials, both of Washington, D.C.

At the local government level, revocation of property-tax exemptions is occurring more frequently, as cash-strapped agencies question whether tax-exempt organizations deserve that exemption. Or else payment in lieu of taxes is being negotiated, as tax-exempt groups try to find a middle ground without setting costly long-term precedents. But when such activity occurs, organizations sometimes threaten to move elsewhere, taking jobs with them. Some carry through with the threat. Gaul and Borowski estimated that in Philadelphia alone, nonprofit organizations owned property that would have generated close to $100 million annually for the city government if taxed.

The IRS traditionally has done almost nothing to examine the truthfulness of a tax-exempt organization's stated mission, although the agency has become aggressive about looking for unrelated business income and determining whether groups continue to deserve their tax-exempt status. More than 95 percent are granted tax-exempt status as long as the forms are complete and the fee is paid. Later, most are never scrutinized beyond seeing whether the blanks are filled in, and non-filers often escape notice. After a federal tax-exemption is granted, groups can usually gain exemptions from local property taxes, state income taxes, local and state sales taxes and borrow money through tax-exempt bonds. They can use the U.S. mail at reduced rates. Those who make donations to tax-exempt groups generally do not have to pay taxes on those donations.

Journalists who check with enough regulators might find somebody scrutinizing filings. For instance, this wording appeared on a recent solicitation from the American Civil Liberties Union (I have omitted the addresses):

> A copy of the last Financial Report and Registration filed by this organization may be obtained by contacting one of the following: American Civil Liberties ... Office of Charities Registration, Albany, N.Y. ... Office of Secretary of State, Annapolis, Md. ... State Division of Consumer Affairs, Department of the Secretary of State, Olympia, Wash. ... Pennsylvania Department of State. ... Florida Division of Consumer Services. ... Secretary of State, Charleston, W. Va. Registration with any of these governmental agencies does not imply endorsement by the state.

Some tax-exempt organizations escape regulation altogether, especially the estimated 300,000 to 400,000 churches and religious-based cults in the United States. Their unreported, unregulated activities range from local bingo games—a form of gambling often allowed in jurisdictions where other types of gambling are illegal—to multimillion-dollar operations of television evangelists. Books by journalists that can shed light include Charles E. Shepard's "Forgiven: The Rise and Fall of Jim Bakker and the PTL Ministry," Charles M. Sennott's "Broken Covenant" and Samuel G. Freedman's "Upon This Rock: The Miracles of a Black Church." A few organizations that can help provide perspective are the Evangelical Council for Financial Accountability, Washington, D.C., and the National Council of Churches, New York City.

Summing Up: Boys Town and the Sun Newspapers

Paul Williams, whose thoughts on investigative journalism have been praised throughout this book, was an editor at the Sun Newspapers in metropolitan Omaha. He decided that his tiny staff should scrutinize Boys Town, the sprawling, famous (because of the Spencer Tracy–Mickey Rooney movie) home away from home in Omaha for wayward boys.

For decades, Boys Town had operated in financial secrecy, keeping regulators and journalists at a distance. Nobody was inclined to push very hard to pierce the veil—until Williams. He believed that all major institutions—governmental and private-sector—ought to be examined in depth.

As the Sun staff slowly pieced together the puzzle, it became increasingly obvious that Boys Town had more money than it could use, yet kept soliciting more through heart-rending mailings. How to learn the exact amount of the institution's assets was eluding Williams, though.

As the staff discussed how to proceed, a local financier who served as Sun Newspapers board chairman mentioned something called an IRS Form 990. He guessed that Boys Town would be exempt from filing the form because of its church affiliation, but it might be worth checking. The form was previously unknown to Williams, but why not try, he thought. He called a freelancer of his acquaintance in Washington, D.C. She made an inquiry at the IRS; it took the agency about three weeks to retrieve and deliver the 94-page filing.

When Williams received the document, he was amazed to find the institution's net worth listed. He was even more amazed at the number on the page—$191 million, and growing by about $17 million annually. That sum could run Boys Town for years and years. So why were millions of pleading letters going to potential contributors, suggesting an institution near poverty? Needless to say, Williams had his story.

Chapter 14

INVESTIGATING HEALTH CARE

*A*mericans spend more than a billion dollars each day for a health-care system they fail to understand and that might fail them. In fact, "health" care sometimes is a misnomer; too often "sick" care is more accurate.

The beat is filled with investigative potential. Journalists who understand the system will know where to look for overpriced hospitals releasing patients quicker and sicker; health maintenance organizations driven by greed, where preventive medicine is more joke than reality; nursing homes that warehouse residents who eventually stop caring whether they live or die; doctors and nurses who are uncaring, incompetent or incapacitated by drugs; pharmacists, drug companies and medical device manufacturers interested in maximum profits first, alleviating disease and pain second; and, as covered in Chapter 15, insurance companies that withhold coverage when the patient needs it most.

As the health-care system has grown, so have the records that explain it. Almost every procedure generates a record. Almost every provider of medical services is licensed or otherwise regulated by a government agency. Every patient is the subject of personalized files. A great deal of the documentation, in the aggregate, is public, although records on individual cases can be difficult to obtain unless the patient is dead, alive and cooperative, or involved in litigation.

The trouble is, much of the documentation is difficult to understand. With help from an array of secondary materials, primary documents and human sources, understanding will come.

No single investigation, no single aspect of the health-care system, can be representative. The system is so vast; there are so many stories to tell. What follows is one of those stories, reprinted (in an edited version) from the IRE Journal. The authors are Chris Szechenyi, then of WRC-TV, Washington, D.C., and Elliot Jaspin, then directing the Missouri Institute for Computer-Assisted Reporting:

Imagine calling an ambulance when someone in your family has a heart attack. The medics arrive with a machine that is supposed to jump-start the heart with a powerful electric shock. But when they try to deliver a charge from the briefcase-sized device, it will not work. There is no power. They try again. Nothing. Your loved one dies.

That has happened at least 512 times during the past six years, according to U.S. Food and Drug Administration records. In those fatal cases, the FDA found defibrillators—the machines designed to jolt the heart to life—disabled by design flaws and errors by incompetent medics.

When a 17-year-old man was rescued from drowning in a swimming pool, bystanders performed CPR, and medics tried defibrillation several times. But the machine would not charge or transfer the electric shock and the young man died, an FDA report says.

In some defibrillator failures, the machine is faulty, but in others the machines have been poorly maintained or used improperly by medics. Defibrillators made by various companies are carried on ambulances throughout the United States, and their misuse and malfunctions present potential stories for journalists concerned with health and safety.

Defibrillator failures are only a fraction of the toll caused by a variety of defective devices, ranging from faulty syringes to unreliable breathing monitors, all of which may be good subjects for journalists.

An investigation by WRC-TV and the Missouri Institute for Computer-Assisted Reporting uncovered 3,328 deaths and 52,000 injuries associated with medical devices during a six-year period.

Pacemakers, ventilators, heart valves and other devices designed to save lives are in fact losing lives. One company's heart valve has fractured and killed at least 250 people during the last 10 years, and thousands of people still live with the uncertainty of their valve breaking suddenly. The company stopped production after 150 people had died from valve fractures. But that was too late to save some victims. "Someone, for the sake of money, took away from me a woman who was just very outstanding," said one victim's husband, whose legal action against the manufacturer has been settled.

There's ample evidence in FDA reports, General Accounting Office studies, congressional hearings, court records and other public documents for reporters to dig up dozens of new stories in this field. The traditional way of getting started is to talk to local doctors, biomedical engineers and hospital officials to identify a local medical-device manufacturer that may be producing questionable equipment.

But, thanks to computers, there is an easier, more comprehensive approach to getting leads. By law, medical-device manufacturers must report deaths and injuries to the FDA within 15 days if there is a reason to believe they were caused by the device. The FDA later investigates those reports during plant inspections and determines whether the device or user was the cause of the death, injury or malfunction. Since 1984 the FDA has accumulated reports, which it keeps on a computer.

To do the series on defective medical devices, WRC and MICAR purchased a copy of the computer tape from the National Technical Information Service, part of the U.S. Commerce Department. In addition to a description of the problem, each computerized record contains the name and address of the manufacturer. That means if reporters in Michigan want to find local companies with a history of problems, they can ask the computer to print the names of all manufacturers who list Michigan as their address.

Finding problem companies, however, is only the first step. As well as the manufacturer's name and address, the database lists the kind of medical device that caused the problem, categorizes each incident as a "malfunction," "serious injury" or "death," gives a description of the problem and, if the FDA has finished its investigation, identifies whether the device itself was at fault.

A reporter in Minneapolis checking into a hometown medical manufacturer would have found 211 deaths and 2,014 injuries associated with the company's products, primarily cardiac pacemakers. The reporter could break down the data by year and device to look for trends, and find out how many times the FDA blamed deaths and injuries on the device in its final assessment.

A reporter curious about a particular device can get a count from the database of deaths and injuries linked to each manufacturer, then compare one company to another to see whether one stands out. We found one company accounted for 442 of the 512 deaths associated with defibrillator problems. The company had about 80 percent of the defibrillator market at the time.

Using a computer, however, is not without its problems. The tape was easy to obtain from NTIS, which took the order by telephone. The staff was extremely cooperative. But the first few tapes we obtained had serious problems. Not only was the record layout incorrect, but the government programmers had made a mistake when they copied the information; some fields were gibberish. It was only on the third try that the government was able to produce a useable computer tape.

The computer analysis is only the first step in the reporting process. Once a product that is causing problems has been identified, the next step is to find out if there have been any recalls. The recall information is essential for fleshing out the statistics in the database; it can be obtained from the FDA. Recall notices say what is wrong with devices, how many were distributed, and what the company is doing to correct the problem. The defibrillator company we scrutinized had 16 recalls in the past decade.

FDA inspections of a company's plant may reveal poor manufacturing practices, quality control deficiencies and other details. These reports and the recalls may be obtained through the FDA's field offices more quickly than from its Washington, D.C., headquarters.

Correspondence between the FDA and a manufacturer is also important to request. We found letters in which the problem company resisted the FDA's attempt to recall defective defibrillators. The FDA said the machines had a faulty relay that could prevent defibrillators from working. The agency called it a life-threatening situation. The company, however, opposed a recall, asserting that medics could go for a backup unit if a defibrillator failed. Unfortunately, few ambulances carry spare defibrillators, which cost about $8,000 each. Also, there may not be time to set up a spare defibrillator as every minute counts when someone is having a heart attack. The FDA finally forced the company to recall the devices.

Behind the statistics and records are tragic human stories. Court records are the best source to find the victims. Consider the case of a 21-year-old woman who had a heart attack in her doctor's office during a prenatal checkup in St. Paul. Her doctor quickly began CPR. When medics arrived minutes later, they were "unable to use the defibrillator" because of a "malfunction," an ambulance report says. The medics rushed the woman to the hospital. She was six months pregnant. It was too late. She died nine minutes after doctors delivered her baby in an emergency cesarean-section operation. The baby was being supported by a respirator and a feeding tube and may have suffered brain damage.

WRC-TV learned that just days before paramedics tried to save the woman with the defibrillator, the company had recalled the model because the devices "failed to deliver an electrical charge" due to "two defective components."

Knowing from the WRC-TV experience and other journalistic exposés that medical devices frequently malfunction, U.S. News and World Report requested the FDA's complete computerized database tracking problems. As a staff writer studied the database, looking for patterns, he and his team members realized penile implants were showing up again and again. They had the focus of their project.

Hospitals

A great deal of information about local hospitals is available in state capitals. For example, the Missouri Bureau of Hospital Licensing and Certification monitors acute-care community hospitals, ambulatory surgical centers and abortion facilities. The agency checks not only quality of medical care, but also fire safety, environmental hazards and dietary services. If the hospital accepts federal money for treating Medicare patients (and most do), the state agency helps monitor Medicare providers and suppliers. Those providers and suppliers include independent laboratories, physical and occupational rehabilitation facilities, end-stage renal disease services, portable X-ray centers, screening mammography operators, rural health clinics and hospital long-term care units.

What a journalist can find by searching files at the state agency overseeing hospitals is just the beginning. The Joint Commission on Accreditation of Healthcare Organizations, Chicago, or the American Osteopathic Hospital Association, Washington, D.C., has probably paid a visit in the past three years. If so, the accreditation report will be rich with details. If the commission has not visited, a journalist should find out why. The commission has its critics. Health-care consumers say it gives so much advance warning of an inspection that any hospital can mask its shortcomings temporarily, then almost always gives hospitals the benefit of the doubt, thus devaluing the meaning of accreditation. Furthermore, the commission's board has multiple slots reserved for American Hospital Association members, and the AHA pays more than half of the commission's budget. But accrediting standards are often strict, and the details in an accreditation report are useful to journalists—even if overall the hospital should happen to receive unjustifiably high marks.

That accreditation is too easily granted appears to be the case if Medicare validation surveys by the U.S. Health Care Financing Administration have any meaning. Congress mandated the surveys as a follow-up to accreditation by JCAHO. Despite being accredited, between one-fourth and one-third of the hospitals inspected by the less-beholden HCFA are found lacking in some aspect of their care for Medicare patients.

Quality of patient care is a major concern of the accrediting team. Their concern is shared by the peer review organization (PRO) in each state. Created by federal legislation, peer review organizations study whether admissions to hospitals are appropriate, whether longer-than-average stays are justified, whether diagnoses are coded incorrectly to justify overcharges and numerous other matters. Few journalists know that peer review organizations exist in their state; even fewer mine the expertise found there.

In my state, for example, the PRO is called the Missouri Patient Care Review Foundation and is located in Jefferson City. It handles individual complaints about hospital care, including premature discharges of patients. In addition, it tries to work with hospitals in local projects that result in better care, then suggests similar procedures to hospitals statewide. Journalists should find out whether any local hospitals are involved in such projects, then monitor the results.

Reading the PRO's regular reports can tip off journalists to story ideas and documents. A recent report from the Missouri PRO mentioned the Medicare Hospital Information Project, which predicts death rates of Medicare patients hospital by hospital, then compares the predicted rates to actual rates. The PRO report said each hospital had received its mortality profile, as well as profiles of other hospitals for comparison purposes. Obtaining those projected and actual death statistics could be the beginning of a compelling investigation.

To reach their conclusions, peer review organizations can calculate a hospital's performance according to each of the nearly 500 medical procedures identified by the government. Each procedure is known as a diagnostic-related group (DRG). The federal Medicare program has set payment schedules for each DRG. Because Medicare does not pay the full cost of care for some procedures, many hospitals release patients sooner than they should. That phenomenon gave rise to the aphorism of patients going home "quicker and sicker."

Knight-Ridder Newspapers' Washington Bureau was among the early news organizations to use PRO statistics. Reporters there performed a computer analysis of deaths seemingly connected to coronary artery bypass surgery at hospitals nationwide. They discovered that 44 hospitals rang up death rates at least twice the national average. It appeared that as many as 1,000 Medicare patients in just one year suffered preventable deaths during or after surgery. PROs can collect information more subtle than death rates. For instance, "adverse patient occurrences" can include unplanned returns to the operating room, infections, unexpected cardiac or respitory arrest, negative reactions to drugs and more.

Employers frequently supplement PRO studies. Because they spend so much money on health insurance, employers are naturally curious about comparing hospitals. They often find wildly varying rates for the same medical procedures, different philosophies on how long a patient needs to be hospitalized, employee dissatisfaction with individual physicians and inflated charges to recover payments for equipment (helicopters, open heart surgery rooms, brain scanners and the like) that unnecessarily duplicate what is already available at other hospitals. Sometimes employers use their findings to pressure local hospitals to change their ways. When a journalist gets wind of such pressure, it can be the beginning of a good story.

U.S. News and World Report magazine relies on a mix of sources to rank "America's best hospitals" on an annual basis, including death rates from all causes, as reported by the U.S. Health Care Financing Administration; whether the institution had earned membership in the Council of Teaching Hospitals; ratios of hospital beds to registered nurses (many of whom are being laid off as hospitals try to cut expenses in the age of managed care); board-certified specialist physicians; medical trainee residents/interns; inpatient surgeries; discharge services, such as social workers and patient representatives; high technology services, such as sophisticated imaging devices; specialized geriatric care; specialized outpatient services, such as substance-abuse, AIDS care, genetic counseling, fertility counseling and home health care.

Aggregate statistics provide context, but sometimes medical records of individual patients are necessary to nail down a project. Journalists should ask patients themselves, family members and lawyers representing patients for access to case histories, fees and correspondence with hospitals. Many individuals will say yes. If a lawsuit is already filed, detailed individual medical records and hospital treatment studies might be available.

Examination of any individual's hospital bill is bound to raise questions; experts are almost unanimous in agreeing that paying patients' hospital bills are routinely increased to subsidize non-paying patients. Sometimes the bills are just plain wrong or ludicrous. Items to look for include double billing for tests, with each entry rendered in slightly different language; fees charged automatically even when the procedure was not performed, such as sedation for childbirth when none was administered; unrequested items, such as toothbrushes and toothpaste; human error in keyboarding that turns a $10 item into a $100 item.

While some hospitals are slow to correct their billing mistakes, they are often fast at trying to collect from patients when insurance companies reimburse less than the full amount. A journalist can ask whether local hospitals use outside bill collection agencies. If so, do the bill collectors illegally resort to verbal threats or physical intimidation? Do local hospitals place liens on the residences of patients who have yet to pay or try to garnish their wages? Life magazine provided a pictorial illustration of why bills are often so high, picturing the 105 hospital employees involved in a heart operation, for which the patient received a bill of $63,000. The total annual salary of the 105 employees equalled $3.6 million.

Some experts believe quality of care is tied to cost of care. Any hospital's budget is also rich with details: what percentage of revenue comes from patient fees, the amount of writeoffs for indigent care and uncollectible bills, how much is spent on new equipment and how different departments within the hospital fare. In Missouri, basic financial information on every hospital is available from the state Center for Health Statistics. Similar agencies in other states also generate hospital by hospital statistics. If a hospital wants to spend money on capital improvements, in many states it must obtain a certificate of need from a state agency. In Missouri, that agency is the state Health Facilities Review Committee.

If the hospital is owned by a for-profit corporation whose stock is publicly traded (see Chapter 12), financial information might be available at the U.S. Securities and Exchange Commission or the state securities department. If the hospital operates on a not-for-profit basis, it might have to disclose finances to the Internal Revenue Service on Form 990.

Andrew Caffrey of WBUR-FM Radio, Boston, routinely read tax returns of not-for-profit hospitals (also mentioned in Chapter 13). His accumulated knowledge led to a story about insider loans from hospital treasuries to senior executives and doctors. As Caffrey explained in the form accompanying his award-winning IRE contest entry,

> The loans were often at interest rates several points below what an average consumer would get from a commercial lender. The story pointed up how well-paid top people in the nonprofit medical world were getting special perquisites . . . while consumers were footing the bills for ever-higher health-care costs.

Supplementing budget documents are Medicare and Medicaid cost reports required by federal and state governments paying for treatment of elderly, low-income and disabled patients. The reports are kept by the hospital, the government agency paying the bills (at the federal level, usually the Health Care Financing Administration, part of the Health and Human Services Department) and the company (often a nearby Blue

Cross plan) administering the program day to day, deciding which bills to pay in full and which to question.

The Chicago Reporter used financial statements and cost reports filed at the Illinois Health Facilities Planning Board to calculate the amount of indigent care provided by each hospital. Unsurprisingly, the reporter found that inner-city, public, not-for-profit hospitals provided more indigent care than suburban, private, for-profit hospitals. What surprised the reporter, though, were the huge variations among the not-for-profit hospitals, leaving her the task of investigating whether the variations were accidents of geography or by design. Health-care facilities that have accepted federal government money for construction and modernization under the Hill-Burton Act agree to provide a reasonable amount of services to persons unable to pay. Journalists should ask HHS which hospitals have filed an allocation plan, and whether they are living up to their commitments to serve low-income patients. What happens in the community when the hospital has met its annual allocation? Does HHS allow some allocations to be set too low?

Minimal indigent care by not-for-profit hospitals raises a legitimate question of whether they have paid back the community adequately for property tax waivers and other special treatment. The situation is likely to worsen as hospitals treating only subacute patients or only head injuries spring up in a fragmented health-care system. Those hospitals skim off the most profitable patients, leaving old-line inner-city hospitals to provide necessary, expensive, money-losing services such as emergency rooms. A useful book about access (and lack of access) to indigent treatment is Laurie Kaye Abraham's "Mama Might Be Better Off Dead: The Failure of Health Care in Urban America."

A federal law called the Emergency Medical Treatment and Active Labor Act attempts to ban patient dumping. That occurs when a hospital inappropriately turns away an emergency case based on lack of health insurance or some other inability to pay. A hospital receiving a patient dumped by another institution is supposed to notify the U.S. Department of Health and Human Services within 72 hours. Journalists should request those notifications from the federal agency, then determine if any follow-up occurred. The Health Letter, a muckraking publication of Public Citizen Health Research Group, Washington, D.C., does an excellent job of tracking violators, listing every hospital and doctor or other health-care professional cited by HHS. Hospital insiders warn, though, that what at first looks like dumping might be just a matter of sloppy paperwork. Hospitals sometimes find themselves caught in a bind between the patient dumping rules and insurance companies. Journalists should look for situations like this: A patient comes to a hospital emergency room because of sudden heart pains. The doctor on duty runs expensive but necessary tests to learn if a heart attack has occurred. If the tests had not been done, or if the doctor had sent the patient elsewhere, it might have been a violation of the dumping law. But the insurer will not pay, because the patient's HMO does not have a contract with that hospital or that doctor. So either the patient pays the bill, or the hospital eats the cost.

When skilled journalists take the time to dig deep into any one aspect of hospital care, what they find is often alarming. Dave Davis and Ted Wendling of the Cleveland Plain Dealer had no idea they would be digging deep when they received a daily assignment to cover a spill of radioactive phosphorus-32 at a Cleveland hospital. But their suspicions kicked in when hospital officials refused to identify a nearby music school that had been contaminated.

As the duo began reading documents and asking questions about hospital radiation safety programs, they started learning about deaths from radiation overdoses across the nation. They tapped into a computer database at the U.S. Nuclear Regulatory Commission on radiation overexposures. Eventually the reporters identified more than 40 deaths attributable to radiation deaths in hospitals, many of them followed by falsified records and other cover-ups. Another environment-related violation that's common is burning medical waste and releasing residues into the air. Journalists should track the path of amputated limbs, scraped warts, blood, used bandages, syringes and scalpels. Does any agency license and regulate incinerators and landfill disposal?

Journalists should be asking how well hospitals prevent drug thefts and other losses. Hospitals are supposed to report the losses to the U.S. Drug Enforcement Administration. The local police department or the state narcotics agency might also know about specific instances of theft.

Even when drugs are all accounted for, there can be other types of trouble. At the Pittsburgh Post-Gazette, reporter Steve Twedt found that hospital patients sometimes died or were crippled because they receive the wrong medication or the wrong dose of the correct medication. Twedt wondered why the patterns showed up in hospital after hospital. He concluded that the information network had failed: "Only a fraction of the errors are ever published in professional journals and even when they are, it is hard to know where to look. . . . There is no requirements for hospitals in most states . . . to share or analyze information on errors."

Like all top-notch investigators, Twedt found sources that others would have ignored. For example, he conducted a national survey of pharmacists who are employed by hospitals. The 250 respondents said that in just one year they saw more than 16,000 medication errors resulting in more than 100 deaths and 300-plus serious injuries. But transgressors rarely received punishment, Twedt found:

> Sometimes a medication error might be referred to a licensing board for discipline against a pharmacist, doctor or nurse. Or a coroner's office will be told about a death. But those agencies have narrow responsibilities, such as

the revocation of a license or determination of criminality. It is not their job to look for patterns among errors. And even when mistakes are reported there is no central agency, governmental or private, that systematically seeks out and analyzes the information to alert other hospitals.

In an interview with the journalism publication Prize Press, San Jose, Calif., Twedt said he had to pull together information from a variety of sources:

> We checked civil lawsuit records. We went to the American Trial Lawyers Association. They could, in some cases, give us citations. We checked the professional journals. . . . You have an incident involving a drug. It could turn up in a nursing journal, it could turn up in an anesthesiology journal, it could turn up in a medical journal. We had to check all of these, one by one collect all these separate cases. Other sources we went to were medical boards. I contacted every medical board, nursing board and pharmacy board in every state and asked them for copies of any board actions involving a medication error. . . .
>
> We looked for newspaper clippings in a variety of databases, and we also had some record checking with the U.S. Food and Drug Administration's adverse drug reaction database. We used the newspaper accounts as kind of a signal that there was a case out there. We did not write about them unless we had some backup verification from the center where it happened or from someone who was directly involved.
>
> We might have a copy of a three-paragraph newspaper account in the Midwest of someone who was accidentally given potassium chloride and died. And from that newspaper account, you just go through all the steps—you contact the hospital. You get the coroner's report. From the coroner's report you have names of family members and you follow that. . . . You try and track down names of practitioners involved and see if they would be willing to talk.

Almost every sin that can be committed by a hospital—medication errors and otherwise—is exposed in Walt Bogdanich's book "The Great White Lie: How America's Hospitals Betray Our Trust and Endanger Our Lives." A historical look at why hospitals became the subjects of exposés is Charles E. Rosenberg's "The Care of Strangers." Susan Garrett, a former hospital administrator, provides a different perspective in "Taking Care of Our Own: A Year in the Life of a Small Hospital." Other valuable books are more narrowly focused, such as Lisa Belkin's examination of hospital ethics committees, "First, Do No Harm," and B.D. Colen's look at a surgery unit, "O.R." The American Hospital Association, Chicago, and its related state and metropolitan groups can provide perspective. Dozens of publications, such as Hospital Litigation Reporter, Atlanta, supply additional information. The Hospital Literature Index, compiled by the American Hospital Association, covers thousands of books and articles in every issue.

Veterans Administration Hospitals

These hospitals, operated by an arm of the federal government, constitute one of the largest health-care networks in the world. But that size has not always been a blessing—VA hospitals are known for long waits, complicated paperwork, high death rates and medical malpractice, consequences of which are paid for by U.S. taxpayers rather than individual malpractice insurance policies. If taking apart the operation of an entire hospital is overwhelming, a journalist can concentrate on one aspect. That is what the Fort Lauderdale Sun-Sentinel did to produce a series on high death and injury rates in VA hospital heart surgery units.

Veterans hospitals are supposed to be visited by accrediting teams every three years, just like private-sector hospitals. If the accrediting report is withheld by the local VA hospital, a journalist should request it from the U.S. Department of Veterans Affairs, Washington, D.C. The agency's inspector general and the U.S. General Accounting Office, an arm of Congress (see Chapter 6), audit VA hospitals on an occasional basis. KTBS-TV, Shreveport, La., relied heavily on VA inspector general audits to tell viewers about shoddy medicine at the local hospital. Those audits might lead to congressional hearings by the appropriate committees in the U.S. House and Senate. Veterans groups such as the American Legion, Washington, D.C., might have their own ratings of VA hospitals.

When trying to learn about individual cases, journalists might benefit from requesting a patient injury control report on DVA Form 10-2633. PrimeTime Live, an ABC-TV News program, used patient records—some obtained from family members—to check tips from former VA doctors and nurses about alleged inadequate care.

Emergency Medical Services

Ambulances and other emergency services are often tied closely to hospitals, which at the very least end up caring for the individuals transported. Journalists should determine which part of each county is covered by which ambulance service. Are they so competitive that a service that has staked out a certain part of the county will fight off another service, even if the competitor can arrive more quickly? On the other hand, are some portions of the county underserved because of their remoteness, bad roads, racial composition or high crime rate? Are some sick people refused a ride because they are uninsured? If the ambulance is owned by a hospital, do all riders end up at that hospital, even if some other facility is better suited to treat the patient?

Journalists should study ambulance response times. A study in one city showed nearly one-fourth of the ambulance runs did not begin until seven minutes after receipt of the emergency call. Experts say critically ill people should be picked up within six minutes. Are qualified drivers and paramedics on duty at all hours or is the service cutting costs by letting all drivers and paramedics go home at certain hours? If possible, a journalist should calculate response times independently based on a combination of ambulance company records and 911 system dispatches.

WBRZ-TV, Baton Rouge, received a tip about slow response times. When its reporters had finished their research, they described their findings on an IRE awards entry form:

> The public service, designed to treat on the scene and hand off noncritical patients to private ambulance companies, was now carrying noncritical patients so they could bill their insurance companies. While the ratio of transports rose, response times fell. The tax revenues were no longer sufficient, and city officials were breaking a promise not to send bills. Emergency room doctors were critical of the medical direction and were fighting over who controlled the service.

What is the cost of an ambulance ride? Is it substantially higher or lower than in other cities? Does the city, county or state government regulate the rates ambulance services can charge? Does any governmental body license personnel, require certain equipment be on board and require also that the equipment pass tests regularly?

When air ambulances (helicopters) are involved, is there any regulation involved other than through Federal Aviation Administration pilot licenses? If an air ambulance service contract is awarded by a hospital or a government entity to an outsider, is the award based solely on price? Or is the air ambulance service's safety record considered? A journalist can check the National Transportation Safety Board for crash records.

In Missouri, the state government's Bureau of Emergency Medical Services is a good place to start on the paper and people trails. The agency handles ground and air ambulance licensing, emergency medical technician and paramedic licensing, poison control programs, trauma center inspections, plus head and spinal cord injury registries. In Missouri, there were recently 227 ambulance services with 804 licensed vehicles. Advanced life support was provided by 185 services. Ten helicopter and eight fixed-wing air ambulance services were licensed to operate.

Health Maintenance Organizations

HMOs arose to encourage preventive care by charging a low, flat fee for routine wellness visits. That is still a distinguishing feature of HMOs. But in an age of health-care reform, they have become the center of controversy over managed care. Are HMOs practicing impersonal, assembly-line medicine to cut costs? Are insurance company representatives, looking to save money, making the key decisions about expensive referrals to specialists, hospitalization and drug prescriptions, rather than the doctors and nurses who are medically qualified to make such a determination?

As journalists investigate HMOs, they should ask questions about accreditation. The National Committee for Quality Assurance, Washington, D.C., is an HMO accrediting organization, but its coverage is not complete. Will it be eventually? At what intervals will HMOs be inspected and with what rigor? In some states, health and insurance departments exercise jurisdiction over HMOs. If an HMO wants to be reimbursed for Medicare patients, it must be certified by the Office of Prepaid Health Care, part of the U.S. Health and Human Services Department. The Health Care Association of America, Washington, D.C., a trade association of HMOs, can provide perspective.

Journalists can gather some figures on their own. What is the ratio of doctors to patients at local HMOs? In the United States as a whole, there are about 400 patients per doctor. Many HMOs have a ratio closer to 1,000 to one. How does any given HMO's ratio compare to private-practice doctors' offices? Do patients suffer through long waits? Are they able to visit the same doctor every appointment if they so desire? If the HMO says patients can choose from among 500 doctors, a journalist should request the list. If 500 names appear, the journalist should verify their affiliation. If only 200 names are on the list, contrary to the HMO's advertising, that is an automatic story. If the list lacks specialists, how stingy will the HMO be about patients visiting outside specialists?

At the Fort Lauderdale Sun-Sentinel, Fred Schulte and Larry Keller ran an advertisement in their own newspaper asking readers to share their views on HMOs covering Medicare recipients. Discussing the project in the IRE Journal, Schulte said:

> Of the 353 people who wrote us, 48 percent were negative, 39 percent were positive; the rest voiced no opinion. Most letters were highly literate, detailed and forcefully written. . . . Thirty-eight percent of the unhappy group blamed cost-cutting by a Medicare HMO for causing the death of, or serious injury to, a loved one. The anger aimed at the HMOs startled us. So did the common story threads. For example, some people said HMOs failed to spot cancers promptly because they limited diagnostic testing or were reluctant to send patients to specialists.

Schulte and Keller asked for information from the U.S. Health Care Financing Administration, eventually receiving "an obscure Medicare data set called the Beneficiary Tracking and Information System." It allowed the reporters to "document more than 10,000 patient complaints filed against eight South Florida HMOs in recent years, grievances ranging from improper enrollments to failure to pay medical bills" as well as "rapid disenrollment rates at various HMOs, an indicator of patient dissatisfaction and perceived low quality." Some of the HMOs had drop-out rates more than four times the national average.

The Florida insurance department also yielded patient complaints. Schulte said,

> We discovered hundreds of examples in which HMOs brazenly refused to pay legitimate medical bills, leaving patients to be hounded by collection agencies. We even found a few cases in which health plans hand-delivered letters to hospitalized patients directing them to check out by a set date or foot the bill themselves.

Some local patients choose a middle ground between HMOs and individual physicians, joining preferred provider organizations. Health-care providers began PPOs in response to what they considered to be the HMO threat. For a monthly fee, PPOs offer more comprehensive benefits than traditional insurance, but less than HMOs, if subscribers are willing to visit only certain doctors and certain hospitals. Subscribers can visit doctors and hospitals outside the PPO network, but must pay extra. The American Association of Preferred Provider Organizations, Washington, D.C., can provide perspective. PPOs and physician-hospital organizations (PHOs) raise interesting regulatory questions. Should they be regulated as insurance companies, since they are offering insurance-type contracts? If they are not regulated, do they gain unfair advantage over traditional insurance companies? What if a PPO or PHO has inadequate reserves to handle all payouts to its subscribers? Who would provide the safety nets similar to those provided by state insurance departments?

Nursing Homes

The Joint Commission on Accreditation of Healthcare Organizations is spotty when it comes to nursing homes, and state regulation varies greatly in quality and quantity. Rather than falling under the state health department, in Missouri nursing homes are regulated by the Social Services Department's Division of Aging. It inspects and licenses adult day care centers, adult residential care homes, intermediate care and skilled nursing facilities. Journalists have access to complaint investigation forms, as well as the "Statement of Deficiencies and Plan of Correction." The agency also licenses nursing home administrators, rules on construction and equipment requests and establishes nursing home Medicare and Medicaid eligibility. City or county departments play a role, too, checking kitchen sanitation, fire, electrical and other building codes.

Nursing homes do file certain reports similar to those filed by hospitals: U.S. Securities and Exchange Commission documents if part of a publicly held company; IRS Form 990s if operating under certain tax-exempt sections of the law (many nonprofit nursing homes, a minority in the industry, belong to the American Association of Homes for the Aged, Washington, D.C.); Medicare and Medicaid cost figures. Somewhere in those papers investigators might find clues to the self-dealing that infects the industry, such as what Mark Lagerkvist of WZZM-TV, Grand Rapids, Mich., discovered.

Reading files at the state public health department on a specific nursing home, Lagerkvist noticed the owner and leaser of the facility had the same address. With more research, he determined the owner had established a dummy corporation to run the home, then billed Medicaid for the rental fees paid by the dummy. The total amount of fraud at just the one home topped $3 million, with taxpayers taking the hit.

State governments pay large portions of nursing home billings through Medicaid. With an increasing number of patients being moved from hospitals to nursing homes, states are trying to reckon with increased costs. As a result, state executive branch agencies and legislatures might be generating more studies and hearings than in the past. Journalists should explore whether relatively well-to-do families are spending down their assets to qualify for Medicaid in nursing homes. Should not only the patient but also the spouse and children have to become impoverished before state Medicaid payments kick in? After the nursing home patient dies, are state governments going after the estate's assets to help pay off Medicaid costs? What is the average annual cost of nursing home care? How much does it vary home by home, city by city, state by state?

Journalists visiting nursing homes for themselves will walk away with useful impressions, as well as promotional literature to compare with the reality, plus interviews with administrators, doctors, nurses, patients and family members. Those visits might lead to projects like the one done by Gannett News Service, Washington, D.C. The reporter used numerous sources for a series with this opening:

> Thousands of violent criminals, thieves and bullies work in the nation's nursing homes, left to care for people too old, sick or disabled to care for themselves.... When their abusive natures surface, usually as scars on the frail bodies and psyches of patients, many aides move on to new nursing homes and, sometimes, new targets.

To conduct the investigation, a Gannett database editor asked state regulators for computerized registries of nursing home aides; federal law mandates that those registries be kept. Every state except Louisiana cooperated. Gannett then combined the registries to create a single list of aides designated as abusive. That list also pinpointed aides who were found to be abusive in one state and who ended up with certification to work in a different state. The series suggested questions to ask about the staff of any nursing home: Are criminal record checks performed on every potential employee? Are references from previous employment sought? How many nurses and nursing aides per bed are on duty during a given shift? How closely are they supervised and by whom? What is their hourly wage or annual salary? What is their turnover rate? How many positions are currently unfilled?

The Miami Herald began an investigation after the nursing home death of a neglected quadriplegic. The newspaper found many more avoidable deaths, as well as cover-ups. In an IRE contest entry form, the reporter commented that

> proper postmortem investigations are rare, and rarer still are the prosecutions of culpable caregivers. . . . The Herald found shoddy police investigations of suspicious adult deaths, health-care workers who tampered with medical documents to hide neglect or poor medical care and doctors who failed to properly report suspicions of abuse.

At the Record, Hackensack, N.J., Gale Scott, Barbara Gardner and Bruce Locklin started their investigation as the result of a telephone call about how residents at a nursing home were in danger of dying because the owner refused to fix an air conditioner during a heat wave. As the Record team searched obituary notices from the newsroom library, they noted people who had died at the nursing home being investigated, then contacted survivors and pulled death certificates.

Checking for lawsuits turned up wrongful death allegations against the nursing home. As Scott and Locklin wrote in the IRE Journal:

> The lawyers in those cases had valuable medical records from the nursing home, such as schedules showing which hours nurses worked and patients' medical records. We scrutinized those records and found instances where nurses who were on the schedule as working were not the same nurses who allegedly signed patients' medical records. That finding supported our charges that records were falsified to cover up the fact that basic care was not given.

For perspective, journalists can turn to groups such as the National Citizens Coalition for Nursing Home Reform, the American Health Care Association and the Hospice Association of America, all of Washington, D.C.; publications such as McKnight's Long-Term Care News, Deerfield, Ill.; and books such as Timothy Diamond's "Making Gray Gold: Narratives of Nursing Home Care"; Nancy Foner's "The Caregiving Dilemma: Work in an American Nursing Home"; and Mary Adelaide Mendelson's "Tender Loving Greed."

Mental Health Institutions

Deinstitutionalization should have altered the coverage of mental health forever. With more and more mentally retarded or mentally unstable people working productively in the community—or wandering the streets aimlessly, or jailed over and over as nuisances—journalists cannot handle the mental health beat merely by visiting the state asylum every once in awhile.

Time has proven that the wonder drugs leading to deinstitutionalization are no panacea. Many patients spend their lives going from mental hospital to inadequate community placement to the street and back to the hospital. Journalists should ask how well the release of mental patients has worked locally. What do outpatient treatment specialists at mental hospitals say about broken appointments and failures to adhere to medication regimes? Are there enough supervised community residences locally? Do patients receive counseling or mostly watch television? How qualified are the supervisors? Is taxpayer money lining the pockets of supervisors' friends and family in the form of inflated rents and unnecessary, expensive supplies?

Because the old-line mental health institutions are still part of the picture, they must be scrutinized, too. In Missouri, for example, the Department of Mental Health directs three state hospitals, nine mental health centers, three children's facilities and contracts with 23 private, not-for-profit mental health agencies to help meet needs of the population.

Some lack enough beds or enough employees. Other centers have an overabundance of beds, and so they bend the rules to accept patients involuntarily committed. As employers reduce or eliminate mental health benefits, the centers will probably receive fewer referrals. As the number of beds filled drops further and staff layoffs seem likely, psychiatric hospitals might start paying fees to clergy, parole officers and corporate employee assistance personnel for referrals resulting in new patients.

Finding current or former patients to interview can be difficult because of privacy considerations and doctor-patient confidentiality. Previous local newspaper articles or television features might mention specific names of patients who can later be contacted.

The St. Petersburg Times learned about such patient brokers after receiving a tip that a local drug treatment center flew in pregnant addicts from the northern United States. The center then enrolled the patients in Florida's Medicaid system so that taxpayers would absorb costs. In their IRE contest entry form, the reporters said the patient brokers

can collect thousands of dollars per head in kickbacks for referring unsuspecting patients to drug treatment or psychiatric care they may not need. Patient referral services are run by ex-cons and drug addicts who use phony credentials to gain credibility. . . . Such patient brokers are completely unregulated; few states have laws banning the practice.

Some of the psychiatrists and other so-called professional staff lack credentials altogether or come from the bottom of the employment barrel because the work is so draining and frustrating. Because mental illness is so difficult to even classify properly, poorly trained staff members complicate an already bad situation. The field's bible "Diagnostic and Statistical Manual of Mental Disorders," compiled by the American Psychiatric Association, identifies about 300 conditions. Separating one from all the possibilities, then treating it effectively, is no job for the incompetent.

Organizations providing perspective include the American Mental Health Counselors Association and the National Association of State Mental Health Program Directors, both of Alexandria, Va.; National Alliance for the Mentally Ill, Arlington, Va.; American Psychiatric Association, American Psychological Association, Mental Health Law Project and National Association of Private Psychiatric Hospitals, all based in Washington, D.C.

The U.S. government publishes SAMHSA News, from the Substance Abuse and Mental Health Services Administration. Useful books include Joe Sharkey's "Bedlam: Greed, Profiteering and Fraud in a Mental Health System Gone Crazy"; Lisa Berger and Alexander Vuckovic's "Under Observation: Life Inside a Psychiatric Hospital"; and Michael Winerip's "9 Highland Road," based on two years of immersion journalism in a state-financed group home for the mentally ill.

Home Health-Care Companies

Home health-care workers can be angels of mercy, allowing elderly or chronically ill patients to stay in their own homes instead of unfamiliar nursing homes, or they can be workers from hell, abusing patients and stealing their belongings. Home health care is growing as Medicare administrators and private insurance companies push patients to shorten hospital stays. Are problems growing, too?

At Scripps Howard News Service in Washington, D.C., reporters ran across high medical bills for in-home intravenous drug treatments, some of which were for the wrong disease. The reporters had heard the conventional wisdom that home health IV companies were transforming medical care in new, positive ways, but their suspicions led them to dig into the subject. As they said in their IRE awards contest entry, they

> documented home charges four or five times greater than the highest hospital charges; found many IV companies using unskilled or undertrained nurses

with some patients being seriously harmed; uncovered massive kickbacks being paid to physicians who prescribed home IV for patients who did not have the illness being treated, such as Lyme disease.

Major home health-care companies paid bribes to physicians to prescribe home intravenous therapy. Paying for legitimate referrals is permissible; what is out of bounds is treatment that occurs because of potential profit rather than medical necessity. The National Alliance for Infusion Therapy and the Home Health-Care Association of America, both of Washington, D.C., might be helpful in weeding out the sleazy providers.

When investigating home health-care providers, journalists should ask whether they have submitted their services for national recognition from the Joint Commission on Accreditation of Healthcare Organizations. Then they should ask about state scrutiny. In Missouri, for instance, the Bureau of Home Health Licensing and Certification is supposed to oversee 235 home health agencies and 33 hospices; that scrutiny is supposed to qualify the providers for billing the government under Medicare. Does the state collect financial information? A financially troubled home health-care company might be cheating patients on the number of visits, paying minimum wage to unqualified nursing aides or taking other shortcuts.

Medical Laboratories

A reporter at WRC-TV, Washington, D.C., knew that medical laboratories wanting federal payments for testing Medicare patients had to undergo periodic inspections. So he obtained inspection reports from the U.S. Health Care Financing Administration. They showed quality-control violations at 40 percent of the Washington-area laboratories. Because such violations often have real-world consequences, the reporter decided to seek lawsuits against the laboratories. He found them, including one filed by a teenager incorrectly diagnosed as having gonorrhea, a man falsely informed that he had AIDS and a woman given a hysterectomy because of a mistaken cancer test reading.

The Wall Street Journal found frequent incorrect readings of Pap smear tests by laboratories. The result: Women dying of cervical cancer who could have been saved through early detection. As the newspaper delved into the reasons, it found technicians paid by the number of slides they read per hour, leading to carelessness, low pay (despite the harried pace) and lack of supervision.

Only some states regulate laboratories. If that is the case, are labs in hospitals and physicians' offices covered or exempted? If nobody is inspecting those labs, journalists should look for medical board complaints and lawsuits. In states that do provide regulation, journalists should study the inspection reports lab by lab. In states that do not regulate labs, journalists should ask why not?

Like many other types of Medicare providers, laboratories sometimes cheat the federal government by charging higher fees than they charge to hospitals, health maintenance organizations or private physicians. One technique is unbundling tests that are otherwise offered as a package for a flat fee. By charging the Medicare program separately for each unbundled test, the laboratory increases its profits. Some laboratories simply do no analysis, dumping blood and urine samples into a drain. The labs then charge the government as though they had performed sophisticated analyses.

Blood Banks

At Dateline NBC, a producer was analyzing a U.S. Food and Drug Administration recall database when he noticed a reference to a blood recall. Not knowing what that meant, he began asking questions. The result: A story about how blood banks frequently had to call back blood already released for use in transfusions. Why? It had been taken from high-risk donors or had not been properly tested for diseases or had tested positively for AIDS-related HIV, but had been circulated anyway.

The Philadelphia Inquirer began a project after a reporter's routine donation of blood. As the reporter lay still, he wondered where the blood would go after it left his body. How would it be processed? Who would decide where it got sent after processing? How much would it cost a patient receiving it during surgery? Eighteen months later, the newspaper published its series, "The Blood Brokers." It made for unsettling reading. The reporter found local blood shortages caused by mismanagement, not donor reluctance. He found blood banks with shortages buying pints from overstocked banks, all without donor knowledge, government regulation or price controls. The American Association of Blood Banks, Bethesda, Md., provided perspective.

Drug Companies

For many patients, drugs have been a curse, not a cure. Women took Diethylstilbestrol (DES) because drug companies told physicians, and physicians told their patients, that it would prevent miscarriages. It worked as prescribed, sometimes. But it also produced a generation of women with a higher than normal risk of vaginal cancer. When such situations occur, do drug manufacturers voluntarily remove the product from the market? Or must they be forced by the government? When the government intervenes, are its procedures adequate to restrict the drug immediately or do adversary proceedings continue for years while the offending compound is still available? If a drug company loses its domestic market, does it then sell the same product overseas without appropriate warnings?

The U.S. Food and Drug Administration keeps records on premarket testing of specific medications, as well as any adverse reactions reported. The most egregious cases usually find their way into the government periodical FDA Enforcement Report. FDA clinical investigator files might help a journalist prove that the tests have been conducted by self-interested researchers at universities or supposedly independent private laboratories. Sometimes the researchers are honest but their scientific methods are flawed. In any case, even the most upright drug companies tend to fund research that has the potential to find or increase a market for the product. As for drug experience reports showing adverse reactions—which also might show up at the federal Centers for Disease Control and in state health departments—they are sporadic at best. Drug companies do not encourage a centralized network. When they are forced by the FDA to add warnings to the package inserts, the serious consequences might be buried in a long list of normally trivial side effects. Even if the warning is clear, physicians might not read it. As a result, physicians might not know what they are seeing. Pharmacists, less captive of drug manufacturers, are far more likely to contact the FDA about problems than are physicians.

The Eugene Register-Guard started a project after a reporter saw a death notice for a seven-year-old boy in foster care. Curious, she requested the medical examiner's report, which pinpointed a prescription drug as the cause. FDA files indicated at least 80 similar child deaths, but the agency said it had never compiled the statistics in that way, so had missed the big picture.

When a drug is effective and safe, is it affordable? Drug prices are controversial. The industry says it needs money to develop new medicines. But promotion, advertising, lobbying and campaign contribution expenses top those for development. Much of the promotion budget is for well-paid sales representatives, who travel the nation calling on individual doctors. Only a small percentage of the representatives have training in pharmacy or pharmacology; their primary purpose is to sell, not to inform. There is nothing the FDA can do to control the problem, given the private, one-on-one nature of the meetings. A journalist trying to understand the cost equation would be wise to travel with a drug company representative for a few days. Manufacturers of generic drugs hope to keep costs down after receiving FDA approval for their formulas. The recipes, however, sometimes fail to work when made in large batches. In at least a few cases, generic drug makers knowingly failed to follow the approved recipes to cut costs. The result: sick or dead consumers of the flawed generics.

As for advertising, studies of drug company paid advertisements in medical journals have shown about one-third of the claims are misleading and nearly half would lead to improper prescribing practices. Yet many doctors rely heavily on such advertisements. Journalists can check FDA sources to learn if the agency has warned or sanctioned any drug advertisers for misleading claims. When journalists write articles about so-called wonder drugs, they must be careful to ask the right questions. Are studies purporting to validate drugs' effectiveness part of the official clinical trials submitted to the FDA? Is the compound used in the trials more potent than what will be marketed? Has the drug so bothered some people in the trial sample that they have dropped out before the final results are tabulated? Will the drug have even broader, more serious adverse effects if used in unapproved ways?

It is difficult for patients to buy the least expensive, most effective prescription drug because it is the doctor who chooses the therapy. Because of that, the normal supply-demand curve is fractured. Physicians who prescribe the newest, most costly drugs on the theory that there must have been improvements made are not only encouraging inflation, but also using medications with the least reliable histories.

Barry Werth's book "The Billion-Dollar Molecule: One Company's Quest for the Perfect Drug" explains the industry well. The "Physicians' Desk Reference" is probably the most comprehensive guide to prescription drugs. It is published by Medical Economics Data, of Montvale, N.J. The same company publishes companion guides to nonprescription drugs, drug interactions and side effects.

Pharmacies

How far do pharmacists go in counteracting the dangerous prescription practices of physicians? If a pharmacist suspects a particular medication will have adverse effects on a specific patient, does the pharmacist speak up? What if the medication seems sensible, but the dosage appears too high? Strictly on a cost basis, do pharmacists have the authority under state law to substitute generic drugs when there is a choice (not all drugs have generic equivalents) for name brands without physician approval? If they have the authority, do they use it regularly? If they lack the authority, why is that?

Pharmacies must submit ownership information to the FDA. Are any local physicians on the list of officers and directors? If so, do they require prescription drug buyers to use that particular pharmacy, even though a different pharmacy might have a different selection or better prices? Speaking of conflicts, what financial inducements are offered to pharmacies by drug makers to stock certain medicines and sway customers to those brands?

Some of the organizations that can provide perspective are the Pharmaceutical Manufacturers Association, American Pharmaceutical Association and Nonprescription Drug Manufacturers Association, all of Washington, D.C.; National Association of Retail Druggists and National Association of Chain Store Druggists, both of Alexandria, Va.; National Wholesale Druggists Association, Reston, Va.; and American Society of Hospital Pharmacists, Bethesda, Md. Thomas Maeder's book "Adverse Reactions" is a useful overview of how one drug rose and fell, helping many patients and killing others.

Medical Device Companies

The opening anecdote in this chapter demonstrates the impact medical device manufacturers can have, and how investigators can dig into their operations. The possibilities are numerous. When a freelance magazine writer wanted to know about wheelchairs made by a major company, she obtained files from the appropriate branch of the Food and Drug Administration. The existence of documents for any given medical device can be gleaned early in the process by regular reading of the Federal Register. The documents—clinical data, test results, labeling requirements, promotional materials, progress reports, adverse reaction data and correspondence—told of an electric wheelchair that caught fire, killing its quadriplegic occupant. But no agency was empowered to punish anybody.

The situation has improved little. One private organization, the Emergency Care Research Institute, Plymouth Meeting, Pa., investigates medical device accidents and tries to keep track of litigation involving the devices. Its publications, Health Devices Alert and Health Devices, are worth reading. Two industry groups, the Health Industry Manufacturers Association, Washington, D.C., and the National Association for Medical Equipment Services, Alexandria, Va., can provide perspective.

Individual Health-Care Providers

Most individuals who are health-care providers are licensed by one or more government agency and by professional organizations. Chapter 11 of this book covers licensed professionals, providing an investigative paradigm that cuts across all occupations. The remainder of this section will focus more intensively on the different types of individual health-care providers.

Medical doctors are the most obvious subjects of journalistic inquiry because of their life-and-death powers, their wealth and the political influence they have when they choose to exercise it. Their licensing, performance standards, ethics codes, discipline and professional associations all received attention in Chapter 11. In this chapter on the broader health-care system, it is relevant to mention the claims to knowledge that split medicine.

The split sometimes is found along specialist lines. The professional interests and practice patterns of surgeons, pathologists and pediatricians, to name a few, occasionally diverge. Such divergence is played out starkly when in-hospital peer review panels suspend a physician's privileges; the targeted physician might fight back, with the dispute spilling over into court. Journalists can learn a lot from those intramural disputes. When it so often seems as if medicine speaks with one voice, the fissures are educational. Journalists should be sure to cultivate sources at each of the medical specialty organizations, such as the American College of Obstetricians and Gynecologists. The American Board of Medical Specialties and Marquis Who's Who (part of Reed Reference Publishing) compile "The Official ABMS Directory of Board Certified Medical Specialists," covering allergists, anesthesiologists, colon surgeons, dermatologists, emergency medicine practitioners, family practice doctors, immunologists, internal medicine specialists, medical geneticists, neurological surgeons, nuclear medicine practitioners, obstetricians, gynecologists, ophthalmologists, orthopedic surgeons, otolaryngologists, pathologists, pediatricians, physical and rehabilitation specialists, plastic surgeons, preventive medicine practitioners, psychiatrists, radiologists, thoracic surgeons and urologists.

The biggest splits are between the physicians with MD (and, increasingly, DO) after their names, and others who usually call themselves doctors—especially chiropractors and homeopaths. As journalists try to explain which medical care works and which does not and why, they should explore the realms of so-called alternative medicine. Assuming that all chiropractors and homeopaths are unscientific charlatans is unacceptable, because millions of patients testify about being cured. On the other hand, some chiropractors and homeopaths are quacks or at least incompetent, just as some MDs and DOs are.

The American Chiropractic Association, Arlington, Va., and the National Center for Homeopathy, Alexandria, Va., can provide perspective, as can the American Academy of Physician Assistants, Alexandria, Va., plus the American Medical Association and American Osteopathic Association, both based in Chicago. The American Medical Association publishes "Reader's Guide to Alternative Health Methods" edited by Arthur W. Hafner; a less conventional approach is taken by Mark Kastner and Hugh Burroughs in their book "Alternative Healing: The Complete A-Z Guide to Over 160 Different Alternative Therapies."

Greed is one trait that unites some doctors across specialties and schools of thought. Doctors as entrepreneurs refer patients to their own profit-making hospitals, infertility clinics, imaging centers, diagnostic laboratories and the like. Journalists can document the abuses of self-referral by thinking of doctors as businesspeople, then running the corporate paper trails discussed in the first section of this book, as well as in Chapter 12.

Trying to profit from government medical care is another avenue for greed. Journalists can ask state government Medicaid administrators how much money any individual doctor earned the previous year, and where that amount ranked statewide among doctors certified to see Medicaid recipients. The top earners might have stimulated the curiosity of the Medicaid fraud unit. One Michigan doctor brought unwanted attention to himself by billing Medicaid for 96,000 home visits over a two-year span. The Detroit News found that in a 21-month period, at least 30 Medicaid patients had died at least partly because doctors had prescribed too many drugs. Why were doctors overprescribing? Because they could bill Medicaid for the drugs.

On behalf of the federal Medicare program, the Health and Human Services Department inspector general publishes a list of doctors suspended from receiving Medicare payments. Journalists should check the list on a regular basis for local names. Some of those same names might have already appeared on the investigations list of the state medical board, which the journalist should be monitoring regularly. But other names on the Medicare list will not have yet come to the attention of the state board.

Dentists, a kind of doctor that needs to be scrutinized separately—partly because the dental insurance system is usually separate from the rest of health insurance—usually escape the attention of journalists. That is a mistake on the part of journalists.

Tracy Barnett of the Columbia Daily Tribune looked where few other journalists look after hearing from a Medicaid recipient that a local dentist planned to pull seven of her teeth. Barnett's investigation revealed that the dentist often performed questionable procedures just so he could submit hefty bills to Medicaid. In an extreme case, Susan Crain Bakos wrote a book, "Appointment for Murder," about a dentist who was a serial killer but continued to practice for an unconscionably long period. The American Dental Association, Chicago, National Dental Association (for black dentists), Washington, D.C., and National Association of Dental Laboratories, Alexandria, Va., are among the organizations that can provide perspective.

In many medical settings, nurses play as important a role as doctors. Peter Elkind wrote a book, "The Death Shift," about a pediatric nurse who murdered babies in hospitals. A look at nursing from the inside comes from Echo Heron, in her autobiographical books "Intensive Care" and "Condition Critical." At the state level, journalists will find licensing/disciplinary boards and support agencies such as the Missouri Bureau of

Community Health Nursing. Groups like the American Nurses Association and American College of Nurse-Midwives, both in Washington, D.C., can provide perspective.

■ GENERAL REFERENCE SOURCES

The Index Medicus covers more than 3,000 biomedical journals, in print or on-line. In their health chapter for an earlier edition of this book, Penny Loeb and Dolly Katz called it

> the medical field's equivalent to the Reader's Guide to Periodical Literature. You will find studies and articles on almost any subject you are investigating—physician incompetence, unnecessary surgery, dumping of poor patients on public hospitals, or variations in death rates among hospitals. Moreover, you will find excellent commentaries on the articles in often-pithy letters to the editor, which the Index also chronicles. You will find doctors calling each other names and attacking each others' studies in remarkably frank language. Even if the articles do not answer your questions, they will tell you who the experts are, and you can ask them yourself.

Medline is a computerized government database that will search Index Medicus as well as other on-line resources. Searching the federal government's National Library of Medicine using Grateful Med software will yield names of organizations offering expert advice, drug effects and a chemical dictionary, among other resources.

The National Institutes of Health, Bethesda, Md., is a federal agency consisting of subagencies that concentrate on specific diseases, including diabetes, allergies, arthritis and more. The federal government's publication Morbidity and Mortality Weekly Report covers the occurrence of disease and death from all causes in the United States. Every disease has its own set of interest groups, such as the American Cancer Society. The National Association of Consumer Agency Administrators, Washington, D.C., publishes a multivolume bindered set called Health Fraud Information Exchange.

Independent publications, such as medical journals, can help journalists understand what is considered acceptable medical theory and practice. The answers are not always clear-cut. As Loeb and Katz said, refereed journals tend to be the most dependable. But even when experts review the soundness and importance of research before publication, confusion might reign. Loeb and Katz mention one issue of the New England Journal of Medicine containing "two conflicting studies on estrogen, a hormone commonly prescribed for postmenopausal women. One, by the eminent researchers of the Framingham Heart Study, concluded that estrogen greatly increases the incidence of heart disease. The other, by equally distinguished Harvard researchers, said that giving estrogen to postmenopausal women reduces their risk of heart disease." The newsletter Public Health, Alexandria, Va., tries to track state legislative developments.

Books about health care in general, and specific aspects of it, abound. A few of the best are Paul Starr's "The Social Transformation of American Medicine"; Jeanne Kassler's "Bitter Medicine: Greed and Chaos in American Health Care"; Randy Shilts' "And the Band Played On"; Ruth Macklin's "Enemies of Patients"; Steven R. Eastaugh's "Health Care Finance: Economic Incentives and Productivity Enhancement"; "Introduction to Reference Sources in the Health Sciences" by Fred W. Roper and Jo Anne Boorkman; and "Getting the Most for Your Medical Dollar: A Consumer's Guide to Affordable Health Care" by Charles B. Inlander and Karla Morales of the People's Medical Society, Allentown, Pa.

Chapter 15

INVESTIGATING INSURANCE

*I*nvestigative journalists, beat reporters and editors tend to ignore insurance companies and regulators. Why insurance is undercovered by most journalists cannot be explained logically. The cases they could be examining involve people from all walks of life, usually in moments of suffering. To guard against economic devastation caused by suffering, individuals pay for personal insurance—life, health, automobile, homeowners—or wish they could. Businesses pay, too—for workers' compensation and unemployment insurance, as well as protection against flooding and other disasters of nature, crop failures, bridge collapses, malpractice claims, libel, product liability lawsuits and more. Federal and state governments, meaning hundreds of millions of taxpayers, pay for Medicare and Medicaid insurance coverage, as well as contracting with insurance companies to provide care for the employees who staff the government.

Insurance companies, part of the private sector already covered in Chapter 12, divide along three lines: life, health and property-casualty (liability) insurance. Some companies form subsidiaries to sell every kind of insurance. This chapter focuses on how investigators can scrutinize those companies and their agents.

There is plenty to scrutinize. While paying hundreds of billions of dollars in premiums each year, many individuals and businesses gripe about the product. They think insurance is overpriced, sold by untrustworthy people and rarely pays off when needed. Insurance companies could be more socially conscious, pushing harder than they do for safer workplaces, homes, highways, automobiles and better health care to reduce the claims against them, the critics add. Instead, they too often simply raise prices to cover their liability.

Several studies indicate that the average U.S. family spends about 12 percent of its income on insurance. Many families spend more money on health insurance alone than on food. They have no idea how to comparison shop, since understandable information about specific companies, agents and policies may be nonexistent. So they buy on the basis of name brand or a reassuring-sounding promise ("You're in good hands" and "Like a good neighbor") or because they know a local insurance agent or because they are swayed by high-pressure sales tactics.

Government is of little help. Regulation by state agencies tends to be lax; federal regulation is minimal. Meanwhile, fraud is rampant, often perpetuated by those outside the insurance industry who are looking to enrich themselves illegally. In that way, the insurance industry is like the savings and loan industry—there is so much money in the till every day, it is going to attract people who intend to misuse it.

All that sounds like investigative nirvana. Instead, insurance has been an investigative wasteland in most news organizations. This chapter is meant to change the equation.

Investigating the Sellers: Insurance Companies and Agents

Annual statements filed by insurance companies with state insurance departments are probably the most detailed disclosure of income, expenditures and assets required of any institution by any government agency. Yet most journalists have never seen an insurance company annual statement. Investigators who read every page carefully will find kernels of many stories concerning the vast real estate holdings of the company, how it invests money from policyholders, whether its reserves are adequate to pay claims in a timely manner and much more.

Part of the challenge is determining the true state of the company's financial health. Insurers like to use accounting rules to mask their profits, thereby avoiding price decreases when state regulators mention the possibility. Andrew Tobias, one of the few journalists to write frequently about insurance in a clear-eyed way for a general audience, explains the financial shenanigans in a chapter of his book, "The Invisible Bankers." The chapter's title tells a big part of the story: "By Popular Demand: A Very Short Chapter on Insurance Accounting—How to Take in $52 Million, Pay Out $6 Million and Report a Loss."

One journalist was wandering around a county government building one day when he decided to sit in on a case of a large insurance company challenging its $31 million property tax assessment for a downtown building. The insurer wanted the assessment reduced to $20 million. A check with the state insurance commissioner showed that for asset valuation purposes, the company considered the building to be worth $27.4 million. Another building showed up as a $78 million asset on the report to the state, but the company was asking the assessor to reduce his valuation from $62 million to $37.2 million.

Investigators should look for insurance companies involved in lines of business unrelated to insurance, such as computer software subsidiaries or real-estate development companies. Do such subsidiaries yield financial gains for insurance company executives who are charging the main company outrageous management and equipment fees to line their own pockets? As with any business, investigators should check for inflated executive salaries and benefits and favored treatment for directors, such as millions of dollars of company-related legal work going to the lawyer on the board.

In trying to interpret the insurers' own numbers, journalists can rely on examinations conducted by state insurance departments at routine intervals or in response to perceived problems. Furthermore, journalists can read through complaints against insurance companies filed with state regulators by policyholders. Any given individual complaint might lead to a larger story. Multiple complaints against the same company about the same practice might be the first step in documenting a pattern of illegal or unethical behavior.

Scrutiny is especially important because life and health insurance company insolvencies have increased threefold in recent years. Many that are technically solvent are in weak condition, especially a substantial percentage of Blue Cross health plans, which collectively make up the country's largest health insurer. An investigation of Empire Blue Cross and Blue Shield by the New York Times showed starkly how much can go wrong, and why.

Empire's filings with state regulators seemed to inflate losses on policies for high-risk individuals and small groups—rates on those policies came under state control, and the supposedly not-for-profit insurer wanted to charge more. At the same time, the insurer appeared to understate losses on large business accounts, which were unregulated and desirable from Empire's standpoint. The legislature, believing all the figures, did Empire's bidding by requiring for-profit insurers to write health policies for high-risk applicants or stop selling in the state.

State guaranty funds designed to pay policyholders caught in insolvencies are working poorly in many instances. Those funds often provide no relief for persons covered by Blue Cross, health maintenance organizations and self-insured businesses. Even when guaranty funds do make policyholders whole, everybody pays because guaranty funds are financed by insurance premium increases and general tax dollars.

When journalists are finished scrutinizing the corporate suites of insurers, they should next turn their attention to the street-level sellers, known as agents. Some agents sell exclusively for one company as employees. Other agents are independents representing numerous insurers. How honestly is price represented? Forbes magazine priced 250 term life insurance policies for a 45-year-old male nonsmoker who wanted $1 million of coverage. The 10-year total bill ranged from $16,200 to $94,100.

Investigators should determine how much commission agents receive on each type of policy sold. Does the level of commission influence what they push to customers? By selling a certain whole-life policy, an agent can earn $550 on a $1,000 premium; an annuity policy, on the other hand, will earn only a $20 commission.

When checking agents, investigators should ask whether they have achieved the rank of chartered life underwriter, chartered financial consultant, chartered property-casualty underwriter or certified financial planner. Attaining those ranks cannot guarantee honesty, but such attainment shows that the agents sought advanced training.

State insurance departments, which license agents, might issue a notice of regulatory activity against a specific agent based on investigations of outside complaints or suspicions within the department. The notice shows the reason for disciplinary action and the disposition. A monetary fine, license suspension or license revocation are the most common penalties. The process tends to be reactive. In Missouri, for example, with about 68,000 agents, there is no individual review at license renewal time. That gives journalists all the more reason to initiate investigations. Some state insurance departments will provide complaints against agents even when no discipline resulted.

The New York Times investigated sales pitches by agents from a major insurer who pushed term life to every customer, no matter how varied their situations. The reporter determined that some of the agents were improperly licensed and used misleading comparisons. For example, in denigrating whole-life policies, the agents showed no dividends, arguing that was fair because dividends were not guaranteed. But the whole-life policy in question had paid dividends every year.

When agent deception occurs, journalists should document whether it is the result of a few bad apples or if it reveals a central strategy encouraged by the company. What happens to the insured if an agent embezzles the premium or misplaces the application, which then never gets to the home office? As journalists interview sources and review documents, they should determine whether checks are payable to the company or, at their insistence, to the agent. That can be an indicator of fraud.

Redlining is a conspiracy involving insurers and agents to exclude certain people in designated neighborhoods, often predominantly black or some other minority, from coverage. The worst problems seem to be with automobile and homeowners insurance. To investigate redlining allegations, journalists should check sales and claims data by ZIP code, plus check whether agents' offices are absent from certain neighborhoods while thick in more affluent sections. Another test is whether a black person pays a premium comparable to that paid by whites if the black person lives in a mostly white neighborhood, but pays more for less coverage when moving to a larger house in a mostly black neighborhood. CNN pulled together evidence of redlining for the cable network's projects reports.

One irony is that insurance companies and agents might be hurting themselves financially while breaking the law by redlining. The Missouri Insurance Department conducted a study showing much higher percentage payouts to white policyholders than to blacks, because whites were more likely to file claims.

Health and Disability Insurance

Of all insurance policies worth investigating, health coverage is frequently the most compelling. The stories literally involve life and death on a daily basis.

Because so much health insurance is employment based, journalists should be delving into the coverage provided by local employers, large and small. Do they offer adequate and equal coverage for all employees at a reasonable price? Inadequate coverage might include some of the very illnesses usually related with that type of workplace—repetitive motion injuries in a meatpacking plant, for example. Unequal coverage might mean an employer excludes a worker with a pre-existing kidney problem or charges higher rates than others covered by the group policy are charged. An unreasonable price might mean that some workers cannot afford their share of the premium, so go without coverage. The federal government and state governments are restricted from regulating employer health insurance plans if the employers are self-insured—that is, those who refrain from paying premiums to commercial insurers.

About 37 million Americans lack health insurance; they are likely to be unemployed or part-time workers, part of a minority group or foreign born. A reporter should locate local residents who are uninsured, then seek documentation of what steps they may have taken in an attempt to resolve their problem. Have employers and insurers acted illegally or unethically in denying coverage? Is there a government-run insurance pool for those unable to obtain coverage any other way? Are the policies offered through the pool affordable and adequate in their coverages? Joel Weissman and Arnold M. Epstein collected huge amounts of data as they wrestled with answers to those questions. Their findings are in their book "Falling Through the Safety Net: Insurance Status and Access to Health Care." As more and more employer and government insurance plans move patients into managed care (especially health maintenance organizations), procedures routinely performed by doctors and hospitals are being denied coverage. Or, if coverage is finally approved by the insurer affiliated with the HMO, it comes only after delays during which the patient's condition deteriorates.

Technology has aggravated the conundrums. If, according to high-technology testing, a patient has a tendency toward a genetic disease, but shows no overt signs of it, should an insurer be able to deny coverage without penalty? Some insurers will pay for prenatal testing only if the parents agree to abort should certain diseases, such as cystic fibrosis, show up. What about ending or reducing coverage when a person already covered is diagnosed with an AIDS-related disease? Cancer coverage is a similar problem, especially if the treatment is deemed experimental by the insurer, and thus excluded.

The questions worthy of investigation seem endless: When so much health insurance is employer-based, should a worker lose coverage if the job is lost? What about higher premiums based on age? Is that fair? But if all premiums are level for the same coverage, no matter what the covered person's age, should healthy younger people in effect have to subsidize less healthy older people?

The New York Times investigated the case of a California couple whose already insured daughter started suffering from kidney trouble at age three, although she was able to lead an active life. Their group health insurance, purchased through a university alumni association, could not arbitrarily exclude coverage, so the insurer began doubling premiums every year, the maximum yearly increase allowed by state law. When the annual premium reached $16,000, the moderate-income couple could no longer afford to pay. No other insurer would offer a policy covering the kidney problem.

Disability insurance is a more limited health policy, designed mainly to replace lost income. In scrutinizing such insurance coverage, a journalist should ask whether it excludes certain causes of injury, especially those most likely to befall the policyholder. Will it pay benefits if the policyholder can do some work, but not at the previous occupation? Will it pay benefits for enough weeks or months to matter? Will it kick in only after a certain number of months or years, leaving the policyholder vulnerable during the waiting period? As insurance companies become more aggressive fighting disability claims, journalists can find more and more complaints filed by policyholders with state insurance commissioners, as well as more and more lawsuits pitting disability insurers against individuals trying to collect after being injured. Insurers believe up to 25 percent of all disability claims are fraudulent; the insurers are also receiving large numbers of claims for disabilities almost unheard of a decade ago, including carpal tunnel syndrome, the Epstein-Barr virus, stress-related disorders and AIDS. On the other hand, insurers have themselves to blame as a result of aggressively marketing policies with broad benefits to persons who were questionable risks.

The Detroit News exposed auto dealers—none of which were licensed as insurance agents—selling credit life and disability policies to car buyers at huge mark-ups, adding as much as $7,000 to the cost of a $15,000 vehicle. When the policyholders became disabled or died, their insurance often paid nothing, since the insurance companies could say the sales had been made by unlicensed persons. The state attorney general said he had filed no charges because he was waiting for the insurance commissioner to request action. The insurance commissioner said he had not filed a complaint because laws regulating auto dealers were outside his jurisdiction.

■ JAMES NEFF ON MEWA FRAUD

Fraud emanates from many quarters when so much money is involved. Freelance journalist James Neff wrote for the IRE Journal about a kind he labeled "insurance racketeering," otherwise known as "MEWA fraud."

MEWA stands for Multiple Employer Welfare Arrangement, a collection of small companies or labor unions combining their resources to buy coverage from a local health insurer. The insurer self-pays smaller claims and protects itself against large claims with a stop-loss policy at a big insurance company. In most states, MEWAs fall through regulatory cracks, so are not required to maintain a legally mandated minimum cash reserve or disclose finances.

The fraud often starts like this: A small company or union local loses its insurance from a big provider trying to rid itself of less profitable accounts or faces an unaffordable rate hike from Blue Cross. It is suddenly susceptible to an insurance racketeer who offers a plan that looks like it provides the same benefits for a lower cost. Some of these racketeers drum up business by going to an industrial park and making cold calls business to business. The small company or local union, crushed by high health costs and needing to care for its workers, buys the new plan.

Now all kinds of tricks can happen, based on the time lag between when workers pay premiums and when they need medical bills picked up by the MEWA. Some crooked MEWAs use a Ponzi scheme—taking in cash premiums, paying off early claims to win additional health insurance business with small companies, then disappearing with the money. Some of these crooked MEWAs are reinsured with phony offshore companies that have organized-crime ties. The workers are stuck paying all of their medical bills, in addition to having lost their premium payments.

Sometimes a MEWA crook will promise a kickback to a union official who shifts the local's health plan to the MEWA. The official will claim he did it to save money or was unaware he was recommending a shaky health plan. MEWA operators move in and out of states so fast that nothing effective can be done to hold them accountable.

Complicating the situation are the supposedly legitimate insurance agents who, along with their other policies, sell MEWA packages at hefty commissions. When the MEWAs fold, disappear or pay out substandard benefits, the agents claim they had no idea they were pushing faulty benefits packages. While all this is occurring, government regulators do little or nothing, hampered by lack of authority and inadequate staffing.

CNN put together a compelling series on MEWA troubles, showing family after family that had been defrauded of their premium payments, then found themselves in debt for tens of thousands of dollars because of uncovered major medical problems.

Life Insurance

Life insurance is often advertised as a savings tool, so journalists should determine whether the investment and savings features really pay. Would the policyholder be better off putting the money in a lower-risk bank certificate of deposit or in a government savings bond, then buying term life insurance for its death benefit only?

Universal life was the rage for awhile, as agents promised huge earnings tied to rising interest rates. But when interest rates fell, policyholders had to pay additional premiums. Next came variable life, tied to mutual fund performance. That meant policyholders became the captives of stock market performance. A project combining investigative reporting and service journalism could focus on one or more policyholders who volunteer to provide quarterly updates on life insurance earnings. The reporter could compare the earnings with alternative investments. The focus on the volunteer policyholders could be supplemented by complaints filed at the state insurance department, lawsuits plus other paper and people trails.

When life insurers are defrauded by consumers, the cases tend to be dramatic. That is because they involve economically motivated murders or staged deaths. The book "Death Benefit," by David Heilbroner, explains how a lawyer helping a fellow church member collect a death benefit on her daughter uncovered a serial killer motivated by life insurance benefits on her victims.

Automobile Insurance

A seminal question is whether the state requires proof of automobile insurance before it will issue a driver's license or license plates. If coverage is not mandatory, why not? Who has successfully opposed it? If coverage is supposedly mandatory, how many uninsured motorists are driving nonetheless, with or without valid licenses and plates? There is no way to obtain precise numbers, but journalists can talk to sources at the state insurance department, state motor vehicles division, state highway patrol, other agencies and insurance companies, then supplement what they learn from those sources by looking for lawsuits involving uninsured drivers.

If a motorist without automobile coverage suffers physical or vehicular damage because of another uninsured driver's negligence, do both parties refrain from reporting the accident because they are insurance-law violators? If one party does report the accident, are police empowered to make arrests on the suspicion of insurance-law violations?

Another type of fraud is the staged accident. Those accidents usually involve a lawyer and doctor, a middleperson who hires the driver and passengers and those who put their lives in danger. The target will probably be a well-insured driver, who can then be sued or whose insurance company will be vulnerable. The most desperate daredevils are willing to crash into 18-wheel trucks on interstate highways. Other times, crashes are staged at low speeds, with both vehicles involving people in collusion. Still other times, the accidents exist only on paper, as a team at WAGA-TV, Atlanta, found after infiltrating a medical clinic filing claims for fictitious automobile accident victims. Those claims might be bolstered with phony X-rays created by a corrupt radiologist. The crooked doctors are often linked to crooked lawyers, who use the fictitious medical records to file claims against the insurance companies unfortunate enough to have written the policies in force.

Journalists who understand the anatomy of fraud will look for suspicious circumstances in police reports and lawsuits. Those journalists will also talk regularly to insurance company investigators who can direct them to compelling stories. The insurance industry established the National Insurance Crime Bureau in Palos Hills, Ill., to help investigators uncover policyholder fraud, as well as to aid in auto theft prevention and recovery. (Uncovering stolen car fraud is handled more fully in Chapter 9 of this book.)

Several hundred NICB agents work with law enforcement agencies to solve cases. The group's computer databases can help detect fraud by spotting false claim patterns. After the bombing of New York City's World Trade Center, one of the databases played a key role. The FBI found a partial vehicle identification number (8 of 17 digits) on a twisted metal fragment. An NICB computer operator was able to fill in the remaining digits, then trace the vehicle to a rental agency. When law enforcement officers visited the rental agency, they learned it had received a report earlier in the day from the renter that the vehicle had been stolen.

If an insured motorist suffers property damage or personal injury because of an uninsured or underinsured driver's negligence, does the insured motorist receive payment from the insurance company without being penalized through higher premiums? Is the experience significantly different in states with actual or modified no-fault automobile insurance than in states still using the traditional fault-based system? When state legislators try to approve no-fault auto insurance, what groups oppose it?

In states still using the fault system, at least one-third of all two-party crashes end up being litigated for pain and suffering. The litigation costs and awards end up raising auto insurance premiums for everybody, even those with flawless driving records. Is that fair?

Geographic distinctions, type of car driven, number of miles driven in an average week for what purposes, age of the driver, health—all might be factors in determining rates. Is that fair? Should a motorist with a perfect driving record in, say, Massachusetts have to pay much heavier premiums than a comparable driver in Kansas? Because of such rate differentials, how many motorists live in, say, New York, but insure their car in New Jersey to get lower rates?

Should a motorist living in a high-crime area of Boston pay far more for auto insurance than someone living a few miles away in a lower-crime neighborhood? Should where they drive and their safety record be used as the gauge of premium levels, rather than place of residence?

Does the medical portion of the auto insurance policy pay the bulk of the bills? Studies say no. How do the medical portion of auto insurance and other health insurance policies mesh or fail to mesh?

Investigating Homeowners and Other Property Insurance

Should people who live in high-risk weather or crime areas be excluded from coverage by insurers or have to pay higher premiums than they would for the same coverage in a different locale? If the local building code is lax in its standards or its enforcement, homes (and commercial buildings) are likely to suffer more damage than if they were more soundly constructed and inspected. In such circumstances, should insurers be able to pull out of the market or charge policyholders more? Should insurers be allowed to avoid all applicants from certain ZIP codes or census tracts? To reject all applicants who live in homes that are 50 years old or older, even if the homes are in good condition? Are some of these conditions meant to exclude applicants on the basis of race or ethnicity?

Homeowners' policies usually cover damage to the building, theft of its contents and legal liability for bodily injury or property damage of others. Within each of those categories, are there exclusions that mean the policyholder has less coverage than is expected? For example, does the liability category exclude injuries incurred while rollerblading on the property? When damage occurs to the structure or contents are stolen, does the policy provide enough coverage to rebuild or replace with comparable quality, thanks to inflation protection combined with a replacement value provision? Or will the policyholder be surprised to learn that the insurer will pay only the original cost minus depreciation because the contract contains an actual cash value clause?

As with other types of policies, fraud against insurance companies is common, too. Journalists should be alert for civil lawsuits and criminal cases aimed at policyholders trying to bilk insurers by staging burglaries; overvaluing stolen contents; claiming money for preexisting damages; backdating policies; inflating property repair costs; and paying somebody to fake an injury on the property, collect damages, then split the award later. The most insidious fraud involves arson because it often results in death, serious injury and damage to the property of innocent parties. (Arson investigations are treated more fully in Chapter 9.)

Investigating Commercial and Professional Insurance Policies

Things are not always as they seem. In Florida, insurance companies writing medical malpractice policies were pushing for the authority to charge higher premiums. But the Orlando Sentinel showed that insurers were misleading the public about a widespread medical malpractice crisis. It turned out that 3 percent of all doctors in Florida accounted for half the malpractice claims paid by insurers. Instead of dealing with that tiny minority, insurers wanted to raise rates for all doctors.

Another type of professional liability insurance for journalists to monitor covers officers and directors of businesses. How much do local employers pay for that coverage? Is the price so high that it significantly affects retail and wholesale prices charged to customers? Have local employers invoked their officers' and directors' coverage as the result of lawsuits filed against them? Have the insurers writing the coverage paid?

There are dozens of types of commercial insurance, including ocean marine, inland marine, earthquake, glass and machinery policies. Each type spawns its own series of questions. To help answer those questions, state insurance departments issue number-laden reports on specific lines of commercial and professional liability insurance, such as Missouri's report showing a substantial profit on medical malpractice for most insurers during the period studied. When the profit diminishes because of a state court system with juries and judges making huge punitive awards to plaintiffs, insurance companies sometimes leave forever.

As with every other type of insurance, the probability of fraud by policyholders is worth investigating. Property/casualty insurance companies estimate that about 10 percent of annual payouts, running into the billions of dollars, are the result of inflated or fabricated claims. Businesses carrying commercial and professional liability constitute a huge part of overall insurance fraud—the amounts of money are usually much larger than with personal insurance policies, so criminals find that the risks are more palatable.

Corrupt adjusters employed by the insurers are often part of the fraud; their inside knowledge makes detection difficult. If given access to unsolved suspicious claims files, journalists can look for clues. One clue is a photograph submitted by the claimant that fails to show the exact damage being reported. An inside adjuster who is part of the scheme might stick such a photograph in the file so that a casual inquiry will uncover no wrongdoing.

Another clue that fraud might be present is the involvement of outside "public" adjusters, who receive a percentage of the eventual insurance settlement. Their participation might signal inflated monetary claims, an unusually large number of water damage reports, and the like. The National Insurance Crime Bureau can provide perspective.

Investigating the Regulators: State Insurance Commissioners

Fraud is so rampant and state insurance departments are usually so understaffed that the regulators are forced to be reactive. Because they cannot investigate all complaints thoroughly, they sometimes miss individual gems and fail to detect patterns of fraud. Knowing that, journalists should eagerly and regularly seek access to complaint files.

Health insurance, one of the biggest stories of the decade, is barely policed by state agencies, especially if the insurance is provided by employers. That is because court rulings have held that employer-sponsored health insurance falls under the federal Employment Retirement Income Security Act (ERISA). Unfortunately for employees, ERISA is a 1974 law that never contemplated the importance of health insurance as a benefit and so lacks regulatory bite. The National Journal reported a case of an employee insured by her employer who checked out of a hospital after learning her health insurance would not pay for care during a difficult pregnancy. Instead, the insurer said, it would pay for less costly monitoring at home. Two weeks later, the unborn fetus died.

The insurer had ignored the advice of two doctors. But when the patient sued for wrongful death, the court held that she had no right to sue under state law. As for suing in federal court under ERISA, well, ERISA provided no remedy.

The decision was not just a wrinkle in an otherwise smoothly functioning system. As noted throughout this chapter, there is almost no federal monitoring of insurance unless Medicare is involved. At the state level, monitoring is often split among several agencies—the Insurance Department is supposed to oversee insurance companies, while state medical boards are supposed to oversee physicians. Health maintenance organizations often fall through the cracks of regulation, even though they might be controlled by insurance companies.

Sometimes the best consumers—and journalists—can hope for is statistics rather than regulation. State insurance departments report on the number of complaints by company, type of insurance and reasons, which number in the dozens. While studying the nature and number of complaints, journalists can try to determine whether the state department is handling even a small percentage of them effectively. One measure: What is the department's budget per complaint investigation (an average of $250, according to one study) or per company examination (an average of $4,000). Can the job be done properly on such budgets?

When an insurance company insolvency occurs on the state's watch, should regulators have seen trouble coming? Had they conducted a thorough examination of the company within the past few years, as prescribed by law? If so, what warning signs did the examination contain? If none showed up, why not? If regulators identified trouble spots, did they feel constrained by lack of jurisdiction? After the insolvency, did the state department work effectively to make the maximum number of policyholders whole? Did the federal and state governments receive priority over other creditors, leaving individual policyholders impoverished?

Unless insurance commissioners in every state agree on a new rule, there will be gaps and loopholes allowing the insurance industry to circumvent reform. Noting that the Kansas City–based National Association of Insurance Commissioners lacks enforcement power as an organization, Newsweek finance writer Jane Bryant Quinn commented, "If the NAIC approves a paragraph that key insurance companies hate, they will turn loose their lobbyists in the state capitals to excise the offending words." That is especially easy for insurers to accomplish when a significant number of state legislators are insurance agents, as is the case in many capitals. As an example, Quinn noted a model NAIC regulation that companies writing credit insurance pay out at least 60 cents in claims for every dollar collected. But only four jurisdictions met that standard.

Some state insurance commissioners are appointed by the governor with legislative consent; others are elected. Each system has its strengths and weaknesses. Appointed commissioners might feel less accountable to policyholders, who are unable to directly vote them out of office. On the other hand, elected commissioners tend to be in the debt of insurance industry contributors to their campaigns. How many commissioners go to work for insurers immediately after leaving their state job? How many of their assistants do the same? How many state regulators came from the industry originally? That path is a way to gain intimate knowledge of the industry, but it might also lead to a pro-insurer, anti-policyholder mindset.

As journalists explore the regulatory side of the industry, they should ask: What is the appropriate level of regulation? Should states be able to force insurers to write policies for all applicants, require renewals, micromanage rates? Journalists should find out whether consumers at large are represented by a public advocate on rate increase requests. If so, how effective is the public advocate? If there is no public advocate, why not? A study of public advocates in other states can provide perspective.

Investigating the Government as Insurer

When a government agency steps in to supplement or preempt the private insurance market, some good usually results, such as broader coverage at affordable prices. But a less positive result is almost certain; fraud and inefficiency will run rampant, while taxpayers carry large burdens to support targeted segments of the populace.

The National Flood Insurance Program is an example. Most private insurers sensibly stay away from writing policies for people who insist on building homes and businesses in flood plains. But the federal government decided that residential and commercial development of flood plains was worth certain risks. As a result, it pays certain policyholders again and again as water washes over the structures and the fields. Newsweek told of an Illinois resident along the Mississippi River who had paid $6,000 in premiums over two decades, but had collected payouts totalling $24,000 after four different floods.

Veterans benefits are another example, but are discussed mainly in the previous chapter, in the section on veterans hospitals. Unemployment insurance, another program with heavy government involvement, is dealt with largely in Chapter 12.

Medicare

Medicare is in essence partial universal health insurance for persons 65 or older. Its acceptance and overall success make the current debate over universal coverage seem superfluous: it has been shown to work most of the time. Medicare Part A covers inpatient hospital expenses; it is financed by payments of workers and employers, based on a percentage of gross income. Elderly recipients pay no premiums and incur just one annual deductible. Part B covers other health-care expenses, financed 75 percent by general tax revenues and 25 percent by individual premiums upon application; recipients pay a bit more through a deductible.

Because Medicare is such a huge part of the federal budget, journalists have plenty of reason to ask questions. Are hospitals ripping off the government for outpatient expenses? Payments for in-hospital care are limited to amounts set by the government according to 491 diagnostic-related groups (commonly called DRGs). They are usually below rates charged to non-Medicare patients, so taxpayers are not being victimized often. So far, though, outpatient expenses have escaped DRG limits.

Are private-practice physicians charging Medicare for patients never seen, or for treatments never administered, hoping the huge amount of claims processed by the government will cause the fraud to be overlooked? Are medical equipment suppliers (wheelchairs, oxygen tanks and the like) submitting padded or otherwise fraudulent bills? Journalists should begin their inquiries by examining cases of fraud and abuse filed by the federal government against specific health-care providers. Those cases are only a small percentage of the total problem, but they tend to be accessible and well-documented. The Federal Register will contain notices of specific cases; other sources could include the nearest U.S. attorney, the Medicare legal staff, congressional committees with jurisdiction over Medicare appropriations, and state medical licensing boards.

What about local physicians who refuse to participate? Their complaints usually include inadequate compensation, retroactive denial of claims and insurer interference with medical decisions. Are those complaints justified? Journalists should listen carefully, then investigate. If the physicians are correct, that could lead to a good story about an overbearing government. If the physicians are exaggerating, their failure to participate on the basis of mistaken perceptions is a good story, too.

Medicaid

Medicaid is usually more troubled than Medicare, yet most journalists look the other way. Medicaid involves federal money and federal rules, but is operated day to day by the state government. It is meant to help low-income and disabled families and individuals. But in many locales it is hemorrhaging money through inefficiency and fraud, providing subquality care for those it reaches and failing to reach many people who need help. The Congressional Research Service summarized some of the craziness in the preface to its "Medicaid Source Book," prepared for the U.S. House subcommittee on health and the environment:

> To many, the program is an enigma. The program's complexity surrounding who is eligible, what services will be paid for and how those services can be paid is one source of confusion. State Medicaid plan variability is the rule rather than the exception. For example, income eligibility levels vary, the services covered vary, and the amount of reimbursement for the services varies from state to state.
>
> The program acts as a form of health insurance providing access to health services traditionally covered by private health insurance. However, it also provides payment for services such as nursing homes and community-based long-term care, services that have traditionally been outside the umbrella of

private insurance. Furthermore, Medicaid is a program that is targeted at individuals with low incomes. But not all the poor are covered, and not all who are covered are poor.

The Chicago Tribune spent years investigating the Medicaid system. The nine-part series covered nearly every angle that journalists should be examining in their own hometowns. Here is a summary.

Part One. "Storefront Medicine: A Prescription for Failure." This overview shows why Medicaid bills are approaching $200 billion annually. The Tribune reporters found urban patients waiting hours to see doctors working outside their specialties or doctors who were wholly incompetent. Low-income rural patients had to drive 50 miles or more to find a doctor who would accept a Medicaid card.

Part Two. "Paying the Bills: System Dispenses Millions Blindly." Medicaid's administrators pay for prescription drugs without knowing who ordered them, for emergency room visits when the patient has nothing more than a common cold. Claim forms that are obviously inaccurate are accepted without further inquiry.

Part Three. "Doctors: Poor Often Face Turnstile Medicine." The Tribune found that although 24,000 Illinois doctors are certified to treat Medicaid patients, about 240 of those doctors handle 40 percent of the business.

Part Four. "Shoppers: How Hustlers Milk Medicaid." Many patients obtain medicine and medical equipment free, then sell them illegally on the street.

Part Five. "Walter: A Legend at Work—$100,000 in Bills." The Tribune found a Medicaid recipient who cost taxpayers more than $100,000 during one year, even though he never entered a hospital. Remarkably, he gave permission for the Tribune team to tag along with him for two weeks as he collected prescription drugs.

Part Six. "Policing: Bad Doctors Hide in Vast Maze." Doctors who break the rules are either never caught or continue to profit for years while the case drags through the disciplinary machinery.

Part Seven. "Rural Plight: Long-Distance Health Care." Although Medicaid helps with transportation costs, the services generally run only during daytime on weekdays. After normal business hours and on weekends, the poor without transportation suffer, unless an ambulance is available.

Part Eight. "Budget: Medicaid Gobbles Money." Expenses are so out of control that the state has cut its budget for other programs, including public schooling.

Part Nine. "Solutions: No Cheap Cure and No Quick Fix."

Journalists can get a quick understanding of how any given state's Medicaid procedures compare to other states by consulting the U.S. Department of Health and Human Services, Health Care Financing Administration, Medicaid Bureau. One of many helpful reports is "Medicaid: Characteristics of Medicaid State Programs, Volume II, State-by-State Profiles."

Sources to help ferret out Medicaid fraud can be found at the National Association of Attorneys General, Washington, D.C., and its affiliated organization, the National Association of Medicaid Fraud Control Units. The book "Prescription for Profit: How Doctors Defraud Medicaid" by Paul Jesilow, Henry N. Pontell and Gilbert Geis examines one source of fraud in depth.

Workers' Compensation

Workers' compensation insurance provides health care for job-related injuries. It started out as a no-fault system: The worker received payments underwritten by the employer, after agreeing to refrain from suing the employer. But workers started hearing from lawyers wanting to represent them. The lawyers started filing litigation against employers and the state based on pain and suffering, rejected or delayed payments and inefficient, ineffective medical care.

Gradually, a no-fault system turned into a plaintiff lawyer's dream. The litigation, combined with endemic fraud, have led to out-of-control insurance programs in many states, ripe for exposure by journalists.

After Brant Houston of the Hartford (Conn.) Courant and David Armstrong of the Boston Herald exposed workers' compensation frauds in separate locales, they combined to write an article for the IRE Journal. It is reprinted here, lightly edited:

> A Connecticut state employee is arrested for prostitution while out of work because of a supposed back injury. Another injured employee is arrested for drug dealing and yet another is arrested on 185 counts of forgery and larceny. In Massachusetts, a prison guard off the job with an injured left knee wins a state bodybuilding title. A second injured state worker operates a laundry business and runs for political office while out with a strained groin muscle.
>
> In both Connecticut and Massachusetts, allegedly injured state workers perform vigorous activities and earn healthy incomes while being paid thousands of dollars in injury benefits.
>
> All of these examples originated from examining what initially appears to be a complex topic: workers' compensation insurance. In fact, the idea of doing an article on workers' compensation makes most reporters want to file a stress claim themselves. But we have found and published dozens of good stories on the subject, and each of us put together a three-part series about snafus and fraud in our state.
>
> While workers' compensation systems differ from state to state and involve arcane insurance terms, each system ultimately boils down to blood,

money and justice. Workers' compensation is supposed to pay medical expenses and replace the lost wages of an employee injured on the job. Sometimes, though, the system delays or denies fair benefits to legitimately injured workers while letting fakers collect from employers and taxpayers. In your state, both of those problems quite likely exist.

In states where benefits are generous, you will hear plenty of tales of fraud and abuse from employers and insurers. In the public employee part of the system, records will be easier to find than in the private sector.

Look at the state or municipal budget [workers' compensation] increases over the years. Talk to the administrators of the local or state program. They are generally livid about the abuses, which they can do little to stop. They can point you to compensation case files of employees—at least part of those files should be public—showing the kinds of injuries claimed, the money spent and the contesting of the injury claims. In Connecticut, we have found numerous state and municipal employees who have had more than 10 injury claims and cost taxpayers $50,000 or more.

If the case files are partially closed, there should be some documentation at the compensation board [usually in the state capital] where contested cases are heard. In addition, there may be labor-relations documents in which injury claim information is revealed when the government tries to fire an employee. Public governments are finally realizing how high the costs of workers' compensation are and probably have hired consultants to tell them what to do. Consultant reports are full of clues to problems in the system created both by employers and employees.

When looking at state employees, keep an eye out for unusual benefits. For instance, in Connecticut and Massachusetts state employees who are injured by an inmate or a patient are entitled to 100 percent of their wages tax-free while out with an injury. That means they can earn 20 percent to 30 percent more by *not* returning to work.

Numerous injuries do not necessarily mean bad employees. They also can mean employers and managers do not care about the employees. Ask for documents on accident prevention programs (also known as loss control) and programs to reduce dangers in the workplace (also known as risk management). The state of Connecticut spends only a fraction of what it should on preventing injuries, and it shows. Other places to look for documents on workplace safety are the U.S. Occupational Safety and Health Administration's local office (for private employers) and the agencies (sometimes the state's Department of Labor) responsible for safety of public employees. This also is the time to contact local union or employee representatives who will be willing to point you to cases and give you tours of workplace dangers. In many states, there is a chapter of Injured Workers United Inc. Nationally, there is the National Association of Federal Injured Workers.

While the insurers may do a poor job of helping injured workers, they are also occasionally victimized by the system. In Massachusetts, insurers writing workers' compensation policies lost $1 billion in the past four years. As a result, the insurers are writing fewer policies and more employers are being tossed into an assigned-risk pool. The assigned-risk pool drives up insurance rates and sours employers already embittered by the high cost of workers' compensation. The frustrated employers, in turn, often take out their anger on the injured workers.

For information on workers' compensation insurance, check with the National Council on Compensation Insurance in Boca Raton, Fla. Also, state insurance regulators usually keep information on premium rates and insurers who have been sanctioned.

For doctors, chiropractors, rehabilitation clinics and nursing services, the field of workers' compensation is a potential gold mine. Companies and states are just starting to tighten up on medical costs of workers' compensation. One critic called workers' compensation "the Cadillac" of medical benefits because the fees for treating injured workers are seldom limited. You will probably find that certain doctors and clinics get repeat business and that employees know which doctors and clinics to go to.

Check the state agency charged with setting the rates for workers' compensation medical costs. The rate structure will give you a hint of which practitioners stand to profit from treating injured workers. In Massachusetts, the rates are unattractive for some specialists, who usually spurn workers' compensation cases. Chiropractors, however, are able to bill at attractive rates and actively seek this business in television and print advertising.

Lawyers often collect one-third of the final settlement in a disputed workers' compensation claim so there is a hefty profit involved. You will find there are certain lawyers who specialize in workers' compensation; often they push new legislation increasing benefits or oppose legislation to decrease benefits. Bad lawyers may be teaming up with the bad doctors, as they have in more traditional insurance fraud cases.

In some systems, lawyers are paid a fee based on how many hearings, conferences and trials their client can obtain. As a result, some lawyers drag out cases and file needless litigation. Honest attorneys can point out their less scrupulous brethren.

Also, find out how long it takes to resolve disputes in workers' compensation cases in your state. Often, there are lengthy delays strangling a system gasping for air.

Often the commissioners who hear disputed cases are politically appointed. Are they qualified? It depends. In Massachusetts, judges need not be lawyers or medical specialists. In fact, there are no qualifications for judges. Can they be arbitrary, even crazy, in their decisions? Yes. Do they often let cases drag on? Yes. Do they fail to penalize insurers or employers who fight legitimate claims? Definitely. Furthermore, these offices are generally understaffed and underfunded, meaning that employees lose their cars and houses while waiting for their cases to be heard.

Commissioners' offices should contain documents on contested hearings and maintain some kind of reports for statistical studies. Make sure you spend some time in the courtrooms where workers' compensation cases are heard. You may find the delays in the system are simply the result of judges and clerks not working a full day.

When looking for trends, check the U.S. Chamber of Commerce analysis of workers' compensation systems. While the report represents a business point of view, it does track costs and benefits. The Workers Compensation

Research Institute in Cambridge, Mass., also performs studies on national trends and frequently examines state systems. The National Safety Council in Chicago puts out annual reports. Actuarial and Technical Solutions of Patchogue, N.Y., undertakes yearly studies of the cost of compensation systems nationwide.

If you can get workers' compensation data in computerized form, you have a terrific start on your stories. Computers allow you to sort through cases quickly and find the oddities and trends. In Connecticut, the Courant obtained 40,000 injury cases on computer diskette. As a result, the newspaper was able to pinpoint locations with the highest rate of injuries, the kind of injuries and the expense of injuries. On the absurd side, several workers had collected compensation for paper cuts. On the serious side, some workers had been stabbed or badly beaten by inmates or patients at mental institutions.

Do not completely trust the data, however. Use common sense when analyzing it. In Connecticut, it appeared prison guards were more often injured by each other in fights than by inmates. Not true. Data entry clerks had been incorrectly coding injuries when typing the information.

Also, try for computerized records from the agency responsible for administering the workers' compensation courts. These records could allow you to figure out who the big money compensation lawyers are and if they are working in tandem with certain doctors.

Besides following the advice of Houston and Armstrong, journalists can explore whether participation in the state plan is compulsory. When it is, employers frequently complain about high premiums, usually calculated in cost per $100 of payroll. But sometimes costs have risen in part because employers are cheating the system by understating payrolls (upon which rates are based), misclassifying the type of business (claiming that roofers, for whom rates are expensive, are actually clerical workers, for whom rates are lower) and underreporting losses.

If participation in the state system is not compulsory, how many employers have decided to self-insure? Have the arrangements led to safer workplaces, fewer injuries and monetary savings? A key to companies succeeding as self-insurers, they say, is deciding which doctors an allegedly injured worker can consult. That restriction will indeed cut the number of fraudulent claims approved by dishonest physicians taking kickbacks from patients. On the other hand, will the approved doctors deny certification of legitimate injuries to stay in the employer's good graces?

Journalists can also look for doctor and diagnosis shopping. If a worker seeks medical care under an employer's health plan, the worker must pay for part of the bill because of deductibles. But workers' compensation often has no deductibles or other co-payments, which encourages those injured to undergo multiple medical tests. Such shopping around means it will be easier to find a physician or chiropractor who will validate an injury, even though it is concocted.

As state workers' compensation fraud runs rampant, so do the federal Social Security disability trust fund and Supplemental Security

Income program for the poor. The federal government received nearly 3 million disability applications in a recent year, almost double the number of applications from four years earlier. A journalist should examine the original disability claims to see whether they are too easily granted by entry-level processors working for the government. When granted, is the level of benefits too high considering the claimant is also receiving workers' compensation payments and money from a job-related or personal disability insurance policy? Journalists can often consult a fuller record when claims are rejected at the first level, because the allegedly disabled person often appeals. That might mean a full on-the-record hearing before a Social Security administrative law judge. When a claim is granted at the first level or on appeal, is the Social Security Administration reviewing cases to determine if claimants can return to their jobs? Or do disability payments continue long after the disabled person's health is restored?

Insurance Sources to Use Over and Over

Ratings agencies study the financial condition of insurance companies, then grade them publicly. One such agency is A.M. Best, Oldwick, N.J., which additionally publishes the magazine Best's Review. The magazine has one edition covering property-casualty, another for life-health insurers.

Other major agencies that rate insurance company finances are Moody's, New York City; Standard and Poor's, New York City; Duff and Phelps, Chicago; and Weiss Research, West Palm Beach, Fla. Weiss' seems to be the most skeptical of insurance company projections. Before relying too heavily on ratings, journalists should ask which of the agencies require payment from insurers for a rating, which give advice to insurers on what they must do to achieve a better rating, which will not publish a rating contested by an insurer, which have given the highest rating to insurers that then failed the same year.

Financial analysts at stock brokerages often track insurance company conditions as carefully as the ratings agencies do.

Consumer groups with insurance expertise include the National Insurance Consumer Organization, Alexandria, Va. (recently renamed the Insurance Group of the Consumer Federation of America) and Consumers Union, Mount Vernon, N.Y., publisher of Consumer Reports magazine.

Trade associations that will provide perspective include the Alliance of American Insurers, Schaumburg, Ill., and Insurance Information Institute, New York City (both property-casualty); Independent Insurance Agents of America, Alexandria, Va.; Society of Chartered Property and Casualty Underwriters, Malvern, Pa.; the American Academy of Actuaries, American Council of Life Insurance, Mortgage Insurance Companies of America and Health Insurance Association of America, all headquartered in Washington, D.C.

Publications such as Business Insurance, Chicago, abound. Lexis and Nexis, among other on-line databases, have libraries devoted to insurance.

Congressional hearings and reports, state legislative hearings and reports, as well as studies from their research arms, provide regular leads for investigations. A book from the National Conference of State Legislatures, "The State of Workers' Compensation," is helpful, as are General Accounting Office booklets.

A few other books can help immensely: "The Life Insurance Game" by Ronald Kessler; "The Invisible Bankers" by Andrew Tobias; "Winning the Insurance Game" by Ralph Nader and Wesley J. Smith; as well as noncritical consumer guides such as "The Guide to Buying Insurance: How to Secure the Coverage You Need at an Affordable Price" by David L. Scott.

State insurance departments, for all their shortcomings, continue to be the best place for one-stop shopping.

Chapter *16*

INVESTIGATING FINANCIAL INSTITUTIONS

Banks, Savings and Loans, Credit Unions, Investment Companies and Their Mutual Funds

*D*ay-in, day-out, financial institutions have a bigger impact on cities and many of their residents than any other private-sector business or any governmental agency. The failure of so many news organizations to see the big picture during the collapse of the savings and loans is an obvious reason to learn more about the beat, as soon as possible.

Banks, savings and loans, credit unions and—increasingly—investment companies decide whether they will make money available for a business to begin or expand, a family to buy or repair a home, an individual to acquire an automobile, one company to purchase another, residents in a largely minority subdivision to join the mainstream of society. If a financial institution follows unreasonable or illegal lending practices, the harm done can be great. If the financial institution is so badly managed or corrupt that it fails, individuals and businesses might be without checking accounts and might lose some of their savings.

Yet most journalists, most newsrooms, fail to cover financial institutions in a consistent, meaningful way. That means if any given financial institution in town is in danger of failing, illegally discriminating in its loan policies, making dangerous loans to its own directors, laundering money for criminals, miscalculating interest rates on savings and checking accounts, thousands (or maybe millions) of local residents will be ignorant of the situation.

Many journalists say, quietly and privately, that they stay away from covering financial institutions because the terrain is so difficult to understand. Besides, they add, such sensitive private-sector institutions are secretive, too hard to penetrate. Those are irresponsible—and, given financial institutions' impact, dangerous—copouts. The complexity is no greater than on any other beat covered thoroughly. As for the secretiveness, much information is available about financial institutions along the paper and people trails, as specialized publications like American Banker and National Thrift News have demonstrated for decades.

Mary Fricker of the Santa Rosa Press Democrat in California has been a leading spokesperson within IRE for regularly scrutinizing local financial institutions. Co-author (with Stephen Pizzo and Paul Muolo) of the book "Inside Job: The Looting of America's Savings and Loans," Fricker has worked tirelessly within to spread knowledge. This chapter owes an especially large debt to her.

Government Regulators as Sources of Information

Every bank, savings and loan or credit union is supervised by at least one state or federal agency. The Federal Reserve Board and its 12 district banks regulate state-chartered banks that are members of its system. Many state-chartered banks, in addition, are scrutinized by a state agency. The U.S. Office of Comptroller of the Currency, part of the Treasury Department, regulates the several thousand nationally chartered banks. The Federal Deposit Insurance Corp. tries to guarantee depositors will be protected against total loss if a bank fails; the agency also possesses some supervisory powers. If the financial institution is part of a holding company or a corporation selling stock broadly, the U.S. Securities and Exchange Commission and state securities departments might require filings. Savings and loans are usually regulated by the U.S. Office of Thrift Supervision and the FDIC. Credit unions fall under the jurisdiction of the National Credit Union Administration. The federal agencies have regional offices that often have documentation more readily available than headquarters in Washington, D.C.

Examiners tend to look at similar criteria no matter what type of financial institutions they are inspecting. One useful acronym for journalists is CAMEL: Does the financial institution have adequate and stable Capital, high quality of Assets, a Management with competency and integrity, high-quality and sufficient Earnings, plus the necessary Liquidity? There are dozens of textbooks, such as "The Economics of Money, Banking and Financial Markets" by Frederic S. Mishkin, that can help journalists better understand those measurements.

Many stories about financial institutions, such as discriminatory mortgage lending, cut across regulatory lines, applying to banks, savings and loans, credit unions and even nonbank financial institutions equally. Other stories are more about one type of financial institution than other types because of different traditions and regulatory treatments. This chapter concentrates first on the stories relating to each type of financial institution, then moves to the common-denominator stories.

Banks

Federal regulators rate banks in one of five categories: well capitalized, adequately capitalized, undercapitalized, significantly undercapitalized and critically undercapitalized. Banks in the last category are likely to be seized by the government or merged with a healthier bank.

Sometimes the ranking information is available directly from regulators through leaks or documents filed in a legal proceeding; other times private-sector bank rating services will know in which category a bank falls. Those services include Veribanc Inc., Wakefield, Mass.; Sheshunoff Information Services Inc., Austin, Tex.; Bauer Financial Reports, Coral Gables, Fla.; Weiss Research Inc., West Palm Beach, Fla.; W.C. Ferguson Inc., Irving, Tex.; and SNL Securities, Charlottesville, Va.

Using data collected by the Federal Deposit Insurance Corp., sold by the National Technical Information Service on nine-track tape and reformatted for ease of use by one of the private bank-rating services, Dan Woods at the Raleigh News and Observer ranks banks and savings and loans annually. Woods says: "Almost everyone does business with some kind of bank and it is hard to find a topic that readers care about more than their money."

Banks regulated federally are supposed to be inspected at least once annually by one or more examiners working from Washington, D.C., or a district office. Although objective criteria play a major role in the examination, to some extent a bank's report will reflect the personality of the individual federal examiner.

There is an informal network among financial institutions about which examiners are lenient, which are strict but fair and which are considered unreasonably demanding. By developing sources over time, a journalist can mention in stories which examiner is at the local bank during a given week and how that examiner is viewed by the industry.

There are similar networks that can inform journalists about state bank examiners. In Missouri, for example, any of the state-chartered banks and trust companies might be visited by a general examiner, consumer credit examiner or trust examiner.

When a journalist has reason to believe a bank is in danger of being taken over by regulators, arrangements should be worked out with clerks at local motels and copy shops to call if they book room reservations or receive a rush job from Federal Deposit Insurance Corp. inspectors. This is also the time to be especially alert for a change in outside auditors, either because they quit or are fired.

Even the most secretive banks must make some financial information public. The "call report," compiled quarterly, can be studied by journalists. Major changes in any figures from quarter to quarter should be questioned. Some of the key statistics subject to fluctuation are amount of deposits, brokered deposits (which tend to be riskier than those coming to the bank in more traditional ways), jumbo deposits (defined as those over $100,000; too many can make a bank overly dependent on a few people or institutions), net interest income, provision for loan losses, quantity of insider loans, net profit or loss, net income per share, amount of investments in real estate, U.S. Treasury instruments and other securities. Shorter versions of the call report are imbedded in the balance sheet and the income statement.

Knowing such figures allows a journalist to ask some meaningful questions.

What percent of a bank's loans are nonperforming, meaning at least 90 days overdue and otherwise not in compliance with contract language? If the figure is higher than 5 percent, there perhaps is reason to be wary. How many loans have already been written off as uncollectible? What other assets are nonperforming? If the aggregate is higher than 3 percent, there might be cause among depositors and borrowers for concern. How many loans are being made outside the metropolitan area? Such loans, especially on real estate, can be difficult to monitor adequately.

Is the bank lending enough of its deposits locally to keep the community healthy? If local loans are a relatively low percentage of deposits, the bank is perhaps too conservative. If, on the other hand, the percentage is much higher, the bank might face cash flow difficulties. Some experts believe 80 percent is a sensible level in most circumstances. Is the fair market value of current loans equal to the value of the loans when originally made? If loan values are declining, why?

Have some real-estate loans been made on the basis of inflated values, perhaps because the borrower and a land appraiser are in cahoots? As a check on inflated appraisals, a journalist interested in a particular parcel can determine what similar properties nearby sold for in the same six-month period.

Is the bank offering interest rates higher than local competitors? If so, that might indicate a need for cash.

Most of those questions apply to savings and loans and credit unions, too.

Besides financial statements, journalists should ask banks themselves or regulators for these documents when relevant: examination reports, available about once a year; supervisory letters, warning management to change its ways; supervisory agreements, in which a bank signs binding terms to make changes mentioned in supervisory letters; cease and desist orders, stated in stronger terms than supervisory agreements; announcements that officers and directors have been removed; applications to open new branches or buy subsidiary companies.

One big change in the banking environment is Congress and regulators allowing regional and national branches. That change has led to a bank holding company in, say, California, buying all the banks of another company in, say, Florida. When that happens, Florida journalists should be especially alert for the new owners allocating the bulk of Florida deposits to loans in California, thus draining an important source of money from the local economy. Another change to look for: less involvement by local bank officials on community boards of directors, reduced contributions to neighborhood philanthropic groups.

Perspective is available from the American Bankers Association, Bankers Association for Foreign Trade, Conference of State Bank Supervisors, Consumer Bankers Association, Independent Bankers Association of America, National Bankers Association, Association of Bank Holding Companies and Mortgage Bankers Association of America, all of Washington, D.C., plus the American Society of Bank Directors, Alexandria, Va., and the Bank Administration Institute, Rolling Meadows, Ill.

Some of the best books exposing banking practices are "Funny Money" by Mark Singer; "In Banks We Trust" by Penny Lernoux; and "False Profits" by Peter Truell and Larry Gurwin. The newspaper American Banker, New York City, is filled with useful stories every issue.

Savings and Loans

Information available from the Office of Thrift Supervision, part of the Treasury Department, is almost the same as that which can be obtained from the regulators of commercial banks: summaries of cease and desist orders, quarterly reports and applications, challenges, exhibits and so on. The regulatory agency has jurisdiction over several thousand federal and state-chartered savings and loans whose deposits are guaranteed by the Savings Association Insurance Fund. The agency is being folded into the Federal Deposit Insurance Corporation.

State regulators have a role as well. In Missouri, for instance, the Division of Savings and Loan Supervision within the Department of Economic Development oversees a few dozen financial institutions as well as licensed mortgage brokers. State regulators, as a general rule, seem more susceptible to corruption than federal regulators, maybe because their salaries tend to be lower and because they are less sophisticated in their training. The IRE Resource Center contains investigations of state regulators accepting—sometimes even soliciting—favorable loans or other favors from the financial institutions they oversee.

The increase in recent years of savings associations converting from mutual form (ostensibly owned by the depositors) to stock form has resulted in more savings and loans being subject to SEC filing requirements. Many SEC reports, such as the 10Ks and 8Ks (see Chapter 12), may be on file with OTS. Savings and loans are required to file certain reports with the Federal Deposit Insurance Corp., including applications for deposit insurance, mergers with noninsured institutions and insurance fund conversions.

The Resolution Trust Corp. appeared on the scene in the wake of the savings and loan debacle specifically to liquidate failed institutions on behalf of taxpayers, who were already paying for losses totaling tens of billions of dollars. According to many experts, the RTC has turned into a typical federal bureaucracy, hidebound by rules and shot through with corruption. That makes it a suitable subject for an investigation, as well as a repository of information about specific defunct savings and loans. It is headquartered in Washington, D.C., but like most federal agencies has regional offices scattered around the nation.

Journalists throughout the country have shown that the RTC, along with the FDIC, have failed time and again to bring the top executives of failed savings and loans to justice, failed to sell assets for anywhere near their market value, failed to show concern for small depositors and borrowers who lost everything they owned through no fault of their own. Journalists chronicling the aftermath of a savings and loan closing can often tell the story effectively through specific examples—for instance, tracing one piece of property as the RTC dawdles putting it on the market, rejects what seems to be a fair price, lets it sit, then finally sells it to an investor for a penny on the dollar. That investor often resells the property soon thereafter for many times the amount paid for it. Some property sales go smoothly—those can also be followed from beginning to end.

Numerous books by investigative journalists have chronicled the savings and loan scandal. A few of the best are "S&L Hell: The People and the Politics Behind the $1 Trillion Savings and Loan Scandal" by Kathleen Day; "Trust Me: Charles Keating and the Missing Billions" by Michael Binstein and Charles Bowden; and "The Daisy Chain: How Borrowed Billions Sank a Texas S&L" by James O'Shea.

Perspective is available from the American Council of State Savings Supervisors, American League of Financial Institutions, Association of Thrift Holding Companies, all of Washington, D.C., plus U.S. League of Savings Institutions, Chicago. The Federal Home Loan Mortgage Corp.

(Freddie Mac) is chartered by the U.S. Congress and owned by savings and loans to create a secondary market for conventional residential loans. The Federal National Mortgage Association (Fannie Mae) is a congressionally sanctioned private corporation that purchases mortgage loans from financial institutions. National Thrift News, New York City, is a valuable publication to read regularly.

Credit Unions

Credit unions are likely to be regulated at one or both of two levels: the National Credit Union Administration, with main offices in Washington, D.C., and regional branches, or a state regulatory agency. The National Credit Union Administration oversees federally chartered or federally insured credit unions; state agencies are the primary regulators of a much smaller number of state-chartered credit unions or ones that carry no federal insurance. In Missouri, for example, the Division of Credit Unions in the Department of Economic Development oversees a couple hundred state-chartered groups.

Banks and savings and loans are increasingly at odds with credit unions as traditional boundaries blur. A journalist can explore whether local credit unions are expanding beyond their original geographic, employment or other well-defined boundaries to win customers away from banks and savings and loans.

Clues might be found in the "Financial and Statistical Report," commonly known as a "call report," which must be submitted by credit unions of a certain size to either federal or state regulators every six months. Federally insured state credit unions are supposed to supply a financial statement, income and expense statement, statistical loan information, statistical share information, line of credit information and miscellaneous data. Federally chartered credit unions supply essentially the same information, but in a different format.

The financial statement includes information about loans to members; loans purchased from liquidating credit unions; allowances for loan losses; net loans outstanding; cash and petty cash; investments broken down by passbook accounts, certificates of deposit and government obligations; loans to other credit unions; land, buildings and other fixed assets; accounts payable; statutory reserve; special reserve for losses; and reserves for contingencies. The income and expenses statement includes interest on loans, income from loans, interest on real estate loans, income from investments, employee compensation, employee benefits, travel and conference expenses, association dues, office rent and supply expenses, educational and promotional expenses, professional and outside services costs, insurance costs, annual meeting expenses and the allocation of net gains or losses that year to dividends, statutory reserves and undivided earnings.

Regulators often add requirements for additional disclosure to obtain information they deem necessary to address emerging problems in the industry. The Credit Union National Association, Madison, Wis., offers perspective, as do the National Association of State Credit Union Supervisors and the National Association of Federal Credit Unions, both of Arlington, Va.

Farm Credit Banks

WSMV-TV, Nashville, investigated loan fraud at a Tennessee Production Credit Association, a little-known organization that is part of the federal farm credit system. The story showed that the association had approved millions of dollars in loans to an egg company in which the PCA president held a financial interest and in spite of warnings that the company had serious difficulties. To make matters worse, the PCA shifted liability for the loans to local poultry farmers by tricking them into co-signing legal papers.

The U.S. Farm Credit Administration, McLean, Va., is supposed to regulate the components of the system, which includes not only Production Credit Associations, but also Farm Credit Banks, Banks for Cooperatives, the National Bank for Cooperatives, Federal Land Bank Associations, Agricultural Credit Associations and Federal Land Credit Associations.

Mutual Funds and Other Investment Company Products

Investment companies, especially mutual funds, are a large force in the business world. More and more well-to-do but not wealthy individuals are entrusting their money to these companies, which in turn pour that accumulated money into a variety of investments. Because mutual fund investments are not insured by the federal government—unlike deposits in banks, savings and loans and credit unions—citizens are at greater risk when they place money there. Some of them have no idea their funds are uninsured. Their vulnerability is reduced only somewhat by the Securities Investor Protection Corp., a nonprofit organization created by Congress to serve as a safety net for the public.

Investment companies have two theoretical advantages over individual investors trying to profit on their own: professional research and enough money to diversify broadly as a hedge against a few poor-performing choices. Their critics, however, point out that these companies often do no better than individual investors making educated guesses. Local investigative journalists might want to explore specific mutual funds if they are either headquartered there or if large numbers of area residents have put savings into those funds.

Because of financial market uncertainties affecting mutual funds combined with the potential for out-of-control management fees, the Securities and Exchange Commission requires them to file extensive reports, starting with a detailed prospectus for potential investors.

The mutual fund industry suggests that potential investors look for 17 important pieces of information in a prospectus. They include a fund's statement of investment objectives; the industry recognizes 22 different phrasings. At bottom, there are three key goals. One is stability, defined as protecting the amount invested from the risk of loss. A second is growth, defined as increasing the value of principal through capital gains. A third is income, defined as a steady stream of income payments through dividends.

Another of the 17 pieces is the fee table. All fees charged by a mutual fund to an investor are summarized in a table at the front of the prospectus. The first section of the table summarizes an investor's transaction expenses for purchases, exchanges or redemptions. The second section summarizes the mutual fund's operating expenses. The third section is a hypothetical example of how such fees reduce earnings over periods of one, three, five and ten years. Located near the fee table is the per-share table, actually a condensed financial statement, that illustrates how well the fund has been doing with investors' money for the past ten years.

In addition to overseeing the prospectus, the SEC regulates the activities of investment advisors to mutual funds and conflicts of interests involving fund managers. Potential and real conflicts are receiving more attention from mainstream investigative journalists. As Diana B. Henriques wrote in a New York Times series, "fund managers, operating with little oversight by regulators, are investing in companies that employ executives, advisors or underwriters with whom they have close ties. Often, those deals have left the funds holding securities of dubious value."

As mutual funds take more and more money away from savings institutions, those institutions are seeking legislative and regulatory authority to compete. When traditional financial institutions like banks sell mutual funds in their lobbies, do they make it clear to consumers that the funds are not federally insured against loss or collapse? Some mutual fund industry sources believe that if banks are going to enter the fray, then their trust departments ought to be scrutinized under federal securities laws. So should insurance companies. In other words, the same rules should apply to every institution with decision-making power over pooled investments.

The Investment Company Institute, Washington, D.C., represents mutual funds. Perspective is also available from the Futures Industry Association, Washington, D.C.

Redlining by All Types of Financial Institutions

When the U.S. Justice Department filed lending discrimination charges against a Maryland bank recently, it set new rules on loan discrimination—rules that should suggest investigations by journalists in city after city. The government said that by virtue of having all its branches and mortgage-origination offices in majority white neighborhoods, the bank had failed to give minority groups the opportunity to seek loans on an equal basis. To make its case, the government cited two laws unused in previous lending discrimination cases, the Fair Housing Act and Equal Credit Opportunity Act. As part of the settlement, the bank agreed to distribute its lending offices more equitably.

More traditionally, journalists have relied on two other laws to study redlining. The Home Mortgage Disclosure Act pinpoints one type of loan. Lending institutions fitting certain criteria keep application data by race, gender and income level. The law requires depository institutions with assets of more than $10 million and at least one branch in an urban area to disclose their number and total dollar amount of mortgage loans made. Part A of the statement reports loans written, organized by census tract and listed by type of loan, number of loans and total dollar amount. Types of loans include those involving the Farmers Home Administration and Department of Veterans Affairs, home improvement, non-occupant, multifamily dwelling and conventional. If the financial institution has redlined any neighborhoods, the first indication might show up in Part A as portions of census tracts in which it has made few or no loans. Part B reports on mortgages purchased from other institutions. It tells how much business a particular financial institution is doing in the secondary market.

The Community Reinvestment Act (CRA) is broader than the Home Mortgage Disclosure Act. CRA requires financial institutions to ascertain and meet credit needs of minority and low-income areas near their branch locations. This should be of interest to journalists in all locales. Financial institutions must make available a list specific enough to identify residential loans for one- to four-dwelling units, small business loans, housing rehabilitation loans, farm loans and commercial loans. The CRA statement is available to anyone, on request. A file must be kept of signed comments received from the public within the previous two years that specifically relate to the CRA statement or to the lender's performance in meeting the credit needs of the community, together with any responses the lender wishes to make.

The CRA encourages lenders to include a description of their efforts to evaluate and meet community credit needs, including efforts to offer and publicize special credit-related programs. Although these activities are encouraged rather than required, government examiners take the lender's efforts into consideration when deciding whether to grant approval on applications for facility expansion or new services.

Because lots of mortgage lending is now done by non-bank financial institutions, including huge brokerages like Merrill Lynch, information available under current banking laws fails to provide a complete picture of redlining, if any, in a community. Lawmakers and regulators are considering whether all lenders ought to report their practices. In the meantime, journalists will have to obtain whatever data they can from lenders exempt from disclosure.

The data are computerized and available on tapes from the federal government. As a result, computer-assisted reporting has been employed for many years now on redlining projects. A 1988 computer-assisted project at the Atlanta Journal-Constitution is most frequently cited as encouraging other journalists to jump in. It began with a casual remark to a reporter by a white housing developer, who said he was having trouble building homes in a largely black section of the city because banks would not make the loans he needed.

The newspaper encountered objections from lenders, objections that have been repeated over the years. Lenders say the higher percentages of rejections for blacks have nothing to do with race or neighborhood, and everything to do with creditworthiness. Many journalists have found, however, that rejection rates are greater for high-income blacks and Hispanics (household income of $75,000 annually) than for middle-income whites ($30,000 annual household income). Furthermore, the Orange County Register has documented how black and other minority neighborhoods tend to lack loan offices, while white areas have easy accessibility to such offices. Uplink, the newsletter from the National Institute for Computer-Assisted Reporting at the University of Missouri School of Journalism, has published articles explaining how to best use the massive amounts of information available from the federal government.

Most of the investigations have focused on loan rejection rates, because they are the most readily available. A better test might be to combine loan rejections with loan applications. After all, raw rejection rates tell nothing about applicants' credit or income histories—nobody is advocating that lenders provide mortgages almost sure to go into default. Loan application statistics have their flaws, too. But if a financial institution is receiving proportionally equal numbers of applications from all races and ethnic groups, it is probably trying to do the right thing.

A Wall Street Journal investigation used loan application data. In an explanation of its methodology, the Journal said it merged information from 2.25 million loan applications and U.S. census data on racial makeup of neighborhoods:

> The Journal first counted the number of applications each lender received on property in all U.S. census tracts. It also calculated the number of applications a lender received on property in census tracts where blacks make up at least 75 percent of the population. The Journal next computed the percentage, or share, of applications a lender garnered in all states in which it operated, and then the share of applications a lender received from census tracts with a black population of 75 percent or more.
>
> For each lender, a share ratio was derived by dividing its percentage of predominantly black-area applications by its overall share of applications. A ratio of one indicates equal penetration in black and nonblack areas. A ratio less than one shows less marketing penetration in black areas than white, and a ratio greater than one shows more penetration in black areas.

Blacks submitted just 128,000 (5.6 percent) of the 2.25 million applications; only 25,000 came from blacks in mostly black neighborhoods. Unlike most previous investigations, the Journal's covered largely unregulated non-bank mortgage lenders as well as traditional commercial banks and savings and loans. Some of the non-bank mortgage lenders, though, are the unregulated subsidiaries of commercial banks and savings and loans.

Perspective on how financial institutions are doing when it comes to insider transactions, lending diversity or many other measures can often be gained by reading reports from the Federal Financial Institutions Examination Council, Washington, D.C., especially its "Uniform Bank Performance Report."

Insider Transactions

How do officers, directors, major customers, politicians and other influentials benefit in ways unavailable to the average customer from a financial institution? Using documents filed with regulators, plus human sources, journalists should be able to piece together salaries paid to officers, fees paid to inside and outside directors, loans made to officers and directors or their companies, rent paid to insiders who own the financial institution's building or land, remuneration to insiders who broker loans and mortgages, legal or accounting or other professional fees to insiders.

Because financial institutions control so much money, they attract a lot of unsavory characters with questionable pasts. Even when insiders look clean on paper, they might have a history of greed that will show up in civil lawsuits or emerge through extensive interviewing of friends and enemies. When Mary Fricker and her partners were looking at savings and loan fraud on a national scale, they discovered that the same sleazy insiders showed up as directors, officers or borrowers at institution after institution despite the efforts of government regulators to police the situation.

The Detroit News looked at the directors of a savings and loan. The newspaper discovered one who had voted in favor of lending money to a business partner for a housing development; other directors making real-estate deals with officers and borrowers, public officials serving on the board while accepting campaign contributions from borrowers, a lease for a yacht to be used by the institution with the president and a rent agreement between the institution and a director, who eventually sold the space to the savings and loan for a profit.

The IRE Resource Center is filled with other projects documenting the activities of greedy insiders at financial institutions.

High-Risk Transactions

Derivatives are relatively new, complicated financial instruments that banks, savings and loans and other trusted institutions have begun buying and selling. Banks have to report their derivative holdings in their call reports, on special schedules. They must list the dollar amount of their holdings in collateralized mortgage obligations, interest-rate contracts and foreign exchange rate contracts. Journalists should determine what percentage of a financial institution's assets are tied up in derivatives. How well do the institution's officers understand the derivatives they have bought? Have they been conned by securities dealers who are looking to dump derivatives that more sophisticated investors avoid? What is the long-term earning record of the derivatives owned by the financial institution? Have they traditionally earned well in early years, then taken a nosedive?

How exposed is the financial institution when it comes to government-guaranteed loans? For example, the U.S. Small Business Administration loan guarantees enable financial institutions to make loans they might otherwise avoid. But how sound are the loans? Are the borrowers likely to default? The same questions are relevant for loans guaranteed by other government agencies.

Investments in U.S. Treasury securities would seem to carry little risk, but there are risks. Financial institutions sometimes fail to set aside capital to cover losses from Treasury securities, so when interest rates rise and the value of the securities drops, reserves might be drained. Futhermore, the losses might be masked because the institutions do not have to report losses unless they actually sell the securities. All this should teach a journalist to ask whether local financial institutions are overextended in U.S. Treasury securities.

■ MONEY LAUNDERING

Not all money laundering involves banks or other financial institutions, but sometimes they are accomplices in helping drug dealers and other criminals move the huge amounts of cash they accumulate.

Regulated financial institutions by law are supposed to complete IRS Form 4789 every time a depositor brings in cash of $10,000 or more. Those currency transaction reports have discouraged the kind of brazen money laundering that used to occur. But financial institutions that care little about the law will work with launderers to break up the cash deposits into amounts under $10,000. Some dishonest bankers will also look the other way when huge amounts of cash come in from retail businesses that realistically would not generate that amount of money.

A typical scenario would be for a drug ring to buy a jewelry store, then create fake invoices allowing dirty money to be disguised as revenue from sales of diamond rings and the like. Other scenarios, as summarized in Business Week magazine, include:

Launderers buying money orders locally, which are then deposited in a bank or wired across the country to a fellow launderer who does not need identification to cash them.

Dishonest offshore insurance brokers who accept cash from launderers, buy large annuities from U.S. insurance companies, cancel the annuities and obtain cash in the form of a refund check.

Launderers who buy postal money orders, which are exempt from currency transaction reporting rules, then redeem them at foreign banks.

Currency exchange shops, sometimes called casas de cambios, take cash from launderers, then deposit the money in regulated financial institutions. When the institutions file currency transaction reports, the exchange shops show up, not the launderers. John P. Caskey's book "Fringe Banking: Check-Cashing Outlets, Pawnshops, and the Poor" can provide further information.

Journalists should be alert for such dishonest players. Furthermore, if a local bank has a correspondent relationship with an offshore bank, especially in the Caribbean, journalists should explore why. The newsletter Money Laundering Alert, Miami, can help journalists understand the culture. Books on money laundering include Ann Woolner's "Washed in Gold" and Robert E. Powis' "The Money Launderers."

■ When a Financial Institution Collapses

Mary Fricker and other journalists suggest these story possibilities after a local financial institution has collapsed:

When the Resolution Trust Corp. is involved, its mission is to dispose of the assets, including loans, real estate and other investments. It is a huge task. What kind of return per dollar is the agency getting for depositors, creditors and taxpayers? How long is it taking? How much is going to outside lawyers, accountants and other nongovernment personnel in fees? How are those outsiders chosen: Are they improperly connected to RTC personnel or politicians in a position to influence RTC decision makers?

When the institution remains open under interim management, who chose those interim managers, and how? Are the new managers doing a responsible, effective job? Or are they losing even more money?

If the Federal Deposit Insurance Corp. hires private lawyers to sue officers, directors and others involved in the collapse, are the lawyers charging the government more than they win in judgments? Are they falsifying time sheets? Are the Federal Bureau of Investigation and U.S. Attorney's Offices cooperating with the outside lawyers?

When a healthy financial institution receives permission from the government to take over the failed one, what are the sale terms? Is it a sweetheart deal that rips off depositors and taxpayers?

What happens to legitimate, honest local builders and homebuyers who had depended on loans from the failed institution? Have their loans been smoothly assumed by a healthy successor? Or are the builders and homebuyers financially ruined?

Chapter 17

INVESTIGATING ENERGY AND COMMUNICATIONS UTILITIES

*T*he companies that supply electricity and gas for heating, lighting and cooling; water for drinking, bathing and gardening; local and long-distance telephone service; and cable television programming and transmission are vital to modern existence. So why do most journalists ignore them most of the time?

The primary answer seems to be that such businesses are too complicated to understand, so let's not bother. That is a big mistake.

The confusion starts with the terminology. The companies are often called "public utilities," even though some are investor-owned private businesses while others are indeed owned by governmental units. In this book all are referred to simply as "utilities," with no potentially misleading adjective.

A utility is a business allowed to operate as a monopoly or near monopoly in exchange for offering its services to everybody in a defined geographic area for a reasonable price—reasonable to consumers and the utility—subject to public review. In addition to opening its finances to public review, utilities undergo more scrutiny than the average business concerning safety and adequacy of service.

Utilities usually are regulated in the states where they do business, in addition to coming under scrutiny by one or more federal agencies. The National Association of Regulatory Utility Commissioners, Washington, D.C., can provide an overview of who oversees whom.

In almost every state, one agency takes the regulatory lead. For example, the Missouri Public Service Commission regulates rates, service and safety for investor-owned electric, gas, telecommunications, sewer and water companies. It also has limited jurisdiction over rural electric cooperatives and municipally owned electric utilities. The five commissioners, appointed by the governor with state Senate consent, and a professional staff intersect with federal regulators frequently, especially the Federal Energy Regulatory Commission and the Federal Communications Commission.

As is often the case with agency appointees, there are obvious and not-so-obvious conflicts of interests. Some have long experience in the industry being regulated, meaning they have deep-seated loyalties to accompany their invaluable knowledge. Some intend to return to the industry, meaning they might be reluctant to anger future employers. Others have no previous ties to the regulated industry but, as a result, lack the understanding they ought to have to decide complex issues.

What residential and commercial customers must pay for their utilities is determined in part by the state public service commission. The process begins either with a utility asking to raise its rates or the commission moving to decrease rates. Utilities adhere to their own tailored accounting standards, as is the case with other industries. A textbook such as "Accounting for Public Utilities" by Robert L. Hahne and Gregory L. Aliff can help journalists determine whether companies are masking financial difficulties or outright fraud.

Detailed hearings, in the capital city or elsewhere in the state, usually follow a rate increase or decrease petition. Decisions are sometimes appealed to the state courts. Besides studying the big rate cases, journalists can get a feel for whether hardships are occurring by looking at individual consumer complaints filed with the commission.

In Missouri, the general public is supposed to be represented at the commission by the Office of the Public Counsel, an independent agency. It is involved in every rate case, but does not represent individual consumers with complaints. Similar offices in other states have banded together to form the National Association of State Utility Consumer Advocates, Washington, D.C.

In a few states, consumers are also represented by citizen utility boards. The boards consist of dues-paying members who have received authority from a legislature or regulatory agency to routinely intervene in utility cases. Furthermore, the boards are allowed to insert membership cards and informational literature in state mailings such as motor vehicle registrations, tax forms and benefit payments.

Consumers need all the help they can get because of the frequently cozy relationships between state regulators and utility officials, who depend on each other so much they tend to let lines blur between right and wrong. The New York Times chronicled the influence peddling of a lobbyist for an East Coast energy utility. Her contributions to legislators and regulators were so blatant that she ended up facing a prison sentence. The ultimate losers were the utility's customers, who paid higher rates to absorb the gifts and bribes. The influence cycle involving regulators and the regulated is usually more subtle, and thus difficult to document convincingly. At the Minneapolis Star Tribune, a project about payoffs to state public utilities commissioners by the utilities they regulated began with a phone tip. The caller said utilities had provided commissioners with tickets to sports events. That brief story spawned more tips, until reporters couldn't ignore the possibility of a pattern. Eventually, to answer the question "so what?", the paper's team decided to examine whether the telephone company had received better rate treatment than in other states. The team devised 14 measures to help make comparisons valid, including basic residential rates, the percentage of utility requests approved by public utility commissioners and authorized profit levels. Only Minnesota came out above average on favorable treatment of phone companies on every measure.

Within the federal government, a key agency is the Federal Energy Regulatory Commission, housed inside the Cabinet-level Energy Department. It rules on rates for the transportation and sale of natural gas as well as oil that moves through pipelines, the transmission and sale of electricity and the licensing of hydroelectric power projects, some of which are operated by the federal government itself through regional administrations in Oregon, Georgia, Alaska, Oklahoma and Colorado. The Tennessee Valley Authority is kin to the regional administrations, serving as a wholesale power supplier for local municipal and cooperative electric systems in parts of seven states. As with many other government projects, when these electric power agencies lose money from operations and therefore receive subsidies, all federal taxpayers are charged for low-cost energy that benefits a relative few.

Other bureaucracies within the U.S. Energy Department play a role in tracking utilities. The Energy Information Administration's Office of Coal, Nuclear, Electric and Alternate Fuels publishes documents such as Financial Statistics of Selected Publicly Owned Electric Utilities and Financial Statistics of Major Investor-Owned Electric Utilities. More general EIA publications include Annual Energy Review, Annual Energy Outlook, Petroleum Supply Annual, National Gas Annual and Electric Power Annual.

Private-sector groups that can provide perspective on electric power include the Electricity Consumers Resource Council, National Independent Energy Producers, American Public Power Association, Edison Electric Institute, Electric Generation Association, all of Washington, D.C.; Electric Power Research Institute, Palo Alto, Calif.; and the American Bar Association's Section of Public Utility, Communications and Transportation Law.

Private-sector organizations supplying information on oil, coal and natural gas resources—the key fossil fuels used to make electricity—include the American Gas Association, Arlington, Va.; National Propane Gas Association, Lisle, Ill.; National Coal Association, Natural Gas Supply Association, American Independent Refiners Association, Independent Petroleum Association of America, American Petroleum Institute, Gas Research Institute, Association of Oil Pipe Lines, Interstate Natural Gas Association of America, all of Washington, D.C.; American Public Gas Association and Service Station Dealers of America, both of Fairfax, Va.

McGraw-Hill's Energy and Business Newsletters division, New York City, covers virtually every power resource with one or more publications. Public Utilities—From the State Capitals is published by Wakeman/Walworth Inc., Alexandria, Va. Groups promoting alternate energy sources include the Council on Alternate Fuels, Arlington, Va.; American Wind Energy Association and Solar Energy Industries Association, both of Washington, D.C. The Public Utility, Communications and Transportation section of the American Bar Association, Chicago, can suggest specialized lawyers to interview. David Howard Davis' book "Energy Politics" explains how and why each type of fuel is regulated, as well as delving into the regulation of electricity, which after all is the result of fuel use.

The Nuclear Regulatory Commission licenses construction of nuclear power plants, then inspects them regularly. Each of the more than 100 nuclear plants nationwide is staffed by resident NRC inspectors. Journalists should make their acquaintance, then determine whether the resident inspectors are vigilant and aggressive or if they have been compromised by the nuclear plant culture that envelops them every day. Of all federal agencies, the commission produces some of the most understandable and accessible information, including its annual report, its telephone directory, a compilation of its rulings, a quarterly report to Congress of abnormal occurrences and a plant-by-plant status summary report.

A Licensee Event Report is supposed to be filed whenever an unusual occurrence takes place at a plant. Thousands are filed annually, but the NRC asks for remedial action only about 1 percent of the time. It classifies events from Level One, the most serious, to Level Five, the least serious.

Much of the valuable information is on-line in the Nuclear Document System database, often referred to as NUDOCS. It covers more than electricity generating plants run by utilities; the NRC also oversees research activities involving nuclear materials at universities, hospitals and industrial corporations. NUDOCS is available at no cost; even the connecting telephone call can be made on a toll-free 800 number. Private-sector resources include the American Nuclear Energy Council, Nuclear Energy Institute and Nuclear Information and Resource Service, all of Washington, D.C.

The Rural Electrification Administration, inside the Agriculture Department, assists rural electric and telephone utilities when they need financing. Some of its recipients are profit-making commercial enterprises; others are not-for-profit consumer cooperatives or government units. The National Rural Electric Cooperative Association, Washington, D.C., can provide perspective.

The nation's public utility holding companies file certain records with the SEC. These electricity and gas corporate structures have only one purpose—to hold stock in companies that actually provide the services. Privately owned utilities outnumber the public holding companies by about five to one, but the relatively small number of holding companies control a significant minority percentage of the nation's energy generation. The SEC becomes involved when the purchase or sale of a holding company's securities or assets is under consideration. Intrasystem transactions, service and management arrangements also might fall under SEC scrutiny.

The Federal Communications Commission is the national government agency regulating cable television, as well as other electronic mass media. Local governments award licenses to cable companies that must abide by federal rules. Some state governments have created cable television commissions to promote uniform franchising requirements in every city where cable operators want to do business. The National Cable Television Association and Alliance for Community Media, both of Washington, D.C., and the Cable Telecommunications Association, Fairfax, Va., are among the most significant private-sector groups. The FCC also takes the lead in regulating interstate telephone service; state public utility commissions oversee intrastate service. Leading private-sector groups include the U.S. Telephone Association, National Telephone Cooperative Association and Competitive Telecommunications Association, all of Washington, D.C.

Anne C. Roess' book Public Utilities: An Annotated Guide to Information Sources covers energy companies, their industry groups, their academic chroniclers and their regulators with admirable breadth. Up-to-date rulings by regulatory authorities at every level are compiled in publications from Public Utilities Reports, Arlington, Va.

Heating and Cooling Utilities

The U.S. electric power industry is a combination of electric utilities (some owned by profit-seeking private investors, some owned by governmental units, some owned by cooperatives consisting of consumers) and nonutility producers of power. Only one state has no investor-owned energy utilities; only one other state has no publicly owned utilities.

There are far more governmentally owned and cooperative-owned than there are privately owned utilities, but the private companies have historically accounted for the vast majority of sales and revenues because they dominate in large urban areas. Investor-owned utilities have traditionally participated in all three aspects of providing energy: generation, transmission and distribution.

Federal laws and regulations have recently ended monopolies on power generation. Transmission has opened up to some extent, as utilities must now carry other utilities' electricity on their lines for a fee. That means some consumers are able to negotiate with distant utilities for better rates, and those distant utilities now have a means to deliver their product. Some large business consumers are even building their own power plants. A narrative account of how monopoly service has been loosened is "Dynamos and Virgins" by David Roe.

All of those traditions play into contemporary coverage. At the San Francisco Examiner, a reporter wondered why heating and cooling bills were rising so rapidly. Rates for residences and businesses were much lower in some nearby jurisdictions as well as in some other states. Furthermore, disparities between commercial and residential rates were less pronounced in other places. (The disparities frequently favor commercial users, who receive discounts based on volume. In other words, individual homeowners and renters subsidize businesses, many of which are inefficient in their energy usage.) The reporter found that management at the monopoly investor-owned utility had become fat and inefficient. State government regulators had an inkling of the problems, but were having so much trouble keeping up with routine rate-hike requests that they had little time to deal with structural questions.

To piece together his articles, the reporter used California Public Utility Commission audits, company studies on costs and salaries, depositions from lawsuits, reports of campaign contributions to elected officials and required filings by lobbyists for the utility. On the people trail, he talked to current and former state utility regulators, legislators, industry analysts, executive compensation experts and consumer watchdog groups.

As the reporting indicates, the tradition of monopoly utilities is changing in the energy industry. There are numerous reasons. First, the monopoly status of utilities has been premised on government rate regulation. As the philosophy of deregulation took hold, it became clear that government would have to loosen its reins, giving competitors the potential to enter the field. Second, environmentalism led to questioning of utilities using more and more nonrenewable natural resources (coal, gas, uranium) to sell more power to make more money. Third, some utilities spent lots of money building nuclear power plants, thereby losing millions and requesting rate hikes that ran way ahead of inflation.

As noted by reporter Gregg Easterbrook in Atlantic Monthly, "Once utility managers began to make significant blunders about matters like nuclear expansion, the public perception of them changed, from that of far-seeing technocrats to that of fat cats with legal sanction to reach into people's pockets. Economists argued that presumptuous utilities needed competitors."

Journalists should determine whether electric utilities are cutting rates on their own as they compete against alternate power sources that allow big manufacturers and other major customers to generate their own heating and cooling. If they are cutting rates, are they laying off workers, reducing salaries or executive positions to stay profitable? How are the changes affecting day-to-day service in the average home and small business, customers that lack the bargaining clout of huge manufacturers? Are electric utilities also involved with natural gas sales to weather the changes?

Are regulators looking out for special categories of gas and electricity consumers by requiring lower rates for low-income households or those with elderly residents on fixed incomes? Are regulators encouraging efficiency by requiring consumers to pay more for use at peak hours? The theory is that if consumption can be spread more evenly throughout the 24-hour cycle, utilities can refrain from building expensive, polluting plants merely to meet peak demand. Do regulators require utilities to offer and promote conservation measures to business and residential users to cut consumption not only at peak hours, but also at all other hours? Is anybody pushing utilities to increase efficiency by storing excess electricity on site, to be retrieved as needed?

Cooperatives should not be ignored. They are no longer do-gooder institutions serving isolated farmers and ranchers who would lack electricity otherwise. Cooperatives receiving aid from the Rural Electrification Administration now serve suburbs of cities like Dallas and resort towns like Aspen. Should taxpayers nationwide be subsidizing federal low-interest loans or loan guarantees for profitable cooperatives?

■ NUCLEAR POWER PLANTS

Nuclear power plants are often owned and operated by old-line utilities, but are regulated separately from other utilities' operations because of their special characteristics. Many states have no nuclear plants; other states have only one. A few states have more than one. Overall, nuclear plants generate about 20 percent of the nation's electricity.

The problems at the Three Mile Island nuclear plant in Pennsylvania during 1978 left the impression among many people that nuclear power plants are especially dangerous. The industry has sought to build few new nuclear plants since. Many plants already on-line are aging dangerously. Journalists need to ask what the local utility and regulators plan to do about the plant when it can no longer produce power ("decommissioning" is the catchword), because the dangers from the radioactivity in the vicinity will last many centuries. The NRC requires a decommissioning plan at the time of original licensing. Is that plan still valid, or is it obsolete? Does it involve quick dismantling of the plant, which means letting the surrounding land sit idle for at least six years after operations cease because of radioactivity levels? Or is the alternative strategy being pursued, which means sealing off the plant intact for at least 50 years before dismantling?

Plants that continue operating face serious questions about how and where to store the spent radioactive waste. Journalists near a nuclear plant can check how many times it has requested permission from the Nuclear Regulatory Commission to store more spent radioactive fuel rods in water-filled storage pools than originally planned. Has the NRC granted permission without hesitation? Or granted it with reservations? Or denied permission? Has the utility received permission to store spent rods in even more controversial above-ground silos? Is the utility doing anything to deal with the problem in a meaningful way long-term? To seek a more stable, industry-wide solution, Congress created an independent Office of Nuclear Waste Negotiator. The goal: find a locale interested, for economic reasons, in serving as a waste repository site. Journalists can ask whether local nuclear utilities have been involved in that search. Transportation of nuclear waste off-site means hauling dangerous materials through populated areas that could be contaminated for decades if an accident occurred. (The topic is dealt with more fully, in a different context, in Chapter 18.)

Jim Morris at the Houston Chronicle has spent time with nuclear industry whistleblowers. They are everywhere, he says, because the industry has so many problems that it ignores or tries to cover up. A utility might lose $1 million a day if a nuclear plant must close for repairs because of problems reported by employees. In a talk at an IRE national conference, Morris made these observations, which have been edited for this book:

> Covering nuclear power need not be limited to rewriting utility press releases and attending protests. . . . Reporters and editors are put off by the difficulties of the subject matter, the lack of cooperation by utility officials and the plodding pace of regulatory investigations. . . . The owners and operators of these plants, by and large, like it this way. . . . They . . . want to tightly control . . . information . . . ostensibly to keep the public from panicking about "minor" incidents. Reporters who persist are forced to plow through dull inspection reports and interview engineers who talk like engineers. Rather than say "[the plant] damned near melted down last week," they will use cryptic terms like "unusual event," "turbine projectile" and "SALP report."
>
> There is another way. You can get a good sense of what is happening inside a plant by talking to whistleblowers. Initially, this may not seem appealing. Before . . . I thought of whistleblowers as disgruntled, somewhat eccentric people who hated their bosses and were looking for ways to get even. In some cases, this is true. After interviewing more than 50 of these people, however, I found that the vast majority were well-educated, conscientious utility or contractor employees who had devoted many years to the power industry and were strongly pro-nuclear. They merely wanted their bosses to follow the rules.

Water Utilities

In the Wall Street Journal, an in-depth story told about a Pennsylvania city where the residents paid the highest water use rates in the state. But those residents complained regularly about the awful taste, the way the water turned whites yellow in the laundry, about how once it caused widespread intestinal illness. Meanwhile, the state public utility commission fined the company, reluctantly granted its rate-increase requests, and warned it to use the money from the increases to upgrade equipment and repair old pipes.

That was a controversy over water quality. Sometimes the controversies center on water availability and pricing, especially in the dry Southwest and West. In many locales, citizens take their drinking, washing, outdoor and toilet water for granted. They barely even glance at the monthly bill, worrying far more about their heating and cooling charges. They should be paying more attention, as water-borne illnesses increase, availability of groundwater diminishes and water-carrying infrastructures crumble.

Of all the utility sectors, the water industry is perhaps the least understood and least visible, partly because of how most journalists ignore it. In journalists' defense, coverage is made more difficult by the atomized nature of the industry. Of tens of thousands of U.S. water systems, only a few dozen, at most, are publicly owned. The others are run by local governments or private developers. Though vital to the relatively compact areas they serve, they escape the scrutiny of national and regional news organizations. It took minority politicians to organize a concerted attempt to gain control of certain California water boards for most journalists to pay attention. Those tiny districts spent about $10 million every month on construction, not to mention their influence on water allocation and price. Robert Gottlieb, a California freelance investigative journalist, said in his book "A Life of Its Own: The Politics and Power of Water" that the water industry

is a combination of private interests and public agencies. The private groups, led by agriculture, have dominated over the years, with other contending parties—including recreation, mining and energy, navigation and, more recently, urban-development interests—also playing critical roles. These groups are the beneficiaries of water development, taking advantage of its generous subsidies and extensive facilities.

The public agencies, on the other hand, predominate in supplying this most basic resource. They are organized in a variety of forms, from municipal water and sewer departments to county water authorities and irrigation districts [numbering hundreds in some states], each of which has varying powers, from the ability to levy taxes and charge user fees to the ability to make formal or informal land-use decisions. Water agencies, in fact, function at times as de facto land planners for their service areas.

Polluting the Environment

An especially contentious environmental debate involves electromagnetic fields created by outdoor power lines and indoor appliances. Investigative journalist Paul Brodeur's book "The Great Power-Line Cover-Up" has been hailed by some as a convincing exposé of how people living near electric substations or high-current wires develop cancer at abnormally high rates. Some utility regulators, environmental bureaucrats and scientists believe Brodeur's investigation is flawed—that view is summarized well in the book "Health and Low-Frequency Electromagnetic Fields" by William Ralph Bennett Jr. As is often the case with a controversy, specialized newsletters have sprung up. They include EMF Health Report, Philadelphia, and EMF Litigation News, Chelfont, Pa. Micro-Wave News, New York City, is not quite so specialized, but has covered the controversy for many years.

As energy utilities worry about profitability, they must simultaneously worry about polluting the water and air. Journalists should question utility managers dependent on coal, which fuels about half of all U.S. electricity, about whether the pollution that results is morally as well as economically justified. When pollution costs are factored in, is coal still economical? Is the utility using available technology to convert the coal to a gas before burning, a process that often reduces pollution? If the local utility is polluting less than federal guidelines allow, is it part of the program selling sulfur dioxide "pollution rights" to utilities elsewhere that are heavier polluters? If such sales are occurring, what is the local utility receiving in return? If local utilities that are above government levels are spending lots of money on pollution rights, would it be wiser to buy permanent pollution-control equipment? Are state legislators and regulators revolting against the federal system, making utilities prove their trades will not result in additional pollution within state borders?

What about utilities that generate power by using hydroelectric dams? The water is a renewable resource, an environmental plus. But are the dams themselves or the way they are operated damaging fish populations, including endangered species? Are they interfering with the recreational activities of canoeists, rafters and other boaters?

Water utilities should be questioned about contamination of surface water and groundwater. Surface water has been the focus of environmentalists in many locales because when it is polluted everyone can see the problem. But the majority of the country's water systems depend on groundwater, meaning the supplies are in underground aquifers not visible to the naked eye.

A journalist can get a rough gauge about the public's confidence level in local tap water quality by charting sales of bottled water. While charting sales, a journalist should also explore the source of the bottled water. In many instances, the company selling bottled water is obtaining it from the same source as the local utility, the only differences being more extensive treatment combined with image advertising.

Communications Utilities

In many states, the same underfunded agency regulating energy utilities also regulates rates charged by telephone companies for intrastate service. The term "telephone" is no longer simple. Telephone companies are divided into local and long-distance carriers, and both have the ability to provide video along with voice. Furthermore, cable television utilities, usually awarded a franchise at the city rather than state or federal level, know how to provide telephone service to accompany their pictures. Computer manufacturers supply components to both telephone and cable companies.

The Federal Communications Commission headquarters or its regional offices should be checked on any story, because its licensing, annual report, inspection and disciplinary files might provide insights into a regional utility, insights unavailable in state capitals. It can use any of nine enforcement methods when there is cause for concern. Those methods include an admonishing letter asking for an explanation; a consent order negotiated after an alleged violation is designated for hearing; a cease-and-desist order; a monetary fine; court action; conditional license renewal; short-term license renewal; denial of license renewal; or license revocation.

State utility commissions unable to keep up with the changes brought by technology often impede efficient, innovative, affordable service by restricting local telephone companies from certain activities and refusing to drop old-fashioned rate-of-return regulation based on the past monopolistic system. Because telephone service is available to just about anybody who desires it, and because most incoming and outgoing calls are handled efficiently, price has become the focus. Journalists can dissect phone bills, explaining how separate, sometimes masked charges for directory listings, operator-assisted calls, credit-card calls, call-waiting, call-forwarding, separate lines and so on can baffle consumers. Long-distance calling from pay phones and hotel rooms is especially confusing, as consumers often know nothing about the carrier owning and operating those phones. The charges are far more expensive than they would be if the callers had used access codes to tie into their usual long-distance service.

In rural and even some suburban areas, Rural Electrification Administration telephone subsidies helped develop quality service, but taxpayers far away from the areas served paid billions of dollars. Journalists can search for REA subsidies to telephone companies that would be profitable in any case but which use access to government-backed funding to obtain unjustifiably low interest rates at the public trough.

Telephone rates to households and businesses are based on many factors, including salaries of phone company officials, rents paid on phone company buildings and lavish advertising budgets. Journalists can examine which expenses state regulators allow and which, if any, they disallow when considering requests to hike rates. By doing just that, the Denver Business Journal discovered that a telephone company was paying millions of dollars above market rates to rent some of its buildings. The company planned to soak telephone users for the inflated rental costs.

As for long-distance telephone service, what are consumers to make of promises by competing companies? If a consumer switches long-distance carriers only to find the new firm is more expensive rather than less expensive, to whom should the consumer complain? Do consumers ever receive refunds or monetary damages as a result of misleading long-distance company statements? What about cellular telephone companies? Is the FCC working to ensure the availability of the technology at competitive prices?

How the telephone utilities and their regulators got to this confusing, more competitive juncture is explained in Steve Coll's book "The Deal of the Century: The Breakup of AT&T." A book by William J. Baumol and J. Gregory Sidak, "Toward Competition in Local Telephony," is also helpful.

Logically, cable television would seem to be exempt from federal regulation, and in fact cable systems do not need a FCC license to begin business because they have no need of scarce over-the-air frequencies. Channels 14 and above on a cable system use a different frequency altogether, which means there has to be special connection run by wire to a traditional television set. A cable company must run wire along a public right-of-way to accomplish the hook-up, which is where local jurisdiction enters. The right-of-way is, after all, public.

After covering the awarding of a cable franchise, journalists should check periodically to see whether the operator is requesting modifications in the contract. For instance, some cable companies have sought permission to convert one or more public access channels—free to citizens and nonprofit groups, including governments, to air their views—to for-profit channels after securing what is in effect a cable monopoly.

As for renewal negotiations, they often begin several years before actual expiration. The FCC's involvement covers programming content, signal carriage, rates, service guarantees and ownership restrictions. The restrictions are meant to prohibit the same persons from controlling a community's cable system while also controlling the telephone service, over-the-air television, multichannel, multipoint distribution services and satellite master antenna services.

Coverage of cable television utilities should raise questions of efficiency and availability as well as questions about pricing. Millions of consumers lack access to cable television systems because the companies will not wire certain geographic areas and regulators cannot force them to do so. When service is available, it is often difficult to obtain a hook-up and begin service, which might itself be inept. As for rates, many customers become upset at complicated and sometimes hidden charges.

When my cable company recently decided to charge an extra $1.16 per month for "expanded basic" service, its notice said "You have the right to file a complaint with the FCC about any changes in service or price on the expanded basic tier within 45 days from the time these charges appear on your bill."

Regulation leads to situations such as cable operators petitioning the FCC to change its definition of "small" from systems with under 15,000 subscribers to the Small Business Administration standard of less than $11 million in annual revenue. Any cable operator gaining the "small" designation would be exempted from rate reductions of 17 percent mandated by the FCC.

Writing in the IRE Journal, James Neff suggested covering local cable television utilities more aggressively and meaningfully. A few of his suggestions:

> *Rate increases.* Often viewers are gouged as rates rise faster than inflation. Compare the past five years of cable increases with inflation. What is the company's explanation? Today some cities are so strapped that elected officials just wink when companies raise rates because they know that franchise fee revenue will go up.
>
> *Renewal term.* Most franchises were awarded years ago. Now systems are coming up for renewal. Typically, terms had been for 15 years, but some cities are moving to five-year renewals, which hold companies more accountable. Is your city asking for shorter contract terms? If politicians seem like pushovers, look for ties between the cable company principals and elected officials or their family members. Have the politicians benefitted from campaign contributions from the cable owners?
>
> *Community programming.* Does anyone ever use the community-access studios other than elected officials? Why not? Are higher rates absorbing the costs of free studio time for elected officials?
>
> *The public file.* It is kept at the local cable company. It should include complaints, correspondence between the FCC and the company and other public records required by the FCC.

Other matters covered in the public file include finances and equal employment opportunity compliance.

A textbook covering communications utilities comprehensively is "Electronic Media and Government: The Regulation of Wireless and Wired Mass Communication in the United States" by F. Leslie Smith,

Milan Meeske and John Wright. Among other questions, it is bound to make investigators curious about how the government—with the FCC in the forefront—will divvy up the electromagnetic spectrum among competing interests. Those interests are lobbying for more than their fair share, and are willing to pay large sums to win. The players include radio and television stations, cellular telephone and pager companies and firms that sell garage door openers. Will the government exact promises of programming and product quality from the winners? Or will the government simply sell to the highest bidders, then step aside? These will be fascinating questions for journalists to investigate.

Chapter 18

INVESTIGATING TRANSPORTATION

*R*eaders, viewers and listeners have to think about transportation every day. Can they get from here to there on time, safely and affordably? Journalists are among those commuters—by private automobile, taxi, bus, subway, train, airplane, ferry, helicopter, bicycle or on foot. Yet most journalists never investigate transportation providers or the government transportation bureaucrats who help or hinder getting around. Nor do journalists normally investigate the freight transporters—especially trucks, trains, ships and barges—that move commodities so vital to daily life.

The most compelling transportation investigations tend to be about safety. Delays and other inefficiencies in the system are important, but not as important as life and death. There are two times to conduct transportation safety investigations: after injury or death occurs or before tragedy strikes. The preventive investigation is without question preferable, yet few journalists make the effort.

An exception was a joint project of Cox News Service, Washington, D.C., and the NBC-TV news magazine Dateline that investigated bridge safety in every state. The nationwide scope came from a computer tape called the National Bridge Inventory, supplied by the Federal Highway Administration.

The journalists supplemented the computerized data by examining paper copies of federal, state and local bridge inspection reports, scientific studies, lawsuits, General Accounting Office findings, congressional hearings and National Transportation Safety Board (NTSB) investigations. Human sources included current and former government and private industry bridge inspectors, structural engineers, bridge collapse victims and their lawyers. The reporters studied investigations of bridges that had already collapsed, then looked for records in the computer database identifying bridges with similar characteristics.

One problem in the weakening of bridges nationwide turned out to be trucks carrying more weight than allowed by law. The extra weight had a cumulative weakening effect, hastening collapses. But most states were levying such light fines against overweight trucks that their owners paid, then continued their practices. Another problem: some bridges with low ratings were not repaired because government agencies said they lacked money. As a result, those bridges deteriorated until they fell, until someone died. Then, somehow, too late, money was found.

Transportation safety investigations can begin with day-to-day observation. Journalists riding around with local highway engineers, taxi drivers and ambulance personnel can gain special insights. Which streets are filled with potholes and bumps that lead to vehicle damage or accidents? Which are so poorly lit at night that they become dangerous? Where does it flood worst after a rain? Where is the sun's glare a potentially deadly hazard? What are the especially dangerous spots when ice is on the roadway? Which intersections are so poorly designed that drivers take chances to get across? What do police and sheriff reports show about accident frequencies at various locations? Compiling a top ten accident location list every month would be a service to the audience and might help bring about change.

Besides the infrastructure's safety, what about the vehicles? Is a particular model of car, truck, bus, motorcycle, boat, ship, barge, helicopter or airplane designed unsafely, manufactured shoddily, easy to operate irresponsibly? What about the operators of those vehicles? If they drive under the influence of alcohol or other drugs, how frequently are they caught? Are they punished appropriately? The IRE Resource Center is filled with investigations about the failure of drunk driving prevention and enforcement, leading to thousands of deaths, tens of thousands of nonfatal injuries and millions of dollars of property damage.

■ GOVERNMENT AND TRANSPORTATION

Journalists could serve the public interest simply by following up on recommendations from the National Transportation Safety Board, which investigates certain types of accidents. Manufacturers and regulators frequently ignore or try to reverse NTSB recommendations. They would probably be less likely to do so if journalists were asking questions.

In an impressive feat of anticipatory journalism, Keith Epstein of the Cleveland Plain Dealer used NTSB reports, court records, cockpit recordings and other sources to examine delays in implementing agency recommendations meant to improve airline safety. He showed how minutes before takeoff, a flight headed from New York City to Cleveland had ice on its wings. The pilots knew a last de-icing would be useful, but there was pressure to take off on time and no regulator absolutely required such a final de-icing.

As Epstein reported, the pilots "did not realize just how precarious their situation was. The federal government knew for seven years. U.S. safety officials repeatedly had pinpointed the cause of nine crashes of planes similar to that of Flight 405—the wing's high vulnerability to trace amounts of ice. Yet Washington had done nothing to require simple, proven remedies advocated for years, such as checking the wings by hand or spraying with a stronger antifreeze just before takeoff."

Epstein discovered similar lack of government forcefulness, combined with private-sector refusal to make safety improvements on its own, in other types of situations. For example, commuter airplanes were crashing on routine approaches to airports in part because the government refused to mandate the type of low-altitude alarms used on large jets. Single-engine planes fell to earth after the motor sputtered, something that perhaps could have been avoided by requiring an inexpensive remedy for carburetor flaws.

On the ground, tractor-trailer trucks traveling interstate highways maimed motorists partly because government regulators refused to require antilock brakes and automatic brake adjusters. Drivers ended up decapitated after their cars slid under the rear of large trucks while the government refused to mandate a protective guard. Riders on school buses died because the government did nothing about making an extra emergency exit standard. Freight train crews died in collisions despite the existence of automated warning systems that the government failed to require.

One former NTSB chairman told Epstein, "We know when we investigate an accident we are going to see it [the same cause] again." Summarizing his research, Epstein wrote, "Transportation experts describe a bureaucracy increasingly paralyzed by fear of lawsuits from regulated industries, hobbled by conflicts with other agencies, buffeted by meddling members of Congress and political appointees and crippled by weak leadership unable to choose priorities or stick to deadlines."

The U.S. Transportation Department, part of the president's Cabinet, is supposed to establish overall policy. The NTSB is part of the department, as are the Coast Guard, Federal Aviation Administration, Federal Highway Administration, Federal Railroad Administration, Federal Transit Administration, Maritime Administration, Office of Hazardous Materials Safety and Office of Pipeline Safety.

The Interstate Commerce Commission, a self-contained federal agency directed by five presidential appointees, plays a role in overseeing surface transportation that crosses state lines, with an emphasis on trucks, railroads, buses, barges plus some coal and chemical pipelines. There is overlap between ICC programs and Transportation Department units, meaning journalists frequently can consult government sources with differing perspectives.

State governments also oversee transportation. In Missouri, for example, the Department of Highways and Transportation uses money from motor vehicle fuel taxes, licenses and fees to build and repair roads and bridges. Simply reading a description of the agency's responsibilities in the state government manual raises many questions, such as how are multimillion dollar contracts awarded? Once awarded, how are they monitored? For instance, the manual says the Division of Materials and Research "tests and inspects all materials used in the construction and maintenance of the state highway system." Is that word "all" accurate? How frequently does the division reject materials? If never, why not? If rejections occur, what happens then?

The Division of Right of Way acquires land for road building. What happens when the agency decides residences, commercial buildings or productive farmland must be destroyed to build roads? Do the landowners have any recourse? Is payment equitable? What happens when the agency decides previously purchased land is no longer needed? Is it sold at market price to anybody who bids or is there a closed system favoring influential people?

Within the Division of Transportation, the aviation section inspects publicly and privately owned airports to determine safety and efficiency. How often are the reports negative? What happens when they are?

Just as there is overlap among federal transportation agencies, there is overlap between state and federal agencies. The multiple sources can be used to advantage as one is played off another to obtain sensitive documents or verbal comments. The Missouri State Water Patrol is a scaled-down version of the U.S. Coast Guard. The Missouri Division of Highway Safety in many ways mirrors the National Highway Traffic Safety Administration. The Missouri State Highway Patrol has much in common with the FBI.

Private-sector groups can add perspective. For instance, the International Institute for Safety in Transportation, New York City, tries to publicize hazards in all modes of transportation. Among its publications are the Safety Activist and Transportation Safety Newsletter.

Land Transportation

When people travel long or short distances in the United States, the automobile is the predominant mode. It accounts for about 81 percent of intercity travel, according to federal studies. Airplanes account for another 17 percent. Buses and railroads split the remaining 2 percent.

All that auto travel requires interstate and state highways, county roads, local streets. Roadbuilding at all levels of government is partly a story about contracts—who decides where the pavement should go and its design; who is willing to bid; whether contractors collude to rig bids, thereby spreading out the business (with designated "losers" receiving subcontracts later from the winner) and driving up costs to taxpayers; whether public officials awarding the contracts accept payoffs, steer awards to relatives or business partners.

The Independent in Durham, N.C., showed how campaign contributors to legislators ended up with the roads they sought—one bypassing a country club so that its wealthy members could play golf without traffic noise distracting them. The series also documented how campaign contributors to the governor bought their way onto the state transportation board, which allocated several billion dollars of road money annually.

Most of the board members had occupations that benefitted directly from the roads they voted for themselves: land developers, contractors, bankers, lawyers, rock quarry owners, engineers, trucking company executives and automobile dealers.

The Phoenix Gazette focused on the most expensive land purchases by the state transportation department to demonstrate how the agency was wasting taxpayer money by overpaying for property owned by speculators who had bought it in the first place to make a profit from road-building. Abuses included the agency paying $350,000 an acre for vacant land and more than $1 million an acre for desert brush in freeway corridors. Appraisers and county assessors had judged the land to be worth much less.

The St. Louis Post-Dispatch determined that Illinois highway officials frequently awarded contracts without competitive bidding, costing taxpayers millions of dollars annually in unnecessary expenses. The reporters made the discovery by analyzing a Federal Highway Administration computer tape with information on every highway construction project involving U.S. government money for five years. The tape showed location, date of contract award, completion date, estimated cost, final cost, identity of contractor—and number of bidders. Private toll roads are being built in some areas, as investors see ways to make profits while governments struggle to pay for needed repairs, leaving new construction on the planning boards. Private roads might save taxpayer dollars and relieve traffic congestion. But the developers still need government approvals, which open the potential for bribes and other unsavory deals. Journalists should not become less vigilant simply because the private sector is taking the lead.

Perspective is available from the American Association of State Highway and Transportation Officials plus the American Road and Transportation Builders Association, both of Washington, D.C. The National Conference of State Legislatures publishes a booklet titled State and Local Highway Finance: Where Does the Money Come From and Why Isn't There Enough?

Not all newsworthy decisions are made at the local and state levels. Journalists should ask how federal highway trust fund money is allocated by U.S. government officials in a local area. Are local members of Congress able to dip into the trust fund for pork-barrel highway projects that fail to meet the criteria of the interstate highway program? Gasoline taxes are allocated to the fund. (There are similar trust funds for air travel, inland waterways and harbors.) The Federal Highway Administration says the money is supposed to be spent on "making highway improvements that are the highest priority needs in each state, adherence to environmental requirements, improving the safety design of new highways, correcting highway hazards of existing roads, reducing traffic congestion and facilitating the flow of traffic." Wasteful or corrupt projects are undesirable. On the other hand, if trust fund money generated by users is not being spent to improve the particular mode of transportation, are legislatures breaking promises to the public? What is happening? A U.S. government publication available by subscription, Public Roads: A Journal of Highway Research and Development, might suggest answers.

Speaking of spending for safer highways, what about toll roads? What happens to the quarters and dollar bills collected from every driver passing through toll gates day and night, every hour of the year? Does the time ever arrive when tolls are no longer needed or are at least reduced? The International Bridge, Tunnel and Turnpike Association, Washington, D.C., can answer such questions.

When documenting problems spawned by a geographic area's dependence on automobiles, journalists can find a wealth of information at the state motor vehicles department in the capital. Questions to ask include: Does the state require that drivers carry automobile insurance? If so, how is the law enforced? How many drivers find ways to evade the law? How do they accomplish the evasion and what are the consequences? How often do drivers have to renew their licenses? Is an on-the-road test part of the renewal requirement? If not, why not? Does the vehicle have to be inspected for safety on a regular basis? For polluting emissions? Who does the inspecting, and are they susceptible to payoffs or known for shoddy work?

The Raleigh (N.C.) News and Observer compared local inspection stations licensed by the state. At one, 90 percent of inspections led to approval. At another, two miles away, only 20 percent of inspections led to approval. Tire stores with inspection authority found tire problems more often than nontire store inspection sites. Muffler shops found muffler problems more frequently. Maybe the specialists spotted problems more often because of their expertise. Or maybe they were hoping to increase sales.

What is the percentage of drivers who pass their written test on the first try? What about pass rates for on-the-road tests? How long must applicants who fail wait before a retest? Are the written and on-the-road tests valid enough so that they screen out drivers who should not be licensed? What kind of training is required of those who administer on-the-road tests? Does the state ever use inspectors to pose as applicants, fail the examination, then offer bribes to test examiners' honesty? Are drivers with certain restrictions, adverse health or of a certain age retested more frequently than other drivers? What does it take, how may points, to have a license revoked? Is the point system sensible—does the punishment fit the crime? After revocation occurs, what measures are taken to ensure that the person penalized refrains from driving?

If a person is caught driving after revocation, what happens? How efficiently does the state share its revocations with other states, in an attempt to keep a dangerous driver from receiving a license elsewhere? How are driving-while-intoxicated cases handled?

The answers to such questions are frequently alarming. Even though drunk drivers are operating deadly weapons, many police officers, legislators, prosecutors and judges refuse to take the offense seriously. The Dayton Daily News found a man convicted of drunk driving 19 times; he was out of jail and driving again. The Atlanta Journal-Constitution found more than 83,000 offenders with at least three charges against them, and 43 with at least 15 convictions. Reporters should ask whether the state has begun confiscating vehicles of drunk drivers, revoking license plates and destroying registrations, rather than merely suspending a driver's license temporarily. Does the state highway patrol publicize an 800 phone line that motorists can call when they spot a dangerous driver? That tactic is increasingly effective as more cars are equipped with cellular telephones. Do bar and restaurant owners have legal liability if they serve drivers to the point of intoxication? H. Laurence Ross' book "Confronting Drunk Driving: Social Policy for Saving Lives" looks at the big picture.

What are the requirements to obtain and retain a taxicab or limousine license? The Washington Post documented corruption among cab drivers as well as on the commission licensing and overseeing them. Examinations for prospective drivers were available for a price; safety inspectors accepted bribes to approve unsafe cabs; drivers without a valid license or an insurance policy stayed on the road without detection. In the rare instance when the commission levied fines against cab companies or drivers, the fines frequently went unpaid without further penalty.

U.S. News and World Report looked at cabbie scams in ten cities. By taking lots of cab rides, plus interviewing drivers, fleet owners, dispatchers, taxi commissioners, police, hotel doorkeepers and airport officials, the team documented rigged meters that ran faster than allowed by law or added charges illegally; allegedly broken meters used as an excuse to charge flat fares far above the actual cost; impermissible baggage fees; drivers pretending to be lost while the meter ran; low-pressure rear tires that added revolutions per mile as the charge on the meter rose faster than it should; drivers picking up passengers headed for different locations, then charging each the full fare, even though passengers dropped off after the first should be charged the differential only; racial, ethnic, physical and geographic discrimination, as drivers illegally refused to pick up passengers based on appearance, confinement to a wheelchair or destination. Because so many cab drivers are robbed, shot or in a hurry to transport the quickest, most lucrative-looking fares, their discrimination is justifiable in their own minds, but it is still illegal. The International Taxicab and Livery Association, Kensington, Md., can provide perspective.

What are the requirements for a commercial truck driver's license? For hauling hazardous materials? For a school bus license? Are there special requirements for a motorcycle license? Is there a mandatory helmet law for motorcycle riders? A mandatory seat belt law for other drivers and passengers? If so, are the helmet and belt laws enforced? If not, why not? What are the penalties for violations? The American Association of Motor Vehicle Administrators, Arlington, Va., can provide perspective, as can the American Automobile Association, Washington, D.C., and the Motorcycle Industry Council, Arlington, Va. For perspective about how to decrease dependence on dangerous, polluting motorized travel, the Bicycle Federation of America, Washington, D.C., is one of many groups that can help. Are government agencies pushing established automakers or encouraging entrepreneurs to develop electric vehicles or other alternatives to current polluting cars? Are governments buying lesser-polluting vehicles to provide a market and set a good example? If not, why not?

The safety of the cars being driven, including the tires, is monitored by the National Highway Traffic Safety Administration. The agency issues general standards, rates specific models for crashworthiness and fuel economy plus tests tires for treadwear, temperature resistance and traction. If enough problems appear, the agency can order the manufacturer to take corrective action, often through a nationwide recall.

Sometimes manufacturers contest a recall within the executive branch or in court. Other times, they quietly make the repairs without issuing a recall. As explained by Clarence Ditlow and Ray Gold in their book "Little Secrets of the Auto Industry," manufacturers will authorize local dealers to make repairs, but only if consumers demand the work. Journalists in any locale can explore whether dealers are involved in such questionable arrangements. Providing perspective are individual companies as well as their groups the American Automobile Manufacturers Association, Detroit; the National Automobile Dealers Association, McLean, Va.; National Institute for Automotive Service Excellence, Herndon, Va.; National Tire Dealers and Retreaders Association, Washington, D.C.; Center for Auto Safety, Washington, D.C.; and Insurance Institute for Highway Safety, Arlington, Va., among others. The magazine Automotive News, Detroit, is among those covering the industry.

Most people who think about truckers picture operators of tractor-trailers barreling down interstate highways at 80 miles per hour, leaving terrified drivers of passenger cars in their wake. There are indeed reckless truck drivers. But journalists too often fail to consider other trucking stories.

For instance, most cities are home to trucking companies that haul vital goods in and out, transport hazardous materials, employ hundreds or thousands of people, engage in litigation as plaintiff or defendant, do (or do not) hire drivers who care about safety, do (or do not) conduct safety training programs. Any local trucking company can be investigated by using the Interstate Commerce Commission (ICC) and state regulatory records, locating lawsuits, plus developing current and former human sources. Enterprising journalists might find sources who will supply falsified drivers' daily logs, falsified because employers push them to drive more hours at higher speeds every week than allowed by law.

Technology to minimize falsification exists in the form of on-board recorders. But government regulators beholden to business owners refused to require on-board recorders or cut back on the hours that can legally be driven per week.

The Los Angeles Times assigned a reporter to ride with an independent trucker. As they approached a weigh station, the trucker swerved onto a gravel back road, passed through a tiny town, then through a larger downtown before picking up the interstate again. He knew if he had stopped at the weigh station, as required, he would have been fined for a missing mud flap, a blown tire, a log book that was many days behind and for possessing an illegal radar detector.

The Federal Highway Administration plays a role in all of this. The agency maintains a national network for trucks allowing the biggest vehicles with the heaviest loads to travel without regard to individual state size and weight restrictions. Those state restrictions have a sound basis, which means journalists should be asking the consequences of overriding them. For example, how much pavement damage results?

There are plenty of trucking incidents to investigate. WCCO-TV, Minneapolis, received a tip from a truck driver that his employer made him operate unsafe vehicles. He had reported the company to state regulators, but nothing happened. WCCO found the problem was not isolated. As explained on an IRE awards entry, the series "showed that one out of three trucks inspected on Minnesota highways is so unsafe it should be pulled off the road; some truck companies tolerate shoddy maintenance, routinely allowing their trucks to operate with defective brakes, no lights and missing safety gear; trucks routinely dodge state inspections; judges and prosecutors have allowed companies and drivers that cause serious accidents to go virtually unpunished."

Journalists wanting to better understand the commerce and culture of long-distance trucking can contact the American Trucking Association, Alexandria, Va.; Owner-Operator Independent Drivers Association, Oak Grove, Mo.; and read "Pedal to the Metal: The Work Lives of Truckers" by Lawrence J. Ouellet.

When considering buses, journalists need to think along three different lines: school buses, charter buses that must be reserved and commercial buses running on public routes. Stories about school bus safety and drivers' records are explored in Chapter 8. The School Bus Manufacturers Institute, Bethesda, Md., can answer questions.

Charter buses are regulated to some extent, but in most states are not watched carefully. Journalists tend to check only when disaster strikes. After 21 elderly persons died because their tour bus drove off the road into a river, the Sacramento Bee found that lax state regulation combined with charter company greed led to unsafe vehicles operated by unfit drivers. The Bee used state laws, driving records of individual operators obtained from the state motor vehicles department, inspection records from the state highway patrol, licensing records from the state public utilities commission, regulations from the Interstate Commerce Commission and laws approved by Congress. James S. Kunen, author of "Reckless Disregard: Corporate Greed, Government Indifference and the Kentucky School Bus Crash," used NTSB reports to show how the deaths of 24 children and three adults traveling in an old school bus acquired by a church for chartered excursions could have been prevented by more effective regulation.

As for commercial buses, intrastate companies tend to be watched less carefully than the interstate carriers, which are dominated by Greyhound. Journalists should inquire about who is building buses used on intrastate and interstate commercial routes, who is inspecting them and how often, who licenses the drivers and how frequently they are retested. Are all drivers checked for alcohol-related arrests before they are hired and then checked periodically afterward? Are they regularly tested for drug use? How often does equipment fail, leading to late arrivals, canceled routes or accidents? Are rates reasonable given the level of service? Where Greyhound and other intercity bus companies refuse to provide service, have van or limousine companies filled the void? If so, who regulates them, and how carefully? Such vehicles normally carry a placard inside, in a prominent spot, showing the most recent inspection date. Looking at the placard can be the starting point. The American Bus Association, Washington, D.C., can answer questions.

Journalists who work in locales that depend on railroads for freight hauling, employment and passenger service ought to keep up with ICC publications and develop human sources within the agency. The agency can provide information about the financial health of railroads, mergers, new construction and repair, abandonments that can leave a community without traditional shipping services, rates, and attempts to begin or improve commuter and long-distance passenger service.

What should be a big story in many communities is the fate of short-line railroads, which can make or break small businesses that must ship goods medium or long distances. The ICC has encouraged nonrailroad entrepreneurs to buy troubled short lines that major railroads threaten to abandon. But labor unions oppose sales to entrepreneurs because the ICC refuses to protect union jobs in such circumstances. Those elements would make for interesting projects, yet many journalists are unaware of short-line railroads in their backyards.

Sharing jurisdiction with the ICC on some issues is the Federal Railroad Administration, which is supposed to concentrate on safety, including track maintenance, equipment standards and operating practices. Perspective is available from the Association of American Railroads, the American Short Line Railroad Association, the Railway Labor Executives' Association, the National Association of Rail Shippers and the National Association of Railroad Passengers, all of Washington, D.C.

Railroad crossings are a problem in many locales, as poor markings (no flashing lights or warning bells), visual obstructions (such as un-trimmed trees), inadequate restraints (such as no gates), plus risk-taking drivers, bicyclists and pedestrians lead to death. When the Lansing State Journal in Michigan started investigating the death of a teenager at a rail-road crossing, the reporter learned the state was supposed to oversee about 5,500 crossings. She showed that recommendations from rail inspectors received no attention, or met with delays running into years. It took a death to make a difference.

One important railroad (and trucking) story involves transportation of nuclear wastes from power plants and other producers. It is not always possible to route the dangerous waste through unpopulated areas, which means residents are in danger if an accident occurs—residents who frequently have no idea such shipments are passing by their backyards. Sometimes nuclear waste is shipped by truck, which means it might be passing through downtowns and residential areas. U.S. Transportation Department regulations require heavily populated areas be bypassed whenever feasible. Is that happening? Journalists should check with local power plant operators and the U.S. Nuclear Regulatory Commission about the timing and routing of shipments.

To do its investigation, the Cleveland Plain Dealer used a computer database called Transnet, developed by Sandia National Laboratories, Albuquerque, under contract with the U.S. Energy Department. It shows shipments and accidents in the transportation of radioactive materials; Transnet also offers routing models that allow users to plan the safest highway and rail lines for shipping hot material. The Los Angeles Times used a different computer tape, the U.S. Transportation Department's Hazardous Material Incident Reporting System, to cull compelling examples from the tens of thousands of shipments. Specialized publications such as Hazardous Materials Transportation newsletter, Arlington, Va., can be valuable resources. The National Conference of State Legislatures has published a booklet, Hazardous Material Transport: Closing the Information Gap.

Mass transit is another category worth investigating. In cities, suburbs and rural areas with subway or bus systems, the Federal Transit Administration pays a portion of construction and operating costs. Journalists should explore whether systems serve all neighborhoods equally, or whether there is a modified type of redlining at work. For instance, do routes in the wealthier sections of town get the newest equipment, the best trained and most courteous drivers? Are some neighborhoods bypassed altogether, as occurred in the Washington, D.C., subway system? Are there provisions to transport wheelchair-bound passengers on the buses and subways? Trade groups that can provide perspective include the American Public Transit Association, United Bus Owners of America and the Association for Commuter Transportation, all of Washington, D.C. Mass Transit magazine, Melville, N.Y., covers most sectors of the industry.

Air Transportation

The book "Unfriendly Skies: Revelations of a Deregulated Airline Pilot" appears sensationalistic at first, written as it is by an anonymous pilot identified only as Captain X (with assistance from author Reynolds Dodson). But it is a sober, informative look at getting from here to there at speeds that leave no margin for error. It will give a journalist points of reference when delving into airline safety *before* the next crash.

How well do the pilot, co-pilot and flight engineer know one another? If they have never flown together, or if they have but are incompatible, trouble is more likely. The Federal Aviation Administration (FAA), the agency licensing airline personnel, often fails to detect lies. The Cleveland Plain Dealer discovered the pilot of a cargo jet that crashed at the local airport had lied about his job experience. In an awards entry to IRE, the newspaper said it had discovered a major airline's mechanic "who had fabricated experience fixing jets to qualify" for a license. When the FAA finally caught him, it revoked the license but never notified the airline because of a policy meant to protect the violator's privacy rights. "We found a Florida pilot who wanted to fly for an airline so badly he made up experience to get a license to haul passengers. To punish him, the FAA took away his right to fly"—for 10 weeks. The Plain Dealer obtained much of its raw data from the FAA's computerized accident/incident data subsystem, complemented by its enforcement information subsystem.

More questions to ask: Is the pilot familiar with the airport where the plane will land, especially with any unusual local weather patterns? If not, chances for trouble are increased. Is the airport designed sensibly? Captain X explains, for example, why the approach and runway patterns at the Atlanta airport (a pilot favorite) are safer than at the airports pilots dislike most (Washington, D.C., National; New York LaGuardia, San Diego and Los Angeles). If there are noise pollution regulations for that particular airport, do they affect takeoff procedures adversely? If there is a large population of small private airplanes (many without two-way radios or transponders that transmit their altitudes) taking off and landing, how much do they increase the danger for commercial airliners?

Is the pilot experienced flying the type of airplane in service that day? Not all planes handle the same. Did the pilot have military flight experience before joining a commercial airline? Most do not anymore, because of military cutbacks. But many experienced pilots believe those with military training tend to be the best. The International Air Line Pilots Association, Washington, D.C., can provide perspective.

Is the air traffic controller in the tower experienced and alert? Pilots and controllers rarely meet face to face, but they (and the passengers) have a life-and-death bond. The Cleveland Plain Dealer found that a new radar system meant to help controllers worked poorly, despite a $1 billion cost to taxpayers. The newspaper relied on complaints filed by controllers with their union and the FAA; the stories provided figures for individual airports. The union involved, the National Air Traffic Controllers Association, Arlington, Va., can provide perspective.

Are the maintenance crews on the ground careful about every procedure, or are they told to ignore certain "little" matters to get the plane back in the air as soon as possible. As Captain X says, "They are not the big items we call the 'no-go' or 'kill' items . . . they . . . are small ailments which are ultimately important but which are not that essential to a particular day's flight operations . . . nicked panels . . . levers with knob ends missing . . . fraying and chipping and rattling and lightbulbs missing." The Wall Street Journal reported how the FAA suspended the mechanic's certificate of a maintenance supervisor for a major airline who admitted allowing a plane to fly despite a malfunctioning warning system. He did it, the supervisor said, to save money for his employer.

Airlines that are losing money tend to skimp on maintenance, so journalists concerned with safety need to study corporate bottom lines. Aaron Bernstein's book "Grounded: Frank Lorenzo and the Destruction of Eastern Airlines" provides insights into airline economics, as does "Rapid Descent: Deregulation and the Shakeout in the Airlines" by Barbara Sturken Peterson and James Glab. Before federal airline deregulation, everything worked better, Captain X says. Every system was checked and rechecked. As deregulation encouraged more competition based on price, profit margins eroded; so did ground maintenance, flight crew training and the overall safety cushion.

Journalists should inquire at the FAA about alcohol and drug prevention and testing programs, airline by airline. If no pilots or other crew have been sanctioned, something is almost certainly wrong because at least a few are bound to be substance abusers. If lots have been sanctioned, something is probably awry in hiring and training procedures. Are airlines complying with federal rules on crew fatigue? Crews are supposed to be on the ground a certain number of consecutive hours after a certain number of airborne hours. During that stretch on the ground, crews are supposed to have the opportunity for adequate sleep. John J. Nance's book "Blind Trust" is especially useful in its explanation of how human error affects airline safety. "Collision Course: The Truth About Airline Safety" by Ralph Nader and Wesley J. Smith is another useful book.

Some airplanes have design or manufacturing flaws. That means journalists investigating safety must develop sources within companies that design and manufacture airplanes, be on the alert for litigation, plus check airworthiness certifications granted or denied by federal inspectors.

Many airlines are flying planes longer than intended by manufacturers. Journalists should interview manufacturers about dangers associated with longer-than-expected usage, then check specific airlines and planes for reports of those dangers. Age-related cracks and corrosion lead to aborted takeoffs, unscheduled landings and canceled flights. Landing gear, radar, hydraulic systems and cabin pressure are especially vulnerable to problems.

At the Dallas Morning News, a reporter wanted to follow an NTSB investigator from beginning to end of a fatal crash inquiry. Agency officials agreed to cooperate and designated an investigator for the News to follow. Six months later, the reporter received his call that a fatal crash had occurred. Nearly two years after that, his series appeared. Infused with death, it is also filled with insights into government bureaucracies, airplane manufacturers and air safety. The series is reprinted in the book "The Pulitzer Prizes 1989," edited by Kendall J. Wills.

The plane involved in the News investigation was a private aircraft owned by a multinational corporation. It carried seven people the day of the crash. Private planes have some of the same safety problems as large commercial airliners. But sometimes journalists must raise different questions about manufacturing, maintenance, pilot competence, airport factors and air traffic controller conduct than with large commercial airliners. Standards and training are more lax for aircraft that fly fewer than 30 passengers.

Journalists should seek out airlines that remove seats specifically to avoid being governed by the more stringent standards. The pilots tend to be younger, less experienced, fly more hours per week (sometimes on schedules that allow for little sleep), are poorly paid compared to pilots of large commercial carriers and expected to underwrite their own training, which costs thousands of dollars. Journalists should ask legislators, regulators and commuter airline officials why they resist safety measures. Twenty-five deaths is obviously not as large a disaster as hundreds of deaths on a jumbo jet. But are those 25 lives valued so cheaply that commuter airlines should be exempt from certain safety standards simply to make money? A U.S. News and World Report team found that the largest airlines flying the largest planes averaged 2.9 accidents per million departures; regional airlines, flying mostly turboprops of up to 75 seats, 5.1; commuter airlines with 30 seats or fewer, 6.6.

After a commuter airplane crashed in Minnesota, the St. Paul Pioneer Press found out the deceased pilot had failed six flight checks in a 13-year stretch, punched his first officer while in the air, sought turbulent pockets so passengers would complain to the airline he hated so much and verbally abused passengers. If journalists checked pilot records routinely, they could have warned potential passengers before it was too late.

Airplanes operated for government officials need close scrutiny: the planes and the pilots are exempt from some safety procedures that govern commercial and private aviation. Hearst Newspapers documented crashes and emergency landings involving government airplanes. In one, the governor of South Dakota died. At least 180 other deaths had occurred in the span of a decade. Separately, the magazine Aviation Week and Space Technology, Washington, D.C., reported how two planes operated by the FAA for agency travel had been involved in fatal crashes.

Helicopters raise their own questions, especially when they are operated commercially as part of commuter and tourist services. New York magazine documented the fatal crash of a sightseeing helicopter. The crash occurred right after takeoff, near the heliport, but the private company had no rescue equipment ready and no experience with emergency procedures. One of the surviving passengers, whose son died, later learned the company had reported eight crashes in 15 years, four involving deaths. The pilot, who survived, had a record of driving a car while intoxicated. The company had been in bankruptcy court. The American Helicopter Society, Alexandria, Va., can provide perspective.

The FAA will often be the most valuable resource on air transportation investigations. Its center in Oklahoma City has licensing, ownership and inspection information on pilots and airplanes. The data are so vast that private services set up shop there. For example, the Aircraft Owners and Pilots Association has a staff in Oklahoma City to do customized searches for members.

Among the customized reports it produces is a title search, listing current ownership of the aircraft and whether the FAA knows of any liens against the owner. An airworthiness directive search is based on the plane's serial number. If the frame or engine used on the plane has caused problems, they should show up. A service difficulty report is related to airworthiness. The report will list malfunctions submitted to the FAA by pilots, mechanics, inspectors and maintenance shops concerning the plane's frame, powerplant, propeller and components.

Checking FAA databases is necessary; in theory, they should contain the ultimate primary information about pilots, crew, mechanics and aircraft. But experienced journalists know to doublecheck primary sources. A Cleveland Plain Dealer reporter tested the FAA system meant to inform callers whether an individual held a valid pilot or mechanic license. First, he requested information about 13 pilots whose licenses he knew had been revoked and never reinstated. In 12 cases, the FAA said those pilots had valid licenses. Why? The agency's computer system was not appending revocations to the licensing file. Then the reporter checked the license status of six pilots who had died in crashes. Five of them were alive and licensed, the FAA center told the reporter. Service difficulty reports on file at the FAA often fail to delineate the seriousness of the specific safety problem. Journalists have found far more such reports in the files of airplane manufacturers and operators than they have found at the FAA. That said, the service difficulty reports are a logical place to begin when trying to quantify problems with a type of plane or a specific part that might fatally malfunction.

Many private databases contain information on airplane manufacturers, owners, pilots and performance. For instance, Aviation Data Service (sometimes called AvData), Wichita, maintains computerized lists of turbine business aircraft, turbine and piston helicopters and turbine-powered commercial aircraft. Other groups maintain databases, which may or may not incorporate FAA-generated information. The Aerospace Industries Association of America, Washington, D.C., represents manufacturers of commercial, business and military aircraft. The Air Transport Association of America, Washington, D.C., represents scheduled airlines; the Regional Airline Association, Washington, D.C., handles representation for carriers of planes with 60 or fewer seats. The Aircraft Owners and Pilots Association, Frederick, Md., represents those involved with smaller planes, often used for pleasure. The Aeronautical Repair Station Association, Alexandria, Va., represents certified mechanics' garages. The Association of Flight Attendants, Washington, D.C. and the Aviation Safety Institute, Worthington, Ohio, can also provide perspective.

Airports raise safety questions, as already noted, but the questions do not end there. Airport costs to flyers and to taxpayers in general should be scrutinized more than they are. In many cities, airports are subsidized heavily by governments. Those airports might serve a relatively small number of travelers, but governments (and those travelers, who tend to be influential in the community) believe operating an airport is a matter of prestige, besides being necessary to attract new employers and retain long-time employers. The American Association of Airport Executives, Alexandria, Va., can provide perspective.

Those assumptions about airport costs and benefits might be correct, but then again they might be flawed. Journalists should be checking the conventional wisdom by studying budgets, calculating subsidies and conducting interviews. Is the nearest small city part of the federal "essential air service" program, created by Congress to appease locales in the wake of airline deregulation? Because deregulation meant market forces would eliminate air service to some small cities, Congress jumped in. Some of the preserved routes benefitted enough taxpayers to justify assessing everybody, but other routes were boondoggles. According to Martin L. Gross in his book "The Government Racket": "One 'essential' flight is from Washington, D.C., to the luxurious Homestead resort in Hot Springs. The hotel, which charges $335 a day, has one of the richest clientele in the world, including businessmen, conventioneers, Washington politicians, lawyers and lobbyists." Without the subsidy, travelers would have had to fly to a different airport, then drive 45 miles to the resort. James Kaplan's book "The Airport: Terminal Nights and Runway Days at John F. Kennedy International" provides useful information.

No matter how many or few airport flights, how expensive or inexpensive, travelers hope for on-time service. A Detroit Free Press reporter noticed one airline trumpeting its on-time ranking. Because he often flew on the airline, he noticed he often arrived early. The newspaper bought on-time computer tapes from the U.S. Transportation Department. Calculating predicted and actual departures and arrivals, the reporter determined that the airline allowed itself more time than its competitors. That meant passengers did not reach their destinations faster, but were more likely to be "on time."

Water Transportation

The U.S. Maritime Administration tries to help commercial shipping by subsidizing private companies, collectively called the merchant marine. The Federal Maritime Commission, an independent agency, shares jurisdiction, with an emphasis on setting rates and licensing ocean freight businesses. Journalists in locales with large merchant marine employers can inquire about subsidies for construction and repair of private vessels as well as the building and maintenance of port facilities.

One justification for the subsidies is job protection in the face of competition from other nations, whose governments supposedly support their maritime industries more vigorously. To test the justification, a journalist can divide the total subsidy to an employer by the jobs that otherwise would cease to exist. If the subsidy is tens of thousands of dollars per saved job, it is worth exploring whether retraining those workers might be more sensible.

Journalists in port cities should pay attention to the ships coming and going. Many are staffed by international crews who know little about their rights, are cheated out of their wages, receive substandard food and are generally treated like slaves by tyrannical captains. Some of the worst ships are owned by U.S. corporations; no matter what nationality the ownership, the mistreatment is taking place in U.S. waters. Paul K. Chapman's book "Trouble on Board: The Plight of International Seafarers" provides background. Eric Nalder's book "Tankers Full of Trouble" concentrates on the perils of shipping oil. It demonstrates how some ship owners put profit first, safety and the environment last. Given its job description, it is a wonder journalists tend to ignore the Coast Guard. Besides serving as a law enforcement agency, the Coast Guard, according to the federal government manual,

> is charged with formulating, administering and enforcing various safety standards for the design, construction, equipment and maintenance of commercial vessels of the United States. . . .
>
> The program includes enforcement of safety standards on foreign vessels subject to U.S. jurisdiction. Investigations are conducted of reported marine accidents, casualties, violations of law and regulations, misconduct, negli-

gence and incompetence occurring on commercial vessels subject to U.S. jurisdiction. Surveillance operations and boardings are conducted to detect violations. . . . The Coast Guard administers a system for evaluating and licensing of U.S. Merchant Marine personnel. This program develops safe manning standards for commercial vessels. . . .

The Coast Guard is responsible for enforcing the Federal Water Pollution Control Act and various other laws relating to the protection of the marine environment. . . . U.S. and foreign vessels are prohibited from using U.S. waters unless they have insurance or other guarantees that potential pollution liability for cleanup and damages will be met. Other functions include providing a National Response Center to receive reports of oil and hazardous substance spills, investigating spills, initiating subsequent civil penalty actions when warranted, encouraging and monitoring responsible party cleanups and, when necessary, coordinating federally funded spill response operations. The program also provides a National Strike Force to assist federal on-scene coordinators in responding to pollution incidents.

As the Coast Guard missions illustrate, the fit among various transportation modes shows up over and over, demonstrating how journalists cannot be bound by bureaucratic boundaries. An example: 47 people died as a National Railroad Passenger Corp. (Amtrak) train derailed on tracks that were out of alignment. The misalignment happened after a towboat accidentally rammed a railroad bridge while trying to pass under it. The National Transportation Safety Board investigated. The U.S. transportation secretary proposed more stringent licensing requirements and route restrictions for towboat operators as well as beefed-up Coast Guard inspections. The Coast Guard also planned to upgrade standards for radar and other navigational aids on towboats. Meanwhile, the Federal Railroad Administration sought new ways to examine the structural integrity of bridges and warn train engineers when tracks were out of alignment.

Increased enforcement is needed to monitor recreational boating. It is a puzzle why states and the federal government consider automobile recklessness to be worth monitoring closely, while reckless boating is barely monitored at all. Journalists should ask whether the states they cover require boat drivers to obtain a license based on passing a safety course. Does the state require boaters to wear life jackets? After an accident, do boat drivers have to submit to alcohol and drug tests? If not, why not? The National Conference of State Legislatures publishes a useful primer, Recreational Boating Safety: State Policies and Programs.

Private sector sources abound. Fairplay Information Systems, Germantown, N.Y., maintains a database of merchant vessels. The American Maritime Congress, Washington, D.C., can provide perspective on issues facing U.S. flag carriers, as can the Shipbuilders Council of America, Arlington, Va. The union viewpoint is represented by the AFL-CIO Maritime Committee, Seafarers International Union of North America and Marine Engineers Beneficial Association. The American Waterway Operators, Arlington, Va., consists of commercial shipyard owners and operators of barges, tugboats and towboats. Those interests have some common ground with the American Association of Port Authorities, Alexandria, Va. Recreational interests are represented by the Boat Owners Association of America, Alexandria, Va.

People will always have to get from here to there; no matter how much technology changes the means for doing that, journalists will always be able to scrutinize those means on grounds of safety, efficiency and cost.

Chapter *19*

INVESTIGATING REAL ESTATE

Housing, Commercial Uses and Zoning

*I*n most newsrooms, there is no overall real estate beat. Nor do narrower beats exist for housing, commercial property or zoning. That is difficult to understand, because land literally undergirds where people live and work. Who owns it and how it is used define a geographic area.

Writing in Columbia Journalism Review, Mary Ellen Schoonmaker put it well:

> Real estate is a wonderful beat. It is the heart of a city, its glamour and grit, its skyscrapers and slums, its elite inner circle and its grass-roots demanding change. In its fullest definition it touches on housing, neighborhoods, finance, planning, local government and politics. . . . At its core, it is about power— who has it, who does not, what is being done with it by the few and how it affects the many.

When George Kennedy of the Columbia Missourian wrote the chapter titled "Tracing Land Holdings" for an earlier edition of this book, he began by quoting a slogan of real estate developers: "Land endures." That is true. Some of Kennedy's chapter endures in this version of the book. Though land endures, how a piece of land is used can change. Ownership changes. Zoning changes. So does market value. Good journalists search out the corruption and favoritism that often accompany big developments, zoning changes and land purchases by public agencies. Such investigations yield important stories.

Projects just as important are being written by small numbers of reporters who realize the need to examine the broader issues of land-use policies and patterns. These stories are usually based on information from public records: housing starts, resales of existing homes, the pace of apartment and commercial building, census data, ownership records, zoning files, building permits, inspection reports and court cases.

Most land records are so easily accessible once a journalist knows how the system works that they can be used on quick-breaking stories, too. At the Portland Oregonian, Dee Lane was following up the shooting of a five-year-old boy. The suspect was a teenage gang member who had been showing off a gun on the neighboring property when it discharged. "We're trying to get in the habit of finding out who owns a house whenever there is a fire or shooting," Lane said. "We're basically looking for slumlords."

Using the county government's assessment and taxation database, Lane found the owners' names. She then searched for other properties owned by the same couple. She found 25, most in the same part of the city and acquired during a buying spree that lasted two years—clues that she might be dealing with landlords who had overextended themselves, letting their rental properties become slums. She checked the assessed valuation of the properties, finding they were on the low end of the scale. She also found building code violations tagged by city inspectors. To learn more about the two owners, Lane consulted the motor vehicles department. They owned 10 cars, including a Mercedes Benz and a Cadillac, plus a motorcycle.

At city hall, Lane found a letter issued to the owners under a local drug-house ordinance. The letter showed her that the owners were aware illegal drugs had been dealt on the property where the fatal shooting occurred. Lane later learned that neighbors had complained to the owners about drug dealing, and police had arrested a gang member in the house's basement. Records showed the owners evicted numerous tenants from their properties, but never attempted an eviction from the house involved in the shooting.

Sometimes a real-estate story is so big nobody sees it at first. That was the case in Saginaw, Mich. The Saginaw News conducted record checks for what was intended to be a story on sleazy landlords. But as a reporter studied computerized data from the city on rental properties, the figures on demolitions—not something he had intended examining—looked staggering. Landlords were tearing down rental properties rather than repairing them. Sectors of the city had been razed, leaving tracts of weeds and concrete slabs.

The newspaper set out to answer the question: Why? The answers emerged after two months of reorganizing the city's records, followed by extensive interviewing and visiting the abandoned neighborhoods to examine condemned homes. The answer encompassed an incompetent housing inspection department, destructive tenants, plus a mixture of inexperienced and exploitive landlords. The reporting included analysis of housing department inspection records, census reports, court files on landlord-tenant disputes, fire department logs, old city directories and histories, ordinances and city council minutes. Human sources included national experts on housing decay, tenants, landlords, inspectors, city and state officials, neighborhood leaders and former residents. Instead of exposing one lazy inspector or one sleazy landlord, the newspaper coupled computer analysis with street reporting and had the vision to see how the facts added up to a pattern of municipal self-destruction.

The Detroit Free Press looked at housing city-wide because a columnist thought he was noticing more abandoned houses than before. The newspaper's team began by driving each of the city's streets—about 2,300 miles—to count abandoned homes and buildings. The count topped 15,000, three times more than city officials had estimated. The team then turned to property ownership records, demolition files and police reports to figure out why so many abandoned structures remained standing and how often they became sites of crimes. Even one abandoned home should raise questions, such as why the owner or the mortgage holder has done nothing to sell it, secure it or tear it down. What impact does the vacant building have on the neighborhood? Have neighborhood residents been rebuffed in their efforts to minimize the negative fallout? What do police say about the use of empty buildings by drug users and other criminals?

The Independent of Durham, N.C., also wondered about local real estate. The alternative weekly examined property tax reassessments in Durham County, finding that not all reassessments were created equally. The stories documented how the homes of the wealthy tended to be assessed at a lower percentage of market value than homes of the poor and middle class. That meant the wealthy were paying less than their fair share for public schools, garbage pick-up and other services that depend on property taxes. After compiling the statistics, journalists should talk to assessors and appraisers in government and the private sector about idiosyncracies in the data and unexpected explanations.

The increasing emphasis on stories that analyze systems does not mean exposure of malfeasance or corruption are unimportant. As Bob Greene of Newsday told an IRE conference, "Like the hustlers say on TV, dealing in real estate is still one of the quickest ways to make a buck. And you can make money even faster if you're willing to bend the rules a bit."

The IRE Resource Center contains land and building investigations under numerous categories, including Conflicts of Interests, Developers, Homeless Persons, Housing, Landlords, Property Taxes, Real Estate, Urban Renewal and Zoning.

Who Owns the Land?

Finding the owner of land might take five seconds, five minutes, five hours, five days or five months. A lot depends on the recordkeeping system of the county, where land ownership is normally recorded. A lot also depends on whether the owner is trying to mask his or her identity through a straw party, corporate name or land trust.

In some newsrooms, like the Miami Herald's, journalists can start with an in-house computer database derived from government records but enhanced to increase its power. Access can be by name, address, folio number, subdivision or other starting points. Searchers can pull up categories of properties within a city, as well as recent sales of properties comparable to the subject property. Many newsrooms are not so well-equipped. Even the best-equipped will not always yield the desired answers for every piece of land. So there is virtue in knowing about searching methods that are more labor-intensive.

When the only information an investigator possesses is an address, it makes sense to begin with the city directory. It is not a primary document, and is sometimes unreliable or out of date. But if the parcel-by-parcel listing in the directory shows a resident's name, that is a name to start with at county repositories holding the primary documents.

In cases where the city directory is no help, the county assessor might yield the answer. The assessor knows who receives the tax bill on every parcel. Traditionally, the assessor files parcels by legal description. But many assessors cross-file by address.

If a legal description is needed, the reporter can visit the recorder of deeds, planning or public works department to view plat maps. A parcel of land on the plat map might have a legal description like this: "Bluestone subdivision, Block 10, Lot 17." If the property is in an unincorporated area, the maps will probably consist of ranges, townships and sections, the units used to divide county land. The description might read: "The northwest quarter of the southwest quarter of Section 11, Township 41, Range 15." A section contains 640 acres. One-fourth of that is 160; one-fourth of that is 40. So, in addition to eventually yielding the address, the legal description of some parcels will reveal the number of acres.

Sometimes investigators want to document the history of a parcel: Who did the current owner buy from, when and at what price? The county recorder's office normally keeps information on every land purchase or sale the parties choose to file. There is a double-entry by buyer and seller, called the "grantee" and "grantor" in legal terminology. After the filing of the legal document, the recorder furnishes the information to the assessor to keep tax records current. An efficient way to trace a parcel's history is to obtain the abstract. They are not normally kept in a public repository, but an investigator can ask either the holder of the mortgage, the title company that verified ownership or the landowner herself. The American Land Title Association, Washington, D.C., can help, as can how-to books such as Sally Light's "House Histories: A Guide to Tracing the Genealogy of Your Home."

Liens filed with county offices establish legal liability and name the owner responsible for satisfying the lien. If a property owner has failed to pay taxes, the appropriate government agency might file a tax lien that clouds legal ownership of the property. If a contractor hires a subcontractor to do work on a building, the subcontractor is quite likely to file a mechanic's lien that stays attached to the property until all bills are paid. There is a reason for every lien. When a commercial property runs into financial difficulties, journalists should start delving into why. Each case has its idiosyncracies, but enough failures in a downtown or a mall or a suburb should suggest the possibility of a pattern. A journalist who discerns that pattern might have a major story.

Unpaid liens frequently mean repossession of the property by the lender or a government takeover. Such property foreclosures can be important stories on their own or can be key evidence in a larger project. Yet many journalists unwisely pay no attention to foreclosures. If the property is eventually sold at auction by the county sheriff or some other government agent because of lagging monthly payments or back taxes owed, the journalist should be alert for a set-up: Sometimes the high bidder is a straw party for the previous owner. To reduce such set-ups, in some states property foreclosures must be handled by a judge in a formal court setting. Journalists should know whether their state is a judicial or nonjudicial foreclosure jurisdiction.

When the title is unclouded, mortgage documents can help solve the mysteries of ownership and price. Relatively few buyers of homes, commercial buildings or tracts of land pay the full cost upfront. So they borrow from a lender who is supposed to disclose the terms, including upfront settlement costs, before the papers are signed. The lender records the loan for legal protection. That paperwork is usually in the county recorder's office. If an investigator knows the mortgage amount, that piece of information might lead to a reasonable guess about total sales price. On the other hand, people sometimes borrow more than the purchase price, if, for example, extensive renovation will be required.

Talking to the lender can be difficult on at least two counts: First, many lenders hide behind the self-imposed confidentiality of financial transactions. Second, it can be difficult to determine who actually owns the mortgage until it is paid in full. Until recent decades, the local lender owned the mortgage until the borrower had made all payments. But local lenders have entered the secondary market, selling mortgages to investors around the nation. The secondary market, besides masking mortgage holders, influences how much money is available locally and at what rate.

One engine of the secondary market is the Federal National Mortgage Association, often called Fannie Mae. It is chartered by the federal government but owned by stockholders and listed on the New York Stock Exchange. It purchases mortgages for its own portfolio; it also issues and guarantees securities backed by mortgages. The Federal Home Loan Mortgage Corp. (Freddie Mac), McLean, Va., is also congressionally chartered. It purchases loans from financial institutions, then sells securities backed by those mortgages to investors.

The two corporations have standardized loan criteria, so investors in their securities anywhere in the nation believe the mortgages are good risks. An investor in Sacramento figures that a bank there will be using the same underwriting criteria as a bank in Miami, so buying the securities no longer has to be done close to home. Fannie Mae and Freddie Mac have no desire to own mortgages if the homes involved have problems, such as inadequate sewer systems. In places like Boone County, Mo., owners wanting to sell rural homes are being pressured to replace environmentally unsound septic tanks with more effective, higher-cost alternatives. The pressure is not coming from county inspectors nor directly from local lenders; instead it is coming from the federally chartered organizations to whom local lenders want to sell mortgages.

When mortgage rates drop, as they do cyclically, borrowers refinance at lower rates. Such refinancings generate documents that might help journalists track ownership. Furthermore, refinancings might lead to the involvement of mortgage brokers, who help homeowners shop for the lowest rates among competing lenders. Mortgage brokers can be excellent sources. They might also be appropriate subjects of investigations, because in many states they are unlicensed and unregulated. In some states, there is not even a net worth requirement for entering the mortgage broker business. Some are dishonest, some just incompetent or so busy that documents are filed too late to take advantage of the lower rates. As states move to regulate mortgage brokers, legislatures are requiring posting of a bond to pay customers who have been cheated.

Sales and refinancings can involve escrow companies, which hold cash as middlemen while the deal takes final shape. New Times of Phoenix documented fraud by an escrow company that left thousands of property buyers, sellers and refinancers holding worthless checks when the state banking department seized the company. The money had been embezzled rather than safely invested. After a home loan is final, a different kind of escrow scam might kick in. The borrowers living in the home pay monthly fees to the mortgage company for property taxes. The mortgage holder often collects more than it needs for the escrow account, uses the excess without paying interest, and maybe even is delinquent with the property tax payment, thus harming the borrowers' credit ratings and causing difficulties on income-tax returns. Yet government regulators almost never penalize mortgage lenders for escrow abuses.

When the identity of the owner is unclear from documents in the recorder's or assessor's offices, other documents might establish who is behind the corporate name or straw party. Building permits, fire safety or health inspections, Uniform Commercial Code forms, lawsuits, federal or state tax liens, utility bills, doing-business-as filings, rezoning applications and bankruptcy records are some of the possibilities. A home inspector might have been hired by a potential buyer; a journalist who tracks down the inspector might learn the owner's name. The American Society of Home Inspectors, Arlington Heights, Ill., can help. Termite exterminators, lawn service crews, landscape architects, heating and air conditioning services, plumbers, electricians, interior designers and tree trimmers, among others, might know who owns the property—or at least who does the hiring and pays the bills. When buildings, either residential or commercial, change hands, lawsuits sometimes result, especially concerning inadequate disclosure by the seller of defects in the structure. Journalists who track such lawsuits in local courts will have a steady supply of individual stories or a critical mass for a project.

A Chicago Sun-Times reporter heard that a mayor thought to be corrupt but nonetheless known for his unpretentious lifestyle owned a summer home in Michigan. By visiting the Michigan county, the reporter determined the owner was an Illinois corporation known as Elard Realty. He later calculated the "El" came from the first name of the mayor's wife, the "ard" from the last syllable of the mayor's first name. Further investigation showed Elard Realty was a land trust concealing the true owners' names. Running the trust was an accountant, friendly with the mayor, who had received contracts from the city. The book "Who Owns Appalachia?: Land Ownership and Its Impact," by the Appalachian Land Ownership Task Force, shows how much work is involved in tracking control of real estate—and how worthwhile that work can be.

How Much Is the Land Worth?

Journalists should never assume the sales price of a home is unavailable. For example, my wife and I bought our house from an estate. Although most home sales in Missouri require no declaration of the sales price when documents are filed at the recorder's office, the estate selling to us did file a piece of paper attesting to the fair market value of the house. There was the exact amount we paid, a public record for anybody to see. Sales price might or might not approximate market value. Perhaps, for example, the seller was under duress. When no such magic document exists, one route is to call real estate agents. They frequently know the sales price firsthand or can find out what it was with one call to a colleague or competitor. The National Association of Realtors and Society of Industrial and Office Realtors, Chicago, plus the National Home Buyers and Home Owners Association, Washington, D.C., can provide help. Cross referencing documents can help, too. A Lexington (Ky.) Herald Leader reporter found a hotel owner claiming a $3 million value in a lawsuit over damage caused by nearby blasting. But in a separate proceeding to reduce his property taxes, the hotel owner was claiming a $1.5 million value.

Determining the fairness of property tax assessments should be a staple of investigative journalism. If certain persons or institutions are receiving unwarranted favorable treatment, all individual taxpayers and organizations dependent on property-tax revenue are damaged. In Columbia, S.C., The State newspaper showed how officials gave up millions of revenue dollars by allowing developers to abuse a tax break meant to help farmers. No farming was taking place on the land, but developers called the tracts "farms" and nobody called them on it. Honest taxpayers—or those unaware of the loophole—ended up subsidizing the crafty ones.

Are assessors in the field acting on orders to render favorable treatment? Are the assessors dishonest or incompetent? What is their training? Must they seek continuing education? Is one assessor's valuations consistently out of line with her colleagues' judgments? Perspective is available from the American Society of Appraisers, Herndon, Va., and the Society of Real Estate Appraisers or the International Association of Assessing Officers, both in Chicago.

Is reassessment done only when a property changes owners? If so, reporters will find nearly identical neighboring buildings with wildly varying taxes. Such a system operates to the advantage of long-time residents and merchants, as well as those able to hold their land for development. Is there a provision for assessing apartment buildings and other commercial properties based on their revenue generation? If so, how is the income verified? If not, why not?

Who is appealing their assessments? An Ann Arbor News project looked at property owners asking for reductions based on some sort of hardship. It turned out that many of the requesters owned second homes, not exactly an indicator of hardship. Is the percentage of appeals higher or lower than in surrounding counties or other states? Who decides the appeals? In the county where I live, it is the Board of Equalization. How often do those appealing prevail, and why? In Missouri, the state Tax Commission, appointed by the governor, supervises lower-level boards of equalization and accepts appeals from taxpayers.

How many properties in the county are tax exempt? A reporter can examine applications for tax exemptions, then determine if the information was truthful at the time and is still valid. For example, if a church completed an application decades ago because its principal place of worship sat on a specific parcel, the property-tax exemption was almost surely valid then. But suppose the church is now using the land for a profit-making subsidiary without notifying the assessor: That should be grist for a journalist.

■ LANDLORDS AND TENANTS

The most egregious violations of residential housing ordinances tend to occur in rentals. Landlords frequently trample the economic, social and civil rights of tenants who have no other place to sleep. Violations include overcharging on rent, repairs and utility bills; refusing to make repairs until after the tenant complains to government inspectors, a step that might place the tenant on an undesirable list kept by landlord associations; requiring deposits that are never refunded; revoking a lease without notice; inspections that violate tenant privacy; and refusal to rent to certain types of persons or families.

At the Buffalo News, housing court records formed the backbone of a project identifying the most heavily prosecuted landlords and the streets with the highest percentages of substandard units. The stories established a link between poor conditions and absentee landlords. As for the housing court, its judges fined or jailed only three percent of defendants charged by government inspectors. The Village Voice found a housing court judge soliciting bribes from landlords in exchange for guaranteed favorable verdicts on eviction cases.

One obvious investigation is to check for complaints of rental or sales discrimination at local, state and federal civil rights commissions, tenants associations and courthouses. In addition to checking for existing complaints, news organizations can send journalists (or non-journalists) of different races to real estate agents and property managers. Are prospective renters and buyers of different races but otherwise similar demographics treated similarly? The IRE Journal published an article explaining how the Miami Herald conducted such an investigation.

On the flip side, tenants rip off landlords by lying about employment and income, damaging property, refusing to pay for needed repairs or their contracted-for rent. Landlord-tenant disputes also occur in commercial buildings; news organizations pay too little attention to sleazy business-district and shopping-center landlords.

How vigilant are city and county residential and commercial building inspectors? Do they conduct unannounced inspections? Or do they wait for complaints to arrive, complaints that tenants might be reluctant to file, knowing that their names will be revealed to landlords? Do they look for dangerous lead paint, ventilation to avoid carbon monoxide poisoning from heating systems, violation of air pollution standards and compliance with fire safety codes? Are the inspectors screened and paid well enough that they turn down favors and bribes? Are the inspectors and their supervisors themselves landlords whose properties fail to measure up? How about when a government agency owns the properties? A Newsday investigation found a city government failing to meet its own housing code for apartment units that had come into its possession. Is special attention paid to mobile homes? They are often dangerous, lacking fire prevention devices and safeguards against high winds. Furthermore, mobile home park residents are frequently poorly educated with little income, making them especially vulnerable to landlords and park managers.

Useful books include "Where We Live: A Social History of American Housing" by Irving Welfeld; "The Suburban Racial Dilemma: Housing and Neighborhoods" by W. Dennis Keating; and "Community Versus Commodity" by John I. Gilderbloom. Perspective is available from the Apartment Owners and Managers Association of America, National Apartment Association and American Society of Home Inspectors, all in Washington, D.C.

When soundness of construction is an issue, the National Conference of States on Building Codes and Standards, Herndon, Va., can help, as can the magazine Engineering News-Record, New York City, and the books "House" by Tracy Kidder and "Why Buildings Fall Down" by Matthys Levy and Mario Salvadori. Construction standards are especially important in commercial buildings that serve large numbers of people, as well as in hurricane and earthquake zones.

The rise of walled-in private housing developments with their own governing boards and security forces raises questions about constitutional rights of the residents as the boards restrict what can be built, what can be displayed in yards, and the like. Restricted entry to the developments raises constitutional questions for those on the outside. Evan McKenzie discusses the dilemmas in his book "Privatopia: Homeowner Associations and the Rise of Residential Private Government."

Changing How the Land Is Used: Zoning and Rezoning

Many zonings and rezonings are smart public policy done aboveboard. The same is true for building permits granted to structures out of character with their surroundings. But in other instances, there is reason for suspicion. As with many potential projects, the experienced journalist asks early who are the winners and who are the losers? Issuance of building permits and rezoning decisions often helps the few to the detriment of the many, so there is temptation to bypass majority sentiment by greasing the process.

Such bypasses are usually accomplished with help from an elected politician or appointed member of the planning and zoning board who secretly gets something of value for approving an unpopular application. The heat of the opposition might determine the size of the bribe. That officials vote for a rezoning, variance or building plan despite seeming widespread opposition does not automatically mean they are taking bribes. They may be voting for something that will benefit the whole community in the face of opposition from folks who think only in terms of their own property. But a pattern of such rezonings is suspect, especially if they violate the master plan for the community hashed out in political forums, or alter previously approved subdivision plans submitted by developers.

Sometimes the bias in favor of developers is out in the open. The Orlando Sentinel showed how local officials approved almost every development proposal from builders, leading to new schools that were overcrowded before opening, traffic jams, polluted rivers, visual blight, backed-up sewer systems, wholesale destruction of trees and poor or nonexistent utility service. When developers propose drastic changes, it is useful to determine if they live in the area and whether they plan to stay. When the developers are already local citizens, it is interesting to document how many are former planning and zoning commissioners, attorneys and elected officials.

Sometimes developers are a moral force, as when they agree to build rental or owner-occupied units for low-income or moderate-income families in exchange for interest-rate breaks from the government. When that happens, local zoning officials sometimes try to change the parcel's designation under pressure from long-time residents who stereotype the intended occupants. Those officials always deny that racial or economic discrimination is behind the decision.

If massive development is going to occur, journalists should ask whether the granting authority requires builders to pay for part of the infrastructure, the environmental mitigation and provide jobs to local workers. Such payments are referred to as "exactions." If the answer is no, why not? If the answer is yes, do consumers end up paying higher prices for their homes because of the exactions? Does the government reduce or waive exactions if the developers promise to build housing for lower-income buyers? If not, why not?

The following methods illustrate ways politicians and bureaucrats have been bribed for favorable votes on development plans, variances and rezonings (the county where I live has 19 different zoning designations):

1. Straight cash, often the most effective because it is tough to trace.
2. A collateral deal. A member of the zoning board in, say, Minneapolis, at the suggestion of a Florida developer wanting to build up north, buys a piece of Tampa land for $10,000. The board member then votes favorably on the Minneapolis rezoning sought by the Florida developer. Two months later, through a well-disguised corporation, the developer buys the Florida land for $110,000. The Minneapolis zoning board member thus receives a $100,000 bribe that can be reported as a capital gain on an income tax return.
3. Ownership. The developer wanting the rezoning gives the board member stock in the corporation that owns the rezoned land or stock of equal value in one of his other corporations.
4. Favorable business dealings. The developer wanting a rezoning agrees to buy insurance, construction bonds, building supplies, engineering, architectural, drafting or design services from a firm owned by the board member or a relative.

5. Fringe benefits. The developer provides the zoning board member with gifts or the vacation use of a San Diego condominium. At the Detroit News, a suburban reporter decided to delve into the seemingly obvious: how suburban growth was draining people and wealth from the city. The findings were anything but obvious: Suburban public officials had hidden interests in real estate. They used their government positions to benefit themselves, business partners and family members. Developers made large contributions. A judge who was a land speculator used his authority to change the landscape to his benefit. The newspaper used computer databases to look for linkages among 2,000 corporations, 35,000 licensed builders and real estate agents.

Homeowners might violate zoning rules by renting out part of their home in a single-family zone or by conducting business from that home. Do zoning restrictions make sense? Are accessory apartments actually less disruptive than allowable apartment complexes? Do at-home businesses mean more eyes on the street, which can lead to inexpensive crime prevention? In many neighborhoods, those who talk about "quality of life" (often defined by them privately as exclusivity for the wealthy) oppose at-home businesses. The rules typically say that the principal use of a house must be residential, the casual observer should not be able to tell there is a business inside (which means no signs) and there must be no negative impact on the neighborhood, from traffic or noise.

Established residents in a neighborhood might dream of cashing in when developers eye the area. Fortunes can be made by those who have advance knowledge of designs affecting the value of land, such as master plans or locations of exits to a superhighway planned by the government. Suppose, for example, a developer is tipped that a new community master plan will allow high-rise apartments in a previously low-density residential area. The developer can buy the best land in the area quickly, then sell it at five times the price to prospective apartment builders when the master plan is made public. Or suppose the state wants to build a limited access superhighway through what is now largely farmland. The exits will be 15 miles apart. A land speculator is tipped to the exact locations of the exits, then buys the land around them. The farmers who sell know nothing about the planned exits, so they accept a low price. When the highway is completed, the speculator makes a bundle selling or leasing the land around the exits for gas stations, motels and fast-food restaurants.

There are many questions to ask: Who owns the tract the city plans to buy for a landfill? For an airport? Who owns adjacent land, which will increase in value once the new facility is built? The Urban Land Institute, Washington, D.C., is one of many organizations that can assist in answering the questions. Especially in the American West, there are lots of land controversies revolving around low sales prices and rents paid by ranchers, miners, timber interests. Those ridiculously low fees are granted by the federal government, in accordance with congressional policy as carried out by the Bureau of Land Management. The reason behind the low fees seems to be political clout rather than sound economic or environmental policy. Richard Rhodes' book "Farm" touches on issues such as the abuse of farmland while raising crops and livestock; temporary loss of productive land to gain government payments for not growing crops; permanent loss of productive land to build homes, office complexes, retail stores or factories. John Opie's "The Law of the Land: 200 Years of American Farmland Policy" is also valuable.

Leonard Downie Jr. researched a classic investigative book, "Mortgage on America: The Real Cost of Real Estate Speculation." A few of the many helpful interest groups are Associated Builders and Contractors, the National Home Builders Association, the American Institute of Architects, the American Resort Development Association, the National Trust for Historic Preservation, Preservation Action, the American Farm Bureau Federation, the National Farmers Organization, and the American Planning Institute, all of Washington, D.C.; the National Roofing Contractors Association, Rosemont, Ill.; the Mechanical Contractors Association of America, Rockville, Md.; the National Farmers Union, Denver. The magazine Professional Builder and Remodeler, Newton, Mass., is one of many periodicals to consult. Richard F. Babcock's book "The Zoning Game" is a standard. Babcock also wrote "The Zoning Game Revisited" with Charles L. Siemon. Terry J. Lassar's book "Carrots and Sticks: New Zoning Downtown" is another useful title. Sometimes zoning has nothing directly to do with big-bucks development. Instead, it is used to keep out "undesirables"—unpopular religious sects that want to build a church, halfway houses for ex-convicts, group homes for the mentally ill, housing for lower-income residents, and the like.

Low-Income Housing and Homelessness

The least desirable residential sites in a geographic area tend to be chosen for public housing. Superficial daily articles about degraded life in public housing projects are common. Many of the stories are marred by the presumption that public housing has to be that way. They are also marred by lack of history and perspective. Who chose the site and why? Who designed the project so stupidly? Who won the building contract and why? Were the bids competitive? Who holds the maintenance contract and why? Are the volunteer board members conscientious and honest? Why would they want such a seemingly thankless duty? Is there profit to be made somehow? Who chose them and why? Is the public housing security force composed of local police department rejects who are prone to brutality? Why does the housing authority manage the project the way it does? Has criticism from below (the tenants) and above (the U.S. Department of Housing and Urban Development regional office) been on target? Has anybody locally made any changes as a result?

So many opportunities exist for corruption. The Fort Lauderdale Sun-Sentinel told of a housing inspector working with local contractors to fix bids on repairs to low-income homes in return for a cut of the inflated price. The money to play with came from a $1 million annual government program to help low-income residents improve their living conditions. When a house needed work, the corrupt inspectors chose from a rotating list of six contractors who supposedly bid competitively. But a corrupt inspector was guiding the bidding so the winner padded it by 10 percent. The inspector and contractor split the overcharge.

Journalists often fail to detect such chicanery. They missed a HUD scandal that continued for years, centered on well-connected presidential campaign contributors and friends of Cabinet secretaries winning contracts for meritless projects. The trade publication Multi-Housing News published some details the earliest. The Washington Post and other major news organizations wound up embarrassed. Irving Welfeld's insider book, "HUD Scandals: Howling Headlines and Silent Fiascoes," tells part of the story. The Washington Post's Howard Kurtz relates the lapses in his book "Media Circus."

Some journalists, on the other hand, have found low-income housing scandals in their backyards. The Philadelphia Inquirer caught speculators selling homes to poverty-stricken buyers by falsifying applications for loans backed by HUD. The federal examiners were so stupid, careless or corrupt that they approved a loan to a four-year-old girl. Unsurprisingly, the unqualified mortgage holders would default after the speculators had grabbed their profitable fees. The U.S. government would then have title to houses few would want to own; as neighborhoods filled with such properties, they became less and less livable.

The federal housing program called Section Eight is supposed to subsidize rentals of existing apartments by low-income persons. But it has done less than promised partly because many landlords refuse to be subjected to federal inspections that might lead to costly and time-consuming repairs. In locales where few landlords participate, the number of qualifying affordable apartments fails to meet the demand.

To supplement HUD programs, the U.S. Farmers Home Administration (FmHA) provides loans for rural housing. That agency is, unfortunately, also susceptible to dishonest contractors and speculators. FmHA is dependent on local offices in which farmers can influence who receives assistance. Many states supplement federal efforts to provide affordable housing. In Missouri, for example, the state Housing Development Commission issues tax-exempt bonds to increase availability of moderately priced places. But the commission is not divorced from politics, consisting as it does of the governor, lieutenant governor, attorney general, treasurer and six gubernatorial appointees. The National Association of Housing and Redevelopment Officials, National Council of State Housing Agencies, Public Housing Authorities Directors Association and National Low-Income Housing Coalition, all of Washington, D.C., are among the organizations that can provide perspective.

No matter how much low-cost housing is available, most communities will have to deal with homelessness. Some homeless people are mentally ill; others are mentally sound, but destitute; still others have money, but no will to find shelter on their own. A story in any locale is how police and other government officials deal with the homeless. Are they arrested and jailed? Are they transported to public and private-financed shelters? Are they taken for a ride, then dumped outside the county line? Are they provided with a one-way bus ticket? One book written by a homeless person is "Travels With Lizbeth" by Lars Eighner. One of many academic studies is "A Nation in Denial: The Truth About Homelessness" by Alice S. Baum and Donald W. Burnes. The National Coalition for the Homeless, Washington, D.C., and the Partnership for the Homeless, New York City, are some of the organizations devoted to the topic.

Land and Housing Fraud

Swindles encompass selling land that does not exist, land owned by someone else and land without clear title. Swindles also can involve misrepresenting the value or utility of the land that is sold. The outright swindle is obvious; misrepresentation can be more subtle. Is someone selling desert land without adequate water? Forest land miles from the nearest road or electric wires? Are prospective customers shown artists' renderings of never-to-be-built swimming pools, golf courses and clubhouses promised as part of the dream community they are being hustled to buy?

If land is being sold across state lines, the seller is supposed to register with the U.S. Department of Housing and Urban Development. The law and federal regulations contain numerous exemptions, but if registration is indeed accomplished, the documents can be revealing.

Then there is the problem of shoddy construction: What happens if a home has defects and the builder will not make good on repairs? Journalists can look for lawsuits versus builders. They can also check warranties offered by builder consortiums. Groups such as Home Owners Warranty Corp., Arlington, Va.; Residential Warranty Corp., Harrisburg, Pa.; Home Buyers Warranty Corp., Aurora, Colo.; and United Homeowners Association, Washington, D.C., a consumer group, can provide guidance. Journalists can check Federal Housing Administration and Department of Veterans Affairs loans, which allow lower down payments if a warranty exists. Housing bureaucrats within those two agencies might have heard about warranty scams that make lower down payment provisions a cruel joke.

Chapter 20

INVESTIGATING ENVIRONMENTAL ISSUES

*I*nvestigating environmental degradation is complicated. It requires an understanding of technical matters, training most journalists lack. Experience covering private-sector businesses, lobbyists, government regulatory agencies, legislatures and research institutes is required for maximum insight. It requires delving into risk—just how dangerous is dioxin, anyway, in what doses, under what conditions and to whom?—while listening to scientists with equally impeccable credentials on opposing sides. Furthermore, environmentalists expect journalists to be on their side—after all, who can oppose clean water, soil and air?—while many businesses expect to be identified as polluters no matter what they say and do. Much of the space for longer articles about environmental issues is allocated by magazines owned and operated by organizations with specific agendas. All the expectations about who will or will not be pro-environment polarize sources, making information-gathering more difficult than it ought to be. Even when opposing sources agree to talk, the journalist too often ends up with a story of dueling quotes, leaving unequipped audiences aware of a controversy but ultimately baffled about what to believe.

That happened in an otherwise admirable in-depth Wall Street Journal page-one story under the headline "Cancer Scare/How Sand on a Beach Came to Be Defined as Human Carcinogen/Tests Using Common Silica Spark a Scientific Clash Over Safety, Procedures/Sounding Grass-Roots Alarm." The sources included:

A young girl's father who was shocked to see the warning label on a bag of sand he had purchased for her backyard play area;

The owner of the store that sold the sand;

A National Cancer Institute researcher;

A U.S. Geological Survey scientist;

The widow of a former quarry worker seeking compensation for his lung cancer allegedly caused by working around silica;

U.S. Occupational Safety and Health Administration data;

A National Institute for Occupational Safety and Health bureaucrat;

Information from multiple California regulatory agencies;

A community activist;

A source at Pacific Gas and Electric Co.;

Medical doctors;

A researcher at Western Consortium for Public Health;

A researcher at Los Alamos National Laboratory;

A World Health Organization research team;

A McGill University professor;

The fire chief of an Ohio town;

Plus industry sources at the Chemical Manufacturers Association, National Industrial Sand Association and National Stone Association.

To complicate matters, there is increasing evidence, after decades of "the sky is falling" environmental stories, that the sum of the parts does not add up to disaster. As Los Angeles Times media writer David Shaw reported in a series titled "Living Scared: Why Do the Media Make Life Seem So Risky?" life expectancy is up, infant mortality down, death rates from many diseases dropping.

There are many big-picture books that discuss overall degradation of the environment: air, water, land and under the ground. Some of the most interesting are "A Fierce Green Fire: The American Environmental Movement" by Philip Shabecoff; "Forcing the Spring: The Transformation of the American Environmental Movement" by Robert Gottlieb; "Environmental Politics: Domestic and Global Dimensions" by Jacqueline Vaughn Switzer; and "Mortgaging the Earth: The World Bank, Environmental Impoverishment and the Crisis of Development" by Bruce Rich.

Many of the difficulties can be overcome by practicing techniques that would work well for any subject. Michael Fabey of the Fayetteville Observer-Times discussed many such techniques at an IRE conference emphasizing agricultural investigations that include environmental issues. Here are some excerpts:

Do not try to cover the environment or agriculture from the office; you will never have a true idea of what is going on. You have to go out there and trod through the soil with a farmer as the planting season starts or choke on the dust during a summer drought. Meet the people, feel the dirt. These are beats about the outdoors and humankind's desire to use or misuse nature. Get out there. . . .

Who is testing what and how are they doing it? Are the researchers' methods valid? When you refer to a study, make sure it has been published in a reputable journal and reviewed by the researchers' peers. Otherwise, the research may be suspect. . . .

Get to know the history. Obtain and read all available reports—such as Environmental Impact Statements—on the topic. Go through the files of every agency involved. One time, I searched through a state agency's files and found a confidential EPA report the state folks had misfiled. It was a Page-One story. . . .

Keep it simple . . . that includes numbers, too. Take the phrase "parts per million." Most people have no idea what that means. It is a penny out of $10,000. It is a minute out of two years. It is an inch out of 16 miles. . . . Also remember that while these numbers may seem small, it may only take those minute amounts to do damage. You should tell your readers how the chemicals affect the environment and people. Which organs are affected? How much of a danger is there? Do the chemicals break down into other substances that are dangerous?

The IRE Resource Center is filled with environmental investigations. The Society of Environmental Journalists, Philadelphia, has an extensive, more targeted resource center, a superb magazine and a useful membership directory. The Science Journalism Center at the University of Missouri School of Journalism also maintains a resource service and publishes how-to accounts for reporters and editors.

Government Regulation of the Environment

Potential and actual polluters come under scrutiny from city, county, state and federal government agencies. Because many journalists feel inadequate evaluating risk and hard science, they rely more heavily on government regulators as sources than on many other beats.

As always, it makes sense for journalists to think about levels and branches of government. At the federal level, the most obvious place to go for documents, computer tapes and human sources is the Environmental Protection Agency in the executive branch. Journalists should study EPA organizational charts in the U.S. Government Manual plus read the agency's annual and periodic reports to find project possibilities. Journalists can base projects on seminal questions, such as whether the agency is using criminal prosecutions against offenders rather than civil suits. Without a criminal conviction, the agency cannot ban violators from seeking government contracts.

Besides the EPA, there are many executive branch agencies with some jurisdiction over environmental enforcement, including the Army Corps of Engineers, Council on Environmental Quality, Nuclear Regulatory

Commission, as well as various bureaucracies within the Agriculture, Energy and Interior departments. To find the relevant agency within larger agencies, a journalist might have to peel away several layers of bureaucracy.

For example, the obviously relevant National Institute of Environmental Health Sciences is part of the National Institutes of Health, which in turn is part of the Public Health Service, which is a unit of the Health and Human Services Department. The Securities and Exchange Commission is requiring publicly held companies under its jurisdiction to disclose environmental information; that has led the Institute of Internal Auditors, Altamonte Springs, Fla., to publish reports such as "The Role of Internal Auditors in Environmental Issues."

Because so many environmental controversies revolve around endangered animal species, the U.S. Fish and Wildlife Service takes on exaggerated importance in the minds of many naturalists, laborers, businesspeople and legislators. The agency's rulings determine whether corporations will have to change their ways to accommodate the survival of an obscure type of owl, frog or snail. The Endangered Species Act, a federal law, is seen by some citizens as a godsend, by others as an anti-people, anti-job farce. Books such as Kathryn Phillips' "Tracking the Vanishing Frogs: An Ecological Mystery," combining depth journalism with sound science, can help generalist journalists grasp the complexities.

Within the legislative branch, numerous House and Senate committees have jurisdiction over environmental matters. An example is the House Public Works and Transportation Committee, which holds hearings on relevant issues and publishes documents such as its "Compilation of Selected Water Resources and Environmental Laws." Support arms such as the General Accounting Office and Office of Technology Assessment generate studies. In the judicial branch, courts regularly decide environmental lawsuits, some of which are argued by the Justice Department, some by the solicitor general. Rosemary O'Leary's book "Environmental Change: Federal Courts and the EPA" can provide understanding.

At lower levels of government, the pattern is similar. In Missouri, for example, the lead executive branch agency is the Department of Natural Resources, which includes the divisions of environmental quality, energy and state parks. It generates reports such as "Confirmed, Abandoned or Uncontrolled Hazardous Waste Disposal Sites in Missouri," with a detailed narrative about each location. Besides bureaucrats in their capital city offices, human sources include state conservation agents, who see a lot in the field.

State legislatures, like Congress, have multiple committees with environmental jurisdiction; the state courts, like their federal counterparts, hear environmental cases; some of them are argued by the state attorney general. The National Association of Attorneys General, Washington, D.C., can provide information about where responsibility for environmental prosecution resides, state by state; the group also publishes a newsletter about significant cases. Evan J. Ringquist's book "Environmental Protection at the State Level: Politics and Progress in Controlling Pollution" is helpful.

Sometimes, as with every issue, legislators, regulators and judges are part of the problem rather than part of the solution. The revolving door between public and private sectors, covered most thoroughly in Chapter 7, is a problem. The Austin American-Statesman documented relationships between polluting industries and the state Air Control Board. Former board officials routinely went to work for companies interested in finding less costly ways to comply with the rules, or evade the rules.

The National Law Journal documented government complicity in environmental racism caused by siting hazardous waste dumps in low-income and minority neighborhoods. The reporters knew, as they said in their IRE Awards entry form:

> for more than a decade, activists in both the environmental and civil rights movements have argued that minority communities have become a hazardous pollution dumping ground. Enough evidence emerged for the Environmental Protection Agency to admit that minority communities do bear a disproportionate share of pollution risks. Still lacking was scrutiny of what role, if any, the federal government played in creating this imbalance. The greatest journalistic challenge was to find a way to quantify in hard numbers whether EPA was culpable.

The reporters obtained a computer diskette of 1,177 toxic waste sites and 1,214 civil lawsuits brought by the EPA concerning those sites, among other information. After detailed analysis of the data combined with extensive interviewing, the reporters concluded

> a community's color influences the way the federal government cleans up toxic waste sites and punishes polluters. When the EPA goes after violators in court, it gets as much as 500 percent more in money fines against polluters of white communities than those who have contaminated minority communities. In some regions, cleanup of the most serious abandoned hazardous waste dumps (so-called Superfund sites) begins three years later in minority areas than in white areas. In fact, minority communities wait a year longer than white communities for their toxic sites even to gain Superfund status. EPA fails to select the Superfund law's preferred clean-up method in minority areas, choosing more often merely to cap or isolate the pollution. In white areas, it more often attacks pollution directly, as the law requires.

The attention to the long-standing problem led to a White House executive order on environmental justice for minority and low-income populations. But as is so often the case, the expression of national will has led to little action satisfactory to residents of contaminated areas. Detailed information is available in a book edited by Robert D. Bullard, "Unequal Protection: Environmental Justice and Communities of Color," and in Michael B. Gerrard's book "Whose Backyard, Whose Risk: Fear and Fairness in Toxic and Nuclear Waste Siting."

In such geographic areas, cancer clusters or other pockets of disease are common. Proving that such diseases are directly linked to environmental hazards is difficult. The Toxic Release Inventory (TRI) kept by the EPA, as mandated by the Emergency Planning and Community Right-to-Know Act, can be a sensible starting point. Data submitted to the EPA on Form R include names and addresses of factories that manufacture, process or otherwise use any of hundreds of toxic chemicals. Discharges into water, air and soil are documented. By law, the agency makes the information available on a computer database. The main outlet is the Toxicology Data Network (TOXNET), from the National Library of Medicine. State agencies often make TRI data available more quickly than TOXNET does.

By using TRI, journalists can answer such questions as how much benzene industrial plants in a particular county released into a particular river, the names and addresses of a particular city's steel plants importing lead or the amount of chlorine gas released by a particular company into the air.

Brant Houston and Kenton Robinson of the Hartford Courant wrote in Uplink about how they used the Toxic Release Inventory to discover that Connecticut manufacturers had failed to report millions of pounds of emissions required by law to be disclosed; that of the emissions reported, ozone-eating Freon was on the increase, despite pledges by industries to cut back; that some factories were dumping toxic chemicals into city sewage treatment plants; and that the state environmental agency had inaccurately reported emissions to downplay the magnitude of the problem.

After becoming proficient with the EPA information, Houston and Robinson said they "matched the database with a state database on pollution from sewer treatment plants, used our database for daily stories and for a longer story on ozone-eating chemicals, gave information from it to many bureau reporters, and analyzed transfers of chemicals to landfills and private disposal treatment companies."

Writing in a later issue of Uplink, Adam Berliant, then a Seattle freelancer, discussed how he went beyond federal Toxic Release Inventory data to study state hazardous waste manifests meant to track toxic material shipped from an institution's premises. The Resource Conservation and Recovery Act requires shippers to complete a uniform hazardous waste manifest:

> Despite the name, there is no such thing as a standardized form. Some manufacturers actually generate their own forms. However, the law does specify reporting requirements. The manifest must not only describe hazardous

material in superb detail, but also must specify who is transporting the material, where it is going (even if out of state), when the material is shipped and just about anything else you would want to know about the material's transport, delivery and disposal.

Air Pollution

There are so many manifestations of air pollution that journalists find it difficult to track them all. As a result, it makes sense to single out one aspect and master it before moving to the next manifestation. For example, in some locales acid rain is an obvious topic. Under the federal Clean Air Act, EPA headquarters, its regional offices plus state pollution agencies compile information about locations of hazardous substances as well as emissions from specific work sites. The Alliance for Acid Rain Control and Energy Policy, Washington, D.C., can provide details. The depletion of the ozone layer and endangered airborne species are two other results of air pollution. The Association of Local Air Pollution Control Officials, Washington, D.C., can provide information about the leading troubles in any given geographic area. Such sources can discuss solutions, too. For example, are some governments trying to reduce transportation pollution by pushing fuels that pollute less than traditional gasoline, requiring commuter car pooling, mandating emission inspections every time a driver's license or license plate is renewed, among other possibilities? If nothing innovative is happening, why not? The book "Vanishing Air," researched in the late 1960s by Ralph Nader's Study Group on Air Pollution and written primarily by John C. Esposito, shows that in many important ways, little has changed. A more recent exposé is Michael H. Brown's "The Toxic Cloud: The Poisoning of America's Air."

Indoor air pollution can be a problem in homes, offices and public buildings. Regulations from the Occupational Safety and Health Administration have spawned legal battles about whether building owners or tenants have responsibility for compliance. Is better ventilation provided by the owner the answer, or should workers change their routines and update their equipment? What about smoking and secondhand smoke? Roberta Altman's "The Complete Book of Home Environmental Hazards" covers lead, asbestos, radon and other elements. Journalists can explore whether real estate agents, landlords and homeowners are living up to their obligations to warn tenants and buyers under the Residential Lead-Based Paint Hazard Reduction Act. The Village Voice reported on the health threats caused by a chemical emitted from dry cleaning establishments. People living or working in buildings shared with dry cleaners might inhale air with more of the chemical than deemed healthy. Noise pollution is a type of airborne pollution little noticed by journalists.

The Noise Regulation Report, Silver Spring, Md., is useful for its story suggestions.

Water Pollution

As with every type of pollution, water coverage revolves to a large extent around sweeping federal laws, in this instance the Clean Water Act and Safe Drinking Water Act. Factories, sewage treatment plants and other facilities are supposed to report discharges into waterways. Documents generated by the process include national pollution discharge system permits, discharge monitor reports, quarterly noncompliance reports, violation warnings, violation notices and orders to cease.

When the Fort Wayne Journal-Gazette received a tip about local companies discharging chemicals into the municipal sewer system without adequate government monitoring, a reporter found a list of companies tied into the system, their discharge permits, inspection reports by the city, court records of companies fined and the sewer department's annual reports. With that information in hand, he had his story.

Journalists can look close to home for unsafe water. The editor of the Daily News in Washington, N.C., was paying his water bill when he noticed a statement on the back about the town's drinking source being tested for chemicals. Curiosity spawned persistent reporting that turned up a scandal: Local officials had known for eight years that the local drinking water supply contained amounts of elements that might be causing cancer, but had said nothing publicly.

The Progressive magazine found about 30,000 small water systems serving fewer than 3,000 customers each, mostly in rural areas. Some of them had never installed equipment to bring drinking water up to minimum federal standards, but regulators had done nothing to force compliance. When WAGA-TV, Atlanta, explored local water-borne disease, it found a municipal plant with operators unlicensed or sleeping on the job. Consumer Reports magazine found higher levels of lead in water than previously found by cities' own tests.

The Maine Times found towns having trouble with sewer systems after heavy rains. Rainwater runoff was overflowing into streams and rivers without being treated first. As water shortages reach many locales, some treat waste water heavily, then use it as drinking water. Is that happening? If so, is the treatment process considered safe by relatively unbiased experts outside the locale? Has the citizenry been informed?

Agricultural land close to home is sometimes the source of pollution, as pesticides, fertilizers and other chemicals applied to the soil run off into the water. Scientists and government bureaucrats sometimes refer to that as nonpoint source pollution because its origin cannot be traced to a single pipe or other obvious outlet. Wetland areas, meant to naturally filter water, sometimes become the center of controversy because farmers want to use the land to plant and developers want to drain the land for apartments, offices or residential subdivisions. The National Conference of State Legislatures provides perspective in its publication "Wetlands Protection and the States."

The operation of dams by the U.S. Army Corps of Engineers or other government entities is yet another possible cause of environmental degradation. Sometimes dams lead to new recreation areas. Journalists near water recreation areas can examine how much pollution comes from pleasure boaters, many of whom never think of themselves as polluters. The Environmental Protection Agency has recognized pleasure boats as a source of water and air pollution.

So many groups can provide perspectives. In Washington, D.C., are Clean Water Action, American Rivers, National Ocean Industries Association, International Association of Fish and Wildlife Agencies and National Association of Water Companies. The Water Environment Federation, Alexandria, Va.; National Fisheries Institute, Arlington, Va.; and Ducks Unlimited, Memphis, Tenn., are a few other groups that can help journalists on water pollution stories.

Soil Pollution

The term "Superfund" is shorthand for a program created by Congress and implemented by the Environmental Protection Agency as part of the Comprehensive Environmental Response, Compensation and Liability Act. The purpose was to identify, seal off and cleanup sites laced with toxic wastes. The identification process seems to work well, giving journalists the opportunity to find out about sites in their locales. But the sealing and cleaning portions have gone less well. A Lexis database search of Superfund sites can be done by name of the responsible party, county, state, congressional district or specific locale.

A reporter at the Burlington Free Press in Vermont knew a barge canal site had been on the Superfund list for years. She decided to check on the cleanup's progress. She read documents at the EPA regional office and the state natural resources agency and conducted interviews. She found bungled scientific studies, inexplicable delays and cost estimates that had jumped from $3 million to $50 million.

Journalists should find out whether the EPA has asked site owners and managers to complete "information requests" to identify "potentially responsible parties" for cleanup costs. If a cleanup has begun, who won the contract and how? Who is auditing that company's performance and what auditing reports are available? Among the books that can help are

"Superfund: The Political Economy of Environmental Risk" by John A. Hird and "Cleaning Up the Mess: Implementation Strategies in Superfund" by Thomas W. Church and Robert T. Nakamura.

Beyond the draconian designation of Superfund site, there are other dangers to the soil. Pesticides, insecticides and fertilizers used in agriculture often increase yields per acre and improve the outward appearance of produce, but the downside can be serious for the environment. Rachel Carson's 1962 book "Silent Spring" still reverberates, as can be seen from the title of a congressional committee report, "Thirty Years After 'Silent Spring': Status of EPA's Review of Older Pesticides."

Soil might undergo long-term contamination, with consumers who eat the produce grown in that soil ingesting harmful substances that can cause or hasten a variety of ailments, including cancer. The Federal Insecticide, Fungicide and Rodenticide Act requires producers of the substances to file reports with EPA. Another federal law, the Toxic Substances Control Act, triggers reporting requirements, too. The cumulative effect is shown by no-till farming: It has cut back soil erosion by leaving the previous season's fields undisturbed. That in turn has reduced pesticide runoff into nearby streams. But to increase crop yields in an untilled operation, farmers have started using more herbicides.

Because so much controversy exists over what is dangerous and at which levels, sometimes the best that journalists can do is report the various sides of the debate, making sure to consult a broad range of qualified sources, delving into their ulterior motives (if any) and evaluating the soundness of measurements used. Sources include the National Association of Conservation Districts, National Agricultural Chemicals Council and National Coalition Against the Misuse of Pesticides, all of Washington, D.C., plus National Pest Control Association, Dunn Loring, Va. The book "Circle of Poison" by David Weir and Mark Schapiro demonstrates the dangers of exporting marginal pesticides for use by farmers with no training in handling them safely.

There is more than toxic material to monitor. Solid waste disposal of nontoxic trash is taken for granted by most journalists. Like other citizens, they leave their daily trash for somebody to cart away. But they should be asking questions. Controversy exists about the appropriate siting of landfills, whether incineration is more evil than good, how much landfills pollute subsurface water and whether locales ought to have unrestrained access to dumping garbage across municipal, county or state lines. Is the waste handled by government employees or private companies? Whatever the answer, do the workers have the training to handle the waste in accordance with the law? Is the current service more cost-effective than the alternative? Is the garbage subject to local flow-control laws that force all pick-ups in a defined geographic area into a government dump? When governments create such monopolies, they often charge higher fees than would be the case if competition existed. As a result, court challenges arise. If the challenges succeed, local governments might be stuck with underused, money-losing facilities.

When governments raise taxes and user fees because the dump is full or a source of pollution or both, journalists rarely ask questions. Yet much of what the citizenry believes about garbage disposal is myth. For instance, plastic is not the item slowest to degrade. Newsprint and other types of paper (including discarded telephone directories) are bigger problems. Recycling programs, either voluntary or mandated, sound good from an environmental standpoint and often are. But journalists should document the true costs to taxpayers who participate, as well as to those who do not. If the program loses money to the extent that governments cut back other services, attractiveness starts looking relative. On the other hand, maybe governments should subsidize recycling, much as they subsidize mass transportation. Journalists should examine the claims of businesses that say their products are recyclable. Technically, almost any product—including disposable diapers—can be recycled, but only if the right conditions exist. State attorneys general sometimes cite businesses for making exaggerated claims for recycling.

Is incineration a sensible alternative? Burning to save space in the landfill sounds good until citizens learn about the air pollution that results. The Reporter Dispatch, White Plains, N.Y., found a garbage-burning plant exceeded federal limits. Instead of working toward compliance, government officials tried to raise permissible emission levels. If an incinerator is being used, how does it compare in cost-effectiveness and pollution control to a cement kiln? Both technologies yield amazing results, according to their proponents. It is up to journalists to measure those claims as accurately as possible.

An element of any investigation into waste disposal should be spending lots of time at the dump to see what really is discarded, how it is handled by the employees and how little space is left. Another technique: Follow waste from its source. WFAA-TV, Dallas, did that to document illegal practices of waste disposal companies draining restaurant grease into sewers, dumping it on private property and mixing it in hazardous chemicals.

Military bases are exempt from some laws and regulations; even when they are subject to the rules, they often act as if they were not. Journalists near military bases should inquire who collects the toxic and nontoxic wastes generated there and where it goes. Then journalists should ask for ride-alongs to verify what they are told. The IRE Resource Center contains an entire section on military mishandling of wastes. Seth Shulman's book "The Threat at Home: Confronting the Toxic Legacy of the U.S. Military" contains background. Other federal lands are also polluted heavily, including mines, oil and gas wells, irrigation drainage canals and factories manufacturing radioactive materials.

Understanding the leading federal law, the Resource Conservation and Recovery Act, can help journalists sort through the issues; knowing state and local law is also important. Sources include the Association of State and Territorial Solid Waste Management Officials, the Council on Plastics and Packaging, the Institute of Scrap Recycling Industries and the National Solid Wastes Management Association, all of Washington, D.C. The book "Global Dumping Ground," a collaboration between the Center for Investigative Reporting and Bill Moyers, exposes dangerous methods for disposing trash that ought to be handled more responsibly. "Rubbish!: The Archaeology of Garbage" by William Rathje and Cullen Murphy explodes myths about solid waste. Also useful is Jennifer Seymour Whitaker's book "Salvaging the Land of Plenty: Garbage and the American Dream."

Extracting natural resources such as coal, copper and gold from the ground causes its own brand of environmental degradation. Numerous mining laws and regulations are supposed to minimize long-term damage, but sometimes are ineffective. Groups that can provide perspective include the National Coal Association, United Mine Workers of America, American Mining Congress, American Petroleum Institute and American Forest Council, all of Washington, D.C., and the Society of American Foresters, Bethesda, Md. The book "Public Domain, Private Dominion: A History of Public Mineral Policy in America" by Carl J. Mayer and George A. Riley is one of several primers.

■ PAPER AND COMPUTER TRAILS AND HUMAN SOURCES

The Toxic Release Inventory is only one of many resources available to journalists embarking on environmental projects. Connected to the inventory are toxicological profiles for many of the hazardous substances involved. The Agency for Toxic Substances and Disease Registry, connected to the U.S. Public Health Service, publishes the profiles.

Another rich resource cutting across boundaries is the environmental impact statement for a specific project.

Whenever federal money is involved in a project that could have negative environmental impact, a journalist should assume an impact statement is available until specifically learning otherwise. The Federal Register is filled with notices of impact statements being initiated or finished. They emanate in such places as the Federal Highway Administration when it helps finance a new road in Tennessee or the Fish and Wildlife Service when it alters the habitat of an endangered species. Completed reports are available from the agency; they are frequently filed in local public libraries, too.

The federal government publishes Access EPA, available in hard copy or on-line. The reference work explains how to find information within the EPA on every environmental topic. Because technology and general science knowledge are so vital to the environmental beat, journalists can broaden their base by consulting bibliographies such as Information Sources in

Science and Technology by C.D. Hurt. Other useful reference works include The Environmentalist's Bookshelf: A Guide to the Best Books by Robert Merideth and Environmental Encyclopedia from Gale Research.

A complete list of organizations housing environmental experts would take many pages of this book. A few of the most useful are the Federal Energy Bar Association, Friends of the Earth, the American Council for an Energy-Efficient Economy, the Citizen/Labor Energy Coalition, Worldwatch Institute, the Environmental Law Institute, the National Audubon Society, Resources for the Future, the World Wildlife Fund and Wilderness Society, all of Washington, D.C.; the Sierra Club, San Francisco; the Union of Concerned Scientists, Cambridge, Mass.: the American Academy of Environmental Engineers, Annapolis, Md.; Environmental Action, Takoma Park, Md.; the Izaak Walton League of America, Arlington, Va.; the Natural Resources Defense Council and the Environmental Defense Fund, New York City.

Many of these groups publish magazines that circulate widely beyond the membership. Other environmental magazines are not affiliated with activist groups, such as Garbage, E and Outside. Environmental newsletters abound, including those from the Bureau of National Affairs, Washington, D.C., and Business Publishers Inc., Silver Spring, Md.

Journalism organizations whose members specialize in environmental coverage include the Society of Environmental Journalists, Philadelphia; Science Journalism Center, Columbia, Mo.; as well as the Council for the Advancement of Science Writing and National Association of Science Writers, both of Greenlawn, N.Y.

Chapter *21*

INVESTIGATING THE WORLD OF THE DISADVANTAGED

*O*ne cliché of investigative journalism is the importance of comforting the afflicted and afflicting the comfortable. Many of the afflicted are poor. Many of the afflicted poor are racial and ethnic minorities. Many are also women, juveniles, the aged and the physically disabled.

Uncovering and explaining welfare, poverty, poverty-related crime, child abuse and neglect are touched on many other places in this book. Social services are delivered through the schools and health-care system, so chapters 8 and 14 contain material related to this chapter. Because governments are usually in the middle of poverty and discrimination controversies, chapters 6 and 7 have special relevance, too. Because so much race, ethnicity, gender, age and physical disability discrimination is connected to the workplace, Chapter 12 covers those topics. This chapter expands on references in earlier chapters as well as introducing new areas of discussion.

The discussion of investigating the disadvantaged begins with an article that Robin Palley of the Philadelphia Daily News wrote for the IRE Journal. At the top of the article was a passage about Eugene Roberts, then editor of the Philadelphia Inquirer, that inspired Palley. The passage reflects Roberts' belief that the best investigative journalists should be "zigging when everyone else is zagging." The key, he said, "is to pry reporters away from officialdom and get them out there with real people, where they can find stories that 'do not break . . . but trickle, seep and ooze.'"

Here we pick up Palley's piece:

Roberts is right about ooze. The poverty beat is that way. Nobody announces what is going on. Sure, people will summon you when they release studies or announce hot programs. Information comes in regularly from Washington think tanks and local agencies.

But basically, the poverty story isn't there. It is on the street. The poverty beat is a beat without paid spokespeople, and by nature, it is about those who have little or no voice in our society. The story of poverty over the past decade, the feminization of poverty, did not even ooze efficiently. It did not reach public consciousness—if it even has now—until after the rate of increase of poverty among female-headed households leveled off. During the period of change, we blithely went on reporting as we always have about that famous Family of Four, Living Below the Poverty Level (mostly mentioning them in eligibility requirement stories). Ask audience members who makes up that family. They will probably say a mother, father and two children rather than the more common one-parent and three-child family. The nature of the families to be served changed, while the nature of programs (originally set up to help the main wage earner regain work while the spouse cared for children) has not changed much.

Traditionally, journalists listen to the advocates for the poor, like social workers, to government agencies or to adversaries who want to cut this or that program, to academics and to occasional whistleblowers with important stories to tell of bureaucracies run amok. Those tips yield some good stories, but they are second-generation stories, once removed from the subject.

Studies and census data eventually pointed to the feminization of poverty, but an ear to neighborhoods where block after block are inhabited by nearly all women and children would have told us sooner, and in a way audiences can relate to better.

Looking and listening—the things we should do best—would have been faster than reporting through traditional approaches, like covering poverty through gloves. Here's how it goes too often: A reporter making a middle-class-or-better salary listens to a bureaucrat or social service professional making a middle-class-or-better salary and reports through a middle-class filter—relying on a lot of telephone reporting and visits to office buildings. Such reporting often misses the point.

The point, to my eyes, is where the giant pyramid of programs and services comes to rest. Picture this pyramid, all the programs in your city, inverted. Its point at the bottom sits on the shoulders of a child, or an adult, or a family. It may not matter if there are 150 or 1,050 programs in place to help them at great cost to taxpayers and volunteers, while supporting an army of do-gooders.

It may not matter because, listening to poor women for a year, we [Palley and her colleagues on the project] found that most often the intended recipients of these services cannot find access to the right programs. The poor spend days getting the paperwork together to meet program criteria. Or they show up for regular monitoring appointments while spending bus fare of $1.50 each way for the adult, plus the kids' fares. Simply being poor takes up every waking moment and every spare dollar. We saw women who showed us that poverty is their full-time job, with survival leaving no time for real job training toward real economic progress. Every appointment took hours, every bill to pay meant a half-hour line.

In an effort to stay afloat, people "game" the system, getting into more programs than they need just to extract the appropriate supportive parts they seek. Or they find ways to cheat enough to stay out of homeless shelters or maintain access to vital Medicaid health protection for themselves and their children.

Research again and again points up a lack of coordination of services, when services are viewed by the recipient rather than the provider. Too often stupid glitches botch up otherwise well-planned efforts. Some are simple: The case of the voice-mail system that answers the phone with instructions on what buttons to push for which services while most callers have dial, or rotary, telephones. Some are complex, like Medicaid rules that cover only certain costly treatments for people who are hospitalized and will not cover the same treatment for them if they must be home to care for children or aged relatives.

We can report on holes in the safety net with the same vigor we normally reserve for busted bureaucracies and wasted dollars. To do this with maximum effectiveness, here are some practical steps.

On Appearance

Do not create additional distance between yourself and your subject, beyond the unavoidable. That is, if you are lucky enough to drive a midlife-crisis red sportscar, do not drive it to the housing project. Take the bus, take a company car, do anything but look like a rich kid arriving in povertyland.

This seems obvious. In real life it is not. I have seen reporters make dumb mistakes. In the course of reporting my project, I took off my wedding ring. I learned not to carry a pocketbook for my money, driver's license, keys and press card. Instead, I stashed them in my pocket or wore a belt pouch that I would never have to keep an eye on. Clutching a bag close looks like you do not trust anyone. Putting it down anywhere invites its disappearance.

Accessories I wear daily were not right on this beat. One day in front of a shelter for the homeless, a woman I had been working with said, "Look at you, hon, the way these junkies do. You want them to talk to you? Do not tempt them." She looked at my black plastic watch: "That's a three-cap watch." My oldest cloth sneakers she dubbed "two-cap shoes." And, she added, "That haircut looks like a downtown job. . . . People think you are a social worker or a cop."

On Social Worker Syndrome

Figure out what social workers and cops wear, and do not wear that. For me it meant changing from long floppy skirts and leather flats to jeans, T-shirts and sneakers. Too many women asked me whether I was there to take their children away. It made them terribly uncomfortable and did not leave me feeling much better. No need to create extra hurdles to interviews. That goes for the reporter in the tweed jacket and shirt and tie, too.

On Cop Cars

If your company has company cars, and those cars have numbers on the back, be prepared to be seen as an undercover cop. Make it clear that you are not, right away. It gets in the way of reporting and can be downright dangerous. A clipping with my byline seemed to work better than a press pass with the people I dealt with. The press pass was too much like flashing a badge, one woman told me.

On Checkbook Journalism

Poor people we wanted to interview wanted to get paid much of the time. Obviously, that does not go. But if it is permissible to take a corporate type out for a business lunch, why not a poor person who is just as much a source? A photographer and I took several good sources out for working lunches and found food to be an effective way to say thanks without doing anything unethical.

Also, we would go out with a stack of the day's Daily News in the car. Whenever we would knock on a door, we would have one tucked under one arm. We'd leave it when we departed and would offer it to the interviewee. They were great for building goodwill.

On Skepticism

Real people with real stories who have so little income that they have gotten by on their wits and their words for years are every bit as sharp as the sharpest public relations person. They know how to present their stories to their best advantage. You may be off guard. That baby is so cute, that story so compelling. Listen with empathy and connection. But at every turn, ask, "How do you know that? Did you see that yourself? Can you take me to the person who did? Do you have the paper they gave you when they turned you down?" You need to know whether this source has ever used drugs or has been in jail recently. Do not let people ply you with great stories and perfect quotes that might be balderdash.

The Give and Take

You want something. You have to give something to get it. You can deliver in many ways: the information trade (maybe you can get help with this problem here, and here is the main phone number of the agency). Or offer to hold the baby while the woman chases the toddler who has just dashed into the street.

I once had to help a woman fry fish at dinner time for her children and grandchildren so she would not have to tell me to leave so she could get her work done. My job was to report the story. Hers was to fry the fish. If you are in the way, you are part of the problem. Get out of the way and into the pace. Yes, this is unorthodox. I'm not sure that maintaining appropriate distance from subjects is possible on this beat. When you schedule a day shadowing an executive to write about the duties of being CEO, he or she delegates like crazy to a secretary and aide to make room for your demand on the day. With the poor, that is impossible. I have done interviews on buses on the way to pick up children at day care and in welfare offices waiting for checks.

On Confidentiality

Revealing the new address of a battered woman whose abusive spouse still seeks her could cost her life. Revealing the names of recovering drug addicts and their children can bring them prejudice in the housing and job markets and cost them their roof or livelihood. Be sure, even more than usual, that the rules of what is on the record, off the record and on but not for attribution are clear. If you gain access, as I did, to confidential therapy sessions, explain the rules of how you will clear material for use with participants. Do not make pledges too easily, and once made, never violate them.

Your Own Eyes

Some of what happens to the poor is inconceivable to people who have grown up in the middle class. I went with a woman to a housing office and saw how she was treated. My dog would have been treated better. I waited with women for three to four hours in clinics for their sick babies to be seen.

Do not report on these things from a distance. Go with someone. Watch what happens when their speech or dress indicate their class. See what happens in the same office if you step to the desk with the same request (without identifying yourself as a reporter, which would obviously distort the entire interaction).

While the ethics code in your newsroom may not allow you to go undercover, you will gain an incredible sensitivity to your subject after seeing his/her life through your eyes. Things so normal that your subject will not even mention them to you will slap you in the face.

A Word on Safety

Look yourself in the eye. Fear will not work in these situations. You are going into dangerous turf? The people you want to talk to live there every day.

Find yourself a protector. Ask around for the neighborhood grandmother or church lady, the beat cop, youth worker or anyone who can put out the word on you. Meet that person first. You will need a reference in new territory.

When possible, the reporter and photographer need to work together so one can watch while the other shoots or writes. Carry a mobile phone if your paper supplies one. Have the phone number of someone at the paper already programmed in so one touch of the "send" button will get your call through. Make sure he/she has, in writing, where you are, who you are seeing, and what time you expect to check in.

Selling the Stories

Editors and news directors are often turned off by down-and-out hard-luck stories. Why would they want to read or view them? Why would anyone? If the poor already know they are living this life and the wealthier are too depressed by the first few sentences to finish, why bother?

Because human nature is about moving along with hope, toward somewhere. Find the hope, the joy in the misery. Find the common human element. Go for the emotional center of the story. This is the key to your selling job: the hope, the triumph, along with the horrible and the tragic. We told the story of an addicted family in rags, the kids in filthy diapers, the suicidal young mother stinking, and the grandmother who led them all to the mayor's office to beg for help. The office of the woman who heard their story had to be disinfected after they left. But we did not tell the story at that point. We followed the family for months and told the story of their recovery and return to life in the mainstream.

Ordinary people become extraordinary heroes every day in neighborhoods where survival requires that heroism be mundane. Find these quiet leaders and tell their stories, using them as a window on the lives of others. Through the person of a grandmother who took in a stranger's child in the projects one night, I told the story of that child and her family that had gone up in a smoky drug haze. By coming at the story through the older woman, I was able to tell a tale of hope.

Sure, you cannot do that when a life of promise is snuffed out in a corner shootout. But usually there is a silver lining in a story, somewhere. It is the key to involving your audience and insulating them a little against the pain.

At times like this, propose a new format. Do not use an anecdotal lead and a statistical nut graph, followed by an overview of the scope of the problem. Blow up that anecdotal lead like popcorn to be the whole story, with a nut graph for context divided into little phrases scattered throughout the first section of the story. Put the statistical backdrop and scope of the issue in the sidebar or related video clip. Readers and viewers love it that way; they write wonderful letters about how the stories have touched their lives.

On Persistence

A story about an unpopular subject that does not appear to have a strong statistical basis, written in an unconventional format, will not make you a newsroom hero. But if you know that your material is strong and that the person whose story you are telling is truly representative of a large class of people, set a bulldog jaw; convince people that what you have seen is not the worst story on earth you could find, but an alarmingly typical one. Get an editor to meet a subject, if necessary. Drag one to the rehabilitation center graduation or the homeless shelter for a brown-bag lunch.

Tom Brune of the Chicago Sun-Times expanded on Palley's themes in an IRE conference handout suggesting the range of human sources who can be consulted on poverty and discrimination projects.

1. Community organizations. These groups include the most active residents of an area. The activists in turn know people whose stories can illustrate your story.
2. Legal aid groups, such as legal assistance foundations, public defenders, public guardians and public interest law firms. These groups have clients who often want to tell their stories.
3. Local and federal court officials and the files they keep.
4. Churches and church-based agencies such as Catholic Charities, Lutheran Social Services and the Jewish Federation. They deal directly with people you might want to interview.

5. Other charities, such as United Way, that provide direct services or are active in the issues of race and poverty.

6. Social workers at welfare agencies. They have many cases to choose from if they want to provide information. (In Missouri, each Division of Family Services county office is supposed to consult with an advisory commission appointed by elected officials; two current or former welfare recipients should be part of each county advisory commission.)

7. Interest groups, such as organizations created to push for better housing.

8. Human relations commissions, part of a local or state government structure.

9. Persons who write letters to the editor of the local newspaper.

10. Cold calls into a neighborhood based on names from the city directory or some other source.

Documenting the World of Poverty

The advice from Palley and Brune is applicable to any topic involving coverage of those dependent on government assistance meant to help those below the poverty line. The most pervasive term used to describe the poverty umbrella is "welfare." That general term carries lots of negative connotations. Linda Gordon, author of the book "Pitied But Not Entitled: Single Mothers and the History of Welfare," commented that in the past 50 years, the meaning of the word has reversed from prosperity and social respect to poverty and social disrespect.

Writing in Ms. magazine under an assumed name, a former welfare recipient told of the daily humiliation, much of which could be documented by alert journalists. A white woman with three children, the author said she had to apply for welfare after her husband of 14 years abandoned the family, then quit his job and left the state rather than pay child support. The eight-by-ten foot apartment she had to accept for the family was crawling with maggots and had no heat. By the third week of every month, welfare benefits had run out, making it difficult to feed the family even one nutritious meal a day.

When she visited the welfare office, the staff phrased their questions in insulting ways: "Do you know who the father of your children is?" rather than "Who is the father of your children?" She looked for a job with the understanding she would receive subsidized child care. She got a job. Then she learned about 700 names were on the subsidized child-care list before hers. It would take years before her name rose to the top. She kept the job anyway. It paid $7 an hour. Of that, $4 went to child care,

$1 to taxes. That left net pay of $2 an hour, $288 a month. She had been receiving twice that much from Aid to Families With Dependent Children. "I had no choice but to quit," she wrote.

Journalists can document such situations by working through the local government assistance office to find recipients willing to subject their lives to sustained observation. If nobody at the assistance office will help make contact, a journalist can approach recipients outside the office, post signs near the offices or at local supermarkets and place advertisements in newspapers.

To capture the world of welfare recipients and government bureaucrats, a journalist posed as an applicant while on assignment for the Los Angeles Times magazine. He found a police-state atmosphere at welfare offices, applicants who lied on their applications while bragging about their deceptions to strangers waiting in lines and bureaucrats who seemed scared and burned out.

Some programs are funded entirely by the federal government; those tend to be administered more or less uniformly by state government welfare bureaucracies under contract to the U.S. Health and Human Services Department. Additional programs are largely paid for by the states without federal involvement. Finally, there is the patchwork of "general assistance" programs, many at the county level with no statewide uniformity. In a few places, those localized programs carry the name "poor relief." Other descriptions include "home relief" and "emergency aid."

The earned-income tax credit is an attempt to help low-income working families with children, but journalists should question the Internal Revenue Service and the congressional tax writing committees about whether it helps families in meaningful ways. One problem is the complexity of tax law. Many eligible families are unaware of the tax credit, cannot understand forms they must complete to claim the credit or are afraid of dealing with the IRS. Many make so little money they would never have to file tax forms except for the earned-income credit. If they overcome all those hurdles, they still do not receive immediate assistance in the form of a larger paycheck. Instead, they receive a lump sum after the IRS processes the paperwork. A lump sum is better than nothing, but often is out of synch with when the family needs the money. Journalists should look not only for ways to gauge the program's effectiveness, but also at whether the government ever acts on fraudulent claims. Some of the fraud schemes include husband and wife filing separately, as if divorced, thus both receiving payments; people underreporting income; and single parents pretending they are paid to care for each other's children.

Covering welfare-related stories takes understanding, compassion, commitment and skepticism. There are many sources available to help. The American Public Welfare Association, Washington, D.C., can provide perspective, including why some recipients leave the welfare system. According to several studies by academics, slightly less than half who leave become ineligible because of increased earnings. Other reasons include an increase in non–work related income, changed circumstances connected to marriage or remarriage, moving in with family or friends, departure of a child who was the reason for eligibility and a move to a different state with different requirements.

Top-notch books about the big picture of poverty include "The Promised Land: The Great Black Migration and How It Changed America" by Nicholas Lemann; "There Are No Children Here: The Story of Two Boys Growing Up in the Other America" by Alex Kotlowitz; "Within Our Reach: Breaking the Cycle of Disadvantage" by Lisbeth B. Schorr with Daniel Schorr; "The Truly Disadvantaged: The Inner City, the Underclass and Public Policy" by William Julius Wilson; and "Living on the Edge: The Realities of Welfare in America" by Mark Robert Rank.

Aid to Families With Dependent Children

Unlike many government assistance programs available to everybody with certain attributes (Social Security, home mortgage tax deductions, farm subsidies), AFDC is means tested and morals tested. Applicants must prove poverty not only initially, but also repeatedly; if they earn enough to cross the poverty line—though they may still be hungry—they lose AFDC benefits. They must satisfy government bureaucrats that their housekeeping, childrearing and sexual behavior are satisfactory, giving up their privacy to unannounced home inspections. Social Security recipients, on the other hand, can be dissolute millionaires who spend their government payments on illegal drugs—without any questions from the agency dispensing the money.

There are two major story streams emanating from AFDC. The first is fraud. Here is an excerpt from a report by the U.S. House Government Operations Committee, "Managing the Federal Government: A Decade of Decline":

> AFDC . . . is a lifeline for many Americans. Unfortunately, scarce resources are being lost in overpayments to beneficiaries because of weak oversight [by the U.S. Health and Human Services Department] of the state agencies that administer the program . . . [HHS] has not established uniform procedures to hold states accountable for their overpayment collections, and to help them determine when it is no longer cost effective to pursue debtors. Finally, it does not require states to match overpayment files with earnings records to identify former recipients who are employed and possibly able to repay their debt.

That is not the only kind of fraud. The Eagle-Tribune of Lawrence, Mass., documented fraud by employees of the state public welfare department. The most outrageous examples included two female employees personally involved with two male career criminals who were collecting benefits illegally and an employee trading food stamps for heroin who retained his state job. The series also portrayed employees who did nothing to bring illegal recipients to justice because it took extra work to do so, then misled the public about the fraud rate.

To report the series, the newspaper conducted numerous interviews, checked state agency vendor payments, budgets, annual reports, employee time sheets and interoffice memos. The newspaper then cross-checked the agency's internal information with arrest logs, conviction records, business licenses, abandoned building rolls, rosters of school bus and taxi drivers. The team entered cases filed with the state industrial accident division into a computer, then looked for matches of individuals collecting welfare and workers' compensation simultaneously.

The other major story stream is the inadequacy of child care, jobs and assistance payments for parents (frequently single mothers) trying to forge decent lives for their children. One place for a journalist to begin learning is the local Head Start program. Head Start is more than preschool for three- and four-year-old children from poor families. Head Start usually requires parents to become involved in running the preschool while also making sure they take advantage of medical, dental and nutritional assistance. Head Start parents on AFDC thus receive child care while trying to enter the workforce as well as picking up life skills that might make obtaining a job more likely.

Journalists can observe Head Start centers to document the level of parent involvement. While doing that, journalists can try to determine how many eligible three and four year olds are turned away due to lack of funding or never attend because their families know nothing about Head Start. Many Head Start programs run only nine months of each year and provide only half-day care—lack of funding, again. So a journalist is likely to see parents who try to work full-day, year-round jobs rather than stay on AFDC rolls placed at a disadvantage when affordable child care is unavailable.

AFDC is filled with counterproductive incentives and disincentives reflecting the difficulty of reforming the welfare system. Unmarried mothers without good jobs obviously need cash. But cash payments from the government might lower their incentive to marry, enter the workforce and stop bearing children. Those same mothers obviously need health care for themselves and their children. Yet providing them with health care through Medicaid lowers the incentive to leave AFDC and accept a low-paying job without health-care benefits.

Funding inadequacy leads to convoluted situations, as when a single parent is receiving AFDC, has been honest about the identity of the absent parent and that absent parent is making child-support payments. The absent parent makes payments to the state government, which sends $50 a month to the custodial parent and keeps the rest to reimburse the AFDC treasury. That scenario encourages dishonesty. The absent parent would rather pay nothing to the state, naturally. So if the custodial parent says the identity of the spouse is unknown, the absent parent has to pay nothing to the state, the custodial parent still receives AFDC and might get under-the-table payments from the absent parent of more than $50 monthly. Even if no money is arriving from the absent parent, the $50 monthly from the state is too small to provide an incentive for the custodial parent to tell the truth. If the absent parent were to find out the custodial parent had informed to the state, there might be violence or a worsened relationship between the absent parent and the children. When journalists find troubled AFDC programs, they often find abuse of a related program, Supplemental Security Income. Originally established to help elderly persons ineligible for Social Security, government bureaucracies have extended SSI eligibility to middle-aged and young persons who claim mental disorders, including hard-to-prove (or disprove) anxiety attacks and depression. Using appeals files at the Social Security Administration and word-of-mouth in neighborhoods, the Baltimore Sun produced a series following case histories of SSI recipients, complete with real names and specific income figures.

Child-Support Enforcement

The federal government, state governments and local governments have all tried innovative ways to collect delinquent child-support payments on behalf of custodial parents. Nothing has worked well on a regular basis. In Missouri, for example, the task falls to the Division of Child Support Enforcement, part of the Department of Social Services. The state division sometimes contracts with county governments to handle enforcement. The government will try to locate the absent parent, establish paternity when necessary, set a payment level, monitor compliance and disburse any money collected. To force payment, the government agency can garnish wages, intercept tax refunds, slap a tax lien on property and, if necessary, refer a case to the local prosecutor for court action. Many custodial parents the state tries to help are AFDC recipients. Parents who are more well-to-do frequently bypass the executive branch bureaucracy by going directly to court to press their collection battles.

A controversial question is whether to imprison violators. If imprisoned, how can they earn money to make payments? On the other hand, if they are chronic violators, does it make sense to let them keep their liberty and continue breaking the law? Missouri recently began experimenting with imprisonment if a parent has the ability to pay and owes more than $5,000 or misses six payments during a year. The first offender sentenced to prison in my home county under the new law had previously pled guilty to nonsupport. At that time, he received a suspended six-month prison sentence and probation. When he still refused to pay, the judge revoked his probation.

Food Stamps

The U.S. House Government Operations Committee report cited earlier said this about the Agriculture Department's handling of the food stamp program, which serves tens of millions of people annually: "Food stamps are issued through state welfare agencies and can be used at authorized retail stores, which turn them in to local banks, which in turn redeem them at the Federal Reserve. The program is losing at least $1 billion annually because the department and the states that administer the program have not prevented cheats from abusing it."

Fraud encompasses ineligible recipients, authorized retailers selling unauthorized nonfood items (from toilet paper to cocaine) for the stamps, retailers exchanging stamps for cash and persons setting themselves up as "stores" that redeem stamps working from a private residence. Journalists can spend time at food stamp pick-up points if they are interested in documenting fraud. A San Francisco Bay Guardian reporter accompanied a recipient to a check-cashing store to pick up the monthly food stamp allotment. That same outlet was a regular site of food stamp-related criminal activity: recipients being robbed of stamps as they left the store, offers of cash for coupons at 50 cents on the dollar, trades of drugs for the stamps. After visiting distribution sites, journalists can walk down the street to retailers authorized to redeem stamps. Does it appear the retailer qualifies on the basis of staple foods accounting for more than 50 percent of sales? As food stamp recipients enter and leave the store, are they offered cash, drugs or other commodities for stamps? Some states are trying to combat fraud by instituting an electronic benefits transfer program. Having recipients use a computerized card at the cash register leaves a paper trail and reduces street trafficking. Journalists can inquire whether that anti-fraud technique is being tried in their jurisdiction.

If no fraud is involved, journalists can write provocative stories about aspects of the program when it is running the way it is supposed to. A story could cover filling out application forms that go on for 45 pages, contain questions that tax the understanding of a college graduate and erase any semblance of privacy. One state's form I studied asked food-stamp applicants to bring these items, for every household member, to the eligibility interview after completing 20 pages of questions:

Proof of identity, age and citizenship (the form does not specify what constitutes proof)

Proof of Social Security numbers

Pay stubs from employers, if any

Federal income tax returns as well as tax-related records from self-employment

Proof of income from rental property or sales contracts, if any

Award letters for Social Security, Supplemental Security Income, workers' compensation, pensions and similar revenue sources

Proof of support or alimony payments, if any

Statements for accounts at banks, credit unions, savings and loans, certificates of deposit, stocks or bonds, if any

Rent receipts or mortgage payments, including insurance and taxes

Utility payments

Medical expenses

Child-care payments

Insurance premium payments

The dozens of sweeping questions include "Has anyone borrowed money or received money from friends, relatives, etc., this month? If yes, explain if money was borrowed or received and the purpose."

Another example:

> Does anyone receive any of the following types of income? If yes, enter the code that describes the type of income and the monthly amount for each person . . . Aid to Families With Dependent Children, assistance payments from another state, Bureau of Indian Affairs, blood/plasma income, emergency assistance cash payment, foster-care payment, general assistance, housing authority, negative rent or energy credit, workers' compensation, insurance payments, interest, royalties, dividends, Job Training Partnership Act, land lease, military allotment, mortgage/sales contract income, rental income, retirement pension, Supplemental Payments Program, strike pay, tuberculosis control, vocational rehabilitation, gambling or lottery winnings, other.

Jeffrey M. Berry's book "Feeding Hungry People: Rulemaking in the Food Stamp Program" contains useful perspective, as does "Let Them Eat Promises: The Politics of Hunger in America" by Nick Kotz.

Child and Family Nutrition Programs Other Than Food Stamps

While checking the functioning of the food stamp program, journalists can ask recipients whether they are able to combine food-stamp assistance with other assistance to feed their families nutritious meals every day. The answer is often no. Most food-assistance programs grew up pretty much independently of each other. That means, depending on the point of view, either many opportunities for the needy to find a program that helps avoid starvation or a senseless bureaucratic morass. Each program is worth investigating separately or in tandem.

The National School Lunch Program is supposed to provide balanced, nutritious, reduced-cost or free meals during the school day to children from low-income families. Journalists can ask numerous questions, some of which they can answer based on extended observation in school lunchrooms: Are eligibility forms reaching families like they should? Is assistance available for families that have trouble understanding the forms? Are schools charging the allowable maximum set by the federal government for reduced-price lunches, or giving low-income families a break by charging less than the allowable maximum? Are the five required meal components present, in the mandated amounts? Are the lunches overly high in cholesterol and too low in fiber? What is the mix between food from surplus commodities virtually given away by the U.S. Agriculture Department and other food purchased locally by the school district? How does that mix affect nutrition, quality and price? How much of the food is fresh, as opposed to frozen or powdered? What kind of enforcement, if any, exists at junior and senior high schools, where students tend to eat unhealthy fast food away from school property if allowed to do so?

The Special Supplemental Food Program for Women, Infants and Children (WIC) program began as a response to studies showing that permanent harm is often caused to the unborn children of malnourished pregnant women. Recipients receive vouchers for use on specific items at grocery stores and farmers' markets. Coverage extends beyond pregnancy for women, as well as for children to age five. The program contains an educational component about nutrition and limited health care. A question for journalists to ask is how many needy women are excluded locally because of funding limitations. Unlike many other hunger and poverty programs, WIC is dependent on annual appropriations, rather than serving everybody who meets objective requirements.

Journalists can observe the other feeding programs aimed at the needy: the School Breakfast Program, Child and Adult Care Food Program, Summer Food Service Program, Special Milk Program, Commodity Supplemental Food Program, Pregnant and Lactating Student Meal Supplement Program, Child Nutrition Homeless Demonstration Project, Nutrition Education and Training Program, Emergency Food Assistance Program, Emergency Food and Shelter Program, Food Distribution Program on Indian Reservations, Nutrition Program for the Elderly, Commodities for Charitable Institutions and Summer Camps, Soup Kitchen and Food Bank Program, Expanded Food and Nutrition Education Program, plus Community Food and Nutrition Program. One of the best studies of the programs is "Hunger in California: A State of Need," from the California-Nevada Community Action Association, Sacramento.

Most private-sector programs aimed at feeding the needy are well-intentioned and many are effective. But like other charitable organizations (see Chapter 13), they ought to be scrutinized by journalists. Even if everybody working at food banks, food pantries, soup kitchens and food cooperatives is honest, at minimum journalists can show how the efforts are never enough, how for-profit businesses that could help choose to do nothing or how lack of public transportation prevents potential recipients from reaching their destination and receiving available benefits.

■ GOVERNMENT SOCIAL SERVICE BUREAUCRACIES

The sprawling bureaucracy approach gained favor in past generations as governments tried to alleviate problems linked with poverty, discrimination and aging. How a government bureaucracy is organized might seem academic, but some experts believe the all-in-one approach has led to less help for the needy. An article in Governing magazine concluded that the approach "never seems to work, either administratively or politically. In response, some are looking away from integration and back toward the decentralization of an earlier day."

The U.S. Health and Human Services Department is an example of the sprawling bureaucracy approach. It contains six major program divisions: aging, Social Security, public health, health care financing, civil rights, children and families. The divisions are further divided into smaller bureaucracies meant to assist Native Americans, developmentally disabled, refugees waiting for resettlement, the mentally ill, drug abusers and single parents whose spouses refuse to pay child support.

If divisions are spun off to become their own agencies, they might be more responsive to those they serve as well as more efficient with budget dollars. Greater equity among states' agencies would reduce the problem of efficient, higher-benefit states serving as a magnet for the poor, while inefficient, lower-benefit states become sites of misery for those who cannot move elsewhere. On the other hand, spinoffs from all-in-one bureaucracies might result in the same kind of patchwork system that integration was meant to replace. Separate agencies might mean separate bureaucracies feuding over who has jurisdiction over what.

■ Children and Families

Not all investigations that need to be done about children and families center on poverty programs administered by sprawling bureaucracies. Because so many children cannot provide for themselves, they suffer abuse and neglect at all income levels. Yet few journalists delve into children and family issues, among rich or poor, on a sustained basis. Writing in Nieman Reports magazine, Carol Kreck of the Denver Post commented that

> abuse and neglect tended to be covered, death by death, by general assignment reporters; gangs and crack babies by urban affairs writers; infant mortality and AIDS babies by medical writers; deteriorating test scores by education writers. Since child care, child support and child protection were not in anyone's bailiwick, they were given short shrift. Children's issues at the state house and in Congress were given no shrift at all.

Handed the children's beat, Kreck realized she had a blank check: "Played the right way, all the beats were mine—health care, courts, cops, the legislature, Congress, education, urban affairs. So were the big stories of our time. After all, AIDS is a children's issue, not to mention poverty, homelessness, welfare reform, gun control, prenatal drug abuse and foster care."

Since Kreck helped pioneer the children's beat, the Casey Journalism Center for Children and Families has come into existence at the University of Maryland. The center is helping the beat grow as well as documenting its growth. Some of the dilemmas it addresses are whether journalists should be advocates for children, and, if so, where they should draw the line. Should journalists publish the names of children in trouble? How should journalists handle sensitive information coming from interviews with unsophisticated children, especially if the information reflects negatively on others?

Martha Shirk of the St. Louis Post-Dispatch has developed answers to difficult questions during her years on the beat. Speaking to an IRE national conference, Shirk emphasized the importance of getting access to case files—from parents, social workers, judges—even if it means promising to keep individual names out of the finished stories.

"Some of you may think that is too high a price," Shirk said.

> In the end, I decided it did not matter that I could not report the names of kids I write about, because it was not the names that were important. The issue was how well the system we have . . . is working. Could I have gotten the case histories simply by interviewing juveniles who had come through the . . . system? I do not think so.
>
> The reason is that on these issues, more than almost any other, people lie. People tell you they have not been abusing their children, when the medical evidence shows they have. People tell you they have not signed over custody to their child's father, when the divorce records show they have. People tell you they are paid up in child support, when the circuit clerk's records show they are not. People tell you they have been arrested once or twice, when the court records show they have been arrested 15 or 20 times. . . . Even people

who call themselves children's advocates lie. Just because someone calls himself a children's advocate does not mean he is not willing to stretch the truth or cook the numbers to strengthen his case. Question every number every children's advocacy group puts before you.

The Casey center's first year of awards indicates how much territory the children/family beat can cover. Here is a summary of the winning entries:

Television features. WFAA-TV, Dallas, delved into the state's child protective services agency, following caseworkers to show how they handled problems.

Television investigations. ABC News Day One showed how a for-profit psychiatric hospital chain mistreated teenaged patients while milking the insurance policies of the teenagers' families.

Television documentaries. Wisconsin Public Television traced the journey of a woman and her family from a violent Chicago public housing project to a new life in Madison, Wis.

Radio reporting. Children's Express, Washington, D.C., discussed how homeless teenagers tried to survive on the streets.

Daily newspapers. The Charlotte Observer exposed a foster-care system riddled with abusive homes unexamined by social service bureaucracies and judges. The Modesto (Calif.) Bee looked at teenaged runaways. The Bristol Press in Connecticut delved into small-city gang life.

Magazines. U.S. News and World Report documented discriminatory practices in school district special education placements.

The range of stories that could be done is vast. At what point should social workers and judges combine to remove a child from a biological parent? When that happens, what is the probability that a foster home, orphanage or other refuge will do a better job than a loving but down-and-out parent? Should parents ever be sterilized? If so, at what point?

The IRE Resource Center and other journalism organizations' files contain accounts of projects shedding light on family issues. Inquiry, the publication from the Science Journalism Center at the University of Missouri, contained an article by Lynne Ohman about a foster-care investigation at the Star Tribune, Minneapolis. She based much of her account on comments by reporters Allen Short and Paul McEnroe:

When Short and McEnroe first found that the state placed many abused children in abusive foster-care homes, they knew they had a good story. But when they discovered that Minnesota granted foster-care licenses to persons with known criminal records, they had a great story. . . .

Negative action letters received from the Minnesota Department of Human Services proved the reporters' original hypothesis that children pulled from abusive homes had been placed with abusive foster-care parents. . . .

[As they delved further], they quickly found that laws designed to protect foster children also acted as a shield for abusive foster parents. . . .

Short and McEnroe then visited district courts throughout Minnesota. They pored over civil and criminal court cases looking for litigation against foster parents. . . . The depositions taken from charged foster parents, coupled with police reports and medical records, provided Short and McEnroe with material to write detailed narratives about abusive parents and the children they abused. . . .

Although McEnroe and Short had a wealth of information on a foster-care system that failed to protect some children, it was an offhand comment during a perfunctory interview that alerted them to the licensing of criminals as foster parents.

There are many more shocking stories out there waiting for journalists. A few of the private umbrella organizations ready to provide perspective are the Children's Defense Fund and Coalition for America's Children, both of Washington, D.C.; the Child Care Action Campaign, New York City; and the National Center for Prosecution of Child Abuse, Alexandria, Va. Useful books not already mentioned in other chapters include "When Home Is No Haven: Child Placement Issues" by Albert J. Solnit, Barbara F. Nordhaus and Ruth Lord; "Making an Issue of Child Abuse: Political Agenda Setting for Social Problems" by Barbara J. Nelson; "Mothers on Trial: The Battle for Children and Custody" by Phyllis Chesler; "Wounded Innocents: The Real Victims of the War Against Child Abuse" by Richard Wexler; and "Lead Us Not Into Temptation: Catholic Priests and the Sexual Abuse of Children" by Jason Berry.

PART THREE

Putting It
All Together

Chapter 22

WRITING COMPELLING PROJECTS

*H*undreds of books have been published about journalistic writing. They explain grammar. They distinguish between hard news and features. They discuss whether to write in first person or not. Those matters are all useful to investigative journalists. But few books or even chapters of existing books are devoted to composing compelling, in-depth, hard-edged projects.

This chapter tries to fill the gap by staying narrowly focused. Call it a chapter on composing the literature of fact. The goal is to help project reporters and editors captivate like the most artful novelist while telling the truth as well as humanly possible. To delve into this special brand of writing, it makes sense to turn to the IRE Journal. What follows is from the article "Remembering the Outrage: How to Stop Drawing Indictments and Start Telling Stories" by Ron Meador, projects editor at the Star Tribune of the Twin Cities.

> Suppose you catch your state-run vocational schools putting out phony placement statistics, luring job-hungry hopefuls to courses that tout 90 percent success but deliver less than 50.
>
> You prove this using the school's own data, taken from computer tapes and analyzed with expert help. You find juicy examples of duplicated and wasteful programs that violate state efficiency rules but serve the pork-barrel interests of legislators and local school boards. You publish this in the paper with sidebars and pictures and color graphics in the very week the legislature is reviewing budgets for all college and vocational programs.
>
> And your story sinks like a set of car keys.
>
> Legislators ask the program chiefs a few questions and let the budgets go forward. Dozens of vo-ed students write to thank you, and so do several academics, but nobody else pays much attention. The schools adopt a few internal reforms—but also stop collecting the data you used to prove their misdeeds.

Can you imagine how this might feel? I know, because it happened at the Star Tribune, and it was my fault.

I've read this project many times since then. I'm always impressed. By all the usual measures, it was a very solid piece of work. The findings were important and presented authoritatively and were never challenged. The stories were clear and crisp even by the usual high standards of their author, David Peterson. Graphics and sidebars added depth and detail.

I had assumed that readers would flock to a series showing that a $160-million-a-year, tax-financed educational system was ridden with waste and deception. But they didn't. Why? I can see now that many of the stories ran very long, covering multiple topics. We probed issues exhaustively, but said too little about people. Some graphics tried to make so many points that it was hard to see any of them. We took a tone of informing and educating our readers rather than talking to them, provoking them, engaging them.

The lesson of this experience? We investigative types have to stop drawing up indictments and start telling stories. This is a big challenge, a continual struggle. I certainly don't have all the answers, but I have a few suggestions.

Keep the Outrage in Sight

There has been a transformation in investigative journalism in the last decade or so, a shift from nailing individual bad guys to dissecting failing systems. Sometimes in our absorption with documenting these dysfunctional systems, we forget that actual people are getting screwed, that other people are screwing them or letting it happen. We forget the outrage that first moved us, and we lose the aspect that can move our readers.

We ran a series by Joe Rigert and Maura Lerner showing that more than 200 nursing-home patients are strangling each year in vests and belts intended to keep them from harm. Worse, the primary manufacturer of these "protective restraints" had known about the deaths for years, and government regulators turned aside persistent signs of trouble. Documenting this indifference made the story much more compelling.

A different project contradicted the folk wisdom that readers are capable of outrage only over death, injury and wasted tax money. Rigert and Tom Hamburger did a quick project on the Federal Reserve Bank's efforts to replace its 18-year-old, state-of-the-art Minneapolis headquarters with a $110-million palace. They found that the bank had exaggerated the existing building's repair problems and used some questionable financial analysis to make a case for abandoning it.

Rather than count on readers to be outraged by the waste of semipublic money—$110 million is just a big abstraction—we built our lead on the threatened destruction of a unique, expensive architectural landmark that had become part of the soul of Minneapolis, where pride in such things runs high.

Put People in the Foreground

There is a tradition in project writing that puts the issues and findings in the main pieces, individual human stories in the sidebars. Our shop talk reflects that thinking: This is a Numbers Story, this is the Policy Story, these are the People Stories over here. Numbers are essential, people are optional.

When people show up in a Numbers Story or a Policy Story, it is usually as a three-paragraph anecdote leading off the piece or one of its subsections. The idea is to use a bit of pungent humanity to lure readers into the hard stuff. This sort of journalistic bait-and-switch is cheap and cynical. Readers deserve more respect. They care about issues but are impatient with abstraction. They want to see problems and conflicts in the flesh. They want to make a personal connection, to imagine how this outrage would feel to them.

I think we have to find ways to weave human experience throughout our stories. The heavier and harder a story is, the more humanity it needs.

Allen Short and Donna Halvorsen wrote a three-day series about predatory sex offenders and how the courts fail to protect us from them. The main findings were about numbers and policies—high recidivism rates, lenient sentencing patterns, failed treatment programs—but each day's presentation gave equal prominence to powerful portrayals of sex crimes, of the men who commit them, of the women and children whose lives have been shredded by rape.

That approach made us work harder to avoid redundancy, to give each story a unique identity. But we decided we did not want any reader to be able to lose sight, even for a moment, of the horrors being endured by women and children while the public policy debate drones on.

Talk to Readers—Do Not Lecture Them

Imagine sitting down on the bus, turning to your fellow commuter and saying, "A U.S. Air Force pilot shot down over Laos in 1968 and listed as missing in action, whose widow has repeatedly received evidence that he might still be alive, was almost certainly killed in the crash, the Star Tribune has learned after an exhaustive review of military records and interviews with the pilot's squadron commander, who acknowledged lying about the incident."

I cannot say nobody will read a story that starts that way. All our newspapers keep running endurance tests like that, and we get enough calls and letters to know that some people keep reading past them. But there is a better way. We can write for our readers the way we talk to our neighbors. We can stop using newspaperese and start using conversational English.

We can stop cramming sentences so full of facts and figures that we need to wrap them with bungee cord to keep them from bursting. We can kill all those wooden quotes, partial quotes and long-winded quotes that are paraphrased. We can get rid of jargon and other language that has meaning only for insiders and newspapers junkies. We can strip away clichés.

We can introduce Bob Ehlert's MIA story by saying, "For nearly 22 years, Richard Walsh's family has waited for him to come home, alive or dead, from the jungles of Southeast Asia. All because of a lie."

That will get a few more sinners into the tent, I think.

Let Graphics Carry More of the Load

We are all using graphics these days. When they are good, they are very, very good. When they are bad, they say the same thing as the story, only not as clearly.

We have two rules for our graphics:

1. Each one has to make its own point. The point must be sharp enough to be conveyed in a short declarative sentence. This sentence focuses the content and design of the graphic, and often becomes the headline. Not "Patterns of Crime," but "Sex Criminals Commit Multiple Offenses." Not "Treatment and Recidivism Rates," but "Treatment Shows Little Benefit."
2. Graphics must stand on their own, just like sidebars. They exist to make or develop their own point, which may have been mentioned in a story only briefly, or not at all. They are not there to say in pictures what we have already said in words.

When Rigert and Bob Franklin wrote a series on cheating, skimming and theft in Minnesota's $1-billion-a-year charitable gambling industry, we faced a big challenge: How to expose the wrongdoing while simultaneously introducing the complicated, unfamiliar system that was being abused.

Our solution was a front-page graphic titled, "A Catalog of Cheating." It showed how the system worked, with pull-tabs moving from distributors to bars to players, as money flowed from players to gambling operators to charities. At the same time, it showed how crooks siphoned off a share at each stage.

From the Beginning, Think of the End

As my colleague and design guru, Tim Bitney, has often said, the problem with a lot of projects is that we spend nine months making the parts for a '55 Ford pickup, and then decide to build a Porsche 911—in two weeks.

We have a simple strategy for avoiding that horror. As soon as we possibly can, we form a team of writers, researchers, data analysts, photographers, illustrators and designers to start talking about how we will present the story.

The team meets infrequently in the early stages of reporting, talking about story concepts and presentation styles. Writers offer photo possibilities, photographers suggest sidebars, designers propose targets for data-crunching. The project editor periodically distills that thinking into a memo that records where we are and lets fellow editors know what is going on.

What does this have to do with storytelling? Everything. A story is not just words. It is also pictures, graphics, page design. All of these elements can bring readers into a story or drive them away. All are worth thinking about from the moment a project starts taking shape.

At Every Step, Remember the Interested, Impatient Reader

Perhaps there was a day when we could throw our evidence of waste and fraud and wrongdoing before our readers like so much raw meat, then sit back and watch them feed. If so, it certainly is long gone. Readers are much more demanding now, and they're getting more sophisticated all the time.

I do not believe, as some journalists do, that readers are losing interest in issues these days. I do believe they are losing patience with newspapers that force them to work too hard and make them care too little. Readers do not like dense, endless stories. They do not like graphics that read like income-tax forms. They do not like getting the same point over and over in a story, sidebar, graphic, cutline, blurb. They do not like to be lectured.

I do not have a prescription for styling investigative stories. Some demand a narrative. Some need a more traditional, newslike structure. Some require an analytical approach, some rest squarely on the facts.

But I do have one last tip. When you have got the project drafted, ask a half-dozen uninitiated readers to look it over and react. You can use people from around the newsroom, or people from outside who can be trusted with the secrets. We have done it both ways, with good results.

Odds are they will show you a lot of things that could be done better. This is not always welcome news in the last weeks of getting a project ready for print. But if you are turning off your readers, it is better to know it before the papers are out the door.

All of this may sound terribly obvious and ordinary, the kind of thing everybody already knows and everybody already does.

I wish that were so. I really do. But the mail brings a lot of projects to my office, from a lot of great newspapers, and a lot of them are long and dull. Gray. Preachy. Too hard. Too complicated. Too dry.

I cannot get through these projects. That makes me sad, because I know there is good work in them. If I cannot read them, on a Thursday afternoon, in my office, when I am hungry for ideas and scouting for techniques to steal—well then, imagine how these projects fare with Mr. or Mrs. Average Reader on a Sunday morning, when the kids are fighting or brunch is arriving or the yard work has to get done.

Our work is too important to be laid aside.

Getting the Details While Reporting

To meet Meador's standards, an investigative story should answer the "so what" as well as the who, what, when, where, why and how. The answers are usually in the details. The reporter and editor should think about collecting details not only for their content, but also for how those details can work to illustrate the project's theme, make audience members angry, sad, relieved and/or more informed about a topic that touches their lives.

Throughout the earlier chapters of this book, investigators have been encouraged to notice details on their own, to ask questions of sources that will elicit details. Rather than ignoring the "obvious," top investigators are perpetually amazed by it. They collect details that nobody else notices. Edna Buchanan of the Miami Herald once wrote about a murder of a man who had been dumped into the street by the driver of a pickup truck. It was only later, after publication, that Buchanan learned the dead man was wearing a black tafetta cocktail dress and red high heels. When she questioned the detectives about why they never told her this, they replied, "You didn't ask." She started asking after that.

All details that find their way into the published or broadcast project should have meaning. Relevant details can make all the difference in a lead. Donald Murray, in "Writing for Your Readers," includes an exercise that adds details to a hard-news lead. The original sentence read "The body was discovered in the kitchen of the Dorchester Street house." By the time Murray is finished adding relevant details, the sentence reads "Steam still rose from the hamburg simmering for homemade spaghetti sauce after the 23-year-old mother's body was discovered in the kitchen of her Dorchester Street house."

Walt Harrington of the Washington Post magazine tells of a writer capturing a country doctor driving to the scene of an accident where a tree has fallen on a man. Several miles before the doctor reaches the victim, he begins beeping his car horn at short intervals. It can be heard throughout the countryside. An observer might assume the doctor is emulating, as best he can, an ambulance siren, hoping other motorists will clear the way. The investigative journalist assumes nothing. She asks the doctor, why are you beeping your horn? The doctor answers that the man pinned by the tree might hear it, know help is on the way, be filled with hope and thus hang on to life. As Harrington explains, "The doctor's motive tells us a great deal about the doctor—his sensitivity and empathy, his desire to grasp even the slimmest advantage in his effort to save a life. Yet it is easy to imagine any fairly good journalist describing that scene, but missing its dramatic and fully subjective meaning by forgetting to ask the last simple and obvious question—what does it mean?" If the pinned man lives, the reporter should ask if he heard the horn and what he thought.

> Was he conscious and filled with hope as the doctor had imagined? Or was he unconscious and the doctor's effort went for naught? Or did he hear the horn but have no idea that the blare and the doctor were linked? These layers of connected subjective meaning are not simply nice touches meant to make the providing of information more palatable to the reader. They are the story itself. . . .
>
> So if a policeman you are profiling has a do-dad of some sort stuck to his dashboard, you can simply report it as a piece of color—or you can ask him where he got it. Perhaps it is not his, was there when he inherited the squad car. But perhaps it was a gift from his mother on her death bed. Or a good-luck charm of an old partner who was killed in action. You just never know.

Harrington uses his handwritten notes, his memory, a tape recorder and photographs (from the interviewee, from his own camera, from the camera of a professional photographer) to help capture detail. Only details that move the story forward should survive the writing and rewriting, though. The surviving details should form a chain of facts, rather than a stack of facts. Much of Harrington's wisdom can be found in his book "American Profiles: Somebodies and Nobodies Who Matter."

Avoiding Stereotypes While Collecting Details

Screening out inappropriate or misleading details is difficult. It means contradicting the natural tendency for journalists to see what they expect to see. Donald Murray warns against clichés of vision:

> The more professional we become the greater the danger that we will see what we expect to see. Experience, of course, is an advantage, but it has a dark side. It may keep us from seeing the real story—the cause that does not fit the stereotype, the effect that is not predictable, the quote that we do not hear before our question is answered. The effective writer must always have an essential naivete; skepticism must be balanced by innocence. The reporter must be capable of seeing what is new. Clichés of language are significant misdemeanors, but clichés of vision are felonies. Too often editors punish each misdemeanor but advocate the commission of felonies.

Murray illustrates his point with an example that rings so true it is bound to make countless journalists blush with shameful recognition:

> A young man has run amok in the neighborhood, killing eight and maiming 15. The man is described as quiet, studious, polite to the neighbors, good to his mother, neat, mild-mannered and the last person in the world you would have expected to do anything like that. . . . He is the cliché killer, and the reporter is happy to find him. There is no problem writing the story; it has been written before, and before, and before. The neighbors all fall into the stereotype. They are not lying, but they are shocked; they do like the mother; they want to avoid responsibility for what they have overlooked the last twenty years.

If the audience is fortunate, at least one reporter will refuse to be blinded by such clichés of vision. Murray says, optimistically, "Some good, hard-edged reporting will discover that neighborhood pets have been disappearing for years, the nice young man was seen cooking pigeons when he was three years old . . . that his father, two brothers and three sisters have refused to live at home with him; that the studious young man has the reading level of a nine-year-old; and that his mother has fought a guerrilla war against getting psychiatric help for him since he was three years old."

The project reporter who refuses to be trapped by clichés of vision is also likely to chronicle the larger context, the universal themes. Those themes might include how the case concerns not only death but also love, how the materialistic culture in which the death occurred is an integral part of the story.

Writing From an Outline, a Chronology or Both

As the details accumulate, experienced investigators find the way to manage the information is to build a chronology. The virtues of a chronology are explained in the introduction of this book. The chronology is more than an information-management tool, though. It is also a writing tool. Whether I am investigating an individual, institution or issue, I build a chronology from the first week. After each interview, I decide what to include in the chronology and what to temporarily file without mention. I include more than facts. I include revealing direct quotations, relevant physical descriptions—anything that might help make my story compelling as well as accurate. As I write drafts every week to test my original thesis, determine gaps that need filling, look for subplots or new angles, I use the chronology as my basic text. That saves me rereading massive files, trying to separate the wheat from the chaff.

In the early stages, when I know there will be holes that need filling, I sometimes write without the chronology or any other notes. Writers should trust the subconscious. What it remembers is probably worth including; what it forgets perhaps should be forgotten.

Writing drafts from a chronology or from memory, though, is no substitute for an outline. One way to test the logic of a draft is to outline it after composition. Does each major point of the project deserve its own roman numeral? If not, something is awry. Do the secondary points designated by capital letters, grouped together under each roman numeral, derive in a natural way from the major point? Do those secondary points fit together naturally in a grouping or do they need to be separated, perhaps placed elsewhere in the outline?

Some journalists construct their outline first, then compose their text roman numeral by roman numeral, capital letter by capital letter. I find that writing from a chronology (but not necessarily chronologically) first gives projects a more natural flow; the outline comes later, as a check on my work rather than the ruling document.

Tension and Resolution

Even the best outline cannot overcome a fuzzy focus, though. Journalists should hone the focus by writing and rewriting a one-sentence statement of no more than 35 words. When Laura Sessions Stepp of the

Charlotte Observer was trying to find an appropriate lead for a series on occupational hazards in the textile industry, she found herself struggling. Her supervisor asked her to summarize the months-long project. "Cotton dust is killing people," Stepp said. She had just verbalized the focus, which eventually came out in print as "Cotton dust is a killer in Carolina's mills."

Inherent in any focus statement should be tension and resolution. The tension might be between individuals, between an individual and an institution (such as an employer), an individual and the larger society, entrenched belief and newly discovered fact, what is being done versus what should be done.

Harrington says, "Introduce tensions early that will be resolved by the end. If possible, let your subjects seem to gain insight and self-awareness in the course of your story. This sounds impossible, but with proper in-depth interviewing it happens most of the time. Of course, it will not just happen if you have not anticipated and chronicled this growth or change while reporting."

Sometimes, resolution is real; other times it is an imposed dramatic device. In Madeleine Blais' article "Zepp's Last Stand," a Harrington favorite, the resolution is real: the old man wins the honorable military discharge he has sought for decades. But if he had not received it, Blais still could have brought dramatic closure to her story. Harrington's guess is she would have argued that by failing to clear his name, Zepp continued to have reason to live.

Perhaps the best-known apostle of the complication-tension-resolution model is Jon Franklin, in his book "Writing for Story: Craft Secrets of Dramatic Nonfiction by a Two-Time Pulitzer Prize Winner." He says almost any project can be described like this: "A sequence of actions that occur when a sympathetic character encounters a complicating situation that he confronts and solves." Franklin suggests avoiding projects that lack a basic complication of significance to the audience. A stolen car is not much of a complication to a wealthy person who can pay cash the next day for a new vehicle. But it will be a complication to a poverty-stricken, single-parent family whose head of household depends on the car to drop the children at day care before using it all day to reach housecleaning jobs scattered throughout neighborhoods lacking public transportation.

Journalists usually notice a complication first, then determine if there has been a resolution. Franklin suggests avoiding projects that lack a resolution because that absence makes telling an interesting story more difficult, if not impossible: "Most people are confused, and they stay confused. Most want more money, and don't get it. Most people want to win lotteries, but don't. Many people never even manage to clearly recognize the complications that face them, so they don't have a prayer of dealing with them. These complications without resolutions are worse than useless to the writer. Not only do they make poor stories, they often have the ability to mesmerize; the apprentice writer may expend copious amounts of mental energy trying to make them into stories."

On a more upbeat note for journalists who want to write compelling projects, there are many resolutions to choose from: Police solve a crime. A corrupt politician is removed from office. A business goes bankrupt. When such matters are the subjects of hard-news stories, Franklin says, they are usually "endings without beginnings attached." The projects reporter will tell the story of the actions that led to the ending: the apprehension of the criminal, the exposed political corruption, the bankruptcy. The tone can be upbeat as well as downbeat. For instance, a story about successful apprehension of a criminal can concentrate on the criminal (the downbeat) or on the honest, fearless detective who made the arrest (the upbeat).

Leads: The Opening Sentences

The first paragraph is in many ways the most important of a project. That said, Franklin suggests writing the ending first: "The story doesn't pivot on the beginning, it pivots on the ending. So write that first. That way you know exactly what it is that you need to foreshadow."

When journalists are finally ready to craft the opening, they will find that sometimes hard-news leads work best on complicated projects. Paul Williams believed a hard-news, summary lead worked on a complex project if an overwhelming revelation, supported by unequivocal evidence, stood out after the reporting had been completed. "Cotton dust is killing people" was one such revelation. Another came after Tom Braden looked into the public housing authority for the Columbia Missourian. His opening sentence: "The city's biggest landlord also may be the worst." When that kind of straightforward news-summary lead is impractical, there are other possibilities. Just about every kind of lead imaginable is demonstrated in Carole Rich's primer, "Writing and Reporting News: A Coaching Method." Through no fault of Rich's, the demarcations are often blurry. For example, what Rich calls descriptive leads, narrative leads and anecdotal leads are often interchangeable, and any of the three can focus on an individual, even though Rich also has a category called focus-on-a-person leads.

After eliminating a hard-news summary lead from consideration, journalists might have difficulty deciding between a news-feature lead and a softer lead. Harrington says, "The difference between news features and features is the difference between the humanized overview takeout on, say, mainstreaming handicapped children in the public schools versus telling the in-depth bittersweet story of one handicapped child who has been mainstreamed for the first time." Leads that focus on a person can be anecdotal or narrative or both. The key element, however, is the use of one person as the connecting thread for the entire project. That is different from opening with one person, using her as a symbol for a few paragraphs, moving to the summary (sometimes called the "so what") paragraph, then dropping all mention of that person for good or until a tie-back ending.

Skillful project journalists can tell a sweeping story through a particular person by including context. As author Tracy Kidder says, "You pluck a guitar string and another one vibrates." Maureen Dowd of the New York Times says a sweeping story can be told by delineating one person's character:

> I have always thought that covering the person—I would not call it character, really—is as important as the policies, because politicians change their policies. I mean, with [President George] Bush, you knew he had made a sort of Faustian bargain to be president, and he had no compass in terms of principles, and he had traded away a lot of what he believed in. So you could hang on to that, and that would help you explain a lot of what he did. And with [President Bill] Clinton I think it is the same. Every time the country has gotten into really deep trouble—the Bay of Pigs, Vietnam, Watergate—all these things have come from the president's personal characteristics.

Occasionally a project can open with a direct quotation. My mentor, Thomas G. Duffy, in his book "Let's Write a Feature," used an example from an investigation about substandard student housing in a university town. It began with this quotation: "'I stay at the library until it closes,' the woman said, shivering. 'Then I come home and go to bed fully dressed.'" The relevance of the quotation? The dingy apartment had a defective heating system that left tenants nearly freezing during winter.

Whatever type of lead is chosen, the writer can use Murray's 30 questions to gauge its effectiveness. Some of the most pertinent questions for investigative projects are "What one thing does the reader need to know more than any other?"; "What surprised me when I was reporting the story?"; "Where is the conflict?"; "What is the appropriate voice for this story?"; "What point of view should the story be told from?"; Can the essence of the story be captured by an anecdote, image, metaphor, quotation?

Middles: Flow and Momentum

Middles of stories receive little attention in many writing books, overshadowed by discussions of leads and endings. A punster might say that too many projects consist of a beginning, a muddle and an end. Journalists writing projects filled with dense information must not flag in the middle.

Part of the trick is grounded more in common sense than literary skill. For example, handling boring but important elements, like numbers, well can keep a project from losing momentum. Yet many projects do nothing to give life to numbers. When discussing a federal agency boondoggle as part of an overall budget topping $1 trillion, a writer should never assume that amount can be understood without help. A sentence explaining that it would take 31,688 years to produce a trillion dollars at the rate of a dollar per second is bound to aid understanding. If there is a 250 square mile oil slick off the California coast, a writer can explain that is about twice the size of San Francisco.

Using literary skill to craft interesting middles eventually must enter the discussion. Part of the problem is that discussions of middles get caught up in discussions of leads: Sometimes the most appropriate lead begins in the chronological middle of a narrative; members of the audience might not know right away precisely what is occurring, but need to know enough to be intrigued.

Franklin's book is one that pays lots of attention to middles. Using the Franklin formula, the middle of the story can be built around the actions the main character takes on the way to resolving the complication, the changes in the character wrestling with the problem, the insight (perhaps a flash, perhaps a slow unfolding) that leads directly to the resolution. Some of those actions might be internal—how does the character view the complication?—as well as external. Those internal thoughts will probably lead the journalist into the character's past: How did the character come to think the way he or she does?

One technique for maintaining interest during the middle portions is writing in scenes. Scenes that are done well show rather than tell, entertain as well as explain, involve audience members as if they were there. A project about unsafe bridges could include a scene of a school bus filled to capacity crossing one of those unsafe bridges day-in, day-out. To make audience members feel as if they are on the bus, the reporter would make the trip multiple times before composing the scene.

The opposite of scene-setting is just-the-facts exposition. A just-the-facts approach might read: "A businessman facing thousands of dollars in payroll taxes stemming from an unemployment claim shot his former receptionist outside an unemployment office, then killed himself at his home after fleeing." Scene-setting, on the other hand, might begin with a description of the bullets entering the receptionist's body. The description could be based on a combination of her recollections, accounts from eyewitnesses, police reports and hospital records.

Scenes can be thought of as chapters in a book. For his book "The Work of Human Hands," G. Wayne Miller describes a pregnancy in which an ultrasound test disclosed serious problems early. Miller ends a chapter (a scene) this way: "This was several weeks before another ultrasound would disclose an unidentified mass inside Lucy, and long before her parents would ever hear the word 'cloaca.'" The ending of that scene builds tension—what is the unidentified mass? What is cloaca?—by fore-shadowing worse trouble. It also sets the stage for the book's main char-acter, a physician who is an expert at combatting the dread birth defect.

Whatever techniques journalists use to craft effective middles, tran-sitions are mandatory. Transitions from sentence to sentence and para-graph to paragraph are taught in almost every university journalism course, illustrated in almost every book on effective nonfiction writing. Writers implicitly know why they place sentence B after sentence A, paragraph D after paragraph C. But the logic might be less obvious to the audience. Transitions make the logic clear. A transition can be accom-plished by repeating a word or phrase in paragraph D that appeared in paragraph C. A transition can be as simple as one word ("however," "then") or as complex as several sentences. Each is a conscious act by the writer, but should appear seamless and effortless. Transition is easier said than done, but it must be done.

Metaphors, similes and allusions are writing techniques that assist in showing rather than telling. But they are taught with less frequency than transition is. George Kennedy, Daryl R. Moen and Don Ranly provide pertinent examples in their book "Beyond the Inverted Pyramid: Effective Writing for Newspapers, Magazines and Specialized Publications."

A metaphor suggests that two things are alike. A physically imposing person with an imposing personality might be described as "a sequoia in a room full of saplings." A simile compares the familiar with the less familiar and uses "like" or "as." County commissioners trying to delib-erate in an ostensibly public meeting could be described as "huddling like football players." An allusion is a literary device allowing comparisons with few words. An allusion by Saul Pett of the Associated Press in a proj-ect about government bureaucracy reads like this: "It is one of the ironies of history that a nation born of a deep revulsion for large, overbearing government is itself complaining, from sea to shining sea, about large, overbearing government." The allusion "from sea to shining sea" will be recognized by many readers as a lyric from a well-known patriotic song.

Pacing is a key element in writing effective middles. Varying the lengths of sentences improves readability generally and can help set the appropriate tone for the events described. The lead-in to paragraphs de-scribing an act of murder might consist of mostly long sentences (35 to 50 words) explaining the backgrounds of the killer and the victim as well as how they came together. But the action paragraphs depicting the violent act will almost surely be more effective if it is short (10 to 15 words).

Harrington and other stylists read aloud, looking for pacing problems and, Harrington says, "for words that do not roll off the tongue, rhythms that clash, clichés that must be rephrased, language that is encrusted with the made-up words of bureaucrats and social scientists, attributions that give long, meaningless job titles instead of conversational job descriptions." Several editors have told me they can go into a newsroom and pick out the best writers by watching whose lips move as they type at their computer terminals.

Skillfully rendered dialogue can make a middle seamless. Harrington says such dialogue creates the sense of real life, while quotations from sources speaking to no one but the reporter work against the sense of real life. In novels, subjects do not talk to the omniscient narrator—they talk to each other, in their own special language. Handling attribution gracefully is one of those "little things" that matters. When one source dominates an extended portion, "he saids" and "she saids" should be used as little as possible. If she says during an interview that she hitchhiked from Connecticut to California at age 16 and that can be verified, there is no reason to write "She says she hitchhiked." Instead write, "She hitchhiked." The same is true of factual material; there is no reason to write "He says the condemned building has broken windows" unless the investigator is unable to verify the building is condemned or unable to see the windows are broken.

Internal monologue should be considered by any writer thinking about effective middles. It is a way to reveal characters' thoughts; generally internal dialogue is not punctuated by quotation marks. In his book "The Right Stuff," Tom Wolfe describes an astronaut in orbit viewing the earth. Wolfe could have quoted the astronaut directly, based on tapes kept by mission control: "I thought I could see the outline of Cuba, but I was not sure." Or Wolfe could have employed traditional journalistic exposition: "He thought he could make out the perimeter of Cuba, but was not positive." Instead, Wolfe interviewed the astronaut, interviewed those around him, then composed this interior monologue:

> He tried to find Cuba. Was that Cuba or wasn't that Cuba? Over there, through the clouds.... Everything was black and white and there were clouds all over.... There is Bimini Island and the shoals around Bimini. He could see that. But everything looked so small! It had all been bigger and clearer in the AFLA trainer, when they flashed the still photos on the screen. ... The real thing did not measure up. It was not realistic."

Foreshadowing, flashbacks and other temporal devices must be used judiciously. Amateur foreshadowing can destroy the tenuous bond between writer and audience members. Foreshadowing is a literary device that gives the audience a taste of what is to come, while simultaneously promising more later. In "Beyond the Inverted Pyramid," the authors use an example involving college roommates Deana and Tricia. Tricia talked regularly about committing suicide; Deana preached against it. Angry about the preaching, Tricia threw a wine bottle at Deana. She narrowly missed; the full bottle shattered against the wall. Tricia says something menacing. The writer ends that section of the story like this: "That was when Deana began to be scared of her own roommate." Audience members ought to be hooked at that point. Will Deana escape unharmed? Will

Tricia hurt Deana or kill herself, or both? Will the underlying causes of Tricia's problems be revealed? If so, will they be mundane or shocking?

Flashbacks, unlike foreshadowing, are rarely imbued with such drama, but they can serve a purpose. In a Washington Post magazine piece, a writer told of a black man who had lost his job because of workplace bias despite his unquestioned capability. Throughout the story, the writer flashes back to the man sitting in a bathtub, thinking as he symbolically tries to wash away his troubles. Occasionally, straight chronology—no literary devices such as foreshadowing and flashbacks—is the best way to handle an investigative project. Chronologically is the way many audience members think. That approach also has the virtue of making cause and effect clear, because the cause appears unambiguously before the effect. Cause and effect is a way of emphasizing the "why" in the how, what, when, where, who and why formula of journalistic writing.

Finding the Appropriate Point of View and Tone

Point of view has a dual meaning. It can signify conclusions reached by the reporter after gathering information. It can also signify from whose vantage point the story will be narrated. Walt Harrington often writes the story from inside the head of a main character. He wants to understand and portray people as they understand themselves. Not as they say they understand themselves, but as they really understand themselves, as when they say their prayers in a quiet room. Harrington warns against the pose of the judgmental journalist, the self-righteous crusader. He prefers the motivation of the anthropologist or the novelist.

Tracy Kidder describes his battle with point of view as he worked on "Among Schoolchildren," his book about an inner-city elementary classroom:

> I had spent a year inside her classroom. I intended, vaguely, to fold into my account of events . . . a great deal about the lives of particular children and about the problems of education in America. I tried every point of view that I had used in previous books, and every page I wrote felt lifeless and remote. Finally, I hit on a restricted third-person narrative.
>
> That approach seemed to work. The world of that classroom seemed to come alive when the view of it was restricted mainly to observations of the teacher and to accounts of what the teacher saw and heard and smelled and felt. This choice narrowed my options. I ended up writing something less comprehensive than I had planned. The book became essentially an account of a year in the emotional life of a schoolteacher.
>
> My choice of the restricted third person also obliged me to write parts of the book as if from within the teacher's mind. I wrote many sentences that contained the phrase "she thought." I felt I could do so because the teacher had told me how she felt and what she thought about almost everything that

happened in her classroom. And her descriptions of her thoughts and feelings never seemed self-serving. Believing in them myself, I thought that I could make them believable on the page.

Point of view normally is chosen before tone. Possibilities for tone include formal, conversational, dramatic, skeptical, flippant, apocalyptic and heart-rending. When Bruce DeSilva worked at the Providence Journal, he reported a story about what looked like medical malpractice. In the book "How I Wrote the Story," edited by Christopher Scanlan, De-Silva revealed how he thought about the tone. Should he write a detailed account of the deceased's final days or a more traditional investigative article documenting inadequate treatment? He decided against the investigative, accusatory model. "This was the case of a single mistake by a single physician," DeSilva said. "Turning the full wrath of the Providence Journal on him seemed a bit ridiculous—like nuking a shoplifter. . . . There was too much more in the story that intrigued me. I loved the characters, the ironies, the sights and sounds of the hospital, the dramatic moments."

Endings

If possible, an ending should leave deep thoughts and emotions in the minds of audience members, without editorializing or preaching. Unfortunately, many endings to investigative pieces do editorialize or preach. Many other endings fizzle. The best many investigators do is pull a punchy quotation from their notes, letting somebody else's words do all the work. Other investigators work hard to close the circle: They begin the story with an anecdote involving one person. That person then drops from sight—until the final paragraph, when the character is resurrected as a tieback to the lead. I have written too many endings like that. They probably work for audience members who are not deep thinkers. But they fall into the category of artificial device, and they fail to respect the integrity of the person who ends up as a wispy opening and closing.

Some reporters work hard to find clever endings, reaching into their files for a gem of a surprise. But too often they overreach or make mistakes in judgment. For example, I read a project about the unjustly convicted that focused on a woman who advocates their release. The writer saved a surprise for the end—she is no bleeding heart, as shown by how she turned in her own son for selling drugs. He served eight years alongside some of the inmates his mother was trying to assist. My reaction: Wow! But why did the writer fail to develop that point? Should it have been the lead? Probably.

There is room for improvement. Reporters should stretch less, using the most obvious ending as the most appropriate. A story of a life can end in death. A story of a day in a life can end at midnight. When there is a tieback to the lead, it should be organic instead of artificial. Here is how Walt Harrington opened and closed his inquiry into the career and personal life of investigative journalist Jack Anderson with a focus that neither expected when the research began—Anderson's relationship with his father. In the lead, Anderson is showing Harrington through the family home in Utah. The father had bought a home so big they could not pay the mortgage alone. So the Andersons lived in the basement while renting the rest of the home. The opening anecdote ends with Anderson thinking about his now elderly father and saying "He was a weird guy." Throughout the story, Harrington refers to the rocky father-son relationship as an ambiguous spur to Anderson's career.

At the end, Harrington shows Anderson making a rare visit to his father, who after a lifetime of finding his famous son wanting, compliments him and cries in Anderson's presence for the first time. Anderson hugs his father, trying to comfort him. Harrington's final sentence about Jack Anderson, perceived as a champion hard-boiled muckracker: "Then Jack falls silent, fighting back his own deep tears."

■ STORY STRUCTURES

Story structures must be thought about, even if they do not have names. Jack Hart at the Portland Oregonian says "I think we are lexicon impoverished. We haven't had many names for story structures. I am a firm believer that if you walk through the woods and you know the names of all the plants, you will see a lot more. A lot of writers get halfway through a story and do not realize that they are writing in a particular structure."

In her textbook "Writing and Reporting News," Carole Rich tries to expand the lexicon. The Inverted Pyramid organizes information from most important to least important. The advantage for audience members is that they receive the highlights quickly. The disadvantage is that audience members have little incentive to finish the story.

The High Fives Formula is a variation on the Inverted Pyramid. Its five elements include the News (what happened or is happening), Context (the background of the event or trend), Scope (is the local event part of a national event or trend), Edge (where is the news leading, what happens next) and Impact (why should anyone care).

Rich next describes the Wall Street Journal formula, which goes from the specific to the general. There is a soft lead, a summary paragraph, a backup for those two elements, supporting points, explanations and an ending that ties back to the lead.

The Hourglass story provides the most important news at the top, then proceeds chronologically. The Pyramid structure frequently is the most appropriate for an investigative piece, consisting as it does of the lead, fore-shadowing, chronological storytelling and the climax.

The Sections structure is akin to well-crafted book chapters, with a lead, body and kicker. At the end of each section, audience members should be compelled to move to the next section. The List technique introduces and summarizes key points.

Other structures, not specifically identified by Rich, are Function and Organic. A project reporter examining a massive institution such as the U.S. Agriculture Department or the military might dissect it function by function. For the Agriculture Department, that might mean part one focused on meat inspection, part two on farm supports, part three on rural housing assistance. For the military, that might mean looking first at air defenses, then sea power, then land forces.

Franklin says dramatic stories usually consist of three major parts. The first and last parts consist of a single major focus; the middle part generally houses three major focuses. The opening major focus in part one is the complication. The three focuses in the middle part describe the main character's actions as he tries to resolve the complication. The final focus, in part three, is the resolution. An example: Complication—company fires Joe. Development—depression paralyzes Joe; Joe regains confidence; Joe sues company. Resolution—Joe regains job.

Whatever the structure of the in-depth piece, writers and editors must decide whether to present the material all at once or whether to divide it into a series appearing on separate days. Bruce DeSilva, a writing specialist at the Hartford Courant, suggests avoiding series except under three conditions: "1) When you have a tightly focused question that you can express in a sentence, but which has an answer too complex to be expressed in a single story." DeSilva uses an example of a project that started out as a "condition of higher education" assignment. The reporters and editors finally decided to narrow the question to "How are recent changes in finances and demographics affecting college teaching, research and access to higher education?" Each part of the three-part series focused on one aspect of that question. "2) When you have an old-fashioned serial—a tale with a plot so intriguing that readers will be frantic to see how it turns out." DeSilva tells of a multipart story about an FBI agent posing as a money launderer in an attempt to cripple an international cocaine ring. Readers began calling the writer in the middle of the series to ask how it would turn out because they could not stand the suspense. "3) When you can send your reporter on an adventure that the reporter can write about in installments as he or she goes along."

Literary Journalism as a Discipline

The work of Franklin plus several dozen other practitioners and scholars has created a body of work that could be called the literature of literary journalism. Besides the books already mentioned in this chapter, print and broadcast journalists can benefit from the theories, explanations and examples found in these titles, among others: "Writing Creative Nonfiction" by Theodore A. Rees Cheney; "The Literary Journalists" edited by Norman Sims; "A Sourcebook of American Literary Journalism" edited by Thomas B. Connery; "The Art of Fact" by Barbara Lounsberry; "The Reporter as Artist: A Look at the New Journalism Controversy," edited by Ronald Weber; "The New Journalism" by Tom Wolfe; "From Fact to Fiction: Journalism and Imaginative Writing in America" by Shelley Fisher Fishkin; "The Art and Craft of Feature Writing" by William E. Blundell; "The Heart Is an Instrument: Portraits in Journalism" by Madeleine Blais; "Coaching Writers: The Essential Guide for Editors and Reporters" by Roy Peter Clark and Don Fry; and "Editing for Today's Newsroom: New Perspectives for a Changing Profession" by Carl Sessions Stepp.

Chapter 23

THE ETHICS AND ACCURACY OF INVESTIGATIVE JOURNALISM

As investigators gather information, they need to think about more than how they will structure the story. They also need to make sure the compelling story they write will avoid breaches of ethics, fairness and accuracy. Those are qualities that must be planned for and pursued; they do not occur automatically.

Most ethical situations are not unique to investigative journalists. Furthermore, many of those situations are covered by a consensus. For example, journalists—whether project reporters or sports writers—should never accept tangible gifts, travel or free meals from sources. Journalists should also never make up facts, quotations or entire stories. Nor should they plagiarize. They should not make promises to sources that they cannot keep. This brief section will emphasize matters with a special impact on investigative journalists. At the end of this section is a list of books on journalism ethics that treat just about every situation imaginable.

If journalists work in newsrooms with ethics codes, those codes should be studied. If journalists have questions about, or disagreements with, newsroom-specific codes, they should start a discussion about making changes. If journalists are working for print or broadcast outlets without codes, they might want to read model codes from the Society of Professional Journalists, the Associated Press Managing Editors or other groups to stimulate thinking. Ethics topics with special resonance for investigative journalists are discussed below.

Pretending to Be Other Than a Journalist

The Chicago Sun-Times received a tip from a government official, who refused to be identified in print or help further, that clinics were falsely telling women they were pregnant, then charging them for phony abortions. The newspaper could have informed health or law enforcement authorities at that point, but did not. The newspaper could have made major efforts to obtain evidence from current and former clinic employees. Instead, the newspaper practiced deception by sending investigators as "patients" to the clinics. The patients carried urine samples from males. When the clinic found those samples to show pregnancy, the newspaper heightened its deception by placing journalists in jobs at the clinics—as receptionist, counselors and nurses' aides. The investigators provided no false information in their job interviews, but omitted any references to their journalism connections. For months, the journalists knew women were being harmed through phony abortions, but kept collecting evidence without informing authorities. The collection of evidence included illegally photocopying files of patients.

Another project, same newspaper: When the Chicago Sun-Times set up a phony bar, playfully named the Mirage, to document corrupt behavior by public officials making life difficult for small businesspeople, was that good journalism or entrapment? The journalists involved denied charges of entrapment, saying they were giving officials a chance to demonstrate their normal talent for lawbreaking. Does that ring true to journalists? Is it likely to ring true to members of the audience?

There are hundreds of other examples involving journalists going undercover. Does that behavior harm the credibility of a specific story? Of journalists in general? Is going undercover never justified? Occasionally justified? Usually justified? What guidelines should be used to determine never, occasionally or usually? If journalists can show convincingly that they tried but failed to document wrongdoing through traditional reporting methods, is deception then justified without exception? Or still never or only occasionally justified?

Obtaining Information Covertly

Sometimes journalists identify themselves accurately, but fail to inform sources that information is being captured through hidden cameras or secret audio taping.

Such conduct raises many of the same questions as in the previous section. How much trust is destroyed among specific sources and the bigger audience when journalists resort to subterfuge? Journalists need to search their souls: Is the hidden camera or tape recorder the only way to gather the information? Is the information that might be captured vital to the story, or is it largely glitz? Is the story worth doing given the possibility for eroding trust? If the answers to all those questions are yes, journalists should next consider the middle ground of relying on the information gathered without actually broadcasting any of it. That middle ground will reduce or eliminate charges of sensationalism. When deception is used after deep thought, the audience ought to receive an explanation as part of the story.

Ambush Interviews

Sometimes journalists identify themselves accurately and have their recording equipment in plain sight, but still spawn ethical dilemmas by catching sources unaware, usually in a public place, then acting rudely. The shorthand for this phenomenon is the loaded term "ambush interview."

Ethical dilemmas can be alleviated if journalists have been persistent in requesting interviews of the source in more traditional, polite ways: office or home visits, telephone calls, letters, faxes, telegrams, and the like. The attempts should be documented; for example, a letter can be sent registered, with a return receipt requested.

Only when all those attempts fail to produce an interview with a key source does it make sense to attempt an ambush interview. If the ambush produces no more than a no comment or a rude rejection from the source, why broadcast that footage? Many audience members will attribute broadcasting it to sensationalism, and they might be correct. All that said, when journalists broadcast ambush interviews, they should at the least explain to the audience all of the previous, more traditional attempts made to reach the source. Another category of ethically questionable interviewing technique is to contact the source an unreasonably brief time before publication or broadcast. Most projects worthy of the name take weeks or months of reporting and writing. So why should audience members consider journalists ethical when the sources are refused adequate time to prepare?

Exposing Private Behaviors of Public Figures

Does it matter when an elected politician is involved in extramarital sexual affairs? What if the politician is so involved, but with the permission and knowledge of one or both spouses? Does it matter if the extramarital affairs involve not an elected official but an appointed agency head, such as a Cabinet secretary or a police chief? A judge? A university president? A high school principal? The chief executive of a local employer?

How about if the private behavior involves not sex, but rather alcohol consumption, drug use, failure to pay bills on time, a divorce or a personal bankruptcy filing? What if the errant behavior involves not the powerful figure but that person's spouse or child or parent?

The easy answer to all those questions is to publish or broadcast only if the private behavior clearly affects public performance or the larger society in some demonstrable way. But, like all seemingly easy answers, it is usually difficult to document the behavior without invading privacy, and just as difficult to show its impact in an unambiguous manner. Yet investigative journalists cannot always look the other way simply because it is less complicated to do so. The conventional wisdom is usually correct in this case—better to err on the side of disclosure than on the side of concealment.

Unidentified Sources

The sensitive matter of publishing accusations based solely on information from sources who refuse to be identified publicly will never go away. But the controversy would be less intense and pervasive if journalists would take three steps. First, they should try harder to find the information from on-the-record human sources and from documents; based on my experience, at least half the time the information is available. Second, they should try harder to persuade the original off-the-record source to go public; many will when asked the right way. Third, when nothing else works, they should explain much more fully than they do now why the source has requested and been granted anonymity while defaming other human beings.

Bob Woodward, book author and Washington Post staff member, is probably the most successful, best known and perhaps most talented investigative journalist in the last quarter of the twentieth century. His extensive, largely unquestioning use of anonymous sources in sensitive situations has lent poignancy to the debate. Woodward routinely grants anonymity to government officials, who are paid with tax dollars. Why should they ever be granted anonymity by any journalist who believes government officials in the legislative, executive and judicial branches should be accountable to the citizenry for their thoughts and actions? That is just one of many ethical questions, the answer to which carries profound consequences for investigators and their audiences.

The Golden Rule

In making ethical judgments, journalists should consider applying the golden rule. How would they feel about a member of a media critics' organization applying for and obtaining a newsroom reporting job with the express deceptive purpose of collecting information about the decision-making process, information that would end up in a report critical of the news organization? How would journalists react if that infiltrator made and used copies of internal memos between reporters and editors working on a sensitive investigation? How would journalists feel about being criticized by unnamed sources in, say, the Columbia Journalism Review for their inaccuracies?

Besides applying the golden rule, journalists should apply the rule of harm when deciding whether to begin an investigation and how to conduct that investigation. Can the harm to an individual, institution or society at large be justified by the good that comes to society at large? Can any damage to a journalism organization or to journalists in general be justified by the public service rendered from broadcast or publication of the exposé?

Edmund B. Lambeth addresses these questions and many more in his book "Committed Journalism: An Ethic for the Profession." It is highly recommended for two reasons. First, its chapter devoted to investigative journalism is superb. Second, Lambeth mixes timeless, classical ethical theory with contemporary journalism conundrums as well as any author I have encountered.

Lambeth begins by explaining why journalists require philosophic reflection more practical and adaptable than what had emerged in decades past. He follows that argument with critiques of classical ethical theories as journalists could apply them in contemporary situations. Next, Lambeth chooses values from a variety of ethical theories, mixes them coherently and then explains them in situations that required close calls by journalists. By the time Lambeth reaches Chapter 12, on investigative journalism, he has given readers a broad and deep framework for viewing special ethical dilemmas in new ways. After reading Lambeth, few journalists will feel the need to say "Well, it all depends"—an escape valve that in the past got trotted out under the grand title of "situational ethics."

Additional useful books about ethics, picked partly because they deal with investigative reporting, are "Feeding Frenzy: How Attack Journalism Has Transformed American Politics" by Larry J. Sabato; "Media Ethics: Cases and Moral Reasoning" by Clifford G. Christians, Kim B. Rotzoll and Mark Fackler; "The Virtuous Journalist" by Stephen Klaidman and Tom L. Beauchamp; "The News at Any Cost: How Journalists Compromise Their Ethics to Shape the News" by Tom Goldstein;

"Drawing the Line: How 31 Editors Solved Their Toughest Ethical Dilemmas" edited by Frank McCulloch; "Ethical Journalism" by Philip Meyer; "Ethics for the Media" by William L. Rivers and Cleve Mathews; "Media Ethics: Issues and Cases" edited by Philip Patterson and Lee Wilkins; "Doing Ethics in Journalism" by Jay Black, Bob Steele and Ralph Barney; "Groping for Ethics in Journalism" by Gene Goodwin and Ron F. Smith; "Responsible Journalism" edited by Deni Elliott; "Press Watch" by David Shaw; and "An Ethic of News: A Reporter's Search for Truth" by Wesley G. Pippert.

The Journal of Mass Media Ethics is a useful periodical; most other periodicals aimed at journalists publish pieces about ethics on a frequent basis. One of the most apt ethics books by a nonjournalist is Sissela Bok's "Secrets: On the Ethics of Concealment and Revelation"; her book "Lying: Moral Choice in Public and Private Life" is a useful companion.

■ Fairness, Accuracy and the Law

If a journalistic practice is legal, is it automatically ethical? In Minneapolis-St. Paul, two major newspapers handled the same story in opposite ways. Both were within the law. But could both have acted ethically? The story involved a high-school athlete who hanged himself in a school building. One newspaper published a story but withheld the name on the grounds that the suicide was a private act. The other news-paper published the name, partly because of a similar previous incident and partly because the editors considered the hanging a public act in a public place. Both decisions were legal. Could both be considered ethical?

The point should be obvious: Just because something is legal does not mean it is ethical. But journalists cite law so often because it is usually more clear-cut than ethical codes. Knowing the laws applying to libel, privacy and infliction of emotional distress is important for investigators. It is better to operate from knowledge than from ignorance. There are dozens of books about what statutory and case laws apply to journalists, such as "Major Principles of Media Law" by Wayne Overbeck and Rick D. Pullen. Those books contains lots of cautions that ought to be considered. That said, journalists should not refrain from investigating individuals, institutions and issues merely because they might be sued.

The unfortunate truth is that anybody can file a lawsuit against journalists. Even if the lawsuit is obviously frivolous, the defendants will have to spend a minimum of a few months and thousands of dollars to win a summary judgment. More often, winning takes years and hundreds of thousands of dollars. Reporters and editors so uncomfortable living with the reality of being sued that they hold back should find another way to make a living. If plaintiffs can stifle investigative journalism by threatening or filing litigation, they have won even if they eventually lose in a courtroom.

The best journalists can do is to be so fair, thorough and accurate that they discourage potential plaintiffs from seeking a lawyer. If the potential plaintiff is so blindly enraged as to seek a lawyer anyway, the journalist will have to hope the fairness, thoroughness and accuracy will be so evident that no lawyer would want to waste time on the case. If a determined plaintiff finds an equally determined lawyer, the journalist can still take solace in knowing that the fairness, thoroughness and accuracy are likely to impress judges and jurors.

Prepublication Review

Thoroughness has been an underlying theme of this entire book. Thoroughness takes a journalist a long way toward fairness and accuracy, too, but there are extra steps journalists can take to be paragons of fairness and accuracy. I am convinced that the most important step is to give sources the chance at prepublication review. I am in a distinct minority, although the minority is growing. At least a few of my colleagues think I am preaching a dangerous gospel. I, in turn, suggest that they try prepublication review before continuing their criticism. After all, I have practiced it in conjunction with every long-term project I have written since the early 1980s. Not once has it backfired. Almost every time, it has improved fairness and accuracy.

It was in 1978 that I began to question the conventional wisdom about prepublication review. I was investigating wrongdoing at a large law firm. Understandably, some of my key sources were reluctant to be quoted by name. Some were nervous about providing details even off the record. I understood their reluctance—their reputations among their colleagues were on the line. Some of them were worried about losing their jobs if they talked. So I asked them if I could do anything to reduce their apprehensions.

We trust your work, they responded, but this project might place our livelihoods in jeopardy no matter how good a job you do. We would like to read what you write before it goes into the newspaper. Maybe we can minimize our problems by discussing the story at that stage. Well, why not, I thought. It seemed like a reasonable request given the circumstances.

When the experiment worked, I decided to expand its usage. Gingerly at first, more confidently later, I began offering the privilege of review—for accuracy only—to a variety of reluctant sources involved in my newspaper, magazine and book projects.

Before expanding on the benefits of the procedure, I will convey the objections I have heard, accompanied by rebuttals.

Objection Number One: Sources will have the chance to deny the quotations attributed to them or shoot down other information.

Rebuttal: Before I conduct prepublication review, I make it clear, in writing, that the source is checking for accuracy only. If something is demonstrably inaccurate, I will change it. All other requests for change are just that—requests. I make the decision. If a source denies a quotation attributed to him, I either have it on tape or in my verbatim notes. After any objection, I recheck the tape and the notes. If I have made a mistake, I correct it. If I am correct, I share the recording or the notes with the source. Sometimes the words are correct, but the source objects to the context. I am willing to engage in that dialogue. We regularly miscommunicate with our spouse, our children, our parents. So why should we expect perfect communication with a source we barely know?

If the context needs changing, I change it. If the source is acting in a self-serving way that impedes rather than serves truth, I change nothing. In any case, discussion before publication is preferable to publishing an out-of-context remark. It is also preferable to hearing from an angry source after publication, a source who had no opportunity to review the manuscript and who is now threatening a lawsuit. Never has a source who had an opportunity to review the manuscript threatened to sue me after publication. Furthermore, not once have I made a change against my better judgment.

Objection Two: Sources might successfully pressure higher-ups in the news organization to revise or kill a piece.

Rebuttal: Yes, that could happen, although it has never happened to me. If my editor or publisher betrayed the truth that way, I would never work for them again. I would also use journalism magazines and organizations such as IRE to publicize their shameful conduct.

Objection Three: Sources might threaten to sue after reading the manuscript.

Rebuttal: So what? Courts have almost always refused to engage in prepublication suppression. Besides, if a source is angry enough to make such a threat, the same source will quite likely sue after publication—whether or not there was a prepublication review. Should that occur, I suspect most judges and jurors would be impressed by a reporter so eager to be accurate that he or she conducted a prepublication check.

Objection Four: Prepublication review is unprofessional. Competent journalists get their information right the first time.

Rebuttal: This is wishful thinking. Look at the corrections appearing in the best newspapers and magazines. (Most broadcast outlets almost never air corrections, but that is a result of arrogance, not inerrancy.) Listen to people who are experts on a subject or have attended an event in the news. Almost without exception, they complain about errors and out-of-context information. I once interviewed 40 newspaper editors about how mistakes occur. Everyone of them said they had been misquoted—

often in their own publications. During the seven years I directed IRE, I was a quoted source almost every week, sometimes every day for weeks on end. I cannot remember any story that had everything correct. While I was researching my Armand Hammer biography, I found errors of fact and interpretation in almost everything written about him, covering thousands of newspaper articles, magazine pieces, broadcast clips and books.

Many journalists conduct interviews without tape recorders and without knowledge of shorthand. If any reporter believes that notetaking (minus shorthand) can capture quotations fully and accurately, I invite that reporter to interview me for 15 minutes, taking notes. I will tape the interview. Then we will compare the notes to the tape. The reporter is likely to be chagrined, maybe even shocked, at the discrepancies.

The benefits of prepublication review might be clear by now. First, it sometimes catches errors—the primary purpose of the exercise. Second, it builds trust with sources. Next time I go to those sources, their doors are likely to be open. Furthermore, they will tell future sources about my desire for accuracy, opening additional doors. Third, previously cooperative sources recall new information while reading the manuscript. One such source wrote me an eight-page, single-spaced letter filled with gems while reading a manuscript chapter on Armand Hammer. I had interviewed him multiple times; he has been a fount of information. But reading the manuscript opened a section of his memory that had been closed until that point. Fourth, previously uncooperative sources are so impressed by the procedure that they warm up. On the Hammer book, a key source who had told me little, and that off the record, granted a full interview— for attribution.

The Line-by-Line Accuracy Check

While at the Star Tribune in Minneapolis, projects editor John Ullmann refined the line-by-line procedure to near perfection. Here is an explanation adapted from Ullmann's book "Investigative Reporting: Advanced Methods and Techniques."

> Near the end of each project, we go over every word of every line to check for accuracy, fairness and context. . . . I take a draft of the first story, starting at the top, and the reporter goes back to the original documentation to check out each fact. When we come to quotes, the reporter reads the quotes from the computer where the transcribed interviews reside. This is our last chance to make sure everything is right and it is a much more thorough method than any lawyer's. We wait until near the end because most problems arise not from the facts we use but in the words used to characterize them, as in adverbs and adjectives. How we say something is as important as what we

say. . . . We are not just looking for simple things, such as is the name spelled correctly or is the date of birth right.

Ullmann then explains that the line-by-line procedure is also meant to spot logical inconsistencies or information gaps. He provides three extended examples. Here is an adapted version of one, involving an investigation of 22 children who had died from abuse, neglect or other suspicious circumstances.

All of the children had been known to authorities as being in problem homes, but the system had failed to protect them. Most did not live to their first birthday. The project team concluded that these deaths showed a system out of control. But against what standard?

It can be argued that the death of one child is one child too many, but can we conclude the system is a failure? During this same period, the system handled some 20,000 cases. Did 22 deaths make the system a failure? Looked at another way, did the 20,000 or so child survivors make the system a success? How about another measure—the success/failure rate of other states? Depending on how it is measured, Minnesota was about average or among the best. What, then, could reasonably be concluded from the facts we had dug up?

By taking the cases and poring over them anew, a different pattern emerged. In every case, when the person taking care of the child wanted to avoid supervision, it had been ridiculously easy for him or her to do so. The parent would move a lot. Or, in at least one case, when the social worker came to the door and was told to come back because the child was sleeping, the compliant and overworked case officer failed to return before the child's death.

Another clear pattern showed that the system never integrated observations of doctors, police and case workers until after the death, thus severely reducing the chance, in many cases, of exposing the fact that the child was in danger. This was coupled with some underused research the team had dug up. A researcher in Chicago had made a statistical profile of the child most likely to be at risk, a profile that fit most of our children like a glove. That is, these were children who should have benefitted from the most aggressive intervention, but had not. This was a system seriously out of kilter and in need of reform.

Ullmann ends his section on line-by-lining with this thought: "No one I ever worked with likes going through the line-by-line procedure, including me, but they and I like the feeling before publication that every single thing we published has a reason to be believed."

Bibliography

*T*his chapter-by-chapter bibliography is selective, consisting of books only. Why only books? Because they are usually easily accessible and comprehensive. The right book will give investigators more information on an individual, institution or issue than often difficult-to-obtain newspaper, magazine, newsletter or broadcast pieces will.

The books mentioned ought to be available in at least one of these locations: newsrooms, the publisher, new or used bookstores, collections of friends and relatives, and public libraries. Systematic browsing in those locations will undoubtedly yield books mentioned nowhere in this book. Studying the subject categories of Books in Print should yield additional relevant titles as well. Once a useful book is in hand, an investigator can locate its Library of Congress subject heading, then search for other useful titles under the same designation. That useful book might also contain a bibliography, endnotes and footnotes with titles worth checking.

Books about the law of a topic are likely to yield valuable information as well as additional titles. For example, an up-to-date, accurate, well-written book about environmental law might answer most of an investigator's questions. Its endnotes and footnotes will undoubtedly contain references to more books, some of them highly specialized, that this bibliography has omitted because of space constraints.

For reasons of space, neither the text of this book nor this bibliography mentions every good book—or even a majority of the useful books—about a given topic. Most of the books listed in this bibliography are also mentioned in the text at the appropriate place. When mentioned in the text, books are presented with their main titles and subtitles. Subtitles are omitted in this bibliography because of space constraints.

A caveat about accuracy: Many of the publishers mentioned have since moved to new cities, been swallowed in mergers or gone out of business. The information for each book is presented as it was at the time of the book's appearance.

Most of the non-narrative reference books mentioned in the text of this book do not appear in this bibliography. Reference books are revised and republished so frequently that bibliographic references to them are often outdated. Furthermore, reference books usually cannot be checked out of libraries, are not carried in most retail stores, and are too expensive for many readers of this book to purchase. Every reference book named in the text is described fully enough that investigators should be able to locate it in libraries or, if necessary, order it through a retailer, wholesaler or directly from the publisher.

Books mentioned in more than one chapter of the text appear only once in the bibliography. That appearance comes in the most appropriate chapter. Such an arrangement will mean some readers will occasionally have to search a few minutes outside the chapter they are reading at the time. For that, my apologies, but no arrangement is perfect.

A final thought: As noted, this bibliography does not list already published or broadcast investigative projects found in the IRE Resource Center. That is not meant to devalue Resource Center items. I use the Resource Center for every project I report. It is a unique, unmatchable repository of investigative journalism. Readers of this book wanting to find a specific resource mentioned in the text but absent from the bibliography have enough information to locate it at the news organization's library, on an electronic database or within IRE files. Those locations will often yield resources even more useful than those mentioned in this book—there are many superb investigations that I either have not seen or could not mention for reasons of space.

If a reader of this book becomes interested in conducting an investigation of a specific topic, IRE holds other resources that will help. Does a passage in Chapter 14 about the conduct of a hospital plant a seed? The IRE Journal has published articles about investigating hospitals; speakers at IRE national conferences have given advice preserved on audio tape; and panelists at all manner of IRE workshops have presented handouts on file.

INTRODUCTION

Anderson, Jack, with James Boyd. "Confessions of a Muckraker." New York: Random House, 1979.

Beaty, Jonathan, and S.C. Gwynne. "The Outlaw Bank." New York: Random House, 1993.

Behrens, John C. "The Typewriter Guerillas." Chicago: Nelson-Hall, 1977.

Benjaminson, Peter, and David Anderson. "Investigative Reporting." Ames: Iowa State University Press, 1990.

Bernstein, Carl, and Bob Woodward. "All the President's Men." New York: Simon & Schuster, 1974.

Binyan, Liu. "A Higher Kind of Loyalty." New York: Pantheon, 1990.

Brady, Kathleen. "Ida Tarbell." New York: Seaview/Putnam, 1984.

Buchanan, Edna. "The Corpse Had a Familiar Face." New York: Random House, 1987.

Buchanan, Edna. "Never Let Them See You Cry." New York: Random House, 1992.

Campbell, Richard. "Sixty Minutes and the News." Urbana: University of Illinois Press, 1991.

Cheshire, Maxine. "Maxine Cheshire, Reporter." Boston: Houghton Mifflin, 1978.

Cook, Fred. "Maverick." New York: Putnam, 1984.

Cottrell, Robert C. "Izzy." New Brunswick, N.J.: Rutgers University Press, 1992.

Davidson, James West, and Mark Hamilton Lytle. "After the Fact." New York: Knopf, 1985.

Downie, Leonard Jr. "The New Muckrakers." Washington, D.C.: New Republic Books, 1976.

Duzan, Maria Jimena. "Death Beat." New York: HarperCollins, 1994.

Farber, Myron. "Somebody Is Lying." Garden City, N.Y.: Doubleday, 1982.

Filler, Louis. "The Muckrakers." University Park: Pennsylvania State University Press, 1976.

Fischer, David Hackett. "Historians' Fallacies." New York: Harper & Row, 1970.

Gaines, William. "Investigative Reporting for Print and Broadcast." Chicago: Nelson-Hall, 1994.

Gross, Ronald, ed. The Independent Scholar's Handbook. Berkeley, Calif.: Ten Speed Press, 1993.

Gunther, Marc. "The House That Roone Built." Boston: Little, Brown, 1994.

Havill, Adrian. "Deep Truth." New York: Birch Lane/Carol Publishing, 1993.

Hume, Brit. "Inside Story." Garden City, N.Y.: Doubleday, 1974.

Kaplan, Justin. "Lincoln Steffens." New York: Simon & Schuster, 1974.

Keeler, Robert F. "Newsday." New York: Arbor House/Morrow, 1990.

King, Dennis. "Get the Facts on Anyone." New York: Prentice Hall, 1992.

Kroeger, Brooke. "Nellie Bly." New York: Times Books, 1994.

Kurtz, Howard. "Media Circus." New York: Times Books, 1993.

McWilliams, Carey. "The Education of Carey McWilliams." New York: Simon & Schuster, 1979.

Meyer, Philip. "The New Precision Journalism." Bloomington: Indiana University Press, 1991.

Miraldi, Robert. "Muckraking and Objectivity." Westport, Conn.: Greenwood Press, 1990.

Mitchell, Dave, Cathy Mitchell and Richard Ofshe. "The Light on Synanon." New York: Seaview Books, 1980.

Mitford, Jessica. "Poison Penmanship." New York: Knopf, 1979.

Mollenhoff, Clark. "Investigative Reporting." New York: Macmillan, 1981.

Nerone, John. "Violence Against the Press." New York: Oxford University Press, 1994.

`aret Jones, and Robert H. Russell, eds. "Behind the Lines." New
nbia University Press, 1986.

Have I Got a Tip for You." New York: Dow Jones, 1994.

rnelan, James. "Scandals, Scamps and Scoundrels." New York: Random House, 1982.

Pileggi, Nicholas. "Blye, Private Eye." Chicago: Playboy Press, 1976.

Protess, David, Fay Lomax Cook, Jack C. Doppelt, James S. Ettema, Margaret T. Gordon, Donna R. Leff and Peter Miller. "The Journalism of Outrage." New York: Guilford, 1991.

Ricchiardi, Sherry, and Virginia Young. "Women on Deadline." Ames: Iowa State University Press, 1991.

Rivera, Geraldo, and Daniel Paisner. "Exposing Myself." New York: Bantam, 1991.

Rose, Louis J. "How to Investigate Your Friends and Enemies." St. Louis: Albion Press, 1992.

Schorr, Daniel. "Clearing the Air." Boston: Houghton Mifflin, 1977.

Steffens, Lincoln. "The Autobiography of Lincoln Steffens." New York: Harcourt, Brace, 1931.

Stocking, S. Holly, and Paget H. Gross. "How Do Journalists Think?" Bloomington, Ind.: ERIC Clearinghouse, 1989.

Taibbi, Mike, and Anna Sims-Phillips. "Unholy Alliances." San Diego: Harcourt Brace Jovanovich, 1989.

Tarbell, Ida. "All in the Day's Work." New York: Macmillan, 1939.

Thiem, George. "The Hodge Scandal." New York: St. Martin's, 1963.

Thompson, Josiah. "Gumshoe." Boston: Little, Brown, 1988.

Thompson, Loren B., ed. "The Defense Beat." New York: Lexington Books, 1991.

Ullmann, John. "Investigative Reporting." New York: St. Martin's, 1994.

Wallraff, Gunter. "Wallraff, the Undesirable Journalist." Woodstock, N.Y.: Overlook Press, 1979.

Wendland, Michael F. "The Arizona Project." Kansas City: Sheed Andrews & McMeel, 1977.

Williams, Paul N. "Investigative Reporting and Editing." Englewood Cliffs, N.J.: Prentice Hall, 1978.

Yocum, Robin, and Catherine Candisky. "Insured for Murder." Buffalo, N.Y.: Prometheus Books, 1993.

CHAPTER 1

Mann, Thomas. "A Guide to Library Research Methods." New York: Oxford University Press, 1987.

Maxwell, Bruce. "Washington Online: How to Access the Federal Government on the Internet." Washington, D.C.: Congressional Quarterly, 1994.

Reddick, Randy, and Elliot King. "The Online Journalist." Fort Worth: Harcourt Brace, 1995.

Semonche, Barbara P., ed. "News Media Libraries." Westport, Conn.: Greenwood Press, 1993.

CHAPTER 2

Johnson, Richard S. "How to Locate Anyone Who Is or Has Been in the Military." Fort Sam Houston, Texas: Military Information Enterprises, 1991.

Lesko, Matthew. The Federal Data Base Finder. Kensington, Md.: Information USA, 1990.

Morehead, Joe, and Mary Fetzer. "Introduction to United States Government Information Sources." Englewood, Colo.: Libraries Unlimited, 1992.

Robinson, Judith Schiek. "Tapping the Government Grapevine." Phoenix: Oryx Press, 1993.

Schick, Frank L., Renee Schick and Mark Carroll. "Records of the Presidency." Phoenix: Oryx Press, 1989.

CHAPTER 3

Berkman, Robert I. "Find It Fast." New York: HarperCollins, 1994.

Branscomb, Anne Wells. "Who Owns Information?" New York: Basic Books, 1994.

Haines, Gerald K., and David A. Langbart. "Unlocking the Files of the FBI." Wilmington, Del.: Scholarly Resources, 1993.

CHAPTER 4

Bell, Barbara L. An Annotated Guide to Current National Bibliographies. Alexandria, Va.: Chadwyck-Healey, 1986.

Dubro, Alec, and David Kaplan. "Yakuza." Reading, Mass.: Addison-Wesley, 1986.

Eakle, Arlene, and Johni Cerny, eds. The Source. Salt Lake City: Ancestry Publishing, 1984.

Hersh, Seymour. "The Samson Option." New York: Vintage/Random House, 1993.

Jackson, Paul. British Sources of Information. New York: Routledge & Kegan Paul, 1987.

Jennings, Andrew, and Vyv Simson. "The Lords of the Rings." London: Simon & Schuster, 1992.

Kaminkow, Marion J. Genealogies in the Library of Congress. Baltimore: Genealogical Publishing, 1981.

Overbury, Stephen. Finding Canadian Facts Fast. Toronto: Methuen, 1985.

Shannon, Elaine. "Desperados." New York: Viking, 1988.

Smith, Allen. "Directory of Oral History Collections." Phoenix: Oryx Press, 1988.

CHAPTER 5

Biagi, Shirley. "Interviews That Work." Belmont, Calif.: Wadsworth, 1992.

Brady, John. "The Craft of Interviewing." New York: Vintage, 1977.

Domhoff, G. William. "Who Rules America Now?" New York: Simon & Schuster, 1983.

Fitzgerald, A. Ernest. "The Pentagonists." Boston: Houghton Mifflin, 1989.

Glazer, Myron Peretz, and Penina Migdal Glazer. "The Whistleblowers." New York: Basic Books, 1989.

Harrington, Walt. "American Profiles." Columbia: University of Missouri Press, 1992.

Killenberg, George M., and Rob Anderson. "Before the Story." New York: St. Martin's, 1989.

Maas, Peter. "Serpico." New York: Viking, 1973.

Metzler, Ken. "Creative Interviewing." Needham Heights, Mass.: Prentice Hall, 1989.

Pankau, Edmund J. "Check It Out!" Chicago: Contemporary Books, 1992.

Ricci, David M. "The Transformation of American Politics." New Haven, Conn.: Yale University Press, 1993.

Smith, James A. "The Idea Brokers." New York: Free Press, 1991.

Trounstine, Philip J. "Movers and Shakers." New York: St. Martin's, 1982.

CHAPTER 6

Aberbach, Joel D. "Keeping a Watchful Eye." Washington, D.C.: Brookings Institution, 1990.

Arnold, R. Douglas. "Congress and the Bureaucracy." New Haven, Conn.: Yale University Press, 1979.

Biersack, Robert, Paul S. Herrnson and Clyde Wilcox, eds. "Risky Business?" Armonk, N.Y.: Sharpe, 1994.

Birnbaum, Jeffrey H. "The Lobbyists." New York: Times Books, 1992.

Bryner, Gary. "Blue Skies, Green Politics." Washington, D.C.: Congressional Quarterly, 1992.

Cohen, William S., and George J. Mitchell. "Men of Zeal." New York: Viking Penguin, 1988.

Cohodas, Nadine. "Strom Thurmond." New York: Simon & Schuster, 1993.

DeLeon, Peter. "Thinking About Political Corruption." Armonk, N.Y.: Sharpe, 1993.

Drew, Elizabeth. "Politics and Money." New York: Macmillan, 1983.

Drew, Elizabeth. "Senator." New York: Simon & Schuster, 1979.

Fenno, Richard F. Jr. "The Emergence of a Senate Leader." Washington, D.C.: Congressional Quarterly, 1991.

Fenno, Richard F. Jr. "Learning to Legislate." Washington, D.C.: Congressional Quarterly, 1991.

Fenno, Richard F. Jr. "The Making of a Senator." Washington, D.C.: Congressional Quarterly, 1989.

Fenno, Richard F. Jr. "When Incumbency Fails." Washington, D.C.: Congressional Quarterly, 1992.

Forgette, Richard. "The Power of the Purse Strings." Westport, Conn.: Praeger, 1994.

Fox, Harrison W. Jr., and Susan W. Hammond. "Congressional Staffs." New York: Free Press, 1977.

Gross, Martin L. "The Government Racket." New York: Bantam, 1992.

Hamilton, James. "The Power to Probe." New York: Random House, 1976.

Hickok, Eugene W. "The Reform of State Legislatures and the Changing Character of Representation." Bethesda, Md.: University Press of America, 1992.

Jackley, John L. "Hill Rat." Washington, D.C.: Regnery Gateway, 1992.

Jackson, Brooks. "Honest Graft." Washington, D.C.: Farragut Publishing, 1990.

Kelly, Brian. "Adventures in Porkland." New York: Times Books, 1993.

Kirchmeier, Mark. "Packwood." San Francisco: HarperCollins West, 1995.

Loftus, Tom. "The Art of Legislative Politics." Washington, D.C.: Congressional Quarterly, 1994.

Makinson, Larry. "Follow the Money Handbook." Washington, D.C.: Center for Responsive Politics, 1994.

Malbin, Michael J. "Unelected Representatives." New York: Basic Books, 1980.

Manley, John F. "The Politics of Finance." Boston: Little, Brown, 1970.

Martin, Janet M. "Lessons From the Hill." New York: St. Martin's, 1994.

Mosher, Frederick C. "The GAO." Boulder, Colo.: Westview Press, 1979.

Mosher, Frederick C. "A Tale of Two Agencies." Baton Rouge: Louisiana State University Press, 1986.

Munson, Richard. "The Cardinals of Capitol Hill." New York: Grove Atlantic, 1993.

Overacker, Louise. "Money in Elections." New York: Macmillan, 1932.

Page, Benjamin I. "Who Gets What From Government." Berkeley: University of California Press, 1983.

Peters, Charles. "How Washington Really Works." Reading, Mass.: Addison-Wesley, 1980.

Redman, Eric. "The Dance of Legislation." New York: Simon & Schuster, 1973.

Reid, T.R. "Congressional Odyssey." New York: W.H. Freeman, 1980.

Roberts, Jerry. "Dianne Feinstein." San Francisco: HarperCollins West, 1994.

Roderick, Lee. "Orrin Hatch." Placerville, Calif.: Gold Leaf Press, 1994.

Sabato, Larry J. "Feeding Frenzy." New York: Free Press, 1993.

Schneier, Edward V., and Bertram Gross. "Congress Today." New York: St. Martin's, 1993.

Schoenbrod, David. "Power Without Responsibility." New Haven, Conn.: Yale University Press, 1993.

Smist, Frank J. Jr. "Congress Oversees the United States Intelligence Community." Knoxville: University of Tennessee Press, 1989.

Stedino, Joseph, and Dary Matera. "What's In It for Me?" New York: HarperCollins, 1992.

Thompson, Dennis F. "Political Ethics and Public Office." Cambridge, Mass.: Harvard University Press, 1987.

Waldman, Steven. "The Bill." New York: Viking, 1995.

Zilliox, Larry Jr. "The Opposition Research Handbook." McLean, Va.: Investigative Research Specialists, 1993.

CHAPTER 7

Adams, Gordon. "The Iron Triangle." Washington, D.C.: Council on Economic Priorities, 1981.

Axelrod, Donald. "Shadow Government." New York: Wiley, 1992.

Bailey, Thomas A. "Presidential Saints and Sinners." New York: Free Press, 1981.

Bamford, James. "The Puzzle Palace." New York: Penguin, 1983.

Bell, Griffin, and Ronald Ostrow. "Taking Care of the Law." New York: Morrow, 1982.

Berman, David R., ed. "County Governments in an Era of Change." Westport, Conn.: Greenwood Press, 1993.

Beyle, Thad L. "Governors and Hard Times." Washington, D.C.: Congressional Quarterly, 1992.

Burnham, David. "A Law Unto Itself." New York: Random House, 1989.

Caro, Robert A. "The Power Broker." New York: Knopf, 1974.

Carter, Stephen L. "The Confirmation Mess." New York: Basic Books, 1994.

Cogan, John F., Timothy J. Muris and Allen Schick. "The Budget Puzzle." Stanford, Calif.: Stanford University Press, 1994.

Collender, Stanley E. "The Guide to the Federal Budget." Washington, D.C.: Urban Institute Press, 1995.

Edwards, George C. III. "Implementing Public Policy." Washington, D.C.: Congressional Quarterly, 1980.

Fritschler, A. Lee. "Smoking and Politics." Englewood Cliffs, N.J.: Prentice Hall, 1989.

Goodsell, Charles T. "The Case for Bureaucracy." Chatham, N.J.: Chatham House, 1994.

Henriques, Diana B. "The Machinery of Greed." Lexington, Mass.: Lexington Books, 1986.

Holloway, Harry, and Frank S. Meyers. "Bad Times for Good Ol' Boys." Norman: University of Oklahoma Press, 1993.

Kerwin, Cornelius M. "Rulemaking." Washington, D.C.: Congressional Quarterly, 1994.

Koch, Ed, and Daniel Paisner. "Citizen Koch." New York: St. Martin's, 1992.

Light, Paul C. "Monitoring Government." Washington, D.C.: Brookings Institution, 1993.

McElvaine, Robert S. "Mario Cuomo." New York: Scribners, 1988.

Noonan, John T. Jr. "Bribes." New York: Macmillan, 1984.

Osborne, David, and Ted Gaebler. "Reinventing Government." Reading, Mass.: Addison-Wesley, 1992.

Payne, J. Gregory, and Scott C. Ratzan. "Tom Bradley." Santa Monica, Calif.: Roundtable Publishing, 1986.

Roberts, Robert N. "White House Ethics." New York: Greenwood Press, 1988.

Ross, Shelley. "Fall From Grace." New York: Ballantine, 1988.

Schick, Allen. "The Federal Budget." Washington, D.C.: Brookings Institution, 1994.

Shropshire, Mike, and Frank Schaeffer. "The Thorny Rose of Texas." New York: Birch Lane/Carol Publishing, 1994.

Stanton, Thomas H. "A State of Risk." New York: HarperBusiness, 1991.

Sternberg, William, and Matthew C. Harrison Jr. "Feeding Frenzy." New York: Holt, 1989.

Yancey, Dwayne. "When Hell Froze Over." Dallas: Taylor Publishing, 1990.

Young, Coleman. "Hard Stuff." New York: Viking, 1994.

CHAPTER 8

Banks, James A., and Cherry A. McGee Banks. "Multicultural Education." Needham Heights, Mass.: Allyn, 1989.

Banks, Jeri. "All of Us Together." Washington, D.C.: Gallaudet University Press, 1994.

Biklen, Douglas. "Schooling Without Labels." Philadelphia: Temple University Press, 1991.

Brint, Steven, and Jerome Karabel. "The Diverted Dream." New York: Oxford University Press, 1991.

Chernoff, Michael L., Paula M. Nassif and William P. Gorth. "The Validity Issue." Hillsdale, N.J.: Erlbaum, 1987.

Collins, Catherine, and Douglas Frantz. "Teachers Talking Out of School." New York: Little, Brown, 1993.

Cookson, Peter W. Jr. "School Choice." New Haven, Conn.: Yale University Press, 1994.

Dreyfuss, Joel, and Charles Lawrence III. "The Bakke Case." New York: Harcourt Brace Jovanovich, 1979.

Farber, Barry A. "Crisis in Education." San Francisco: Jossey-Bass, 1991.

Freedman, Samuel G. "Small Victories." New York: Harper & Row, 1990.

French, Thomas. "South of Heaven." New York: Doubleday, 1993.

Greenspan, Stanley I., and Jacqueline L. Salmon. "Playground Politics." Reading, Mass.: Addison-Wesley, 1993.

Griffin, Robert S. "Underachievers in Secondary Schools." Hillsdale, N.J.: Erlbaum, 1988.

Hanson, F. Allan. "Testing, Testing." Berkeley: University of California Press, 1993.

Hyman, Irwin A. "Reading, Writing and the Hickory Stick." Lexington, Mass.: Lexington Books, 1990.

Kerr, Clark, and Marian L. Gade. "The Guardians." Washington, D.C.: Association of Governing Boards of Universities and Colleges, 1989.

Kidder, Tracy. "Among Schoolchildren." Boston: Houghton Mifflin, 1989.

Kimball, Roger. "Tenured Radicals." New York: Harper & Row, 1990.

Kluger, Richard. "Simple Justice." New York: Knopf, 1976.

Kozol, Jonathan. "Savage Inequalities." New York: Crown, 1991.

Leap, Terry L. "Tenure, Discrimination and the Courts." Ithaca, N.Y.: ILR Press, 1993.

Lehne, Richard. "The Quest for Justice." New York: Longman, 1978.

Lickona, Thomas. "Educating for Character." New York: Bantam, 1991.

Loewen, James W. "Lies My Teacher Told Me." New York: New Press, 1994.

Manshel, Lisa. "Nap Time." New York: Zebra Books, 1991.

Miracle, Andrew W. Jr., and C. Roger Rees. "Lessons of the Locker Room." Buffalo, N.Y.: Prometheus Books, 1994.

Nelson, Jack, and Gene Roberts Jr. "The Censors and the Schools." Boston: Little, Brown, 1962.

Nord, Warren A. "Religion and American Education." Chapel Hill: University of North Carolina Press, 1994.

Nuwer, Hank. "Broken Pledges." Atlanta: Longstreet, 1990.

Olevnik, Peter P., et al. "American Higher Education." Westport, Conn.: Greenwood Press, 1993.

Owen, David. "None of the Above." Boston: Houghton Mifflin, 1985.

Powell, John W., Michael S. Pander and Robert C. Nielsen. "Campus Security and Law Enforcement." Woburn, Mass.: Butterworth-Heinemann, 1994.

Rosenberg, Michael S., and Irene Edmond-Rosenberg. The Special Education Sourcebook. Bethesda, Md.: Woodbine House, 1994.

Rossell, Christine H. "The Carrot or the Stick for School Desegregation Policy." Philadelphia: Temple University Press, 1990.

Sachar, Emily. "Shut Up and Let the Lady Teach." New York: Simon & Schuster, 1991.

Sadker, Myra, and David Sadker. "Failing at Fairness." New York: Scribners, 1994.

Sizer, Theodore R. "Horace's School." Boston: Houghton Mifflin, 1992.

Smith, Sally L. "Succeeding Against the Odds." Los Angeles: Tarcher, 1992.

Sykes, Charles J. "Profscam." New York: St. Martin's, 1988.

Tyson, Harriet. "A Conspiracy of Good Intentions." Washington, D.C.: Council for Basic Education, 1988.

Weber, Don W., and Charles Bosworth Jr. "Secret Lessons." New York: Onyx, 1994.

Wheelock, Anne. "Crossing the Tracks." New York: New Press, 1992.

Woodbury, Marda. "A Guide to Sources of Educational Information." Arlington, Va.: Information Resources Press, 1982.

Wortham, Sue C. "Early Childhood Curriculum." New York: Macmillan, 1993.

Zigler, Edward, and Sally Styfco, eds. "Head Start and Beyond." New Haven, Conn.: Yale University Press, 1993.

CHAPTER 9

Abadinsky, Howard. "The Criminal Elite." Westport, Conn.: Greenwood Press, 1983.

Anderson, David C. "Crimes of Justice." New York: Times Books, 1988.

Belenko, Steven R. "Crack and the Evolution of Anti-Drug Policy." Westport, Conn.: Greenwood Press, 1993.

Benedict, Helen. "Virgin or Vamp." New York: Oxford University Press, 1992.

Blau, Robert. "The Cop Shop." Reading, Mass.: Addison-Wesley, 1993.

Blumenthal, Ralph. "Last Days of the Sicilians." New York: Times Books, 1988.

Coleman, James William. "The Criminal Elite." New York: St. Martin's, 1994.

Count, E.W. "Cop Talk." New York: Pocket Books, 1994.

Dunham, Roger G., and Geoffrey P. Alpert, eds. "Critical Issues in Policing." Prospect Heights, Ill.: Waveland Press, 1989.

Fletcher, Connie. "What Cops Know." New York: Villard, 1990.

Flynn, Kevin. "The Unmasking." New York: Free Press, 1993.

Gelman, Mitch. "Crime Scene." New York: Times Books, 1992.

Golab, Jan. "The Dark Side of the Force." New York: Atlantic Monthly Press, 1993.

Greene, Melissa Fay. "Praying for Sheetrock." Reading, Mass.: Addison-Wesley, 1991.

Gugliotta, Guy, and Jeff Leen. "Kings of Cocaine." New York: Simon & Schuster, 1989.

Hazelwood, Robert R., and Ann Wolbert Burgess. "Practical Aspects of Rape Investigation." Elkins Park, Pa.: CRC Press, 1987.

Hosansky, Tamar, and Pat Sparling. "Working Vice." New York: HarperCollins, 1992.

Humes, Edward. "Murderer With a Badge." New York: Dutton, 1992.

Jones, Ann. "Next Time, She'll Be Dead." Boston: Beacon Press, 1994.

Knoedelseder, William. "Stiffed." New York: HarperCollins, 1993.

Kwitny, Jonathan. "Vicious Circles." New York: Norton, 1981.

Larson, Erik. "Lethal Passage." New York: Crown, 1994.

Levine, Michael. "Deep Cover." New York: Delacorte Press, 1990.

Marion, Nancy E. "A History of Federal Crime Control Initiatives." Westport, Conn.: Praeger, 1994.

Marx, Gary T. "Undercover." Berkeley: University of California Press, 1988.

Micheels, Peter A. "Heat." New York: St. Martin's, 1991.

Middleton, Michael L. "Cop." Chicago: Contemporary Books, 1994.

Neff, James. "Unfinished Murder." New York: Pocket Books, 1995.

Noguchi, Thomas T., and Joseph DiMona. "Coroner." New York: Pocket Books, 1984.

O'Neill, Hugh, Hy Hammer and E.P. Steinberg. "Police Officer." New York: Arco, 1994.

Osterburg, James W., and Richard H. Ward. "Criminal Investigation." Cincinnati: Anderson Publishing, 1992.

Perez, Douglas W. "Common Sense About Police Review." Philadelphia: Temple University Press, 1994.

Reuter, Peter. "Disorganized Crime." Cambridge, Mass.: MIT Press, 1983.

Sasser, Charles W., and Michael W. Sasser. "Last American Heroes." New York: Pocket Books, 1994.

Sellers, Steve. "Terror on Highway 59." Austin: Texas Monthly Press, 1984.

Sherman, Lawrence W. "Policing Domestic Violence." New York: Free Press, 1992.

Simon, David. "Homicide." Boston: Houghton Mifflin, 1991.

Skolnick, Jerome H., and James J. Fyfe. "Above the Law." New York: Free Press, 1993.

Stutman, Robert M., and Richard Esposito. "Dead on Delivery." New York: Warner, 1992.

Swindle, Howard. "Deliberate Indifference." New York: Viking, 1993.

Trojanowicz, Robert, and Bonnie Bucqueroux. "Community Policing." Cincinnati: Anderson Publishing, 1993.

Woolner, Ann. "Washed in Gold." New York: Simon & Schuster, 1994.

Wright, Richard T., and Scott Decker. "Burglars on the Job." Boston: Northeastern University Press, 1994.

Ziegenmeyer, Nancy, and Larkin Warren. "Taking Back My Life." New York: Summit Books, 1992.

CHAPTER 10

Adler, Stephen J. "The Jury." New York: Times Books, 1994.

Baker, Thomas E. "Rationing Justice on Appeal." St. Paul: West Publishing, 1994.

Bass, Jack. "Taming the Storm." New York: Doubleday, 1993.

Brill, Steven, ed. "Trial by Jury." New York: American Lawyer/Simon & Schuster, 1990.

Brown, Edmund G., and Dick Adler. "Public Justice, Private Mercy." New York: Weidenfeld and Nicolson, 1989.

Caplan, Lincoln. "Skadden." New York: Farrar, Straus & Giroux, 1993.

Caplan, Lincoln. "The Tenth Justice." New York: Knopf, 1987.

Coffin, Frank M. "On Appeal." New York: Norton, 1994.

Couric, Emily. "The Trial Lawyers." New York: St. Martin's, 1988.

Daly, Kathleen. "Gender, Crime and Punishment." New Haven, Conn.: Yale University Press, 1994.

Denniston, Lyle W. "The Reporter and the Law." New York: Columbia University Press, 1992.

Dickerson, Thomas A. "Class Actions." New York: New York Law Publishing, 1988.

DiIulio, John J. Jr. "Courts, Corrections and the Constitution." New York: Oxford University Press, 1990.

DiIulio, John J. Jr. "Governing Prisons." New York: Free Press, 1987.

DiIulio, John J. Jr. "No Escape." New York: Basic Books, 1991.

DiPerna, Paula. "Juries on Trial." New York: Dembner, 1984.

Drechsel, Robert E. "News Making in the Trial Courts." New York: Longman, 1983.

Earley, Pete. "The Hot House." New York: Bantam, 1992.

Elias, Stephen, Albin Renauer and Robin Leonard. "How to File for Bankruptcy." Berkeley, Calif.: Nolo Press, 1993.

Faux, Marian. "Roe v. Wade." New York: Macmillan, 1988.

Feld, Barry C. "Justice for Children." Boston: Northeastern University Press, 1993.

Forer, Lois G. "Criminals and Victims." New York: Norton, 1980.

Forer, Lois G. "A Rage to Punish." New York: Norton, 1994.

Forer, Lois G. "Unequal Protection." New York: Norton, 1991.

Friedman, Lawrence M. "Crime and Punishment in American History." New York: Basic Books, 1993.

Ganey, Terry. "St. Joseph's Children." New York: Lyle Stuart, 1989.

Garrison, J. Gregory, and Randy Roberts. "Heavy Justice." Reading, Mass.: Addison-Wesley, 1994.

Goulden, Joseph C. "The Benchwarmers." New York: Weybright and Talley, 1974.

Goulden, Joseph C. "The Million-Dollar Lawyers." New York: Putnam, 1978.

Hillman, William C. "Personal Bankruptcy." New York: Practising Law Institute, 1993.

Jacobs, Mark D. "Screwing the System and Making It Work." Chicago: University of Chicago Press, 1990.

Kramer, Rita. "At a Tender Age." New York: Holt, 1988.

Lewis, Anthony. "Gideon's Trumpet." New York: Random House, 1964.

Loftus, Elizabeth, and Katherine Ketcham. "Witness for the Defense." New York: St. Martin's, 1991.

Lotz, Roy Edward. "Crime and the American Press." New York: Praeger, 1991.

Maas, Peter. "Marie." New York: Random House, 1983.

MacLean, Harry N. "Once Upon a Time." New York: HarperCollins, 1993.

Mann, Coramae Richey. "Unequal Justice." Bloomington: Indiana University Press, 1993.

McGough, Lucy S. "Child Witnesses." New Haven, Conn.: Yale University Press, 1994.

Mitford, Jessica. "Kind and Usual Punishment." New York: Vintage Books, 1974.

Morris, Norval, and Michael Tonry. "Between Prison and Probation." New York: Oxford University Press, 1993.

Noonan, John T. Jr., and Kenneth I. Winston, eds. "The Responsible Judge." Westport, Conn.: Praeger, 1993.

Perlin, Michael T. "The Jurisprudence of the Insanity Defense." Durham, N.C.: Carolina Academic Press, 1994.

Phillips, Steven. "No Heroes, No Villains." New York: Random House, 1977.

Protess, David, and Rob Warden. "Gone in the Night." New York: Delacorte, 1993.

Radelet, Michael L., Hugo Adam Bedau and Constance E. Putnam. "In Spite of Innocence." Boston: Northeastern University Press, 1992.

Rideau, Wilbert, and Ron Wikberg. "Life Sentences." New York: Times Books, 1992.

Ross, Lynne, ed. "State Attorneys General." Washington, D.C.: Bureau of National Affairs, 1990.

Saldana, Richard H. "Crime Victim Compensation Programs." Bountiful, Utah: QuartZite Publishing, 1994.

Salokar, Rebecca Mae. "The Solicitor General." Philadelphia: Temple University Press, 1992.

Savage, David G. "Turning Right." New York: Wiley, 1992.

Schwartz, Ira M., and William H. Barton, eds. "Reforming Juvenile Detention." Columbus: Ohio State University Press, 1994.

Sherrill, Robert. "Military Justice Is to Justice as Military Music Is to Music." New York: Harper & Row, 1970.

Steinberg, E.P. "Correction Officer." New York: Arco, 1994.

Stewart, James B. "The Prosecutors." New York: Simon & Schuster, 1987.

Stumpf, Harry P., and John H. Culver. "The Politics of State Courts." New York: Longman, 1992.

Sullivan, Timothy. "Unequal Verdicts." New York: Simon & Schuster, 1992.

Terr, Lenore. "Unchained Memories." New York: Basic Books, 1994.

Thaler, Paul. "The Watchful Eye." Westport, Conn.: Greenwood Press, 1994.

Touhy, James, and Rob Warden. "Greylord." New York: Putnam, 1989.

Urofsky, Melvin I. "A Conflict of Rights." New York: Scribners, 1991.

Wicker, Tom. "A Time to Die." Lincoln: University of Nebraska Press, 1994.

Williford, Miriam, ed. "Higher Education in Prison." Phoenix: Oryx Press, 1994.

Woodward, Bob, and Scott Armstrong. "The Brethren." New York: Avon Books, 1981.

Wright, Lawrence. "Remembering Satan." New York: Knopf, 1994.

Yant, Martin. "Presumed Guilty." Buffalo, N.Y.: Prometheus Books, 1991.

CHAPTER 11

Bakos, Susan Crain. "Appointment for Murder." New York: Putnam, 1988.

Barnhart, Phillip A. The Guide to National Professional Certification Programs. Amherst, Mass.: Human Resource Development Press, 1994.

Cottell, Philip G. Jr. "Accounting Ethics." Westport, Conn.: Quorum/Greenwood Press, 1990.

Englade, Ken. "A Family Business." New York: St. Martin's, 1992.

Gorlin, Rena A., ed. "Codes of Professional Responsibility." Washington, D.C.: Bureau of National Affairs, 1990.

Greising, David, and Laurie Morse. "Brokers, Bagmen and Moles." New York: Wiley, 1991.

Gross, Stanley J. "Of Foxes and Henhouses." Westport, Conn.: Quorum Books, 1984.

Kultgen, John. "Ethics and Professionalism." Philadelphia: University of Pennsylvania Press, 1988.

CHAPTER 12

Avrutis, Raymond, and Geraldine S. Wulff. "How to Maximize Your Unemployment Benefits." Garden City Park, N.Y.: Avery, 1994.

Barlett, Donald L., and James B. Steele. "America: What Went Wrong?" Kansas City: Andrews & McMeel, 1992.

Barlett, Donald L., and James B. Steele. "America: Who Pays the Taxes?" New York: Simon & Schuster, 1994.

Barlett, Donald L., and James B. Steele. "Empire." New York: Norton, 1981.

Brill, Steven. "The Teamsters." New York: Pocket Books, 1979.

Brodeur, Paul. "Expendable Americans." New York: Viking, 1974.

Broehl, Wayne G. Jr. "Cargill." Hanover, N.H.: University Press of New England, 1992.

Browne, Harry, and Beth Sims. "Runaway America." Albuquerque: Resource Center Press, 1993.

Cohen-Rosenthal, Edward, and Cynthia Burton. "Mutual Gains." Ithaca, N.Y.: ILR Press, 1993.

Coleman, Charles J., and Theodora T. Haynes, eds. Labor Arbitration. Ithaca, N.Y.: ILR Press, 1994.

Commons, Dorman L. "Tender Offer." Berkeley: University of California Press, 1985.

Crowe, Kenneth C. "Collision." New York: Scribners, 1993.

Daniells, Lorna M. Business Information Sources. Berkeley: University of California Press, 1993.

Delgado, Hector L. "New Immigrants, Old Unions." Philadelphia: Temple University Press, 1993.

Dorsey, David. "The Force." New York: Random House, 1994.

Hawkes, Ellen. "Blood and Wine." New York: Simon & Schuster, 1993.

Hernon, Peter, and Terry Ganey. "Under the Influence." New York: Simon & Schuster, 1991.

Joel, Lewin G. III. "Every Employee's Guide to the Law." New York: Pantheon, 1993.

Kluge, Pamela Hollie, ed. "The Columbia Knight-Bagehot Guide to Business and Economics Journalism." New York: Columbia University Press, 1991.

Levitt, Martin Jay, and Terry Conrow. "Confessions of a Union Buster." New York: Crown, 1993.

Lofgren, Don J. "Dangerous Premises." Ithaca, N.Y.: ILR Press, 1989.

Lydenberg, Steven D., Alice Tepper Marlin and Sean O'Brien Strub. "Rating America's Corporate Conscience." Reading, Mass.: Addison-Wesley, 1986.

Mintz, Morton. "At Any Cost." New York: Pantheon, 1985.

Mokhiber, Russell. "Corporate Crime and Violence." San Francisco: Sierra Club Books, 1988.

Morgan, Dan. "Merchants of Grain." New York: Viking, 1979.

Nader, Ralph, and William Taylor. "The Big Boys." New York: Pantheon, 1986.

Neff, James. "Mobbed Up." New York: Atlantic Monthly Press, 1989.

Page, Joseph A., and Mary-Win O'Brien. "Bitter Wages." New York: Grossman, 1973.

Parker, Robert E. "Flesh Peddlers and Warm Bodies." New Brunswick, N.J.: Rutgers University Press, 1994.

Sack, Steven Mitchell. "The Employee Rights Handbook." New York: Facts On File, 1990.

Schilit, Howard M. "Financial Shenanigans." New York: McGraw-Hill, 1993.

Schor, Juliet B. "The Overworked American." New York: Basic Books, 1991.

Shapiro, Joseph P. "No Pity." New York: Times Books, 1993.

Shostak, Arthur B. "Robust Unionism." Ithaca, N.Y.: ILR Press, 1991.

Sloane, Arthur A. "Hoffa." Cambridge, Mass.: MIT Press, 1991.

Stevens, Mark. "The Accounting Wars." New York: Macmillan, 1985.

Stevens, Mark. "The Big Eight." New York: Macmillan, 1981.

Terkel, Studs. "Working." New York: Pantheon, 1974.

Trost, Cathy. "Elements of Risk." New York: Times Books, 1984.

Turner, John A. "Pension Policy for a Mobile Labor Force." Kalamazoo, Mich.: Upjohn Institute, 1993.

Vedder, Richard K., and Lowell E. Gallaway. "Out of Work." New York: Holmes & Meier, 1993.

CHAPTER 13

Beck, Roy Howard. "Prophets and Politics." Washington, D.C.: Institute on Religion and Democracy, 1994.

Bennett, James T., and Thomas J. DiLorenzo. "Unfair Competition." Lanham, Md.: University Press of America, 1988.

Bennett, James T., and Thomas J. DiLorenzo. "Unhealthy Charities." New York: Basic Books, 1994.

Bookman, Mark. "Protecting Your Organization's Tax-Exempt Status." San Francisco: Jossey-Bass, 1992.

Boyle, Patrick. "Scouts Honor." Rocklin, Calif.: Prima Publishing, 1994.

Brilliant, Eleanor L. "The United Way." New York: Columbia University Press, 1990.

Freedman, Samuel G. "Upon This Rock." New York: HarperCollins, 1993.

Gaul, Gilbert M., and Neill A. Borowski. "Free Ride." Kansas City, Mo.: Andrews & McMeel, 1993.

Glaser, John S. "The United Way Scandal." New York: Wiley, 1993.

Hopkins, Bruce R. "The Law of Tax-Exempt Organizations." New York: Wiley, 1993.

Sanders, Michael I., and Celia Roady. "Completing Your IRS Form 990." Washington, D.C.: American Society of Association Executives, 1990.

Sennott, Charles M. "Broken Covenant." New York: Simon & Schuster, 1992.

Shepard, Charles E. "Forgiven." New York: Atlantic Monthly Press, 1989.

CHAPTER 14

Abraham, Laurie Kaye. "Mama Might Be Better Off Dead." Chicago: University of Chicago Press, 1993.

Berger, Lisa, and Alexander Vuckovic. "Under Observation." New York: Ticknor & Fields, 1994.

Belkin, Lisa. "First, Do No Harm." New York: Simon & Schuster, 1993.

Bogdanich, Walt. "The Great White Lie." New York: Simon & Schuster, 1991.

Colen, B.D. "O.R." New York: Dutton, 1993.

Diamond, Timothy. "Making Gray Gold." Chicago: University of Chicago Press, 1992.

Drake, Donald, and Marian Uhlman. "Making Medicine, Making Money." Kansas City: Andrews & McMeel, 1993.

Eastaugh, Steven R. "Health Care Finance." New York: Auburn House, 1992.

Elkind, Peter. "The Death Shift." New York: Viking, 1989.

Foner, Nancy. "The Caregiving Dilemma." Berkeley: University of California Press, 1994.

Garrett, Susan. "Taking Care of Our Own." New York: Dutton, 1994.

Hafner, Arthur W., ed. "Reader's Guide to Alternative Health Methods." Chicago: American Medical Association, 1992.

Heron, Echo. "Condition Critical." New York: Fawcett Columbine, 1994.

Heron, Echo. "Intensive Care." New York: Ivy Books, 1988.

Inlander, Charles B., and Karla Morales. "Getting the Most for Your Medical Dollar." New York: Pantheon, 1991.

Kassler, Jeanne. "Bitter Medicine." New York: Birch Lane, 1994.

Kastner, Mark, and Hugh Burroughs. "Alternative Healing." La Mesa, Calif.: Halcyon, 1993.

Kidder, Tracy. "Old Friends." Boston: Houghton Mifflin, 1993.

Klaidman, Stephen. "Health in the Headlines." New York: Oxford University Press, 1992.

Macklin, Ruth. "Enemies of Patients." New York: Oxford University Press, 1993.

Maeder, Thomas. "Adverse Reactions." New York, Morrow, 1994.

Mendelson, Mary Adelaide. "Tender Loving Greed." New York: Knopf, 1974.

Miller, G. Wayne. "The Work of Human Hands." New York: Random House, 1993.

Roper, Fred W., and Jo Anne Boorkman. "Introduction to Reference Sources in the Health Sciences." Metuchen, N.J.: Scarecrow Press, 1994.

Rosenberg, Charles E. "The Care of Strangers." New York: Basic Books, 1987.

Sharkey, Joe. "Bedlam." New York: St. Martin's, 1994.

Shilts, Randy. "And the Band Played On." New York: St. Martin's, 1987.

Starr, Paul. "The Social Transformation of American Medicine." New York: Basic Books, 1984.

Werth, Barry. "The Billion-Dollar Molecule." New York: Simon & Schuster, 1994.

Winerip, Michael. "9 Highland Road." New York: Pantheon, 1994.

Wolinsky, Howard, and Tom Brune. "The Serpent on the Staff." New York: Tarcher/Putnam, 1994.

CHAPTER 15

Heilbroner, David. "Death Benefit." New York: Harmony Books, 1993.

Jesilow, Paul, Henry N. Pontell and Gilbert Geis. "Prescription for Profit." Berkeley: University of California Press, 1993.

Kessler, Ronald. "The Life Insurance Game." New York: Holt, Rinehart and Winston, 1985.

Nader, Ralph, and Wesley J. Smith. "Winning the Insurance Game." New York: Doubleday, 1993.

Scott, David L. "The Guide to Buying Insurance." Old Saybrook, Conn.: Globe Pequot Press, 1994.

Tobias, Andrew. "The Invisible Bankers." New York: Linden/Simon & Schuster, 1982.

Weissman, Joel S., and Arnold M. Epstein. "Falling Through the Safety Net." Baltimore: Johns Hopkins University Press, 1994.

CHAPTER 16

Binstein, Michael, and Charles Bowden. "Trust Me." New York: Random House, 1993.

Caskey, John P. "Fringe Banking." New York: Russell Sage Foundation, 1994.

Day, Kathleen. "S&L Hell." New York: Norton, 1993.

Greider, William. "Secrets of the Temple." New York: Simon & Schuster, 1987.

Lernoux, Penny. "In Banks We Trust." Garden City, N.Y.: Anchor/Doubleday, 1984.

Mishkin, Frederic S. "The Economics of Money, Banking and Financial Markets." New York: HarperCollins, 1994.

O'Shea, James. "The Daisy Chain." New York: Pocket Books, 1991.

Pizzo, Stephen, Mary Fricker and Paul Muolo. "Inside Job." New York: McGraw-Hill, 1989.

Powis, Robert E. "The Money Launderers." Chicago: Probus, 1992.

Singer, Mark. "Funny Money." New York: Knopf, 1985.

Truell, Peter, and Larry Gurwin. "False Profits." Boston: Houghton Mifflin, 1992.

CHAPTER 17

Baumol, William J., and J. Gregory Sidak. "Toward Competition in Local Telephony." Cambridge, Mass.: MIT Press/American Enterprise Institute, 1994.

Bennett, William Ralph Jr. "Health and Low-Frequency Electromagnetic Fields." New Haven, Conn.: Yale University Press, 1994.

Brodeur, Paul. "The Great Power-Line Cover-Up." Boston: Little, Brown, 1993.

Coll, Steve. "The Deal of the Century." New York: Atheneum, 1986.

Davis, David Howard. "Energy Politics." New York: St. Martin's, 1993.

Gellhorn, Ernest, and Richard J. Pierce Jr. "Regulated Industries." St. Paul: West Publishing, 1986.

Gottlieb, Robert. "A Life of Its Own." San Diego: Harcourt Brace Jovanovich, 1988.

Hahne, Robert L., and Gregory L. Aliff. "Accounting for Public Utilities." New York: Bender, 1983.

Mueller, Milton L. "Telephone Companies in Paradise." New Brunswick, N.J.: Transaction Publishers, 1993.

Roe, David. "Dynamos and Virgins." New York: Random House, 1984.

Roess, Anne C. Public Utilities. Metuchen, N.J.: Scarecrow, 1991.

Smith, F. Leslie, Milan Meeske and John W. Wright II. "Electronic Media and Government." White Plains, N.Y.: Longman, 1995.

CHAPTER 18

Bernstein, Aaron. "Grounded." New York: Simon & Schuster, 1990.

Chapman, Paul K. "Trouble on Board." Ithaca, N.Y.: ILR Press, 1992.

Ditlow, Clarence, and Ray Gold. "Little Secrets of the Auto Industry." Wakefield, R.I.: Moyer Bell, 1994.

Kaplan, James. "The Airport." New York: Morrow, 1994.

Kunen, James S. "Reckless Disregard." New York: Simon & Schuster, 1994.

McShane, Clay. "Down the Asphalt Path." New York: Columbia University Press, 1994.

Nader, Ralph, and Wesley J. Smith. "Collision Course." New York: McGraw-Hill, 1993.

Nalder, Eric. "Tankers Full of Trouble." New York: Grove, 1994.

Nance, John J. "Blind Trust." New York: Morrow, 1986.

Ouellet, Lawrence J. "Pedal to the Metal." Philadelphia: Temple University Press, 1994.

Peterson, Barbara Sturken, and James Glab. "Rapid Descent." New York: Simon & Schuster, 1994.

Ross, H. Laurence. "Confronting Drunk Driving." New Haven, Conn.: Yale University Press, 1992.

Troitsky, M.S. "Planning and Design of Bridges." New York: Wiley, 1994.

Wills, Kendall J., ed. "The Pulitzer Prizes 1989." New York: Touchstone/Simon & Schuster, 1989.

X, Captain, and Reynolds Dodson. "Unfriendly Skies." New York: Doubleday, 1989.

CHAPTER 19

Appalachian Land Ownership Task Force. "Who Owns Appalachia?" Lexington: University Press of Kentucky, 1983.

Babcock, Richard F. "The Zoning Game." Madison: University of Wisconsin Press, 1966.

Babcock, Richard F., and Charles L. Siemon. "The Zoning Game Revisited." Boston: Oelgeschlager, Gunn & Hain, 1985.

Baum, Alice S., and Donald W. Burnes. "A Nation in Denial." Boulder, Colo.: Westview Press, 1993.

Beatley, Timothy. "Ethical Land Use." Baltimore: Johns Hopkins University Press, 1994.

Downie, Leonard Jr. "Mortgage on America." New York: Praeger, 1974.

Eighner, Lars. "Travels With Lizbeth." New York: St. Martin's, 1993.

Gilderbloom, John I. "Community Versus Commodity." Albany: State University of New York Press, 1992.

Gilderbloom, John, and Richard Applebaum. "Rethinking Rental Housing." Philadelphia: Temple University Press, 1988.

Jacobs, Jane. "The Death and Life of Great American Cities." New York: Random House, 1961.

Keating, W. Dennis. "The Suburban Racial Dilemma." Philadelphia: Temple University Press, 1994.

Kidder, Tracy. "House." Boston: Houghton Mifflin, 1985.

Lassar, Terry J. "Carrots and Sticks." Washington, D.C.: Urban Land Institute, 1989.

Levy, Matthys, and Mario Salvadori. "Why Buildings Fall Down." New York: Norton, 1992.

Light, Sally. "House Histories." Spencertown, N.Y.: Golden Hill Press, 1989.

McKenzie, Evan. "Privatopia." New Haven, Conn.: Yale University Press, 1994.

Opie, John. "The Law of the Land." Lincoln: University of Nebraska Press, 1987.

Rhodes, Richard. "Farm." New York: Simon & Schuster, 1989.

Sullivan, Arthur O., Terri A. Sexton and Steven M. Sheffrin. "Property Taxes and Tax Revolts." New York: Cambridge University Press, 1995.

Welfeld, Irving. "HUD Scandals." New Brunswick, N.J.: Transaction Publishers, 1992.

Welfeld, Irving. "Where We Live." New York: Simon & Schuster, 1988.

Wright, Robert R. "Land Use." St. Paul: West Publishing, 1994.

CHAPTER 20

Altman, Roberta. "The Complete Book of Home Environmental Hazards." New York: Facts On File, 1991.

Barlett, Donald L., and James B. Steele. "Forevermore." New York: Norton, 1986.

Brown, Michael H. "Laying Waste." New York: Washington Square Press, 1981.

Brown, Michael H. "The Toxic Cloud." New York: Harper & Row, 1987.

Bullard, Robert D., ed. "Unequal Protection." San Francisco: Sierra Club Books, 1993.

Carson, Rachel. "Silent Spring." Boston: Houghton Mifflin, 1962.

Center for Investigative Reporting and Bill Moyers. "Global Dumping Ground." Washington, D.C.: Seven Locks Press, 1990.

Church, Thomas W., and Robert T. Nakamura. "Cleaning Up the Mess." Washington, D.C.: Brookings Institution, 1993.

Esposito, John C. "Vanishing Air." New York: Grossman, 1970.

Gerrard, Michael B. "Whose Backyard, Whose Risk." Cambridge, Mass.: MIT Press, 1994.

Gottlieb, Robert. "Forcing the Spring." Covelo, Calif.: Island Press, 1993.

Hird, John A. "Superfund." Baltimore: Johns Hopkins University Press, 1994.

Hurt, C.D. Information Sources in Science and Technology. Englewood, Colo.: Libraries Unlimited, 1994.

Logan, Robert A., Wendy Gibbons and Stacy Kingsbury. "Environmental Issues for the '90s." Washington, D.C.: Environmental Reporting Forum/Media Institute, 1992.

Mayer, Carl J., and George A. Riley. "Public Domain, Private Dominion." San Francisco: Sierra Club Books, 1985.

Merideth, Robert. The Environmentalist's Bookshelf. Thorndike, Maine: G.K. Hall, 1993.

O'Leary, Rosemary. "Environmental Change." Philadelphia: Temple University Press, 1994.

Phillips, Kathryn. "Tracking the Vanishing Frogs." New York: St. Martin's, 1994.

Rathje, William, and Cullen Murphy. "Rubbish!" New York: HarperCollins, 1992.

Rich, Bruce. "Mortgaging the Earth." Boston: Beacon Press, 1994.

Ringquist, Evan J. "Environmental Protection at the State Level." Armonk, N.Y.: Sharpe, 1994.

Rosenbaum, Walter A. "Environmental Politics and Policy." Washington, D.C.: Congressional Quarterly, 1995.

Shabecoff, Philip. "A Fierce Green Fire." New York: Hill & Wang, 1993.

Shulman, Seth. "The Threat at Home." Boston: Beacon Press, 1992.

Switzer, Jacqueline Vaughn. "Environmental Politics." New York: St. Martin's, 1994.

Weir, David, and Mark Schapiro. "Circle of Poison." San Francisco: Institute for Food and Development Policy, 1981.

Whitaker, Jennifer Seymour. "Salvaging the Land of Plenty." New York: Morrow, 1994.

Young, Gordon J., James C.I. Dodge and John C. Rodda. "Global Water Resource Issues." New York: Cambridge University Press, 1994.

CHAPTER 21

Bane, Mary Jo, and David T. Ellwood. "Welfare Realities." Cambridge, Mass.: Harvard University Press, 1994.

Berry, Jason. "Lead Us Not Into Temptation." New York: Doubleday, 1992.

Berry, Jeffrey M. "Feeding Hungry People." New Brunswick, N.J.: Rutgers University Press, 1984.

Chesler, Phyllis. "Mothers on Trial." San Diego: Harcourt Brace Jovanovich, 1991.

Dash, Leon. "When Children Want Children." New York: Penguin, 1989.

Funiciello, Theresa. "The Tyranny of Kindness." New York: Atlantic Monthly Press, 1993.

Gordon, Linda. "Pitied But Not Entitled." New York: Free Press, 1994.

Kotlowitz, Alex. "There Are No Children Here." New York: Doubleday, 1991.

Kotz, Nick. "Let Them Eat Promises." Englewood Cliffs, N.J.: Prentice Hall, 1969.

Lemann, Nicholas. "The Promised Land." New York: Knopf, 1991.

Nelson, Barbara J. "Making an Issue of Child Abuse." Chicago: University of Chicago Press, 1984.

Rank, Mark Robert. "Living on the Edge." New York: Columbia University Press, 1994.

Schorr, Lisbeth B., and Daniel Schorr. "Within Our Reach." New York: Doubleday, 1988.

Solnit, Albert J., Barbara F. Nordhaus and Ruth Lord. "When Home Is No Haven." New Haven, Conn.: Yale University Press, 1992.

Wexler, Richard. "Wounded Innocents." Buffalo, N.Y.: Prometheus Books, 1990.

Wilson, William Julius. "The Truly Disadvantaged." Chicago: University of Chicago Press, 1987.

CHAPTER 22

Blais, Madeleine. "The Heart Is an Instrument." Amherst: University of Massachusetts Press, 1992.

Blundell, William E. "The Art and Craft of Feature Writing." New York: New American Library, 1988.

Brooks, Brian S., George Kennedy, Daryl R. Moen and Don Ranly. "News Reporting and Writing." New York: St. Martin's, 1992.

Cheney, Theodore A. Rees. "Writing Creative Nonfiction." Berkeley, Calif.: Ten Speed Press, 1991.

Clark, Roy Peter, and Don Fry. "Coaching Writers." New York: St. Martin's, 1992.

Connery, Thomas B., ed. "A Sourcebook of American Literary Journalism." Westport, Conn.: Greenwood, 1992.

Duffy, Thomas G. "Let's Write a Feature." Columbia, Mo.: Lucas Brothers, 1969.

Fishkin, Shelley Fisher. "From Fact to Fiction." Baltimore: Johns Hopkins University Press, 1985.

Franklin, Jon. "Writing for Story." New York: Atheneum, 1986.

Kennedy, George, Daryl R. Moen and Don Ranly. "Beyond the Inverted Pyramid." New York: St. Martin's, 1993.

Lounsberry, Barbara. "The Art of Fact." Westport, Conn.: Greenwood Press, 1990.

Murray, Donald. "Writing for Your Readers." Old Saybrook, Conn.: Globe Pequot Press, 1992.

Poynter Institute for Media Studies. "Best Newspaper Writing." St. Petersburg, Fla.: Poynter Institute, 1994 (annual publication with different editors back to 1979).

Rich, Carole. "Writing and Reporting News." Belmont, Calif.: Wadsworth, 1994.

Scanlan, Christopher, ed. "How I Wrote the Story." Providence, R.I.: Providence Journal Publishing, 1986.

Sims, Norman, ed. "The Literary Journalists." New York: Ballantine, 1984.

Stepp, Carl Sessions. "Editing for Today's Newsroom." Hillsdale, N.J.: Erlbaum, 1990.

Weber, Ronald, ed. "The Reporter as Artist." New York: Hastings House, 1974.

Wolfe, Tom. "The New Journalism." New York: Harper & Row, 1973.

Wolfe, Tom. "The Right Stuff." New York: Farrar, Straus & Giroux, 1979.

Zinsser, William. "Writing to Learn." New York: Harper & Row, 1988.

CHAPTER 23

Black, Jay, Bob Steele and Ralph Barney. "Doing Ethics in Journalism." Greencastle, Ind.: Sigma Delta Chi Foundation, 1993.

Bok, Sissela. "Lying." New York: Pantheon, 1978.

Bok, Sissela. "Secrets." New York: Pantheon, 1983.

Christians, Clifford G., Kim B. Rotzoll and Mark Fackler. "Media Ethics." New York: Longman, 1991.

Elliott, Deni, ed. "Responsible Journalism." Beverly Hills, Calif.: Sage, 1986.

Gillmor, Donald M. "Power, Publicity and the Abuse of Libel Law." New York: Oxford University Press, 1992.

Goldstein, Tom. "The News at Any Cost." New York: Simon & Schuster, 1985.

Goodwin, Gene, and Ron F. Smith. "Groping for Ethics in Journalism." Ames: Iowa State University Press, 1994.

Klaidman, Stephen, and Tom L. Beauchamp. "The Virtuous Journalist." New York: Oxford University Press, 1987.

Lambeth, Edmund B. "Committed Journalism." Bloomington: Indiana University Press, 1992.

Littlewood, Thomas B. "Coals of Fire." Carbondale: Southern Illinois University Press, 1988.

McCulloch, Frank, ed. "Drawing the Line." Washington, D.C.: American Society of Newspaper Editors Foundation, 1984.

Merrill, John. "The Imperative of Freedom." New York: Hastings House, 1974.

Meyer, Philip. "Ethical Journalism." New York: Longman, 1987.

Overbeck, Wayne, and Rick D. Pullen. "Major Principles of Media Law." Fort Worth: Harcourt Brace, 1995.

Patterson, Philip, and Lee Wilkins. "Media Ethics." Dubuque, Iowa: Brown & Benchmark, 1994.

Pippert, Wesley G. "An Ethics of News." Washington, D.C.: Georgetown University Press, 1989.

Rivers, William L., and Cleve Mathews. "Ethics for the Media." Englewood Cliffs, N.J.: Prentice Hall, 1988.

Shaw, David. "Press Watch." New York: Macmillan, 1984.

Index

Note About the Index: Included in this index are as many main entries and cross-references as space permits: Readers should be able to find terms easily in a reference book. Specific terms are cross-referenced to general terms if the cross-reference provides closely related additional information ("income tax. *See also* taxes"). Items are not cross-referenced if the link is obvious ("age discrimination" is not cross-referenced to "discrimination").

Most proper names mentioned in the text are excluded for reasons of space. Many superb journalists and news organizations are not mentioned in the text because I could cite only so many examples. That means many deserving reporters, editors and news organizations do not appear in the index. By omitting all names from the index, a certain justice is achieved: If the book cannot recognize all good investigative work, it shouldn't call special attention to just a small portion.

The names of most institutions are excluded, but topics of an institution's work are included. Geographic locations are omitted, too. Books and other specific resources generally are not listed by title but appear in subject matter entries.

wiretapping, 203, 221. *See also* privacy;
  surveillance
witnesses, 110, 190, 192, 207, 209, 215,
  217, 223–25, 228, 231, 233, 237–40,
  245, 268. *See also* courts; crime;
  hearings, legislative
wives. *See* spouses
women, 77, 186, 187, 219, 284, 305–8,
  449–66. *See also* sex discrimination
workers. *See* employees
workers' compensation insurance, 18,
  33, 36, 119, 120, 189, 285, 298,
  367–72, 458, 461. *See also* employees;
  employers; insurance
workplaces, 70, 114, 137, 195, 257,
  279–308, 326
  safety of, 4, 231, 285, 286, 292, 296–99,
    305, 351, 367–70, 436, 437, 441, 449,
    477
  See also employees; employers

work release. *See* probation
writing, 7, 8, 13, 15, 147, 157, 438, 453,
  454, 469–87. *See also* investigative
  reporting; schools
wrongful convictions, 201, 239–41. *See
  also* prosecutors
wrongful terminations. *See* firings

X–rays, 359. *See also* radiologists

yachts, 37, 385. *See also* personal
  property; transportation
yearbooks, 5, 23. *See also* individuals;
  schools

ZIP codes, 51, 95, 98, 354, 360
zoning, 7, 18, 206, 364, 421–35. *See also*
  developers; flooding; land
zoos, 126. *See also* animals